PRICE THEORY AND APPLICATIONS

Prentice-Hall, Inc., *Englewood Cliffs, New Jersey 07632*

JACK HIRSHLEIFER

University of California, Los Angeles

second edition

PRICE
THEORY
AND
APPLICATIONS

Library of Congress Cataloging in Publication Data

Hirshleifer, Jack.
  Price theory and applications.

  Includes bibliographical references and index.
  1. Microeconomics.   I. Title.
HB171.5.H66 1980   338.5   79-21355
ISBN 0-13-699710-4

Editorial/production supervision by Paul Spencer
Cover and interior design by Judith Winthrop
Manufacturing buyers: Edmund W. Leone and Gordon Osbourne

PRICE THEORY AND APPLICATIONS, *second edition*

Jack Hirshleifer

Printed in the United States of America
10 9 8 7 6 5 4 3 2

PRENTICE-HALL INTERNATIONAL, INC., *London*
PRENTICE-HALL OF AUSTRALIA, PTY. LTD., *Sydney*
PRENTICE-HALL OF CANADA, LTD., *Toronto*
PRENTICE-HALL OF INDIA PRIVATE LIMITED, *New Delhi*
PRENTICE-HALL OF JAPAN, INC., *Tokyo*
PRENTICE-HALL OF SOUTHEAST ASIA PTE. LTD., *Singapore*
WHITEHALL BOOKS LIMITED, *Wellington, New Zealand*

CONTENTS

PREFACE   *xi*

PART ONE
introduction

1

THE NATURE AND SCOPE OF ECONOMICS
(Core Chapter)   *3*

2

WORKING TOOLS
(Core Chapter)   *25*

PART TWO
preference, consumption, and demand

3

UTILITY AND PREFERENCE
(Core Chapter)   *61*

4

CONSUMPTION AND DEMAND

(Core Chapter)

87

5

**MEASURES AND DETERMINANTS
OF DEMAND**

(Core Chapter)

125

6

**APPLICATIONS AND EXTENSIONS
OF DEMAND THEORY**

(Supplementary Chapter)

155

PART THREE
equilibrium and exchange

7

**EQUILIBRIUM, EXCHANGE, AND THE
GAINS FROM TRADE**

(Core Chapter)

189

8

**COSTS OF EXCHANGE AND THE ROLE
OF MONEY**

(Supplementary Chapter)

228

PART FOUR
the firm and the industry

9

THE BUSINESS FIRM
(Core Chapter)   259

10

COMPETITIVE SUPPLY, AND
EQUILIBRIUM IN THE PRODUCT MARKET
(Core Chapter)   303

11

MONOPOLY AND THE QUESTION
OF ECONOMIC EFFICIENCY
(Core Chapter)   331

12

PRODUCT AS A VARIABLE
(Supplementary Chapter)   365

13

OLIGOPOLY
(Supplementary Chapter)   388

PART FIVE
factor markets, distribution, and intertemporal analysis

14

THE DEMAND FOR FACTORS
OF PRODUCTION
411   *(Core Chapter)*

15

FACTOR SUPPLY, FACTOR-MARKET
EQUILIBRIUM, AND INCOME
DISTRIBUTION
446   *(Core Chapter)*

16

INTERTEMPORAL CHOICE: SAVING,
INVESTMENT, AND INTEREST
486   *(Supplementary Chapter)*

PART SIX
political economy

17

WELFARE ECONOMICS: THE THEORY
OF ECONOMIC POLICY
519   *(Supplementary Chapter)*

18

GOVERNMENT AND THE ECONOMY:
A POSITIVE ANALYSIS
(Supplementary Chapter) 552

ANSWERS *578*

INDEX *611*

PREFACE TO THE SECOND EDITION

The generally favorable reception of the first edition of *Price Theory and Applications* has confirmed my belief that there is a market for a text in microeconomic theory that, without multiplying elegant niceties or losing touch with the world of applications, will challenge students at all levels.

There are two opposed pedagogical difficulties in presenting price theory. The student's initial interests are almost always not in theoretical questions but in concrete facts and specific problems, both societal and personal. On the societal level these might include the energy crisis, the burden of government, or the persistence of poverty. On the personal level the typical student will have an understandable interest in the very practical problem of improving his or her financial prospects—making a wise choice of occupation, for example. But the student will find that the solutions to these questions are not found by simple recital of the facts. Instead, he or she must learn to approach problems of choice in a more roundabout "theoretical" way, to deal with an abstract version or "model" at some distance from direct reality. On the other hand, economics is *not* a branch of mathematics, a body of abstract theorems deduced purely from given postulates without any necessary connection with reality. Unfortunately, one sometimes encounters intellectually muscle-bound theorists, overtrained virtuosos who may be knowledgeable about Frobenius matrices and conditions of multidimensional dynamic stability, but are at a loss to explain why vegetables are cheaper after the harvest than before. *Economics is a science designed to explain the nature of the real world.* Consequently, it is not only duller but fundamentally misleading to present "theory" in the absence of "application." *Theory is justified only by its power of application in the world of reality.* The intent here is to keep the integration of theory and application always before the student.

Two specific methods of integrating students' understanding of theory and application are especially prominent in this text. First, scattered throughout the book are dozens of brief discussions of real-world "Examples," designed both to display the relevance of the theory and to provide some expository change of pace. In addition, a number of applied topics—such as import quotas, the negative income tax, rationing, subsidy versus voucher support for education, monopolistic suppression of inventions, and investment in human capital—are discussed in more extended fashion. Users of the first edition found both of these devices to be very helpful, judging from letters received. In this second edition I have (where required) updated the Examples and the extended discussions, and have added to their numbers as well.

A great expository problem for authors of microeconomics textbooks is the level of difficulty to aim at. Some students will already have taken a full-year basic economics course and additional applied-area studies before approaching intermediate theory; others may have no more than a single-semester "elements" course as background. In some cases the previous courses may have been demanding, in other cases perhaps too easy. As for the price theory course itself, some colleges cover it in a single term, while others may devote an entire year. A price theory course offered by a graduate school of business or of public administration will encounter students already mature, with considerable experience of the world, but the book should also remain accessible to undergraduates at the sophomore level. Apart from use as text in a course, the book ought to be capable of serving as general reference and guide for later study and review.

It is evidently impossible to meet all these requirements. The particular compromise adopted here is as follows: First of all, and taken as a whole, *this is not a minimal book.* The intent was to build a growth potential into the text that would match the student's later deepening understanding of economics. *But it is not absolutely necessary to take the book as a whole.* A book-within-the-book exists in the form of the series of marked *Core Chapters* (Chapters 1-5, 7, 9-11, 14, and 15). This constitutes a nucleus to which, depending upon the severity of time and other constraints, other material can be added. In addition, a number of more difficult or ancillary topics, not essential for logical continuity, are relegated to special (asterisked) sections or sub-sections within chapters.

To some degree these objectives were, it seems, met by the first edition. In basic courses instructors concentrated on the Core Chapters, with individual variations in response to particular needs and interests. The enriched coverage beyond the core material was appreciated by students in intensive or more advanced microeconomics courses, and in addition the book was found serviceable as supplement or self-study guide in a variety of contexts.

However, nothing is perfect in our imperfect world. As Dr. Samuel Johnson said of one of his productions, the first edition contained "a few wild blunders, and risible absurdities, from which no work of such multiplicity was ever free." My thanks go to the many correspondents, students as well as professional economists, who have helped me correct a number of these blunders and absurdities, and to make a variety of other improvements in exposition and content.

The weightiest change from the first edition is a revision in sequence of topics. In the first edition explicit coverage of production theory was deferred to the chapter on demand for factors, appearing relatively late in the book. While this innovation was welcomed by some, the majority opinion seems to have gone against it. As the test of experience must govern in such matters, I have returned in this edition to something closer to the traditional order of topics in microeconomics. Specifically, after the introductory material in Part One, the topics of consumer preference and demand are covered in Part Two; equilibrium and exchange in Part Three; production, the firm, and industry supply in Part Four; demand for and supply of factors, distribution, and general equilibrium in Part Five; and political economy in Part Six.

A number of other changes, apart from general rewriting, have been introduced in the interest of avoiding needless difficulty and making the book more easily accessible to undergraduate students of varying backgrounds. The first edition contained an Appendix on equations of general equilibrium which was perhaps out-of-place in a book on the intermediate level, and which has therefore been omitted from this edition. Among the steps taken to improve exposition and facilitate comprehension in this edition were the following: (1) Explanatory descriptive legends are now provided for the diagrams. (2) Each chapter is followed by a Summary. (3) Questions at the end of chapters are divided into a first group mainly for review, and a second group for further thought and discussion; answers are provided in the back of the book for selected questions (about half of them).

This book contains a number of textual features intended as improvements upon conventional treatments of microeconomics:

> 1. Traditional intermediate texts are silent or evasive on the price-theoretic underpinnings of *money*. In Chapter 8, the analysis of exchange as an actual (and therefore costly) economic activity provides the foundation for understanding the function of a monetary commodity. Similar reasoning serves in Chapter 9 to explain the existence of the business firm as another institution called into being by the costliness of exchange.

> 2. The traditional topic of "monopolistic competition" is presented here as only one instance of a more general issue—*variation of product*. Topics covered under this heading include optimal product assortment and equilibrium level of quality. Product variation can of course emerge from monopolistic, competitive, and other market structures apart from the special case of monopolistic competition.

3. Chapter 16 is devoted to the topic of intertemporal choice, leading to a theory of investment and saving decisions. This is a helpful bridge to macroeconomics, and also to the business-finance literature.

4. After a treatment of traditional welfare economics in Chapter 17 ("The Theory of Economic Policy"), Chapter 18 provides a *positive* analysis of government. The apparatus of the state is treated as consisting of human agents responding to motivations of individual advantage. Government is shown to be an institutional alternative to the market, but one whose functioning and performance are still analyzable by economic techniques. More generally, market and non-market institutions are seen to be differentiated not by "higher" or "lower" motivations, but by the rules governing the processes of human interaction.

One point always in contention is the degree of command of mathematics to expect of readers. By now a good fraction, though still a minority, of undergraduate courses in microeconomic theory require elementary calculus as prerequisite. In this text calculus techniques and notations are used only in marked "mathematical footnotes." But the delta (Δ) notation employed in the definitions of "marginal" concepts will be naturally interpretable in differential or derivative terms by the student equipped with calculus. No use is made of integrals or matrices. The instructor should, of course, warn serious students that further command of college mathematics is a necessity for study of economics beyond the intermediate level.

Whether a proper balance has been struck between coverage and simplicity, between theory and application, between technical accuracy and suggestive exposition, only the reader can judge. I will be grateful for guidance on this point from instructors and students, as well as for specific corrections where errors appear.

ACKNOWLEDGMENTS

Many colleagues provided helpful reviews and suggestions for the initial edition. In this group I would like to mention especially Professors Robert Dorfman (Harvard), Ross Eckert (U.S.C.), David L. McNicol (Pennsylvania), Edwin Mills (Princeton), R. Charles Moyer (University of Houston), and Lloyd M. Valentine (University of Cincinnati). Extremely valuable corrections and comments were received from so many readers that it is impossible to list their names here. But I would like to express my gratitude for the more extended reviews and guidance provided by Professors Allen R. Sanderson (College of William and Mary) and Daniel S. Christiansen (University of Rochester). None bears any responsibility for any remaining errors or omissions. Particular thanks are due to my research assistants over the years who have helped develop the examples used in the text and suggested many of the questions which appear at the end of each chapter: Charles Knoeber (now a faculty member at North Carolina State University) for the first edition, and for the second edition Ralph Cole, Gary Galles, David A. Hirshleifer, Carroll Shelor, M. Holly Shissler, Shirley Svorny, and Richard Tontz. Typing and editorial assistance of an exceptional order was provided by M. Lorraine Grams. The index for the second edition was prepared mainly by Charles Morris.

PRICE THEORY AND APPLICATIONS

PART ONE
Introduction

1.A   ECONOMICS AS A SOCIAL SCIENCE, 5

   1.A.1   Is Economics Scientific? 5

   1.A.2   The Scope of Economics, 8

   1.A.3   Normative versus Positive Analysis, 14

1.B   THE INVISIBLE HAND, 14

1.C   ELEMENTS OF THE ECONOMIC SYSTEM, AND THE CIRCULAR FLOW OF ACTIVITY, 15

   1.C.1   Decision-Making Agents in the Economy, 16

   1.C.2   Scarcity, Objects of Choice, and Economic Activities, 17

   1.C.3   The Circular Flow, 18

1.D   MICROECONOMICS AND MACROECONOMICS, 19

1.E   ANALYTICAL TECHNIQUES OF ECONOMICS, 20

Examples

   1.1   HYDROLOGY VERSUS ECONOMICS, 6

   1.2   SALARIES, 7

   1.3   RATIONAL PSYCHOTICS? 9

   1.4   RATIONAL CRIMINALS? 12

THE NATURE AND SCOPE OF ECONOMICS

Core Chapter

Actions have good and bad effects—pros and cons, benefits and costs. Taking up tennis may be good for your figure, but bad for your studies. Someone who buys a cheap product is likely to find its quality low as well. Defending an allied nation against aggression may help the cause of freedom but involve the horrors of war. Economics develops methods for the systematic assessment and comparison of such favorable and unfavorable aspects of all proposed decisions. And it explores the often surprising outcomes that emerge when individuals' private actions interact on the social scene.

Your study of economics should make your private decisions more effective, and your views on social issues more subtle and balanced. It may not make you more popular, however. Economics has been called "the dismal science" because economists are always telling people what is wrong with superficially attractive solutions to social problems. Mr. A would like to ease his financial burdens by drastic cuts in taxes—the economist tells him that he must then probably expect less police and fire protection, or poorer public schools for his children, or curtailment of public library and playground hours. Mrs. B would cure unemployment at home by banning the import of cheap foreign goods—the economist tells her that our export industries depend on sales to these same foreigners, and we'd clearly all be worse off if countries could not specialize in the production of goods. Mr. C would eliminate poverty by guaranteeing a high income to all—the economist tells him that this would gravely weaken the incentive to work, and that we cannot in aggregate consume what we do not produce. Ms. D wants to encourage women to overcome female stereotypes and make a career outside the home—the economist tells her that as more women seek non-home employments, female wage rates will tend to fall (relative to men's wages). The economist might personally favor any or all of these proposals, but emphasizes that they all have costs that must be weighed against their actual or seeming benefits. Unfortunately, when people become committed to policies they generally don't want to hear of possible disadvantages.

The economist's set of mind is thus diametrically opposed to that of the *advocate,* who looks only for arguments buttressing one side of an issue. Of course, in a particular situation the advocate may be right. He or she might with some justice complain that the economic mentality, always considering the pros and cons, may paralyze needed action. ("The native hue of resolution is sicklied o'er with the pale cast of thought"—*Hamlet.*) Nor can the economist replace the *prophet* and *poet* who inspire us to aim at ideal goals; economics does not give us our goals but only weighs the consequences of trying to achieve them. Prophets and poets, men and women of action, and even advocates are needed elements in society. But so are economists.

ECONOMICS AS A SOCIAL SCIENCE

It may have struck you that the outlook attributed to the economist is essentially the same as that of the *scientist.* And indeed this book is an introduction to economics as a science: as a body of analytical models (theories) that yield verifiable implications about the real world. More specifically, economics is a *social* science; it aims to explain how human beings interact with one another in the world of affairs.

Economics claims to be a social science. That it concerns behavior in human society no one will deny. But can it be a science? Cynics cite two important pieces of evidence to the contrary: (1) On any issue one can find economists on either side of the argument; indeed, they always seem to disagree. (2) If economics were really a science, economists would be able to predict commercial and financial affairs and so should be (but visibly are not) all rich! Each of these contentions is worthy of serious attention.

As to differences among economists, individuals disagree in all aspects of life—and in science as well. To mention only a few great scientific debates: In astronomy the geocentric model of Ptolemy was opposed by the newer heliocentric model of Copernicus; in chemistry Priestley supported the phlogiston theory of combustion while Lavoisier propounded the oxidation theory; and in biology the creationism of earlier naturalists was countered by Darwin's theory of evolution. It is not universal agreement, but rather the willingness to consider evidence that signals the scientific approach. For Galileo's opponents to disagree with him about Jupiter's moons was not unscientific of itself; what was unscientific was their

1.A.1
Is Economics Scientific?

Chapter 1
THE NATURE
AND SCOPE OF
ECONOMICS

5

refusal to look through his telescope and see. An inspection of economic texts and journals will reveal that current great issues, whether it be the monetarist vs. fiscalist hypotheses in macroeconomics, or the determinants of labor's share in distribution theory, or the effectiveness of centralized planning versus *laissez faire* for achieving economic growth, are under continuous scientific evaluation. Failure to arrive at a general scientific consensus[1] may be due to the complexity of the problem or to the incompetence of the investigators, but there will always be unresolved issues in any living science.

Are there, however, any *resolved* issues in economics? This book will highlight a great many, in the area of price theory or microeconomics. (For some comments on *macro*economics, see Section D below.) There is little remaining disagreement on essentials of such topics as the impact of taxes or subsidies upon prices and outputs, the implications for consumers of competitive vs. monopolistic market structures, the effects of reducing tariffs, etc.

Observers often exaggerate not only the extent of disagreement among economists, but also the degree to which the natural sciences (sometimes miscalled the "exact" sciences) have mastered their respective fields of inquiry. Few topics have been so well studied as strength of materials in applied physics. Yet engineers, after going through their calculations, commonly add on a huge safety factor (50% or even 100%) before undertaking construction of a bridge or a dam. And even so, bridges still collapse and dams wash away. If economists predicting the rate of inflation were permitted as wide a safety factor as engineers, they would rarely go astray.

EXAMPLE 1.1
HYDROLOGY
VERSUS
ECONOMICS

In 1955 the Board of Water Supply of New York City projected that the city's future rate of water use would reach 1320 MGD (million gallons per day) as of 1960, rising further to 1500 MGD by 1970. "Safe yield" (a hydrologic concept supposedly representing a reliable minimum supply) from existing water sources was pegged at 1550 MGD throughout. With only a thin safety margin (1550 − 1500 = 50 MGD) anticipated as remaining by 1970, the Board of Water Supply decided to acquire a new water source to come into service before that date.

A team of economists reviewed this decision in 1960. They concluded that the Board's projections of water use were much too high; the economists' prediction was that actual water use in New York City would surely not reach 1500 MGD by 1970, if ever. Since the "safe yield" supposedly guaranteed by hydrologic science already equalled 1550 MGD, the economists concluded that provision of a new supply was not warranted.

After 1960, the economists' predictions about actual use were borne out. Water consumption in New York City stabilized well below 1300 MGD, far under the Board's projected rate of 1500 MGD, and never came anywhere near the supposed "safe yield" of 1550 MGD. So all should have been well. Instead, the city was hit by a catastrophic water shortage. What had happened? Throughout the early 1960's the *actual* yield of water sources

---

[1]*Scientific* consensus need not imply general agreement as to *policy*, however. See the discussion of "Normative versus Positive Analysis" in Section 1.A.3 below.

was far, far below the hydrologists' alleged "safe yield." In the four successive years 1962 through 1965, the *highest* actual water yield was only 1204 MGD. The projections of economics, one of the social sciences, thus proved to be immensely more reliable than those of one of the vaunted natural sciences.[2]

COMMENT: In making policy recommendations, the economist may be in a position of having to evaluate the reliability of other sciences as well as his own.

[2]For a discussion, see J. Hirshleifer and J. W. Milliman, "Urban Water Supply: A Second Look," *American Economic Review*, v. 47 (May 1967), pp. 169–78.

What about the charge that if economics were truly a science, economists would all be rich? To this several answers, not all mutually consistent, are commonly offered. It is sometimes argued that a scientific knowledge of economics ought *not* to be expected to lead to financial success. If Henry Aaron had studied the aerodynamic equations governing the motion of spheroidal missiles, would that have helped him beat Babe Ruth's home-run record? This argument should not be pressed too far, however. After all, what is the use of economics (or of aerodynamic knowledge, for that matter) if it does not lead to *some* practical result? In the case of economics this usefulness is surely in understanding market phenomena, which ought to be convertible, at least to some extent, into higher cash income. While the general run of people can hardly be expected to match the achievements of geniuses like Henry Aaron in his field or J. Paul Getty in his, there ought to be some observable effect of economics training upon income. And indeed, it seems, to some degree there is!

The table below shows salaries for college instructors in a number of selected fields.

EXAMPLE 1.2
SALARIES

Salaries of University or College Instructors with Ph.D.'s (1975)

FIELD	MEDIAN SALARY
Engineers	$18,900
Medical Scientists	18,700
Economists	18,400
Agricultural Scientists	18,200
Oceanographers	18,100
Computer Specialists	18,000
Statisticians	17,800
Physicists	17,700
Earth Scientists	16,900
Psychologists	16,900
Mathematicians	16,800
Sociologists/Anthropologists	16,800
Social Scientists, other than Economists or Sociologists	16,800

Chemists	16,600
Biological Scientists	16,200

Source: National Science Foundation, 1975 Surveys of Science Resources Series, *Characteristics of Doctoral Scientists and Engineers in the United States*, pp. 112–113.

COMMENT: Economists rank near the top of teaching salaries in the U.S., third in this table. The only academic fields with more earning power, according to these data, are engineering and medicine. Both these other fields (and, to a lesser extent, economics as well) are characterized by excellent opportunities outside of college teaching, in business employment or independent professional practice. As we shall see in Chapter 14, employers of teachers must compete against all other possible employers of trained professionals so that salaries in teaching are influenced by these outside opportunities.

Nevertheless, the data in Example 1.2 do not prove that it is *the economics training* that leads to the higher incomes reported. There are other possible explanations of income differentials. It might be that economics is so unpleasant that its practitioners must be offered added financial compensation—rather like sewage workers or hangmen. Or perhaps the higher salaries economists earn are only normal rewards for those exceptional talents necessary to understand economics in the first place.

The following quotation from Aristotle (384–322 B.C.) is also of some relevance. Aristotle is discussing his predecessor Thales (approx. 636–546 B.C.), considered to be the first Greek philosopher and scientist.

Thales . . . was reproached for his poverty, which was supposed to show the uselessness of philosophy; but observing from his knowledge of meteorology (so the story goes) that there was likely to be a heavy crop of olives, and having a small sum at his command, he paid down earnest-money, early in the year, for the hire of all the olive presses in Miletus and Chios; and he managed, in the absence of any higher offer, to secure them at a low rate. When the season came, and there was a sudden and simultaneous demand for a number of presses, he let out the stock he had collected at any rate he chose to fix, and making a considerable fortune he succeeded in proving that it is easy for philosophers to become rich if they so desire, though it is not the business which they are really about. (Aristotle, *Politics*, I.)

Thales was renowned not only as a meteorologist but as an astronomer, mathematician, and statesman. Still, we may doubt Aristotle's assertion that "it is easy for philosophers to become rich if they so desire"—unless, like Thales, a philosopher happens to be a pretty good economist as well.

1.A.2
The Scope of Economics

Economics is not the only social science. Sociology, anthropology, political science, social psychology, and even social biology have much to contribute to our understanding of how humans behave in relation to their fellows. No absolute boundaries can be drawn between the topics covered by economics and those addressed by her sister social sciences. That the boundaries are indistinct is actually a healthy intellectual situation, since the modes of attack of different disciplines can then compete over the bordering territories. It is useful to think of economics as having a central nucleus, plus outlying extensions into the domains more usually associated with other disciplines. The nucleus of economics covers a limited range of human activity: that characterized by *rational behavior* on the part of individuals, interacting upon one another through a particular social mechanism, *the market*.

The concept of "rational behavior" turns out to involve some difficulties. There are two main meanings of rationality, the first running in terms of *method* and the second in terms of *result*. In terms of method, rational behavior is action selected on the basis of considered thought; in terms of result, rational behavior is action that is in fact well designed to achieve your goals. But we know that good method sometimes leads to bad result: "The best laid schemes o' mice and men / Gang aft a-gley" (Robert Burns). And Nature often has evolved effective strategies for animals possessing very limited capacity for thought. Anyone who has chased a fly with a swatter knows that the insect, despite its tiny brain, may defeat us and achieve its goal of survival. And disease germs may destroy us, though they have no brain at all. But in general, on the human level we expect that considered thought will indeed lead to better action.

Everyone behaves irrationally to some extent—out of passion, thoughtlessness, mental defect, or just plain perverseness. Some do so to such a degree that they are institutionalized for their own or others' protection. In view of the prevalence of human irrationality, how can rationality be postulated in economics? Clearly, only to the extent that the assumption works in providing usable predictions of social phenomena. Rational behavior is systematic and purposive, whereas irrational behavior tends to be unpredictable and erratic. Since it is the aggregate behavior of a great number of individuals that determines social results, the cumulative effect of even a limited degree of rationality tends to dominate over the unsystematic irrational elements. Predictions of social phenomena in terms of rational responses do tend to work, often in surprising ways (see the "Rational Psychotics?" example below). And yet economics as a science is not irrevocably wedded to the rationality postulate. When an alternative that proves more usable for predictive purposes comes along, it will be adopted instead.

With 44 female psychotics (primarily schizophrenics) as experimental subjects, the psychologists T. Ayllon and N. H. Azrin studied responsiveness of patients in a mental institution to changes in systems of reward for services. Prior to the beginning of the experiment patients were allowed to choose among a variety of tasks (laundry service, dietary service, etc.) for which they were to be rewarded. The reward took the form of tokens, which were

EXAMPLE 1.3
RATIONAL
PSYCHOTICS?[3]

[3]Discussion based upon T. Ayllon and N. H. Azrin, "The Measurement and Reinforcement of Behavior of Psychotics," *Journal of the Experimental Analysis of Behavior*, v. 8 (Nov. 1965).

convertible into commissary articles (clothing, toiletries, cigarettes, etc.) or into hospital privileges (e.g., privacy, leave from the ward).

During the first 20 days patients were rewarded with tokens only upon completion of their tasks—a system the psychologists term "contingent reinforcement." After 20 days it was announced that the same number of tokens as before would henceforth be paid each patient automatically, *whether or not the tasks were performed*—in psychological jargon, a shift to a system of "non-contingent reinforcement." On an average day in the first period of "contingent reinforcement" (that is, where wages were paid for services rendered), the 44 patients worked 45 hours in total, just a bit over one hour per patient per day. After the shift to "non-contingent reinforcement" (i.e., to the free gift of tokens) the total number of hours worked by the 44 patients declined to 35 on the first day and to 20 hours on the third. Shortly afterward the bottom dropped out, and close to zero hours were worked thereafter.

Then, at the end of a second period of 20 days, the earlier system of "contingent reinforcement" was reinstated. The total number of hours worked jumped immediately to 45 hours per day, and remained near that level to the end of the experiment 20 days later.

CONCLUSION: The experimental subjects may have been psychotic, but they were not stupid. They showed an ability to adapt to systems of rewards in their society. If working was necessary to earn these rewards, they worked; if the rewards came without working, they chose not to work.

Rationality is an instrumental concept. It requires the prior existence of goals aimed at. The economist, by and large, regards the process whereby individuals somehow become pointed toward particular desired ends as outside his sphere of competence. He is only interested in the net result of this process, the patterns that he calls *tastes* or *wants* or *preferences*. These are, from his point of view, arbitrary. In one society individuals may protect children but eat cattle; another society may protect cattle but expose unwanted infants. Either way, the scientific economist is prepared to make predictions about the social consequences of the given preferences.

This undoubtedly leaves a great territory, including what are perhaps the most important aspects of social phenomena, for other sciences to study. Goals and preferences are not determined randomly. Psychology brings explanations to bear in terms of primitive instincts, as reinforced or suppressed by socialization processes. The anthropologist analyzes the relevance of culture for goal formation, and the sociologist the relevance of class or other group identification. Social biologists have shown that human goals must have tended over evolutionary time to promote the survival of the individuals concerned and their offspring, since otherwise the process of natural selection would have eliminated them in the long period of development of the human species. The economist has allowed this division of intellectual labor to operate, leaving the explanation of the formation of tastes and goals as a task for these other social sciences.

The economist's mode of procedure inclines him to suppose that preferences are generally quite *stable*, only rarely constituting the dynamic element in social changes. If a tax on liquor is imposed, his analysis will almost automatically assume that the desire to drink is just as great—only that the tax makes it more expensive to indulge that desire. For the economist this represents a possible blind spot, and scientific caution is indicated. Take liquor: Without any change in taxes the temperance campaign of Father Mathew around 1850 in Ireland reduced that country's consumption of spirits from 12,000,000 to 5,000,000 gallons per annum (but only temporarily). And if there is a higher tax on liquor, its imposition may itself reflect a change of tastes in the form of increased revulsion against drinking. Nor is the assumption of unchanging tastes very helpful for analyzing the element of fashion and style in consumption. Far more important, many of the really great social changes in human history have clearly stemmed from shifts in people's goals for living. Indeed, the economist is in danger of trivializing these fundamental values and goals by suggesting that they are merely arbitrary "tastes." From the prophets of ancient Israel to the ministry of Jesus to the recent decline in effective belief in God, the changes in the kinds of rewards that people seek from life have had enormous effect upon the shape of the social system of the West. The ethical messages of Buddha and Confucius have perhaps had similar impacts upon the civilization of the East. The areas the economist leaves out of his cognizance are therefore at least as important as those he feels equipped to examine.

It is sometimes charged that economics also postulates that people's preferences are completely selfish. This is an uninformed criticism. It is true that, observing facts as they really are, the economist ordinarily operates on the premise that individuals seek their own advantage. "It is not from the benevolence of the butcher, the brewer, or the baker, that we expect our dinner, but from their regard to their own interest."[4] That this is a main truth about human activity it would be absurd to deny. Nevertheless, charity is an important feature of economic life; people have, in a sense, a taste for benevolence. Even so, the economist is likely to say, if benevolence were made less costly (for example, if the Internal Revenue Service permitted more ample deductions for charitable giving against income tax), we would see more of it. As another example, the economist can hardly explain the economic relations between parents and children—parental expenditures for protection and education, and provision for inheritance—with a postulate of complete selfishness. But again, if we want to elicit a higher degree of love and care on the part of parents, a financial inducement would help.

In addition to the postulate of individual rational choice, the sensible selection of means for achieving given ends, the nucleus of economics has also specified something about the ways in which people's rational decisions interact. If consumer A wants bread from baker B, it may seem like rational behavior for A to get a job and earn the price of a loaf. But it may also be rational, in certain circumstances, for A to simply steal the bread from B. Alternatively, A might organize a political party with the object of passing laws dictating that B must give bread to A. Or, A might attempt to persuade B that it is the latter's charita-

[4]Adam Smith, *The Wealth of Nations*, Book I, Chap. 2.

ble duty to help out hungry A's. Economics concentrates upon the first of these forms of interaction: i.e., the integration of individuals' separate goal-seeking activities *through the market*. For the most part crime has been left to sociology, the uses of state power to political science, and techniques of persuasion to psychology. But the vigor and rigor of economic science are proving increasingly useful in these related areas. Economics has tended, therefore, to overflow these boundaries, as the following example shows.

EXAMPLE 1.4
RATIONAL
CRIMINALS? Crime may well be, in certain circumstances, an effective way of achieving one's goals without using the market. (That is, without bothering to offer something in exchange for what one wants to get.) The dominant opinion in modern criminology (a field of study which, up to quite recently, made no use of economic analysis) had been that criminals were best thought of as individuals with "deviant" motivations. The solution to crime, it was therefore inferred, should be sought on the psychological level (for example, by improving the mental health of potential criminals, or providing them with better role models to follow). Economic analysis, without necessarily denying that criminals are psychologically "deviant" in some ways, suggests nevertheless that they may still (like the psychotics in Example 1.3 above) respond to changes in incentives in a way that could be regarded as rational.

These responses have been studied by Isaac Ehrlich in several papers. One of these related the rates of commission of major felonies to the punishments and rewards for crime in the different states of the U.S.[5] As economists would expect, the crime rate tended to be lower the more effective the punishment. The rate of commission of robberies, for example, decreased about 1.3% in response to each 1% increase in the proportionate *probability* of punishment and also decreased about .4% for each 1% increase in the *severity* of punishment (length of imprisonment). Another seemingly rational response was that the *property crime* rate in a state tended to be higher where average income and inequality of income were both high. Presumably, in those states criminals were relatively poor individuals living in an environment containing many attractive targets.

The most controversial of Ehrlich's results concerned the effect of capital punishment in deterring murder. Concentrating emphasis upon the abnormal psychology of murderers, the standard view in criminology had been that murderers are surely too "deviant" to be deterred by the threat of execution. Yet Ehrlich's investigation indicated very big deterrent effects: according to one set of data each execution was associated with 7 to 8 fewer murders, according to another set 20 to 24 fewer murders.[6]

These inferences were, however, based upon complex statistical manipulations, to which a number of more or less serious reservations or objections

[5]I. Ehrlich, "Participation in Illegitimate Activities: A Theoretical and Empirical Investigation," *Journal of Political Economy*, v. 81 (May/June 1973).

[6]I. Ehrlich, "The Deterrent Effect of Capital Punishment: A Question of Life and Death," *American Economic Review*, v. 65 (June 1975), p. 414 and "Capital Punishment and Deterrence: Some Further Thoughts and Additional Evidence," *Journal of Political Economy*, v. 85 (August 1977), p. 779.

were raised by critics. A panel of the National Academy of Sciences, mainly consisting of non-economists, was set up to review the conclusions of Ehrlich and the broadly similar results reached by other economic investigators into crime. The panel, while conceding that the evidence tended to support the deterrence hypothesis, nevertheless regarded it as still unproven.[7] As more data are accumulated and more accurate analytical techniques are devised, we can expect this scientific disagreement ultimately to be resolved.

[7]Panel on Research in Deterrent and Incapacitative Effects, *Deterrence and Incapacitation: Estimating the Effects of Criminal Sanctions on Crime Rates* (National Academy of Sciences, 1978).

These results suggest that economic analysis is applicable also to non-market interactions. And indeed, even the social inter-relationships of animals (which do not ordinarily engage in anything recognizably like exchange) are beginning to be analyzed by biologists in economic terms.[8] One important human non-market form of interaction is *politics,* a topic that will be examined from the economic point of view in Part Six of this book.

Returning to market interactions among people, these have distinctive characteristics that set them apart from other forms of human transactions. *The market relation is mutual and voluntary*. Theft, a non-market interaction, is clearly *involuntary* on one side. The gift relation, another non-market interaction, is voluntary but not *mutual*. Two different objections can immediately be raised on this score. First, if A is hungry and B has bread, can their relation really be voluntary? Must not the A's of this world be "wage slaves" of the B's? Then how does the market differ from coercive dominance? Second, suppose some highwayman declares to his victim, "Your money or your life!" Isn't he offering a voluntary deal? Then how can criminal transfers be distinguished from market exchange?

The explanation of these puzzles turns on the legal concept of *property*. To take up the highwayman first, he is indeed proposing a market deal: to "sell" the victim back his or her own life, in exchange for money. But under our legal system each person has property in his or her own life. The seemingly voluntary transaction proposed by the highwayman is premised upon his seizing power over something he has no right to—his victim's life. As for the "wage slave" contention, it is of course true that those endowed with more valuable property will be better off in the market than those possessing little in the way of resources. But there is a vast difference between laborers possessing property rights in their own labor power, in a position to bargain with alternative employers for the best available terms, and slaves. The latter have no property; indeed, they are property. They cannot market or trade their labor power, for it is not legally theirs to dispose of.

[8]Martin L. Cody, "Optimization in Ecology," *Science,* v. 183 (March 22, 1974); David J. Rapport and James E. Turner, "Economic Models in Ecology," *Science,* v. 195 (January 18, 1977).

In its scientific aspect economics is strictly *positive*. It answers the question "What is reality like?" But *normative* issues in public policy, turning upon the question "What *should* be done?", also always require economic analysis. Given the social objective aimed at (with which they might in fact personally disagree), scientific economists can use their knowledge of reality to analyze the problem and suggest efficient means for attaining the desired end. This book will touch upon many policy issues, but always emphasizing the positive point of view.

When economists disagree on policy issues, it may be because they are seeking divergent goals; one may be more concerned with achieving social equality, another with promoting individual freedom. Where the divergence is indeed on such a philosophical plane, even the most complete scientific understanding of economic reality will not resolve the conflict. But it is often the case that variance of opinion among economists is over *means* rather than *goals*. Further scientific progress in positive economics will, over time, tend to eliminate this source of disagreement.

1.B

THE INVISIBLE HAND

As astronomy has Newton's principle of universal gravitation, and biology Darwin's principle of evolution through natural selection, economics also has a great unifying scientific conception. Its discovery was, like Newton's and Darwin's, one of the important intellectual achievements of humanity.

Adam Smith's *The Wealth of Nations* appeared in 1776. The key idea is suggested by the following quotation:

> But it is only for the sake of profit that any man employs his capital in the support of industry; and he will always, therefore, endeavour to employ it in the support of that industry of which the produce is likely to be of the greatest value, or to exchange for the greatest quantity either of money or of other goods. . . . he is in this, as in many other cases, led by an invisible hand to promote an end which was no part of his intention. Nor is it always the worse for the society that it was no part of it. By pursuing his own interest he frequently promotes that of the society more effectually than when he really intends to promote it.[9]

We can amplify this, in more modern language, as follows. People will be motivated by rational self-interest to employ the resources under their control wherever they can get the highest possible price. But high prices reflect scarcity of supply relative to intensity of consumers' demands. Hence the private incentives will work continuously to overcome scarcity and meet consumer demands, i.e., to direct resources to the employments most suited for satisfying consumers' desires.

This seems obvious enough, though it was not so obvious two centuries ago. At that time it was commonly believed that untrammeled selfishness must lead to

[9]Book IV, Chap. 2.

mutual harm, if not to total chaos. Even today many people hardly understand how, for example, the city of New York can be regularly fed by convergence of food shipments from all corners of the earth—without any governing plan to make sure that the Kansas farmer, the New England fisherman, and the Florida orange-grower actually deliver to the hungry city. Yet the city is fed, although none of its suppliers need be motivated by any particular love and concern for New Yorkers. Kansas farmers simply find it more profitable to ship to New York than to eat their own wheat, and similarly for the others.

To quote *The Wealth of Nations* still once more: "In civilized society [man] stands at all times in need of the cooperation and assistance of great multitudes, while his whole life is scarce sufficient to gain the friendship of a few persons."[10] The Invisible Hand is what leads an individual to work for the good of other persons, practically all unknown to him, in a vast interlocking network of *spontaneous order* that has arisen without anyone's planning it that way.

Adam Smith's object in composing *The Wealth of Nations* was largely policy-oriented or *normative*; he opposed the then politically dominant "mercantilists,"[11] arguing instead in favor of a policy of "natural liberty."[12] But it is not his policy recommendations that will mainly concern us. For our purposes, his key conception is that *the economy is an integrated system whose behavior follows scientifically determinable laws*. In early times, the motion of the planets was so incomprehensible that it was thought they were pushed in their courses by angels. The development of astronomy eventually led to the scientific idea of gravitation as the integrating mechanism that explains these motions. Similarly today, all too many people find it utterly incomprehensible why (for example) water is cheap and diamonds expensive, a strange situation that they are all too likely to attribute to the actions of angels or devils. We owe to Smith the conception of the market economy as a self-regulating mechanism, harnessing as motive power the self-interest of participants, yet so integrating their activities that each is led to serve the desires of the others. How this leads to water being cheap and diamonds expensive we shall see in the pages to come.

1.C

ELEMENTS OF THE ECONOMIC SYSTEM,
AND THE CIRCULAR FLOW OF ACTIVITY

That *there is an economic system*—that there are laws of economics—is the first message to learn. We can now survey some of the necessary elements going into the make-up of the economic system.

[10]Book I, Chap. 2.

[11]The mercantilists believed that a nation's well-being could best be furthered by accumulation of gold and silver, to be achieved by systematic government interventions designed to encourage exports and restrain imports.

[12]Smith recommended free trade among nations and *laissez faire* within.

Economics concerns the making of rational decisions, as well as the social interactions of the choices so made. What are the active entities to be regarded as engaging in the process of choice? We shall deal in this book with three main categories of decision-making units: individuals, firms, and governments.

Individuals are the ultimate active members of social systems, the only agents said to have goals or *preferences* and to engage in the process of *consumption* (to be discussed in Part Two). Actually, recognizing the mutual support and cohesiveness of the family some economists prefer to consider the ''household'' to be the effective consumptive unit. Except where otherwise specified, the individual here will be understood as making decisions for his or her family or household.

The business firm is an artificial unit; it is ultimately owned by or operated for the benefit of one or more individuals. Surprisingly, this fact is often not appreciated. It is sometimes argued, for example, that ''soulless corporations'' can be taxed without cost to the people. But of course taxing a corporation will hurt some people: the company's owners will suffer reduced profits, its workers may find it harder to get wage increases, its customers are likely to find that prices of its products have been increased. (At the same time, the taxes paid will allow government to provide assistance to other people—as usual, every choice of policy involves both costs and benefits.) The economist finds it convenient to think of firms as distinct agents specialized in the process of *production*, the conversion of resource inputs into desired goods as outputs. Firms will be the center of attention in Part Four of the text. In point of fact, however, much production actually takes place within the household; cooking, gardening, and home maintenance are examples.

Individuals and firms are not the only economic decision-making agents. A third category, government, is of great and growing importance. Governments, like firms, are artificial groupings; they differ from firms by not being owned by individuals, and also by having powers to take property involuntarily, yet legally (as by taxing). From the economic point of view governments are agencies engaging in a number of collective productive and consumptive activities, the scope of which is determined by a political rather than a market process. Perhaps even more important, government establishes the legal framework within which the entire economy works. Just as ownership of valuable resources (economic power) leads some individuals to superior outcomes through the market mechanism, similarly possession of influence over government policies (political power) can be expected to lead others to superior outcomes through the political mechanism. (The role of government is examined specifically in Part Six.)

In complex modern economies there are still other ''collective'' decision-making units, in which people get together for undertaking some form of united action. Trade unions and cartels are of particular interest as representing organizations of buyers or sellers in markets, and will be discussed in the text below. Of lesser economic importance are voluntary associations like clubs, foundations, and religious institutions, which can be regarded as instrumentalities whereby individuals combine for certain collective consumption choices.

someone else must have more. Thus, exchange is a kind of transfer. But it is a mutual and voluntary transfer; *all* parties involved are satisfied. The objects of choice in exchange activities may be either consumption goods and services or production goods and services.

1.C.3
The Circular Flow

In a simplified world with only two types of economic agents, individuals and business firms, the relations between them can be pictured as in Figure 1.1. Individuals and firms have dual aspects, and thus transact with one another in two distinct ways. Individuals are in one aspect *consumers of goods*, while firms are *producers of goods*. Thus, the diagram shows a "real" flow of consumption goods (solid upper channel) from firms to individuals. But the goods must be produced. To permit this there must be a "real" flow of productive services (solid lower channel), from the individuals in their second aspect as *owners of resources* to the firms as *employers of resource services*.

Figure 1.1
The Circular Flow of Economic Activity

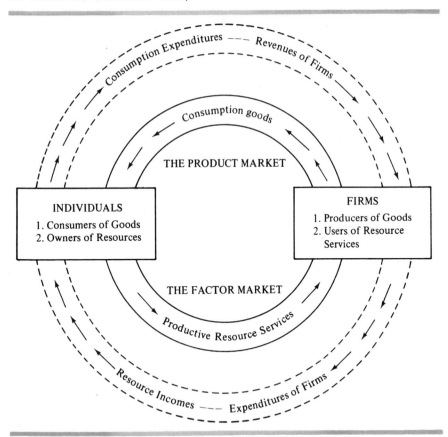

The all-pervasive economic problem is that of *scarcity*. Not all desired things are available to individuals, the ultimate decision-making agents, when and as desired. Even if all desired physical commodities were present in unlimited quantities, we would not have enough *time* to enjoy them all. And, in addition, we all desire things other than material commodities: power, love, prestige. There can never be enough of these. It is the fact of scarcity that forces us to make economic decisions, that is, to organize our efforts for production and/or to engage in trade with a view toward obtaining desired objects.

Setting aside the desire for social relations and distinctions like affection or prestige, which we will not attempt to cover in this text, the entities that we usually think of as the objects of economic choice are called *commodities*, or *goods and services*. Goods as distinguished from services are physical things (wares or merchandise). Services represent a flow of benefits over a period of time, derived either from physical goods (like the shelter service provided by a house) or from human activities (like the entertainment service provided by concert performers). The distinction between wares and services will not be essential for us until the discussion of resources and production in Part Five. For the present, therefore, we will think of commodities or goods as synonymous words covering also desired consumption services.

Consumption of commodities or goods represents one of the main economic activities. The consumptive decisions of particular individuals will range over the various goods available, attempting to pick out assortments within their means that best accord with their given tastes. We shall say that goods are the *objects of choice* for the consumption decision.

Production is another main economic activity. We shall sometimes find it convenient to regard it as engaged in by individuals, and sometimes by firms. We usually think of production as the physical conversion of inputs into outputs, i.e., of resources (or the services of resources) into consumable goods. More fundamentally, production is any transformation adding to the social totals of some desired goods at the expense of a reduction in the amount of others. Production might represent a transformation *of physical form*, as in the conversion of leather and human labor into shoes, but not necessarily so. Transformations would still be regarded as productive if they took place *over space* (shipment of oranges from Florida to Maine) or *over time* (storing of potatoes after harvest so as to distribute consumption over the year).

Of course, to be economically rational production should represent a conversion from a less desired to a more desired configuration. To burn an antique Chippendale chair for heat is a kind of production, but ill-advised under ordinary conditions. (On the other hand, an individual on the point of freezing to death might find the conversion from chair to warmth exceedingly advantageous.)

The third main economic activity is *exchange* (to be discussed in Part Three). For the individual, exchange is also a kind of conversion—he or she trades away some objects for others. But from the social point of view, exchange is distinguished from production in that the totals of commodities are unaffected; goods and services are reshuffled in trade, but wherever one person has less,

In a command economy these flows of goods and resources would be directly ordered by a dictator. But in a private-enterprise economy the relations are based on exchange and so must be mutual and voluntary. Hence, offsetting the "real" flows are reverse "financial" flows of claims that in a modern economy normally take the form of money payments. The consumers' financial expenditures on goods (dashed upper channel) become the receipts or revenues of the firms. The exchange of consumption goods between individuals and producing firms, and the balancing financial payments, take place in what is abstractly termed "the product market." (Actually, there will of course be a host of separate product markets, one for each distinct consumption good.)

The revenues from sales to consumers provide the firms with the wherewithal to buy productive services from resource owners (dashed lower channel). This closes the circle, as the firms' payments for productive services become income to the individuals, available once more for consumption expenditures to begin the next cycle. The purchase and sale of productive services take place in what is abstractly called "the factor market," again, really a number of distinct markets for the various types of productive services.

Looking within the box representing the firms as economic agents, what takes place there is the process of *production*, i.e., the physical transformation of resources into products. Within the box representing individuals, *consumption* of the produced goods takes place. Here again, the circle is closed by the fact that consumption is necessary to recreate the main productive resource—labor power—for the next cycle.

MICROECONOMICS AND MACROECONOMICS

A distinguished professor of logic, deploring the division of his subject between deductive reasoning and inductive reasoning, once declared: "In our textbooks on deduction we explain all about logical fallacies; in our textbooks on induction, we then commit them." In economic theory as well, we have an as yet unresolved split of the subject—microeconomics versus macroeconomics. In microeconomics we see how and why the Invisible Hand operates (how and why self-interest leads each person toward a spontaneous system of productive cooperation); in macroeconomics we examine the consequences of its failing to do so!

An easy explanation of this unsatisfactory state of affairs is not available. Suffice it to say, for our purposes here, that microeconomics concentrates mainly upon equilibrium states of particular markets, presuming an equilibrium of the market system as a whole. But it seems to be the case that the equilibrium of the market system as a whole is not as robust as might be hoped. The circular flow of economic activity may become disorganized, to greater or lesser degree, without any significant disequilibrium in particular markets. Some types of disturbance may generate self-reinforcing aggregate movements (e.g., the Keynesian "multiplier'') likely, at least for a time, to lead the system of the circular flow away from rather than back to an equilibrium condition. It is these disequilibria of the system as a whole that macroeconomics studies.

For some period of time, starting in the 1930s, macroeconomists attempted to develop modes of reasoning largely independent of any microeconomic foundation; some theorists went so far as to dismiss classical microeconomics as obsolete or irrelevant. It is now generally recognized that this attempt has failed. Significant recent progress in macroeconomics has been made precisely by improving the logical connection of the subject with the microeconomic theories of production, consumption, and exchange. So if we cannot give answers to the key questions of macroeconomics here, we can still with some confidence assure students that their study of microeconomics will also promote their understanding of the former subject.

1.E

ANALYTICAL TECHNIQUES OF ECONOMICS

In any intellectual discipline, partially informed individuals, i.e., students, are liable to moments of despair. They will have acquired many bits of knowledge and technique, yet the subject in its entirety can remain a buzzing, blooming confusion; the parts may not come together into a meaningful whole. In economics, as has already been mentioned, students can keep hold upon a key unifying concept: the Invisible Hand. They can recall that they are studying the market system as one way of solving the economic problems of society, a way that (at least, when working ideally) harnesses individual self-interest to achieve a kind of mutual cooperation in the face of scarcity.

In addition (and this should really be good news), it is a remarkable fact that the great bulk of economic reasoning makes use of only two analytical techniques: (1) *optimization*, and (2) *determination of equilibrium*. In facing any question, the student who asks, "Is this an optimization problem, or an equilibrium problem?" will rarely go astray.

Optimization occurs at the level of the decision-making agent. What signals an optimization situation is the appearance of the word "best." In his consumption decision the individual wants to determine the best package or combination of goods to purchase out of his income. In his resource–supply decision he wants to find the best employment of his resources—in particular, of his labor power—taking into account the alternatives available. The business firm, engaging in the process of production, is presumed to decide upon the nature and quantities of commodities to be produced and of resources to be employed in order to achieve a best possible outcome for its owners.

Mathematically, the process of optimization can be formulated as finding a maximum (or minimum) of some desired (or undesired) *criterion*. This is the standard problem of the calculus. In this book calculus techniques are not explicitly used (except in specified mathematical footnotes). Economists have devised a variety of methods for optimization, turning upon the idea of "marginal" quantities, which amount to being able to do calculus without necessarily knowing it! As for the criterion measures, we say that the individual maximizes "utility" while the firm maximizes "profits." The nature and use of these criteria will be explained in Part Two (covering the decisions of the individual) and Part Four (covering the decisions of the firm), respectively.

Equilibrium is a property of the interaction of economic agents in markets. A system is in equilibrium when the forces acting upon it are so balanced that there is no net tendency to change. When the price is such that the quantity supplied equals the quantity demanded, conditions are in balance and there is no tendency for price or for quantity to change—the market is in equilibrium. The process determining an equilibrium can be formulated mathematically as a conditional equation (or system of equations). The student is assumed in this book to have the ability to understand and solve simple equations. Where complications or tricky features arise, however, explanations will be provided.

This chapter discusses the relevance and scope of economic analysis, introduces the unifying idea of the "Invisible Hand," and previews the analytical techniques used in the text and in economic theorizing generally.

Economics is a social science, whose nucleus is the study of the *rational behavior* of economic agents interacting through *market exchanges*. Rational behavior is the appropriate choice of means for achieving given ends—always involving comparison of benefits and costs, the advantages and disadvantages of alternative courses of action. Economists do not ordinarily attempt to go behind the ends sought by individuals, their tastes or wants or desires, but rather take these as given and relatively stable facts which are to be explained (if at all) by the other social sciences. Individuals can achieve their desires in human society in a number of ways, among them persuasion, force, theft, or use of government power. But economics mainly studies interaction through market relations, the process of mutual voluntary exchange.

Adam Smith's principle of the Invisible Hand indicates how individuals interacting through markets are led to cooperate, simply in their own self-interest. The Invisible Hand makes the economy a system of spontaneous order, an integrated arrangement whose behavior follows scientifically determinable laws.

The main agents (acting units) in the economic system are individuals (possibly acting on behalf of their families or households), firms, and governments. Individuals are the only agents who consume. Individuals may directly produce, but also do so indirectly by creating business firms, artificial agents that specialize in production. The activity of production, which transforms some goods and services into others, must be distinguished from exchange—which reshuffles goods and services among the economic agents without changing the social totals thereof.

A very important and simplifying feature of microeconomics is that it mainly makes use only of two analytical techniques: optimization, and determination of equilibrium. *Optimization*, which takes place on the level of the economic agent, is the choice of the best procedure for achieving a given end, corresponding analytically to maximizing some criterion or objective subject to the applicable constraints. *Equilibrium* occurs when the interaction of the various agents has achieved a market balance so that there is no further tendency to change. The determination of equilibrium corresponds analytically to the solution of simultaneous equations.

QUESTIONS FOR CHAPTER 1

Mainly for Review

*R1. In what respects can it be said that economics is a science? Give an example of a prediction that modern economic science can confidently make. Are there predictions that economic science has not yet shown itself competent to make?

*R2. What is rational behavior? Give examples of rational and of irrational behavior. Can the economist's postulate of rationality be useful even when irrational elements strongly influence behavior?

R3. Does the economist assume stable preferences? Give an example of a change in preferences that has had important economic effects.

R4. Does the economist assume that everyone is selfish? Give an example of an area where unselfish behavior has important economic consequences.

R5. Market transactions or exchanges are said to be both *mutual* and *voluntary*. Give an example of a non-market interpersonal transaction that is not voluntary. Of one that is voluntary but not mutual.

R6. What are positive issues in economics? Normative issues? Give an example of each.

*R7. How does the "Invisible Hand" lead individuals in a market economy to cooperate for mutual advantage even without any definite intention on their part to do so? Would self-interested behavior lead to mutual advantage in a monastic economy where all income is equally divided? In a dictatorship where the political authorities confiscate the lion's share? In an economy with no property, so that any person could take what he needs from any other person?

R8. What are the most important classes of decision-making units in a modern economy? In what types of activity do they engage? In what sense are firms and governments "artificial" units?

*R9. In the circular flow of economic activity, distinguish between the "real" and "financial" circuits of flow. What is the relation between the two? Distinguish between the "product market" and the "factor market." How are these connected?

R10. "The principle of the Invisible Hand asserts that self-interested behavior on the part of resource-owners leads inevitably to chaos." True or false, and why?

*The answers to asterisked questions appear at the end of the book.

R11. What are the two main analytical techniques used in economic reasoning? Which concerns the decisions of rational economic agents? Which concerns the interactions of their decisions through the market process?

R12. What is the difference between production and exchange?

For Further Thought and Discussion

*T1. Other things being equal, would you expect the murder rate to be lower in jurisdictions applying capital punishment? If the income-tax exemption granted for each child were increased, would you expect the birth rate to rise?

*T2. The psychiatrist T. S. Szasz argues that what is called "mental illness" is the result of rewarding people for disability. Not only is the patient motivated to become "ill," but there is a financial advantage to the healing professions in declaring personal problems to be "illnesses." How could mental illness be made less "rewarding"? Would doing this result in less mental illness?

T3. If government were to increase relief payments to the unemployed, would you expect unemployment to rise?

T4. In terms of the circular flow of economic activity, explain what determines the fact that some individuals are wealthy (in a position to consume a great deal in the product market) and others are poor.

*T5. If the Invisible Hand leads individuals to serve their own interests by serving others, why are some people led to a life of crime? Why do some corrupt politicians find it advantageous to serve themselves at the expense of their constituents? Why are dictators motivated to seize power? [*Hint:* Does the principle of the Invisible Hand apply to all kinds of social interactions, or does it hold only when individuals interact in a particular way?]

*T6. Would an effectively enforced law requiring drivers to wear seat belts tend to reduce driver deaths? Pedestrian deaths?

*T7. Dr. Samuel Johnson: "There are few ways in which a man can be more innocently employed than in getting money." Charles Baudelaire: "Commerce is satanic, because it is the basest and vilest form of egoism." What do you think each had in mind?

T8. Classify each of the following statements or propositions as either *positive* or *normative*. (Does the classification "positive vs. normative" have any bearing upon truth or falsity?)
   a. Smoking in enclosed public spaces should be banned.
   b. Prohibiting smoking in public places would reduce the demand for cigarettes.
   c. Proposed legislation to limit the places in which smokers may indulge in their habit would elicit opposition from the tobacco industry.
   d. Non-smokers' rights to breathe clean air are more important than smokers' rights to pollute the air.
   e. Anti-smoking laws will have no effect on sales of cigarettes because smokers will light up just as much as before but confine their puffing to legal areas.

T9. It may soon become possible to predict the place and time of earthquakes, weeks or even months before their occurrence. Some influential writers have argued that such predictions should be kept secret, or even that investigations leading to such predictions should be banned. Allegedly, the panic caused by predicting an earthquake would be more damaging than the earthquake itself. What does this view imply as to individual rationality? Would you be for or against banning earthquake prediction?

2.A   SUPPLY–DEMAND ANALYSIS, 27

    2.A.1   Equilibrium of Supply and Demand, 27

    2.A.2   Comparative Statics of Supply and Demand—Shift of Equilibrium, 29

    2.A.3   An Application: Effects of a Tax on Transactions, 36

    2.A.4   Algebra of Supply–Demand Analysis, 37

    2.A.5   Interferences with Equilibrium, 40

2.B   THE RELATIONS AMONG TOTAL, AVERAGE, AND MARGINAL MAGNITUDES, 44

Examples

    2.1   CATHOLICS AND FISH, 32

    2.2   POTATOES, 32

    2.3   HEATING OIL, 33

    2.4   BRIDES, 34

    2.5   COMPUTING POWER, 35

    2.6   REPRESSED INFLATION AND TREKKING, 41

    2.7   AGRICULTURAL ''PARITY'' PRICES, 43

    2.8   BIRDS DO IT! 50

    2.9   THE OIL ENTITLEMENTS PROGRAM, 53

    2.10   TAXES, 54

WORKING TOOLS

2

Core Chapter

At the end of Chapter 1 the student received possibly surprising, but surely encouraging news: that the great bulk of economic reasoning makes use of only two analytical techniques. One of these conceptual techniques is *optimization*, attainment of a best or preferred position by a decision-making agent. The other is *determination of equilibrium*, the condition of balance in the market when all the individual decisions interact together.

Each of these techniques employs a characteristic working tool. To analyze equilibrium problems the student must be able to use *supply–demand analysis*. To solve optimization problems, he or she will have to have an understanding of *the relations among total, average, and marginal magnitudes*. Almost all students will have already had some exposure, in introductory economics courses or elsewhere, to these working tools. What is provided in this chapter is therefore mainly a review, together with some indication of the many applications of these tools.

Chapter 2
WORKING
TOOLS

26

Consider the supply–demand diagram of Figure 2.1. The horizontal axis represents the quantity Q of some good or service. In accordance with the idea of the economy as a circular *flow* of activity, it is sometimes important to think of quantity as a continuing stream of production or consumption over time. Thus, we should speak of quantity per month or per week, etc. That quantities represent flows over time, however, will be taken as understood throughout this book.

The vertical axis of the diagram represents price P. *Price is a ratio of quantities:* the amount of some other good Y that must be given up to obtain a unit of a desired good X. Thus, one can speak of the price in cigarettes of a hat, or the price in labor-hours of a loaf of bread. However, in modern economies price is normally quoted in terms of *money*,[1] a "medium of exchange." Consequently, the dimensionality of the vertical or price axis in Figure 2.1 is stated in the diagram as the ratio $\$/Q$.

The demand curve DD shows, for each price P, the quantity that purchasers choose to take from the market. Its negative slope is to be accepted for the moment as an empirical fact: Buyers are willing to purchase more, the lower the

Figure 2.1

Demand and Supply. The equilibrium at point E determines the price P^* and quantity Q^* where supply and demand are in balance.

[1]The nature and role of the institution of money will be explained in Chapter 8.

price. (*Verification*: We often observe sellers trying to win more customers by claiming to be offering unusually low prices. Do sellers ever try to attract customers by asserting that their prices are exceptionally high?) Similarly, the positive slope of the supply curve SS asserts as an empirical fact that sellers will offer more the higher the price. Supply and demand curves will be derived analytically from more fundamental determinants in later chapters, where further light will be cast upon their normal shapes.

In Figure 2.1 market equilibrium is represented by the intersection point E of SS and DD, whose coordinates are the quantity Q^* and price P^*.[2] The justification for the assertion that the intersection of the supply and demand curves is an equilibrium position for the market will be familiar from elementary economics. Suppose the market price were momentarily at any price higher than P^*, such as P' in the diagram. At that price the quantity along the demand curve, the number of units Q_d' that consumers are willing to purchase, is less than Q_s', the number of units that suppliers offer on the market. Not all the suppliers can find customers. What will then happen? It is reasonable to suppose that some suppliers will quote lower prices rather than be left with undesired stocks of goods. Thus, the excess of the supply-quantity Q_s' over the demand-quantity Q_d' generates *downward* pressure on price, indicated in the diagram by the arrow pointing downward from the horizontal line representing the price P'.

What if market price were momentarily at some level lower than P^*, such as P'' in Figure 2.1? Then the quantity demanded would be Q_d'', in excess of the supply-quantity Q_s'' offered on the market. Not all demanders would be able to find the number of units they desire to purchase, and hence some of them will start to bid up the price. Here there is *upward* pressure on price, indicated in the diagram by the arrow pointing upward from the horizontal line representing the price P''.

Clearly, one or the other process will always be at work so long as price is not at the equilibrium P^*. Only at P^* are the demand-quantity Q_d and the supply-quantity Q_s equal to one another, so as to rule out any upward or downward pressure on price. When Q_d equals Q_s, we have the market equilibrium quantity Q^*.

How realistic is this picture? What we are dealing with here is a *model* of reality, not reality itself. It is a model (as will be explained later) of perfect competition among individuals interacting in a perfect market. The question of scientific interest is not the literal *truth* of the model but rather its usability for understanding reality and predicting the consequences of change. This is the subject of the next section.

CONCLUSION: The intersection of demand and supply curves determines the equilibrium values of price and quantity exchanged.

[2]In this text we will generally follow the convention of designating solution values (values of the variables associated with equilibrium or optimum positions, as the case may be) by asterisks.

Equilibrium was determined, in the picture of Figure 2.1, by the intersection of *given* supply and demand curves. But the concepts of supply and demand are mainly used to analyze the consequences of *changes* in economic data, affecting the relative scarcities of economic goods. Such changes can be interpreted as shifts or displacements of either the supply curve of the good, of its demand curve, or both at once.

Suppose, for example, that buyers suddenly wanted to consume more of the commodity in question. (The underlying change here is in consumer preferences.) Then more of the good would be purchased at each possible price. This is called an *increase of demand*. As shown in Figure 2.2, the demand curve shifts *to the right* (from a position like D_1D_1 to D_2D_2). Where the old equilibrium price was P_1^* and quantity Q_1^*, the new equilibrium price and quantity are P_2^* and Q_2^*.

How does the revision of the equilibrium position actually come about? We might describe the process somewhat as follows. Suppose the price were originally unchanged at P_1^* after the demand curve shifted to D_2D_2 in Figure 2.2. Then consumers would want to purchase the quantity Q_d' which exceeds Q_1^*. But at price P_1^* suppliers would still be offering only the quantity Q_1^*. There is an excess of quantity demanded over quantity supplied, leading to upward pressure on price. In a free market, price will respond to this pressure and continue to move upward until Q_d equals Q_s at the new equilibrium price P_2^*.

Figure 2.2

Increase of Demand. When consumers' preferences change in such a way that they desire to purchase more at each price, the demand curve shifts to the right from D_1D_1 to D_2D_2. Equilibrium price and equilibrium quantity both increase.

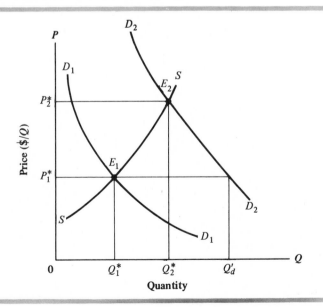

While this description of the process of price–quantity adjustment to change is plausible, it is not the only possible scenario of events. Nor is it entirely free of problems. For example, some transactions might actually take place at "wrong" prices (before P_2^* is reached), and these "wrong" transactions might in turn affect the supply or demand curves. That is, the final equilibrium reached might conceivably depend upon the path for getting there. Issues of this kind are studied in the branch of economics called *dynamics*. We will, except where the contrary is indicated, waive consideration of such problems. Thus, we limit ourselves to comparisons of the initial and the final equilibrium situations. This is called *the method of comparative statics*. While some aspects of reality cannot be successfully modeled without use of dynamics, the relatively simple tools of comparative statics can still tell us a great deal about real-world phenomena.

Our basic technique, then, in analyzing the consequences of some change in market circumstances will be to ask: Is the change reflected in a shift of supply, or a shift of demand (or, possibly, of both)? It will be immediately evident from Figure 2.2 that *an increase in demand alone leads to an increase in both equilibrium price and equilibrium quantity*. An increase in *supply* (see Figure 2.3) is to be interpreted as a *rightward* displacement of the supply curve (from S_1S_1 to S_2S_2), since at each price a larger quantity is offered. (*Warning*: A common slip is to think of an "increase" of demand or supply as an *upward* shift of the corresponding curve; this is correct for the demand curve but incorrect for the supply curve.

Figure 2.3

Increase of Supply. When a change in conditions induces sellers to offer more at each price, the supply curve shifts to the right from S_1S_1 to S_2S_2. Equilibrium quantity increases, but equilibrium price falls.

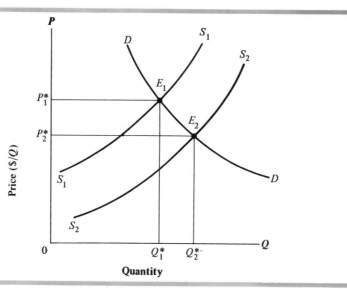

The student can avoid error by thinking of an "increase" always as a *rightward* shift of the corresponding curve.) *An increase in supply thus leads to an increase in equilibrium quantity, but to a decrease in equilibrium price.* (*Question for the student*: What can be said if both supply and demand increase together?)

PROPOSITION: If demand increases, equilibrium price and quantity *both* rise. If supply increases, equilibrium quantity rises but equilibrium price falls.

Any change in economic data affecting market equilibrium can be expressed as a shift in demand or in supply (or both), upward or downward. But what are the sources of these shifts? It is sometimes useful to distinguish between those sources of change originating "outside" and those originating "inside" the economic system. The "outside" sources of variation include: 1. *Changes in tastes*: A temperance campaign may alter a population's willingness to consume hard liquor. 2. *Changes in technology*: Eli Whitney's invention of the cotton gin vastly increased the market availability of cotton. 3. *Changes in resources*: An important oil discovery will enlarge the world's supply of petroleum. 4. *Changes in the political–legal system*: "Decriminalization" of the trade in marijuana can be expected to increase both the market supply and the market demand for that substance. All these changes can be regarded, in some degree at least, as originating autonomously rather than in response to economic factors.[3]

Displacement of equilibrium in a particular market may, however, also stem from movements "inside" the economic system as a whole. The "inside" or economic variations that may affect the price–quantity equilibrium of a particular good or service include: 1. *Changes in prices (or quantities) of goods related in demand*. An increase in the price of butter (however caused in terms of the ultimate or "outside" sources of variation) will tend to raise the demand for margarine. 2. *Changes in prices (or quantities) of goods related in supply*. A rise in the production of wool will almost necessarily increase the supply of mutton on the market. 3. *Changes in levels of income*. The higher incomes recently received by petroleum-exporting countries would be expected to raise their demands for a variety of consumption goods.

It is of considerable importance for the student to develop his or her intuition by analyzing a number of situations in which the price–quantity equilibrium of particular markets is observed to vary over space or time.

---

[3]There is no hard-and-fast rule as to what elements lie "outside" and what "inside" the economic system. Rates of change of resources like petroleum reserves or even of population (labor supply) do actually respond to economic incentives. The pace of technological change, also, is dependent upon the economic effort applied to the process of invention. Similar statements can be made about the other elements conventionally considered as originating independently of economic factors; the broader the concept of the scope of economics, the fewer the elements determined "outside" the system.

EXAMPLE 2.1
CATHOLICS AND
FISH For over a thousand years, the Roman Catholic Church required believers to abstain from consuming meat on Fridays. But a liberalization of the regulations of the Church abolished this requirement for American Catholics as of December 1966 (except for Fridays falling within Lent).

Frederick W. Bell studied the impact of the liberalization upon the price of fish in New England (population approximately 45% Catholic). The study compared a ten-year period before the liberalization with the nine-month period just after (excluding Lenten months). In estimating the shift of the demand curve (price paid for given quantities of fish landed by New England fishermen), it was necessary to adjust for a number of economic factors: imports of fish, prices of closely competitive foods (poultry and meat), cold storage holdings, and personal income among them. Having made these adjustments, the effect of the liberalization on fish prices can be seen in the following table.

Prices of Fish, Monthly Data, 1957–67

SPECIES	PERCENT CHANGE DUE TO LIBERALIZATION
Sea scallops	−17%
Yellowtail flounder	−14
Large haddock	−21
Small haddock (scrod)	− 2
Cod	−10
Ocean perch	−10
Whiting	−20

Source: F. W. Bell, "The Pope and the Price of Fish," *American Economic Review*, v. 58 (Dec. 1968), p. 1348.

The results show that, for any given quantity of fish landings (and after adjusting for the other variables mentioned above), the prices received for fish of all seven species were lower after the liberalization than before.

The "Catholics and Fish" example clearly represents a *decrease* in the demand for fish. (The demand curve for fish shifted leftward, rather than rightward as in Figure 2.2.) The source of the variation would seem to lie clearly "outside" the economic system, since the modification in Church regulations was not in any evident way a response to market factors.

EXAMPLE 2.2
POTATOES That vegetables are cheap at harvest time may well have been the first law of economics observed in primitive society. In the case of potatoes there is some production throughout the year, but the major crop is harvested in the Fall. The table below shows the average U.S. prices and production of potatoes in the various seasons of the year during the period from 1968 to 1970.

Prices and Production of Potatoes, 1968–70

SEASON	AVERAGE PRODUCTION IN CWT.	AVERAGE PRICE RECEIVED BY FARMERS, $/CWT.
Winter	3,765	2.09
Early Spring	5,154	2.48
Late Spring	20,977	2.71
Early Summer	13,483	2.73
Late Summer	29,790	2.07
Fall	237,391	1.90

Source: Data from U.S. Dept. of Agriculture, *Agricultural Prices, 1970 Annual Summary,* p. 22; *Crop Production,* July 9, 1971, p. A2, July 10, 1969, p. 2.

What we see here is obviously an *increase in supply* (rightward shift of the supply curve as in Figure 2.3) in the main Fall harvest season. Quantity is biggest, and price is lowest, in that season. It is perhaps surprising that the price variation is so small, given the enormous production swings over the year. The main reason is that potatoes are *stored* from harvest on. Therefore, price is still relatively low in the Winter season just after the Fall harvest, even though production is at a minimum in the Winter. As stored holdings are gradually consumed, price rises steadily over the year until the new crop begins to arrive in the Late Summer and Fall seasons.

The original source of agricultural supply variation over the year is the "outside" element of God-given seasonal climate. But note that the "inside" element of storage activity greatly modifies the force of the external factors. Other economic activities like improvements in transportation, changes in agricultural practices, and development of new seed varieties may also be at work to minimize the impact of seasonal variation of supply.

The supply of petroleum is relatively constant over the year, but there is substantial seasonal variation in demand. Gasoline purchases tend to be highest in the summer months, and of course heating oil is most required during the winter.

The first column of the table is an index of monthly consumption of heating oil during the period 1960–1966. (The index figure of 100 represents average consumption over the entire year.) A slight adjustment has been made in the data to account for the differing numbers of days in the months. The second column is a similar index of the monthly prices per gallon of heating oil at retail. Here an adjustment has been made in the data to eliminate the effect of continuing inflation, which tends to make all end-of-year prices higher than beginning-of-year prices.

EXAMPLE 2.3
HEATING OIL

Indexes of Retail Sales and Prices, Fuel Oil No. 2, In the United States, 1960–1966

MONTH	INDEX OF AVERAGE CONSUMPTION (MILLIONS OF BBLS, ADJUSTED FOR NUMBER OF DAYS IN MONTH)	INDEX OF AVERAGE PRICE (PER GALLON, RETAIL, ADJUSTED FOR INFLATION)
January	153	102.3
February	143	102.5
March	121	101.8
April	90	100.5
May	74	99.2
June	68	98.3
July	64	98.2
August	68	98.2
September	76	98.5
October	83	99.4
November	111	99.9
December	149	101.1

Source: Indexes calculated from data in American Petroleum Institute, *Petroleum Facts and Figures, 1971 Edition,* p. 452; U.S. Department of Commerce, *Survey of Current Business,* March 1961 through April 1967.

Consumption of fuel oil varies widely over the year, with December and January by far the highest months. Evidently, the demand curve is greatest (farthest to the right) in those months. Increased demand is also accompanied by higher prices, as would be expected. On the other hand, it is surprising that the price swings are so small. Here once again, the explanation is that storage over the year permits a build-up of stocks to meet the peak winter demand. As another factor in the situation, refineries in winter months can produce larger fractions of heating oil and smaller fractions of gasoline from their petroleum input, since demand for gasoline is less in those months. So a rightward shift of heating oil supply partially offsets the increase in demand. The storage feature is also reflected by the way the price index lags slightly behind the quantity index. In early winter, December is a high-consumption month, but price is still moderate because stocks tend to be ample. By February consumption has begun to decline; nevertheless, prices are high in February since inventories have been drawn down to their lowest levels.

EXAMPLE 2.4
BRIDES

Among the Sebei in Uganda, husbands obtain wives by purchase. The anthropologist Walter Goldschmidt secured data on bride-prices paid by husbands in two communities: the cattle-herding district of Kapsirika and the farming district of Sasur.

The Kapsirika herders pay higher prices for brides than the Sasur farmers, even though the herders are not generally wealthier. The rate of polygyny (plural wives) is also higher among the Kapsirika; their wife/husband ratio is 1.52, whereas among the Sasur farmers it is only 1.17.[4] There is a substantial intermarriage rate, but it takes entirely the form of herder husbands buying farmers' daughters. Thus, the herders' demand curve for brides seems to be higher; they pay more, and so they get more.

[4]Walter Goldschmidt, "The Brideprice of the Sebei," *Scientific American*, v. 229 (July 1973), pp. 74–85.

The "Brides" example shows how supply–demand analysis can be used to interpret changes over space or across communities as well as over time within a given community. In the example, the herders' demand curve for brides can be regarded as greater than (lying to the right of) the farmers' demand curve. The *source* of the difference might seem to be just the "outside" factor of differential preferences for brides on the part of the males in the two communities. An alternative explanation is that wives are better "productive assets" for herders than for farmers among the Sebei. One interesting question is why any bride-price difference persists: if Kapsirika herders and Sasur farmers compete to buy wives, why don't they end up paying about the same? The answer appears to be that intermarriage takes only the form of the Kapsirika "importing" wives; it seems that the "importers" must pay some kind of premium in order to overcome unwillingness of brides to move from one community to the other.

An outstanding instance of technological advance in recent decades has been the development of the computer. It is difficult to directly show changes in computer prices (actually, large computers are usually rented, so the "price" is an annual or monthly rental) over time because quality has improved so drastically. Gregory C. Chow developed an index for the quantity of *computing power* represented by the physical stock of computers in existence at any moment of time. Taking account of the improvements in quality variables like multiplication time, memory size, and access time, he expressed this quantity in terms of 1960 rental equivalents. Associating the quantity index with the current prices of computing power for each year led to the results shown in the table.

EXAMPLE 2.5
COMPUTING
POWER

Quantity and Price of Computing Power

YEAR	QUANTITY (THOUSANDS OF 1960 RENTALS)	ABSOLUTE PRICE INDEX
1954	370.26	3.2554
1955	991.67	2.9610
1956	2389.9	2.5336
1957	5087.6	2.3168
1958	8362.0	2.0342
1959	12549.	1.5884

1960	19072.	1.0716
1961	38264.	.9042
1962	64349.	.6873
1963	95815.	.5712
1964	136845.	.4186
1965	194136.	.3416

Source: Gregory C. Chow, "Technological Change and the Demand for Computers," *American Economic Review,* v. 57 (Dec. 1967), p. 1124.

Between 1954 and 1965 the quantity of computing power rose over fifty-fold, while the unit price fell to around 10.5% of its original level. Since the rise in the general price level due to inflation between 1954 and 1965 was some 20%, in real terms the fall in the price of computing power was even greater.

In the "Computing Power" example, technological advances brought about an increase in supply, a rightward shift of the supply curve, leading to an increase in quantity and fall in price. At the same time, business firms were in the process of learning about what computers could do, and so the demand curve was surely also shifting to the right. This makes the drastic reduction in price all the more remarkable, since the demand shift considered separately was placing *upward* pressure on price. The increase in supply due to technological advances in the computer industry was therefore the dominant element in the picture. Technological improvement is sometimes regarded as an "outside" source of variation. But in this case advances in computer power emerged for the most part in response to profit incentives—the conflicting efforts of firms to get ahead of the hot quality competition in the computer industry.

2.A.3
An Application: Effects of a Tax on Transactions

The familiar sales tax is an example of a tax on transactions. Consider what is sometimes called an "excise tax" levied upon *sellers,* in the form of a fixed dollar charge per unit of commodity exchanged, say, T per unit. The situation is portrayed in Figure 2.4 where, for simplicity, the supply and demand curves are all shown as straight lines. We can think of the tax as shifting the original supply curve SS *upward* (recall that an upward shift of the supply curve is *not* an "increase of supply") by the amount T, to the position $S'S'$. Why? The original SS curve specifies the number of units suppliers were willing to provide at any price P. They still must be paid the same *net* "supply price" if they are to supply the same number of units. But if the *net* price is P dollars along SS, the *gross* price per unit ("demand price") must be $P + T$ dollars along $S'S'$ if the tax is T per unit. Using the symbols P^+ for the gross price and P^- for the net price, we have:

$$P^+ = P^- + T$$

The new equilibrium quantity is determined by the intersection of the shifted supply curve $S'S'$ with the original demand curve DD. Evidently, the equilibrium

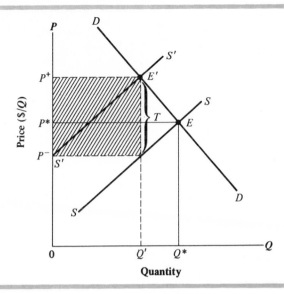

Figure 2.4

A Tax Upon Sales. A tax of $T per unit sold shifts the supply curve (*gross* of tax) upward to $S'S'$. The original SS is the *net* supply curve. The new equilibrium quantity Q' is less than the pre-tax equilibrium quantity Q^*. The equilibrium gross price P^+ (inclusive of tax) is higher than the pre-tax price P^*, but net price P^- (exclusive of tax) is lower than P^*.

quantity Q' bought and sold is less as a result of the tax. What about price? Carelessness can cause confusion here, because the new *gross* price P^+ is higher than the previous equilibrium P^*, but the new *net* price P^- is lower than P^*. One must state *which* price, gross or net, in asking whether price has risen or fallen.

PROPOSITION: A tax on transactions lowers the equilibrium quantity exchanged in the market. The new price *gross* of the tax (the demand price paid by buyers) is more than before; the new price *net* of the tax (the supply price received by sellers) is less than before.

It may seem arbitrary that our analysis here took the form of shifting the supply curve rather than the demand curve. This seems logical if the tax were, legally, levied upon sellers. What if it were levied on buyers instead? It is left for the student to determine, as an exercise, that a shift of the *demand curve* (downward from DD by the vertical distance T) would lead to exactly the same solution as before for quantity and for gross and net prices. So the supply–demand analysis leads to a possibly surprising conclusion: *It makes no difference whether a tax on transactions is formally levied upon buyers or upon sellers*.

We have seen that equilibrium in supply–demand analysis is found geometrically at the point of intersection of the supply curve and the demand curve. It is also useful for the student to be able to solve the equivalent problem algebraically. This is not at all difficult if the demand and supply curves are straight lines, as will be assumed here.

2.A.4
Algebra of Supply–Demand Analysis

Let the equation of the demand curve take the linear form $P = A - BQ_d$, where Q_d is the quantity demanded and A and B are positive constants. Geometrically, A corresponds to the intercept of the demand curve with the vertical price axis (the price so high that purchases are zero); $-B$ is the negative demand-curve slope. Let the supply-curve equation have the linear form $P = C + DQ_s$, where Q_s is the quantity supplied. Here the positive constant C is a vertical intercept (the minimum price below which positive amounts of the good will not be supplied), while the positive constant D represents the supply-curve slope. The condition of equilibrium is that the quantity demanded must equal the quantity supplied:

(2.1) $Q_s = Q_d$

We thus have a system of two simultaneous equations:

(2.2) $\begin{cases} P = A - BQ \\ P = C + DQ \end{cases}$

This is an easy algebraic problem, assumed to be within the capacity of the student to solve. (One way of solving is first to eliminate P by equating the right-hand sides of the two simultaneous equations, thus obtaining an explicit solution for Q in terms of the constants. This solution can then be substituted for Q in either equation to yield a result for P.)

As a numerical example, suppose that in a certain market the demand schedule is given by the linear equation $P = 300 - Q_d$ and the supply schedule by $P = 60 + 2 Q_s$. Thus, the numerical values for the constants in equation (2.2) are $A = 300, B = 1, C = 60$, and $D = 2$. The student should verify that the solution values for price and quantity are $P^* = 220$ and $Q^* = 80$.

More generally, equations (2.2) can be solved algebraically to yield the following expressions for the solution values:

(2.3) $Q_1^* = \dfrac{A - C}{B + D}, \quad P_1^* = \dfrac{AD + BC}{B + D}$

Substituting the numerical values in the example above for A, B, C, and D in these equations provides a check on the answers obtained for P and Q.

Now consider the comparative-statics problem of shifts in the determinants of equilibrium. From the algebraic point of view, we are dealing with "parametric change," i.e., shifts in the constants A, B, C, or D. An increase (rightward shift) in demand can take the form of an *increase* in the intercept A (this is an upward displacement of the demand curve as in Figure 2.2) or a *decrease* in the absolute magnitude of B (this would be a tilting about the vertical intercept making the curve more horizontal). Consider an increase in A, writing $A' = A + \Delta A$, where ΔA symbolizes a positive increment of A.

Then:

$$Q_2^* = \frac{A' - C}{B + D} = \frac{(A + \Delta A) - C}{B + D}$$

Since B and D and ΔA are all positive, Q_2^* is surely greater than Q_1^* in equation (2.3).

Also:

$$P_2^* = \frac{A'D + BC}{B + D} = \frac{(A + \Delta A)D + BC}{B + D}$$

Again, since B and D and ΔA are positive, P_2^* is surely greater than P_1^*.

An increase (a rightward shift) of supply can take the form of a *decrease* in the intercept C (a downward displacement of the curve) or a *decrease* in D (a tilting that makes the curve more horizontal). Let us consider here only the effect of a decrease in C, corresponding to the situation pictured in Fig. 2.3. We can write $C' = C + \Delta C$, where ΔC now represents a *negative* increment.

Then:

$$Q_3^* = \frac{A - C'}{B + D} = \frac{A - (C + \Delta C)}{B + D}$$

Since B and D are positive, but ΔC is negative, Q_3^* is surely greater than Q_1^*.

Also:

$$P_3^* = \frac{AD + BC'}{B + D} = \frac{AD + B(C + \Delta C)}{B + D}$$

Again, since B and D are both positive but ΔC is negative, P_3^* is surely *smaller* than P_1^*.

These results are consistent with those obtained via the verbal and diagrammatic analysis above. An increase in demand (rightward shift of the demand curve) raises both price and quantity; an increase in supply (rightward shift of the supply curve) raises quantity but lowers price.

What of the effect of an excise tax of T per unit, the situation pictured in Figure 2.4? We start once again with equations (2.2), but must now distinguish between the price *gross of tax* (P^+) and the price *net of tax* (P^-), using the relation $P^+ = P^- + T$. The consumers must of course pay the gross price, while the suppliers receive only the net price. Here we have three simultaneous equations:

$$\begin{cases} P^+ = A - BQ \\ P^- = C + DQ \\ P^+ = P^- + T \end{cases}$$

In Figure 2.4 the geometrical solution was found at the intersection of the demand curve with the supply curve, the latter having been shifted upward by the amount of the tax. This corresponds to re-writing the second equation in terms of P^+, making use of the third equation in doing so. The revised second (supply) equation becomes $P^+ = (C + T) + DQ$. Having reduced the three equations to two, we can use the usual algebraic procedures to obtain the solution values:

$$Q_4^* = \frac{A - (C + T)}{B + D}, \qquad P_4^+ = \frac{AD + B(C + T)}{B + D}, \qquad P_4^- = \frac{(A - T)D + BC}{B + D}$$

Since T is necessarily positive, Q_4^* is surely less than Q_1^* in the solution in equation (2.3)—the tax has reduced the volume of transactions. The new gross price P_4^+ is greater than and the new net price P_4^- is less than the old solution price P_1^*, thus confirming the geometrical result.

Continuing with the preceding numerical example, suppose a tax $T = 15$ were imposed. The student should be able to verify that the new solution values are $Q_4^* = 75$, $P_4^+ = 225$, $P_4^- = 210$.

2.A.5

Interferences with Equilibrium

Government policy, as in the case of a tax or a subsidy, may lead to a shift from one equilibrium position to another. The government may also, however, intervene directly in the functioning of markets. Government action may be directed to improving the perfection of the market process. For example, by providing a mechanism for the enforcement of private contracts through the judicial system, the state reduces or eliminates the need for individuals to make costly private enforcement arrangements. This facilitates the process whereby markets attain equilibrium.

Government interventions may, however, be designed to *prevent* markets from reaching equilibrium. It is not our purpose to make normative judgments as to the wisdom of such interventions. Rather, we seek only to show how the tool of supply–demand analysis enables the economist to understand and predict the consequences.

In the current inflationary period, we are all familiar with attempts to hold down inflation by "freezes" or other forms of maximum wage–price controls. In the deflationary period of the 1930s there were similar attempts to prevent a feared downward spiral of prices by *minimum* wage–price controls under the NRA (National Recovery Administration). The extent to which such "price ceilings" or "price floors" can actually cure a general inflation or a general deflation, as the case may be, remains a controversial issue in macroeconomics. We shall not be concerned with the macroeconomic problem, but only with the impacts of control policies upon particular markets.

Apart from the macroeconomic motivation, government may interfere with the equilibrium of markets in order to promote the interests of particular economic groups perceived as particularly deserving of aid (or, perhaps, merely as wielding enough political clout).

Figure 2.5 pictures a "meaningful" ceiling price P'. (To be meaningful, the ceiling must be *below* the equilibrium price P^*.) At the ceiling price, the quantity demanded Q_d' exceeds the quantity supplied Q_s', so there is upward pressure on

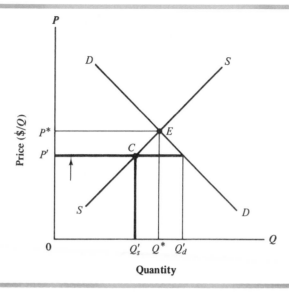

Figure 2.5

A Price Ceiling. Imposition of an effective price ceiling at the level $P' < P^*$ reduces the quantity traded from Q^* to Q'_s.

price, indicated by the upward-pointing arrow. However, the arrow is blocked by the fixed ceiling price P', which remains in effect regardless of the upward pressure. (We do not consider here the possibility of illegal trading at higher prices — black markets.)

What about the actual quantity traded? There is a fundamental maxim of markets, "It takes two to tango." That is, exchange requires willing buyers *and* willing sellers. At the fixed ceiling price P' the sellers are willing to offer only Q'_s. The buyers would be delighted to take this much and any larger quantity up to Q'_d, but they can only find trading partners to the extent of the smaller magnitude. Thus, the position denoted C is the actual price–quantity situation. So the effective price is lower than the unregulated equilibrium P^*, but the effective quantity is also lower than the equilibrium Q^*. This sometimes surprises students, as they expect the quantity traded to be some compromise between the larger quantity demanded Q'_d and the smaller quantity offered Q'_s. But the result is no compromise; *it is the smaller of the desired transaction magnitudes that governs.* This is emphasized in Figure 2.5 by the bold vertical drawn through the point C.

During and after World War II all the major belligerent powers were troubled by severe inflationary pressures. Wartime and postwar needs led to enormous government deficits, covered largely by increased monetary issues. And yet consumer prices were frozen at low ceiling levels. Since the necessities of life were scarce, there was strong upward pressure on prices.

EXAMPLE 2.6
REPRESSED
INFLATION
AND TREKKING

Indeed, often the absolutely minimal needs of life were not legitimately available. In postwar Germany, for example, the official daily ration at one point was down to the incredibly low figure of 1180 calories.

In these circumstances the curious institution of "trekking" developed in a number of different countries. City-dwellers would leave town for a day and scour the nearby countryside for food, making private black market deals with farmers or, indeed, often simply stealing. The more the governments succeeded in controlling prices in the legitimate means of food distribution, the more the abnormal system of trekking flourished. On one single day, it was reported, over 900,000 persons trekked from Tokyo into the countryside.[5] In Germany, the "Erhard reforms" of 1948 abolished price freezes and thus eliminated trekking. But a curious and unexpected consequence was a financial crisis for the State railroads. Shorthaul railroad passenger traffic dropped immediately to less than 40% of its pre-reform volume, evidencing the massive volume of trekking that had previously been going on.[6]

[5]Jerome B. Cohen, *Japan's Economy in War and Reconstruction* (Minneapolis: University of Minnesota Press, 1949), p. 378.

[6]Lucius D. Clay, *Decision in Germany* (Garden City, L.I.: Doubleday, 1950), p. 191.

A meaningful price *floor* is pictured in Figure 2.6. At the legal floor P'' the quantity offered by sellers Q_s'' exceeds the quantity desired by buyers Q_d''. There is downward pressure on price. Here the effective price is higher than the unregulated equilibrium P^*, but the effective quantity is again *lower* than the equilibrium Q^*, as indicated by the bold vertical drawn through the point F. Once more, "It takes two to tango." We see, therefore, that although price ceilings and price floors have opposite effects on price they have similar effects upon the real volume of transactions; *in either case, the quantity exchanged is less than in the unregulated market*. (Again, a kind of black market may come into existence, permitting the trading of somewhat larger quantities at illegally low prices.)

Floors hold up better when they are *supported*. The supply–demand analysis of supported floors shows results drastically different from those of unsupported floors. Support takes the form of a "buyer of last resort"—Uncle Sam in the case of agricultural price supports in the United States. Going back to Figure 2.6, private buyers are only willing to take Q_d'' at the high floor price P''. But now suppose the government as buyer of last resort is available as trading partner for unrequited suppliers. Then the latter *can* actually dispose of their supply-quantity Q_s''; the actual situation is represented by the position G in the diagram. There is no black market problem with a supported floor, as no supplier would let units of the good go for less than the floor price. Instead there is a "surplus" problem. The buyer of last resort finds himself accumulating larger and larger unwanted stocks of the supported community.

CONCLUSION: Meaningful ceilings hold down prices; meaningful floors keep them up. In either case, the quantity exchanged is *less* than in

Figure 2.6

A Price Floor. Imposition of an effective price floor at the level $P'' > P^*$ reduces the quantity traded from Q^* to Q_d''. However, if the floor is "supported" by government purchases, the amount Q_s'' will actually be supplied. The difference between Q_s'' and Q_d'' will be accumulated as a "surplus."

unregulated equilibrium. If, however, the floor is *supported*, quantity will be greater than equilibrium, but the "buyer of last resort" must accumulate inventories.

The U.S. government has attempted since the 1930s to maintain "parity" prices for agricultural products. "Parity" is interpreted to mean the relationship between agricultural and non-agricultural prices that obtained during the years 1910–14, a period of farm prosperity. Throughout the 1950s and 1960s the primary method employed to achieve parity was price support of farm products: a Federal agency called the Commodity Credit Corporation (CCC) stood always ready to buy any unsold fractions of supported crops at 90% of the parity price.

EXAMPLE 2.7
AGRICULTURAL
"PARITY" PRICES

The "surpluses" purchased by the CCC were for the most part kept in storage, the intention being to release them to the market in years of deficient crops. But as parity corresponded to an unusually favorable price relationship from the farmers' point of view, we might expect that in most years the government would have to purchase sizable shares of the supported crops. As indicated in the table, the CCC did purchase enormous amounts in the 1950s. By 1960 the CCC held in storage as much wheat as the entire 1960 crop (not to mention amounts that had previously been disposed of).

With the burden of maintaining such huge stores becoming increasingly intolerable, other methods were turned to. Food stamps and school lunch programs subsidized market demand. More important, under a system of acreage limitations farmers were paid *not* to produce. The consequent increase in demand and decrease in supply cooperated to raise the market prices received by farmers. In addition, the price support levels were adjusted downward. The table shows the resulting reduction of CCC purchases in the 1960s.

Yearly Acquisitions of Three Supported Crops by the Commodity Credit Corporation, Selected Years

| | MILLIONS OF BUSHELS | | |
	GRAIN SORGHUM	CORN	WHEAT
1953	40.9	422.3	486.1
54	110.1	250.6	391.6
55	92.6	408.9	276.7
56	32.5	477.4	148.4
57	279.5	268.1	193.5
58	258.0	266.6	511.0
1963	125.1	17.9	85.1
64	66.8	29.1	86.9
65	85.0	11.2	17.4
66	0.3	12.4	12.4
67	9.1	191.0	90.0
68	13.7	34.4	182.9

Source: Commodity Credit Corporation Charts, Nov. 1972, pp. 49, 75, 115.

2.B

THE RELATIONS AMONG TOTAL, AVERAGE, AND MARGINAL MAGNITUDES

Supply–demand analysis, as just discussed in Section 2.A, represents the main tool employed for the solution of *equilibrium* problems. The other major category of economic problems is *optimization,* where an economic agent seeks a best situation or outcome over the range of choice available. As mentioned in Chapter 1, economists have devised a process of solving optimization questions that does the work of the mathematical calculus without requiring any formal knowledge of calculus techniques. The key to this process is understanding the relationships among total, average, and marginal magnitudes.

It is important to appreciate that these relations are ones of fundamental logic. The principles remain the same, regardless of whether we are thinking of Total, Average, and Marginal *Cost* or of Total, Average, and Marginal *Revenue* or of Total, Average, and Marginal *Utility* (to mention only a few of the variables to which these concepts will be applied in the pages to come). The purpose of this section is to illustrate and review these general logical principles.

Consider Figure 2.7, which represents an assumed straight-line market de-

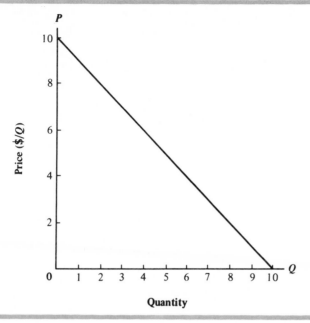

Figure 2.7
A Demand Curve. The demand curve, which shows price as a function of quantity, can also be regarded as an Average Revenue curve, since $P \equiv R/Q \equiv AR$.

mand curve for some good. Hypothetical data underlying this demand curve are tabulated in the first two columns of Table 2.1, representing Quantity (Q) and Price (P) of the good, respectively.

If we multiply Price times Quantity, we obtain definitionally the magnitude economists call Total Revenue or sometimes simply Revenue (R). Thus:[7]

(2.4) $R \equiv PQ$

Total Revenue is tabulated in the third column of Table 2.1, and the corresponding data are plotted in the upper diagram of Figure 2.8.

Revenue R is a *total* magnitude or function of Quantity. And Price P can be regarded as an *average* magnitude. In Table 2.1, for example, at quantity $Q = 2$ Total Revenue R equals 16. If we ask what is the Average Revenue received per unit of quantity when $Q = 2$, the answer is obviously 8, which is, of course, nothing but the price along the demand curve associated with that quantity. Formally, equation (2.5) defining Average Revenue (AR) follows immediately from equation (2.4):

(2.5) $AR \equiv P \equiv \dfrac{R}{Q}$

[7]The triple equality sign $\equiv$ represents *mathematical identity*. This symbol will be used in the text where it is desired to emphasize that both sides of the equality are definitionally equivalent.

Table 2.1
Total, Average, and Marginal Revenue

QUANTITY	PRICE—OR AVERAGE REVENUE (P OR AR)	TOTAL REVENUE (R)	MARGINAL REVENUE— BETTER APPROXIMATION (MR)	MARGINAL REVENUE POORER— APPROXIMATION (MR)
0	10	0	(10)	—
			9	
1	9	9	(8)	9
			7	
2	8	16	(6)	7
			5	
3	7	21	(4)	5
			3	
4	6	24	(2)	3
			1	
5	5	25	(0)	1
			−1	
6	4	24	(−2)	−1
			−3	
7	3	21	(−4)	−3
			−5	
8	2	16	(−6)	−5
			−7	
9	1	9	(−8)	−7
			−9	
10	0	0	(−10)	−9

Dimensionally, Price is measured in terms of *dollars per unit quantity* ($/Q$), whereas Revenue is simply scaled in dollars.

To understand the geometrical relation between total and average magnitudes, it is best to take the *total* measure as the fundamental or primitive concept. In the upper diagram of Figure 2.8, for any level of Q, say $Q = 4$, consider the line from the origin to the curve. The slope of this line is the ratio R/Q—the height R reached along the curve, divided by the horizontal length represented by the distance Q. By equation (2.5), R/Q equals Price P or Average Revenue AR. Numerically, at $Q = 4$ we have $AR = 24/4 = 6$. Consequently, in the lower diagram of Figure 2.8 the Average Revenue AR at $Q = 4$ is shown as equal to 6. By repeating the procedure for all levels of Q, the entire AR curve in the lower diagram can be derived. (*Warning*: The vertical axis of the upper or "total" diagram is scaled in terms of R—in dollars. The vertical axis of the lower diagram is scaled in terms of R/Q—dollars *per unit of quantity*. Total and average magnitudes should never be plotted in the same diagram, since the dimensionality conflicts. Confusion is almost certain to result when this warning is overlooked.)

For the particular data assumed in Table 2.1, the Average Revenue AR is declining throughout (negatively sloped demand curve). Geometrically, we can see that AR must be falling since, in the "total" diagram of Figure 2.8, the slope of the line connecting the origin to points on the Total Revenue curve diminishes in moving to the right along the humped shape of the function.

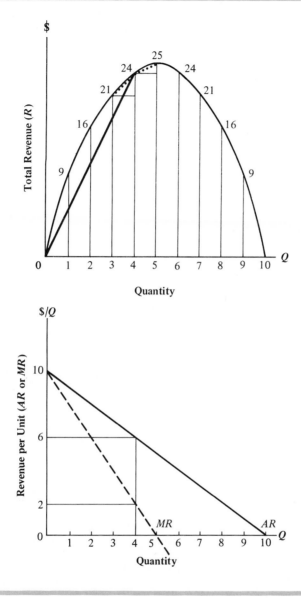

Figure 2.8

Derivation of Average and Marginal Magnitudes from Total Function: Revenue. The upper diagram illustrates the derivation of the magnitudes of AR and MR when $Q = 4$ and $R = 24$. The height of the AR curve in the lower diagram at $Q = 4$ corresponds to the slope of the bold line in the upper diagram, so that $AR = 24/4 = 6$. The height of the MR curve in the lower diagram equals the slope *along* the R function in the upper diagram. At $Q = 4$, it is found by averaging the slopes of the dotted hypotenuses of the two small triangles. Thus $MR = \frac{1}{2} [(25 - 24) + (24 - 21)] = 2$.

Actually, as can be determined from Figure 2.7, the demand curve or *AR* function implied by the given data has the specific algebraic form:

$$P = 10 - Q$$

Since $R = PQ$, the Total Revenue curve satisfies the equation:

$$R = (10 - Q)Q = 10Q - Q^2$$

So much for the connection between average and total magnitudes. The *marginal* function is akin to the average function in that both are measured, geometrically, in terms of slopes derived from a total magnitude. Consequently, marginal and average curves are scaled in the same dimensions (dollars per unit of quantity) and can, without danger of confusion, be plotted in the same diagram. The difference between average and marginal concepts is the following: the *average* function *AR* corresponds to the slope of a line connecting the origin to positions *on* the Total Revenue curve *R*; the *marginal* function *MR*, on the other hand, is defined geometrically as the slope *along* the curve *R* itself.

To approximate the slope along the curve at $Q = 4$, first consider what happens when Q increases by one unit (notationally, $\Delta Q = 1$) from $Q = 4$. The corresponding small vertical change in R is denoted ΔR. The ΔQ and ΔR so obtained are the horizontal and vertical legs of the small triangle shown between $Q = 4$ and $Q = 5$ in the upper diagram of Figure 2.8. The desired slope along the curve at $Q = 4$ is approximated by the slope $\Delta R/\Delta Q$ of the hypotenuse of this small triangle (dotted in the diagram). Numerically, this slope is $\Delta R/\Delta Q = (25 - 24)/1 = 1$. But this slope upward of $Q = 4$ is only an approximation of what we want, which is the Marginal Revenue or exact slope of the Revenue curve *at* $Q = 4$. And it may not be a very good approximation. (In Table 2.1, the *MR* figures derived in this way are tabulated in the last column under the heading "Marginal Revenue—Poorer Approximation.")

What is almost always a better approximation of the *MR* at $Q = 4$ is to take a simple average of two slopes: the one just described between $Q = 4$ and $Q = 5$ (for an upward variation ΔQ) and the one between $Q = 3$ and $Q = 4$ (for a downward variation ΔQ). Geometrically, this is the average of the slopes of the dotted hypotenuses of the two small triangles in the upper diagram of Figure 2.8. The upward variation, as we have seen, implied an *MR* estimate $\Delta R/\Delta Q = 1$. The downward variation leads to the *MR* estimate $\Delta R/\Delta Q = (24 - 21)/1 = 3$. The average is therefore $MR = 2$, which is the figure shown in Table 2.1 in the column headed "Marginal Revenue—Better Approximation." (The figures for integer values of Q, found by an averaging process as just described, are those shown within parentheses in Table 2.1.)

Even the "better approximation" will not in general be precisely correct. However, when (as in this numerical example) the underlying demand curve is linear, it can be shown mathematically that the "better approximation" will indeed be perfect. So $MR = 2$ is the *true* Marginal Revenue at $Q = 4$. More generally, the degree to which the slope represented by the hypotenuse of any small triangle (as in the upper diagram of Figure 2.8), for an upward or downward variation ΔQ, approximates the exact slope along the Total Revenue curve itself (the latter being the true Marginal Revenue) can be improved by taking a smaller and smaller variation ΔQ. This leads to the formal definition of Marginal Revenue as:

$$(2.6) \qquad MR \equiv \lim_{(\text{as } \Delta Q \to 0)} \frac{\Delta R}{\Delta Q}$$

Even though the denominator ΔQ approaches zero in the limiting process, it will in general be the case that the ratio of ΔR to ΔQ approaches some definite number, which is the slope *along* the curve. This ratio is known as the *derivative* in the calculus.[8] In this book we will however think of Marginal Revenue as the ratio of small finite differences (symbolized as $\Delta R/\Delta Q$), which is not quite exact but generally close enough if the "better approximation" is used.

So long as the Total Revenue R is rising as Q increases, it is obvious from Figure 2.8 that the slope along the R curve must be positive; hence the Marginal Revenue MR exceeds zero. When R is decreasing in the region past the hump in the upper diagram of Figure 2.8, however, the slope along the curve and therefore the MR must be negative. Thus we have the following geometrical relations between total and marginal functions:

PROPOSITION 2.1a: *When a total function or magnitude is rising, the corresponding marginal function or magnitude is positive.*

PROPOSITION 2.1b: *When a total magnitude is falling, the corresponding marginal magnitude is negative.*

But when R reaches a maximum it is neither increasing nor decreasing, i.e., it is level. Drawing the obvious inference, we have:

PROPOSITION 2.1c: *When a total magnitude reaches a maximum or a minimum, the corresponding marginal magnitude is zero.*[9]

While the example above applied to a maximum situation, at a *minimum* along any total function the total curve would again be level, so that the corresponding marginal measure would again be zero.[10]

---

[8]*Mathematical Footnote*: Marginal Revenue as a derivative is symbolized dR/dQ and defined as:

$$MR \equiv \frac{dR}{dQ} \equiv \lim_{\Delta Q \to 0} \frac{\Delta R}{\Delta Q}$$

[9]*Mathematical Footnote:* When $dR/dQ > 0$, the Total Revenue function R is increasing; when $dR/dQ < 0$ it is decreasing; and when $dR/dQ = 0$, we have a stationary value of the function, in this case, a maximum.

[10]Some technical qualifications should be made to these assertions. Not all minima or maxima are "flat." In the upper diagram of Figure 2.8, Total Revenue R has an interior maximum at $Q = 5$, for which $MR = 0$. But it also has minima at $Q = 0$ and $Q = 10$ (since revenue R can never be less than zero). But the curve is not flat at those points. In this book we will be dealing almost always with flat minima or maxima, so that Proposition 2.1c holds.

Verifying in Table 2.1, we see that at $Q = 4$ (where the Total Revenue function R is rising), $MR = 2$ is positive. At $Q = 8$, R is in its falling range and $MR = -6$ is negative. Where does the Total Revenue function reach a maximum? In the upper diagram of Figure 2.8, we see that the true maximum of $R = 25$ is reached at $Q = 5$.[11] This is correctly indicated by the figure $MR = 0$ shown in parentheses for $Q = 5$ in the "better approximation" column. Note that the "poorer approximation" column incorrectly suggests that MR equals zero at $Q = 5\frac{1}{2}$, where the Total Revenue function is already beyond its maximum.

In the lower diagram in Figure 2.8, we also see a geometrical relation between average and marginal functions:

PROPOSITION 2.2a: *When the average magnitude is falling, the marginal magnitude must lie below it.*

This can be intuitively appreciated: If adding one more unit to a previous collection reduces the average of some measure, the additional unit or newcomer must have been below average. In Figure 2.8 the Average Revenue AR is always falling, hence the Marginal Revenue MR lies always below it.

EXAMPLE 2.8
BIRDS DO IT!

Critics of academic economics often argue that the theoretical reasoning required to solve optimization problems involves concepts too subtle to be employed in actual decision-making. The *marginal* concept has been an object of particular attack; it has been contended, for example, that businessmen can hardly be expected to compute and employ marginal concepts of revenue or cost in choosing price or output.

Biologists, in contrast, have recently discovered that the adaptive decisions of animals can often be best interpreted in marginal terms. Consider a bird foraging for seeds or insects that are distributed in patches over the environment. The bird must decide when to leave its current patch and fly off to look for another. As it continues to exploit the current patch, food becomes sparser and sparser there—the marginal "revenue" (energy intake) the bird receives per unit of time spent is falling. But if the bird abandons its current patch, it must suffer an entire loss of energy intake in the dead time before it locates a fresh patch. Bioeconomic reasoning in this situation says that the bird should continue to exploit its current patch until the *marginal* "revenue" per unit of time spent there falls to equality with the *average* "revenue" it can attain overall, allowing for the dead time between patches.[12]

Field studies have tended to confirm that foraging birds do indeed behave as if they can solve this economic problem. Under more controlled labora-

[12]Eric L. Charnov, "Optimal Foraging, the Marginal Value Theorem," *Theoretical Population Biology*, v. 9 (April 1976).

[11]*Mathematical Footnote*: If $R = 10Q - Q^2$, then $dR/dQ = 10 - 2Q$. Setting $dR/dQ = 0$ (first-order condition for a maximum), we have $Q = 5$.

What if the average magnitude is not falling but rising? Then we have the analogous proposition:

PROPOSITION 2.2b: *When the average magnitude is rising, the marginal magnitude must lie above it.*

And, of course, Propositions 2.2a and 2.2b together imply:

PROPOSITION 2.2c: *When an average magnitude is neither rising nor falling* (at a minimum or maximum, or other stationary point), *the marginal magnitude must be equal to it.*[14]

Figure 2.8 illustrates only the relation of Proposition 2.2a, since the average magnitude (Average Revenue AR) is a declining function of Q throughout (negatively sloped demand curve). To illustrate Propositions 2.2b and 2.2c as well, we will need a total function that generates also rising and level ranges of the corresponding average magnitude. Figure 2.9 shows, in the upper diagram, a different total function to be frequently employed in this book: a firm's Total Cost C as a function of Quantity Q. Unlike the Total Revenue function R of Figure 2.8, Total Cost C is positive even for $Q = 0$, and rises throughout. The initial positive intercept of the C function is called the "fixed cost." This fixed positive quantity dictates that, at $Q = 0$, the average cost $AC \equiv C/Q$ is infinite. But using the technique of determining AC as the slope of a line connecting the origin with a point along the curve, we can see that as Q increases this slope will first fall (become flatter) but then rise (become steeper). Hence in the lower diagram of Figure 2.9 the AC curve has at first a declining, and then a rising range—so that it must have a minimum in between. The MC curve is of course below AC in the latter's declining range, and above AC in the latter's rising range. Therefore, MC must cut AC at the latter's minimum as asserted in Proposition 2.2c. Note also that the minimum of the MC curve in the lower diagram corresponds to where the

[14]*Mathematical Footnote:* Let us verify Proposition 2.2a of the text, and specifically that MR is below AR when the latter is falling (a declining function of Q). For AR to be falling:

$$0 > \frac{d(AR)}{dQ} = \frac{d(R/Q)}{dQ} = \frac{Q(dR/dQ) - R}{Q^2}$$

This directly implies $dR/dQ < R/Q$, or $MR < AR$. Similar proofs for Propositions 2.2b and 2.2c can easily be shown.

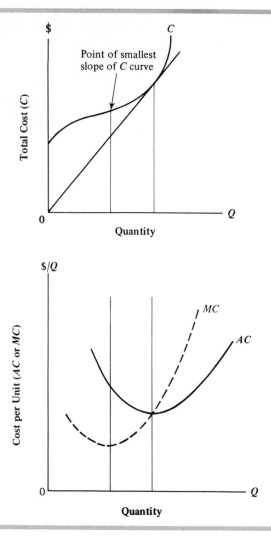

Figure 2.9

Derivation of Average and Marginal Magnitudes from Total Function: Cost. The lower diagram sketches the average and marginal functions AC and MC derived from the Total Cost function C in the upper diagram. Where the slope along the Total Cost function is least, MC is at a minimum. Where the slope of the line drawn from the origin to the curve is least (bold tangent line in the upper diagram), AC is at a minimum. Where AC is falling MC lies below it; where AC is rising, MC lies above it.

slope *along* the C curve is least in the upper diagram; the minimum of the AC curve in the lower diagram corresponds to where the slope of a line drawn from the origin *to* points on the C curve is least in the upper diagram (bold tangent out of origin).

Beginning in 1973 the Organization of Petroleum Exporting Countries (OPEC) was able to effect a startling increase in the world price of crude oil from about $2 to almost $14 per barrel (see the example, "The OPEC," in Chapter 11 below). The United States government, concerned about its balance of payments, immediately began efforts to reduce oil imports. But another aspect of the situation was that the enormous jump in the world price of crude, if allowed to become effective in domestic transactions, would have led to huge profits for American producers of crude oil. United States policy-makers, regarding such profits as inequitable, also wanted to eliminate such "windfall" gains. Unfortunately, the way chosen[15] to achieve the second objective tended to defeat the first, because of the impact upon crude-oil importers' calculations of marginal and average costs.

EXAMPLE 2.9
THE OIL
ENTITLEMENTS
PROGRAM

To prevent domestic producers from reaping windfall gains, the U.S. government froze the price of domestic crude. This immediately caused a problem, because some refiners did and others did not have access to the limited supply of artificially cheap domestic crude. Again in the interests of "equity," the Entitlements Program was undertaken. The basic idea was that every refiner was entitled to buy, at the low frozen price, the nationwide average fraction of cheap domestic oil. This program forced those refiners having more-than-average access to cheap domestic crude to make payments so as to compensate those refiners making more-than-average use of expensive imported crude. The unanticipated effect was to *encourage* rather than discourage imports.

From the point of view of the nation as a whole, the Marginal Cost of crude oil was a rising function, the highest-cost step being the imported crude at $14 per barrel. Had refiners using imported crude been required to pay this full world price, there would have been an incentive to reduce imports. But, under the Entitlements Program, each barrel imported entitled the importer to a great bargain: a certain amount of domestic crude at the cheap frozen price. In effect, all refiners were "equitably" treated by being able to obtain crude at the nation-wide Average Cost, no matter what their source of crude. But, as a result, no refiners were discouraged from using imported crude even though that represented the highest Marginal Cost for the nation as a whole.[16]

---

[15]This is necessarily a very simplified discussion of the enormously complicated and ever-changing details of U.S. oil policy. In particular the legal distinction between so-called "new domestic oil" and "old domestic oil" has been omitted here.

[16]Many discussions of the oil entitlements program are available. See, for example, C. E. Phelps and R. T. Smith, *Petroleum Regulation: The False Dilemma of Decontrol* (Santa Monica, Calif.: The RAND Corporation, 1977).

The unintended effects of government policy illustrated in the preceding example may have stemmed from a failure to distinguish properly between Average and Marginal Cost. Confusion may sometimes exist between marginal and total concepts, as indicated below.

EXAMPLE 2.10
TAXES

The table below shows the personal income tax schedule for single taxpayers in the tax year 1978. For any "Taxable Income"[17] bracket on the lefthand side of the table, the righthand side shows the Total Tax at the bottom of the bracket and the Marginal Tax for increments of income within the bracket. In the $20,200–22,200 income bracket, for example, the Tax Due is stated as $4510 + 36%. Therefore, $4510 is the Total Tax for someone earning exactly $20,200, and $.36 (or 36 cents) is the Marginal Tax per dollar of income thereafter (up to the top of the bracket).

The following fallacy is sometimes encountered. An employee is making an annual income of $20,199 and paying a Total Tax just under $4510. His employer offers him a raise of $1000, which the worker refuses on the ground that it would put him in a higher tax bracket. The worker may think that, in moving up to a higher *marginal* tax rate (36% instead of 34%) he will be taxed more heavily on his $20,199 in addition to whatever tax he must pay on the $1000 raise. This is incorrect. The worker's additional tax would be a trifle under 36% of $1000, or $360. Had he accepted the raise he would be better off by $1000 − $360. His net loss of $640 is one of the costs of being unable to comprehend the marginal concept of economics.

TAXABLE INCOME		TAX DUE	
OVER	BUT NOT OVER	AMOUNT	OF EXCESS OVER
$2,200	$2,700	$0+14%	$2,200
$2,700	$3,200	$70+15%	$2,700
$3,200	$3,700	$145+16%	$3,200
$3,700	$4,200	$225+17%	$3,700
$4,200	$6,200	$310+19%	$4,200
$6,200	$8,200	$690+21%	$6,200
$8,200	$10,200	$1,110+24%	$8,200
$10,200	$12,200	$1,590+25%	$10,200
$12,200	$14,200	$2,090+27%	$12,200
$14,200	$16,200	$2,630+29%	$14,200
$16,200	$18,200	$3,210+31%	$16,200
$18,200	$20,200	$3,830+34%	$18,200
$20,200	$22,200	$4,510+36%	$20,200
$22,200	$24,200	$5,230+38%	$22,200
$24,200	$28,200	$5,990+40%	$24,200
$28,200	$34,200	$7,590+45%	$28,200
$34,200	$40,200	$10,290+50%	$34,200
$40,200	$46,200	$13,290+55%	$40,200
$46,200	$52,200	$16,590+60%	$46,200
$52,200	$62,200	$20,190+62%	$52,200
$62,200	$72,200	$26,390+64%	$62,200
$72,200	$82,200	$32,790+66%	$72,200
$82,200	$92,200	$39,390+68%	$82,200
$92,200	$102,200	$46,190+69%	$92,200
$102,200	———.	$53,090+70%	$102,200

Source: *1978 Federal Income Tax Forms,* Department of the Treasury, Internal Revenue Service, p. 41.

[17]"Taxable Income" is earned income minus the amount of exemptions, deductions, etc., as provided in the tax law.

54

This chapter covers two main topics: supply–demand analysis, and the relations among total, average, and marginal magnitudes.

Supply–demand analysis is the main working tool for solving problems of *equilibrium*. Equilibrium price and quantity are determined by the intersection of a supply curve and a demand curve. Changes in demand and supply are represented by shifts in the positions or shapes of one or both of these curves. An increase in demand (rightward shift of the demand curve) raises both equilibrium price and equilibrium quantity in the market; an increase in supply (rightward shift of the supply curve) raises equilibrium quantity but lowers equilibrium price. A tax on transactions will reduce the quantity exchanged; it raises the *gross price* (the price paid by buyers) but lowers the *net price* (price received by sellers). Price ceilings or floors, if effective, prevent markets from reaching equilibrium. In such cases the quantity exchanged is always the *smaller* of the differing amounts demanded and supplied—except in the case of a *supported* price floor.

The relations among total, average, and marginal magnitudes are essential for understanding problems of *optimization*. Regardless of the variable involved (whether Revenue, or Cost, or Utility, or other), the marginal magnitude is positive, zero, or negative depending on whether the total magnitude is rising, level, or falling. And the marginal magnitude is below, equal to, or above the average magnitude depending on whether the latter is falling, level, or rising.

QUESTIONS FOR CHAPTER 2

Mainly for Review

R1. Supply–demand analysis is the key tool for which of the two main analytical techniques of economics? For what class of problem is the relation among total, average, and marginal quantities the key tool?

*R2. In what sense is price a "ratio of quantities"?

R3. Explain why market equilibrium is determined by the *intersection* of the supply curve and the demand curve.

R4. How does an "increase in demand" shift the demand curve? How does an "increase in supply" shift the supply curve? Do the effects upon equilibrium price and equilibrium quantity go in the same direction in the case of an increase in demand? In the case of an increase in supply?

*R5. In the analysis of a $T per unit tax described in the text, the supply curve was shifted upward by $T to find the new equilibrium. Would the same result have been achieved if instead the demand curve were shifted downward by $T? Explain.

*R6. In each of the following cases, state whether an excise tax will raise the (gross) price *paid* by consumers, or lower the (net) price *received* by sellers, or both.
  a. Supply curve upward-sloping, demand curve downward-sloping.
  b. Supply curve horizontal, demand curve downward-sloping.

*The answers to asterisked questions appear at the end of the book.

c. Supply curve vertical, demand curve downward-sloping.

d. Supply curve vertical, demand curve horizontal.

R7. Suppose that an $S per unit *subsidy* upon sales of a particular commodity is put into effect. What would the implications be for the quantity exchanged? For the gross and the net price?

*R8. What is a "meaningful" price ceiling or price floor? Why is it that meaningful floors and meaningful ceilings both *decrease* the quantity traded? What happens, however, if a price floor is "supported"?

R9. Starting from a given Total Revenue function R, show how the Average Revenue function AR is derived. Show how the Marginal Revenue function MR is derived.

R10. Starting from a given Total Cost function C, show how the Average Cost function AC and the Marginal Cost function MC are derived.

*R11. In terms of the general relations among total, average, and marginal quantities, which of the following statements are necessarily true, and which are not:

a. When the total function is rising, the marginal function is rising.

b. When the total function is rising, the marginal function is positive.

c. When the total function is rising, the marginal function lies above it.

d. When the marginal function is rising, the average function is also rising.

e. When the average function is falling, the marginal function lies below it.

f. When the marginal function is neither rising nor falling, the average function is constant.

*R12. For a Total Revenue function given at integer quantities as in Table 2.1, explain the nature of the "better approximation" of Marginal Revenue that provides a greater degree of accuracy.

For Further Thought and Discussion

*T1. For a particular commodity, suppose that the supply curve is very steep (positively sloped, but almost vertical). Would a $T tax tend to have a relatively large or a relatively small effect on quantity exchanged in the market? Would there tend to be a relatively large or a relatively small effect on the gross price paid by buyers? Upon the net price received by sellers? In terms of the underlying economic meaning, why would these consequences be anticipated if a tax were imposed upon a commodity with a steeply rising supply curve?

T2. Analyze correspondingly the case where the *demand* curve is very steep (negatively sloped, but almost vertical).

*T3. If the price of gasoline rises as a result of a reduction in petroleum supplies, what effect would you anticipate upon the price of automobiles? Upon the relative price of small, light cars versus large, heavy cars?

*T4. What assumptions underlie "the method of comparative statics"? Will these assumptions ever be met in the real world?

T5. During World War II in Great Britain, a ceiling was imposed to hold down the market price of bread. Explain why there was upward pressure upon the price of bread. What consequences of the upward pressure would you anticipate, given continuing enforcement of the ceiling? To help reduce this upward pressure, the British government took fresh bread off the market—all bread sold had to be at least one day old. Would you expect this regulation to achieve the desired effect?

*T6. In the year 302 A.D., the Roman emperor Diocletian "commanded that there should be cheapness." His edict declared:

> Unprincipled greed appears wherever our armies, following the commands of the public weal, march, not only in villages and cities but also upon all highways, with the result that prices of foodstuffs mount not only fourfold and eightfold, but transcend all measure. Our law shall fix a measure and a limit to this greed.

Why do you think Diocletian found food prices higher wherever he marched with his armies? What result would you anticipate from the command that "there should be cheapness"?

*T7. From the tax-schedule data in the text, graph the Total Tax ("tax due") as a function of Taxable Income in the range from $0 to $10,000 of income. Also graph the corresponding Average Tax and Marginal Tax functions. Note that Average Tax and Marginal Tax are percentages. Why?

PART TWO
Preference, Consumption, and Demand

3.A THE DECISION PROBLEM OF THE INDIVIDUAL, 62

3.B LAWS OF PREFERENCE, 63

3.C UTILITY, PREFERENCE, AND RATIONAL CHOICE, 66

3.D UTILITY: CARDINAL OR ORDINAL MAGNITUDE? 67
    3.D.1   Cardinal Magnitudes, 67
    3.D.2   Utility of Commodity Baskets, 71

3.E CHARACTERISTICS OF INDIFFERENCE CURVES FOR GOODS, 74

3.F GOODS, BADS, AND NEUTERS, 78
    3.F.1   An Application of Utility Theory: The Economics of Charity, 81

3.G THE SOURCES AND CONTENT OF PREFERENCES, 83

Examples
    3.1   TRANSITIVITY AND AGE, 64
    3.2   DOES MONEY BUY HAPPINESS? 69
    3.3   THE WEBER-FECHNER LAW, 70
    3.4   PREFERENCES FOR CHILDREN—NUMBER AND SEX, 77
    3.5   BALL-POINT PENS AND FRENCH PASTRIES, 79

UTILITY AND PREFERENCE

Core Chapter

The two basic techniques of analysis over which the student must gain command are *optimization* and *determination of equilibrium*. Here in Part Two, which covers the topics of Preference, Consumption, and Demand, we will concentrate upon the optimization problem of the consumer as decision-making agent.

3.A

THE DECISION PROBLEM OF THE INDIVIDUAL

As the circular flow of economic activity that was pictured in Figure 1.1 shows, the economic problem of the individual is two-fold. Facing the product market as a demander, everyone must decide how to spend his or her income on consumable goods and services. (A person can also save, as will be explained more fully in Chapter 16; however, saving is to be regarded as an indirect purchase of *future* consumable goods.) But a consumer's income does not come down from heaven like manna; it must be *earned*, an activity that also involves a decision-making process. Facing the factor market as a supplier, each person must decide what employments to accept for the resources (labor power, rental property, etc.) that he or she owns. The earnings obtained from such employment become the income for making consumptive choices.

In Part Two, however, we will limit ourselves to the individual as consumer, taking as given the income resulting from whatever decisions may have been made as resource-owner. But it should be kept in mind that in *both* of these aspects, consumer and resource-owner, the rational individual will be optimizing—attempting to make the decision that is best in terms of his or her existing tastes and preferences.

The economist finds it convenient to describe this optimization process as the *maximization of utility*. Utility as a hypothetical magnitude serving as an index for preference will be the central topic of this chapter.

3.B

LAWS OF PREFERENCE

Scientific analysis involves the construction of theories or models which are always, at best, simplified pictures of reality. They can be regarded as idealizations in which irrelevant or unsystematic peculiarities are stripped away to permit concentration upon the dominant features of the situation for the purpose at hand. Such an idealized picture of the individual's preferences for alternative bundles or baskets of consumptive commodities is presented here.

We postulate that the individual's preferences follow two laws:

1. AXIOM OF COMPARISON.   *Any two distinct baskets A and B of commodities can be compared in preference by the individual. Each such comparison must lead to one of the three following results: (i) Basket A is preferred to basket B, or (ii) B is preferred to A, or (iii) A and B are indifferent.*

The Axiom of Comparison is an idealization of reality, in that we suppose that the individual never says "I simply can't compare A and B." Nor is he supposed ever to say "Two-thirds of the time I prefer A, but the other one-third of the time B."[1]

2. AXIOM OF TRANSITIVITY.   *Consider any three baskets A, B, and C. If A is preferred to B, and B is preferred to C, then A must be preferred to C. Similarly, if A is indifferent to B, and B to C, then A is indifferent to C.*

The Axiom of Transitivity is also an idealization, for violations of it no doubt take place. But if an individual were to tell you, "I prefer Apples to Bananas and Bananas to Cherries," and were then to add, "But I'll always take Cherries over Apples!" you'd surely be inclined to regard that person as odd.

Chapter 3
UTILITY AND
PREFERENCE

---

[1]More advanced studies in economics have constructed models of preference that allow for limited or probabilistic comparisons.

EXAMPLE 3.1
TRANSITIVITY
AND AGE

Arnold A. Weinstein administered a questionnaire to experimental subjects asking them for preference rankings over ten commodity bundles, offered as pairs in random order. Among the bundles, all having a market value of around $3 at the time, were items such as: (1) $3 in cash; (2) the three latest Beatles 45-rpm phonograph records; (3) three men's clip-on bow ties, all with red polka dots, one brown, one blue, one gray; (4) a brush-stroke print of El Greco's "View of Toledo"; (5) a vanilla malted milk (two glasses) per day for ten days; and so forth.

The intent of the experiment was to detect possible intransitivities of preference over *triads* of offerings, in the course of the subjects' successive *pairwise* comparisons. An intransitivity would occur if, for example, a particular subject were observed to choose cash over malted milk, malted milk over bow ties, but bow ties over cash. The great majority of the triads showed consistent transitive preferences. An interesting result obtained was that transitivity tended to increase with age, as indicated in the table:

Transitivity Experiment Results

GROUP	PROPORTION OF TRANSITIVE RESPONSES
52 children aged 9–12	79.2%
36 teenagers aged 14–16	83.3
46 high-school seniors aged 17–18	88.0
18 mature adults (mostly teachers)	93.5

Source: Table compiled from data reported in Arnold A. Weinstein, "Transitivity of Preference: A Comparison among Age Groups," *Journal of Political Economy,* v. 76 (March/April 1968), p. 310.

The experimenter's interpretation was that consistency in preference ordering is an acquired skill, hence more difficult for younger people to achieve. More arguably, he concluded that his results lent some support for the legal restrictions and protections placed on youth in our society.

COMMENT: As an alternative explanation, younger persons are more likely to engage in choices that seem inconsistent only because they are really *exploratory* in nature. "Don't knock it until you've tried it" is a dangerous maxim, but one with some appeal. If *all* possibilities are to be tried at least once, some seeming intransitivities of choice are inevitable. Consider the three possibilities: cash, malted milk, and bow ties. If cash is chosen over malted milk and malted milk over bow ties, the only way to try out the bow ties is to choose them when offered next—even over cash. So the Laws of Preference presume an already well-settled pattern of consumer desires.

The Axiom of Comparison and the Axiom of Transitivity taken together lead to the:

PROPOSITION OF RANK ORDERING OF PREFERENCES: *All conceivable baskets of commodities can be consistently ranked in order of preference by the individual.* This ranking is called "the preference function."

Suppose there are only two commodities, X and Y. Amounts x and y consumed by an individual[2] are scaled along the horizontal and vertical axes respectively of Figure 3.1. Four possible combinations of X and Y are being considered by the consumer: the baskets represented by the points A, B, C, and D in the diagram. Notice that basket A represents more of both commodities than basket D. Also, basket A has as much of commodity Y as has basket B, and more of commodity X; in comparison with basket C, basket A has as much of X and more of commodity Y. What do the Laws of Preference tell us about this situation? Only two things: (1) that the individual is capable of ranking all four combinations; and (2) that if, for example, A is preferred to B and B to D, then (by transitivity) A must be preferred to D.

It may seem plausible to assert that the combination A—containing at least as much of either commodity as any other basket, and exceeding every other basket in quantity of X or of Y or both—must be preferred to all the others shown in Figure 3.1. This plausibility is sometimes erected into a principle known as: *More is preferred to less*. But "More is preferred to less" is not an inviolable law of preference. Rather, it can be regarded as the defining characteristic of the sub-

Figure 3.1

Alternative Consumption Baskets. A point like A, B, C, or D represents a combination or basket containing amounts of commodity X and commodity Y. If X and Y are both *goods*, then A is preferred to any of the other marked points.

[2]Capital letters X and Y here designate the two commodities; lower-case letters x and y indicate particular quantities.

class of commodities called *goods*. Undesired commodities, *bads*, also surely exist; household garbage is a homely example. Some commodities, like tapioca pudding, may be goods for some individuals and bads for others. And even for a great many (all?) undoubted goods, beyond a certain point of satiation they would become bads. (See Example 3.5, "Ball-Point Pens and French Pastries.") If disposal of undesired objects were always free, it would do no harm to assume that all commodities were goods. Any bads would be immediately and costlessly discarded. But as a practical matter, disposal is a seriously costly economic activity; more is *not* always better than less.

DEFINITION: A *good* is a commodity for which more is preferred to less.

3.C

UTILITY, PREFERENCE, AND RATIONAL CHOICE

The term "utility" was introduced by the British philosopher Jeremy Bentham. Bentham declared:

> Nature has placed mankind under the governance of two sovereign masters, *pain* and *pleasure*. . . . The *principle of utility* recognizes this subjection. . . . By the principle of utility is meant that principle which approves or disapproves of every action whatsoever, according to the tendency which it appears to have to augment or diminish the happiness of the party whose interest is in question. . . . [3]

For Bentham, then, the maximization of utility is an assertedly true psychological principle—that men avoid pain and seek pleasure or happiness.

While economists have held to the term "utility," they have felt uneasy about erecting the economic theory of choice upon an arguable psychological premise that man's goals are nothing but seeking pleasure and avoiding pain. Economists today simply say that individuals do make consistent choices: that the Laws of Preference of the previous section, while undoubtedly idealized, are a good approximation of actual behavior observed in the world. Since the Laws of Preference are really rules of rational choice, this reduces to the postulate of rationality discussed in Chapter 1.

What modern economists call "utility" reflects nothing more than rank ordering of preference. The statement "Basket *A* is preferred to basket *B*" and the statement "Basket *A* has higher utility than basket *B*" are equivalent. They both lead to the empirical prediction: "Basket *A* will be chosen over basket *B*."

CONCLUSION: Utility is the variable whose relative magnitude indicates direction of preference: In finding the most preferred position, the individual maximizes utility.

[3]J. Bentham, *An Introduction to the Principles of Morals and Legislation* (1823 edition), Chap. 1.

UTILITY: CARDINAL OR ORDINAL MAGNITUDE?

Early writers had no doubt that utility was a quantitatively measurable entity like length or temperature. They would have regarded it as perfectly reasonable to employ a construction like the upper diagram of Figure 3.2 in which any individual's utility (scaled in "utils" according to the vertical column of numbers U in the diagram) is shown as a function of the quantity taken of some generalized consumption good C. Some even believed it possible to add up these "util" numbers interpersonally: that 5 of John Doe's utils could be added to 7 of Richard Roe's so as to make a total of 12 utils for the pair. Jeremy Bentham apparently believed that public policies—for example, whether the state should punish crime more or less severely, whether the rich should be taxed more or less heavily in comparison with the poor—could be determined by summing the utils of everyone involved. This seems to be what Bentham meant in recommending public policies designed to achieve "the greatest good of the greatest number," a mystifying though noble-sounding expression. Economists today generally believe that summation of the utilities of different people is meaningless, and cannot be used as a basis for economic policy.[4]

What do we mean when we say that a variable is "quantitatively measurable"? We do not necessarily mean that there is only a *single* way of measuring or scaling it. Temperature, for example, can be measured according to the Celsius or the Fahrenheit scale; 32° Fahrenheit is 0° Celsius, and each degree up or down of Celsius corresponds to 1.8 degrees up or down of Fahrenheit. The two scales differ, but only in *zero-point* and *unit interval*. Similarly, altitude could be measured from sea level or from the center of the Earth (shift of zero-point) and in feet or meters (shift of unit interval). Both temperature and altitude as quantitatively measurable variables are more technically called *cardinal* magnitudes, variables which have the following property: that, regardless of shift of zero-point and unit interval, the relative magnitudes of *differences* remain the same. In the case of altitude for example, there's a bigger difference between the heights of the base and crest of Mount Everest than between the ground floor and roof of even the tallest man-made building. The difference remains bigger whether we measure altitude in feet or in meters, from sea-level or from the center of the Earth.

In plotting utility as in the upper diagram of Figure 3.2, we are assuming it is a cardinally measurable variable. In doing so it does not matter where we place the zero-point and what the unit interval is for the vertical U scale. What is really being asserted is that it is possible to compare the *relative magnitudes of utility differences*. For example, regardless of how we might shift the zero-point and the unit interval of the U scale along the vertical axis in the diagram, it remains true

[4]The modern approach to interpersonal comparisons will be taken up in Part Six.

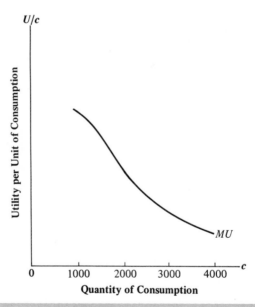

Figure 3.2
Cardinal Utility: Total and Marginal. If utility is "cardinally measurable," Total Utility U can be represented quantitatively as in the upper diagram. Marginal Utility in the lower diagram can be derived from Total Utility as explained in Chapter 2, Section B. Since Total Utility increases but at a decreasing rate as consumption rises, Marginal Utility is positive but declining.

that moving from 1000 to 2000 consumption units yields a bigger utility improvement than moving from 2000 to 3000 units.[5]

Utility in the upper diagram of Figure 3.2 is a *total* function of consumption C. The corresponding *Marginal Utility* function, defined (as described in Chapter 2) as the slope or rate of change of the Total Utility function, is shown in the lower diagram of Figure 3.2. Since Total Utility is shown as rising throughout, by Proposition 2.1a Marginal Utility MU is always positive. But since Total Utility in the upper diagram is increasing *at a steadily decreasing rate*, the MU curve in the lower diagram declines as consumption increases. This property, called *diminishing Marginal Utility*, is unaffected if we change the zero-point or unit interval of the utility scale.[6] Putting it more generally: If the underlying total variable is a cardinal magnitude, it is possible to say when the corresponding marginal variable is an increasing or decreasing function. This is so because marginal quantities are of the nature of differences of total quantities, and the comparison of differences is unaffected by shift of zero-point or unit interval.

The assertion that people are characterized by diminishing Marginal Utility, as consumption income rises, is an empirical one. This assertion was and is widely believed, despite the absence of a generally accepted measuring rod for utilities. It corresponds to our common-sense notion that more income makes us happier, but we usually get more of a thrill from our first million than from our tenth.

While most economists do not believe that there is a valid cardinal scale for utilities, the economist Julian Simon disagrees. He has proposed to measure utility, among other ways, by asking people, "Are you happy?"[7] Psychologists have carried out questionnaire surveys asking people to classify themselves as very happy, pretty happy, or not too happy. The percentage results in the table were obtained from a survey of residents in four small Illinois towns reported in 1965.

EXAMPLE 3.2
DOES MONEY
BUY HAPPINESS?

[7]One of the "other ways" he proposes is to look at the suicide rate. See Julian L. Simon, "Interpersonal Welfare Comparison Can Be Made—And Used for Redistribution Decisions," *Kyklos*, v. 27 (1974).

---

[5]*Mathematical Footnote*: Two utility scales U and U' are cardinally equivalent if measurements along the two scales are related by the linear equation:

$$U' = a + bU \qquad (\text{for } b > 0)$$

The constant a here represents the shift of zero-point and the constant b the change in unit interval. Consider three quantities U_1, U_2, and U_3 along the U scale, where the difference $U_3 - U_2$ exceeds the difference $U_2 - U_1$. Then $U'_3 - U'_2$ also exceeds $U'_2 - U'_1$, as can be verified by direct substitutions. So the *ranking of differences* is preserved for all cardinally equivalent scales.

[6]*Mathematical Footnote*: Since $U' = a + bU$, and b is positive, positive Marginal Utility according to the U scale ($dU/dc > 0$) implies positive Marginal Utility according to the U' scale ($dU'/dc = bdU/dc > 0$). Note that a change in zero-point a does not affect MU at all, and a change in unit interval b changes it only by the same positive multiplicative constant everywhere. *Diminishing* Marginal Utility according to the U scale ($d^2U/dc^2 < 0$) similarly implies diminishing Marginal Utility according to the U' scale ($d^2U'/dc^2 < 0$).

Income and Happiness

INCOME	VERY HAPPY	PRETTY HAPPY	NOT TOO HAPPY	SCORE*
Less than $3000	14%	55%	31%	−.17
$3000–3999	21	63	16	+.05
$4000–4999	27	61	12	+.15
$5000–5999	26	64	10	+.16
$6000–6999	24	65	10	+.14
$7000–7999	30	60	10	+.20
$8000–9999	29	63	7	+.22
$10,000 or more	38	54	8	+.30

Source: N. M. Bradburn and D. Caplovitz, *Reports on Happiness* (Chicago: Aldine, 1965), p. 9.
*Method for computing "Score" is described in text.

In interpreting these data, we still need a numerical utility (happiness) scale. Let us count "very happy" as +1, "pretty happy" as 0, and "not too happy" as −1. The average for each income group is then shown by the column headed "Score." If plotted, the Score data would show (despite some irregularities) a picture not too different from Figure 3.2.

EXAMPLE 3.3
THE
WEBER-FECHNER
LAW

An empirical generalization was developed by the psychologists E. H. Weber (1846) and G. T. Fechner (1860) concerning the relation between degree of stimulus and subjective sensitivity. The assertion is that subjective ability to discriminate is a function of *proportionate* change in the magnitude of stimulus.

Applying this to utility, subjective satisfaction can be regarded as sensitive to *proportionate* changes of income (or material well-being) regarded as stimulus. For example, if an increase in income from $10,000 to $12,000 (i.e., by 20%) is valued as a "one-util" improvement, then a further 20% increase from $12,000 to $14,400 would add a second util and still another 20% increase from $14,400 to $17,280 would provide a third util. If this is the case, utility would be a *logarithmic* function of income. Such a function would accord with the general picture of Figure 3.2, and in particular would imply diminishing Marginal Utility.

The idea of diminishing Marginal Utility has, therefore, some evidential basis. It also provides a way of explaining the fact that, for instance, people *save* more (i.e., buy more *future* consumption) as their wealth increases. If current consumption yields diminishing Marginal Utility, it is reasonable to respond to increments of income by arranging for part of the increment to be spent on *future* consumption. Unfortunately, this argument is not quite iron-clad. For, in general, we would expect the quantity of the one type of consumption to affect the utility of the other. It may be that an extra unit of current consumption *raises* its Marginal Utility but raises the Marginal Utility of future consumption *even more*. So the evidence of saving more as income rises is not conclusive as to diminishing Marginal Utility. What we need is a way of considering utility as depending simultaneously upon the amounts of all the different goods consumed. That is the topic of the next section.

Usually in economics we think of utility as a function of several variables, as depending upon the quantities consumed of a number of different commodities. (It may also depend upon quantities supplied of factor-services like labor effort, but the resource–supply decision is not being considered here.) Suppose we take, for simplicity, a world of two goods X and Y. Here, if the utility scale $U(x,y)$ were cardinal, the total of "utils" would depend upon the quantities consumed x and y. There is likely to be some interdependence in the satisfactions derived from each of the goods. The Marginal Utility a consumer derives from another pound of butter normally depends also upon the person's current rate of consumption of other commodities like margarine (a "substitute") or bread (a "complement").[8]

Figure 3.3 pictures a possible cardinal utility function $U(x,y)$. The quantities x and y are measured along the horizontal axes. Utility is measured in the upward

Figure 3.3

A Cardinal Total-Utility Function of Two Goods. Utility is measured vertically, and the horizontal axes x and y represent quantities consumed of commodities X and Y. The curves OA, PR, SU, and BG along the surface show how Total Utility changes as x rises, holding y constant (at a different level for each curve). Similarly the curves OB, WV, and AG show how Total Utility changes as y increases, holding x constant.

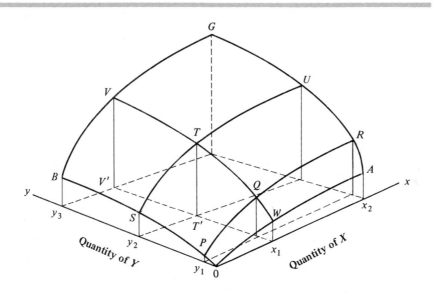

[8]*Mathematical Footnote*: Where Utility $U(x,y)$ is a function of amounts consumed of both X and Y, the Marginal Utilities are defined as *partial derivatives*: $MU_x \equiv \partial U/\partial x$ and $MU_y \equiv \partial U/\partial y$. In general, each Marginal Utility will be a function of both x and y, that is, the cross-derivative $\partial^2 U/\partial x \partial y$ will not ordinarily be zero.

direction, as the height of the surface above the base plane. When $x = x_1$ and $y = y_2$, for example, utility is the height $T'T$. If the quantity of Y is held constant at $y = y_1$, we can see how utility varies with x. This is shown by the curve PQR lying on the utility surface; note that Total Utility rises steadily as X increases. If Y is held constant at $y = y_2$ instead, we obtain a similar curve STU; or if Y is held constant at $y = y_3$, we observe the curve BVG. In each case the curves are rising (Total Utility is increasing) as x increases, and so (in accordance with Proposition 2.1a) the Marginal Utility of X is positive. Similar statements can be made about the Marginal Utility of the other commodity Y. But, in general, the Marginal Utility for *either* commodity depends upon the specific amounts of *both* commodities. For example, the Marginal Utility of X at the point T (i.e., when $x = x_1$ and $y = y_2$), given by the slope at point T in the x-direction along the curve STU, is not necessarily the same as the Marginal Utility of X at the point V (where $x = x_1$ but $y = y_3$), given by the slope at V along BVG. So we see that Marginal Utility of X may depend upon the quantity of Y, and vice versa.

Figure 3.4 is another representation of the same utility surface as Figure 3.3. But, in contrast with the preceding diagram, the curves drawn here on the surface (CC, DD, and EE) are *contours* connecting points of equal altitude on the "utility hill"; in effect, they show slices into the hill at fixed heights parallel to the base plane. These contours therefore are *curves of constant utility*. They were first employed by Edgeworth (1881)[9] who called them *indifference curves*. Any con-

Figure 3.4

Cardinal Utility and Indifference Curves. The surface here is the same as the preceding diagram, but the curves *along* the surface (CC, DD, EE) are contours connecting equal heights (levels of utility). The projections of these curves onto the base plane (C'C', D'D', E'E') are the indifference curves.

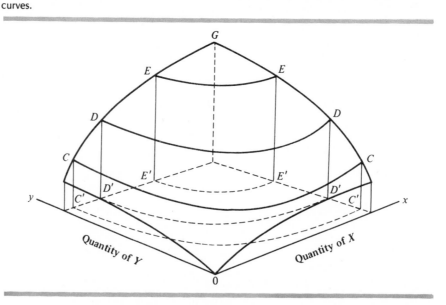

[9]Francis Y. Edgeworth, British economist, 1845–1926.

tour such as CC represents the equal level of utility yielded by a set of alternative consumption baskets (combinations of X and Y) that the consumer therefore regards as *indifferent* to one another. In Figure 3.4, looking through the transparent utility surface we can see on the base plane the *projections* $C'C'$, $D'D'$, $E'E'$ of the various indifference contours.

Next, suppose we simply deleted the vertical dimension of Figure 3.4, so as to leave *only* the base plane. We are left with the pure projection map shown in Figure 3.5. We can now think of the projections of the contours as being themselves the indifference curves; this step was taken by Pareto (1906).[10] Since X and Y are both goods, "More is preferred to less." Hence the *preference directions* are north and east as indicated by the arrows on the diagram. Thus, as between any two indifference curves, the one that can be reached moving northeast of the other is "higher up" on the invisible utility hill. Apart from the indifference curves, the preference directions are all we need to know for evaluating the *relative* preference status of alternative consumption combinations. So long as we know which of two baskets is on the higher indifference curve, we will choose that one over the other.

But if the contour map of indifference curves (with preference directions) fully describes preference, it is unnecessary to think of the invisible vertical dimension—utility—as having any particular quantification (other than *direction* of increase up or down). To put it another way, if the original util scale U is

Figure 3.5

Indifference Curves and Preference Directions—Ordinal Utility. Here the cardinal scaling of utility has been stripped away, and we are left with the indifference curves. These indifference curves, together with the preference directions, give us all the information needed to compare (to rank) alternative consumption baskets in terms of *ordinal* utility.

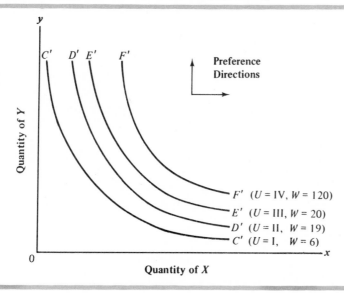

[10] Vilfredo Pareto, Italian economist and sociologist, 1848–1923.

represented by the magnitudes shown in roman numbers I, II, III, IV in Figure 3.5, we can just as well replace these numerical values by the scale W represented by arabic numbers such as 6, 19, 20, 120, respectively. Note that *this is a more drastic change than permitted by "cardinal" quantification*. More than the zero-point and unit interval has been changed as between U and W. This will be evident if we consider the measurement of utility differences. In terms of the original U (roman number) scale, the indifference curves are all equally spaced: the utility differences between successive curves are all 1. But in terms of the new W scale the differences between successive curves vary; in particular, the numerical labels on the two middle curves are much closer together than any other pair. Yet the two scales are equally valid, because the underlying utility concept is an *ordinal* magnitude. For an ordinal magnitude the only meaningful comparisons are equality or else ranking of greatness (*direction* of difference).[11] The two radically disparate preference scales U and W are equally satisfactory, since *they give the same answers as to which baskets are equal in utility* (lie along the same indifference curve) *and as to how baskets that are unequal in utility should be ranked* (direction of preference). This is all we need to know.

3.E

CHARACTERISTICS OF INDIFFERENCE CURVES FOR GOODS

If we are dealing only with *goods*, indifference curves have four crucial properties: (1) Indifference curves are negatively sloped; (2) indifference curves cannot intersect; (3) one indifference curve passes through each point in commodity space; (4) indifference curves are "convex" with respect to the origin (i.e., they bulge toward the origin).

1. *Slopes of Indifference Curves*: For simplicity assume there are only two goods X and Y. We plot their quantities as before in the x,y-plane (the *commodity space*). Then if we consider some initial point like A in Figure 3.6, all points northeast of A (within the upper-right quadrant formed by the vertical and horizontal lines through A) in commodity space represent larger quantities of *both* goods. But for goods, "More is preferred to less." Hence, moving northeast is moving up the invisible utility hill. By a corresponding argument, moving southwest from A is moving down the utility hill to lower levels of satisfaction. It follows that all points *indifferent* to A must lie either to the southeast like points R or Q or to the northwest like points S or T. And

[11]*Mathematical Footnote:* If the two utility scales are only ordinally equivalent, all we can say is that $W = F(U)$ and $dW/dU = F'(U)$, where $F'(U) > 0$. The positive derivative dW/dU always preserves rankings of *magnitudes*: If $U_1 > U_2$, the associated $W_1 > W_2$. Since the second derivative $d^2W/dU^2 = F''(U)$ has indeterminate sign, however, the ranking of *differences* according to the W scale need no longer correspond with their ranking on the U scale.

Figure 3.6
Properties of Indifference Curves. The preference directions indicate that every point in the +
region is preferred to A, while A is preferred over every point in the − region. So any indifference
curves through A must have negative slope. There can be only one indifference curve through A,
since intersecting indifference curves violate transitivity of preference.

so the indifference curve must have a negative slope more or less like U_1 or
U_2 in the diagram.[12]

2. *Non-intersection of Indifference Curves*: Non-intersection is a logical
necessity in a commodity space of goods. Employing Figure 3.6 again, suppose we use the indirect method of proof and tentatively assume that two
indifference curves like U_1 and U_2 can actually intersect as in the diagram.
According to indifference curve U_1, points A and Q are indifferent. According to indifference curve U_2, points A and R are indifferent. By transitivity,
Q and R must be indifferent. But R lies northeast of Q, and "More is preferred to less," so R and Q cannot be indifferent. This logical contradiction
disproves the premise that indifference curves can intersect. Hence the intersection in Figure 3.6 is *not* a valid representation of preference.

[12]*Mathematical Footnote:* In terms of calculus, along any indifference curve utility $U(x,y)$ is constant. So:

$$0 = dU \equiv \frac{\partial U}{\partial x} \, dx + \frac{\partial U}{\partial y} \, dy$$

Then the slope along the indifference curve is:

$$\left.\frac{dy}{dx}\right|_U = -\frac{\partial U/\partial x}{\partial U/\partial y}$$

Since $\partial U/\partial x$ and $\partial U/\partial y$ are both positive (X and Y are both *goods* with positive Marginal Utilities),
the slope is negative.

3. *Coverage of Indifference Curves*: The proposition that one indifference curve passes through each point in commodity space is expressed in compact language as "Indifference curves cover the space." It follows that between any two indifference curves another can always be drawn. A corresponding property is possessed by the real number system. For example, between any two numbers like 17.4398 and 17.4399 we can always find another number like 17.43986 larger than the first and smaller than the second. The coverage property is implied by the first law of preference in Section 3.B above, the Axiom of Comparison. It is assumed *always possible to compare* the preference levels of any baskets of commodities whatsoever. Hence, any describable basket must lie on some indifference curve. Empirically, as already mentioned, this is to be regarded as an idealization rather than a literal description of reality.[13]

4. *Indifference Curves Conves to Origin*: In the two panels of Figure 3.7 we see respectively illustrated the curvatures defined as "convex" and "concave" to the origin. It is the convex curve of Panel (a) that corresponds to the picture of Figure 3.5 and represents the standard assumption applicable

Figure 3.7
Convexity and Concavity. Between two goods, indifference curves must have negative slope. Curvature may be "convex to origin" as in Panel (a), or "concave to origin" as in Panel (b). The convex case is the normally observed situation, even though concavity would not necessarily violate the axioms of rational choice.

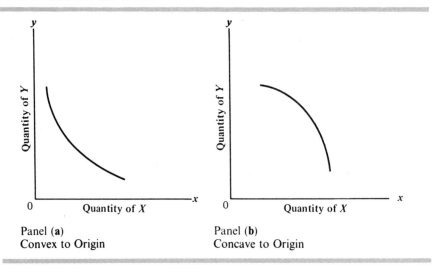

Panel (**a**)
Convex to Origin

Panel (**b**)
Concave to Origin

[13]Psychological experiments indicate that there is a minimum "threshold" below which sensations cannot be distinguished from one another. This suggests that indifference curves have some "width" in actuality, which would not fit very conveniently into our picture. But this is no more disturbing than the fact that Euclid's "lines" (straight curves with no breadth) cannot actually be observed in the world, since the best we can do in line-drawing still leaves some crookedness and some breadth. (Nevertheless, some economists in the interests of a more powerfully predictive theory are currently attempting to construct models of choice that incorporate perception thresholds.)

to indifference curves between two goods. While a common-sense interpretation can be given to this property of indifference curves, in contrast with the previous three properties (negative slope, non-intersection, and coverage) *convexity cannot be proved from the postulates of rational choice*. Rather, it is based upon a well-established empirical generalization about the world called "the principle of diversity in consumption" (to be discussed in Chapter 4).

This common-sense explanation may be convincing, however. Suppose an individual is to be held on an indifference curve (constant utility level) between two commodities like food X and entertainment Y.[14] If his initial position is far to the southeast or lower right on the indifference curve, he is consuming a great deal of food (x is great) but is bored for lack of entertainment (y is very small). Then it is reasonable to expect him to be willing to give up a relatively large amount of his very ample food for even a small amount of fun. So starting at an extreme position toward the southeast, we would expect to be able to find an indifferent point along the same curve that is well to the left (considerably less X) but only a little higher (a bit more Y). This implies relatively flat indifference curves in the southeast sector of the preference map. By a corresponding argument, toward the northwest sector of the preference map indifference curves are likely to be steep. Thus the picture of Panel (a) of Figure 3.7, and not of Panel (b), seems to fit our normal patterns of preference.

The Example following suggests something about the shape of parents' indifference curves between numbers of sons and daughters, regarded as "goods." (These goods happen to be of a kind ordinarily produced at home rather than purchased in the market, but that is quite apart from the preferences that parents might have.)

The table on the next page shows the results of a survey of white families who had two or more children as of 1970. The intention was to determine the proportion of parents who chose to have *more* children, given an initial number of children distributed between boys and girls.

EXAMPLE 3.4
PREFERENCES FOR
CHILDREN—
NUMBER AND SEX

Here the two "goods" are boy children and girl children. The proportion of families who decide to have *more* children can be interpreted as the proportion for whom additional children are still goods, so that the preference directions remain north and east as in Figure 3.5. (Actually, this is a serious underestimate, because some parents might regard additional children as desirable but be unwilling to pay the heavy monetary and psychic costs of having more offspring.)

The table shows that the fraction of parents planning on *more* children is on the whole greatest for those families initially having only two children (regardless of the sex distribution) and least for those families who already have four. But the essential point for our purposes is the somewhat subtler

---

[14]Food and entertainment are aggregations, rather than simple commodities, but this does not affect the point at issue.

Fraction of Families Who Had Another Child—by Number and Sex of Children

NO. OF CHILDREN	NO. OF BOYS	NO. OF FAMILIES	FRACTION WHO HAD ANOTHER CHILD
2	2	35,674	0.56
	1	64,585	0.51
	0	31,607	0.56
3	3	10,431	0.47
	2	26,497	0.44
	1	24,897	0.45
	0	8,948	0.48
4	4	2,619	0.40
	3	8,260	0.40
	2	11,489	0.38
	1	7,527	0.40
	0	2,241	0.41

Source: 1970 Census data reported in Yoram Ben-Porath and Finis Welch, *Do Sex Preferences Really Matter?*. The RAND Corporation Paper Series, P-5560 (December 1975), p. 7.

one that, for any given total number of children, the *families with more balanced sex distributions are notably less interested in having more children*.

Going on, or planning to go on, to have more children evidently signifies dissatisfaction with the present situation. For two-child families 56% of those with unbalanced sex distributions (two boys or two girls) were dissatisfied but only 51% of those with one boy and one girl were dissatisfied. While this difference is perhaps not very large, balanced sex distributions remain preferred over unbalanced distributions for three-child and four-child families as well.

This pattern of choices can be interpreted as showing that indifference curves are *convex* as in Figure 3.5. Recall that a high fraction in the right-hand column of the table expresses dissatisfaction. For any given number of children, the dissatisfaction tends to be greater at the unbalanced positions than toward the middle. With two children, for example, the position (1,1) is preferred to (on a higher indifference curve than) either (0,2) or (2,0). Such a pattern of preferences implies that the indifference curves bulge toward the origin, as in Panel (a) of Figure 3.7.

3.F

GOODS, BADS, AND NEUTERS

As has been suggested above, it is by no means a logical necessity that all commodities of economic significance be *goods*, i.e., desired objects. An obvious example is the problem of pollution. Our society has to choose a combination of industrial production (a *good*) in association with an amount of undesired by-products in the form of contamination of the environment (a *bad*).

One very important application of utility theory in recent years has been to the problem of *portfolio selection*, the balancing of an individual's wealth over such asset types as stocks, bonds, real estate, and so forth. In that application it is standard practice to construct utility functions into which M, the *mean* asset return (average percent yield of the portfolio) enters as a desired feature or good, while the *riskiness S* of the return enters as an undesired feature or bad. That is, investors seem to behave as if they want high average returns and low risk. Figure 3.8 illustrates the indifference map of such an investor. Note that the preference directions here are north and *west*. For the "good" commodity M, as usual more is preferred to less. But for the "bad" commodity S, less is preferred to more. These preference directions imply that the indifference curves have *positive* slopes, as shown in the diagram.

Our everyday experience also tells us that a commodity can be a good up to a point of satiation, and then become a bad if we are forced or pressed to increase our consumption beyond that point.

Figure 3.8
Indifference Curves between a Good and a Bad. Mean Return M (on assets) is a good, but Riskiness of Return S is a "bad." The preference directions are therefore north and *west,* implying that the indifference curves have a *positive* slope.

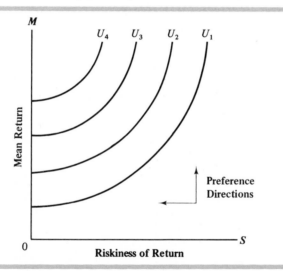

[15] K. R. MacCrimmon and M. Toda, "The Experimental Determination of Indifference Curves," *Review of Economic Studies,* v. 36 (Oct. 1969).

indifference-curve patterns all showed negative slope. The next choice offered was between money and French pastries, with the proviso that the pastries had to be actually eaten on the spot. Not surprisingly, French pastries became a bad after the first one or two; the subjects would eat more only if paid more money for doing so. Consequently, these indifference curves had normal negative slope only in the region marked as Zone I in Figure 3.9, west of the curve drawn through the lowest points of the successive indifference curves. In Zone I the preference directions are north and east as usual. In Zone II, east of the dividing curve, French pastries have become a bad so that the preference directions are north and west, and the indifference curves take on a positive slope.

So long as commodities are definitely goods or definitely bads, there is no problem with the properties of indifference curves: Making the obvious changes where called for by the reversal of preference direction leads to a correct description, whether we are dealing with two goods, two bads, or a bad and a good. What if there were a commodity that was a *neuter*, neither adding to nor detracting from utility? Then the indifference-curve picture will be as in Figure 3.10.

Figure 3.9
Satiation. In Zone I both commodities, Money and French Pastries, are goods so that the indifference curves have negative slope. Zone II is the region of satiation for French Pastries; in this region the preference directions are north and *west*, and the indifference curves have positive slope. In this region an individual would have to be paid to eat another pastry.

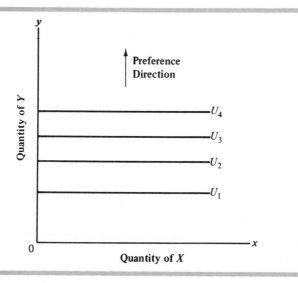

Figure 3.10

A Neuter Commodity. Here *X* is a neuter commodity; regardless of the amount of *Y*, the consumer does not care whether he has more or less of *X*. As the other commodity *Y* is a good, the only preference direction is north. Then the indifference curves are horizontal.

The following observations, among others, can be made about charity: (1) Not everyone makes charitable contributions. (2) But some people do. (3) Those who give charity almost always give to persons poorer than themselves. The problem is to construct an indifference-curve picture or pictures consistent with these observations.

One approach is as follows. Figure 3.11 has as axes "My Income" (measured horizontally to the right) and "His Income" (measured vertically upward)—assuming for convenience that the recipient is one male person. We are thinking solely of "my" preferences, so the feelings of the other individual are in no way involved in the picture. Imagine first that I am completely uninterested in whether he has any income or not. Then "His Income" is a neuter commodity for me; I do not care at all about movements north or south. This is the situation pictured in Panel (a) of Figure 3.11. Since "My Income" is surely a good for me, the only preference direction shown is *east,* and my indifference curves are vertical.

The question is, if my preferences were as pictured in Panel (a), would I give charity to the other individual? That is the same as asking whether I would be willing to move from any initial situation to another involving less income for me but more income for him. If the initial situation were at *E* in Panel (a), I have 1000 units of income and he has zero. Suppose that I could transfer income to him, on a one-for-one basis. In the diagram, this means that I could attain any point along the line *EF*. But any such movement puts me on a lower indifference

Panel (**a**)
Neutral Preferences

Panel (**b**)
Benevolent Preferences

Figure 3.11

Preference and Charity. If my preferences are as pictured in Panel (a), "His Income" is a neuter commodity for me. I would never give charity. But if Panel (b) pictures my preferences, I may give charity to people poorer than myself but never to people richer. ("His Income" is a good for me below the 45° line, but is a neuter commodity for me above the 45° line.)

curve. So I would not give charity. Notice that I am in no way *malevolent* to the other individual here, simply that I am not *benevolent* either.

Panel (b) of Figure 3.11 displays a somewhat more interesting case, where I do have a degree of benevolence. But suppose that observation (3) above applies to me, that I am benevolent only to people poorer than myself. In Panel (b), he is poorer than I am *only below the 45° line* (Zone I in the diagram). In Zone I "His Income" and "My Income" are both goods for me, and the indifference curves have their usual negative slopes. In this range, if my initial situation were at E and I could choose any point along the line EF, I might, as in the diagram of Panel (b), find it advantageous to transfer some income to him (give charity to him). In fact, my optimal solution, in the light of my benevolent preferences, is to transfer just enough income to attain point C^*. If, on the other hand, my initial situation were at a point like M, any charity on my part *would make him richer than me* (would put me above the 45° line, in Zone II). But I do not give charity under these circumstances, according to observation (3). Therefore, my indifference curves in this range must be vertical like those in Panel (a).

THE SOURCES AND CONTENT OF PREFERENCES

Why do people want some things, and not others? Why are our desires for some goods easily satiated, for others not? Can anything be said about how preferences vary among people of different ages, with different ethnic origins, in different circumstances?

As indicated in Chapter 1, individuals' goals and preferences are taken as given in economics; their nature and formation are regarded as falling within the province of our sister social sciences. Yet in some cases the forces involved are clear enough. It is not hard to predict that iced drinks will be more popular in Georgia than in Alaska; that diapers are not a big merchandising item in retirement communities; that bagels sell better in Jewish neighborhoods, and soul food in Harlem. But what are the bases for these common-sense judgments? The economist who intends to apply his discipline should have some knowledge of the deeper forces determining preferences. Even though he takes tastes as given, he should have some appreciation of their actual nature and content—just as an economist wanting to say something about the Gross National Product should have some broad knowledge of the nature and content of the technology that makes modern production possible.

On a very primitive level, humans as organisms choose (and so can be said to have preferences for) objects that will promote their own survival or comfort. We need to keep our skins intact, our body parts connected up nicely, and our blood temperatures not very far from 98.6° Fahrenheit. Physical considerations like these broadly explain the desires for food, for shelter, for protection against injury. But cultural and personal elements are clearly involved in whether these

Chapter 3
UTILITY AND
PREFERENCE

very general desires are translated, more specifically, into preferences for commodities like three-piece suits or levis, pizza pies or *pâté de foie gras*, split-level houses or mobile homes.

Beyond meeting physiological needs, as people grow richer they can afford to indulge their tastes for esthetics, for social distinction, for novelty. These non-material "goods" will therefore tend to become more significant as society becomes more affluent. If economics is to retain its validity for explaining behavior, it will increasingly have to address the question of these non-material tastes and drives.

A very essential element in human society is the extent of help that individuals are willing to give one another, as in the charity behavior discussed above. One observation was already made as to the nature of the "taste" for providing this kind of help: that people will generally give charity to those poorer than themselves, only rarely to those richer than themselves. Another fact about the taste for helping others is even more obvious: that people are inclined to help their own children in preference to almost anyone else. This last fact suggests a biological evolutionary explanation. Organisms that chose to help their own offspring in preference to the offspring of others have tended to leave more descendants over the generations.[16]

The degree to which biology, or ethnic culture, or idiosyncrasies of individual psychology determine the tastes of individuals remains an important topic about which very little is yet known.

SUMMARY OF CHAPTER 3

The individual, in solving his problem of optimization in consumption, is said to maximize his utility. We postulate that his preferences follow the Axiom of Comparison (he can compare all possible pairs of consumption baskets) and the Axiom of Transitivity (if he prefers A to B, and B to C, then he prefers A to C). These together imply that he can rank all conceivable consumption baskets in order of preference.

If utility is quantifiable in the sense of being "cardinally" measurable, statements can be made about the shape of the Marginal Utility curve. In particular, there is some evidence favoring the view that Marginal Utility is a diminishing function of consumption. But for most purposes in modern economics it suffices if utility is only "ordinally" measurable. If one basket is preferred to another we need only say that the utility of the former is greater—how much greater does not matter.

In choosing baskets of two (or more) commodities, cardinal utility would be represented by a quantifiable "utility hill" defined over amounts of the commodities. The ordinal utility interpretation lets us suppress the utility dimension and portray preferences in terms of *indifference curves*—contours connecting consumption baskets yielding equal utility—together with an indication of the *preference directions* (which way is up on the invisible utility hill).

[16]W. D. Hamilton, "The Genetical Evolution of Social Behaviour," *Journal of Theoretical Biology*, v. 7 (1964).

Indifference curves between two goods have three properties that follow from the laws of rational choice: negative slope, non-intersection, and coverage. There is also a fourth property, convexity to the origin, that is based upon observation of choice behavior in the world. In dealing with a *good*, the preference direction indicates that utility increases as the amount increases. For a *bad*, utility decreases with the amount consumed. For a *neuter*, utility is unaffected by the amount consumed.

Although economics takes tastes as given, actual applications of economics often require us to have some understanding of the nature and determinants of preferences for material objects or for non-material ends. As yet very little is known on this subject.

QUESTIONS FOR CHAPTER 3

Mainly for Review

*R1. An individual is offered a choice between a ski trip to Aspen and four cases of Cutty Sark whiskey. Which of the following possible responses violate the laws of preference:
   a. "They're so different, I can't choose."
   b. "I don't care, you choose for me."
   c. "Whichever I choose, I know I'll be sorry."

R2. Name a commodity which is a good for many people, but is a bad for you. Name a commodity which is a good for you, but only up to a point; after that it becomes a bad.

R3. Draw possible indifference maps between:
   a. Two goods.
   b. A good and a bad.
   c. A good and a neuter.
   d. A good and a commodity which is a good up to a point, but then becomes a bad.

*R4. What do modern economists mean by the term "utility"?

R5. From a "cardinal" (quantitatively measurable) Total Utility function, show how a corresponding Marginal Utility function is derived.

*R6. What can be said about the Marginal Utility function if Total Utility is given only in "ordinal" terms?

R7. What are the four essential properties of indifference curves between two goods? Explain the justification for each of the four properties.

*R8. Which of the following requires only *ordinal* utility, which requires *cardinal* utility, and which requires *interpersonal comparability* of cardinal utilities?
   a. Indifference curves can be drawn.
   b. A Marginal Utility function can be used to see numerically how Total Utility changes as consumption of a good increases.
   c. It can be determined which person in a group is most desirous of receiving a particular prize.

*The answers to asterisked questions appear at the end of the book.

*T1. Can you give an exact meaning in utility terms to the expression "greatest good of the greatest number"?

T2. In suppressing the "cardinal" dimension of the utility hill so as to picture preferences only in terms of indifference curves, why is it necessary also to indicate the preference directions?

*T3. An example of an ordinal measure is the military rank system. A sergeant has more authority than a private, a lieutenant more than a sergeant, and so on. Give another example of an ordinal scale of magnitude.

T4. Since you probably would not want to eat pickles and ice cream out of the same bowl, does it follow that your indifference curves between these two goods are concave rather than convex?

*T5. For "His Income" and "My Income" regarded as goods, what shape for the indifference curves would correspond to The Golden Rule ("Love thy neighbor as thyself")?

T6. In the "Economics of Charity" diagram (Figure 3.11), suppose that the initial situation in either panel is point *E* ("My Income" is 1000, "His Income" is 0). If by charitable transfer of income I can attain any position along the line *EMF*, can you see what my preferred position will be if my tastes are represented by Panel (a)? If my tastes are represented by Panel (b)? How much charity will I give in each of the two cases?

*T7. In surveys of income and happiness (see Example 3.2), a puzzling discrepancy has been noted. While there is higher reported happiness with higher income *at a moment of time*, this conclusion does not seem to hold for comparisons *over time*. Even though wealth has risen over the years in the United States all across the scale so that both rich and poor have higher incomes than before, reports on happiness do not average higher than before.[17] The most natural explanation of this paradox is that happiness is more powerfully affected by *relative* income status than by actual consuming power represented by income. The poor are richer than before, but are still on the bottom of the heap in the comparative sense; therefore they may still feel just as unhappy as before. Is this preference pattern consistent with either panel of Figure 3.11? If not, how would you draw the preference map?

[17]See R. A. Easterlin, "Does Economic Growth Improve the Human Lot? Some Empirical Evidence," in P. David and M. Reder, eds., *Nations and Households in Economic Growth; Essays in Honor of M. Abramovitz* (New York: Academic Press, 1974).

4.A THE OPTIMUM OF THE CONSUMER, 88
    4.A.1   Optimum of the Consumer—Geometry, 89
    4.A.2   Optimum of the Consumer—Analysis, 94
4.B VARIATION OF THE CONSUMER'S OPTIMUM, 100
    4.B.1   Income Expansion Path and Engel Curve, 100
    4.B.2   Price Expansion Path and Demand Curve, 108
4.C INCOME AND SUBSTITUTION EFFECTS OF A PRICE CHANGE, 115
4.D FROM INDIVIDUAL DEMAND TO MARKET DEMAND, 117
4.E AN APPLICATION: SUBSIDY VERSUS "VOUCHER", 118

Examples
    4.1   PRISONERS OF WAR—TEA VERSUS COFFEE, 96
    4.2   LUXURIES VERSUS NECESSITIES IN A P.O.W. CAMP, 103
    4.3   POLYGYNY IN MAIDUGURI, 105
    4.4   ENGEL'S LAWS AFTER A CENTURY, 107
    4.5   THE LAW OF DEMAND—ANIMAL AND HUMAN, 112
    4.6   SHOCKING ALCOHOLICS, 113

4

CONSUMPTION AND DEMAND

Core Chapter

In this chapter we will connect the *subjective* patterns of individual preferences with the *objective* observable behavior of consumers in markets. The market behavior of the consumer is summarized, from the viewpoint of the economist, by the responsiveness of consumption decisions to *changes in prices* and to *changes in income*.

4.A

THE OPTIMUM OF THE CONSUMER

As has already been emphasized, two theoretical techniques—optimization, and determination of equilibrium—account for the great bulk of formal economic analysis. Our first application of the technique of optimization will be to the consumption choices of an individual in the product market.

The class of behavior we call "rational" is characterized by a relation between two sets of data underlying an individual's decisions: his *preferences*, and his *opportunities*. The rational individual will, within the opportunities available to him, so arrange his affairs as to best satisfy his preferences. Or with specific reference to the consumption decision, and employing the utility concept introduced in the previous chapter, we can say: The rational individual will select, from among his opportunities, the one consumption basket or combination that *maximizes* his utility. This selection process is called "consumptive optimization"; the position arrived at (the consumption basket chosen) is the *optimum of the consumer*.[1]

Preferences and opportunities are brought together, for a particular individual, as shown in Figure 4.1. Here there are just two commodities, X and Y, both assumed to be *goods*. Consequently the indifference curves U_1, U_2, . . . are negatively-sloped (as in Figure 3.5). This is equivalent to saying that the *preference directions* are north and east. In addition, the indifference curves are shown as *convex* to the origin.

    Since preferences are defined for all conceivable combinations (baskets) of X and Y, the indifference curves should be regarded as covering the entire positive quadrant between the X- and Y-axes. But the range of opportunities of the individual, his *opportunity set*, constitutes only a limited portion of the positive quadrant. We are dealing here with the *market* opportunity set for consumption decisions, the alternative consumption bundles available to the individual through transac-

Figure 4.1

Optimum of the Consumer. The shaded region *OKL* represents the consumer's market opportunity set, bounded by the horizontal and vertical axes and by the budget line *KL*. The position of the budget line is determined by the individual's income *I* and the market prices P_x and P_y. The optimum is the point where the line *KL* touches the highest attainable indifference curve (point *C** on indifference curve U_2); this is the consumption basket yielding the greatest achievable utility.

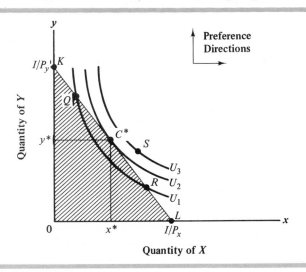

[1]This is sometimes carelessly called the "equilibrium" of the consumer. Such wording blurs the distinction between the two key analytical concepts—equilibrium and optimum—that the student must learn to handle, each in its proper place. An *optimum* is the result of successful goal-oriented choice on the part of an economic decision-maker. An *equilibrium* represents simply a balance of forces.

tions in the product market. In this case, as will be shown below, the opportunity set takes the particular triangular form of the shaded region in Figure 4.1.[2]

The amount of *income*, I, available for spending on consumption is one determinant of an individual's market opportunity set. The *prices* of consumer goods, specifically here the prices P_x and P_y of commodities X and Y respectively, constitute the other determinants. The consumer will ordinarily have obtained income, of course, by selling productive services to business firms.

In a modern economy prices are generally quoted in money terms. And income is also measured as a money flow of earnings from resource services, per unit time. How money functions as a *medium of exchange*, i.e., as a counter whose universal acceptability facilitates the process of trade, will be examined in Chapter 8. For our purposes here we want to "pierce the veil" of money and deal with the underlying *real* magnitudes. Consequently, we will think of prices and income as measured in terms of some standard real good called a "numeraire." Then P_x, the price of X, is the amount of the standard good that must be paid for a unit of X; P_y is the amount that must be paid for a unit of good Y; and income I is the amount earned in units of the standard numeraire good.

Suppose that expenditures on commodities X and Y exactly exhaust income. Then we have the equation:

(4.1) $P_x x + P_y y = I$

This equation is plotted as the straight line KL in Figure 4.1, constituting the northeast boundary of the shaded region. The horizontal intercept of the line equals I/P_x, which is the number of units of X purchasable if the individual were to spend all his income I on commodity X. Similarly, the vertical intercept of the line is I/P_y, representing the number of units of Y purchasable by spending all income on Y. Any mixed basket containing positive quantities of both X and Y will lie somewhere along the line between the two intercepts. The other boundaries of the shaded opportunity set in Figure 4.1 are the horizontal and vertical axes. The economic interpretation is that the quantities purchased of X and of Y can never be negative.

Alternatively, suppose that we wanted to allow for the possibility of not expending all of income on X and Y. This would be expressed algebraically by the condition:

(4.1′) $P_x x + P_y y \leqq I$

The more general expression (4.1′), together with the non-negativity assumptions, describe the entire shaded opportunity region of Figure 4.1.

The northeast boundary KL of the opportunity set, corresponding to the exact equality of equation (4.1), is called the *budget line* of the consumer. Since X

[2]Other types of consumption opportunity sets can also exist. Robinson Crusoe, for example, could be regarded as having an opportunity set as between combinations of commodities like fish and bananas available on his island. Crusoe's consumption opportunity set evidently depends entirely upon his own isolated efforts, and in no way upon the possibility of transactions in markets.

and Y are the only desired goods, and since the preference directions are north and east, in a market situation only this budget line or northeast boundary is of concern to the consumer.[3] (He can get to any position in the *interior* of the shaded region, starting from a point on the budget line, simply by throwing away some X or some Y or both. But with X and Y both goods, he would never want to do so.)

In the analysis of optimization, emphasis will very frequently be placed upon the *slope* of curves or lines drawn on x,y-axes. The slope of a curve or line will be symbolized as $\dfrac{\Delta y}{\Delta x}$, the change in y divided by the change in x. In the case of a line, the slope is of course constant throughout its length. The slope of the budget line specifically, symbolized as $\dfrac{\Delta y}{\Delta x}\Big|_I$, can be expressed as the ratio of the vertical intercept I/P_y to the horizontal intercept I/P_x.

$$(4.2) \qquad \frac{\Delta y}{\Delta x}\Big|_I = -\frac{I/P_y}{I/P_x} = -\frac{P_x}{P_y}$$

This slope carries a negative sign since, along the budget line, an *increase* in x is associated with a *decrease* of y.[4]

Algebraically, equation (4.2) tells us that the slope is also equal to the negative of the price ratio P_x/P_y. This has a natural economic interpretation. Giving up one unit of X is equivalent to moving up to the left along the budget line. How far up? The unit of X foregone makes available the amount P_x for spending on Y, so that the number of units of Y obtainable in exchange is just P_x/P_y. If P_x were 10 and P_y were 2, giving up one unit of X would permit purchase of $\dfrac{10}{2} = 5$ units of Y, so that -5 would be the slope of the budget line.

We have now seen how the market opportunity set depends upon commodity prices P_x and P_y (whose ratio determines the *slope* of the budget line), and upon income I (whose magnitude determines the distances of the intercepts I/P_x and I/P_y from the origin and therefore the *position* of the budget line). With the data both as to preferences and opportunities in hand, we can proceed to the optimum of the consumer.

From inspection of Figure 4.1, it is evident that the consumer's best attainable position along the budget line KL (and, therefore, the best position attainable

---

[3]This statement is valid if there are no *other* imposed constraints upon the consumption decision. It may be that the consumer, while having enough income to purchase certain consumption baskets at currently ruling prices, is barred from doing so on other grounds. One example would be a ration limit upon purchases (discussed in Chapter 6, Section D below).

[4]*Mathematical Footnote:* With the equation of the budget line as $P_x x + P_y y = I$, the slope is found as the derivative:

$$\frac{dy}{dx}\Big|_I = -\frac{P_x}{P_y}$$

Since this derivative is a constant, it equals the ratio of finite increments $\dfrac{\Delta y}{\Delta x}\Big|_I$ in equation (4.2) of the text.

within the shaded market opportunity set) is the point C^*—the consumption combination containing x^* of commodity X and y^* of commodity Y. At C^* the indifference curve U_2 is just *tangent* to the budget line. The geometrical relationships are such that the consumptive optimum must be at a tangency, if a tangency position exists (as discussed below). Non-tangency points like Q and R in the diagram, both lying on indifference curve U_1 at the points where U_1 cuts the budget line, must necessarily be inferior in terms of preference to the tangency point C^* on indifference curve U_2. In terms of the invisible "utility hill" of Chapter 3, Q and R lie along a lower contour than C^*; the highest contour attainable is the one that can just barely be reached at the single (tangency) point C^*. It is true that a point like S on indifference curve U_3 would be even superior to C^*—but the combination S is not attainable since indifference curve U_3 never lies within the opportunity set.

CONCLUSION: The optimum of the consumer is found at the tangency between the budget line and a convex indifference curve (if such a tangency exists).

In Section 3.E the convexity property of indifference curves was asserted to follow not from the logic of the Laws of Preference but rather from observation of behavior in the world. This point can now be demonstrated. Imagine hypothetically that curves of indifference between goods X and Y have negative slope but the opposite concave curvature. Such a situation is pictured in Figure 4.2, where

Figure 4.2

Concave Indifference Curves and Corner Solution. If the indifference curves were negatively sloped but concave to the origin, the best attainable position along the budget line KL must be a *corner solution*, lying along one or the other axis. In this case the corner solution is at C^{**} on the y-axis.

the preference directions, shaded opportunity set, and budget line *KL* remain as in the previous diagram. Here there is again a tangency, the point *T*. But *T* is not the consumptive optimum. Indeed, *T* is the *least* preferred point on the budget line, lying as it does on U_2, the *lowest* indifference curve reached along *KL*. With concave indifference curves, the highest level of preference along a budget line will necessarily be found at the intersection of the budget line with one or the other axis. This means that the best use of income would always be to devote expenditure exclusively to the purchase of one commodity—to consume only one of the two goods available. In Figure 4.2 the optimum position is denoted C^{**} on indifference curve U_4, at point *K* on the *Y*-axis. Such an outcome is called a *corner solution*, as opposed to the ordinary *interior solution* as at C^* in Figure 4.1.

Now in the actual world individuals are observed to *diversify* their consumption, to purchase a *mixture* of many different commodities. Only a convex indifference-curve map like Figure 4.1 can lead to interior solutions and thereby explain this observation.

There is one difficulty with the explanation, however. Let us drop the limiting assumption of exactly two commodities and recognize that the typical individual makes consumption choices among many thousands of alternative goods. We are really dealing with a multi-dimensional preference function, with a separate axis for each commodity available. For three commodities there would be three axes. The three-dimensional indifference contours become indifference *shells*, nested like the skins of an onion. Beyond three dimensions we cannot carry the geometrical representation, but can still imagine the generalization to more commodities. Now in point of fact we actually do observe "corner solutions" with respect to many or even most goods; the typical individual buys positive quantities of only a small number of the distinct commodities that might conceivably be purchased. In some cases this may be because a commodity that is a *good* for some people is a *bad* for others (tapioca pudding). But even among the vast numbers of commodities that consumers recognize as goods, many are not actually purchased. The reason is, of course, that the price is regarded as too high relative to the consumer's desires. You may enjoy the flavor of Beluga caviar, be able to afford at least a small quantity of it, and yet not be willing to pay the steep price required. Thus, you are at a corner solution with regard to the "caviar axis" of your multicommodity utility function.

Observation of actual corner solutions for *some* goods does not, however, require us to abandon convexity to the origin as a property of indifference curves. Figure 4.3 shows in two dimensions how a corner solution can be perfectly consistent with convexity. Here again the most preferred position (highest indifference curve attainable in the market opportunity set) is at C^{**}, reached along the vertical axis at *K*, where only *Y* and no *X* is consumed. We do not have a tangency, but the optimum is the *closest to tangency* (equality of slopes) that the consumer can achieve along the budget line *KL*. Convex indifference curves are thus capable of explaining *both* the observation of interior solutions in some cases and corner solutions in other cases.

We may summarize this geometrical discussion as follows:

Figure 4.3

Convex Indifference Curves and Corner Solution. If indifference curves are convex to the origin, a corner solution is not inevitable, but remains possible. Here the consumer optimum along the budget line *KL* is at point *C*** on the *y*-axis.

GEOMETRICAL OPTIMUM PRINCIPLE: The optimum of the consumer, the position where he maximizes utility or satisfaction subject to his limited income, is the point on the budget line touching his highest attainable indifference curve. With convex indifference curves, the consumer optimum may be an interior solution at a tangency between the budget line and the best attainable indifference curve. Or, it may be a corner solution where the budget line reaches the highest attainable indifference curve along an axis.

4.A.2
Optimum of the Consumer— Analysis

Setting aside geometry, let us now reconsider the problem of consumer choice in terms of underlying concepts. The consumer is seeking to maximize satisfaction, to distribute his given income I optimally over the different commodities he might conceivably purchase, in our example, over the two goods X and Y.

Suppose that we were allowed to think in terms of a "cardinal" preference function, measured in units of utils. Then it would be meaningful to speak of the magnitude of Marginal Utility. The older economists postulated "diminishing Marginal Utility" with respect to additional units consumed of goods like X or Y. Holding Y constant, let the individual increase his consumption of X. Then, assertedly, the additional satisfaction (marginal utils) per unit of X would be steadily falling as the rate of consumption of X increased. Similarly there would be diminishing Marginal Utility for consumption of commodity Y, holding the quantity of the other good X constant.

Given diminishing Marginal Utility for each of the two goods, the consumer will be at an (interior) optimum when the Consumption Balance Equation (4.3) is satisfied:

Chapter 4
CONSUMPTION
AND DEMAND

94

$$(4.3) \quad \frac{\text{Marginal Utility of } X}{\text{Price of } X} = \frac{\text{Marginal Utility of } Y}{\text{Price of } Y} \quad \text{Interior Solution}[5]$$

The explanation is immediate. For any commodity, Marginal Utility divided by price is *Marginal Utility per dollar* spent on that commodity. For the consumer not to want to change his purchase rate of X relative to Y, the Marginal Utility per dollar of X and Y must be equal. The last dollar must yield equivalent satisfaction, whether spent on X or spent on Y. If this were not the case, the consumer would buy more of the commodity for which Marginal Utility per dollar was high, and less of the one whose Marginal Utility per dollar was low. He would continue to reallocate his spending in this way until Marginal Utilities per dollar became equal over all commodities being purchased.

What about the possibility of a corner solution? Suppose that, for some commodity like Beluga caviar, the Marginal Utility per dollar remains lower than that of the other commodity even when zero units of caviar are purchased. Then we would have a corner optimum, which can be expressed (letting X represent caviar) as the inequality:

$$(4.3') \quad \frac{MU_x\,(x=0)}{P_x} < \frac{MU_y\,(y>0)}{P_y} \quad \text{Corner Solution}[6]$$

[5]*Mathematical Footnote:* In optimization problems in economics, a very neat technique called "the method of Lagrangian multipliers" is generally used. Specifically, in the present case we seek to maximize a cardinal utility function $U(x,y)$ subject to the constraint $P_x x + P_y y = I$ (where P_x, P_y, and I are constants). The technique involves setting up an artificial maximand in the following form:

$$\underset{(x,y,\lambda)}{\text{Max}} \; L = U(x,y) - \lambda(P_x x + P_y y - I)$$

The first-order conditions for a maximum are:

$$\frac{\partial L}{\partial x} = \frac{\partial U}{\partial x} - \lambda P_x = 0$$

$$\frac{\partial L}{\partial y} = \frac{\partial U}{\partial y} - \lambda P_y = 0$$

$$\frac{\partial L}{\partial \lambda} = P_x x + P_y y - I = 0$$

The first two conditions imply:

$$\frac{\partial U/\partial x}{P_x} = \frac{\partial U/\partial y}{P_y}$$

This is, of course, the Consumption Balance Equation (4.3). The technique works because in taking the partial derivative with respect to λ we obtain $P_x x + P_y y - I = 0$. This guarantees that the constraint condition (the budget equation) is always met, and also assures that the maximum of the artificial variable L is the same as the desired maximum of U.

[6]If there were many commodities, there might be corner solutions as between some pairs of goods and interior solutions for others. In the case of just three goods, the solution might take the form:

$$\frac{MU_x\,(x=0)}{P_x} < \frac{MU_y\,(y>0)}{P_y} = \frac{MU_z\,(z>0)}{P_z}$$

Here commodities Y and Z, but not commodity X, are being purchased in positive amounts at the consumptive optimum.

In either case, of course, the budget-line condition (4.1) as well as the Consumption Balance Equation (or Inequality, in the case of a corner solution) holds at the optimum of the consumer.[7]

What if utility is an "ordinal" magnitude only? Then we must think in terms of *substituting* Y for X (or vice versa) in the individual's consumption bundle. The rate at which a consumer *can* substitute Y for X in his market purchases, given his fixed income I, is determined by the price ratio P_x/P_y. For example, if $P_x/P_y = 5$, within a total expenditure I he can substitute in his consumption basket 10 units of Y for 2 units of X. More formally, let us define the *Marginal Rate of Substitution in Exchange*, MRS_E, as this ratio governing possible substitutions between X and Y in market exchanges. Then $MRS_E \equiv P_x/P_y$. Since commodity prices are taken as constant by the consumer, MRS_E is a constant. Indeed, we see immediately from equation (4.2) that MRS_E is equal to the absolute value of the constant slope $\left.\dfrac{\Delta y}{\Delta x}\right|_I$ of his budget line.

We thus have a concept explaining the terms according to which the consumer *can* make market substitutions of Y for X in his consumption basket. The next question is, what are the terms on which he would be *willing* to make substitutions of Y for X? More explicitly, what is the ratio $\left.\dfrac{\Delta y}{\Delta x}\right|_U$ at which he would be just willing to make exchanges between X and Y, of small amounts, in either direction? This is defined as the *Marginal Rate of Substitution in Consumption*, denoted MRS_C. The expression "*just willing* to make exchanges in either direction" is equivalent to the expression "*indifferent* between substitutions in either direction." This suggests that MRS_C refers to a small movement along an indifference curve. And indeed MRS_C *is the absolute value of the indifference-curve slope,*[8] *just as* MRS_E *is the absolute value of the budget-line slope.*

Clearly, the consumer cannot be at an optimum position unless the rate at which he is *willing* to make substitutions in his consumption bundle (MRS_C) equals the rate at which he *can* make substitutions via market trading (MRS_E).

EXAMPLE 4.1
PRISONERS OF
WAR—TEA
VERSUS COFEE

The economist R. A. Radford had the unfortunate opportunity of studying, from the inside, social behavior in prisoner-of-war camps in Germany and Italy during World War II. He found that highly active economies functioned in these camps, particularly under the relatively "favorable" conditions that prevailed in the earlier war years.

Cigarettes served generally as the numeraire (or standard good) in terms

---

[7]*Mathematical Footnote*: Since a corner solution is generally not at a tangency, calculus techniques involving equality of derivatives are not applicable; the optimum is not at a point where the indifference-curve slope equals the budget-line slope. Corner solutions arise because of non-negativity constraints. Where such constraints are dictated by the economics of the problem, as in our standard assumption that consumption must be non-negative, the calculus must be used with caution.

[8]*Mathematical Footnote:* In terms of derivatives,

$$MRS_c \equiv - \left.\dfrac{dy}{dx}\right|_U$$

of which prices were quoted. Coffee might go for about 2 cigarettes per cup, a shirt might cost 80, washing service 2 cigarettes per garment, and so on.

In the camp section holding English prisoners, tea was definitely preferred to coffee—and the reverse in the French section. A regular smuggling trade was conducted between the two, permitting prisoners in each section to adjust their consumption choices to the price ratio reflecting the overall supply-demand balance in the camp as a whole.[9]

COMMENT: The two panels of Figure 4.4 illustrate the situations of typical English and French prisoners. In both camp sections prices were quoted, in cigarettes, for coffee (P_c) and for tea (P_t). The efficient smuggling trade between sections prevented disparities from developing between the coffee prices or between the tea prices in the two sections. Therefore, the Marginal Rate of Substitution in Exchange, $MRS_E = P_c/P_t$, was the same for both groups of prisoners. But for the English prisoners, the tangency point C^* where $MRS_C = MRS_E$ was well over toward the tea axis, while for the French prisoners the consumptive optimum lay in the opposite direction, toward the coffee axis.

[9]R. A. Radford, "The Economic Organisation of a P.O.W. Camp," *Economica*, v. 12 (1945). In his enforced period of stay Radford made many other striking observations, some of which will be mentioned below.

Figure 4.4

Coffee versus Tea in a P.O.W. Camp. English and French P.O.W.'s had different tastes for tea relative to coffee. An efficient smuggling system equalized the price ratio P_c/P_t, so both groups of prisoners faced the same MRS_E. For the French prisoners, the consumptive optimum C^* equating MRS_E to MRS_C (the indifference-curve slope) lay toward the coffee axis; for the English prisoners, the solution lay toward the tea axis.

Panel (a)
English Prisoners

Panel (b)
French Prisoners

We see, therefore, that (in the case of an interior solution) the optimum of the consumer occurs where the following condition, the Substitution Equivalence Equation, holds:

$$(4.4) \qquad MRS_C = MRS_E, \quad \text{or equivalently} \quad \frac{\Delta y}{\Delta x}\bigg|_U = -\frac{P_x}{P_y}$$

ANALYTICAL OPTIMUM PRINCIPLE: The optimum of the consumer, the point where the consumer maximizes utility or satisfaction subject to the limitation of income, is characterized by equality between the Marginal Rate of Substitution in Consumption (MRS_C) and the Marginal Rate of Substitution in Exchange (MRS_E). In addition, the amounts spent must exhaust the consumer's budget. These conditions are the equivalent of the geometrical tangency of indifference curve and budget line, and therefore determine an interior optimum. (If MRS_C and MRS_E cannot be equated, i.e., if no tangency exists, they are to be brought as near to equality as possible by reducing the quantity taken of one of the commodities to zero. This is the equivalent of the geometrical corner optimum.)

One important implication of this analysis is that, despite differences of tastes, *on the margin* everyone actually consuming each of two commodities X and Y places the same relative valuation upon them (has the same MRS_C). In our prisoner of war example above, French prisoners preferred coffee and English prisoners preferred tea. Nevertheless, once each group had adapted to the ruling prices, a French prisoner was no more willing than an English prisoner to give up a unit of tea for coffee. Thus, one result of trade is that the "objective" price ratios in the market measure the "subjective" marginal valuations for all the participants.

The Consumption Balance Equation (4.3) applicable for *cardinal* utility, and the Substitution Equivalence Equation (4.4) that remains valid even if utility is only ordinally quantifiable, must of course be closely related. The key to the relationship is that we can think of MRS_C as a ratio of the Marginal Utilities:

$$MRS_C \equiv \frac{MU_x}{MU_y}$$

Suppose, for example, that $MU_x/MU_y = 2$. This says that, in cardinal utility units, the individual gets twice as many utils from a small increment of X as from a small increment of Y. It then follows that the person would be *just willing* to make a small substitution of two units of Y for one unit of X in the consumption basket. But this is exactly the meaning of the concept of Marginal Rate of Substitution in Consumption.[10] Returning to equation (4.3), this can be rewritten as:

[10]*Mathematical Footnote:* Along an indifference curve,

$$0 = dU \equiv \frac{\partial U}{\partial x}\, dx + \frac{\partial U}{\partial y}\, dy$$

$$\frac{MU_x}{MU_y} = \frac{P_x}{P_y}$$

Since we already have defined the price ratio as MRS_E, substituting MRS_C for the ratio of the Marginal Utilities immediately gives us equation (4.4). The upshot is that the Substitution Equivalence Equation (4.4) holds for cardinal utility, but also remains valid even if only an ordinal utility concept is allowed. Since equation (4.3) is meaningful *only* if utility is cardinal, the optimum condition (4.4) is the more general formulation.[11]

In justifying the Consumption Balance Equation (4.3) as optimum condition, the traditional argument used the postulate of diminishing Marginal Utility. A somewhat analogous specification is needed to justify the Substitution Equivalence Equation. That is, we need some kind of additional restriction, not involving any cardinal utility concept, but still assuring that $MRS_E = MRS_C$ actually represents a best position. Geometrically, the tangency position is an optimum given *convexity* of the indifference-curve map with respect to the origin. The analytical equivalent of the geometrical property of indifference-curve convexity is called the postulate of *decreasing Marginal Rate of Substitution in Consumption*. That is, geometrical convexity corresponds to the condition that MRS_C decreases as x increases.[12]

Then:

$$-\left.\frac{dy}{dx}\right|_U \equiv \frac{\partial U/\partial x}{\partial U/\partial y}$$

i.e., MRS_C equals the ratio of the Marginal Utilities of X and Y.

[11]*Mathematical Footnote:* In ordinal-utility terms, let the consumer maximize $V = F[U(x,y)]$, where $F(U)$ is *any* monotonically increasing function of U. That is, $dF(U)/dU > 0$ for all U. Then the Lagrangian artificial maximand and the optimum conditions become:

$$\text{Max } L = F[U(x,y)] - \lambda(P_x x + P_y y - I)$$
$$_{(x,y,\lambda)}$$

$$\frac{\partial L}{\partial x} = \frac{dF}{dU}\frac{\partial U}{\partial x} - \lambda P_x = 0$$

$$\frac{\partial L}{\partial y} = \frac{dF}{dU}\frac{\partial U}{\partial y} - \lambda P_y = 0$$

$$\frac{\partial L}{\partial \lambda} = P_x x + P_y y - I = 0$$

Write the first two conditions as:

$$\frac{dF}{dU}\frac{\partial U}{\partial x} = \lambda P_x \qquad\qquad \frac{dF}{dU}\frac{\partial U}{\partial y} = \lambda P_y$$

Dividing the first by the second, we see that dF/dU cancels out:

$$\frac{\partial U/\partial x}{\partial U/\partial y} \equiv -\left.\frac{dy}{dx}\right|_U = \frac{P_x}{P_y}$$

So condition (4.4) holds for ordinal as well as cardinal utility.

[12]*Mathematical Footnote:* We are dealing here with the *second-order* conditions for a maximum. The condition for indifference-curve convexity is $d(MRS_C)/dx < 0$. Or, recalling that MRS_C is defined as the absolute value of the slope, this can also be expressed as:

$$\frac{d}{dx}\left(\frac{dy}{dx}\right) \equiv \frac{d^2y}{dx^2} > 0$$

VARIATION OF THE CONSUMER'S OPTIMUM

With the data as to *preferences* assumed unchanging, the optimum of the consumer can vary only in response to changes in *opportunities*. The consumer's market opportunity set, we have seen, depends upon two elements: (1) income, and (2) commodity prices. In this section we shall see how the consumer adjusts his or her preferred consumption basket in reaction to changes in these two elements governing market opportunities.

4.B.1

Income Expansion Path and Engel Curve

Let us suppose, to begin with, that income I increases while all prices remain unchanged. Then, in a simplified world of only two commodities X and Y, we can picture the situation as in Figure 4.5. The original consumptive optimum is at point Q, the tangency of the budget line KL with the indifference curve U_0. (This position corresponds to point C^* in Figure 4.1.) Now let income rise from I to I'. Since the intercept of the original budget line KL on the Y-axis was I/P_y and the intercept on the X-axis was I/P_x, an increase in income from I to I' that leaves prices unchanged will increase both intercepts proportionately. Therefore the new budget line, $K'L'$, must be parallel to the original KL. Put another way, the slope of the budget line depends only upon the price ratio P_x/P_y and so any change in the opportunity set that leaves all prices unaffected must keep the *slope* of the budget line the same as before. (A corollary of this is that a proportionate change of *all* prices simultaneously is equivalent to a corresponding change, in the opposite direction, of income.) The new optimum position is shown as point R, where the budget line $K'L'$ is tangent to the higher indifference curve U_1.

A further increase in income from I' to I'' leads to a further expansion of the market opportunity set, as the budget line shifts outward to $K''L''$. Here the consumptive optimum becomes the tangency position S on indifference curve U_2.

---

where dy/dx is the indifference-curve slope usually expressed more explicitly as $\dfrac{dy}{dx}\Big|_U$.

$$\frac{d^2y}{dx^2} \equiv \frac{d}{dx}\left(\frac{dy}{dx}\right) \equiv \frac{\partial}{\partial x}\left(\frac{dy}{dx}\right) + \frac{\partial}{\partial y}\left(\frac{dy}{dx}\right)\frac{dy}{dx}$$

But:

$$\frac{dy}{dx} \equiv -\frac{\partial U/\partial x}{\partial U/\partial y} \equiv -\frac{U_x}{U_y} \quad \text{(in more compact notation)}$$

Then:

$$\frac{d^2y}{dx^2} \equiv -\frac{U_y U_{xx} - U_x U_{xy}}{U_y^2} - \frac{U_y U_{xy} - U_x U_{yy}}{U_y^2}\left(-\frac{U_x}{U_y}\right)$$

$$\equiv \frac{-U_y^2 U_{xx} + U_x U_y U_{xy} + U_y U_x U_{xy} - U_x^2 U_{yy}}{U_y^3}$$

The main significance of this result is to show that diminishing Marginal Utility (U_{xx}, $U_{yy} < 0$) does not *necessarily* imply decreasing MRS_C (positive d^2y/dx^2). For, the cross-derivative U_{xy} has indeterminate sign. So even with cardinal utility, it is indifference-curve convexity rather than diminishing Marginal Utility that should be relied on to define the proper second-order condition for a maximum.

Figure 4.5

Derivation of the Income Expansion Path (IEP). As income increases from I to I' to I'', but with prices P_x and P_y held constant, the budget line shifts outward parallel to itself from KL to $K'L'$ to $K''L''$. The tangency defining the consumer optimum correspondingly shifts from Q to R to S. The Income Expansion Path (IEP) shows all the consumer optimum positions attained as I varies, prices remaining the same.

More generally, if we think of I as hypothetically varying while prices and tastes remain unchanged, an entire curve—an Income Expansion Path (IEP)—will be traced out that connects all the different consumptive optimum positions like Q, R, and S in Figure 4.5. The Income Expansion Path indicates the response of the rational consumer to changes in income alone. It should be kept in mind, however, that the Income Expansion Path as a whole depends upon the price ratio; if prices were held constant but at some differing ratio, a different IEP curve would be obtained. More specifically, a price change leading to an increased ratio P_x/P_y (a steepening of the budget lines KL, $K'L'$, etc.) will have the effect of displacing the entire IEP to the northwest. (The student should check this point to verify his understanding of the nature of the IEP curve.)

What shapes are possible for the Income Expansion Path? Consider the three panels of Figure 4.6. In all three cases the original situation is at the point Q, a tangency with indifference curve U_0 along the budget line KL. Now let income increase, so that the budget line shifts out to the position $K'L'$. In Panel (a), the new tangency R along indifference curve U_1 is within the northeasterly quadrant formed by the vertical and horizontal dashed lines through Q. This means that the quantities purchased of X and of Y have both increased with the rise in income; in this case X and Y are called *normal* goods.

In Panel (b), the new tangency R lies to the northwest of Q, outside the

Figure 4.6

Income Expansion Paths, Three Cases. In all three diagrams the outward shift of the budget line (from *KL* to *K′L′*) represents an increase in income *I*, with prices P_x and P_y held constant. In Panel (a) the upward direction of the Income Expansion Path (IEP) is northeast, so that the new consumptive optimum solution at *R* involves increased purchases of both commodities. Here both *X* and *Y* are normal superior goods. In Panel (b) the upward direction of the IEP is northwest; as income *I* increases more of *Y* is consumed, but less of *X*. *X* here is called an inferior goods, and *Y* an ultra-superior good. Panel (c) is the opposite case, where the upward direction of the IEP is southeast. Here *Y* is inferior, *X* ultra-superior.

normal quadrant; at the higher income, the quantity of *Y* purchased has increased but the quantity of *X* decreased. Thus in Panel (b) the IEP has negative slope through the consumptive optimum positions *Q* and *R*. A commodity like *X* here, whose consumption falls when income rises, is called an *inferior* good.

Unfortunately, there is no terminological agreement as to what to call the other commodity *Y* in this case. The term ''superior good'' refers to any good that is not inferior, i.e., whose consumption rises with income. Hence Y would be regarded as superior in either the situation of Panel (a) or of Panel (b), leaving us still in need of a way to express the distinction between the two cases. Let us adopt the term *ultra-superior* for the good that is a "partner" of an inferior good. Then Y is ultra-superior in Panel (b). The defining characteristic of an ultra-superior good may be expressed as follows: Since less of an inferior good is purchased when income increases, it follows that *more than 100%* of the increase in income has been devoted to additional purchases of the associated ultra-superior good.

Finally, Panel (c) shows the opposite situation where Y is inferior and X ultra-superior. The IEP is again negatively sloped, but the new consumptive optimum position lies to the southeast (rather than northwest) as income rises.

In all three cases, the IEP curve is drawn with an arrowhead pointing in the direction of rising utility (upward on the invisible utility hill). The arrow is convenient in permitting an immediate distinction, by inspection, between the X-inferior [Panel (b)] case and the Y-inferior [Panel (c)] case.

CONCLUSION: A positively-sloped Income Expansion Path, between two goods X and Y, means that consumption of each rises as income grows. Then X and Y are both normal superior goods. Alternatively, if the IEP has negative slope one of the goods must be inferior. The other good must of course be superior, but more specifically may be called ultra-superior as it accounts for more than 100% of the increment of income.

Goods that are predominantly purchased by relatively wealthy people are commonly called luxuries. Correspondingly, a good which accounts for a large portion of the consumption budget of poorer people, the proportion in the budget declining as people become richer, is sometimes termed a "necessity." Standard items of food like bread are generally considered necessities. For, while richer people can afford to and generally do buy more loaves of bread per person than poorer people (i.e., bread is not an inferior good), the *proportion* of the budget spent on bread falls as income rises.

EXAMPLE 4.2
LUXURIES VERSUS
NECESSITIES IN A
P.O.W. CAMP

In the prisoner-of-war economy already mentioned in Example 4.1 above, R. A. Radford[13] also made interesting observations about necessities and luxuries. Toward the end of the war, prisoners were living in severe privation as a result of the steady deterioration of the German economy under bombing and other wartime strains. In August 1944 a further halving of real income rations, the two main items being food and cigarettes, took place. Unexpectedly, cigarettes proved to be more of a "necessity" than food (by the standard definition above). Despite the presence of many non-smokers, in the market as a whole there was a net attempt after real income fell to trade food for cigarettes. As a result, the price of food (in terms of cigarettes) became actually lower than before.

[13]R. A. Radford, "The Economic Organization of a P.O.W. Camp," *Economica*, v. 12 (1945).

The implied shape of indifference curves between cigarettes C and food F at the higher income level (point $Q°$) and the lower income level (point Q'), for a typical prisoner, is indicated in Figure 4.7. The Marginal Rate of Substitution in Consumption, $MRS_c \equiv -\dfrac{\Delta c}{\Delta f}\Big|_U$ is less (the indifference curve has flatter slope) at the lower real-income point.

The analysis to this point has shown the reaction of the consumer's optimum basket of commodities to changes in income—prices and preferences being taken as constant. For any single good such as X, the relation between income and consumption can be summarized in a convenient form for statistical determination known as the *Engel Curve*.[14] A portion of a typical Engel Curve is shown in Figure 4.8. In the case illustrated, the quantity of X consumed rises as income rises, i.e., X is a superior good.

Figure 4.7

Food versus Cigarettes in a P.O.W. Camp. After a halving of cigarette and food rations, the typical P.O.W. was forced from an initial position like $Q°$ to a less preferred outcome Q'. Under these circumstances it was observed that P_f/P_c, the price of food in terms of cigarettes as "numeraire," fell. Since P_f/P_c is the market ratio $\Delta c/\Delta f$ at which cigarettes and food can be exchanged, the MRS_E between cigarettes and food, and since from equation (4.4) $MRS_E = MRS_C$, we know that MRS_C (the indifference-curve slope) must have been less at lower incomes. That is, cigarettes became relatively more preferred as income fell.

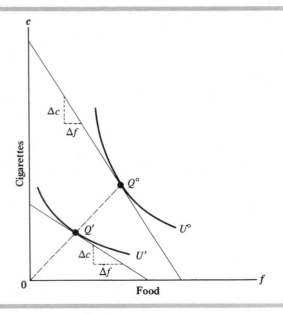

[14]Ernst Engel (1821–1896), German statistician.

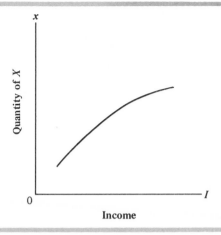

Figure 4.8

Engel Curve. The Engel Curve shows the quantity purchased of any good X as a function of income I. For a superior good, the Engel Curve rises with income as shown here.

EXAMPLE 4.3
POLYGYNY IN
MAIDUGURI

The economist Amyra Grossbard, reviewing data compiled by anthropologists, attempted to estimate a number of the determinants of multiple wives (polygyny) in Maiduguri,[15] a region in Nigeria with an Islamic population. Under the primitive market conditions in that area, income and wealth could not be adequately measured in cash terms. One estimate was provided by an interviewer, who ranked the male subjects on a wealth scale from 1 to 4. It was found that each upward step in rank was associated on average with a .16 increase in number of wives. Several indirect or "proxy" estimates of wealth also were used. For example, it was found that males owning houses had on average .23 more wives than non-owners. And males whose residences had piped water had on average .32 more wives.

COMMENT: No single available measure of income was fully satisfactory, but the different estimates reinforced one another to indicate that wives are a normal superior "good" for Maiduguri males. The Engel curves would therefore be somewhat as pictured in Figure 4.8.

[15] Amyra Grossbard, "An Economic Analysis of Polygyny: The Case of Maiduguri," *Current Anthropology*, v. 17 (Dec. 1976).

In practice we are almost always interested in broader categories or aggregates of consumption like food, clothing, vacation travel, and so forth, rather than in specific single commodities. There is, however, no natural or usable quantity unit for a broad commodity grouping like food or clothing. To handle this, we can replace quantity of X on the vertical axis of the Engel-curve diagram of Figure 4.8

with consumer *expenditures* on X. If X is a single good, expenditures on the good would of course be price times quantity purchased, or $P_x x$. And if X represented an entire grouping of consumption goods $(X_1, \ldots, X_G^G)$, expenditure is $P_1 x_1 + P_2 x_2 + \ldots + P_G x_G$. Or, in more compact notation, $\Sigma_{g=1} P_g x_g$, the sum of the quantities of the separate goods each multiplied by its respective price. The latter version of the income-consumption relation in terms of expenditures may be called the *Engel Expenditure Curve*. Both the simple Engel Curve and the Engel Expenditure Curve represent the same data as the Income Expansion Paths of Figure 4.5 and 4.6, but translated onto different axes. For the former, x is plotted as a function of I; for the latter, $P_x x$ as a function of I.

DEFINITIONS: The *Engel Curve* relates consumption quantity x to income I. The *Engel Expenditure Curve* relates expenditure $P_x x$ to income I.

The Engel Expenditure Curve has the additional advantage (over the simple Engel Curve) of directly displaying the difference between a normal superior good and an ultra-superior good. Indeed, the alternative slopes for the Engel Expenditure Curve in the three panels of Figure 4.9 correspond to the three cases of Figure 4.6. To interpret Figure 4.9, first note the dashed 45° line emerging from the origin. If for any commodity (or commodity grouping) the Engel Expenditure Curve lay along this 45° line, the consumer's entire income would be devoted to purchase of that commodity or grouping. Hence the 45° line constitutes an upper limit for the Engel Expenditure Curve.

In the situation pictured in Panel (a), expenditures on X rise as income I increases. But the slope of the rising curve is less than 45°. This means that expenditures on X have risen by *less* than the rise in income, i.e., some of the increment of income must have been spent on a good or goods other than X. Hence, this corresponds to the "normal" case in Panel (a) of Figure 4.6.

Jumping to Panel (c) of Figure 4.9, we see here that in the range between I' and I'' the Engel Expenditure Curve is rising *more* sharply than the 45° line. Hence more than the total increase in income is being devoted to consumption of X. This means that X is ultra-superior, as in the Panel (c) situation of Figure 4.6. Finally, in the middle Panel (b) of Figure 4.9, expenditures on X actually decline as income rises. Since P_x is constant, the quantity of X taken must have fallen; hence X is inferior, as in the situation pictured in Panel (b) of Figure 4.6.

Recall that the Engel Curve as in Figure 4.8 is a re-plotting of the data summarized by the Income Expansion Path. We know that the IEP will in general shift in response to changes in the price ratio P_x/P_y, and specifically, a rise in P_x (with P_y held constant) will displace the IEP to the northwest. For the Engel Curve, the effect of a rise in P_x will normally be a lowering of the curve, showing that, for any given income I, at a higher P_x less of X will be taken. (See the discussion of the Law of Demand below.) On the other hand, for the Engel Expenditure Curve there are offsetting effects; since P_x rises but the quantity of X falls, the direction of change in $P_x x$ is indeterminate.

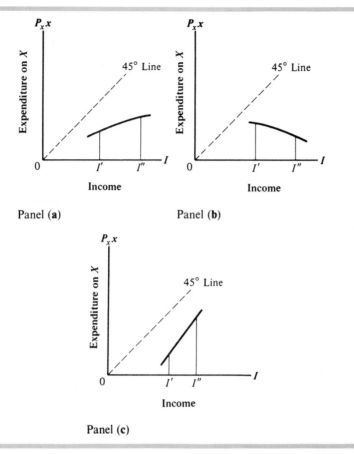

Figure 4.9
Engel Expenditure Curves. An Engel Expenditure Curve shows $P_x x$, the amount expended on good X, as a function of income I (where price P_x is held constant). If the curve were to touch the 45° line, at that point *all* of income would be spent on X. In Panel (a), the expenditure $P_x x$ rises with income but diverges from the 45° line, indicating that more is spent on *other* goods as well, as I rises. In Panel (b) less is spent on X as income rises, so X must be inferior. In Panel (c) more is being spent on X and the curve approaches the 45° line; this means that less is being spent on other goods, so that these other goods must therefore in aggregate be inferior.

EXAMPLE 4.4
ENGEL'S LAWS
AFTER A CENTURY

The 19th-century statistician Engel did more than merely posit a relation between income and consumer expenditures on specific goods or classes of goods. He went on to assert that, as income increases: (1) The proportion of the budget spent on food will fall; (2) the proportions spent on lodging and clothing will remain about the same; and (3) the proportion spent on all other goods will increase.

The table below shows the proportionate expenditures on certain categories of consumer goods, for U.S. urban families in 1960–61 classified by income.

*Distribution of Expenditures**

	FAMILY INCOME LEVEL, AFTER TAXES			
EXPENDITURE CATEGORY	UNDER $2000	$2000– 2999	$3000– 3999	$4000 AND OVER
Food	29.5%	28.4%	25.9%	23.7%
Shelter, fuel, light, refrigeration, water	29.4	24.3	20.6	17.4
Clothing	5.9	8.2	9.0	10.8
Medical care	8.2	8.1	7.3	6.4
Automobile	3.2	6.5	11.3	13.9
All other	23.8	24.5	25.9	27.8
Total	100.0	100.0	100.0	100.0

Source: Bureau of Labor Statistics, "Consumer Expenditures and Income, with Emphasis on Low Income Families," July 1964.

*For a more complete survey, see H. Houthakker, "An International Comparison of House-hold Expenditure Patterns, Commemorating the Centenary of Engel's Law," *Econometrica*, v. 25 (Oct. 1957).

The data confirm Engel in showing a declining proportion spent on food as income rises. But where he predicted constant proportions spent on lodging and clothing, the 20th-century data show a falling proportion in the former and a rising proportion in the latter category. The "All other" category also rises with income, as Engel predicted. One striking feature of the table is the very sharp increase in the proportion spent on the *automobile* as income rises; automobile transportation is evidently a strongly superior good.

4.B.2
Price Expansion Path and Demand Curve

Let us now consider the effect of parametric variation in the other determinant of opportunities—market prices. It will be convenient to hold the price of one of the commodities, P_y, constant. Then variation in prices will take the specific form of changes in P_x, the price of commodity X. Here again the change in data affects the shape of the market opportunity set. But whereas a rise in income leads to a *parallel* outward displacement of the budget line representing the northeasterly boundary of the opportunity set, a change in price leads to a *tilting* of this boundary.

In Figure 4.10, as before, the initial situation is represented by the consumer optimum at Q where the budget line KL is tangent to the indifference curve U_0. Now let the price of X *fall*. Since the intercept of the budget line with the vertical Y-axis is at I/P_y, nothing has changed there; the point K remains as before. But the intercept of the budget line with the horizontal X-axis is at I/P_x, so the fall in P_x is associated with an expansion of the opportunity set taking the form of an outward tilting of the budget line to a new position like KL'. This makes sense, since the

Figure 4.10

Derivation of the Price Expansion Path (PEP). As P_x falls, with income I and the price of the other good P_y held constant, the budget line tilts outward (from KL to KL' to KL''). The consumptive optimum position changes correspondingly from Q to R to S. The Price Expansion Path (PEP) connects all such consumptive optimum positions as P_x varies, the arrowhead on the PEP curve indicating the direction of utility improvement. Normally, the PEP curve moves eastward, and it can never cross above the horizontal drawn through point K. (K is the "corner solution" where, for sufficiently high P_x, none of commodity X would be purchased.)

enhanced market opportunities are associated entirely with the improved terms for purchasing good X. The new optimum of the consumer is then the point R where the new budget line KL' is tangent to a higher indifference curve U_1. And a still further decline in the price P_x leads to a further outward tilting of the budget line, to the position KL''; here the associated optimum of the consumer is at S on the still higher indifference curve U_2.

A curve can now be passed through all possible consumptive optimum positions like Q, R, and S that are generated by changes in P_x (when income I and the price P_y of the other commodity are held constant). The curve so generated can be called, in analogy with the Income Expansion Path (IEP) of the previous section, the Price Expansion Path (PEP). The PEP curve indicates the response of the rational consumer to changes in P_x alone, income I and the price P_y being held fixed. However, just as the IEP curve in its entirety is shifted when prices change, the entire Price Expansion Path will be displaced to a different position if income I changes. Specifically, if goods X and Y are normal, then a parametric increase in income will tend to shift the Price Expansion Path upward and to the right. (Students should check this point to verify their understanding of the PEP curve, and also work out the implications for the PEP of a parametric shift in the price of the *other* commodity.)

A number of aspects of the Price Expansion Path are of interest.

1. As the price P_x falls, the PEP curve enters regions of higher and higher levels of utility. Again, an arrowhead shows the direction of utility improvement along the PEP in Figure 4.10. The level of satisfaction increases since, with income I in numeraire terms held constant, a fall in P_x is equivalent to a rise in *real* income—in the sense of ability to purchase desired commodities.

2. If the PEP curves downward (southeasterly), as in the range between Q and R along the curve in Figure 4.10, at lower prices P_x the consumer purchases more of X but takes less of Y. If the PEP bends upward into a positive slope, as in the range between R and S in the diagram, the consumer is willing and able at the lower price P_x to obtain more X while consuming more Y as well.

3. If there is some price P_x so high that no X is purchased, at that price the optimum of the consumer is a *corner solution* on the Y-axis, as in Figure 4.3. If this condition holds, the Price Expansion Path will have a terminating point on the Y-axis as at K in Figure 4.10. On the other hand, no matter how low the price P_x falls, so long as it does not become negative, the budget line (boundary of the market opportunity set) must lie below the dashed horizontal drawn through K in the diagram. Thus, the Price Expansion Path must also lie everywhere below this horizontal.

4. Astonishing as it may seem, the PEP curve may conceivably curl back so as to be moving for a time in a northwesterly direction, as in the circled region in Figure 4.11. In this region, as price P_x falls the quantity of X consumed also falls! When this condition applies, the commodity is

Figure 4.11

Price Expansion Path—Giffen Case. The Price Expansion Path might conceivably curl back northwest over a limited range (circled region), so that *less* of X is purchased as price P_x falls. In this range X would be called a "Giffen good."

called a "Giffen good"[16] for this consumer. But the Giffen property can only hold over a limited range; with negatively-sloped indifference curves and positive preference directions, the PEP cannot move northwesterly very long and still be entering regions of higher and higher utility. Giffen goods will be discussed further below.

Finally, we can re-plot the data summarized by the Price Expansion Path as a relation between the quantity consumed of commodity X and the price of X, as in the curve dd of Panel (a) in Figure 4.12. This is of course the individual's *demand curve for X*. It will be evident from the derivation that so long as the PEP is moving easterly as in Figure 4.10 (whether southeasterly as in the range KQR, or northeasterly as in the range RS), the demand curve must have a normal negative slope: A lower price P_x is associated with a larger quantity of X entering into the optimum position of the consumer. But if there is a Giffen range in which the PEP curls northwesterly (the circled region in Figure 4.11), then there will be a corresponding range along the demand curve where the demand curve is positively sloped (the circled region in Panel (b) of Figure 4.12). In this range the demand curve has the "Giffen property" that at lower prices a smaller quantity is demanded.

Figure 4.12

Demand Curves—The Law of Demand versus the Giffen Case. Panel (a) pictures a negatively sloped individual demand curve, satisfying the Law of Demand: as the price falls, more of X is purchased. In Panel (b) the demand curve has the exceptional "Giffen" property, more being purchased as prices *rise*, in the small circled region (corresponding to the circled region in Figure 4.11). The Giffen property can only hold, if at all, over a limited range of prices.

Panel (a)
The Law of Demand

Panel (b)
The Giffen Case

[16]Sir Robert Giffen, British statistician and economist (1837–1910).

That the Giffen demand curve is never (or almost never) observed is a principle called the *Law of Demand*. This principle, like convexity of indifference curves with respect to the origin, does *not* follow from the pure logic of choice. Its justification is empirical observation of the world.

<table>
<tr><td>EXAMPLE 4.5
THE LAW OF
DEMAND—
ANIMAL AND
HUMAN</td><td colspan="2">The psychologist S. E. G. Lea reviewed in 1978[17] a number of demand studies from a wide variety of sources—including animal experiments, retailing experiments, and econometric investigations. The following is a summary showing, for each class of study, the number of instances that either support or contradict the Law of Demand, or represent mixed or uncertain results.</td></tr>
</table>

	LAW OF DEMAND SUPPORTED	LAW OF DEMAND CONTRADICTED	MIXED OR UNCERTAIN
Animal Experiments[a] (18)	15	1	2
Retailing Experiments[b] (9)	7	1	1
Selection of Econometric Studies[c] (25)	25	0	0

[a] Estimated visually from Lea, Fig. 1 (p. 447).
[b] Ditto, Fig. 2 (p. 448).
[c] Ditto, Fig. 3 (p. 449).

That demand behavior can be investigated by animal experimentation is perhaps surprising. In these experiments, the commodity "purchased" (called by psychologists a *reinforcer*) was typically "paid for" by presses on a lever. Among the reinforcers used in the experiments surveyed were water, food, sucrose solution, and morphine injections! The animals included rats, mice, monkeys, guinea pigs, and Siamese fighting fish.

COMMENT: The Law of Demand is so firmly believed by economists that there is some danger of distortion of results. An econometric investigator whose data suggest a violation of the Law of Demand is likely to doubt the figures, or to reconsider the methods used, before publishing the study. That even animal experiments conducted by psychologists tend to support the Law of Demand is therefore somewhat reassuring.

[17] S. E. G. Lea, "The Psychology and Economics of Demand," *Psychological Bulletin*, v. 85 (1978).

That the Law of Demand is consistent with the great majority of ordinary consumption decisions of ordinary people probably no one doubts. But perhaps questions might arise in exceptional situations, for example, addicts' demand for narcotics or alcoholics' demand for liquor. Even in such situations, however, the fact that consumption decisions are subject to an income constraint imposes strong pressure in the direction of the Law of Demand. Suppose that an addict were to spend literally all of his income upon drugs, regardless of price. Then by elementary algebra he necessarily must buy less as price rises. On the other hand, in order to support his habit as price increases he might try to acquire more income—by stealing, begging, or even working. But the more income needed, the harder the effort required, and the Law of Demand still tends to hold. So we are not surprised to read, for example, that after Prohibition raised the effective price of liquor in the U.S., there was indeed a decline in consumption. (Indirect evidence: the observed incidence of cirrhosis of the liver declined.)[18]

EXAMPLE 4.6
SHOCKING
ALCOHOLICS

As a portion of an experiment conducted by M. B. Sobell and L. C. Sobell,[19] forty alcoholics who had voluntarily admitted themselves to Patton State Hospital in California were randomly assigned to an experimental or a control group. The twenty patients assigned to the experimental group received, in addition to conventional hospital treatment, a special sequence of sessions. In these sessions liquor was freely available, except that "inappropriate" drinking behavior was punished by an electric shock. Shocks were administered if the patient ordered a drink straight, took too large a sip, ordered drinks less than 20 minutes apart, or ordered more than three drinks in a session. During three of the thirteen sessions, however, no shocks were administered. The overall results were as follows:

SESSIONS	AVERAGE INAPPROPRIATE BEHAVIORS*
With Shocks	2.2
Without Shocks	18.7

*Calculated from Sobell and Sobell, p. 39.

Note that this was a case *without* a fixed constraint on purchasing power. A patient could always "earn" the right to take another drink by undergoing an electric shock. Nevertheless, when the price of drinking was high, less occurred.

COMMENT: An interesting point, touching upon the nature and stability of "tastes" (see Chapter 3, Section G), was observed in follow-up studies at later dates. The experimental group seemed to have better success than the control group in remaining sober afterward. This suggests that life experiences can indeed change attitudes, not a very astonishing conclusion but one that at least superficially appears to be at odds with the standard economic

[19]Mark B. Sobell and Linda C. Sobell, *Individualized Behavior Therapy for Alcoholics: Rationale, Procedures, Preliminary Results, and Appendix*, California Mental Health Research Monograph No. 13 (1972).

[18]H. Kalant and O. J. Kalant, *Drugs, Society, and Personal Choice* (Don Mills, Ontario: Paperjacks, 1971), p. 117.

Since the demand curve is in effect a re-plotting of the data in the Price Expansion Path, and since the latter shifts position as *income I* changes, we would expect a change in income to affect the position of the demand curve for X. If X and the other commodity Y are both normal goods, the quantities consumed at any price ratio will *both* increase as income rises [Figure 4.6, Panel (a)]. Then, as has been mentioned, the entire Price Expansion Path PEP of Figure 4.10 would be displaced upward and to the right (outward from the origin). Considering the effect upon good X alone, it follows that the demand curve for X will be displaced to the right as income rises—dd will shift to a position like $d'd'$ in Figure 4.13, showing that an increased quantity would be consumed at any price P_x. And of course if X is ultra-superior [Figure 4.6, Panel (c)], again dd will shift to the right

Figure 4.13

Effect of Income Shifts on Demand Curve. If X is a superior good (whether normal or ultra-superior), a rise in income implies larger purchases of X at any price P_x; the demand curve shifts to the right (position $d'd'$). But if X is an inferior good, as income increases *less* is purchased at any price P_x; the demand curve shifts to the left (position $d''d''$).

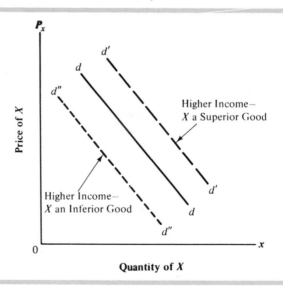

as income rises. But if X is an *inferior* good [Figure 4.6, Panel (b)], the shift of *dd* as income rises will be to the left, to a position like *d"d"* in Figure 4.13; less of X will be purchased at any given price P_x.

INCOME AND SUBSTITUTION EFFECTS OF A PRICE CHANGE

The previous section showed how changes in the two determinants of the opportunity set, *income* and *prices*, affect the optimum of the consumer. However, this classification does not provide a clean separation of the effects of price changes versus income changes upon individual opportunities. For, if income I remains numerically unchanged while the price P_x falls, with the other price P_y held constant, in a sense *real* income has increased. The individual's *market opportunity set* has grown; in terms of Figure 4.10, as P_x falls with I and P_y held constant, we saw that the budget line KL shifted outward to a position like KL' or KL''. Correspondingly, of course, a *rise* in P_x, with P_y and income I held constant, would represent a contraction of opportunities and in that sense a fall in real income.

For some purposes it is desirable to correct for and thus eliminate the real-income effect of a price change upon the consumer optimum. When this is done we are left with what is called the pure *substitution effect* of the price change. The usual method of adjustment, devised by the British economist J. R. Hicks,[20] is illustrated in Figure 4.14. The budget line KL associated with the original price P_x leads to the optimum of the consumer at Q along the indifference curve U_0, where the quantity taken of X is x_0. The budget line KL' reflects a lower price P'_x leading to the new optimum at R along indifference curve U_1, where $x = x_1$. Now construct an artificial budget line $\hat{K}\hat{L}$ (dashed in the diagram) *tangent to the original indifference curve U_0 but whose slope reflects the new price ratio P'_x/P_y.* The tangency of $\hat{K}\hat{L}$ with U_0 is at the point $\hat{Q}$, where $x = \hat{x}_0$.

Between the original consumer optimum Q and the artificial optimum $\hat{Q}$, real income is constant—in the sense that utility is unchanged (the individual remains on the same indifference curve as before). Thus the shift of the optimum from Q to $\hat{Q}$ (or, in terms of quantities of X, the difference $\hat{x}_0 - x_0$), is the pure "substitution effect" due to the price change. The remainder of the movement of the consumer optimum from $\hat{Q}$ to R (or, in terms of X, the difference $x_1 - \hat{x}_0$) is the "income effect." Since $\hat{Q}$ and R are tangencies along budget lines of parallel slopes, the change in the price ratio plays no role between $\hat{Q}$ and R. Thus the income effect isolates the income equivalent of the consumer's gain from the price decrease.

The usefulness of this separation turns upon the qualitatively different elements responsible for the income and the substitution effects. With negatively-

[20]Another method of adjustment, more convenient for some purposes, will be introduced in Chapter 6.

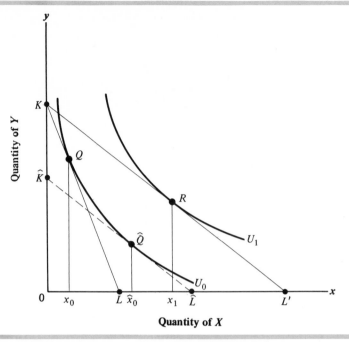

Figure 4.14

Income and Substitution Effects—Hicks Decomposition. A fall in price P_x, with I and P_y held constant, shifts the budget line from KL to KL' so that the consumptive optimum changes from Q to R. As R lies on a higher indifference curve, there has been an increase in *real* income. The "income effect" of the price change can be separated from the pure "substitution effect" by constructing an artificial budget line $\hat{K}\hat{L}$ parallel to KL and tangent to the original indifference curve U_0 (at the position $\hat{Q}$). There is no utility improvement between Q and $\hat{Q}$, only between $\hat{Q}$ and R. The income effect of the price change upon the demand for X is therefore $x_1 - \hat{x}_0$; the pure substitution effect of the price change is $\hat{x}_0 - x_0$.

sloped and convex indifference curves, the substitution effect is always in the normal direction: A *fall* in P_x necessarily leads to a *rise* in the quantity of X taken. For, the fall in P_x flattens the budget line (note that $\hat{K}\hat{L}$ is less steep than KL in Figure 4.14) and so the $\hat{Q}$ tangency along U_0 must be at a point where $\hat{x}_0 > x_0$.

Turning to the income effect, we can see by comparison with the three panels of Figure 4.6 that R might lie to the northwest, northeast, or southeast of $\hat{Q}$. In the normal case [Panel (a)], or if X is ultra-superior [Panel (c)], the income effect (due to the enrichment of the consumer after the fall in P_x) *reinforces* the substitution effect so as to lead to a further increase in consumption of X. (Figure 4.14 illustrates a normal relation between X and Y, and so the income effect $x_1 - \hat{x}_0$ is positive.) But if X were *inferior* [as in Panel (b) of Figure 4.6], the income effect would tend to offset the substitution effect. And indeed it is at least a logical possibility that an abnormal (negative) income effect might outweigh a normal substitution effect. If this occurs a *fall* in price would lead to a net *fall* in quantity purchased; this is the aforementioned "Giffen case."

FROM INDIVIDUAL DEMAND TO MARKET DEMAND

The passage from demand of the individual to the aggregate demand in the market as a whole is simplicity itself. The *individual's* demand function, shown in Figure 4.15 as the curve $d_j d_j$, gives the quantities that would be purchased by a particular consumer (designated as j) in response to any specific price for commodity X ruling in the market. The *market* demand function, the curve DD in the diagram, shows the aggregate quantities that would be purchased by all consumers together at that price. If x_j is the quantity taken by the individual j at price P_x, then the aggregate quantity must obviously be the summation over all such individuals. Symbolically, aggregate quantities will generally be designated by upper-case letters.[21] So we can write:

(4.5) $X = \Sigma_{j=1}^{J} x_j$

Figure 4.15

Individual and Aggregate Demand. To the left of the break in the horizontal axis, the curve $d_j d_j$ shows the demand curve of individual j. Every potential purchaser in the market will have such an individual demand curve. To the right of the break the aggregate demand curve DD, showing the overall quantity X purchased at any price P_x, is the horizontal summation of all the individual demand curves like $d_j d_j$. (The break indicates a considerable distance along the horizontal axis omitted in the construction.)

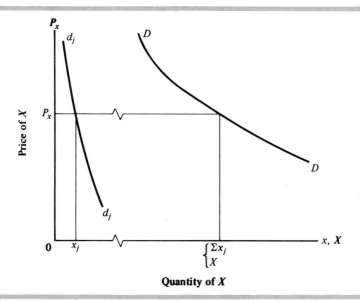

Quantity of X

[21]Symbols like X and Y are used here both as *names* of commodities and as aggregate *quantities* of the corresponding commodities. The ambiguity will not be disturbing, as the meaning will always be clear from the context in which the symbol appears.

This says that the aggregate quantity (along the market demand curve DD) is the sum of the individual quantities, where the subscript j is an index running over all of the individuals $1, 2, \ldots, J$ in the market.

Geometrically, the summation is *horizontal* (i.e., over quantities and not over prices). Note that, in Figure 4.15, the market demand curve has a much flatter *slope* than the individual demand curve. This tells us that if P_x decreases, for example, the quantity increases for the market as a whole will ordinarily be much greater than the increase in quantity consumed by any single individual. However, in terms of percentage changes instead of numerical changes, the *proportionate* increase in X along the aggregate demand curve DD as P_x falls need not be any greater than the proportionate increase along the individual demand curve d_jd_j. This point will be considered further when we take up the concept of "Elasticity" in the next chapter.

An implicit assumption of the foregoing analysis, one which will become the subject of attention in Chapter 7, is that the *same* price P_x is being charged to every individual in the market. Where this assumption is not appropriate, a market demand curve in the ordinary sense cannot be constructed.

CONCLUSION: The market demand curve is the *horizontal* sum of the individual demand curves.

AN APPLICATION: SUBSIDY VERSUS "VOUCHER"

Suppose that the decision-making agencies of government wish to increase consumption of a particular good—education, let us say. There are a number of possible ways to do so. A general *subsidy* to producers or consumers of education is one possibility. (Free public education is of course an extreme kind of subsidy.) But there might be objections on a variety of grounds to a general subsidy. *Voucher* schemes represent a somewhat different technique for achieving the desired end.

In Figure 4.16, E represents education and Z "all other goods." Panel (a) shows the effect of a subsidy to education. The original (unsubsidized) tangency optimum is at Q on indifference curve U_0. A subsidy acts like a reduction in price; it rotates the budget line from KL outward to a new position KL'. The new optimum is at R, on indifference curve U_1. Apart from the unlikely possibility that E is a Giffen good in this range, there will be an increase in the consumer's purchases of education. In the diagram, the increase is the distance $e_1 - e_0$ on the horizontal axis.

Panel (b) of Figure 4.16 shows the effect of a voucher scheme. The initial position Q on indifference curve U_0 is the same as before. The "voucher" is a *gift of income spendable only on the specified commodity E*. The distance KK' on the vertical axis represents the amount of the gift in Z-units, so that the consumer's

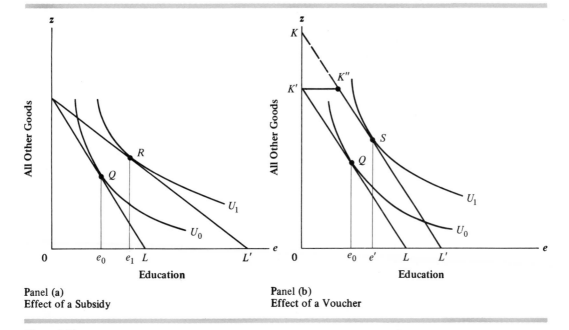

Panel (a)
Effect of a Subsidy

Panel (b)
Effect of a Voucher

Figure 4.16

Subsidy versus Voucher. In Panel (a), a subsidy to consumption of education *(E)* acts like a reduction in price P_e; the budget line shifts from *KL* to *KL'*. At the new consumptive optimum, the quantity purchased of *E* will be greater (unless *E* is a Giffen good in this range, which is highly unlikely). In Panel (b), the "voucher" pictured is a gift of income in the amount *KK'*, but spendable only on good *E*. The budget line shifts to the right, from *KL* to *K'L'*, except that the consumer is not allowed to choose an optimum in the range between *K'* and *K"* (since the full amount of the voucher would not then be spent on purchases of *E*). The new consumptive optimum at *S* will involve increased purchases of *E*, so long as *E* is not an inferior good.

budget line shifts upward from *KL* to *K'L'*. But the gift of *KK'* is only valid to the extent that it is spent on *E*. Note the dashed portion of the new budget line between *K'* and *K"*. This range along the new budget line represents positions for which a lesser amount of income than the voucher gift *KK'* is devoted to purchases of *E* and so is not available to the consumer. That is, the consumer is not permitted to move to a consumption position in this range. (If permitted to do so, the consumer would be converting some of the gift into increased purchases of "other goods" *Z*, which is what the voucher scheme is intended to prevent.) Therefore, the *effective* new budget line is only the range *K"L'* along *K'L'*. In Panel (b) of Figure 4.16 the new optimum is at *S* on indifference curve *U'*. The quantity purchased of commodity *E* will rise ($e' > e_0$) whenever *E* is a superior good (positive income effect).

So far it might appear that there is no great difference between the subsidy and the voucher. The former works through what is in effect a price change, the latter through what is in effect an income change. But the voucher does have a certain special power in the case of a consumer who would *otherwise take very little or nothing* of the commodity whose consumption it is desired to increase.

Consider Figure 4.17. Here the individual is initially at a *corner solution*. That is, at the existing prices (slope of market line KL) the consumptive optimum is the corner point K on indifference curve U_0, where the individual is consuming a zero quantity of commodity E. Even a fairly substantial subsidy, rotating the budget line outward by a considerable angle from K, might have little or no effect on consumption of E. But the voucher displaces the entire budget line upward to $K'L'$ (of which only the solid range $K''L'$ is effective). If free to spend the enlarged income, the consumer might still ideally prefer the new corner point K' on indifference curve U_2. But the farthest the consumer is permitted to go in this direction along $K'L'$ is the point K'', on indifference curve U_1. (Note that the achievable optimum K'' is *not* in general a tangency position.) Here the individual has spent the entire voucher amount on purchases of E, but without spending anything further on E out of non-voucher income. A voucher will almost always be effective in increasing consumption for someone previously not consuming E at all, or previously consuming an amount less than the voucher equivalent. The only exception would be if E is not even a good (i.e., if it is actually a *bad*) from the viewpoint of the consumer. (If E were a bad for an individual, a voucher spendable only on E would simply remain unutilized.)

There are however at least two flaws in this analysis of the effects of a subsidy versus a voucher. First, an implicit assumption was that the market price

Figure 4.17

Corner Solution and Voucher. The initial consumptive optimum is the corner solution at K; none of commodity E is being purchased. A voucher gift of income in the amount KK' leads to a new consumptive optimum at K''. (The consumer would still prefer a corner solution at point K', but this is unavailable.) The voucher leads to increased consumption of E, compared with an initial corner solution, provided only that E is a good for this individual.

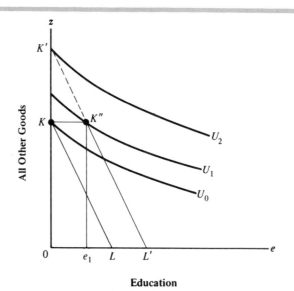

of the good E remained unchanged throughout. This would be a reasonable assumption if the subsidy or voucher were presented only to a single individual, whose own increased consumption would almost surely not significantly affect market price. But if, as is normally the case, the benefit were available to a large class of consumers, supply–demand analysis tells us that a subsidy or voucher would tend to force the previously ruling price upward. Such a price change would shift the *slopes* of the various budget lines in Figures 4.16 and 4.17. Second, the analysis failed to indicate the *source of the funds* needed to finance the subsidy or voucher. Collection of these funds via taxes would reduce the spendable income of some or all consumers, shifting the *positions* of the various budget lines in the diagram. So the previous discussion represented part of the picture, but not the whole story.

The optimum for the consumer involves the interaction of his *preferences* (indifference curves) with his market *opportunities* (budget line). At the optimum position, the budget line bounding his opportunity set touches the highest attainable indifference curve. For an interior solution this would be a tangency point. But if the geometry is such that no interior tangency exists, the highest indifference curve attainable is found where zero quantity of one of the commodities is purchased (corner solution). Indifference curves convex to the origin are consistent with both interior and corner solutions. In the real world, both situations are observed (we consume mixtures of commodities, but do not purchase positive quantities of every possible good), and this is the basis for the assumption of convex indifference curves.

Analytically, the budget line equation for an individual whose income is I, with goods X and Y available at prices P_x and P_y, is:

$$P_x x + P_y y = I$$

The consumptive optimum condition (for an interior solution) can be expressed, if utility is cardinal, as the Consumption Balance Equation:

$$\frac{MU_x}{P_x} = \frac{MU_y}{P_y}$$

That is, marginal utility per dollar (the utility of the last dollar) spent on either commodity is the same. This implies the Substitution Equivalence Equation:

$$MRS_C = MRS_E$$

This latter form is more general, as it does not require that utility be cardinally measurable. MRS_C corresponds to the indifference-curve slope, and MRS_E to the budget-line slope; the equality of the two, together with the equation for the budget line, determine the optimum of the consumer.

As income I increases, with prices held constant, the budget line shifts parallel to itself and outward from the origin. The consumptive optimum positions attained as income varies, for given prices P_x and P_y, are shown by the Income Expansion Path (IEP). If both X and Y are normal superior goods, the IEP has positive slope (the upward direction in utility terms is northeast). If either good is inferior (in which case the other good can be called ultra-superior), the IEP has a negative slope; the upward direction is northwest or southeast, depending upon which good is inferior. The data in the IEP can also be plotted on (I,x) axes as an Engel Curve showing how the quantity of X purchased varies as income increases, or on $(I,P_x x)$ axes as an Engel Expenditure Curve showing how the amount $P_x x$ spent on good X varies as income increases.

As price P_x falls, with I and P_y held constant, the budget line tilts outward while retaining the same intercept on the y-axis. The consumptive optimum positions attained are represented by the Price Expansion Path (PEP). The upward direction along the PEP is (almost) always eastward. When the data represented by the PEP are plotted on (x,P_x) axes as a demand curve, this property corresponds to the demand curve having negative slope; more of X is purchased as P_x falls (the Law of Demand). While the Law of Demand is generally observed in the world, it is conceivable that it may be violated over a limited range of prices (the Giffen case).

A fall in P_x, with I and P_y held constant, implies an increase in *real* income (higher level of satisfaction in utility terms). It is possible to separate the "income effect of the price change" from the pure "substitution effect of the price change." The substitution effect is always in the normal direction; when P_x falls relative to P_y, more of X will be purchased. But the direction of the income effect depends upon whether X is superior or inferior. The Giffen case results when an inferior-good income effect (reducing purchases of X as P_x falls) overbalances the substitution effect.

Market demand is aggregated from individual demands by simply adding up, at each price, the quantities purchased by all the consumers (horizontal summation).

QUESTIONS FOR CHAPTER 4

Mainly for Review

R1. What is the meaning of the expression "the optimum of the consumer"?

R2. In a situation with just two goods X and Y, how does the amount of income I affect the shape of an individual's market opportunity set? How do the prices of the two goods affect the shape?

*R3. What is the "budget line"? What is its equation? What determines the slope of the budget line?

*R4. What is the geometrical condition for the optimum of the consumer? (Distinguish between a corner solution and an interior solution.)

*The answers to asterisked questions appear at the end of the book.

R5. If indifference curves were concave, why would the consumer's optimum never be in the interior?

*R6. What is the Consumption Balance Equation that expresses the optimum of the consumer? Relate this to the Substitution Equivalence Equation. Do the equations hold for an interior solution, a corner solution, or both?

R7. Characterize a normal good, an inferior good, and an ultra-superior good. Give examples of each. For two goods X and Y, which of the above must they be if the Income Expansion Path has positive slope? What can you say if the *IEP* has negative slope?

R8. Prove that if X and Y are goods, the IEP never points southwest.

*R9. A positively sloped Income Expansion Path implies what shape for the Engel Curve? For the Engel Expenditure Curve? If good X is inferior, what can you say about its Engel Curve?

R10. Show how an individual's demand curve can be derived from his Price Expansion Path.

R11. Is there a utility-increasing direction along the IEP? Along the PEP?

*R12. What does the Law of Demand say about the shape of the PEP?

R13. How does the Hicks decomposition separate the "income effect" and the "substitution effect" of a price change?

R14. Using the Hicks decomposition, show that the Giffen condition (violation of the Law of Demand) can hold only for an inferior good.

R15. How is the market demand curve derived from knowledge of individuals' separate demand curves? Can individual demand curves be determined from knowledge of the market demand curve?

*R16. "As compared with a simple subsidy, the voucher scheme is particularly effective for consumers who would otherwise have chosen little or none of the commodity." Illustrate and explain.

For Further Thought and Discussion

*T1. Could you imagine an experiment that might reveal an individual's Marginal Rate of Substitution in Consumption (MRS_C) between two goods? His Marginal Utility for either good?

T2. Why is diminishing Marginal Utility necessary if the Consumption Balance Equation is to express an optimum? Why is decreasing Marginal Rate of Substitution in Consumption necessary if the Substitution Equivalence Equation is to express an optimum?

*T3. Why can the Giffen condition hold only over a limited range of the PEP? Could the PEP ever circle around and rejoin itself at its starting-point on the y-axis?

*T4. Would a change in P_x tend to shift the position of the IEP? Would a change in income I tend to shift the position of the PEP?

T5. If an individual's demand curve cuts the vertical price axis at some finite "choke price" P_x^o, show the equivalent situation in terms of the individual's indifference curves and budget line. Must the consumer's optimum then be a corner solution at price P_x^o?

*T6. Why is the income effect of a price change usually small compared to the substitution effect?

T7. "Since 1900, real income has increased tremendously, yet the average number of children per family has decreased." Consider the following possible explanations, and illustrate in terms of market opportunity sets and family indifference curves between number of children (x) and "all other goods" (y).

a. Children are an inferior good; since we're richer now, we want fewer of them.

b. Children are *not* an inferior good; however, it has become more expensive to bear and raise children.

c. Children are not an inferior good, nor have they become relatively more expensive. What has happened is that tastes have changed; couples today want smaller families than couples did in 1900.

*T8. In the comparison of subsidy versus voucher in the text, it was assumed that in either case the market base price of the good remained unchanged. Would it be correct to anticipate some change of price? In which direction is this likely to go? Show the effect upon the market opportunity set.

T9. Still another consideration is that government expenditures on subsidies or vouchers must ordinarily be financed by taxes. Suppose that the mode of financing works out as a reduction in the typical individual's income *I*. Show the effect upon his market opportunity set of a tax-financed subsidy. Of a tax-financed voucher.

*T10. The following is sometimes given as an example of a Giffen-good situation. A person must make a 1000-mile train trip and has only $100 in funds available. If it is at all possible, he prefers first-class travel to coach travel, but his first priority is to complete his trip. Suppose that first-class travel costs 20¢ per mile and coach costs 5¢ per mile. Then it can be verified that he will travel 333⅓ miles in first class and 666⅔ miles in coach. Now let the price of coach travel rise to 10¢ per mile. Then the traveler cannot afford any first-class miles at all if he is to complete his trip, so the amount of coach travel will rise from 666⅔ to 1000 even though its price has doubled! Question: Is coach travel an inferior good here? (What would happen if the travel budget were to rise above $100?) Under what circumstances will the traveler choose a corner solution with only coach travel? With only first-class travel?

5.A THE ENGEL CURVE AND THE INCOME ELASTICITY OF DEMAND, 126

5.B THE DEMAND CURVE AND THE PRICE ELASTICITY OF DEMAND, 132

5.C CROSS-ELASTICITY OF DEMAND, 135

5.D FITTING A DEMAND FUNCTION, 136
    5.D.1   Slope and Elasticity: Geometry, 136
  *5.D.2   Slope and Elasticity: Analysis, 140

5.E SUBSTITUTABILITY BETWEEN GOODS, 144

5.F DETERMINANTS OF RESPONSIVENESS OF DEMAND TO PRICE, 147

5.G APPLICATION TO GIFFEN GOOD, 149

Examples
    5.1   THE DECLINING PUBLIC-TRANSIT INDUSTRY, 130
    5.2   ELASTICITIES OF ELECTRICITY DEMAND, 135
    5.3   DEMAND FOR DISTILLED SPIRITS, 140
    5.4   MORE ON FISH, 142
    5.5   RATS, 146

MEASURES AND DETERMINANTS OF DEMANDS

Core Chapter

We saw in Chapter 4 that a consumer's demand for any good X depends upon income I, upon the price P_x, and also upon the prices of other commodities. But an important practical question is: How *sensitive* is demand to changes of prices and to changes of income? If it were government policy to reduce gasoline use, for example, among the relevant considerations might be the effectiveness of a gasoline tax (which raises price to the consumer) as well as the degree to which gasoline demand is influenced by fluctuations in business conditions (which raise or lower consumer incomes). This chapter concentrates upon *measures* of the responsiveness of quantity demanded to changes in income and prices, and upon the underlying *forces* that cause strong responses in some cases and weak responses in others.

5.A

THE ENGEL CURVE AND THE INCOME
ELASTICITY OF DEMAND

The most direct measure of the sensitivity of a consumer's purchases of a good X to changes in income I would be the ratio $\Delta x/\Delta I$. For small changes Δx and ΔI, this ratio can be interpreted as the slope of the Engel Curve.[1] In Figure 5.1 a number of alternative Engel Curves, shown as straight lines for geometrical convenience, indicate differing variations of consumption Δx in response to changes of income ΔI.

There is one serious difficulty in the use of the simple ratio $\Delta x/\Delta I$, however: it is affected by the choice of conventional *units of measurement*. If the commodity X were butter, the numerical value of the ratio would vary by a factor of 16, depending upon whether we measured butter in ounces or pounds. And similarly, the ratio would differ depending upon whether income I were measured in cents or dollars. This type of problem arises in many different branches of economics. To eliminate the difficulty, we make use of the concept of *elasticity. Elasticity is a measure of relationship in which the changes in both numerator and denominator are expressed in proportionate or percentage terms*.[2] In this case we are interested in proportionate response of quantity purchased to a proportionate change in income. This concept is called "the income elasticity of demand."

DEFINITION: The income elasticity of demand is the proportional change in the quantity purchased divided by the proportional change in income.

Figure 5.1
Engel Curves and Income Elasticity of Demand. Four alternative Engel Curves, showing consumption of X as income I varies. Income elasticity is the ratio of the slope *along* a curve to the slope of a ray drawn from the origin *to* the curve. Curve I has income elasticity equal to unity, II less than unity, and III greater than unity. Curve IV has negative income elasticity.

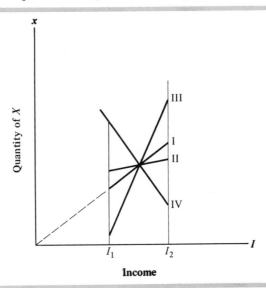

Income

[1]*Mathematical Footnote:* We can write this as the derivative $\partial x/\partial I$, where the symbol ∂ indicates a partial effect of varying one of the underlying parameters with all others held constant.

[2]The student should be warned, however, not to fall into the trap of using proportionate elasticity units in cases when it would be more appropriate to employ the natural physical units.

Symbolizing the income elasticity of commodity X as ϵ_x, this definition is represented by the first ratio in equation (5.1) below.[3] The other two algebraic forms, identically equivalent to the definition of elasticity, are also useful to remember and work with.

$$(5.1) \qquad \epsilon_x \equiv \frac{\Delta x/x}{\Delta I/I} \equiv \frac{\Delta x/\Delta I}{x/I} \equiv \frac{\Delta x}{\Delta I}\frac{I}{x}$$

To illustrate the geometrical significance of the income elasticity of demand, consider the positively sloped line-segment ADB in Figure 5.2. This is an Engel Curve characterized by "unitary income elasticity of demand," i.e., $\epsilon_x = 1$. Note that the two points A and B lie on a straight line through the origin. Then it is evident that the two variables x and I have increased in the same proportion, so that by the definition (the first ratio in equation [5.1]) income elasticity along ADB equals unity. More specifically, we can see this by writing $I_2 - I_1$ as ΔI and $x_2 - x_1$ as Δx, and using x_1 for x and I_1 for I. A geometrical proof could be given making use of the fact that $0AI_1$, $0BI_2$, and ABF are similar triangles. But an easier verification can be found using the middle ratio of equation (5.1). The upper

Figure 5.2

Engel Curve and Unitary Income Elasticity. The straight-line Engel Curve ADB has income elasticity of unity, since the slope *along* the curve is the same as the slope of a ray from the origin *to* any point on the curve. The non-linear Engel Curve CDE, tangent at point D to ADB, therefore also has unitary income elasticity for small changes in the neighborhood of point D. In the range CD the slope *along* the curve CDE is less than the slope of rays from the origin *to* the curve, so income elasticity is less than unity. Correspondingly, $\epsilon_x > 1$ in the range of CDE between D and E.

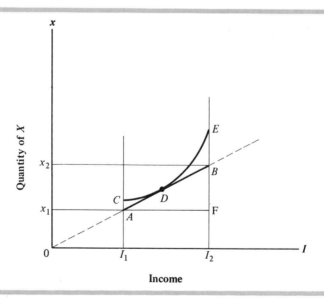

[3]*Mathematical Footnote:* In terms of derivatives, $\epsilon_x = \dfrac{\partial x}{\partial I}\dfrac{I}{x}$.

fraction in this ratio, $\Delta x/\Delta I$, corresponds to the slope *along* the curve ADB. The lower fraction, x/I, corresponds to the slope of a line drawn from the origin *to* points on the curve. Evidently, these fractions are equal and so $\epsilon_x = 1$ for the Engel Curve ADB.

Now consider the curve CDE lying above the line-segment AB but just tangent to it at the single point D. This is an Engel Curve along which the income elasticity of demand is changing. But at the specific tangency point D, we can think of *very small* changes Δx and ΔI as representing a movement *along* the line AB. Thus, the Engel Curve CDE has $\epsilon_x = 1$ in the neighborhood of the point D.

Let us return to the four different examples of Engel Curves distinguished by roman numbers in Figure 5.1. Engel Curve I is like ADB in Figure 5.2; it lies on a line through the origin and so represents unitary income elasticity. Engel Curve II has positive slope, but it is flatter than curve I. It is intuitively evident that this means that x increases in a lesser proportion than I as the latter rises, i.e., $\epsilon_x < 1$. By reversing the argument, we see that the steeper Engel Curve III represents an income elasticity $\epsilon_x > 1$. What of Engel Curve IV? This differs from the others in being negatively sloped. Here x *decreases* as I rises, so X must be an inferior good. Its income elasticity is negative, i.e., $\epsilon_x < 0$.

PROPOSITION: Income elasticity is greater than, equal to, or less than unity depending upon whether the slope *along* the Engel Curve is greater than, equal to, or less than the slope of a ray drawn from the origin *to* the curve. If income elasticity is negative, the Engel Curve has negative slope.

The student should not confuse the geometrical properties of elasticity with slope measures. For *any* positively-sloped straight line through the origin the income elasticity is unity, but such lines can be drawn from very nearly vertical (steep slope) to very nearly horizontal (small slope). It is not the steepness *per se* of an Engel Curve at a particular point that is connected with elasticity, but its steepness at that point *as compared with a line through the origin*.

We have mentioned earlier (in Chapter 2) the distinction between the slope *at a point* along the curve, and the slope over some finite range or *arc* along the curve. Similarly, it is sometimes important to distinguish between elasticity at a point and elasticity over some arc. The definition of income elasticity (5.1), into which the slope enters as the ratio $\Delta x/\Delta I$, is sufficiently general to cover both cases.

Suppose we were interested in the income elasticity ϵ_x over some finite interval along the Engel Curve. Specifically, imagine that 10 units of X are purchased at an income of \$5000 and 14 units at an income of \$6000. Then the increments, for substitution in formula (5.1), are $\Delta x = 4$ and $\Delta I = \$1000$. The only question is what particular values for x and I within the arc to use in the formula. The natural answer is to choose the midpoints of the respective intervals. Then:

$$\epsilon_x = \frac{\Delta x}{\Delta I}\,\frac{I}{x} = \frac{4}{1000}\,\frac{5500}{12} = 1.833$$

This *arc elasticity*, being greater than unity, shows that consumption of X rises more than proportionately with income I in the interval.

It is evident that arc elasticity is a kind of average of the point elasticities along the curve within the range of the arc considered. As the intervals Δx and ΔI shrink down toward zero, their ratio $\Delta x/\Delta I$ approaches a limiting value (the slope of the Engel Curve) that is used in formula (5.1) for determining the point elasticity for a particular x,I combination along the curve.

One simple quantitative statement can be made about income elasticities:

PROPOSITION: On the average over all goods, income elasticity must be unity.

If there is, say, a 10% increase in income, then consumption of some goods may fall and of others rise, by greater or lesser percentages. But since all of the increase in income must somehow be spent, those goods for which consumption rises by less than 10% must be offset by others for which consumption rises by even more than 10%. On the average, consumption must rise by the same proportion as income. If there are just two commodities X and Y, the following equation must hold:

(5.2) $k_x\epsilon_x + k_y\epsilon_y = 1$

Here $k_x \equiv xP_x/I$ is the proportion of the consumer's budget spent on commodity X. Similarly, $k_y \equiv yP_y/I$. These are the weights in the averaging of ϵ_x and ϵ_y that lead to the result of unity.

EXAMPLE 5.1
THE DECLINING
PUBLIC-TRANSIT
INDUSTRY

Table 5.1 illustrates the declining trend of rapid-transit ridership. Generally speaking, ridership declined sharply between 1946 and 1956, and then more slowly between 1956 and 1962. (For some cities, such as Cleveland, the trend is distorted by the opening of new transit lines.) The declining trend in riders has continued since 1962.

The major factor at work has probably been the different income elasticities as between transit and its close substitute—the private automobile. Example 4.3, "Engel's Laws After a Century," indicated the strong positive relationship between income and expenditures on the automobile. In the $2000–2999 income bracket, for example, 6.5% of total expenditure was devoted to the automobile; in the $3000–3999 bracket, 11.3%. Using midpoints of the brackets, the income elasticity of auto expenditures[4] over the arc can be computed as:

$$\epsilon_x = \frac{.113(3500) - .065(2500)}{3500 - 2500} \cdot \frac{3000}{.5[.113(3500) + .065(2500)]}$$

$$= \frac{233}{1000} \cdot \frac{3000}{279} = 2.5 \text{ (approximately)}$$

Table 5.1
Rapid Transit System Ridership (1956 = 100.0)

YEAR	NEW YORK	CHICAGO	PHILADELPHIA	BOSTON	TORONTO	CLEVELAND
1946	151.8	136.8	177.8	185.1		
1950	121.9	95.2	137.3	140.2		
1951	117.5	97.1	126.3	132.3		
1952	114.1	97.0	123.0	127.0		
1953	114.0	96.1	114.8	122.8		
1954	103.9	95.8	109.2	112.1		
1955	101.0	97.2	102.8	103.6	97.0	
1956	100.0	100.0	100.0	100.0	100.0	100.0
1957	99.5	97.2	95.6	96.6	101.0	107.0
1958	96.7	92.8	92.0	94.1	99.1	105.7
1959	97.2	98.1	89.5	92.4	99.1	121.0
1960	98.7	97.6	90.1	91.2	95.7	124.7
1961	100.0	95.2	92.9	—	91.0	120.9
1962	100.5	98.9	89.4	—	91.0	117.5

Source: J. R. Meyer, J. F. Kain, and M. Wohl, *The Urban Transportation Problem* (Cambridge, Mass.: Harvard University Press, 1965), p. 96. (A number of footnotes have been deleted.)

In contrast, the income elasticity of public transit appears to be very low, or even negative. Using degree of housing privacy (multiple, 2-family, and 1-family) as a guide to or proxy for income, Table 5.2 suggests that income elasticity is indeed negative. Regardless of "workplace ring" (distance from central city), the greater the income as measured by housing privacy the less the use of transit.

Table 5.2
Percentage of Detroit White Workers Using Transit

WORKPLACE RING	STRUCTURE TYPE		
	MULTIPLE	2-FAMILY	1-FAMILY
1	60.7	58.7	50.6
2	28.5	28.6	19.5
3	29.4	26.8	18.9
4	27.3	23.1	14.4
5	17.8	11.1	8.4
6	5.8	4.1	3.5

Source: J. R. Meyer, J. F. Kain, and M. Wohl, *The Urban Transportation Problem* (Cambridge, Mass.: Harvard University Press, 1965), p. 132.

[4]We can use auto *expenditures* $P_x x$ in the income elasticity formula since:

$$\frac{\Delta(P_x x)}{\Delta I} \cdot \frac{I}{P_x x} \equiv \frac{\Delta x}{\Delta I} \cdot \frac{I}{x}$$

COMMENT: There have been repeated attempts at encouraging use of public transit in place of the private automobile—to reduce road congestion, to counter "urban sprawl," to minimize air pollution, to save energy, etc. Despite very substantial public subsidies to transit, these efforts seem inevitably to fail. So far, at least, the higher income elasticity of the auto, given the historical trend of rising levels of income and wealth, has defeated efforts to advance public transit.

5.B

THE DEMAND CURVE AND THE PRICE
ELASTICITY OF DEMAND

In the previous section, measures of the responsiveness of consumption to changes in *income* were obtained. Let us now consider the sensitivity of consumption to changes in *price*. Again the most obvious measure would be the ratio of differences $\Delta x / \Delta P_x$.[5] Recall that the demand curve represents the functional relationship between price P_x and the quantity x demanded. For small changes Δx and ΔP_x, therefore, the ratio $\Delta x / \Delta P_x$ corresponds to the *reciprocal* of the slope[6] of the demand curve. The alternative demand curves labelled I, II, III, IV in Figure 5.3 illustrate more and less steep slopes. The steeper the slope, the smaller the numerical or absolute magnitude of $\Delta x / \Delta P_x$. But given the Law of Demand, both the slope and its reciprocal must be negative. (Only in the Giffen case, represented by curve IV in the diagram, would the ratio $\Delta x / \Delta P_x$ be positive.)

As in the case of income, a slope measure like $\Delta x / \Delta P_x$ would be affected by changes in conventional units of measurement in the numerator (e.g., changes from pounds to tons) or in the denominator (e.g., changes from dollars per ton to cents per ton). To avoid this difficulty, we are led once again to an elasticity measure, a ratio of *proportionate* changes. This concept is formally known as "the price elasticity of demand." In common use, the expression "elasticity of demand" standing alone is understood to refer to the price elasticity.

Another very important advantage of the elasticity concept stems from this elimination of dependence upon conventional units of measurement. Comparisons of sensitivity to price changes are often desired between entirely disparate commodities. Since *slope* depends on the units of measurement, it would be meaningless to assert, for example, that the demand curve for wheat is steeper than the demand curve for haircuts, and therefore that the former is less responsive to price changes. The demand curve for wheat could be made to seem as steep or flat as desired, by converting from tons to pounds to ounces as quantity units, or the

[5]*Mathematical Footnote:* In terms of derivatives, this is $\partial x / \partial P_x$.

[6]It is the reciprocal of the slope because economists conventionally draw demand curves with price P_x on the vertical axis.

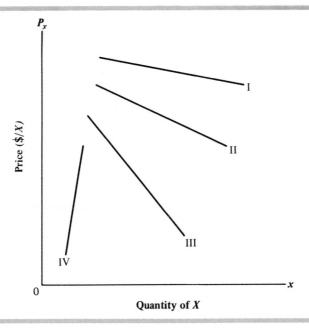

Figure 5.3

Alternative Demand Curve Slopes. Four demand curves, drawn as straight lines, represent different responses of quantity purchased to changes in price. Since demand curves are conventionally drawn with price on the vertical axis, a greater response is represented by a flatter demand curve. The demand-curve slope is negative (the Law of Demand), apart from the exceptional Giffen case (curve IV).

reverse. But it would be meaningful to say that the demand for wheat is *less elastic* than the demand for haircuts, and in that sense less responsive to price changes.

DEFINITION: The price elasticity of demand is the proportional change in the quantity purchased divided by the proportional change in price.

As in the case of income elasticity, there are several ways of expressing the formula for price elasticity of demand. Symbolizing price elasticity as η_x, the definition above is algebraically represented by the first ratio in expression (5.3) below.[7]

$$(5.3) \qquad \eta_x \equiv \frac{\Delta x/x}{\Delta P_x/P_x} \equiv \frac{\Delta x/\Delta P_x}{x/P_x} \equiv \frac{P_x/x}{\Delta P_x/\Delta x} \equiv \frac{\Delta x}{\Delta P_x} \cdot \frac{P_x}{x}$$

The other ratios, all identically equivalent, are also useful to know.

[7]*Mathematical Footnote:* In terms of derivatives,

$$\eta_x \equiv \frac{\partial x/x}{\partial P_x/P_x}$$

When the demand curve is negatively sloped (the Law of Demand), the changes Δx and ΔP_x have opposite signs. Thus, the price elasticity of demand η_x is normally negative. Nevertheless, when we speak of elasticity being "high" we mean large in absolute value, and "low" elasticity means small in absolute value. More specifically, the term "elastic demand" refers to an absolute value of elasticity, symbolized as $\left| \eta_x \right|$, greater than unity while "inelastic demand" means $\left| \eta_x \right| < 1$.

For price elasticity as well as income elasticity, it is sometimes necessary to distinguish the *arc elasticity* over a finite interval of the curve from the *point elasticity* at a single point along the curve. As in the case of the income elasticity definition in equation (5.1), the price elasticity formula of equation (5.3) is sufficiently general to cover both interpretations. For arc elasticity, the finite differences Δx and ΔP_x are employed in the formula, and the specific values used for x and P_x are the mid-points of their respective intervals. For point elasticity, the differences are conceived as shrinking toward zero so that their ratio $\Delta x/\Delta P_x$ approaches a limit—the reciprocal of the slope of the demand curve. This limit is then used in the formula, together with the specific values for x and P_x at the point for which the point elasticity is being computed. Note how in either case the elasticity depends both upon the *slope* of the curve and the *position along* the curve.

There is a well known relation between elasticity of demand and the amount of income spent by the consumer on a good. Suppose the price elasticity is unity (i.e., $\eta_x = -1$, or $\left| \eta_x \right| = 1$). What happens if there is a small decrease in price? From the first ratio in (5.3), we know that with unitary elasticity the proportionate *increase* in quantity $\Delta x/x$ is the same as the proportionate *decrease* $\Delta P_x/P_x$ in price. But since the consumer's expenditure on good X equals $P_x x$, the proportionate increase of x just offsets the proportionate decrease of P_x—so that total expenditure remains unchanged. If the price elasticity is greater than unity ($\left| \eta_x \right| > 1$, or "elastic demand") the proportionate increase in quantity x is larger than the proportionate decrease in price P_x; hence total expenditure $P_x x$ increases when price falls. By a similar argument, if demand is "inelastic," a decrease in P_x leads to a less-than-offsetting rise in x—total expenditure $P_x x$ decreases.[8]

PROPOSITION: A reduction in price P_x will increase, leave unchanged, or decrease a consumer's expenditures $P_x x$ on commodity X depending on whether the demand for X is elastic, of unitary elasticity, or inelastic.

[8]*Mathematical Footnote:*

$$\frac{\partial (P_x x)}{\partial x} = P_x + x \frac{\partial P_x}{\partial x} = P_x + \left(\frac{x}{P_x} \frac{\partial P_x}{\partial x} \right) P_x = P_x \left(1 + \frac{1}{\eta_x} \right)$$

Recall that the sign of η_x is negative. Then the derivative on the left representing the change in expenditure is positive, zero, or negative depending on whether η_x is greater than, equal to, or less than unity in absolute terms.

The demand for a commodity X will generally depend not only upon its own price P_x but upon prices of other goods such as P_y. Here again it is convenient to use the unit-free elasticity measure of responsiveness, called in this case the *cross-elasticity* of demand. The definition is:[9]

$$\eta_{xy} \equiv \frac{\Delta x/x}{\Delta P_y/P_y} \equiv \frac{\Delta x}{\Delta P_y} \cdot \frac{P_y}{x}$$

Cross-elasticity can be either positive or negative. If it is positive the two goods are called *substitutes*; a rise in the price of Y raises the consumption of X. If the cross-elasticity is negative the two goods are called *complements*; here a rise in the price of Y *lowers* the consumption of X. The distinction between substitutes and complements will be discussed in more detail in Section 5.E below.

The table below shows results from an economic study of electricity demand over the period 1946–72. Among the determining variables examined were: (1) electricity price, (2) income, and (3) the price of a competing commodity—gas. It was found convenient to classify the data according to residential, commercial, and industrial use.[10]

EXAMPLE 5.2
ELASTICITIES OF
ELECTRICITY
DEMAND

Elasticities of Electricity Use

WITH RESPECT TO:	ELECTRICITY PRICE	INCOME	GAS PRICE
Residential	−1.3	+0.3	+0.15
Commercial	−1.5	+0.9	+0.15
Industrial	−1.7	+1.1	+0.15

Source: D. Chapman, T. Tyrrell, and T. Mount, "Electricity Demand Growth and the Energy Crisis," *Science*, v. 178 (Nov. 17, 1972), p. 705.

The elasticities of electricity demand with respect to its own price are negative and in the elastic range ($|\eta_x| > 1$), showing a more than proportionate response of consumption to price change. This was the most important result of the study, running counter to the common but uninformed

[10]The industrial and commercial demands are for electricity as a *factor of production* rather than as a consumer good. We have not yet come to the topic of demand for factors of production, but it is of interest to see the comparative data here.

---

[9]*Mathematical Footnote:* In terms of derivatives,

$$\eta_{xy} = \frac{\partial x}{\partial P_y} \frac{P_y}{x}$$

opinion that electricity use is some kind of absolute "requirement" independent of price. The positive elasticities with respect to income show that electricity is a normal superior good. And the positive cross-elasticities with respect to gas price show that gas and electricity are *substitutes*.

COMMENT: The authors of the study emphasize that their results refute the crude techniques for projecting future electricity demands usually employed in "energy crisis" debates. Government planners, industry insiders, and outside critics have often argued as if simple mathematical extrapolations, which compound historically observed rates of demand growth into the indefinite future, represent valid estimates of what will happen in the absence of some extraordinary government intervention. This is surely mistaken; the rate of growth of electricity demand is *strongly* responsive to price. And the price of electricity is bound to increase as fuels become more expensive and as requirements for environmental protection add to cost. (Indeed, since the period of the study electricity prices *have* gone up sharply, with the anticipated discouraging effect upon electricity use.)

5.D

FITTING A DEMAND FUNCTION

The technical statistical problems involved in estimating demand functions from empirical data are studied in courses in econometrics, and will not be considered here. Rather, attention will be devoted to certain theoretical questions involved in making statistical inferences about the nature of the relationship between consumption and its determinants: price, income, prices of related goods, and so forth.

Let us now concentrate upon a single determinant of demand, the price of the commodity itself, in order to focus attention upon the *form* of the relationship. That is, we will suppose that such determinants as income, prices of related commodities, etc., are held constant or statistically allowed for so that we can isolate the price–quantity relationship summarized in the demand curve. What can we say about the shape of the demand curve? In one sense, of course, the statistical data speak for themselves; the curve fitted should be whatever is the best representation of the evidence. Looking at it another way, however, the curve we fit is an artifice. Since it will never *exactly* represent the evidence, there is some choice as to the nature of the approximation to be employed.

5.D.1
Slope and Elasticity: Geometry

In the great bulk of statistical studies, we are constrained to use very simple assumptions about the underlying relationships. The ones most commonly employed are the *linear* demand curve, and the *constant-elasticity* demand curve. They are compared in the two panels of Figure 5.4, as fitted to hypothetical sets of data represented by the clusters of points in the diagrams. The constant-elasticity de-

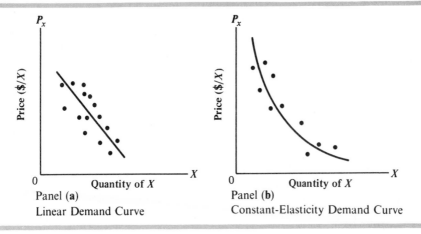

Figure 5.4

Linear and Constant-Elasticity Demand Curves. Simple functional forms are ordinarily assumed in attempting to estimate (to "fit") demand curves, given observed data shown as clusters of points in the diagrams. The functional forms most commonly used are linear demand as in Panel (a) and constant-elasticity demand as in Panel (b).

mand curve is *not* a straight line on X, P_x-axes.[11] Correspondingly, the elasticity *must* change along a straight-line demand curve.

Let us consider the latter point first, in terms of the straight-line demand curve DD' illustrated in Figure 5.5. First of all, from the definition of price elasticity and in particular from the relation $\eta_x \equiv \dfrac{\Delta x}{\Delta P_x} \dfrac{P_x}{x}$ (corresponding to the last ratio in equations [5.3]), elasticity must be zero at the intersection D' with the horizontal axis—since at that intersection P_x is zero. Correspondingly, elasticity is infinite at the intersection D with the vertical axis where X is zero. So, evidently, elasticity rises (in absolute value) as we move upward (northwest) along a straight-line demand curve.

There are several geometrical ways of determining the numerical elasticity at any point along a linear demand curve. Perhaps the simplest is to compare (as in our earlier discussion of income elasticity and the Engel Curve) the slope *along* the curve with the slope of a ray from the origin *to* the curve. We will be using here the third algebraic relation of equations (5.3), $\eta_x \equiv \dfrac{P_x/X}{\Delta P_x/\Delta X}$. The denominator here represents the (ordinarily negative) slope *along* the curve—the constant slope of DD' in Figure 5.5. The numerator is the (necessarily positive) slope of the ray from the origin *to* the curve—the slope of OT, if we are seeking to determine elasticity at point T. Evidently, at T the elasticity of demand is greater than unity, since OT is steeper (in absolute value terms) than DD'—the positive slope of the former is greater in numerical value than the negative slope of the latter.

[11]We use the upper-case symbol X to emphasize that we are now dealing with *aggregate* consumption or demand in the market, rather than with measures derived from choices of an individual.

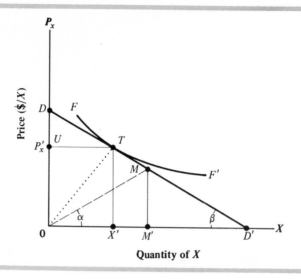

Figure 5.5

Graphical Measure of Elasticity. Elasticity at a point T along a linear demand curve DD' is given numerically by the ratio of the positive slope of OT (the slope of the ray from the origin *to* the curve) to the negative slope of DD' (the slope *along* the curve). Since OT is steeper (slope is larger in absolute value) than DD', elasticity at T is greater than unity. Elasticity equals unity at the mid-point M along a linear demand curve like DD', since OMD' is an isosceles triangle (angles α and β are equal). The elasticity at a point T on the non-linear demand curve FTF' is identical, for small changes, with the elasticity at T along the tangent straight-line demand curve DD'.

A direct corollary of this result is: elasticity is unitary ($\eta_x = -1$) at the mid-point of a linear demand curve. In Figure 5.5, it is geometrically clear that at the mid-point M along DD', the positive slope of OM is equal in absolute value to the slope along DD'. That is, OMD' is an isosceles triangle, determined by the numerically equal angles α and β formed by OM and $D'M$ with the horizontal axis.

This geometrical measure of elasticity along a linear demand curve can be generalized to any demand curve whatsoever. Consider the point T as lying not on DD' but on a *non-linear* demand curve FF' in Figure 5.5. Then DD' could be *constructed* as a line tangent to FF' at the point T. Consequently, at T the slope $\Delta P_x/\Delta X$ along FF' is identical (for small changes) with the slope along DD'. The denominators in the ratio $\eta_x \equiv \dfrac{P_x/X}{\Delta P_x/\Delta X}$ are thus the same for FF' and DD', and since T is on both curves the numerators P_x/X are also evidently the same. So the ratio of the slope of OT to the slope of DD' measures the numerical elasticity of demand at point T for both DD' and FF'.

Let us now consider demand curves along which *elasticity* is constant. Figure 5.6 provides an example, the curve EE', for which the elasticity is in fact *unity* throughout. The point A on the curve is equidistant from the two axes, measuring

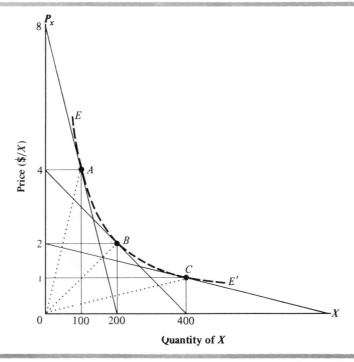

Figure 5.6

Constant-Unit-Elasticity Demand Curve. *EE'* is a demand curve with constant elasticity $\eta_x = -1$. Each point like *A* is the mid-point of a straight line drawn tangent to *EE'* at *A*; it is therefore the apex of an isosceles triangle with one leg along the tangent line and the other along the ray out of the origin. At all points like *A, B, C* along *EE'*, consumer expenditures $P_x X$ equal 400.

along the straight line constructed as tangent to *EE'* at the point *A*. Similarly for the other points like *B* and *C* shown along the curve. Each of the points *A, B, C* is in fact a mid-point like *M* in Figure 5.5, and therefore the apex of an isosceles triangle like *OMD'*—so we see that at every point along *EE'*, $\eta_x = -1$. Using the numbers along the vertical and horizontal axes, note also that the *product* of price times quantity *($P_x X$)* equals 400 for each price-quantity point *A,B,C*. This confirms the Proposition at the end of Section B above, which asserted that a reduction in price leaves consumer expenditures unchanged along a demand curve of unitary elasticity.

So a demand curve with constant elasticity equal to unity must have curvature like that of *EE'* in Figure 5.6. If the demand elasticity were constant but equal to −2 rather than −1, at any point like *A* in the diagram the ray *OA* out of the origin would have to be *twice* as steep as the line tangent to the demand curve at *A*. Such a demand curve would have a curvature generally similar to *EE'* in the diagram, but would have flatter slope throughout. And of course a demand curve with constant elasticity less than unity would be steeper than *EE'* throughout.

A demand curve of constant slope is of course a straight line. It may be expressed in the form of a linear equation:

$$(5.4) \qquad X = A + BP_x$$

Here A and B are constants; B is normally *negative* according to the Law of Demand. When we take into account other determining variables, such as income I and the price of a related good Y, we obtain a generalized *demand function in linear form*:

$$(5.5) \qquad X = A + BP_x + CI + DP_y$$

Here A, B, C, and D are all constants. B is again normally negative. C is the slope of the Engel Curve, and is only negative when X is inferior. The sign of D would be the same as the sign of the cross-elasticity: positive if X and Y are substitutes, negative if they are complements.

A generalized demand function of this form (or, possibly, extended to take into account additional variables) could be fitted statistically to a body of data. Such a fitted function would only be expected to be a reasonable description of the true demand relation within a limited range. Indeed, pushed to extremes it must lead to logical contradictions. For example, equation (5.5) would, for some prices P_x and P_y, indicate a positive quantity X demanded *even when income I is zero*. This is, of course, impossible.[12]

EXAMPLE 5.3
DEMAND FOR
DISTILLED SPIRITS

A study by T. J. Wales employed sales data for different states of the U.S. to estimate demand for distilled spirits.[13] It was found convenient to use a simple linear equation. Straightforward statistical regression led to the equation:

$$X_j = .5084 + .0004079I_j - .1771P_j$$

Here X_j represents the number of cases of spirits per adult resident sold in state j; I_j is the disposable income per adult resident of state j; and P_j is the average liquor price, in dollars, within the state. This equation indicates that, for example, a $1000 increase in average income leads to a consumption increase of about 0.4 cases per adult resident per year. (A case consists

[13]T. J. Wales, "Distilled Spirits and Interstate Consumption Effects," *American Economic Review*, v. 58 (Sept. 1968), esp. p. 858.

---

*The section between the asterisk and the symbol ■ may contain somewhat more difficult or advanced material.

[12]But recall that our model of consumption is timeless. In a multi-period model (to be considered in Chapter 16), the total of consumption expenditures in any single period *may* diverge from income of that period. The difference is accounted for by borrowing and lending between periods, or repayments of previous loans made or incurred.

of 12 fifths, so the increase is about 5 bottles per year.) A one-dollar increase in price leads to a decrease of around .18 case, or around 2 bottles per year.

But Wales was dissatisfied with this result, partly for technical statistical reasons that need not concern us here. He suspected that the data were distorted by failure to allow for liquor sales to *non*-residents crossing state lines to take advantage of lower prices. Correcting for the estimated effect of this factor led to the revised linear equation:

$$X_{jj} = -.4615 + .0004379I_j + .00375P_j$$

Here X_{jj} represents the cases sold in state j to *residents* of that state.

As may be seen, the effect of income differences remains about the same. But the effect of price is much less; demand is now highly price-inelastic. Indeed, these data suggest that the impact of price differences between states is almost entirely limited to the effect upon out-of-state purchasers.

COMMENT: The differences in prices of distilled spirits between states are mainly due to differences in liquor *taxation*. (In some states liquor is a state monopoly, in which case a high monopoly price is substantially equivalent to a high tax.) Very small sensitivity of quantity purchased to price (inelastic demand) is convenient if the purpose of the tax is simply to generate tax revenues. But if the purpose is to discourage consumption, it appears that liquor taxation is not very effective.

A demand curve of constant elasticity also has its own particular algebraic form. This form involves the *logarithms* of quantity and price (and of other determining variables of the demand function). The crucial property of logarithms for our purposes is that equal *arithmetic* steps of the logarithm represent equal *proportionate* steps of the variable. For example, as $\log_{10}X$ (the logarithm of X to the base 10) goes from 1 to 2 to 3, the variable X goes from 10 to 100 to 1000.

For a demand curve of constant elasticity,

$$\eta_x \equiv \frac{\Delta X/X}{\Delta P_x/P_x}$$

is a constant. It follows immediately that the proportionate change in quantity ($\Delta X/X$) is a constant multiple of the proportionate change in price ($\Delta P_x/P_x$) along the demand curve. Using the property that arithmetic changes in the logarithm represent proportionate changes in the variable, we can write:

(5.6) $\Delta(\log X) = b \, \Delta(\log P_x)$

Here b is the constant multiple referred to, which (we can see from the definition of elasticity) must be equal to η_x.

Equation (5.6) is equivalent to:

(5.7) $\qquad \log X = \log a + b \log P_x$

Here $\log a$ is some constant. The linear equation (5.7) in the logarithms implies the previous relation (5.6) between changes ΔP_x and ΔX in P_x and X. It is the linear equation (5.7) that would actually be fitted statistically to the observations reduced to logarithmic form.

Equation (5.7) can be written:

$$\log X = \log (aP_x^b)$$

Taking anti-log on both sides:

(5.8) $\qquad X = aP_x^b$

This is the form of the constant-elasticity demand equation after conversion into natural units. The multiplicative constant a and the elasticity $b = \eta_x$ are the parameters estimated from the statistical data.

Generalizing (5.7), the constant-elasticity demand function (of own-price P_x, income I, and price of some other good P_y) would be expressed in logarithmic form as:

(5.9) $\qquad \log X = \log a + b \log P_x + c \log I + d \log P_y$

Converting to natural units as above, this becomes:

(5.10) $\qquad X = aP_x^b I^c P_y^d$

Here b is as before the price elasticity η_x, c is the income elasticity ϵ_x, and d is the cross-elasticity η_{xy}.

EXAMPLE 5.4
MORE ON FISH

The relaxing of the fish-on-Friday rule for American Catholics led, we saw in Example 2.1 of Chapter 2 ("Catholics and Fish"), to a fall in the price of fish in New England. The same study by F. W. Bell[14] also provided estimates of a number of other parameters of the demand function for fish.

The function fitted in Bell's study was in the logarithmic form of equation (5.9), with two main differences. First, a number of determining variables other than prices and incomes were considered; among them, cold storage holdings, imports, and of course the status of the fish-on-Friday rule. We shall ignore these other variables here. Second, the equation was fitted statis-

[14]F. W. Bell, "The Pope and the Price of Fish," *American Economic Review*, v. 58 (Dec. 1968).

tically with the *price* of fish rather than the *quantity demanded* as the dependent variable on the left-hand side. Thus, Bell's statistically determined equation took the form:

$$\log P_i = \log \alpha + \beta \log Q_i + \gamma \log I + \delta \log P_m + \ldots$$

Here P_i is the price of fish species i (in cents per pound); Q_i is the quantity landed (in thousands of pounds); I is personal income in New England for 1957–59 (in tenths of millions of dollars); and P_m is the consumer price index for a related consumption item, meat and poultry (index based on taking the average 1957–59 price as 100). The study estimated the constants α, β, γ and δ for each of seven fish species. A typical set of results, that for "large haddock," is: $\alpha = -.237$, $\beta = -.460$, $\gamma = +.212$, and $\delta = +.878$.[15]

It is possible to reformulate these results in terms of the constants a, b, c, and d of equation (5.9) that relate to the desired elasticities, by rearranging the statistical equation of the study. Solving the latter for $\log Q_i$, we can write:

$$\log Q_i = -\frac{1}{\beta} \log \alpha + \frac{1}{\beta} \log P_i - \frac{\gamma}{\beta} \log I - \frac{\delta}{\beta} \log P_m$$

But equation (5.9) tells us that $\log Q_i = a + b \log P_i + c \log I + d \log P_m$. Then the desired parameters (apart from the constant term which is not needed) are $b = 1/\beta$, $c = -\gamma/\beta$, and $d = -\delta/\beta$. Remembering that the price elasticity is $b = \eta_i$, the income elasticity is $c = \epsilon_i$, and the cross-elasticity is $d = \eta_{im}$, the results imply that for large haddock:[16]

$$\eta_i = \frac{1}{\beta} = -\frac{1}{.460} = -2.174$$

$$\epsilon_i = -\frac{\gamma}{\beta} = \frac{.212}{.460} = .461$$

$$\eta_{im} = -\frac{\delta}{\beta} = \frac{.878}{.460} = 1.909$$

Thus the price elasticity is in the normal negative range. The positive income elasticity indicates that large haddock is a superior good, though not very strongly superior. And the positive cross-elasticity verifies our presumption that meat and chicken on the one hand, as against fish on the other hand, are substitutes in consumption—a rise in the price of the former leads to a rise in the consumption of the latter.■

[15]*Ibid.*, p. 1348.

[16]For statistical reasons that we need not explore here, these implied estimates are not *exactly* the same as would have been obtained had the equation been initially set up in the form of (5.9), with $\log Q_i$ as the dependent variable.

SUBSTITUTABILITY BETWEEN GOODS

In Section C above, the *cross-elasticity* $\eta_{xy} \equiv \dfrac{\Delta x/x}{\Delta P_y/P_y}$ was introduced as a measure of the demand inter-relatedness of two commodities X and Y. The two were called *substitutes* if the cross-elasticity is positive, *complements* if the cross-elasticity is negative. But cross-elasticity is not a perfectly satisfactory measure of how easily the consumer's preferences allow him to substitute X for Y (or Y for X) and gain equivalent satisfaction. For one thing, as in the ordinary demand elasticity measure η_x there is an "income effect" upon consumption as a rise in price reduces the real income of the consumer or as a reduction in price raises it. For another thing, the formula for η_{xy} is asymmetrical in that only the *quantity of X* and the *price of Y* appear. A more symmetrical formula would involve the quantity and price *ratios* of the two goods.

Consider two commodities that consumers regard as *perfect* substitutes throughout. For example, they might be completely indifferent between 2 nickels and 1 dime, or between 200 nickels and 100 dimes, or between 2000 nickels and 1000 dimes. Then a typical individual's preference map will have the appearance of Panel (a) of Figure 5.7: all the indifference curves will be parallel straight lines. If there were two goods that approached but did not quite attain perfect substitutability, the indifference curves would show a slight degree of normally convex curvature but would be very nearly linear, as in Panel (b) of Figure 5.7. For a particular consumer, bread and rolls might perhaps be so related. The observable market characteristic of strong substitute commodities is: *Small changes in price ratios, with no change in real income, will lead to large shifts in relative quantities purchased.* As can be seen in Panel (b), with the steeper budget line SS' (high ratio of bread price P_b to roll price P_r) the optimum solution S^* is well over toward the northwest of the diagram. But the only slightly flatter budget line FF' (lower ratio P_b/P_r) is associated with a drastically different quantity solution F^* along the same indifference curve U_2 toward the southeast of the diagram.

The opposite of substitutability is called *complementarity*. With perfect complementarity there would be some fixed ratio of quantities (such as one left shoe for each right shoe) of interest to the consumer. If this ratio is departed from, the additional units of whichever commodity is in excess are completely useless. Panel (a) of Figure 5.8 shows the right-angled indifference curves implied by perfect complementarity; the slope of the dashed line through the "elbows" represents the desired ratio of the two commodities. For two goods that approach very nearly to, without quite attaining, perfect complementarity, the indifference map would be as in Panel (b) of Figure 5.8. Possible examples of complementary pairs are bacon and eggs, electricity and appliances, highways and automobiles. The observable market characteristic of strong complementary commodities is: *Large changes in price ratios, with no change in real income, will lead to only small shifts in relative quantities purchased.* As can be seen in Panel (b) of Figure 5.8, along the steeper budget line SS' (representing a high price ratio P_e/P_a) the

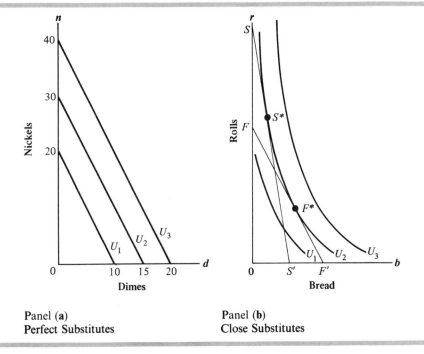

Panel (a)
Perfect Substitutes

Panel (b)
Close Substitutes

Figure 5.7

Substitute Commodities. The parallel straight-line indifference curves of Panel (a) indicate that the two commodities (nickels and dimes) are perfect substitutes. If the price ratio in the market $-P_d/P_n$ diverges from the indifference-curve slope, the consumer will go to a corner solution, buying whichever commodity is relatively cheaper in terms of satisfying his or her preferences. Even a small change in the price ratio, from a slope steeper than to a slope flatter than the indifference-curve slope, would flip the solution over entirely from one corner to the other. In Panel (b) the indifference curves have a slight degree of normal convex curvature, indicating that the two commodities (bread and rolls) are good though not perfect substitutes. A relatively small change in the price ratio (from slope SS' to FF') would then tend to generate a relatively large change in the quantity ratio as the consumptive optimum changes (from $S*$ to $F*$).

tangency solution $S*$ diverges very little from the optimum $F*$ along the flatter budget line FF'.

The substitutability of commodities X and Y in the preferences of a consumer is therefore indicated by the degree of response of the quantity ratio to changes in the price ratio, with real income held constant.[17]

[17]*Mathematical Footnote:* The most commonly used *measure* for this concept of substitutability is called the *elasticity of substitution* (symbolized as σ). The rationale underlying this measure can be indicated as follows. Along any indifference curve, the degree of curvature can be expressed as rate of change of the absolute indifference-curve slope (in economic terms, of the Marginal Rate of Substitution in Consumption, MRS_C) as the ratio y/x varies. Thus, curvature can be represented as $d(MRS_C)/d(y/x)$, remembering that $MRS_C \equiv -\dfrac{dy}{dx}\Big|_U$. But as the degree of substitutability is inversely related to the curvature of the indifference curves (substitutability being greater the closer these curves approach linear form), we are interested in the reciprocal derivative $d(y/x)/d(MRS_C)$. The final step is,

Panel (a)
Perfect Complements

Panel (b)
Close Complements

Figure 5.8

Complementary Commodities. The right-angled indifference curves of Panel (a) indicate that the two commodities (right shoes and left shoes) are perfect complements. A change in price ratio will have no effect upon the quantity ratio chosen, which will always be 1:1 at the best attainable "elbow" point. In Panel (b) the indifference curves are nearly but not quite right-angled: the commodities (electricity and electrical appliances) are strong though not perfect complements. Here a relatively large change in the price ratio (from slope SS' to FF') will bring about only a relatively small change in the quantity ratio as the consumptive optimum changes (from S^* to F^*).

EXAMPLE 5.5
RATS

A team of psychologists and economists investigated the consumptive choices of rats in response to changes in "price ratios" of desired goods.[18] In the first experiment unlimited amounts of water and rat chow were provided, but there were two other commodities—root beer and Collins mix—that each animal could obtain only by pressing one of two levers. The total number of allowed lever presses per day was held fixed as the rat's

[18]J. H. Kagel, H. Rachlin, L. Green, R. C. Battalio, R. L. Basmann, and W. R. Klemm, "Experimental Studies of Consumer Demand Behavior Using Laboratory Animals," *Economic Inquiry*, v. 13 (March 1975).

---

as in all elasticity measures, to deal with *proportionate* rather than absolute changes, in both numerator and denominator. The result becomes:

$$\sigma \equiv \frac{d(y/x)\;/\;(y/x)}{d(MRS_C)/MRS_C}$$

Using the condition that at the consumer's optimum $MRS_C = P_x/P_y$, it can be verified that, if σ is large, then a small change in P_x/P_y will be associated with a large change in y/x along a given indifference curve.

"income." The number of presses needed per ml. of fluid received was the "price." The price ratio was varied by increasing one price and simultaneously reducing the other, so as to hold "real income" approximately constant. Root beer and Collins mix proved to be rather good substitutes for these experimental rats; the consumption ratio changed markedly, in the expected direction, as the price ratio changed.

In a second experiment "free" food and water were no longer provided. Instead, these became the two commodities available only by paying a price (pressing the appropriate lever). When the price ratio was varied, again holding "real income" approximately constant, there was relatively little change in the ratio of quantities consumed. Food and water, it appears, were strong complements for these rats.

COMMENT: In the second experiment, very drastic changes in the prices of food and water led to what the authors' termed "disruptive" behavior. The rats failed to spend all their "income," and began to lose weight. This kind of irrational response to change may be found among humans as well, though not allowed for in standard economic theory.

DETERMINANTS OF RESPONSIVENESS OF DEMAND TO PRICE

As has been remarked at several points above, rightly or wrongly (see the discussion in Chapter 3, Section G), economists seldom concern themselves with the determinants of the basic preferences for goods that underlie consumer demands. A topic that is often considered by economists, however, is why the demands for some goods are strongly and for others are less strongly responsive to changes in price. Here we are dealing not with preferences as such, but rather with sensitivity (in the light of given preferences) to changes in market *opportunities*. As we know, individual responsiveness to price could be measured by the slope $\Delta x/\Delta P_x$, but it is generally more convenient to use the elasticity:

$$\eta_x \equiv \frac{\Delta x}{\Delta P_x} \frac{P_x}{x}$$

Thus the question here can be expressed as: What are the determinants of the elasticity of individual demand? Brief discussions of a number of suggested determinants follow below.

1. *Closeness of Substitutes:* The contention is that demand for a commodity will be more elastic, the more numerous and the closer are the substitutes available. This argument is based upon the "substitution effect" of the

price change (see Chapter 4, Section C). If the preference picture is as in Panel (a) of Figure 5.9 [comparable to the ''close substitutes'' in Figure 5.7, Panel (b)], a tilting of the budget line from KL to KL' would lead to a relatively large change in the quantity of X demanded. Here x_1 is considerably greater than x_0. If the picture were as in Panel (b) of Figure 5.9 [comparable to the ''close complements'' of Figure 5.8, Panel (b)], the corresponding effect on the quantity of X demanded would be much smaller. And so, in Panel (b), x_1 is only a little larger than x_0.

2. *Luxuries versus Necessities:* The contention here is that demand for a ''luxury'' will be more elastic than demand for a ''necessity.'' (As before, a luxury is taken to be a strongly superior good, much more heavily purchased as income rises. A necessity is a good for which almost as much is consumed at low as at high incomes; or even, conceivably, more is consumed at lower incomes.) Thus the argument runs in terms of the *magnitude and direction of the ''income effect''* of price change (Chapter 4, Section C). A fall in the price P_x will tend to enrich the consumer. Then if X is a strongly superior good (a luxury) the income effect will powerfully reinforce the substitution effect so as to augment the increased purchases of X. If X is only weakly superior (a necessity) there will be little reinforcement; if X is actually inferior, the income effect will tend to offset the substitution effect. So the contention is a valid inference from the income effect.

Figure 5.9

Closeness of Substitutes and Demand Elasticity. In Panel (a) the two goods are rather close substitutes. Then a fall in P_x, with consequent shift in the budget line from KL to KL', leads to a relatively large change (from x_0 to x_1) in consumption of X. In Panel (b) the two goods are poor substitutes (strong complements), and a reduction in P_x leads to only a small change in purchase of X.

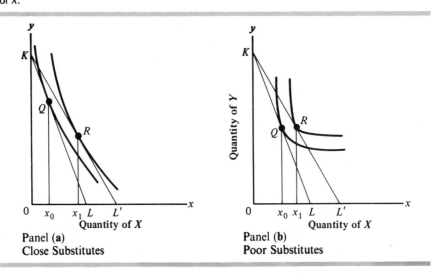

Panel (a)
Close Substitutes

Panel (b)
Poor Substitutes

3. *Importance of the Commodity:* The hypothesis here is that a commodity that is "important," that accounts for a large fraction $k_x \equiv P_x x/I$ of the consumer's budget, tends to have elastic demand. Again we are dealing with the income effect, assumed to be normal in direction (X a superior good). Then it will be evident that the real *enrichment* due to a fall in P_x will be greater, the larger is the consumer's initial expenditure $P_x x$ on commodity X. Thus, the increased purchases due to the income effect will tend to be large simply because of a large real income change as P_x falls. However, this argument is not clear-cut. There is indeed reason to expect a large *absolute* increase in purchases of X after such an enrichment. But elasticity measures *proportionate* increases of consumption. Since the amount of X being consumed may already be large, there is no reason to anticipate that the *proportionate* increase $\Delta x/x$ should be particularly great just because $k_x \equiv P_x x/I$ is large.[19] Thus, a traditional argument given for the *inelasticity* of the demand for salt—that salt accounts for only a tiny fraction of the consumer's budget—is fallacious. The true explanation is that salt is a *necessity*, and has no close substitutes.

4. *High-Priced versus Low-Priced Goods:* The contention here is that high-priced goods tend to have elastic demands, and low-priced goods inelastic demands. A "high" price can be interpreted as one for which the individual's desired quantity approaches zero, i.e., is near the vertical intercept of his demand curve.[20] As shown in Section 5.D.1, if the demand curve actually intercepts the vertical axis the elasticity is indeed infinite at that point. And at an intercept with the horizontal axis where P_x goes to zero, elasticity must be zero. But we also saw, in Figure 5.6, that it is perfectly possible to have a constant-elasticity demand curve, for which elasticity remains constant however closely the axes are approached. (Of course, such a demand curve cannot actually *intersect* either axis.) So the logic of the argument here is less than fully compelling.

APPLICATION TO GIFFEN GOOD

An interesting application of these concepts is to the Giffen case, for which the Law of Demand is violated—a lower price P_x is associated with a *smaller* quantity demanded. It follows that the elasticity η_x has reversed (positive rather than the normal negative) sign.

[19]Consider the special case of an "all-important" commodity, accounting for 100% of the consumer's budget ($k = 1$). For such a commodity the price elasticity of demand is not extraordinarily large. Indeed, the elasticity must be exactly -1.

[20]A demand curve intersecting the vertical axis implies the existence of a "corner solution" at sufficiently high prices.

To have a Giffen good, the income effect must be perverse (negative) and also large enough to overcome the substitution effect, since the latter is *always* in the normal direction. Two elements tend to increase the likelihood of Giffen goods:

1. The larger the proportion of the consumer's budget accounted for by an inferior good (e.g., potatoes as the main staple of life in Ireland), the weightier the perverse income effect relative to the (normal) substitution effect. If, on the other hand, a good accounts only for a small fraction of the budget, the income effect due to a change in its price will be trivial in magnitude—even if in the perverse direction.

2. The Giffen good is likely to have a higher-quality (and dearer) substitute, such that the two are regarded as *closer equivalents at lower incomes than at higher incomes*. In the potatoes example, if the consumer is so poor as to just barely meet minimal calorie needs to stay alive, little importance is attached to the taste superiority of more expensive calorie sources—wheat bread, for example. For minimal survival, it is calorie intake that counts and the cheapest source will be purchased at a corner or near-corner solution. But under more affluent conditions potatoes and bread are not such close substitutes, and an interior solution may be obtained at which fewer potatoes are consumed.

The interaction of these conditions is illustrated in Figure 5.10. On the horizontal axis is quantity of potatoes; on the vertical axis, quantity of bread. At the original high price of potatoes represented by the steeper budget line KL, the consumer's nearly-linear indifference curve U_1 leads him to a near-corner solution at Q. (Potatoes are dear, but still a cheaper source of calories than bread.) Since he is consuming practically all potatoes at Q, any income effect due to a change in the price of potatoes will be large. Now the price of potatoes falls, the new budget line being KL'. The consumer is substantially enriched. However, potatoes are inferior (as can be detected from the fact that U_2 is flatter than U_1 along any vertical line drawn in the neighborhood of the initial solution point Q). Thus the income effect will be both large and negative in direction. This, and the sharper curvature of U_2 (potatoes and bread are weaker substitutes at higher real incomes), constitute the forces leading to an interior solution at R on U_2 *northwest* of Q: fewer potatoes being consumed when the potato price is low than when it was high!

SUMMARY OF CHAPTER 5   The income elasticity of demand for commodity X, denoted ϵ_x, represents the *proportionate* change in purchases of X in response to a proportionate change in income I. The first ratio below represents the definition; the others are useful alternative algebraic forms.

$$\epsilon_x \equiv \frac{\Delta x/x}{\Delta I/I} \equiv \frac{\Delta x/\Delta I}{x/I} \equiv \frac{\Delta x}{\Delta I}\frac{I}{x}$$

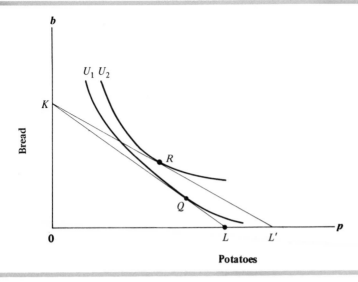

Figure 5.10

Conditions for Giffen Good. This diagram shows how potatoes might have been a Giffen good for impoverished consumers in Ireland. At the initial relatively high potato price P_p, the consumptive optimum is at Q on budget line KL. When the potato price falls, shifting the budget line to KL', the consumer is sufficiently enriched to prefer buying fewer potatoes and more wheat bread at position R. For this to occur potatoes must be strongly inferior, so that the income effect of the price change leads to reduced purchases. In order for the income effect to overcome the pure substitution effect, it is necessary to have the latter become relatively weak as the consumer is enriched. That is, the curvature of U_2 must be greater than that of U_1 (potatoes and bread are closer substitutes for poor consumers than for wealthier consumers).

Income elasticity is positive for superior goods, negative for inferior goods. On the average over all goods, income elasticity must be unity (weighting each elasticity by the proportion of consumer expenditures represented by that good).

The price elasticity of demand for X, denoted η_x, represents the proportionate change in purchases of X in response to a proportionate change in its price P_x. The first ratio below represents this definition, and again the others are useful alternative algebraic forms.

$$\eta_x \equiv \frac{\Delta x/x}{\Delta P_x/P_x} \equiv \frac{\Delta x/\Delta P_x}{x/P_x} \equiv \frac{P_x/x}{\Delta P_x/\Delta x} \equiv \frac{\Delta x}{\Delta P_x} \cdot \frac{P_x}{x}$$

If the Law of Demand holds, price elasticity is negative. Demand is called "elastic" or "inelastic" depending on whether the absolute value of η_x is greater or less than unity. If demand is elastic, a reduction in price is associated with an increase in consumer expenditures $P_x x$; if inelastic, a reduction in price leads to a fall in $P_x x$.

The cross-elasticity of demand η_{xy} is the proportionate change in purchases of X in response to a proportionate change in the price of *another* commodity P_y. The definition and an alternative algebraic form are:

$$\eta_{xy} \equiv \frac{\Delta x/x}{\Delta P_y/P_y} \equiv \frac{\Delta x}{\Delta P_y} \cdot \frac{P_y}{x}$$

If the cross-elasticity is positive the two goods are called *substitutes*, since a rise in the price of Y increases the purchases of X. If η_{xy} is negative the two goods are called *complements*.

Demand functions are commonly estimated from the data ("fitted") by using either linear or constant-elasticity functional forms. The price elasticity of demand increases (in absolute value) moving upward from the horizontal intercept along a linear demand curve. A constant-elasticity demand curve, correspondingly, cannot be a straight line; it must have curvature convex to the origin.

Another concept of substitutability in consumption between commodities X and Y is defined in terms of the *ratios* of price and quantity. Two commodities are called substitutes if, with real income held constant, a relatively small change in their price ratio leads to a relatively large change in the ratio of quantities purchased. If the opposite holds, they are called complements.

The following are often mentioned as causes of high price elasticities of demand: (1) If a commodity has *close substitutes*, the large substitution effect of the price change will lead to strongly increased consumption as its price falls. (2) If a commodity is a *"luxury"* (a strongly superior good), the large income effect of the price change will tend to enlarge its consumption as its price falls. (3) If a commodity is *important* (accounts for a large proportion of the consumer's budget), it is sometimes thought this tends to make the demand elastic. However, this argument is fallacious; even an "all-important" commodity would only have elasticity of unity. (4) At *high prices*, elasticity tends to be large if the demand curve is approximately linear. But since demand curves need not have a linear form, this generalization is not very strongly grounded.

QUESTIONS FOR CHAPTER 5

Mainly for
Review

R1. What is the general definition of all elasticity measures? Why is the income elasticity of demand considered a more useful measure than the simple slope along an Engel Curve? Why is the price elasticity of demand considered a more useful measure than the simple slope along a demand curve? Are elasticity measures always better than the simple measures? (See the question following.)

*R2. Consider this paradox: "Income elasticity is supposed to measure the responsiveness of consumption to changes in income. But income elasticity is unity along *any* Engel Curve which is a straight line through the origin, whether very steep or very flat. Since Engel Curves of different steepness surely show different responses of consumption to income,

*The answers to asterisked questions appear at the end of the book.

how can they all be characterized as having the same income elasticity?"

R3. True or false: "Income elasticity is unity at any point along an Engel Curve such that the tangent at that point extends through the origin." Explain.

R4. True or false: "Since income elasticities must *average* out to unity, any commodity accounting for a very large fraction of income expenditure cannot have an income elasticity very far from unity." Explain.

*R5. What is meant by "elastic demand" and "inelastic demand"? How can elasticity at a point along a linear demand curve be determined by inspection? Along a nonlinear demand curve?

*R6. If the demand curve is $P = A - BX$, where A and B are positive constants, what is the elasticity at $X = 0$? At $X = A/B$? At $X = A/2B$?

R7. If the demand curve is $PX = 100$, what is the elasticity at $X = 10$? At $X = 50$? At $X = 100$?

R8. What is the analytical form of a demand function that is *linear* in both income and price? What is the analytical form of a demand function that has *constant elasticities* with respect to both income and price? Explain the economic meaning of each form.

*R9. If there is a single "all-important" commodity that absorbs all of the individual's income, what is its price elasticity? Income elasticity?

For Further Thought and Discussion

*T1. Prove the proposition that on the average over all goods, income elasticity must be unity.

*T2. The price elasticity of demand for a given commodity is alleged to be greater:

    a. The more numerous and closer the substitutes.
    b. If it is a luxury rather than a necessity.
    c. If it accounts for a large portion of the consumption budget.
    d. At high prices rather than low prices.

    Explain the supporting argument in each case and analyze its validity.

*T3. The American economist Irving Fisher argued in 1891 that a poor community will hardly distinguish quality grades of a commodity like beef, while a rich community would.

> In the country districts of "the west" all cuts of beef sell for the same price (about 10 cts. per lb.). In the cities of the west two or three qualities are commonly distinguished, while in New York a grocer will enumerate over a dozen prices in the same beef varying from 10 to 25 cts. per lb.[21]

Construct the implied indifference curves, at low and high levels of income, between "low-quality beef" and "high-quality beef." Why

[21]Irving Fisher, *Mathematical Investigations in the Theory of Value and Prices* (New Haven: Yale University Press, 1925), p. 74.

should the different beef qualities be better substitutes at low incomes than at high incomes? What would you anticipate about the price elasticity of demand for low-quality beef? For high-quality beef?

T4. Name some goods you expect to have elastic demands. Inelastic demands. Justify your choices.

*T5. Tickets to the King Tut exhibition are available only on a black-market basis. Professor X, calling from out-of-town, gives purchasing instructions to his secretary: "If the price is $30 each, buy one ticket for me; at $20 each, buy 2; if it is $10, buy 3." The secretary says: "Prof, there must be something wrong here. You're saying you'd be willing to pay more in total for 2 tickets than for 3!" Is the secretary correct? Explain.

*T6. For a commodity with "snob appeal," consumers might be willing to buy *more* at a higher price than at a lower price (violation of the Law of Demand). Is this possible or likely? Explain.

*T7. If uninformed consumers judge quality by price, they may also be willing to buy more at a higher than a lower price. Is this possible or likely? Explain.

6.A   SOME SUBTLER APPLICATIONS OF DEMAND THEORY, 156
    6.A.1   The Demand for Charity, 157
    6.A.2   The Demand for Safety, 160
6.B   MULTIPLE CONSTRAINTS, 162
    6.B.1   Rationing, 162
  *6.B.2   Time as a Constraint, 168
6.C   THE "NEW THEORY OF CONSUMPTION," 170
6.D   INDEX NUMBERS, 171
    6.D.1   Index Numbers of Quantity, 172
    6.D.2   Index Numbers of Price, 176
6.E   THE INCOME-COMPENSATED DEMAND CURVE, 179

Examples
    6.1   CHARITABLE GIVING, 159
    6.2   THE VALUE OF SAFETY, 161
    6.3   WARTIME POINT RATIONING, 166
    6.4   TIME-PRICES OF MEDICAL CARE, 169
    6.5   COST OF LIVING IN WARTIME BRITAIN, 178

APPLICATIONS AND EXTENSIONS OF DEMAND THEORY

6

Supplementary Chapter

In this chapter the topics taken up are intended to give the student some further idea of the richness and growing power of the modern theory of consumption and demand. The potential applicability of demand theory to realms of behavior not so far considered, for example, the "purchase" of safety or of charity, will be suggested. And a number of theoretical extensions are analyzed, including the index-number problem and the topic of choice under non-income constraints (as in the case of wartime product rationing).

6.A

SOME SUBTLER APPLICATIONS OF DEMAND THEORY

The previous chapters have covered the theory of choice leading to the determination of market demands for goods. A variety of illustrative applications were described, among them the division of income among major expenditure categories (such as food, clothing, and shelter), and certain aspects of the demands for commodities like electricity, fish, liquor, and so forth. In addition to these rather conventional applications of the theory of consumer choice, to goods that we ordinarily think of as obtained by consumers through the market, some unconventional applications of demand theory were also alluded to. Among these were men's demands for wives, parents' demands for sons versus daughters, and the demands of laboratory animals for a variety of rewards or stimuli.

In this section two such unconventional applications of demand theory, to goods not normally regarded as provided to consumers via a market-like process, are discussed in somewhat more detail.

Panel (b) of Figure 3.11 showed a preference function consistent with the observations that the subject individual: (1) may give charity, but (2) only to persons poorer than himself. This situation is repeated here in the diagram of Figure 6.1. Below the 45° line, "My Income" I is greater than "His Income" H, and so both I and H are goods for me. But above the 45° line, where H exceeds I, His Income is a neuter commodity for me.

We now want to consider charity as the "purchase" of increments to the other person's income H, at the expense of the contributor's income I. Suppose that, to begin with, $I = \$1000$ and $H = 0$, i.e., My Income is $1000, but the

Figure 6.1

Charity and Relative Income Endowments. Below the 45° line His Income *(H)* and My Income *(I)* are both goods for me (my preference directions are north and east). If I can transfer income on a 1:1 basis, the "budget line" *EF* has a slope of 135°. The 1:1 transfer ratio represents a price P_H equal to unity. From any endowment position on *EF*, my preferred combination of *H* and *I* is at *C**. (But since I cannot force him to transfer income to me, this position is unattainable given an initial endowment like *E″*.)

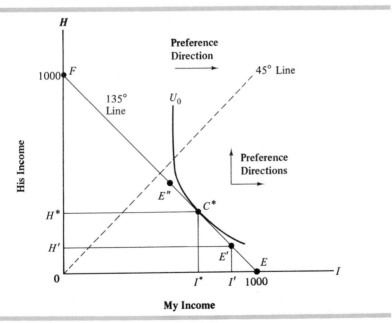

Chapter 6
APPLICATIONS
AND
EXTENSIONS OF
DEMAND
THEORY

157

potential object of charity is absolutely penniless.[1] Then the initial or *endowment* position is at point E on the horizontal axis of Figure 6.1. In the absence of any special tax considerations, I can transfer income to the other person dollar for dollar, i.e., the "price" of H is unity in terms of I. Then EF can be regarded as a *budget line* (in complete analogy with the line KL in Figure 4.1) with a slope of -1, at an angle of 135° from the horizontal. The optimum of the "consumer" (i.e., of "me" as donor) along EF is at C^* in Figure 6.1, with associated quantities I^* for my after-contribution income and H^* for his after-charity income. My donation is of course $1000 - I^*$, which numerically equals his receipt OH^*. Putting this another way, at a "price" P_H of unity, I have purchased H^* units of commodity H, which is a "good" for me in this range of my preference map.

Now consider what would happen if our relative income status were initially different. In particular, suppose that the initial endowment position were at E' rather than at E along the line EF. Here My Income is I', and His Income is H'. The tangency position C^* remains the donor's optimum, but it can now be achieved with a substantially smaller charitable contribution. Specifically, the donor gives only $I' - I^*$, which will equal the charitable receipt $H^* - H'$. What if the endowment position were at E'' along EF, lying beyond (to the northwest of) my tangency optimum C^*? Then, my preferences say that he should make some contribution to me! Unfortunately, however, this decision is not within my control.

In the demand for ordinary commodities, we have seen that the consumer's income I is usually an important determinant. This also undoubtedly holds in the case of demand for charitable giving, which we would expect to be a highly superior or "luxury" good—more being "purchased" as the consumer becomes wealthier. And we would also surely expect to observe reduced charitable giving, other things equal, as the *recipient* becomes richer: the *relative* income status of donor and donee is a major consideration.

Taxes are also a very important element of the situation. In Figure 6.2, we can suppose that the before-tax initial situation is at point E_0 on the horizontal axis. In the absence of taxes the budget line would be E_0F_0, with a slope of 135° as in the previous diagram. The optimum of the consumer would be at C_0^*. But taxes will immediately withdraw a certain amount of income, so that the individual's effective endowment may be only a point like E. Here, other things equal, the optimum along the budget line EF (parallel to E_0F_0) will be somewhere like C^* in Figure 6.2. The amount of charitable giving will surely be less $(H^* < H_0^*)$.

But there is another effect upon the decision as to charitable giving, *if donations are deductible from income before taxes*. In particular, suppose that taxes on income are at a flat rate of 40%, *after* deducting charitable contributions. Then each dollar of H that I "buy" (contribute) costs me only 60 cents. In effect, the tax lowers the "price" of H from $P_H = 1$ to $P_H = 0.6$. In Figure 6.2, the effective (after-tax) budget line becomes steeper, shifting from EF to EF_0. (The absolute slope of EF_0 is $1/P_H = 1/0.6 = 5/3$ whereas the absolute slope of EF is

Chapter 6
APPLICATIONS
AND
EXTENSIONS OF
DEMAND
THEORY

158

---

[1]For convenience, we speak of income as accruing in monetary units in this discussion, but the reader should still be thinking in terms of *real* income.

Figure 6.2
Tax Rates and Charity. Imposition of an income tax at a flat 40% rate shifts the endowment position from E_0 to E, and the consumer optimum from C_0^* to C^*; charitable giving is reduced from H_0^* to H^*. But if donations are deductible against taxes, the effect is to reduce the price of charitable giving from $P_H = 1$ to $P_H = 0.6$. The after-tax budget line becomes EF_0, leading to a consumer optimum at C_1^* with contributions of H_1^*. Deductibility clearly increases the amount given.

unity.) The new optimum is C_1^*, and the associated contribution OH_1^* is now greater than the amount OH^* donated in the no-deductibility situation.[2] As the Law of Demand suggests, the exemption of charitable contributions from tax leads to increased donations in the range where H and I are both goods for the donor.

Robert A. Schwartz studied charitable giving, regarded as a good "purchased" by donors, as a function of a number of variables related to those mentioned in the text above: the "price" of giving P_H (equal to 1 minus the donor's marginal tax rate), the donor's income I, and others' income N. (Unfortunately, a measure of *donees'* income H was not available, and so N representing the per-capita income of all non-donors was used as a very imperfect proxy.) The statistical function fitted was in the constant-elasticity

EXAMPLE 6.1
CHARITABLE
GIVING

[2]With a *progressive* income tax, the price P_H would not be a constant. As the contributor gives more and more, remaining income falls into lower tax brackets. So P_H does not remain quite so favorable as for the first dollar donated. This complication will not be pursued here.

form of equation (5.10), leading to the elasticities given in the following table.

Elasticities of Charitable Donations

INCOME CLASS	"PRICE" (P_H) ELASTICITY	DONOR INCOME (I) ELASTICITY	OTHERS' INCOME (N) ELASTICITY
$0–10,000	−.85	+.19	−.53
$10,000–100,000	−.79	+.76	−.43
Over $100,000	−.37	+.40	−.38

Source: R. A. Schwartz, "Personal Philanthropic Contributions," *Journal of Political Economy*, v. 78 (Nov./Dec. 1970), p. 1279.

The results are all in the directions expected. The lower the P_H, the "cheaper" is charitable giving, and so the greater the contributions (negative price elasticity). The higher the absolute donor income, the more giving (positive income elasticity). But the higher the income of others, the less giving; there is a negative effect on donations, the poorer is the *relative* income status of the donor. One point of interest is the big jump in the donor income elasticity between the top and middle lines of the table. If people are quite poor, a small enrichment will be devoted almost entirely to urgent personal needs. But in the middle income brackets, increments to income are spent in greater degree on behalf of those less well off.

6.A.2
The Demand for Safety

In Chapter 15 we will see just how the decision as to *employment* can be approached with the tools of demand theory. The worker, for example, can be regarded as "buying" consumption income with labor power. But in this section we will be considering only an ancillary aspect of the employment decision: the choice of jobs with more or less safety.

In the job market it is reasonable to anticipate that, other things equal, employments with greater injury or death hazard (lower *safety S*) will offer a higher income return I than safer jobs. A worker choosing between more and less hazardous jobs can be regarded as facing a curve like *AB* in Figure 6.3; there is a choice between a low-income high-safety job toward the southeast end, or a high-income low-safety job toward the northwest end along *AB*. The curve *AB* thus plays the role of a "budget line" bounding the job-seeker's opportunity set. However, we do not know whether *AB* is actually linear in form. (Also, as there are neither *perfectly safe* nor totally *sure-death* jobs, *AB* does not extend out to either axis.) For people with non-pathological preferences, both income I and safety S are surely *goods* (preference directions are north and east). Then, normally shaped (convex) indifference curves can be expected to lead each particular individual to a tangency optimum as at C^* in the diagram. Different workers would, in accordance with their relative preferences for safety and income, distribute themselves at various points along the *AB* opportunity boundary.

Chapter 6
APPLICATIONS
AND
EXTENSIONS OF
DEMAND
THEORY

160

Figure 6.3
The Demand for Safety. A job-seeker making an occupational choice between more and less hazardous occupations can be regarded as "consuming" alternative combinations of the goods Income *I* and Safety *S*. Since, other things equal, riskier jobs offer higher wages, the opportunities available take the form of a "budget curve" *AB*, of negative slope. The optimum is found at *C**, where the highest attainable indifference curve *U* is reached.

A study by Richard Thaler and Sherwin Rosen[3] estimated the amount of income necessary to induce workers to accept higher death hazards. Safety *S* was defined as $1 - p$, where *p* is the *added* annual probability of death due to the job. In current American experience, *p* does not rise to very high levels for any job category employing substantial numbers of people. Among the relatively high-risk jobs are lumbermen ($p = .00256$) and guards, watchmen, and doorkeepers ($p = .00267$). Police and detectives represent a surprisingly safe category ($p = .00078$), with firemen even safer ($p = .00044$). Thus, the data available all fall toward the extreme southeast end of the *AB* curve of Figure 6.3.

Within this limited interval, the income-safety opportunity boundary did not diverge substantially from linear form. The result obtained was that an extra death probability of one-thousandth (.001) per year required an income increment of around $200 per year, in 1967 dollars.

COMMENT: An increment to *p* of .001 means that, for each thousand workers employed, one per year will actually lose his life, on the average. So in a sense $200,000 is the "price of a life"! Needless to say, any such interpretation raises philosophical questions that we cannot take up here.

EXAMPLE 6.2
THE VALUE OF
SAFETY

[3]R. Thaler and S. Rosen, "The Value of Saving a Life: Evidence from the Labor Market," Department of Economics, University of Rochester (Dec. 1973).

MULTIPLE CONSTRAINTS

In Section 4.A, the *budget line* was introduced as the upper (northeast) boundary of an individual's market opportunity set. Or, we may say, the budget line is the binding *constraint* upon the individual's choices. This constraint is due, of course, to the limited income I available for expenditure upon consumption goods.

The familiar equation of the budget line is:

(6.1) $\qquad P_x x + P_y y = I$

The market opportunity set as a whole, the shaded region of Figure 6.4, was previously described as the area bounded on the northeast by the budget line. More precisely, it is the area bounded by the budget line *and the coordinate axes*, the set of points satisfying the inequalities:

(6.2) $\qquad \begin{cases} P_x x + P_y y \leqq I \\ \qquad\quad x \geqq 0 \\ \qquad\quad y \geqq 0 \end{cases}$

The latter two conditions express the physical reality that goods cannot be purchased or consumed in negative quantities.

6.B.1

Rationing

It sometimes happens, however, that the consumer faces constraints upon market decisions apart from limited income. In wartime, for example, a ration limit R_x

Figure 6.4

Market Opportunity Set. The normal market opportunity set is constrained only by income and non-negativity considerations. It is represented as the shaded area bounded by the budget line $P_x x + P_y y = I$ and the vertical and horizontal axes.

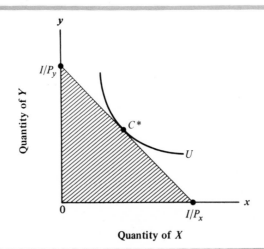

Chapter 6
APPLICATIONS
AND
EXTENSIONS OF
DEMAND
THEORY

might be placed upon consumption of commodity X. Three rationing cases of interest are shown in the three panels of Figure 6.5.

In Panel (a) of Figure 6.5, the ration limit is indicated by the vertical dashed line at the quantity $x = R_x$. Here the ration is so large, relative to the consumer's income that establishes the size of the market opportunity set (shaded area), as to be ineffective. In Panel (b) the ration limit R_x is *potentially* binding; it does bite into (truncate) the market opportunity set so as to reduce the size of the shaded area. However, given the individual's preferences, the ration limit is not *actually*

Figure 6.5

Rationing of One Commodity. In addition to the budget constraint here there is a ration limit R_x (vertical dashed lines) upon purchases of commodity X. In Panel (a) the ration is so large as not to constrain the consumer's choices any more than income does alone. In Panel (b) the ration truncates the market opportunity set, but the consumer's preferences are such that the limit is not actually binding. In Panel (c) the ration limit is binding; it forces a choice of less of X (and more of Y) than the consumer would have otherwise preferred.

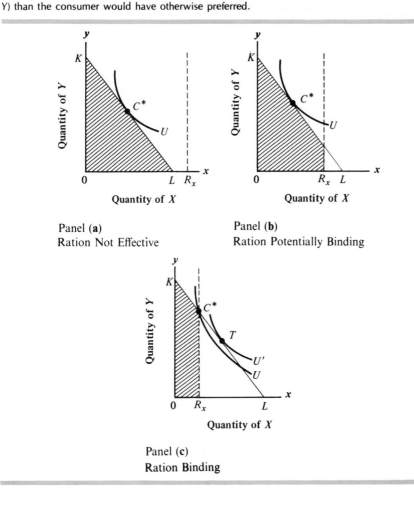

Panel (**a**)
Ration Not Effective

Panel (**b**)
Ration Potentially Binding

Panel (**c**)
Ration Binding

Chapter 6
APPLICATIONS
AND
EXTENSIONS OF
DEMAND
THEORY

binding; the individual does not even want to consume as much of X as the ration permits. Only in Panel (c) is the ration limit R_x actually binding; it dictates a *non-tangency* solution C^*, where, without the ration limit, the consumer would have attained the preferred tangency position T.

As an obvious implication, ration limits are less binding for poorer people, for whom spendable income already serves as a severe constraint. Note also that after imposition of a ration limit upon consumption of some commodity X, consumers' demands tend to "spill over" so that more is consumed of those commodities left unrationed.

What if commodities X and Y were *both* rationed? Here there are a considerable variety of cases, not all of which will be diagrammed. In Figure 6.6 we see only the more interesting situations where both of the ration limits R_x and R_y are at least *potentially* binding, i.e., the market opportunity set is truncated at both ends. Panel (a) shows that even when both ration limits are potentially binding, neither may *actually* be effective at the consumptive optimum position C^*. In Panel (b), only the ration limit R_y for commodity Y is actually binding; it forces the individual to a position C^* inferior to the tangency optimum T that would otherwise be chosen. (There would of course be an opposite case, not diagrammed here, in which the ration limit R_x is the only one binding.) In Panel (c), we see the interesting case in which *both* ration limits are actually effective. Here it is the budget constraint that is not binding. This would correspond to the situation of a rich person, well endowed with income, but unable to legally spend it all in a situation where all desired commodities are subject to severe rationing.

Analytically, it is interesting to interpret these possibilities in terms of opportunity sets. The *market* opportunity set, for which income I is the effective constraint, is the familiar triangular area bounded by the budget line and the axes in the diagrams of Figure 6.6. The *ration* opportunity set, where fixed quantitative limits on both commodities are imposed, takes the form of a rectangle. The lower bounds of the rectangle are the axes, and the upper bounds are the dashed lines $x = R_x$ and $y = R_y$. The *effective* opportunity set, shown as the shaded area in all three situations, is the intersection of the market opportunity set and the ration opportunity set; i.e., it is the collection of all points that satisfy *both* constraints. Formally, the shaded areas are determined by the inequalities:

$$(6.3) \qquad \begin{cases} P_x x + P_y y \leq I \\ 0 \leq x \leq R_x \\ 0 \leq y \leq R_y \end{cases}$$

Chapter 6
APPLICATIONS
AND
EXTENSIONS OF
DEMAND
THEORY

164

The objective of rationing, usually imposed under conditions of special scarcity as in wartime, is ordinarily to assure that people with modest incomes may still be able to purchase at least minimal quantities of essential goods.[4] Figure 6.6 indicates that this objective tends to be achieved. In Panel (a), representing the

----

[4]This of course may not be the only purpose of rationing. In Nazi Germany, for example, smaller rations were assigned to Jews than to Aryans. Similarly, during the "war communism" period 1917–1921 in revolutionary Russia, members of the former upper and middle classes were given smaller rations than individuals of proletarian origin.

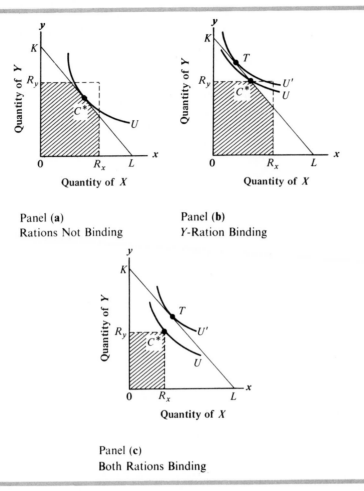

Panel (a)
Rations Not Binding

Panel (b)
Y-Ration Binding

Panel (c)
Both Rations Binding

Figure 6.6
Physical Rationing of Two Commodities—Potentially Binding Cases. Commodities X and Y are both subject to ration limits, R_x and R_y (vertical and horizontal dashed lines). In Panel (a) neither ration limit is binding. In Panel (b) R_y is binding, forcing the consumer to choose less of Y (and more of X) than would otherwise be the case. In Panel (c) both ration limits are binding, and the income constraint on consumption is ineffective.

situation of a relatively poor person, it is only income that constrains consumption. But in Panel (c), representing the situation of a richer individual, the ration limits do force consumption of less than this person would otherwise have purchased—leaving more of X and Y available to others.

Nevertheless, simple quantity rationing is a relatively crude device. Suppose tea and coffee were both rationed. Then consumers whose tastes tolerated both tea and coffee would have an advantage over those strongly preferring one over the other. Someone for whom tea was totally unpalatable, for example, would find a tea ration useless. (*Sale* of ration coupons is ordinarily prohibited.) As a way

Chapter 6
APPLICATIONS
AND
EXTENSIONS OF
DEMAND
THEORY

165

around this objection, in the later years of World War II a number of countries, including the United States, introduced relatively sophisticated rationing systems. Instead of absolute quantity limits like R_x and R_y on specific commodities, a consumer was granted a certain amount of "point income" N that could be spent very much like ordinary income. Rationed commodities were then assigned "point prices" p_x and p_y in addition to money prices P_x and P_y.

Under a point rationing system, the three main possibilities for an individual's effective opportunity set are illustrated in Figure 6.7. In Panel (a) "point income" is so large relative to ordinary income that only the latter constrains consumption. This might be the situation of a poor person. Panel (b) represents the opposite case, a rich person for whom ordinary income is so ample that only points constrain consumption. And finally, Panel (c) pictures a situation where over a certain range ordinary income is binding, but elsewhere point income is binding.

Formally, the opportunity set under point rationing is determined by the inequalities:

$$(6.4) \quad \begin{cases} P_x x + P_y y \leq I \\ p_x x + p_y y \leq N \\ x \geq 0, \quad y \geq 0 \end{cases}$$

In the cases illustrated in Figure 6.7, the income budget line KL is steeper than the point budget line GH. That is, $P_x/P_y > p_x/p_y$. Commodity X is therefore comparatively more expensive in terms of ordinary income, and commodity Y in terms of points. It follows that consumers extremely desirous of purchasing commodity X would tend to find the income constraint binding; those more interested in Y would tend to find the point constraint binding.

EXAMPLE 6.3
WARTIME POINT
RATIONING

Among the commodities rationed by points during World War II in the U.S. were cheese and canned fish. The table below compares the 1942 (pre-rationing) purchases of different income groups with the quantities purchased during 1944 when rationing was effective.

Average Weekly Purchases (lbs.) by Housekeeping Families in Cities

INCOME:	$1000 OR LESS	$1000– 2000	$2000– 3000	$3000– 4000	OVER $4000
1942					
Cheese	.26	.57	.64	.81	1.03
Canned fish	.21	.36	.56	.44	.37
1944					
Cheese	.24	.33	.44	.49	.52
Canned fish	.06	.12	.17	.22	.18

Source: L. A. Epstein, "Wartime Food Purchases," *Monthly Labor Review*, v. 60 (June 1945), pp. 1148, 1150.

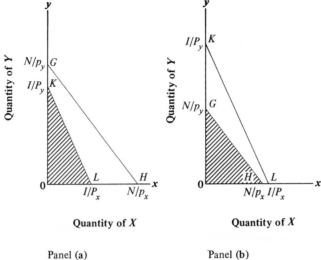

Panel (a)
Income Constraint Binding

Panel (b)
Point Constraint Binding

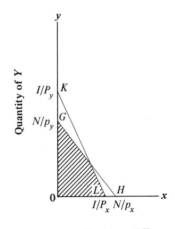

Panel (c)
Both Constraints Binding

Figure 6.7
Point Rationing. Consumption is shown as subject to an income constraint and also to point rationing. Commodity *X* is relatively more expensive in terms of income, and commodity *Y* in terms of points, so the income budget line *KL* is steeper than the point budget line *GH*. In Panel (a) "point income" is so large that only money income is binding; Panel (b) represents the opposite case. In Panel (c) each constraint is binding over a certain range.

Chapter 6
APPLICATIONS
AND
EXTENSIONS OF
DEMAND
THEORY

167

One aspect of interest in this table is the overall binding power of income versus points as constraints. Looking only at the three highest income groups (last three columns), we see that their consumption patterns *in 1944* were almost identical. Hence it appears that consumers in this income range were in the situation pictured in Panel (b) of Figure 6.7—consumption of cheese and canned fish was almost entirely limited by points rather than by income. That the lower income groups and not the upper groups were sensitive to *both* points and income may also be appreciated when it is realized that the dollar price of canned fish relative to cheese approximately doubled between 1942 and 1944. The fish/cheese consumption ratio for the lowest income group consequently fell from .21/.26 to .06/.24, a sharp change indeed. But in the case of the highest income group, the 1942 fish/cheese consumption ratio .37/1.03 remained almost unchanged (at .18/.52) in 1944.

A very important recent development in theoretical and applied work on demand has been the explicit consideration of *time* as well as *income* constraints on consumption. Most consumption activities—playing a round of golf, watching a movie, eating a meal—require significant time inputs as well as cash sacrifices on the part of the consumer.

If time and income were inconvertible, there would be a dual constraint situation like that pictured for point rationing in Figure 6.7. Let t_x and t_y be the time inputs (assumed constant for simplicity) per unit consumed of goods X and Y, respectively. The consumer's effective opportunity set would then have to satisfy not only the income constraint $P_x x + P_y y = I$ but also a time constraint $t_x x + t_y y = T_c$, where T_c is the total time devoted to consumption activities.

But time and income are not inconvertible. Someone who engages in income-earning activities outside the home is reducing consumption time T_c but raising consumable income I. The same can be said if he or she undertakes household activities like home repairs that reduce the need to earn outside income. Since time can be sold to obtain income, the two are convertible into a single constraint upon consumption.[5] Let us suppose that the individual could work any number of hours at a given wage w.[6] Then, in effect, the total "time endowment" T is worth wT in income units. If the person has in addition an ordinary income endowment of I_0, the overall constraint upon consumption choices is given by:

$$(6.5) \qquad (P_x + wt_x)x + (P_y + wt_y)y \leq I_0 + wT$$

Chapter 6
APPLICATIONS
AND
EXTENSIONS OF
DEMAND
THEORY

168

*The section between the asterisk and the symbol ■ may contain somewhat more difficult or advanced material.

[5] In contrast, the sale of "points" for cash was definitely illegal under wartime rationing systems. For law-abiding persons, there was no convertibility.

[6] This is of course a simplification. Shifting an additional hour from consumption to work might actually yield more than the normal wage w (if, for example, overtime work at time-and-a-half is available). Alternatively, the individual might only be able to earn a lower rate of pay for additional hours because of fatigue, or because of the need to take a less desirable second "moonlighting" job. The optimum balance between time and income will be considered further when we analyze the labor–supply decision in Part Five.

It is evident from this formulation that the *effective price* π_x for commodity X is not the money price P_x alone but the expression $P_x + wt_x$, the money price plus the income value of the required time input. And similarly, of course, for commodity Y the effective price is $\pi_y = P_x + wt_y$.

For some purposes it is of interest to distinguish elasticity of demand with respect to the cash component of effective price, $\eta_{x \cdot P}$, from the elasticity of demand with respect to the time element, $\eta_{x \cdot wt}$. The definitions are:

$$(6.6) \qquad \eta_{x \cdot P} \equiv \frac{\Delta x / x}{\Delta P_x / P_x}$$

$$(6.7) \qquad \eta_{x \cdot wt} \equiv \frac{\Delta x / x}{\Delta wt / wt}$$

Since the wage w is assumed constant, (6.7) can be rewritten:

$$(6.7') \qquad \eta_{x \cdot wt} = \frac{\Delta x}{w \Delta t} \frac{wt}{x} = \frac{\Delta x}{\Delta t} \frac{t}{x} = \eta_{x \cdot t}$$

Thus, the wage w cancels out, and we can speak in terms of the "elasticity of demand with respect to time input."

The following proposition can be proved by calculus: The elasticity with respect to cash price $\eta_{x \cdot P}$ will be greater or less (in absolute value) than the elasticity with respect to time input $\eta_{x \cdot t}$, according as the cash price P_x weighs more or less heavily than the income value of the time input wt_x in the sum representing the overall effective price $\pi_x = P_x + wt_x$. For example, if the cash price P_x accounts for more than half of π_x, then $\left| \eta_{x \cdot P} \right| > \left| \eta_{x \cdot t} \right|$.[7]

Jan Acton studied a number of factors determining the demand for medical care on the part of residents of two neighborhoods in Brooklyn, New York—Red Hook and Bedford-Crown. He explicitly distinguished the time input from money price. For medical services, residents of these neighborhoods made substantial use of both (1) free municipal clinics and out-patient

EXAMPLE 6.4
TIME-PRICES OF
MEDICAL CARE

[7]*Mathematical Footnote:* The elasticity of demand with respect to effective price, π_x, is:

$$\eta_{x\pi} = \frac{dx}{d\pi_x} \frac{\pi_x}{x}$$

For *partial* variation of cash price P_x (t_x held constant), $dx/d\pi_x = \partial x/\partial P_x$. Then:

$$\eta_{x \cdot P} = \frac{\partial x}{\partial P_x} \frac{P_x}{x} = \frac{dx}{d\pi_x} \frac{P_x}{x} \frac{\pi_x}{\pi_x} = \eta_{x\pi} \frac{P_x}{\pi_x}$$

Similarly, for partial variation of t_x, $dx/d\pi_x = \partial x/\partial wt_x$. Then:

$$\eta_{x \cdot t} = \eta_{x \cdot wt} = \frac{\partial x}{\partial wt_x} \frac{wt_x}{x} = \frac{dx}{d\pi_x} \frac{wt_x}{x} \frac{\pi_x}{\pi_x} = \eta_{x\pi} \frac{wt_x}{\pi_x}$$

So $\left| \eta_{x \cdot P} \right|$ will be greater than $\left| \eta_{x \cdot t} \right|$ if and only if P_x exceeds wt_x.

Chapter 6
APPLICATIONS
AND
EXTENSIONS OF
DEMAND
THEORY

departments, and (2) private physicians for pay. Data were obtained on the number of visits to both sources of medical care. For the private sources, both a cash payment and a time input were involved. For the free sources, *only* the time input could play a role. (The time input involves both travel time and average waiting time for service; the data in the table below refer to travel time only, however.)

Travel-Time Elasticities for Ambulatory Care

| | RED HOOK | | BEDFORD-CROWN | |
	TRAVEL TIME TO FSMC	TRAVEL TIME TO PPO	TRAVEL TIME TO FSMC	TRAVEL TIME TO PPO
Visits to free sources of medical care (FSMC)	−.958	+.332	−.619	+.137
Visits to private physicians' offices (PPO)	+.640	−.252	+.629	−.337

Source: Jan P. Acton, "Demand for Health Care among the Urban Poor, with Special Emphasis on the Role of Time," The New York City Rand Institute, Report R-1151-OEO-NYC (April 1973), p. 27.

The results for the two neighborhoods are very similar. For both free and paid (private) medical care, the elasticity with respect to the time price (travel time to the source) was negative. For Red Hook the time-elasticity for free sources was −.958; this means that a 1% rise in travel time to free sources was associated with slightly less than a 1% fall in number of visits. The absolute value of this elasticity was much lower for private care, however; for Red Hook, −.252 as compared with −.958. This is evidently explicable in terms of the proposition in the text above. For free sources, the time input is the sole element of effective price. Hence *all* the elasticity of effective price must show up in the time-elasticity. For private sources of medical care, the elasticity with respect to *effective* price will be divided between time-elasticity and elasticity with respect to cash price.

The positive coefficients in the table represent cross-elasticities: the effect on usage of one source of medical care associated with increases in travel time to the other source. The positive elasticities show that the two types of medical services are substitutes, as of course would be expected. ∎

6.C

THE "NEW THEORY OF CONSUMPTION"

In recent years a novel and somewhat richer theory of consumption has been developed by economists. The key idea is a distinction between *market goods* and utility-relevant qualities or *attributes*. In this new approach a market commodity like bread is no longer supposed to be desired in and of itself, but only insofar as it is capable of yielding satisfaction through its attributes: tastiness, calories, proteins, and so on. Similarly an automobile is desired only insofar as it can be the source of transportation, comfort, prestige, and the like. One interesting aspect of this approach is a recognition that often, if not always, the market commodity does not generate its satisfying attributes unaided. Rather, the consumer generally elicits satisfaction from commodities by combining his own time and effort with the market goods themselves. Utility can thus be regarded as generated by activities subject to *income constraints* (upon the purchase of market goods) and *time constraints* (upon the hours to be allocated for their enjoyment), as discussed in the previous section.

We will not attempt to develop the formal theory here, but will point to two interesting implications:

1. Why some market goods are close substitutes, and others are not, becomes much easier to understand in this approach. Bread and potatoes (substitutes) have generally similar attributes; bread and haircuts do not. Substitutability thus, to a considerable extent, becomes an analyzable rather than a merely arbitrary fact.

2. The process whereby market commodities are combined with consumers' time and efforts can be regarded as *production within the household*, analogous to the ordinary productive process within business firms. Indeed, production within the home often competes directly with outside production, as in home washing versus commercial laundries. It is an interesting empirical question how much of the historical advance in standards of living is due to improved methods of business production such as interchangeability of parts, more powerful energy sources, newer and better-yielding crops, and how much is due to improvements mainly in the consumption sphere such as electric light, radio, television, and new fabrics for clothing.

*6.D

INDEX NUMBERS

Suppose we want to know, in comparing two situations, whether consumers are better off in the one or the other. If the commodities involved are *goods* so that "more is preferred to less," this question can be reformulated as: In which situation does the individual get, on the average, a larger quantity of commodities to consume? The average measure designed to answer such a question is called an *index number of quantity*. A closely related question is: In which situation does the consumer, on the average, have to pay a higher price for the goods he consumes? An average measure constructed to answer this question is called an *index number of price*.

* The section between the asterisk and the symbol ■ may contain somewhat more difficult or advanced material.

Chapter 6
APPLICATIONS
AND
EXTENSIONS OF
DEMAND
THEORY

171

Practical applications of index numbers of prices or quantities are almost always associated with problems involving monetary inflation or deflation, i.e., overall swings in the prices of goods measured in money terms. For example, a worker may want to know if his rising money income in an inflationary period has kept up with the rising money prices of the commodities in his consumption basket. Therefore, in this section we diverge from our previous insistence upon dealing in real units only (so as to "pierce the veil" of money). Rather, "income" here is to be understood as accruing to the consumer in the form of a money sum per period (symbolized as I^m). And similarly, prices are to be understood as quoted in money units.[8]

6.D.1

Index Numbers of Quantity

Consider Panel (a) of Figure 6.8. Here a person's levels of satisfaction or "standards of living" in two different time periods (period 0 and period 1) are to be compared by an observer who does *not* have knowledge of the subject's preference map. What the observer knows is that the consumer makes rational choices. He can thus infer that, in the "base year" (period 0), the consumer was at a consumptive optimum combination Q_0 (the corresponding quantities being q_x^0 and q_y^0 of

Figure 6.8

Standard of Living Comparisons. Here $K_0 L_0$ represents the base-year budget line, and $K_1 L_1$ the given-year budget line. In Panel (a) an observer, without knowing the consumer's preferences except that X and Y are both goods, would realize that the standard of living has been improved—since the consumer at Q_1 purchases more of both goods than at Q_0 (Dominant Case). In the Non-Dominant Case of Panel (b), however, preference maps might be constructed for which Q_1 is preferred to Q_0 or *vice versa*.

Panel (a)
Dominant Case

Panel (b)
Non-Dominant Case

[8]An explicit rationale for the existence of money will be provided in Chapter 8 below.

commodities X and Y respectively). This optimum depends, of course, upon base-year income I_0^m and the prices P_x^0 and P_y^0 which enter into the determination of the period-0 market opportunity set and budget line $K_0 L_0$. In the "given year" (period 1) these three determining variables will in general change to new levels I_1^m, P_x^1, and P_y^1, determining a new budget line $K_1 L_1$ and optimum solution Q_1 (with corresponding quantities q_x^1 and q_y^1).

Suppose prices and money income had so changed that the individual's new (given-year) budget line has greater intercepts on both the X- and Y-axes than the old (base-year) budget line. Unlike the picture in Figure 6.8, in such a case the budget line will have shifted completely outward from the origin (not necessarily strictly parallel to its initial position); the market opportunity set will have been enlarged in both the X- and the Y-directions. Since the consumer in period 1 could therefore surely do better than any position attainable along the budget line for the base year, the observer knows that the consumer must be better off in period 1. Similarly, if the budget line were entirely displaced inward, the consumer would surely be made worse off. The difficult case is when income and prices change in such a way that one intercept of the budget line increases while the other decreases. In Figure 6.8, for example, in period 1 the opportunities are greater in the X-direction but poorer in the Y-direction. In other words, the new and the old budget lines intersect.

It is nevertheless possible in some cases to detect immediately an unambiguous improvement or an unambiguous worsening in standard of living. Since X and Y are both goods, the preference directions are north and east. Hence the situation of Panel (a) of Figure 6.8, with the new consumptive optimum at Q_1 lying northeast of the old one at Q_0, represents an unambiguous improvement. We say here that the attained consumption basket Q_1 *dominates* Q_0. Correspondingly, if Q_1 were southwest of Q_0 the new position Q_1 would be *dominated by* the old Q_0, so that an unambiguous reduction in standard of living must have occurred.

In the situation of Panel (b) of Figure 6.8, on the other hand, there is no dominance. With Q_1 lying southeast of Q_0 it would be possible to construct preference maps in which the combination Q_0 is preferred to Q_1, but equally possible to construct maps for which Q_1 is preferred to Q_0. The same would apply if Q_1 were northwest of Q_0. Since the indifference maps are not known to outside observers, no obvious conclusion could be drawn from merely observing Q_0 and Q_1.

However, there is one other consideration that can be brought to bear. Consider now the situation in Panel (a) of Figure 6.9. Here Q_1 lies southeast of Q_0, so this might seem to be a doubtful case. But without knowledge of the preference map the observer can still see that *in period 0, the position Q_1 was attainable*; Q_1 lies within the shaded market opportunity set bounded by the axes and the budget line $K_0 L_0$ that was effective at time 0. Since the basket Q_1 was attainable in period 0 but was *not* purchased and Q_0 was purchased instead, Q_0 must have been preferred to Q_1. On the assumption that preferences have not changed, the observer can infer that the standard of living must have declined between the base year and the given year as a result of the price and income changes. And he can know this even if the indifference map in the diagram were hidden from him.

Chapter 6

APPLICATIONS
AND
EXTENSIONS OF
DEMAND
THEORY

173

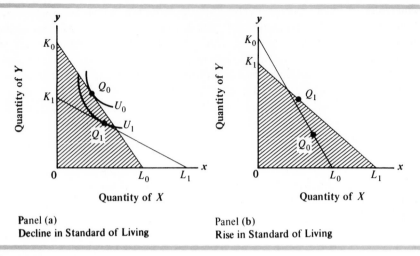

Panel (a)
Decline in Standard of Living

Panel (b)
Rise in Standard of Living

Figure 6.9

Unambiguous Changes in Standard of Living. Here the consumption basket Q_1 does not dominate (contain more of both goods than) Q_0, nor does Q_0 dominate Q_1. Nevertheless, in Panel (a) an observer could detect that Q_0 is preferred to Q_1 even without knowing the preference function. Since Q_1 lies within the $K_0 L_0$ budget line it *could* have been purchased in period 0, but was not. Hence Q_0 must have been preferable. In Panel (b) we see that Q_0 lies within the $K_1 L_1$ budget line and so could have been purchased in period 1, but was not. So here Q_1 must be preferable.

Panel (b) of Figure 6.9 shows the opposite case. As Q_1 lies northwest of Q_0, the *dominance* test in terms of preference directions does not lead to a clear conclusion. But in the given year the shaded market opportunity set, bounded by the axes and the budget line $K_1 L_1$, includes the position Q_0. That is, in period 1 the combination Q_0 is attainable but is *not* being purchased. Hence Q_1 is surely preferred to Q_0, and there has been an improvement in the standard of living.

Looking back at Panel (b) of Figure 6.8, we see that the situation pictured there is not consistent with the diagrams in either Panel of Figure 6.9. This shows that in some cases we simply cannot tell, without knowing the preference function, whether the consumer is better off in period 0 or in period 1.

Let us now consider the problem of constructing an algebraic measure or index that will signify when the basket Q_1 (the consumption combination q_x^1, q_y^1) is on the average greater than—and so, in utility terms is preferred to—the basket Q_0 (the combination q_x^0, q_y^0). There are two standard ways of constructing these averages or indexes: the Laspeyres index ($\mathscr{L}$) using "base-year price weights" and the Paasche index ($\mathscr{P}$) using "given-year price weights."

The Laspeyres index of quantity is defined, where the "sigma" notation for summation provides a helpful shorthand for extending the 2-good geometrical discussion to any number of commodities, as:

$$(6.8) \qquad \mathscr{L}_Q \equiv \frac{P_x^0 q_x^1 + P_y^0 q_y^1}{P_x^0 q_x^0 + P_y^0 q_y^0} \equiv \frac{\sum P^0 q^1}{\sum P^0 q^0}$$

Chapter 6
APPLICATIONS
AND
EXTENSIONS OF
DEMAND
THEORY

174

The Laspeyres index provides an estimate as to whether quantities have increased "on the average" between period 0 and period 1, where, to make the quantity comparison a meaningful one, the same weights (in this case the base-year price weights P_x^0 and P_y^0) are used in calculating the average.

The Paasche index of quantity differs from the Laspeyres only in using given-year price weights instead:

$$(6.9) \qquad \mathscr{P}_Q \equiv \frac{P_x^1 q_x^1 + P_y^1 q_y^1}{P_x^1 q_x^0 + P_y^1 q_y^0} \equiv \frac{\sum P^1 q^1}{\sum P^1 q^0}$$

In Figure 6.10, Panel (a) represents the same situation as in Panel (a) of Figure 6.9. The indifference curves and shading have been suppressed; instead, an artificial budget line represented by the dashed line CC' parallel to the base-year budget line $K_0 L_0$ has been passed through the given-year quantity solution Q_1. The total expenditure (the income I_0^m) represented by the original solution Q_0 at the base-year prices can be written as $I_0^m = P_x^0 q_x^0 + P_y^0 q_y^0$ or $I_0^m = \sum P^0 q^0$. The

Figure 6.10

Unambiguous Changes in Standard of Living—Quantity Indexes. Panel (a) represents the same situation as Panel (a) in Figure 6.9. The artificial budget line CC' has the same slope (represents the same price ratio) as $K_0 L_0$, but is passed through the given-year consumption basket Q_1. CC' corresponds to an expenditure or income $\sum P^0 q^1$ while $K_0 L_0$ corresponds to $\sum P^0 q^0$. Since CC' lies entirely within $K_0 L_0$, the income level represented by the former is effectively lower when evaluated at the prices P^0. Any point like Q_1 along CC' must therefore be less desired than Q_0. So Q_0 must be preferred to Q_1 if the Laspeyres condition $\mathscr{L}_Q < 1$ holds. By a similar argument, the comparison in terms of given-year prices P^1 in Panel (b) shows a situation in which Q_1 must be preferred to Q_0. This is represented algebraically by the Paasche condition $\mathscr{P}_Q > 1$.

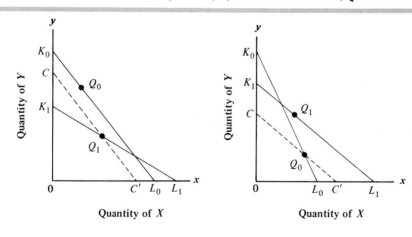

Panel (a)
Decline in
Standard of Living – –
Base–Year Comparison ($\mathscr{L}_Q < 1$)

Panel (b)
Improvement in
Standard of Living – –
Given–Year Comparison ($\mathscr{P}_Q > 1$)

Chapter 6
APPLICATIONS
AND
EXTENSIONS OF
DEMAND
THEORY

new line CC' applies to the *quantities* associated with the given-year solution Q_1, but its slope represents the *base-year* prices. Hence the consumption expenditures associated with CC' can be written in summation notation as $\Sigma P^0 q^1$. In the situation pictured here, at the P^0 prices the basket Q_0 represents a higher expenditure level than Q_1. Hence, in Panel (a) of Figure 6.10:

$$\Sigma P^0 q^0 > \Sigma P^0 q^1 \quad \text{or} \quad \mathscr{L}_Q \equiv \frac{\Sigma P^0 q^1}{\Sigma P^0 q^0} < 1$$

The conclusion is that when the Laspeyres quantity index is *less* than unity, the consumer has surely become worse off in the given year. With the opportunity to buy Q_1 in place of Q_0 in period 0, the consumer chose *not* to do so. And therefore, when actually observed to purchase Q_1 in period 1, he or she must have become worse off than at Q_0 in the previous period.

By a corresponding argument, Panel (b) of Figure 6.10 represents the situation where:

$$\Sigma P^1 q^0 < \Sigma P^1 q^1 \quad \text{or} \quad \mathscr{P}_Q \equiv \frac{\Sigma P^1 q^1}{\Sigma P^1 q^0} > 1$$

The conclusion is that when the Paasche quantity index is *greater* than unity, the consumer has surely become better off in the given year—having in the given year the opportunity of buying Q_0 in place of Q_1, and choosing not to do so.

These conclusions are in each case *sufficient* to determine the direction of improvement, but not *necessary*. If the Laspeyres quantity index is less than unity, the observer knows that the consumer must have become worse off in the given year. But the consumer *can* be worse off without this condition holding. In Figure 6.8, Panel (b), it is not the case that $\mathscr{L}_Q < 1$. Nevertheless, it would be possible to construct an indifference map for that diagram such that Q_1 is inferior to Q_0. Similarly, if the Paasche quantity index is greater than unity the consumer must be better off in period 1—but *can* be better off without this condition holding. Again, it would be possible to show this by constructing a suitable indifference map in Panel (b) of Figure 6.8.

6.D.2
Index Numbers
of Price

We now turn to index numbers of *prices*. Laspeyres and Paasche indexes of prices may be defined algebraically in the same way as for quantities. But here, as it is the prices which are being averaged, the quantities serve as weights. The definitions are:

Chapter 6
APPLICATIONS
AND
EXTENSIONS OF
DEMAND
THEORY

176

$$(6.10) \qquad \mathscr{L}_P \equiv \frac{\Sigma P^1 q^0}{\Sigma P^0 q^0}$$

$$(6.11) \qquad \mathscr{P}_P \equiv \frac{\Sigma P^1 q^1}{\Sigma P^0 q^1}$$

It is useful also to define an index of money-income change as:

(6.12)
$$\mathcal{E} \equiv \frac{\sum P^1 q^1}{\sum P^0 q^0} \equiv \frac{I_1^m}{I_0^m}$$

This is of course simply the ratio of total expenditures in the two periods.

It is intuitively clear that there must be a close connection between the quantity and the price indexes. This connection turns out to involve the index of income change $\mathcal{E}$ as well.

We know from the discussion above that the consumer is surely better off in the given year if $\sum P^1 q^0 < \sum P^1 q^1$ so that the Paasche quantity index is greater than one. Dividing both sides of the inequality by $\sum P^0 q^0$, we have:

$$\frac{\sum P^1 q^1}{\sum P^0 q^0} > \frac{\sum P^1 q^0}{\sum P^0 q^0} \quad \text{or} \quad \mathcal{E} > \mathcal{L}_P$$

Thus, if the income index $\mathcal{E}$ exceeds the Laspeyres index of prices, the consumer is in an improved situation in the given year as compared to the base year. This result is implied by a Paasche index of quantity exceeding unity.

Correspondingly, of course, the consumer is worse off in the given year when the index of income $\mathcal{E}$ is less than the Paasche index of prices, or $\mathcal{E} < \mathcal{P}_P$. This is equivalent to a Laspeyres index of quantity $\mathcal{L}_Q$ that is less than unity.

The economic interpretation of the relation between the income and price indexes is quite direct. If, for example, income has risen more than in proportion to prices, on the average, then the average quantity consumed must have increased. If income has risen less than in proportion to prices, on the average, the average quantity consumed (real income) must have decreased.

CONCLUSION: If the Paasche quantity index $\mathcal{P}_Q$ is greater than unity, the consumer is surely better off in the given year. And then the income index $\mathcal{E}$ exceeds the Laspeyres price index $\mathcal{L}_P$. If the Laspeyres quantity index $\mathcal{L}_Q$ is less than unity, the consumer is surely worse off in the given year. And then the income index $\mathcal{E}$ is less than the Paasche price index $\mathcal{P}_P$.

Exploration of the theoretical niceties of Laspeyres versus Paasche indexes is helpful in forcing students to deepen their understanding of the interrelations among price and income changes. In practice, however, the really important issues do not concern these niceties. The Laspeyres and Paasche indexes will not differ very much, unless indeed an attempt is being made to compare situations so different or so far apart in time or space as to invalidate the *assumption of constant preferences* that underlies the entire analysis. In terms of common sense, the main message to be drawn is that a person whose money-income index has risen, but less than in proportion to the index of money prices (Laspeyres or Paasche makes little difference), is *not* really better off. For such a person, *real* income (index of quantity consumed) has fallen rather than risen.

Chapter 6
APPLICATIONS
AND
EXTENSIONS OF
DEMAND
THEORY

177

But a further warning is also very much in order. Money income may have risen more than in proportion to some official price index, and even so the consumers can really be worse off! For, by accident or design, a host of devices may mask losses in real income during an inflationary period. Most, though not all, of these sources of distortion are connected with the imposition of price controls that prevent legally quoted prices from rising to a higher equilibrium level (see Section 2.A.5). As a result there may be disguised price rises, not registered in the official price indexes, in such forms as: (1) Open or hidden degradation of quality (including range of varieties offered); (2) elimination of customary discounts or special sales, etc.; (3) provision of some portion of goods through illegal black-market or unofficial channels at unreported high prices; (4) forcing consumers to less-preferred combinations, at existing money prices, by such devices as coupon rationing, queue rationing, or simple unavailability of desired goods; (5) fiscal subsidies to those particular commodities appearing in the officially quoted index. (This last is akin to lowering the recorded temperature in a room by pressing an ice cube against the thermometer.)

EXAMPLE 6.5
COST OF LIVING
IN WARTIME
BRITAIN

During World War II the government of Great Britain, like most of the other nations on both sides of that conflict, engaged in inflationary war finance and yet used price ceilings to hold down the prices of consumer goods. Superficially, the latter policy seems to have been successful. The official Ministry of Labor index (based on 1938 prices = 100) of the cost of living for a working-class family rose only from 127 in 1941 to 130 in 1945.

A closer look casts some doubt on this performance, however. To hold the official index down the British government subsidized just those goods whose prices were counted in the statistical averaging process. This led to a divergence between the index as calculated and what it was supposed to measure: the actual cost of maintaining the pre-war standard of living. Estimates based upon an alternative index were reported by Dudley Seers. Some of his data are summarized in the table here.

Cost of Living Indexes

	1940	1945
Official (Working Class)	127	130
Alternative (Working Class)	130.5	149
Alternative (Lower Middle Class)	133	154
Alternative (Upper Middle Class)	139	170

Source: Dudley Seers, ''The Cost of Living 1938–48,'' *Oxford Institute of Statistics Bulletin*, v. 11 (May 1949), pp. 129, 131.

As can be seen, prices rose much faster than indicated by the official index. And yet the results suggest a considerable degree of success, at least for the working class, since even the alternative index shows an increase of only about 14% for them over the four years. (The working class did relatively better, since the goods entering into the official index and therefore chosen for subsidy were predominantly those commodities entering into the consumption baskets of less affluent families.) However, this conclusion must itself be treated with reserve, since even the alternative index fails to allow for the effects of rationing, the necessity to wait in line for goods, or simply unavailability. As shown in the discussion of multiple constraints (Section B above), such limitations on consumption tend to force individuals onto lower indifference curves representing reduced real standards of living—without showing up in any cost of living index based upon averages of price movements. ■

THE INCOME-COMPENSATED DEMAND CURVE

In Chapter 4, Section B.2 the individual's Price Expansion Path (PEP) was derived, as pictured in Figure 4.10, by tilting the budget line outward from KL to KL' to KL'', about the anchoring point K on the vertical Y-axis. The vertical intercept K, corresponding to a Y-quantity equal to I/P_y, is anchored because in deriving the PEP both income I and the price of the "other" commodity P_y are held fixed—with only P_x allowed to vary. The corresponding demand curve, pictured in Panel (a) of Figure 4.12, represented the data of the PEP curve plotted onto x,P_x axes.

In Section C of Chapter 4 it was shown that the consequences of such a reduction in P_x for the consumer's preferred consumption basket could be separated into an *income effect* and a pure *substitution effect*. Figure 4.14 pictured the outward tilting of the budget line (from KL to KL^*) as P_x falls—I and P_y still held constant—and the consequent "Hicks decomposition" of the overall effect of the price change. In this decomposition, the pure substitution effect was obtained by holding real income constant in a particular way: by hypothetically requiring the consumer to choose a new preferred basket along his initial indifference curve after P_x changes.

Here, however, we want to consider a different decomposition, associated with the Russian economist Slutsky.[9] In Figure 6.11, the overall effect of the price change is again represented by a shift of the consumptive optimum from Q_0 to Q_1 as the budget line tilts from KL to KL^* in response to a fall in P_x. But here, in contrast with Figure 4.14, the artificial budget line $K'L'$ parallel to the new budget line KL^* is drawn through the old optimum point Q_0—rather than being made tangent to the old indifference curve U_0. Thus, KL and $K'L'$ both allow the consumer to purchase the original consumption basket Q_0.

*The section between the asterisk and the symbol ■ may contain somewhat more difficult or advanced material.
[9]Eugen Slutsky, 1880–1948.

Chapter 6
APPLICATIONS
AND
EXTENSIONS OF
DEMAND
THEORY

Figure 6.11

Income and Substitution Effects—Slutsky Decomposition. The overall effect of the price change, the shift from Q_0 to Q_1, is decomposed by drawing an artificial budget line $K'L'$ parallel to the new budget line KL^* but through the old optimum point Q_0. Real income is held constant between points Q_0 and Q' in the sense of the Paasche index of quantity (ability to purchase the old consumption basket at the new prices). The Slutsky pure substitution effect of the price change, in terms of purchases of X, is the distance $x' - x_0$; the income effect is the distance $x_1 - x'$.

What is the advantage of the Slutsky over the Hicks decomposition of income versus substitution effects? For one thing, it permits a simple *measure* of the change in real income. For Hicks, the improvement in real income represents only attaining a higher level of utility, a magnitude that is not cardinally measurable. For Slutsky, the real-income change can be measured by the ratio of the expenditures associated with the given-year budget line KL^* (along which the observed Q_1 position falls) to the expenditures associated with the artificial budget line $K'L'$ (along which the observed Q_0 position falls). What is this ratio? It is nothing but the *Paasche index of quantity* defined above in equation (6.9) that will be repeated here:

Chapter 6
APPLICATIONS
AND
EXTENSIONS OF
DEMAND
THEORY

$$\mathscr{P}_Q \equiv \frac{P_x^1 q_x^1 + P_y^1 q_y^1}{P_x^1 q_x^0 + P_y^1 q_y^0}$$

The comparison is of the given-year quantities (consumption combination Q_1) versus the base-year quantities (consumption combination Q_0), averaged in terms of the given-year price weights—represented geometrically by the parallel slopes of KL^* and $K'L'$ in Figure 6.11.

While the Paasche quantity index thus provides us with a measure of the real-income change, we do not yet have a way of separating the *real-income effect* from the *substitution effect* on the basis of the historical observations. Ideally, we would like to know the location of the hypothetical tangency optimum Q' in Figure 6.11 along the artificial budget line $K'L'$. Combination Q' would be the Slutsky analog to the artificial tangency optimum Q' for the Hicks decomposition illustrated in Figure 4.14. Since the Slutsky Q' position is unknowable to an observer (as is the Hicks Q' position), it must be estimated from the observations. This estimation would be based upon the statistical data and the form of the relationship fitted. Suppose, for example, that econometric analysis led to the conclusion that the income elasticity for commodity X (and, therefore, also for Y) is unity. In this case, as explained in Section 5.A, the hypothetical tangency optimum Q' along $K'L'$ in Figure 6.11 would lie on the (dashed) ray drawn from the origin to the point Q_1 along KL^*. If the income elasticity for X were greater than unity, Q' would have to lie along $K'L'$ northwest of the intersection with this ray from the origin; if the income elasticity were less than unity, Q' would lie to the southeast along $K'L'$. But in any case, the statistical evidence would lead to a hypothetical determination of the position of Q'.

As between the points Q_0 and Q', *real income is constant in the sense of the Paasche quantity index* ($\mathscr{P}_Q = 1$). Then the difference between the X-quantities in these consumption combinations can be attributed solely to the effect of the differing price ratios P_x/P_y (budget-line slopes). Plotting the price ratios against the quantities so obtained leads to what is called the *income-compensated* demand curve d^*d^* shown in Figure 6.12. With this is drawn, for comparison, the "ordinary" demand curve dd previously derived (in Chapter 4, Section B).

The two demand curves in Figure 6.12 are shown as coinciding at the initial observed point A, with quantity q_x^0 and price ratio P_x^0/P_y^0, corresponding to the position Q_0 in Figure 6.11. For the ordinary demand curve dd, a point like B is obtained at the lower price ratio P_x^1/P_y^0. As indicated in the discussion of Section 4.B.2, the price-quantity point B corresponds to a position on the individual's Price Expansion Path (PEP) as P_x varies, with income I (in numeraire units) and prices of other goods like P_y held constant. For the income-compensated demand curve d^*d^*, at the lower price ratio the price-quantity point C is obtained. Point C corresponds to the hypothetical consumption combination Q' in Figure 6.11, estimated from the statistical data while holding real income (Paasche quantity index) constant.

A number of aspects of the income-compensated demand curve are of interest.

1. Since the ordinary demand curve incorporates an "income effect of the price change," which the compensated demand curve excludes, it must be that for a normal or superior good dd is flatter than d^*d^*, as drawn in Figure 6.12. When price falls the income effect is positive for a normal good; the ordinary demand, but not the compensated demand, reflects this (point B lies to the right of point C in the diagram). However,

Chapter 6
APPLICATIONS
AND
EXTENSIONS OF
DEMAND
THEORY

181

Figure 6.12

Income-Compensated versus "Ordinary" Demand Curve. Starting from an initial consumptive optimum represented by the price-quantity point A, *dd* represents an individual's "ordinary" demand curve and *d*d** the "income-compensated" demand curve (using the Slutsky decomposition). For the ordinary demand curve, P_y and I are held constant, so that as price P_x (and therefore the price ratio P_x/P_y) falls the substitution effect and the normal income effect combine to increase purchases of X. For the income-compensated demand curve, the income effect is eliminated as P_x/P_y falls, by holding constant the ability to purchase the initial consumption basket. Consequently, if X is a normal good there will be a smaller consumption increment of X along *d*d** than along *dd*.

we saw in Chapter 4 that the income effect *may* be negative, indeed conceivably so much so that the Giffen condition obtains (positively-sloped demand curve within some range). Since the compensated demand curve excludes any income effect, the Giffen possibility is also ruled out.

2. In a many-commodity world, it would be arbitrary to pick out some single other commodity Y whose price P_y would serve as the base of the price ratio P_x/P_y in measuring the change in relative prices. Instead, some general average of prices such as the Consumer Price Index would be used in actual statistical work to "deflate" the observed changes in the nominal money price of commodity X.

3. The great importance of the income-compensated demand curve stems from the fact that, as already suggested, this is the relation that is actually obtained from statistical studies of historical price-quantity observations. In such studies it is almost always necessary to allow for *income differences* by fitting a demand function like that of equation (5.5) or equation (5.10) to the observations. For example, it would hardly be possible to simply fit a demand curve to price-quantity data from both California and

Chapter 6
APPLICATIONS
AND
EXTENSIONS OF
DEMAND
THEORY

182

Mississippi without allowing for the real-income differences between those states. And in time-series analysis, it will similarly be necessary to allow for historical growth of real income over time. But the statistician, in making a separate allowance for differences or changes in real income, is thereby *eliminating the income effect* from the price-quantity data. This necessarily leaves the statistical result an approximation of the "pure substitution effect"—the income-compensated demand curve.

4. It is sometimes thought that the essential distinction between the ordinary and the compensated demand curves is due to money; some authors regard the ordinary demand curve *dd* as one that holds *money income constant* while the compensated demand curve *d*d** holds *real income constant*. This is an understandable confusion, since in modern economies prices are quoted in terms of money. Nevertheless, the existence of money is not the essential here. Suppose money had not been invented so that prices were quoted in terms of some real numeraire commodity. It would still be possible logically to distinguish the "ordinary" demand relation that holds income endowment and other prices constant (see the derivation using the Price Expansion Path of Section 4.B.2) from the "compensated" demand relation that eliminates the income effect of price changes (as derived here and illustrated in Figure 6.11).

5. Nor is it true that the income-compensated demand curve is intrinsically superior to or more valid than the ordinary demand curve (along which consumers' real income rises as price P_x falls). Each has its uses. The ordinary demand curve, for example, is the function that is relevant when a business makes decisions concerning what price to charge. ∎

This chapter, not in the CORE CHAPTER sequence, covers a number of applications and extensions intended to enrich understanding of the standard theory of demand.

One way of expending income is upon charity, which can therefore be considered a *good* demanded by donors. Under normal conditions charity is a superior good (more is contributed as income rises). Also, as the tax rate rises the "price" of charitable giving falls, and so more tends to be given. Similarly, since hazardous jobs pay higher wages a worker can, in effect, spend income to purchase *safety* as a desired good.

A topic with great real-world importance is the decision problem of the consumer subject to constraints apart from income. *Rationing* of one or more commodities, if effective, truncates the consumption opportunity set for the commodities concerned. More sophisticated schemes of "point rationing" in effect impose a dual price scheme—money prices and point prices, subject respectively to constraints on ordinary income and on point income—upon consumers. And, even in the absence of rationing, *time* may be a serious additional constraint upon consumption.

A topic more of technical interest than real-world importance is the theory of index numbers of prices and quantities. The issue here is to determine conditions such that an observer can detect when consumers are better or worse off, *without* knowing their preference functions. In some cases this can be done. In particular, the consumer's situation has surely improved if the Paasche quantity index (which averages consumption quantities using the new prices as weights, and therefore measures ability to buy the old consumption basket at the new prices) is greater than unity. This is equivalent to a Laspeyres price index (which averages prices using the old consumption quantities as weights) having risen by less than the index of income (ratio of new income to old income). However, in some cases the result remains indeterminate. What is probably a more important matter is that if, as often occurs under inflationary conditions, rationing by coupon or by points or by waiting time imposes constraints *other than price* upon consumption decisions, price indexes will very seriously understate the true rise in cost of living.

In investigations of the effects of income changes and price changes upon consumption decisions, it is sometimes convenient to use an *income-compensated* demand curve—that is, a demand curve from which the "income effect" of price changes has been eliminated, leaving only the pure "substitution effect." But in statistical work it is not possible to use the substitution effect derived in Chapter 4 from the Hicksian decomposition of the overall effect of a price change (which was based on finding a hypothetical optimum consumption basket at the new prices while holding utility constant). The Hicksian decomposition requires knowledge of individual preferences. Instead, in empirical work the pure substitution effect is isolated by the Slutsky decomposition: the income effect is eliminated by finding the hypothetical optimum consumption basket at the new prices such that the Paasche quantity index—ability to buy the old consumption basket—is held constant.

QUESTIONS FOR CHAPTER 6

Mainly for Review

*R1. In terms of the example "Charitable Giving," is charitable donation (regarded as a consumption good) a luxury? What is the "price" of charitable giving?

*R2. Gasoline rationing has been proposed as one possible remedy for the recent "energy crisis." If rations were distributed on an egalitarian basis, show the situations of a wealthy and a poor consumer in terms of their opportunity sets for gasoline consumption versus "all other goods." Show typical indifference maps if automobile usage is a luxury. Would permitting sale of coupons be a good idea?

R3. What is the difference between a Laspeyres index and a Paasche index? Show the geometrical meaning of a Laspeyres quantity index that is less than unity. Show the geometrical meaning of a Paasche quantity index

Chapter 6
APPLICATIONS
AND
EXTENSIONS OF
DEMAND
THEORY

*The answers to asterisked questions appear at the end of the book.

that exceeds unity. Can we draw conclusions as to relative well-being in these two cases? If not, why not?

*R4. "If the ratio of new income to old income is greater than the ratio of the new cost to the old cost of the old commodity bundle, the consumer is surely better off." What statement about indexes does this correspond to? Is the statement true?

R5. What is an income-compensated demand curve? How does it differ from the ordinary demand curve? For a normal good (positive income elasticity), which of the two curves is the more elastic?

For Further Thought and Discussion

T1. Suppose that I am an envious rather than a benevolent individual. What would my preference map between "His Income" and "My Income" look like? Would I ever give charity? Might I even be willing to sacrifice income of my own if I could thereby lower the other person's income?

*T2. In wartime rationing situations, purchase or sale of ration allowances for cash, or exchange of ration coupons for other goods, is generally illegal. Is there any justification for this? Are there adverse consequences of forbidding such exchanges?

*T3. It is often thought that the wealthy must have a great deal of leisure. On the other hand, members of present-day richer societies tend to be more harried and pressed for time than were their own grandparents who lacked so many modern time-saving devices. Interpret in terms of the time constraint on consumption.

T4. Since nomadic tribes have a serious portability problem, they are somewhat reluctant to acquire heavy material possessions. Analyze in terms of nomads' income and "carrying capacity" as multiple constraints. What types of goods have high "prices" in terms of carrying capacity?

T5. In the spring of 1979 it became necessary in many areas of the United States to wait on long lines to be served with gasoline. The U.S. Department of Energy had, evidently, set gasoline prices too low to clear the market in those areas—though the problem was also in part due to the same Department's regional allocations of fuel on the basis of historical (and therefore more or less outdated) patterns of usage. If the money price of gasoline was 90¢ per gallon, if the typical consumer had to wait 30 minutes to obtain a refill of ten gallons, and if his time was worth $5 per hour, estimate what the market-clearing money price would have been. Comparing higher money prices versus long waits in line, which system is *relatively* more advantageous for rich people versus poor? For working people versus the retired and unemployed? For owners of cars with large gas tanks versus small?

T6. What would be wrong with an economic system in which everything was allocated by waiting in line rather than by charging money prices? (Hint: Would the Invisible Hand be able to serve its function?)

PART THREE

Equilibrium
and
Exchange

7.A THE FUNDAMENTAL THEOREM OF EXCHANGE, 190

7.B THE EDGEWORTH BOX, THE ADVANTAGE OF TRADE, AND COMPETITIVE EQUILIB-
RIUM, 192

7.C SUPPLY AND DEMAND IN PURE EXCHANGE, 197

7.D EXCHANGE AND PRODUCTION, 203

7.E CONSUMER SURPLUS AND PRODUCER SURPLUS, 212
    7.E.1   An Application: The Water-Diamond Paradox, 213
    7.E.2   Hindrances to Trade, 214
    *7.E.3   Rationale of Consumer and Producer Surplus, 220

Examples
    7.1   ECONOMIC EXCHANGE AND THE AMERICAN CIVIL WAR, 193
    7.2   ANIMAL ROBINSON CRUSOES, 205
    7.3   INTERNATIONAL SPECIALIZATION AND TRADE, 211
    7.4   SUGAR QUOTAS, 219

7

EQUILIBRIUM, EXCHANGE, AND THE GAINS FROM TRADE

Core Chapter

Up to now we have analyzed only the private decisions of individuals (or households)—the ultimate economic agents. In this chapter we make the transition from *individual* behavior to *market* phenomena, with a corresponding shift of emphasis from the technique of *optimization* to the technique of *determination of equilibrium.*

7.A

THE FUNDAMENTAL THEOREM
OF EXCHANGE

PROPOSITION: *Voluntary trade is mutually beneficial* (that is, it increases utility for both parties involved).

This is the Fundamental Theorem of Exchange. An alternative, mistaken view is the "exploitation theory," that in exchange one party's gain is the other party's loss. The proof of the Fundamental Theorem, and disproof of the exploitation theory, would hardly seem to require any long or difficult reasoning. It follows immediately from the postulate of rational behavior. If exchange were not beneficial for both parties, one or the other would refuse to trade. And yet it is astonishing how many misconceptions of economic problems (for example, the most commonly encountered arguments for protective tariffs), rest upon failure to appreciate the obvious truth that exchange is mutually beneficial.[1]

There are, it is true, debatable aspects of this sweeping theorem. (1) Suppose trickery has taken place: A purchaser pays good money for a beachfront lot that turns out to be a mile out to sea. In this case there was no actual *agreement*, no meeting of minds. Hence the transaction was not really a mutually voluntary exchange. (2) More problematically, it may be that the momentary desires on which an exchange is based do not represent an individual's true considered preferences. Esau sold his birthright to Jacob for a mess of pottage, and regretted the transaction afterward. (3) Still more seriously, the question remains as to whether individuals truly benefit from having even their fully-considered preferences satisfied. That a person's desires do not necessarily lead to where true benefit lies has been a theme of moralists through the ages.

While these philosophical questions cannot be studied here, we see that there are possible qualifications to the Fundamental Theorem. Nevertheless, accepting the postulate of rationality, it remains the case that each participant in exchange benefits *according to his own lights at the time of decision*, though possibly not in the opinion of an outside observer (or even in his own opinion at some later date).

There are two distinct elements in the mutual gain from trade. The first element is an *improved allocation of consumption goods* over individuals. Suppose there are two persons, let us call them John and Karl, somehow endowed with equal quantities of tea and coffee (perhaps as a result of a wartime rationing system). If John prefers tea and Karl prefers coffee, the potential gain from trade will be obvious. Nor are differences of taste necessary. Suppose that John and Karl, having the same preferences, find themselves in possession of quantities of bread and butter, except that John has all the bread and Karl all the butter. Again, we see that trade can improve consumptive allocations for both.

The second source of improvement, an indirect consequence of the first, is due to *rearrangement of production* rather than of consumption. In the illustration just given, if John were better at baking bread and Karl at churning butter, the possibility of later trading would permit each to concentrate productively upon the activity for which he is better suited. Improved production would make a greater total of goods available to all, apart from the improved consumptive distributions that trade brings about after the goods are produced.

CONCLUSION: Voluntary trade is mutually beneficial because traders can: (1) reallocate existing stocks of consumption goods so that each achieves a preferred bundle, and (2) specialize in production so as to increase the social totals of goods available.

Sections 7.B and 7.C immediately following concentrate upon the *consumptive* improvement due to trade. Afterward, attention will be turned to the *productive* improvement and to its interaction with the consumptive gains.

[1]This should not be understood as denying the possible validity of more sophisticated arguments for protective tariffs (or for other trade-hindering interventions).

Chapter 7
EQUILIBRIUM,
EXCHANGE,
AND THE
GAINS FROM
TRADE

THE EDGEWORTH BOX, THE ADVANTAGE OF TRADE, AND COMPETITIVE EQUILIBRIUM

How exchange makes possible mutually advantageous improvements in the allocation of consumption goods can be conveniently illustrated by the geometrical device of the "Edgeworth box" in Figure 7.1. This box shows two parties, John and Karl, facing one another in a potential exchange situation. For John, the origin O_j is at the lower-left corner as usual; his preference map (consisting of indifference curves $U_j', U_j'', \ldots$) is drawn upon axes representing his consumption quantities x_j and y_j of commodities X and Y, respectively. For Karl, the directions are reversed.

Figure 7.1

Edgeworth Box. John's consumption of X and Y is measured in the usual way by distances east and north of the origin O_j. For Karl the axes are inverted: his consumption of X is measured by distance west of the origin O_k, and his consumption of Y by distance south of O_k. John's preferences are represented by the indifference curves $U_j', U_j'' \ldots$ with utility increasing moving northeast, Karl's by the curves $U_k', U_k'', \ldots$ with utility rising moving southwest. The overall width of the box corresponds to the fixed social total $\overline{X}$, and the overall height to the fixed social total $\overline{Y}$. Any point in the diagram represents an allocation of these social totals between John and Karl. Starting at the endowment position E, the allocations preferred to E by both parties (on higher U_j and U_k indifference curves) are shown by the shaded Region of Mutual Advantage.

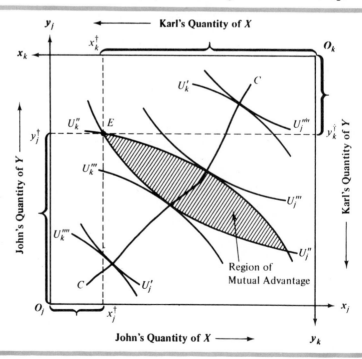

Chapter 7
EQUILIBRIUM,
EXCHANGE,
AND THE
GAINS FROM
TRADE

192

Karl's origin O_k is at the upper-right corner of the box; his indifference curves are drawn with respect to his consumption quantities x_k and y_k. The arrows attached to the axes indicate that, for commodity X, John's quantity x_j is measured by distance to the *right* of O_j and Karl's quantity x_k by distance to the *left* of O_k; similarly, John's y_j is measured *upward* from O_j and Karl's y_k *downward* from O_k.

The width and height of the Edgeworth box are determined by the social totals $\overline{X}$ and $\overline{Y}$ of the two commodities, where $\overline{X} = x_j + x_k$ and $\overline{Y} = y_j + y_k$. The fixed social totals, represented by the dimensions of the Edgeworth box, mean that no production takes place (since production, by its very nature, changes the total availability of some commodities). Thus, in the diagram the individuals' opportunity sets reflect *only* the possibilities of reallocating the fixed social totals of commodities through exchange. It follows that if John's consumption x_j of commodity X increases then Karl's x_k must correspondingly decrease, unit for unit, and similarly for the consumed quantities y_j and y_k of commodity Y.

The initial allocation of the two goods between John and Karl is shown by the *endowment* position E in Figure 7.1. John's endowment consists of the quantities $x_j^\dagger$ and $y_j^\dagger$ measured to the east and to the north, respectively, from his origin O_j. Karl's endowment consists of the quantities $x_k^\dagger$ and $y_k^\dagger$ measured to the west and to the south from his origin O_k. Trading entails a shift to some other allocation of the social totals, i.e., to some position other than E in the box. If X and Y are *goods* for both parties, then each will insist upon receiving more of the one commodity in exchange for giving up some of the other. The allocations permitted by this condition (i.e., achievable by voluntary exchange) are those lying either toward the southeast *or* toward the northwest of the initial endowment position E.

But a still stronger condition can be placed on the mutually advantageous exchanges that are possible. Consider the traders' respective indifference curves U_j'' and U_k'' that pass through the endowment position E. If trade is voluntary and the individuals are rational, neither will ever move to a point at a lower preference level than he has already attained at E. Each will only move "uphill" from E on his utility surface. Consequently, the possible final allocations are only those lying within the shaded lens-shaped region in the diagram between U_j'' and U_k''. This area is called the *region of mutual advantage*.

Before the Civil War, the Northern and Southern states had engaged in a mutually advantageous economic exchange. The South produced a vast surplus of cotton which was sold in the North (and also abroad), the proceeds being used to purchase manufactured products. Less than 10% of the total pre-war (1860) national value of manufactures had been produced in the seceded states.[2]

With the onset of the war, direct North–South trade was interrupted. The interruption hit the Confederacy much harder than the Union. While cotton prices in the North jumped, the adverse impact upon textile availability was

EXAMPLE 7.1
ECONOMIC
EXCHANGE AND
THE AMERICAN
CIVIL WAR

[2]Albert D. Kirwan, ed., *The Confederacy* (New York: Meridian Books, 1959), p. 63.

an inconvenience rather than a catastrophe. But the Union blockade largely prevented the export of Southern cotton, and then took a heavy toll of the limited amounts of manufactured products that could be purchased with the proceeds of the cotton that did slip through. (The small blockade-running traffic was largely used for the import of luxury goods. "When Captain Hobart Pasha of the *Venus* asked a Southern woman in England what was most needed in the Confederacy, she unhesitatingly replied, 'Corsets'.")[3] Despite valiant effort to redirect production, the South was brought to economic and military collapse by its inability to acquire essential manufactured civilian products and implements of war, while huge stocks of unsalable cotton piled up uselessly in her storehouses.

Confederate trade policy was seriously misguided. Export of the huge cotton crops of 1861 and 1862 to earn credits abroad would have been possible, since the Union blockade did not really become effective until later years. The Confederate government discouraged this export. They reasoned that, since "Cotton was King," withholding the crop would force Northern (and foreign) industrial interests to support the secession. Relying on their opponents' loss of the advantage of trade, the South's leaders failed to realize how much more vulnerable their own largely one-crop economy was to the interruption of mutually advantageous exchange.

An even more striking error was the policy of the Confederate government that banned trade through the lines with the North, partly on moralistic grounds, partly again to withhold "King Cotton." This was illogical for several reasons, one of which was that most of the cotton run through the blockade to Cuba or Bermuda was transshipped to the North anyway. But more important, a strict ban on trade through the lines was, for the Union, a logical complement to the sea blockade, a component of the "anaconda" policy of strangling the Southern economy. In contrast, it was in the interest of the South to break this overland ban almost as much as it was to evade the sea blockade. It is true that the cotton and tobacco that could have been sent North would, to some degree, have helped the Northern war economy. But the Confederacy, its economy collapsing because of inability to dispose of its surpluses for needed imports of all kinds, was in a position where it had to grasp every opportunity. Actually, a substantial (though unrecorded) amount of illegal trade did pass through the lines; despite the attempts of officials on both sides to stop the practice, the temptations of corruption and the real needs of the Southern economy at times proved to be an overwhelming combination. Curiously, even today historians commonly take a moralistic attitude on this question, and fail to appreciate the fundamental asymmetry in position that made maintenance of the land blockade a wise policy for the Union, but an unwise one for the Confederacy.[4]

[3]Clement Eaton, *A History of the Southern Confederacy* (New York: Macmillan, 1954), p. 144.

[4]This discussion is based on J. Hirshleifer, "Disaster and Recovery: A Historical Survey," The Rand Corporation Memorandum RM–3079–PR (April 1963), Section IV.

The lens-shaped region of mutual advantage is shown again in Figure 7.2. Suppose that market *prices* are now established, by some impersonal process not dependent upon the decisions of our two individuals John and Karl. We say that each is a *competitive* trader or "price-taker." The price ratio P_x/P_y, we know, is the absolute value of the slope of the budget line in an indifference-curve diagram like Figure 4.1. But the Edgeworth box, Figure 7.2, is a double indifference-curve diagram. Suppose hypothetically that prices are such that the dashed line KL is the budget line. For John, KL passes through his endowment position $E = (x_j^\dagger, y_j^\dagger)$ and represents an upper (northeast) boundary of his market opportunities (just as in Figure 4.1). But in the Edgeworth box KL must also serve as budget line for Karl,

Figure 7.2

Budget Lines and Competitive Equilibrium. Any price ratio P_x/P_y determines the slope of a corresponding budget line through the endowment position E. Each such budget line is a northeast boundary of the opportunity set for John, a southwest boundary for Karl. The dashed budget line KL does not correspond to a competitive market equilibrium for these two traders, since along KL John's optimum Q_j and Karl's optimum Q_k do not coincide. $K'L'$ does correspond to an equilibrium price ratio, since the optimum positions Q_j^* and Q_k^* do coincide. A *mutual tangency* of indifference curves therefore exists at that point. If the endowment position were to vary, any equilibrium solution would still have to be at a point of mutual tangency of indifference curves; the contract curve CC shows all such possible equilibrium solutions.

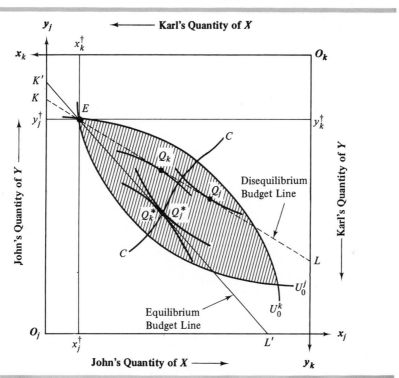

Chapter 7
EQUILIBRIUM,
EXCHANGE,
AND THE
GAINS FROM
TRADE

passing through his endowment position $E = (x_k^\dagger, y_k^\dagger)$. Since Karl's axes are inverted, KL as upper limit for him bounds the market opportunity set toward the *southwest* rather than the northeast.

With KL as budget line in Figure 7.2, John would want to proceed to a consumptive optimum indicated by the position Q_j. Similarly, Karl would want to move to his optimum along KL at Q_k. But the two points Q_j and Q_k do not coincide! This means that the quantity of X that John wishes to purchase, offering Y in exchange in accordance with the price ratio represented by the slope of KL, is *not* equal to the quantity that Karl is prepared to supply at that price ratio. If John and Karl are the only two transactors, the situation is not one of competitive equilibrium. The difficulty is that KL represents a price ratio P_x/P_y such that X is too cheap relative to Y, the buyer (John) seeking to take more of X than the seller (Karl) is willing to offer.

An *equilibrium price ratio* for competitive trading is represented by the steeper line $K'L'$ in Figure 7.2, corresponding to a higher price ratio P_x'/P_y'. At this price ratio both parties are led to *coinciding* preferred positions $Q_j^* = Q_k^*$, meaning that the amount of commodity X offered by Karl equals the amount willingly purchased by John. (Correspondingly, of course, the quantity of Y offered by John in payment must also exactly balance the amount required by Karl.) This discussion can be summed up as follows.

PROPOSITION: In the Edgeworth box, the competitive equilibrium allocation of the two commodities (1) lies in the region of mutual advantage, and (2) represents a mutual tangency of both traders' indifference curves with one another and with a common budget line.

Now imagine a number of possible variations of the endowment position E. For each such E, there will be a different region of mutual advantage and equilibrium budget line. But the only potential competitive equilibria are the points representing mutual tangencies of indifference curves of John and Karl, since only then do the consumptive optimum positions coincide. The curve connecting these mutual tangencies is known as the *contract curve*, shown as CC in both Figure 7.1 and Figure 7.2.

In Section 4.A, the concept of the Marginal Rate of Substitution in Consumption, MRS_C—the rate at which an individual is just willing to make a small exchange of X for Y—was introduced. It was also shown that MRS_C corresponds to the absolute value of the indifference-curve slope between commodities X and Y. Consumptive *optimality* was attained, as indicated in equation (4.4), where $MRS_C = P_x/P_y$, i.e., where the indifference-curve slope equals the budget-line slope. We see from the above discussion that *a condition of competitive equilibrium is that consumptive optimality holds for both traders*:

(7.1) $MRS_C^j = P_x/P_y = MRS_C^k.$

Generalizing, the consumptive optimality condition $MRS_C = P_x/P_y$ (developed

Chapter 7
EQUILIBRIUM,
EXCHANGE,
AND THE
GAINS FROM
TRADE

196

in Chapter 4 for *any single* trader) must, in competitive equilibrium, be holding for *every* trader.

The other formal condition of equilibrium can be expressed as:

$$\textbf{(7.2)} \qquad \begin{cases} x_j + x_k = \overline{X} \\ y_j + y_k = \overline{Y} \end{cases}$$

This corresponds to the requirement that Q_j^* and Q_k^* coincide in Figure 7.2. In general terms, we can say: The equilibrium price ratio is such that the sum of the individuals' desired consumption quantities equals the social total available, for each commodity.

SUPPLY AND DEMAND IN PURE EXCHANGE

The picture of competitive equilibrium is rather artificial in the two-person Edgeworth box diagram, though this diagram shows clearly how trade contributes to mutually desired consumptive reallocations. More familiarly, we think of competitive equilibrium as determined by an intersection of supply and demand curves (as in Section 2.A). The demand–supply formulation overcomes the limitation of the Edgeworth box to two *persons*, but we will continue for the present to maintain the simplifying assumption of only two *goods*.

The elements underlying the equilibrium of supply and demand stand out most clearly if we continue to assume a hypothetical world without production—a world of *pure exchange*. In such a world the only purpose of trade is the reallocation of consumption goods. Each individual i comes to market with an endowment $E_i = (x_i^\dagger, y_i^\dagger)$ of consumptive commodities X and Y; trade redistributes the goods among persons, but there is no change in the social totals of commodities. Later on in the chapter, *production* will be introduced as a process that transforms the social totals of commodities, leading to a generalized conception of supply–demand equilibrium.

We have already seen (in Section 4.B.2) how an individual's demand curve for a commodity X is derived—by parametric variation of his consumptive optimum in response to changes of the price ratio P_x/P_y (or simply of P_x, since P_y can be assumed constant). This process led to the Price Expansion Path (PEP) of Figure 4.10 which, upon translation to x, P_x-axes, yielded the individual's demand curve as in Figure 4.12.

In Panel (a) of Figure 7.3, the derivation of the Price Expansion Path (PEP) looks almost exactly like the picture in Figure 4.10. There is only one novel feature. In the diagram of Chapter 4, as the budget lines tilted (in response to changes in P_x) they all remained anchored to a fixed point K on the vertical axis. This anchoring point corresponded to the quantity I/P_y—the amount of Y purchas-

Chapter 7
EQUILIBRIUM,
EXCHANGE,
AND THE
GAINS FROM
TRADE

Figure 7.3

Price Expansion Paths. Changes in the price ratio are reflected by tilting of the budget lines which, however, must all pass through the endowment positions E_j for John in Panel (a) and E_k for Karl in Panel (b). Since John's endowment is toward the northwest in Panel (a), he will ordinarily be a demander of X from the market (supplier of Y). More specifically, for price ratios leading to points on PEP_j east of E_j, John will be a net demander of X; at the "sustaining" price ratio (budget line $K^\circ L^\circ$) leading to a tangency at E_j itself he will stand pat and not trade; for still higher price ratios he will be a supplier of X (indicated by the range of PEP_j to the west of E_j). A corresponding analysis holds for Karl in Panel (b).

able if none of X is bought. This was a fixed amount, since P_y was assumed not to change and I was the individual's fixed income available for consumption expenditure. Here the situation is slightly different. John comes to market not with a fixed *income I*, but rather with fixed *endowment quantities* of X and Y. Therefore, the anchoring position through which the budget lines all pass is not necessarily a point on the vertical axis; the endowment point E_j may lie anywhere in the diagram. (The previous analysis therefore corresponded to a special case in which the individual had an endowment consisting only of units of Y, none of X.)

This modification has an important consequence. In Figure 4.10 the anchoring point (endowment position) lay along the vertical axis; the individual could only be a demander of X, never a supplier. In Panel (a) of Figure 7.3, we see that John's endowment position E_j lies toward but not quite at the vertical axis; John has a large endowment of Y and only a small endowment of X. We would there-

Chapter 7
EQUILIBRIUM,
EXCHANGE,
AND THE
GAINS FROM
TRADE

198

fore expect him *usually* to be a demander of X from the market, but not necessarily *always*. Since the endowment point E_j is itself a point on PEP$_j$, there is some price ratio P_x/P_y so high (some budget line $K°L°$ so steep) that he will prefer to stand pat with his endowment combination and not make any additional purchases of X. This is called the "sustaining" price ratio. And for even higher price ratios (even steeper budget lines through E_j), John would actually be a net supplier of X to the market—that is, his consumptive optimum position would then be at a point northwest of E_j. (Of course, every time that John is a demander of X from the market he is necessarily a supplier of Y, and *vice versa*.)

Turning to Karl, Panel (b) of Figure 7.3 shows for him a large endowment of X and a small endowment of Y, consistent with his situation as pictured in the Edgeworth box diagrams. A low price ratio P_x/P_y, corresponding to the rather flat absolute slope of the budget line K_0L_0, "sustains" his endowment position E_k; at this price ratio he will stand pat with his endowment at the tangency with indifference curve U_0. At still lower price ratios Karl would even be a net demander of X, as represented by the extension of PEP$_k$ to the southeast of E_k. But more normally, at the higher price ratios reflected in the slopes of budget lines like K_{1L1} and K_2L_2, Karl would move northwest from E_k to an optimum position like R_k or S_k. That is, he would give up some of his ample X-endowment for Y; he would be usually a net supplier of X to the market, and so a net demander of Y.

The next step is the transfer of the data represented by the Price Expansion Paths of Figure 7.3 to generate demand and supply curves on x, P_x-axes. This can be done in two different ways, which we must be careful not to confuse. The first runs in terms of the whole or "full" quantities demanded or supplied, the second in terms of the net or "transaction" quantities. On the demand side, the "full" quantity demanded of good X *includes* the quantity of X endowed—this is the demand concept relevant for purposes of consumption. The "transaction" demand quantity *excludes* the quantity endowed (the quantity self-supplied) and thus represents demand relevant for purposes of market trading. On the supply side, the "full" quantity of good X supplied (in the absence of production) is simply the fixed endowment amount. The "transaction" quantity supplied is that portion of the endowment offered to the market. We can think of the "full" quantities as those demanded from or supplied to the *economy*, while the "transaction" quantities are those smaller amounts demanded from or supplied to the *market*.

The relation between transaction demands and full demands, for any individual i, is given by:

$$(7.3) \quad \begin{cases} x_i^t = x_i - x_i^\dagger \\ y_i^t = y_i - y_i^\dagger \end{cases} \quad \text{Transaction Demands and Full Demands}$$

The first equation of (7.3) says that the transaction quantity of commodity X demanded by individual i from the market, x_i^t, is equal to the full quantity demanded for purposes of consumption, x_i, minus the quantity already in the individual's possession before trading, $x_i^\dagger$. The second equation expresses a corresponding relation for commodity Y. In Panel (a) of Figure 7.3, the *full* quantity of X associated with any consumptive optimum position like E_j, R_j, or S_j along the PEP$_j$ curve is

Chapter 7
EQUILIBRIUM,
EXCHANGE,
AND THE
GAINS FROM
TRADE

199

simply the x-coordinate of that position—the horizontal distance from that point on the PEP_j curve to the vertical axis. The transaction quantity is this horizontal distance *less* the endowed amount $x_j^\dagger$, the x-coordinate of E_j. It follows, of course, that at the price ratio for which E_j is itself the consumptive optimum position (at the sustaining price ratio), John's full demand for X equals $x_j^\dagger$ and his transaction demand for X is zero.

The transaction demands x_i^t and y_i^t in equation (7.3) can be positive or negative. Negative transaction demand is, of course, positive transaction supply. But the full demand magnitudes x_i and y_i and the endowed or full supply quantities $x_i^\dagger$ and $y_i^\dagger$ are necessarily non-negative; neither consumption nor endowment can ever be less than zero.

The distinction between full and transaction magnitudes is important in a number of areas, among them the theory of taxation. A tax on *consumption* of good X is one levied upon the full demands; a tax on *purchases* of X is one that burdens only the transaction demands. Put another way, endowed quantities that are self-consumed escape a "transaction tax" on purchases, but do not escape a tax on consumption. A special case of a transaction tax is a tariff, which burdens international trading but not domestic trading (the latter representing quantities that are "self-supplied" from the viewpoint of the nation as a whole).

One important practical implication is that as transaction taxes become higher, individuals will find it increasingly attractive to self-supply their wants rather than deal in the market. It seems very likely that the growth of the "do-it-yourself" movement is in large part a response to the growing burden of taxes on market transactions.

We can now turn to the geometrical relations between full and transaction demand and supply curves.

Any price P_x (corresponding to a price ratio P_x/P_y, since P_y is assumed constant) is associated with a particular consumptive optimum position along an individual i's PEP_i curve. Plotting the x-coordinate of that position against the price P_x gives a point on his *full* demand curve d_i in Figure 7.4. Speaking more generally, the data represented by the PEP_i curve can be replotted on x, P_x-axes to yield the individual's full demand curve d_i.

The transaction demand curve d_i^t is obtained by simply subtracting (horizontally) the endowment quantity $x_i^\dagger$ from the full demand d_i. We can think of the vertical line, representing the individual's fixed X-endowment $x_i^\dagger$, as his *full supply curve* for X—symbolized as $s_i^\dagger$. Then in correspondence with equations (7.3) relating full and transaction magnitudes we have the geometrical relation:

$$(7.4) \qquad d_i^t = d_i - s_i^\dagger$$

Chapter 7
EQUILIBRIUM,
EXCHANGE,
AND THE
GAINS FROM
TRADE

200

This says that, at any price P_x, an individual's transaction demand equals full demand less full (endowed) supply.[5] Note that at the price $P_x^\dagger$ representing the

[5]In Chapter 4 the individual was endowed with a quantity I of *income* in numeraire units, rather than with specific $x_i^\dagger$ and $y_i^\dagger$ amounts of X and Y. But since P_x was allowed to vary with P_y held constant, in effect the person in Chapter 4 was endowed with I/P_y units of commodity Y and none of X, so that position K on the Y-axis of Figure 4.10 served as the equivalent of an initial endowment position. Hence for the individual in Chapter 4 the full and transaction demands for X were identical.

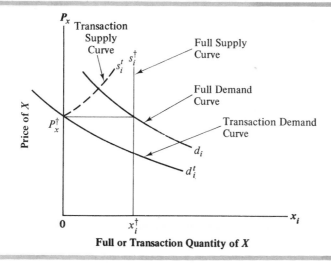

Figure 7.4

Full and Transaction Supply and Demand Curves, in Pure Exchange. For an individual i in pure exchange, the *full demand curve* d_i shows, at any price P_x, the desired consumption quantity. The *full supply curve* $s_i^\dagger$ represents i's fixed endowment quantity. The *transaction demand curve* d_i^t shows, at any price P_x, the amount demanded from the market (horizontal difference between d_i and $s_i^\dagger$). In the range where transaction demand d_i^t is negative, it is usually more convenient to speak of a positive *transaction supply curve* s_i^t. Transaction demand and supply are exactly zero at the sustaining price $P_x^\dagger$.

individual's *sustaining price*, full demand equals endowed supply, so that the transaction demand becomes zero.

At prices *higher* than the sustaining price, the transaction demand curve d_i^t enters a negative region. Rather than deal with *negative transaction demand*, it is usually more convenient to speak of *positive transaction supply*. This is represented geometrically in Figure 7.4 by the dashed curve s_i^t, which is the mirror image of the negative range of d_i^t for prices above $P_x^\dagger$.

We can portray the determination of market equilibrium by letting our two traders John and Karl (for whom PEP curves were pictured in Figure 7.3) constitute the demand and supply sides of a competitive market. Since John is relatively less well-endowed with X, we expect him to be the demander and Karl the supplier of that commodity in the market. Karl's *transaction supply* curve s_k^t, and John's *transaction demand* curve d_j^t, are plotted in Panel (a) of Figure 7.5. John's sustaining price $P_x^\dagger(j)$ is at the point where d_j^t contacts the vertical axis. Similarly, Karl's sustaining price $P_x^\dagger(k)$ is where s_k^t contacts the vertical axis. More generally, of course, *all* the individual net demanders' d_j^t curves would be combined (summed horizontally) into an aggregate transaction demand curve or *market* demand curve D^t, and *all* the net suppliers' s_k^t curves into an aggregate transaction supply curve or *market* supply curve S^t. It is the intersection of D^t and S^t that would determine the equilibrium price and quantity. Henceforth in this chapter the aggregation process will be short-circuited by assuming that the two traders John

Chapter 7
EQUILIBRIUM,
EXCHANGE,
AND THE
GAINS FROM
TRADE

201

Figure 7.5

Supply–Demand Equilibrium. Panel (a) shows a competitive demand–supply equilibrium for commodity X in terms of the *transaction* quantities; Panel (b) pictures the same equilibrium in terms of the *full* quantities. Since John is relatively poorly-endowed and Karl well-endowed with commodity X, the equilibrium in Panel (a) is at the intersection of John's *transaction demand curve* d_j^t and Karl's *transaction supply curve* s_k^t. In Panel (b) the aggregate *full supply curve* S^t to the economy as a whole is the sum of John's s_j^t and Karl's s_k^t. The aggregate *full demand curve* D is similarly the sum of d_j and d_k. The S^t and D curves in Panel (b) must intersect at the same equilibrium price P_x^* as at the intersection of S^t and D^t.

and Karl can serve as a microcosm of the supply and demand sides of the entire market.

Panel (b) of Figure 7.5 shows the other instructive way of looking at the two-person supply–demand equilibrium. Here, instead of net quantities supplied to or demanded from *the market*, we consider the full magnitudes demanded (for consumption) from or supplied (via endowment) to *the economy*. The difference between the two concepts is due to the quantities self-supplied for consumption out of a trader's own endowment. The detailed verification of the pictured correspondence between the two panels is left as an exercise for the reader.

The intersection of S^t and D^t in Panel (a) of Figure 7.5, or of S^t and D in Panel (b), determines the equilibrium for commodity X. But it will be evident that the equilibrium for commodity Y is also being implicitly determined.

Chapter 7
EQUILIBRIUM,
EXCHANGE,
AND THE
GAINS FROM
TRADE

202

CONCLUSION: Competitive supply–demand equilibrium can be expressed in two ways. The intersection of the aggregate *transaction* supply curve and the aggregate *transaction* demand curve determines the equilibrium price and the quantity actually traded in markets. The intersection of the aggregate *full* supply curve and the aggregate *full* demand curve determines the same equilibrium price, but the quantity shown is the entire economy-wide consumption, which must equal the aggregate full amount supplied. (In pure exchange, this quantity would be the sum of the individual endowments.)[6]

We should, of course, be thinking of the equilibrating process as involving not just two commodities X and Y but rather all goods simultaneously. The result is a *general* equilibrium of prices and quantities. However, the underlying principles—individual optimization, and the balance of demand and supply in the market—are in no way different from the principles illustrated in the simplified two-good world.

EXCHANGE AND PRODUCTION

So far in this chapter we have considered trade in a world without production, a world of "pure exchange." Under pure exchange individuals can alter their endowments of commodities *only* through the market process, as illustrated in the Edgeworth box of Figure 7.1. But in the actual world individuals can also modify endowments by *production*, by dealing (so to speak) with Nature rather than or in addition to engaging in transactions with other people. To take the extreme opposite case, Robinson Crusoe (before Friday's arrival) could deal *only* with Nature; he could physically produce and consume, but he could not trade. What we really want to consider, of course, is the interaction of the economic processes of production, consumption, *and* exchange in a multi-person economy.

To begin with, production appears here only in a limited sense that is sometimes called *productive transformation*. This means taking account of production only as offering the physical possibility of alternative "output" baskets of consumptive commodities like X and Y. The role of "factors of production"—commodities not desired in and of themselves, but only as *inputs* for generating consumptive goods—is left in the background. (In Part Four we will take up production as an explicit input-output process that converts factors into products).

In both panels of Figure 7.6, the possible output baskets of commodities X and Y that an individual might be able to produce are shown as the shaded region, called the *productive opportunity set*. Compare its shape with that of the pure-exchange *market opportunity set OKL* in Figure 4.1. The northeast boundary of the market opportunity set in the earlier diagram was the budget line. The northeast boundary QQ of the productive opportunity set here is called the *transformation locus* or *Production-Possibility Curve* (PPC), whose "concave" shape represents diminishing returns in productive transformation. Suppose an individual pro-

[6]We may note that the demand curves entering into the determination of equilibrium are *not* the "compensated" demands (discussed earlier in Section 6.E) but rather the "ordinary" demand curves. It is the ordinary demand curves (and associated supply curves) that summarize the market reactions that lead to equilibrium. The importance of the "compensated" demand functions, as discussed in the preceding chapter, lies in the analysis of the sources of observed historical *changes* in equilibrium positions.

Chapter 7
EQUILIBRIUM,
EXCHANGE,
AND THE
GAINS FROM
TRADE

203

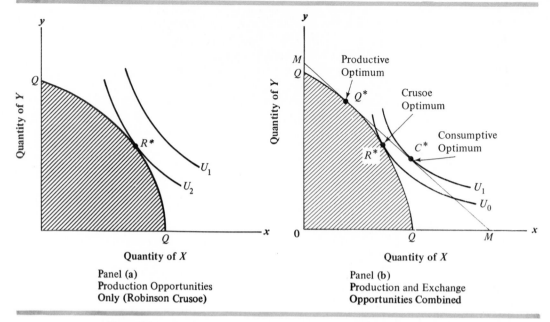

Figure 7.6

Productive and Consumptive Optimum Positions. In both panels the shaded region shows a *productive opportunity set* subject to diminishing returns as the individual specializes in production of either X or Y. Panel (a) is the situation of a Robinson Crusoe, whose best attainable point R^* is a joint productive–consumptive optimum. In Panel (b) the individual has *both* productive and exchange opportunities. The productive optimum is at Q^*, allowing trade to a consumptive optimum at C^*. The final C^* outcome made possible by exchange is superior to the Robinson Crusoe outcome at R^*.

ducer (or a nation) tried to "specialize" by concentrating upon the production of commodity X, i.e., tried to produce a combination well toward the X-axis along QQ. As specialization is pushed further and further, each increment of X requires a greater and greater sacrifice of Y. We say that *increasing opportunity costs*, sacrifices of potential output of the other commodity Y, are encountered. Diminishing returns in productive transformation are not derivable from the pure logic of economic theory; rather, they supposedly constitute an observed fact of Nature. (Concavity of the transformation locus thus rests upon the same observational basis as the convex shape of indifference curves discussed in Section 3.E.)

For a Robinson Crusoe possessing *only* productive transformation opportunities, his optimum consumption basket in Panel (a) of Figure 7.6 is R^*, the tangency of his transformation locus QQ with his highest attainable indifference curve U_0. Since Crusoe cannot engage in trade, R^* represents for him a *joint productive–consumptive optimum*. The tangency condition can be expressed as the equation:

Chapter 7
EQUILIBRIUM,
EXCHANGE,
AND THE
GAINS FROM
TRADE

204

(7.5) $MRS_C = MRS_T$ Robinson Crusoe Optimum

MRS_C, the Marginal Rate of Substitution in Consumption, corresponds as we know to the absolute indifference-curve slope. The new symbol MRS_T stands for the *Marginal Rate of Substitution in Productive Transformation*; more briefly, *Marginal Rate of Transformation*. MRS_T is the absolute slope of the Production-Possibility Curve, the additional amount of Y that can be produced per unit small sacrifice of X. Note how the opposing curvatures (of the transformation locus QQ versus the indifference curves) guarantee that there will be a unique tangency $R*$.[7]

CONCLUSION: A Robinson Crusoe, possessing productive transformation opportunities but isolated from opportunities for exchange with other individuals, would find his joint productive–consumptive optimum at the point where his Marginal Rate of Substitution in Consumption MRS_C equals his Marginal Rate of Transformation MRS_T along the boundary of his productive opportunity set.

Robinson Crusoe situations may seem fanciful, but this is not necessarily so. We might, for example, sometimes want to consider a nation as a whole as an acting entity; history has shown a number of instances in which a nation has isolated itself from external trade.

Trade is a human invention. Since they do not engage in exchange with one another, non-human animals make all their economic decisions under Robinson Crusoe conditions. An example of such a decision is the problem of "optimal diet breadth," which biologists have analyzed in a way that corresponds exactly to Panel (a) of Figure 7.6.[8]

EXAMPLE 7.2
ANIMAL
ROBINSON
CRUSOES

Think of X and Y as two sources of food—for example, two prey species for a predator. Because of diminishing returns the predator's productive opportunity set typically has a shape like the shaded region in the diagram. The more the predator concentrates upon consuming prey species X, the scarcer and harder to capture X becomes relative to the availability of Y (increasing Marginal Rate of Transformation). The predator also has "preferences" as represented by the indifference curves in the diagram. Each such curve represents a set of equally acceptable diets. The convexity of the indifference curves presumably reflects the fact that a variety of foods helps provide the many metabolic inputs required by living organisms. The greater the con-

[8]The discussion here is based on D. J. Rapport, "An Optimization Model of Food Selection," *The American Naturalist*, v. 105 (Nov.–Dec. 1971) and M. L. Cody, "Optimization in Ecology," *Science*, v. 183 (March 22, 1974).

[7]*Mathematical Footnote:* In terms of derivatives, the condition can be expressed as:

$$\frac{dy}{dx}\bigg|_U = \frac{dy}{dx}\bigg|_Q$$

In addition, the individual must be on his Production-Possibility Curve, so that the equation $Q(x,y) = 0$ is satisfied.

sumption of food source X, the harder it becomes to achieve nutritional needs by additional consumption of X as compared to the nutritional benefit of a unit of Y (decreasing Marginal Rate of Substitution in Consumption).

The optimal position for the animal is of course at the "Robinson Crusoe" tangency point R^*, which will ordinarily represent an interior (mixed-diet) solution.

Now let us drop the Robinson Crusoe case and consider an individual having both productive and trading opportunities. We can imagine that Crusoe is discovered by the world and thus is put into contact with a market in which he becomes a competitive trader or "price-taker." Market opportunities are shown in Panel (b) of Figure 7.6 by the line MM just tangent to the transformation locus QQ. The absolute slope of the market line represents the ruling price ratio P_x/P_y. The existence of market opportunities permits a trader to *separate the productive and consumptive decisions*. Specifically, the formerly isolated individual can now attain his consumptive optimum (most preferred combination of x and y) at C^* on indifference curve U_1 by a two-step procedure. First, he moves along QQ to his *productive optimum* Q^*, the tangency of the Production-Possibility Curve with the market line MM. From Q^*, by exchanging X for Y he can move southeast along MM so as to finally achieve the *consumptive optimum* at C^*. A comparison of the Crusoe solution R^* with the improved optimum C^* now attainable reveals the advantage gained from the separation of productive and consumptive decisions made possible by trade.

The productive optimum position Q^* is associated with the equation:

(7.6) $\qquad MRS_T = MRS_E \equiv \dfrac{P_x}{P_y}$ $\qquad$ Productive Optimum Condition

The individual sets the Marginal Rate of Transformation along QQ equal to the Marginal Rate of Substitution *in Exchange*, the absolute price ratio P_x/P_y ruling in the market. This condition in effect moves the individual *onto* the market line MM at point Q^*. The consumptive optimum condition, achieved by movement *along* MM to C^*, is:

(7.7) $\qquad \dfrac{P_x}{P_y} \equiv MRS_E = MRS_C$ $\qquad$ Consumptive Optimum Condition

Chapter 7
EQUILIBRIUM,
EXCHANGE,
AND THE
GAINS FROM
TRADE

206

The latter condition is the same as equation (4.4).

Since (7.6) and (7.7) together imply $MRS_T = MRS_C$, equation (7.5) holds in a world of exchange as well as for an isolated Robinson Crusoe. But for Crusoe MRS_C and MRS_T are equated *at the same point* R^* *along* QQ, whereas for a trader the productive and consumptive solutions are separated. MRS_T is set equal to the price ratio at a tangency along QQ; MRS_C is set equal to the same price ratio at a tangency along an indifference curve. The separation is made possible by trading along the market line MM.

We have not yet discussed the forces that determine the equilibrium price ratio P_x/P_y in a world of production and exchange, and therefore the slope of the market line MM facing particular producer-traders. These forces can be expressed, as usual, in terms of supply and demand.

Just as in the case of pure exchange, it will be useful to distinguish "full" and "transaction" supply and demand concepts. Figure 7.7 is analogous to Figure 7.4, with one important difference. In pure exchange the individual's full supply of X to the economy was simply the given endowed quantity $x_i^\dagger$, independent of price, and therefore represented by the vertical line $s_i^\dagger$ in Figure 7.4. But in a world of production and exchange, an individual's full supply of X is the result of a productive decision in response to the ruling market price. In Figure 7.7, the full supply curve s_i^q represents, for any price P_x, the x-coordinate of the *productive optimum* Q^* in Panel (b) of Figure 7.6. As P_x rises (with P_y held constant), the market line MM in Figure 7.6 grows increasingly steep. The tangency of MM with the transformation locus QQ at Q^* therefore shifts around to the southeast. This

Figure 7.7

Individual Demand and Supply, with Production. For an individual i, at any price P_x (or price ratio P_x/P_y, with P_y fixed), the full supply provided to the economy as a whole is the x-coordinate of the productive optimum Q^* in Panel (b) of Figure 7.6. As P_x rises, an increased quantity of X is produced, so the full supply curve s_i^q is rising. The individual's full demand is the x-coordinate of C^* in Panel (b) of Figure 7.6, which generally decreases as P_x rises. The transaction supply and demand of X are exactly zero at the "autarky price" P_x^o, the price at which the full demand curve and the full supply curve intersect. Above this price full supply exceeds full demand, so there will be positive *transaction supply*—increasing as P_x rises. Below this price full demand exceeds full supply, so there will be positive *transaction demand*—increasing as P_x falls.

Chapter 7

EQUILIBRIUM,

EXCHANGE,

AND THE

GAINS FROM

TRADE

207

shift represents an increased quantity of X produced, thus demonstrating that the individual's full supply curve s_i^q for commodity X is a rising function of price P_x.

The full demand curve d_i of Figure 7.7 similarly represents, for any price P_x, the x-coordinate of the individual's *consumptive optimum* C^* in Panel (b) of Figure 7.6. The relation between the s_i^q curve and the d_i curve in Figure 7.7 reflects the movement of the C^* position and the Q^* position of the previous diagram as price changes. Panel (b) of Figure 7.6 pictures a relatively low price P_x, such that C^* lies southeast of Q^* along the tangent line MM. At that price the individual's full quantity of X demanded exceeds the full quantity he wants to supply. As P_x rises, MM becomes steeper; the tangency Q^* moves toward the southeast (the full-supply quantity rises) and C^* tends to shift toward the west (the full-demand quantity decreases). At some sufficiently high price, called the "autarky price" P_x^o,[9] the productive solution Q^* becomes identical with the Robinson Crusoe solution R^*, in which case the consumptive solution C^* must also coincide at the same point. This means that, in Figure 7.7, the full supply curve s_i and the full demand curve d_i intersect at the autarky price P_x^o. And for prices still higher, the C^* solution would lie to the northwest of Q^* along a very steep market line MM; at those prices the full supply would exceed the full demand.

What about the individual's transaction demand from or transaction supply to *the market*? In parallel with the discussion of the preceding section, the s_i^t curve of Figure 7.7 represents the positive net amounts supplied (for prices higher than P_x^o) and the d_i^t curve the positive net amounts demanded (at prices lower than P_x^o). Of course, at the autarky price itself there is zero net amount demanded and supplied.

Figure 7.7 describes the supply and demand curves for a single person. Equilibrium in the market as a whole is based of course upon balancing the aggregate market or transaction supply and the market or transaction demand of all individuals. This is pictured in Figure 7.8, which simultaneously shows the solutions for: (1) X^*, the full social total of X produced and consumed, and (2) X^{t*}, the transaction amount of X exchanged in the market.

At the equilibrium price P_x, the aggregate quantity *produced* (along the aggregate full supply curve S^q) must equal the aggregate amount *desired for consumption* (along the aggregate full demand curve D). Of course, S^q is the horizontal sum of the individuals' s_i^q curves, and D the horizontal sum of their d_i curves. The same price P_x^* obtains at the intersection of the aggregate transaction supply curve S^t and the aggregate transaction demand curve D^t. Note that for any single individual as in the preceding Figure 7.7, s_i^t and d_i^t intersect only along the vertical axis; no person is ever simultaneously a positive net supplier to and a positive net demander from the market. But at the market equilibrium *some* persons will be supplying and others demanding, so that X^{t*}, the volume of transactions, is positive. The difference between the X^* and X^{t*} quantities represents, as we have

Chapter 7
EQUILIBRIUM,
EXCHANGE,
AND THE
GAINS FROM
TRADE

208

---

[9]The autarky price is analogous to the "sustaining price" $P_x^{\ddagger}$ of pure exchange; each represents the price at which the individual does not participate in trade.

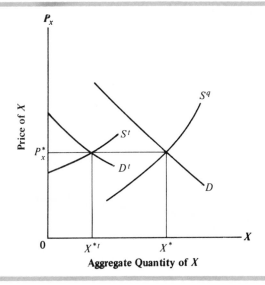

Figure 7.8

Equilibrium of Supply and Demand, with Production. The aggregate full supply curve S^q and full demand curve D represent horizontal summations of the corresponding individual curves of Figure 7.7, and similarly for the aggregate transaction supply and transaction demand curves S^t and D^t. The equilibrium price P_x^* is determined by the intersection of either pair of curves. At the equilibrium, the aggregate full quantity produced and consumed is X^* while the aggregate transaction quantity traded among individuals is X^{t*}. (The difference is the aggregate quantity self-supplied by individuals for their own consumption.)

seen, the amounts of X produced by individuals for personal consumption rather than for trade in markets.

The "transaction" solution in Figure 7.8 (intersection of S^t and D^t) is the analog for a world of production and exchange of the intersection of the correspondingly labelled curves in Panel (a) of Figure 7.5 for the pure exchange case. And the "full" solution of Figure 7.8 (intersection of S^q and D) corresponds to the intersection of S^t and D in Panel (b) of Figure 7.5. This permits us to see how the artificial illustrative world of pure exchange in Section 7.C above can be regarded as a "degenerate" instance of a realistic world in which production and exchange interact. The pure-exchange model simply replaces the upward-sloping supply curve S^q (representing the *productive* response to changes in price) with a fixed vertical supply curve S^t, so as to permit concentration of attention upon the *consumptive* response to changes in price.

The pure-exchange model was appropriate for highlighting one of the two advantages of exchange: the reallocation of existing stocks of goods among individuals so as to achieve a mutually preferred combination. The model of production and exchange now permits us to appreciate the second advantage of exchange:

Chapter 7
EQUILIBRIUM,
EXCHANGE,
AND THE
GAINS FROM
TRADE

209

the fact that greater social totals of goods are generated by *productive specialization*.

In Figure 7.9, the two panels show different shapes of Production-Possibility Curves QQ for John and Karl. The QQ shapes assumed are such that John can more easily or efficiently produce commodity Y, while Karl can advantageously specialize in producing X. Yet, in the absence of trade, their diversified preferences would dictate "Robinson Crusoe solutions" R_j^* and R_k^* that both lie toward the middle of their respective Production-Possibility Curves QQ. To meet his desires for both commodities, each person would have to devote a large portion of his efforts to manufacturing the good that is unsuited to his productive talents.

The opening of trade makes available market lines MM (of slope $-P_x/P_y$) to both John and Karl. The former takes advantage of the market by shifting his productive solution northwest along QQ to Q_j^*, i.e., he now *specializes in producing Y*. And this does not in any way require of him a corresponding loss of "diversity in consumption" (see Section 3.E), for he will trade the excess Y to Karl. Correspondingly, of course, Karl is enabled to become a specialist in the production of X, the excess to be traded to John. It is the adjustment of relative prices P_x/P_y (that reflect relative scarcities of goods in society as a whole), determining the slope of the market line MM, that induces each person (as if led by an "Invisible Hand") to serve the interests of the other in his production decisions.

Figure 7.9

Productive Specialization. In the absence of exchange, John and Karl would each find an optimum productive–consumptive combination at his "Robinson Crusoe" solution R*. The opening of trade permits each to specialize in producing the commodity favored by his transformation opportunities. John's productive solution Q* involves heavier production of Y, Karl's involves heavier production of X. By trading with one another thereafter, each can move along a market line MM to achieve a superior consumption basket C*.

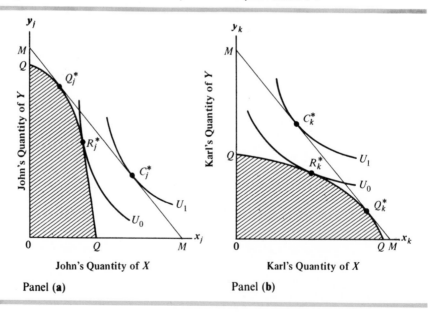

John's Quantity of X

Panel (a)

Karl's Quantity of X

Panel (b)

Chapter 7
EQUILIBRIUM,
EXCHANGE,
AND THE
GAINS FROM
TRADE

210

That both individuals benefit is evident from the superiority of their C_j^* and C_k^* consumptive optimum positions in a world of exchange, in comparison with their "Crusoe" solutions R_j^* and R_k^*. And inspection reveals that the social totals available of *both* X and Y have increased. As a natural application of this conclusion, economists have usually argued that free trade between two nations benefits both of them.

EXAMPLE 7.3
INTERNATIONAL
SPECIALIZATION
AND TRADE

Individuals then to specialize in production but diversify in consumption. We work at just one job, or a very few, but consume hundreds of different products. Should we expect the same thing of countries? To some extent, surely yes. But we would probably anticipate that the degree of productive specialization will be less for *larger* countries, which tend to have more highly varied resources and productive opportunities, and thus are less dependent upon international trade to secure diversity in consumption.

A study by M. Michaely compared the extent of specialization in the exports and imports of 44 countries, in terms of 1954 (or, in some cases, 1953 or 1952) data. The table below shows, for a number of countries, indexes of specialization in exports and in imports. The measure of specialization employed was the "Gini coefficient," which in this case has a possible range of from 8.2 to 100.0.[10] The countries in the table are ranked in decreasing order of export (productive) specialization. As can be seen, the highly specialized group at the top tend to be small countries while the group at the bottom tend to be large countries. No particular pattern is evident in the specialization index for imports, a result consistent with the principle of diversity in consumption.

Indexes of Specialization of International Trade

COUNTRY	EXPORTS	IMPORTS
Egypt	84.2	18.6
Colombia	84.0	23.9
Gold Coast	83.5	21.4
Iceland	80.3	19.1
Finland	38.1	19.2
Mexico	35.0	26.8
Libya	34.1	18.9
Spain	33.9	24.5
Italy	20.5	20.7
U.K.	19.2	16.1
U.S.	18.8	20.5
France	18.0	20.4

Source: Michael Michaely, "Concentration of Exports and Imports: An International Comparison," *Economic Journal*, v. 68 (Dec. 1958), p. 725.

[10]The Gini coefficient for exports is defined as $100 \sqrt{\sum_{i=1}^{n} (x_i/X)^2}$; x_i is a nation's annual value of exports of a particular good i, and X is its total annual value of exports. The goods were classified into 150 categories. If only a single good was exported by a country, the formula would show a specialization index of 100.0. If it exported all 150 goods in equal amounts, the result would be an index of 8.2. The measure of import specialization is similarly defined and has the same range.

CONSUMER SURPLUS AND PRODUCER SURPLUS

According to the Fundamental Theorem of Exchange, trade is mutually beneficial. In practical applications it is very helpful to have a measure of the benefits of trade, scaled in objective units apart from individuals' subjective utilities. *Consumer Surplus* and *Producer Surplus* are such measures. Actually, these terms are misnomers. The benefit in question is due to the act of *trading*, rather than to the mere fact of consumption or production.

The traditional measures of Consumer Surplus (really "buyer surplus") and Producer Surplus (really "seller surplus") are illustrated in Figure 7.10. In this section all supply and demand quantities are to be interpreted as aggregate transaction or *market* magnitudes; the supply and demand curves are thus the S^t and D^t curves of the previous section. This being understood, however, it is convenient to drop the superscript "t" for the remainder of the chapter. The market supply-demand equilibrium is at price P_x^* and quantity X^*. Consumer Surplus is represented by the upper shaded area, lying beneath the demand curve D but above the horizontal line P_x^*B. The general intention is to show *the net advantage to consumer-buyers of being able to buy all their desired units at the ruling price P_x^*,*

Figure 7.10

Consumer Surplus and Producer Surplus – Traditional Measures. At the transaction quantity X^*, Consumer Surplus is the area lying below the demand curve D but above the equilibrium price P_x^*. It is the difference between the aggregate willingness to pay for the quantity X^* (the roughly trapezoidal region $OABX^*$) and the amount actually paid (the rectangle $OP_x^*BX^*$). The Producer Surplus is similarly the area above the supply curve S but below the equilibrium price.

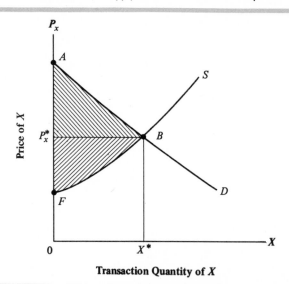

Chapter 7
EQUILIBRIUM,
EXCHANGE,
AND THE
GAINS FROM
TRADE

212

even though they would have been willing to pay higher prices (as shown by the downward-sloping demand curve) for smaller numbers of units. The Producer Surplus is the analogous lower shaded area, lying above the supply curve S but below the horizontal P_x^*B. It shows the net gain to producer-sellers of receiving a price as high as P_x^* for *all* units sold even though they would have been willing to supply smaller numbers of units at lower prices (as shown by the upward-sloping supply curve).

The concepts of *demand price* (height of demand curve for any X-quantity) and *supply price* (corresponding height of supply curve) are useful here. For the very first unit purchased, the demand price in Figure 7.10 is OA. But the price charged is only OP_x^*—hence a Consumer Surplus of $OA - OP_x^* = AP_x^*$ is gained on the first unit bought. Now extend this argument to all successive units. Then, at the aggregate transaction quantity $X = X^*$, the sum of successive demand prices (which may be called the consumers' aggregate *willingness to pay* for quantity X^*) is the roughly trapezoidal area $OABX^*$ in Figure 7.10. Since the aggregate amount charged is only the rectangle $OP_x^*BX^*$, the upper shaded (roughly triangular) area AP_x^*B is the Consumer Surplus.[11] A corresponding argument applies, of course, to Producer Surplus.

7.E.1
*An Application:
The
Water-Diamond
Paradox*

Many people have found it difficult to understand why a truly vital commodity like water is very cheap, while diamonds—satisfying relatively insignificant human needs—are so dear. Of course, comparisons like "cheaper" or "dearer" can be made only in terms of some common unit. It is rather absurd to compare the cost of gallons of water with gallons of diamonds, or carats of diamonds with carats of water. Nevertheless, the conclusion is sometimes drawn that there is something wrong with a market system that makes the less vital commodity, diamonds, so much more expensive. This anomaly leads some people to suspect that market prices are merely arbitrary measurements, imposed in a capricious manner on goods and services.

Elementary textbooks explain the supposed "paradox" in terms of downward-sloping demand curves for both water and diamonds, together with the enormously greater supply available of the former. If water as a necessity of life were also very scarce, it would be far more valuable than diamonds. Thus, using some common physical unit (e.g., gallons) as in Figure 7.11, for equivalent quantities the demand curve for water D_w is surely far higher than the demand curve for diamonds D_d. But at the actual tremendously disparate quantities, the market price of water is lower. A fairly typical retail price of municipal water is $100 per acre-foot, or about 3 cents per hundred gallons. At this price municipal water consumption is commonly about 150 gallons (five-eighths of a ton) per capita *per day*. Diamond quantities are measured in terms of the carat (one-fifth of a gram), and gem-quality prices run upward from $1000 per carat. At such prices (on the order of $20,000,000 per *gallon*) the number of gallons of diamonds demanded per day (or even per year or per lifetime) is small.

Chapter 7
EQUILIBRIUM,
EXCHANGE,
AND THE
GAINS FROM
TRADE

[11]This argument is strictly valid only under certain special assumptions that will be discussed in the optional Section 7.E.3 below.

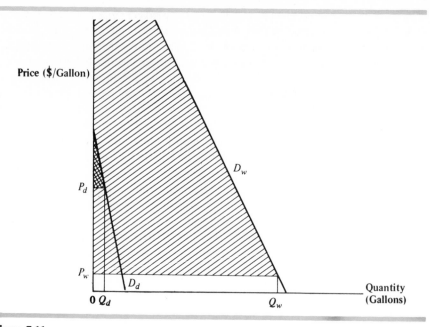

Figure 7.11

The Water-Diamond Paradox. For equivalent quantities (gallons), water is "more valuable" than diamonds, in the sense that the aggregate willingness to pay (total area under the demand curve) for a necessity like water is greater. But the quantity of water available is so enormously great, in comparison to demand, that its *market value* (rectangle of width Q_w and height P_w) is small. Purchasers therefore derive a huge Consumer Surplus (shaded region). For diamonds the quantity on the market is tiny relative to the demand. Compared to the area under the demand curve, the market value of diamonds (rectangle of width Q_d and height P_d) is large and so Consumer Surplus is small.

In terms of the benefits of trade, the Consumer Surplus in water consumption must then be enormously great, not only in comparison with the Consumer Surplus for diamonds (which is only the small hatched area under the D_d curve in Figure 7.11), but in comparison with the actual market value of water bought and sold. This market value, P_wQ_w, is represented in the diagram by the very low, flat rectangle lying just above the horizontal axis. The enormously greater area lying above this rectangle but below the demand curve D_w approximates the Consumer Surplus. Using the instructive terminology of Adam Smith, the aggregate *value in use* of water (total worth to consumers, or willingness to pay) is very, very large in comparison with its *value in exchange*—the difference between the two being the Consumer Surplus. For diamonds, on the other hand, there is comparatively little Consumer Surplus; the market value represents the great bulk of the aggregate value in use.

7.E.2

Hindrances to Trade

In Section 2.A.3, taxes on transactions were analyzed. The conclusion was that, regardless of whether a tax is imposed upon buyers (shifting the demand curve down) or upon sellers (shifting the supply curve up), the effects are identical. As illustrated in Figure 7.12 (essentially equivalent to Figure 2.4), the quantity of X traded falls from a pre-tax amount X^* to a post-tax $X°$. As for price, post-tax, there are *two* prices to consider: a "gross price" P_x^+ inclusive of tax and a "net price" P_x^- exclusive of tax. Buyers would be paying the gross (demand) price, whereas sellers would be receiving only the net (supply) price; hence, it is P_x^+ that is relevant for transaction *demand* decisions and P_x^- that is relevant for transaction *supply* decisions. Figure 7.12 shows that the gross price is higher than, but the net price lower than, the pre-tax equilibrium price P_x^*.

The effects of the tax upon the *gains from trade* can be analyzed in terms of the shaded and dotted areas of Figure 7.12. The entire shaded rectangle, equal to $(P_x^+ - P_x^-)X°$, represents the aggregate tax collections. The upper shaded portion, lying above the previous equilibrium price P_x^*, is at the expense of what was formerly Consumer Surplus (since the buyers now must pay the higher price P_x^+); the lower portion, lying below P_x^*, represents a corresponding loss of Producer Surplus. However, these two losses are offset by whatever benefits stem from the uses government makes of the funds collected. And indeed, measured in dollars, the uses of funds must exactly balance the losses of surplus. Hence, the rectangular shaded area is a *transfer* from buyers and sellers to the beneficiaries of government expenditures.

Figure 7.12

Effects Upon Consumer and Producer Surplus of a Tax on Transactions. A unit tax on transactions lowers the quantity exchanged from X^* to $X°$. The gross price paid by consumers rises from P_x^* to P_x^+ while the net price received by sellers falls from P_x^* to P_x^-. The upper shaded area is a transfer from Consumer Surplus and the lower shaded area a transfer from Product Surplus, the two transfers together constituting the amount of tax collections. The small dotted areas represent losses of Consumer Surplus and Producer Surplus that are not balanced by funds going to beneficiaries of government tax collections.

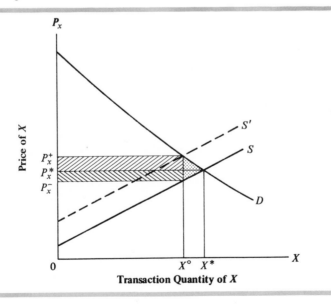

Chapter 7
EQUILIBRIUM,
EXCHANGE,
AND THE
GAINS FROM
TRADE

The dotted areas in Figure 7.12 represent something quite different. The triangular upper dotted area is a *net loss* of Consumer Surplus, and the corresponding lower area a *net loss* of Producer Surplus. Here there is no gain to any other party offsetting the loss to traders. The tax, by raising the effective price to buyers and lowering the effective price to sellers, *has reduced the volume of transactions* and the benefits derived from trade. The dotted areas therefore represent deadweight losses. Their aggregate magnitude constitutes the *efficiency loss* due to the tax.

But it cannot therefore be inferred that taxes should be abolished. The transfer (shaded rectangular area) represents an equivalence *in numeraire terms* between losses in Consumer and Producer Surplus on the one hand, and gains to beneficiaries of government expenditures on the other. The deadweight loss (dotted area) represents an additional loss of surplus, but it cannot be said that the "social value" (a term not defined here, and perhaps undefinable) of the government expenditures is necessarily less than the sum of the transfer and deadweight losses to traders taken together. It cannot even be proven that government revenue "should" be acquired in a way that minimizes these deadweight losses, though the analysis here is perhaps suggestive in that direction. (What economics can say about such policy issues will be examined in Part Six following.)

PROPOSITION: Taxes imposed on transactions reduce both Consumer Surplus and Producer Surplus. Some of the loss takes the form of a revenue transfer from consumers and producers to the beneficiaries of government expenditures. But there is also a deadweight or efficiency loss, due to the reduction in the volume of trade.

Taxes hamper trade through their effect on *prices*, more specifically, by driving a "wedge" between the gross price P_x^+ effective for buyers and the net price P_x^- effective for sellers. *Quantitative* restrictions on trade, to be considered next, operate somewhat differently.

Using Figure 7.13, suppose that a *quota* equal to $X' < X^*$ were imposed on the amount of commodity X that could be supplied to the market—with no restriction upon demand. The reduced quantity X' would then be sold at "whatever price the market will bear," determined along the demand curve D at the level P_x'. We want to compare this outcome with the unregulated equilibrium at price P_x^* and quantity X^*. The upper transfer (shaded) rectangle $(P_x' - P_x^*)X'$ is a loss of Consumer Surplus that now goes *to the suppliers* rather than to government. (And, of course, the suppliers retain the lower shaded area.) It follows that suppliers in the aggregate *may* benefit from the quantitative restriction on trading; they will do so if their transfer gain (upper shaded area) is more than their deadweight loss from the reduced volume of transactions (lower dotted area). The buyers, on the other hand, upon the imposition of a supply quota suffer *both* a transfer loss and a deadweight loss (just as in the case of a tax on transactions).

Now consider a quantitative restriction $X'' < X^*$ on the demand side, such as *rationing*. This is akin to a "quota" restricting demand rather than one limiting supply. If only those possessing ration tickets were allowed to buy, the demand

Chapter 7
EQUILIBRIUM,
EXCHANGE,
AND THE
GAINS FROM
TRADE

216

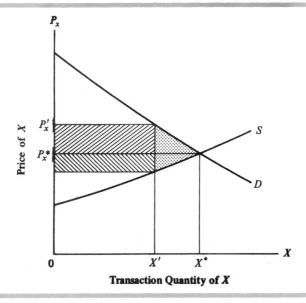

Figure 7.13

Effects Upon Consumer and Producer Surplus of a Quota Limit on Supply. Market supply is limited to the "quota" X', so price rises from P_x^* to P_x'. As before, Consumer Surplus is reduced by the upper shaded area (a transfer) plus the upper dotted area (an efficiency loss). But here the transfer is received *by the sellers*. If the transfer (upper shaded area) exceeds the sellers' efficiency loss (the lower dotted area), the sellers benefit from imposition of the quota. But buyers and sellers, considered together, lose by the amount of the dotted areas representing the combined efficiency losses.

curve would, as shown in Figure 7.14, in effect drop vertically from the point H representing the ration quantity X''. The effective price would be P_x'' along the supply curve in Figure 7.14. An exactly corresponding analysis will show that then the buyers *may gain* on balance, though the suppliers *must lose*.

There is one important respect, however, in which these analyses of quantitative restrictions are misleading. The cases just discussed are "ideal" limiting situations; in general, the deadweight losses due to quantitative restrictions upon trade will really be *much greater* than has been indicated. Let us reconsider Figure 7.14, showing consumption rationing that limits demand to the quantity X''. At the price P_x'' that suffices to elicit the desired quantity X'' from suppliers, the cross-hatched area in Figure 7.14 would represent the total Consumer Surplus in the "ideal" case just analyzed. But at a price as low as P_x'' the buyers are desirous of purchasing not X'' but the much larger X'''. Somehow or other the ration tickets must be distributed so as to validate no more than X'' of the X''' units demanded. Only if the validated demand units correspond exactly to the most intense demands (as measured by willingness-to-pay, or demand price) will the Consumer Surplus actually remain the shaded area in the diagram.

Consider the single most intensely demanded unit, for which some buyer is willing to pay as much as OA (where the demand curve intersects the vertical

Chapter 7
EQUILIBRIUM,
EXCHANGE,
AND THE
GAINS FROM
TRADE

217

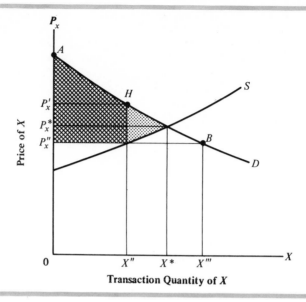

Figure 7.14

Effects Upon Consumer and Producer Surplus of a Ration Limit on Demand. If a ration limit in the amount X'' is imposed upon demand, price falls to P_x''. The cross-hatched area is the Consumer Surplus under rationing which, as a result of the transfer of the lower rectangle from suppliers, may be larger than at the X^*, P_x^* equilibrium. However, the dotted areas still represent an efficiency loss to consumers and producers taken together. (Note: The text indicates that the efficiency losses due to quota limits on supply or to ration limits on demand are generally *greater* than the dotted areas shown here and in the preceding figure.)

axis). It may be that the desirous buyer of this unit *does not obtain even a single ration ticket* and so cannot buy in the rationing situation. In contrast, consider the low-demand-price unit of demand at the point B along the demand curve, where some consumer is only barely willing to offer P_x''. Nonetheless, this last unit may represent demand that is validated by a ration ticket, and thus effective in a rationing situation. Note how rationing of demand, by leading to a low price P_x'', may induce *greater* consumption on the part of those buyers successful at obtaining ration tickets. The upshot, of course, is that the overall efficiency loss is indeed greater than would be indicated by the previous analysis. And an exactly analogous argument holds also for quota limits on supply.

Chapter 7
EQUILIBRIUM,
EXCHANGE,
AND THE
GAINS FROM
TRADE

218

PROPOSITION: Production quotas involve a transfer of surplus from consumers to producers; rationing of demand involves a transfer from producers to consumers. In addition, both cause an efficiency loss due to the reduced volume of trade. There will generally be a further efficiency loss as a result of non-ideal assignments of rights to sell or rights to buy.

Under the Sugar Act of 1948, the availability of sugar in the United States is limited by specific marketing quotas assigned to foreign countries and to domestic production areas. The U.S. market price for sugar is consequently at a substantial premium over the world price: for example, a 35% premium in 1960, 61% in 1968, 40% in 1970.

EXAMPLE 7.4
SUGAR QUOTAS

The effects of the U.S. quota system were studied by Ilse Mintz for the year 1970; the figures here are based upon her "low" estimates.[12] The underlying situation is pictured in Figure 7.15. Panel (a) represents a hypothetical free-market equilibrium that would have occurred in the absence of quotas. The world price is 5.5¢ per pound, and the domestic price would have to equal this. United States domestic production along the supply curve S_{US} is 2.9 million tons at this price, and imports are 8.7 million, making up a total of 11.6 million tons along the curve S_w showing world supply (inclusive of the domestic supply) to the United States. Since this is an equilibrium situation, the U.S. demand curve D intersects S_w at this price. Producer Surplus of the *domestic* producers is the small lower shaded area in Panel (a), and the U.S. Consumer Surplus is the huge upper shaded area (because of the steepness of the demand curve, the latter is shown only suggestively).

The effects of the quotas are shown in Panel (b). The quota assignments (6.0 million tons of domestic supply, 5.2 million tons of imports) aggregate to only a little less than the 11.6 million tons that would have been supplied annually under free markets. But as demand is highly inelastic (price elasticity of -0.1, according to the "low" estimate), the U.S. domestic price is sharply higher at the observed 8.07¢ per pound.

The deadweight loss of Consumer Surplus [the smaller dotted triangle in Panel (b)] is estimated by assuming that the demand curve D is linear between 11.2 million and 11.6 million tons. The area of the dotted triangle is ½(8.07¢ − 5.5¢)(.8 billion pounds) or $10,280,000 per year.

But the most obvious feature of the situation is the tremendous cost increase to consumers due to the price difference calculated upon the 11.2 million tons consumed in either case. This amounts to (22.4 billion pounds) times (8.07¢ − 5.5¢) or $575,680,000 annually.

The increased cost to U.S. consumers, all at the expense of Consumer Surplus, is broken down into four numbered areas in Panel (b). Area 1 is the transfer from domestic consumers to foreign producers, calculated on the basis of the higher price received for the 5.2 million tons they continue to deliver to the U.S. market. This amounts to $267,280,000 per year. Area 2 is the transfer to domestic producers, calculated on the 2.9 million tons they would have delivered in either case. This amounts to $149,060,000 per year. Areas 3 and 4 are equal (assuming for simplicity that the domestic supply curve S_{US} is linear), and amount together to the remaining $159,340,000. However, they are conceptually quite different. The upper area 3, like area 2, is a transfer from Consumer Surplus to domestic Producer Surplus. But the lower area 4 is a deadweight loss. It represents increased cost of produc-

[12]Ilse Mintz, *U.S. Import Quotas: Costs and Consequences*, American Enterprise Institute for Public Policy Research, Washington, D.C. (Feb. 1973).

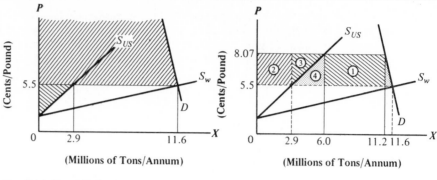

Panel (a) Free Markets   **Panel (b) Quotas**

Figure 7.15

Sugar Supply and Demand. In Panel (a), representing the unregulated situation, the small lower shaded triangle is the annual Producer Surplus received by U.S. suppliers while the large upper shaded area is the annual Consumer Surplus of U.S. purchasers. In Panel (b), imposition of a quota slightly smaller than the equilibrium market quantity (11.2 million tons in comparison with 11.6 million) raises price quite substantially (demand is extremely inelastic). U.S. Consumer Surplus *falls* by the amount of the four numbered areas, plus the small upper dotted triangle to the right. U.S. Producer Surplus *rises* by the amount of the numbered areas 2 and 3, both being transfers from domestic consumers. Area 1 is a transfer from domestic consumers to *foreign* producers. Area 4 is an efficiency loss due to displacement of low-cost foreign production by high-cost domestic production. The small upper dotted triangle is an efficiency loss due to reduced exchange.

tion (higher supply price) on units produced domestically that could have been obtained more cheaply from foreigners. This is the type of deadweight loss, described in the text above, that is due to a *non-ideal distribution* of quantitative restrictions upon trading. Granting that only 11.2 million tons of sugar are to be sold in the United States, there is an additional loss to the extent that quotas are assigned to high-cost domestic rather than to low-cost foreign producers. This additional deadweight loss, the larger dotted triangle in Panel (b), amounts to one-half of $159,340,000—or $79,670,000.

If we regard the transfers as cancelling out, the aggregate of the deadweight losses to the U.S. (the "efficiency loss" due to the sugar quotas) amounts to $89,950,000 per year.

*7.E.3

Rationale of Consumer and Producer Surplus

In the discussion of Section 7.A, the benefits of trade were divided into two categories: those due to improved consumptive reallocations of given commodity totals, and those due to the increased production of consumable goods stemming from the specialization that exchange makes possible. Consumer Surplus measures

* The section between the asterisk and the symbol ■ may contain somewhat more difficult or advanced material.

the first type of benefit, and Producer Surplus the second. But the traditional geometrical representations of these concepts, the shaded areas of Figure 7.10, are precisely valid only under certain restrictive assumptions.

Consider Producer Surplus first. In Figure 7.16 we see an individual's Production-Possibility Curve QQ, market line MM, and productive optimum Q^* (as in Figure 7.6). We now make the following assumptions: (1) Commodity Y represents "all other goods," and serves as numeraire so that price P_y is unity; "surplus" will be measured in terms of units of Y gained or lost. (2) We consider only the individual's productive aspect, summed up in attempting to achieve a productive optimum at Q^*. (In effect, we are assuming that this person will never want to *consume* X at all.) (3) The individual has an initial *endowment* position E on the Y-axis, and therefore can generate units of X only by sacrificing Y along the transformation locus QQ.

In moving from endowment position E to the productive optimum Q^* along QQ, the individual has transformed (sacrificed) EH units of Y to generate the produced-supply x^q. But at the equilibrium price ratio, corresponding to the slope $-P_x/P_y$ of the market line MM (with $P_x = P_x^*$ and $P_y = 1$), the x^q units of X produced have a market value of KH in Y-units. Thus, in Figure 7.16, the individual's Producer Surplus or *net gain in terms of Y-equivalents* is the distance

Figure 7.16

Derivation of Producer Surplus. For any producer of X, the Producer Surplus can be shown as the *difference in market value* (measured in Y-units) of the productive optimum position Q^* over the endowment position E. Since the Y-value of Q^* is OK, and of E is OE, this difference is the distance KE.

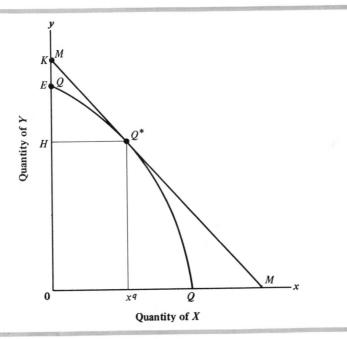

Chapter 7
EQUILIBRIUM,
EXCHANGE,
AND THE
GAINS FROM
TRADE

221

$KE = KH - EH$ along the vertical axis. In order to translate into the picture of Figure 7.10, we can assume that this individual is typical of the supply side as a whole. The distance KH, the worth in Y-units of the X-production at the equilibrium price ratio, corresponds to the price-times-quantity rectangle $OP_x^*BX^*$ in Figure 7.10. The distance EH, the opportunity cost or amount of Y sacrificed in producing X, corresponds to the area $OFBX^*$ lying below the supply curve. The lower shaded area FP_x^*B in Figure 7.10 is thus the analog on the aggregate level of the individual Producer Surplus KE of Figure 7.16.

Now consider Consumer Surplus, illustrated in Figure 7.17. Here we make the following assumptions: (1) Only the individual's consumptive aspect is considered, leading from an endowment position E to a consumptive optimum C^* along budget line EC^*L. (In effect, we assume here that the person does not *produce* X at all.) (2) The endowment position is along the Y-axis, so that the individual can acquire X *only* by paying out "other goods" Y. (3) The preference map is characterized by parallelism in the Y-direction; i.e., for any vertical line in the diagram of Figure 7.17, the indifference-curve slopes encountered along that vertical (whether steep as along $A'B'$ or flat as along $A''B''$) will all be the same. (The significance of this assumption will become clear shortly.)

If the individual in Figure 7.17 could not trade, he would have to remain at endowment position E on indifference curve U_0, and could not attain the position

Figure 7.17

Derivation of Consumer Surplus. For any consumer of X with endowment E on the vertical axis, the Consumer Surplus can be shown as a measure in Y-units of the *difference in utility* between the consumptive optimum position C^* and endowment position E. The vertical distance GE is the "compensation" measure of Consumer Surplus, while the distance C^*D is the "deprivation" measure. If indifference curves are vertically parallel, these two measures will be equal.

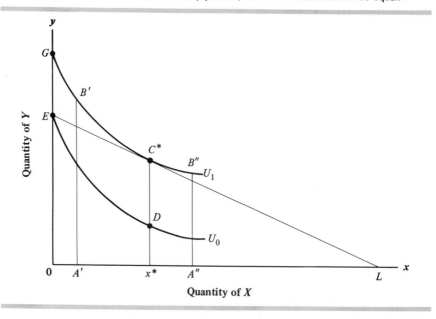

Chapter 7
EQUILIBRIUM,
EXCHANGE,
AND THE
GAINS FROM
TRADE

C^* on indifference curve U_1. Two possible measures, in Y-units, of the gain he derives from trade are the distances C^*D (along the vertical line $x = x^*$) and GE (along the vertical axis $x = 0$).

The distance GE corresponds to what may be called the "compensation" concept of the gain from trade. Consider the question: If the individual at the endowment position E were forbidden to purchase commodity X along the budget line EL, what amount of "other goods" Y would be required just to compensate? The answer is GE, since the position G is at the same U_1 utility level that the individual would have attained by trading from E to the consumptive optimum C^*. The distance C^*D, in contrast, may be called the "deprivation" concept of the benefit of trade. Here the question is: Having attained C^* by trading along the budget line, how many units of Y can the consumer be deprived of and still be no worse off than at E? The answer is C^*D, since the position D is at the same U_0 utility level as the endowment E.[13]

Now we can see the point of the special "Y-parallelism" assumption. First of all, if indifference curves are everywhere vertically parallel then they remain the same vertical difference apart (by the fundamental geometrical property of parallelism). Then the distances GE and C^*D are identical; the compensation and deprivation measures coincide.

Even more important is the following consideration: Y-parallelism means that the Marginal Rate of Substitution in Consumption, MRS_C, is a function only of the X-quantity and not of the Y-quantity. With Y-parallelism, when we move along a vertical and thus hold the X-quantity constant, the indifference-curve slope (whose absolute value is MRS_C) is unchanged. *This is equivalent to assuming that X is a commodity with zero income elasticity*: As the budget line shifts outward with increased income, the consumptive optimum shifts vertically upward. Put another way, *under this assumption the consumer's demand price for any quantity of X is independent of income*. It is this that justifies the simple aggregation of successive demand prices as the traditional measure of the consumer's total "willingness to pay," i.e., as the roughly trapezoidal area $OABX^*$ under the demand curve in Figure 7.10.

What if the demand price for X were *not* independent of income? Specifically, consider the normal case where the consumer's demand price for any X-quantity *rises* with income (positive income elasticity for X). In Figure 7.10, if the individual hypothetically paid OA for the first unit instead of the lower market price P_x^*, this would be an impoverishment. If the income effect is normal, such a person would no longer be willing to pay as high demand prices for successive units as suggested by the heights along the "ordinary" demand curve D in Figure 7.10. Consequently: *For a superior good, the aggregate willingness to pay is less than the area under the demand curve* (less than the area $OABX^*$ in Figure 7.10). Since Consumer Surplus is defined as willingness to pay less actual cost of purchase, it follows immediately that for a good with positive income elasticity, the true Consumer Surplus is less than the traditional roughly triangular area ABP_x^*

Chapter 7
EQUILIBRIUM,
EXCHANGE,
AND THE
GAINS FROM
TRADE

[13]Other measures of the benefit can be defined—for example, in terms of deprivation or compensation quantities of the commodity X itself.

(upper shaded area in the diagram). For an inferior good, of course, the true Consumer Surplus would be larger than the conventional representation.

Nevertheless, the conventional representation is almost always a usable approximation. The reason is that the *income effect*, the enrichment or impoverishment due to changes in P_x, is ordinarily only a minor factor affecting the demand for X itself. (The only exception would be if X accounts for a very large fraction of the consumer's budget).■

SUMMARY OF CHAPTER 7

This crucial chapter examines the equilibrium of markets and the gains from trade. Benefits of exchange fall into two main categories: *reallocation of the existing stocks* of goods to the mutual advantage of all consumers, and the *increased quantities* of goods made possible by specialization in production.

The first benefit can be isolated by assuming fixed stocks of commodities (a regime of pure exchange). As between two traders, the region of mutual advantage in the Edgeworth box shows how both parties can achieve higher indifference curves through exchange. At competitive *equilibrium* in pure exchange, for each trader the Marginal Rate of Substitution in Consumption MRS_C is equal to the price ratio P_x/P_y. This equality corresponds to a mutual indifference-curve tangency in the Edgeworth box.

For any individual, supply and demand curves for commodity X can be derived from the data represented by the Price Expansion Path (PEP). It is useful to distinguish the *full supply* (endowed quantity) and *full demand* (consumption quantity) on the one hand, and on the other hand the *transaction supply* (excess of full supply over full demand) and the *transaction demand* (excess of full demand over full supply). To determine aggregate supply and demand curves for the economy as a whole, the individual curves are summed horizontally. At the equilibrium price P_x^*, the intersection of the aggregate *full* supply and demand curves shows the quantity endowed and consumed; the intersection of the aggregate *transaction* supply and demand curves shows the quantity exchanged.

More generally, individuals will have productive as well as exchange opportunities (regime of production and exchange). Here, in competitive equilibrium, not only the MRS_C but also the Marginal Rate of Transformation MRS_T for each individual will be set equal to the price ratio P_x/P_y. The equality $MRS_C = P_x/P_y$ corresponds to the usual tangency of the budget or market line with the highest attainable indifference curve, representing the *consumptive optimum* position C^*. The equality $MRS_T = P_x/P_y$ corresponds to a tangency of the Production-Possibility Curve with the highest attainable market line, representing the *productive optimum* position Q^*. Unlike a Robinson Crusoe, a producer having also exchange opportunities makes distinct productive and consumptive decisions.

These decisions can again be translated into supply and demand curves. If production can take place, the full supply curve does not represent a fixed endowment amount but rather the increasing quantity of X produced as the price P_x rises. With this modification, the equilibrium is found as before. At P_x^* the aggregate *full* supply and *full* demand curves intersect to show the quantity of X produced and

Chapter 7
EQUILIBRIUM,
EXCHANGE,
AND THE
GAINS FROM
TRADE

224

consumed, while the aggregate *transaction* supply and demand curves intersect at the same price to show the quantity exchanged in the market.

The availability of a market makes it possible for each individual to specialize in production. Anyone with superior ability to produce any commodity can take advantage of that ability; even if he or she wants to consume little or none of the commodity, the excess amount produced can be sold to others in market transactions.

Consumer Surplus is a measure of purchasers' gains from trade; Producer Surplus is a measure of the gain for sellers. Consumer Surplus represents the excess of what consumers would ultimately have been *willing to pay* for any amount of the good, over what they actually *have to pay*. Similarly, Producer Surplus is what sellers *actually receive* in trade over the minimum they would have been *willing to accept*.

The effects of various hindrances to trade—such as taxes, production quotas, or consumption rationing—can be analyzed in terms of Consumer Surplus and Producer Surplus. In general these interferences transfer some of the gains of trade from one side to another (or to a third party like government). But, in addition, the hindrances generally involve some deadweight or efficiency loss, since they reduce the extent of mutually beneficial exchange.

QUESTIONS FOR CHAPTER 7

Mainly for Review

R1. Explain how the possibility of trade can lead both to *consumptive* benefits (preferred allocations of given social totals of goods over the different individuals) and *productive* benefits (larger social totals of desired goods). How is the consumptive improvement illustrated in the Edgeworth box of Figure 7.1? Which diagram illustrates the productive improvement?

*R2. If two persons have identical preferences (indifference-curve maps), does it follow that they cannot trade to mutual advantage? What if they have identical preferences *and* identical endowments in a world of pure exchange? In a world of production, what if they have identical preferences and identical productive opportunities?

*R3. We normally observe a strong tendency toward specialization in production, but diversification (non-specialization) in consumption. What shapes of the individuals' Production-Possibility Curves and preference maps lead to this pattern of behavior? Is trade necessary to bring it about?

R4. What is meant by an individual's "sustaining price" for a particular good? What happens at higher prices? At lower prices? How does the "sustaining price" differ from the "autarky price"?

Chapter 7
EQUILIBRIUM,
EXCHANGE,
AND THE
GAINS FROM
TRADE

*The answers to asterisked questions appear at the end of the book.

R5. What condition must hold for each individual at competitive equilibrium in a world of *pure exchange*? What additional condition characterizes the market as a whole?

*R6. What are the productive and consumptive conditions that must hold for each individual in a world of *production and exchange*? What additional conditions characterize the market as a whole?

R7. Justify the assertion that the *productive* improvement due to trade necessarily implies greater social totals of desired goods. [*Hint*: Consider the two individuals' Marginal Rates of Transformation with and without trade.]

*R8. If market equilibrium takes place at the intersection of the aggregate *transaction* demand and *transaction* supply curves, how can the intersection of the full demand and full supply curves also determine the equilibrium?

R9. "For every individual, the s_i^t and d_i^t curves must intersect along the vertical axis, as in Figure 7.7. It is therefore quite impossible for the aggregate S^t and D^t curves to intersect in the interior, as in Figure 7.8." True or false? Explain.

R10. Why are the deadweight losses due to rationing or quotas likely to be far larger than the simple graphical analysis in Figure 7.14 suggests?

For Further Thought and Discussion

T1. From Omar Khayyam:

> I often wonder what the Vintners buy
> One half so precious as the Goods they sell.

Omar seems to be suggesting that vintners ought not engage in exchange, since wine is more precious than anything else. Does this make sense in economic terms? Interpret.

*T2. Compare the likely effects of a tax upon *consumption*, upon *production*, and upon *exchange* of a commodity.

*T3. Why do we assume diminishing marginal returns in production (diminishing MRS_T) but not in exchange?

T4. It was shown in the text that the opening of trade between two formerly autarkic producers tends to lead to greater specialization in production. The demonstration was based on the premise that preferences are relatively diversified (unspecialized) in comparison with productive opportunities. Show that if, on the contrary, the two traders had relatively specialized tastes (one strongly preferring X, the other Y) and unspecialized productive opportunities, then the opening of trade would lead to a *lesser* degree of productive specialization. Does this mean that there is no productive benefit from trade? Explain.

*T5. From the Report of the President's Water Resources Commission (1950):

> There are many types of public objectives and gains which defy analysis in commercial terms. . . . Market prices reflect scarcity values; thus, if half our forests were burned, the remainder would be worth more money than the existing forests. . . . A commercial property has

Chapter 7
EQUILIBRIUM,
EXCHANGE,
AND THE
GAINS FROM
TRADE

226

dollar value according to scarcity; a Nation's resources have *security* value if they are so plentiful as to be cheap.

What is being assumed here about the elasticity of demand for our forests? Does the quotation make economic sense?

*T6. Imagine an initial Edgeworth-box competitive equilibrium, starting from an endowment position where individual i has all of commodity C (corn) and individual j has all of commodity Y (numeraire). Suppose that i's endowment of corn doubles, everything else remaining unchanged. Can we be sure that i is better off at the new competitive equilibrium? That j is better off? That at least one of them is better off? [*Hint*: Are corn farmers necessarily better off if the crop is large? What about consumers of corn?]

8.A   TRANSFER COSTS VERSUS COSTS OF EXCHANGE, 230

8.B   PERFECT COMPETITION AND PERFECT MARKETS, 232

8.C   TRANSACTION COSTS AND MARKET EQUILIBRIUM, 236

    8.C.1   Proportional Transaction Costs, 237

   *8.C.2   Lump-Sum Transaction Costs, 245

8.D   THE ROLE OF MONEY, 249

Examples

    8.1   Farmer, Consumer, and Middleman, 231

    8.2   Experiments in Perfect and Imperfect Markets, 235

    8.3   Costs of Trading on the New York Stock Exchange, 236

    8.4   Urban–Farm Food Cost Differentials, 244

    8.5   Barter in the East Indies, 253

8

COSTS OF EXCHANGE AND THE ROLE OF MONEY

Supplementary Chapter

Exchange is the very heart of microeconomics. We have seen in Chapter 7 how trade confers benefits upon participants in the form of Consumer Surplus and Producer Surplus, and how hindrances to trade tend to reduce these gains. The specialization in production that makes modern integrated economic life possible without detailed centralized planning, as a system of spontaneous order, is a consequence of market exchange. (On the other hand, productive specialization might also come about as a result of command decisions under a system of centralized planning, as will be discussed further below.)

But the exchange process itself has inevitable costs and imperfections. It is as an attempt to cope with these imperfections that the crucial institution of *money* comes into existence (together with banking, credit cards, and other puzzling phenomena of our modern world). The role of money is generally emphasized as a topic in *macro*economics, an application that lies beyond the scope of the present book. However, the foundations of money as an artificial or invented commodity lie in the *micro*economics of the market process. In this chapter it will be shown how money, serving its classical functions as "medium of exchange" and "store of value," reduces the costs and imperfections of exchange.

TRANSFER COSTS VERSUS COSTS
OF EXCHANGE

At first sight, very large proportions of our resources appear to be devoted to the process of exchange. In 1971 around 19% of the total U.S. employed civilian labor force was reported as engaged in the occupational category Wholesale and Retail Trade. And many workers classified under other headings—e.g., Transportation and Communication; Finance, Insurance and Real Estate; and Services—might also be regarded as associated with the exchange process. This suggests that "middleman" (transaction-facilitating) activities are a truly enormous drain upon the nation's resources. It might seem astonishing that such heavy burdens remain even after the invention of money, banking, and other sophisticated devices designed to economize upon the costs of market exchange.

This initial impression is misleading. From the social point of view, a crucial distinction must be made between two logically distinct classes of interpersonal "transactions." The *trading* of goods and services between self-interested individuals, i.e., the social process of market exchange, is one thing. The sheer physical *transfer* of possession or control of commodities is quite another. Any economy that integrates the activities of a great number of individuals so as to take advantage of productive specialization and the division of labor, whether it be an economy of saints, of monks, of slaves, of ants, or of utility-maximizers under *laissez-faire,* would still involve physical transfer of commodities. *Activities and costs that are intrinsically due to the mere physical fact of transfer must not be attributed to the particular process that achieves interpersonal integration via market trading.*

For concreteness, consider an extreme "command economy" in which all economic decisions are made by a central authority. The economy might be a slave society in which everyone works for the benefit of a single master. Or it might be a total socialist dictatorship, centrally planned (let us say) to achieve popular well-being. (Egypt, after Pharoah assigned authority to Joseph to meet the threat of the seven lean years, might be an example.) To achieve high levels of output in such a command economy, specialization in production still would be essential. But it would be achieved by visible direction rather than by an "Invisible Hand."[1] Farmers would be ordered to grow crops and turn them over to railroads; railroads ordered to ship them to cities, and turn them over to warehouses; warehouses ordered to store them, and turn them over to the next recipients in the chain, and so forth. Every transfer of control of goods would involve costs: handling, shipping, storing, record-keeping, and so forth.

The costs associated with mere physical transfers that would persist even in

[1]We leave aside here the question of "comparative economic systems"—the relative effectiveness of *inducing* interpersonal cooperation through self-interest (the "Invisible Hand") as opposed to *commanding* it by central direction (with suitable provision for enforcement) on the other.

a totally dictated economy fall logically under the economic category of *production* costs rather than exchange costs. This accounts for essentially all transportation services, for one thing. "Adding" transportation to a good so as to physically bring it to a consumer is in principle the same as "adding" baking services to dough so as to make bread that the consumer can eat. The consequence is that *the costs of market exchange as a process are not nearly so great as might have first been thought*. Even wholesaling and retailing expenses, as usually classified, are in large part due to the physical warehousing of goods that would still be needed in a total command economy with no market process at all.

What then are the *costs of exchange* proper? These are the costs, in a non-command or "free" economy, that stem specifically from the contending wills and property interests of the parties. In such an economy physical transfers of commodities take place only if and as consistent with perceived mutual advantage of traders. To arrange transactions, offers must be communicated and alternatives compared. Contracts must be negotiated, and their execution thereafter must be verified. Fraud or other non-performance must be guarded against. All these activities involve costs.[2] All of the expenses of an institution like the New York Stock Exchange, for example, fall under one or more of these headings. (Without private ownership there would be no need for a Stock Exchange, since there would be no corporate shares.) In addition, we shall see that certain "trading inventories" will be held, over and above the necessary stocks of goods that would be carried by an ideal command economy.

"Consumerists" contend that food prices are too high, while farmers can be counted on to complain that the prices they receive are too low. It is natural for both groups to fasten upon the "middleman" as the culprit. And, in fact, payments to middlemen have over the years been accounting for an increasing share of consumer expenditure on food.

But of course middlemen are providing services for the income they receive: processing, transporting, packaging, distributing, and so forth. Over time the middleman services incorporated into food products have been increasing. We have been choosing to consume food that has traveled further, been processed more elaborately, and distributed in more complex ways than in earlier times.

One explanation of this phenomenon is that middleman services are a relatively superior or "luxury" commodity compared to raw farm products themselves. That is, the *income elasticity of demand* (see Section 5.A) for off-farm food services is greater than for farm products alone. Confirming this, one study has indicated an overall income elasticity of demand of .705 for food products—but when this figure is divided between the farm and

EXAMPLE 8.1
FARMER,
CONSUMER, AND
MIDDLEMAN

---

[2]Of course there would also be great communication and enforcement problems in any actual attempt to construct a functioning *command* economy. Again, it is not our purpose here to engage in an analysis of comparative economic systems.

off-farm components, the income elasticity of demand is only .279 for the farm but 1.322 for the off-farm element.[3] So the rising share of the middleman in food sales in the United States is largely a result of rising consumer income, which has permitted an increase in the purchases of middleman services that constitute a relatively superior good as a component of food at the point of consumption.

[3]E. W. Bunkers and W. W. Cochrane, "On the Income Elasticity of Food Services," *Review of Economics and Statistics*, v. 30 (May 1957), p. 217.

8.B

PERFECT COMPETITION AND PERFECT MARKETS

In the preceding chapters, we have been implicitly assuming ideal conditions of exchange: *perfect competition* and *perfect markets*. We also assumed away any costs of the exchange process, except where such costs come artificially into existence as a result of interventions such as the imposition of taxes upon transactions. The absence of costs of exchange is also a kind of "perfection" assumption; this section examines the relation between perfection in this sense and the related ideas of perfect competition and perfect markets.

A competitive trader was described above as a *price-taker*. The terms of exchange facing a price-taker in the market are perceived as fixed; price-takers regard themselves as able to buy or sell any desired quantity at the current ruling price.

There is a paradox here. Suppose individual i is a net demander in the market for a good X, where the *overall* supply-demand equilibrium is as pictured in Figure 8.1, Panel (a). The equilibrium price is P_x^* and aggregate transaction quantity is X^*. Note the normally upward-sloping market supply curve S.[4] But if the individual's own purchases do not affect price, the supply curve S in Panel (b) *as viewed by the individual* is horizontal (at the supply price P_x^*). At this price the individual market demand curve d_i indicates that the person will purchase the quantity x_i^*. But how can a supply curve that is upward-sloping in Panel (a) be horizontal in Panel (b)?

The explanation is simple: The supply curve is not *really* horizontal in Panel (b). However, if an individual i is a negligible element in the overall supply-demand picture, variations in x_i will not noticeably affect the price in equilibrium. In effect, the supply curve viewed by the individual demander in Panel (b) is a very tiny segment of the total supply curve S, lying in the immediate neighbor-

Chapter 8
COST OF
EXCHANGE
AND THE ROLE
OF MONEY

232

[4]In this chapter, and henceforth in the text, supply and demand curves will be understood to be the *transaction* supply and demand curves that were symbolized as S^t and D^t (on the aggregate level) and s^t and d^t (on the individual level) in the previous chapter.

Figure 8.1

A Price-Taker in the Market. Panel (a) shows an ordinary market equilibrium of demand and supply, where X is the aggregate *transaction* quantity. Panel (b) has a different horizontal scale, corresponding to quantity demanded by a single individual i representing a very small fraction of the market. As trader i's decisions do not noticeably affect market price, the supply curve as viewed by him in Panel (b) is effectively horizontal (he is a "price-taker").

hood of the quantity X^* in Panel (a). In shifting from the aggregate X-scale in Panel (a) to the individual x_i-scale in Panel (b), this segment is stretched out horizontally so that in appearance it becomes practically flat. Thus, we see that a competitive demander cannot literally be a "price-taker" in the sense of being able to buy *any* quantity at a given price P_x. Rather, the supply price is effectively constant with respect to the relatively negligible quantities he might be *able and willing* to purchase.

NUMERICAL ILLUSTRATION: Suppose that the market supply equation is $X_s = 10,000P_x$ and the market demand equation is $X_d = 75,000 - 5000P_x$. By letting $X_x = X_d = X^*$, the equilibrium price is seen to be $P_{\ddagger}^* = 5$ and equilibrium quantity $X^* = 50,000$ units. If we imagine that the demand side of the market actually consists of 1000 identical individuals, each has an individual demand function $x_d = 75 - 5P_x$. At the equilibrium price $P_{\ddagger}^* = 5$, each is of course purchasing 50 units.

Now suppose that the purchases of one single demander were reduced to zero. Then the market demand equation becomes $X_d = 999$ $(75 - 5P_x)$, and the equilibrium price falls from $P_{\ddagger}^* = 5$ to $P_{\ddagger}^* = 4.997$. If, on the other hand, the purchases of any single demander were doubled from 50 to 100 units, the equation becomes $X_d = $

Chapter 8
COST OF
EXCHANGE
AND THE ROLE
OF MONEY

233

$100 + 999(75 - 5P_x)$, and the market price rises from $P_{\bar{x}}^* = 5$ to $P_{\bar{x}}^* = 5.003$.

The price shift in either case is negligible, though not literally zero.

The ideal concept of *perfect competition* goes beyond mere price-taking behavior on the part of individual traders, however. It involves *perfect markets* as well. There are three main characteristics of perfect markets:

1. *Perfect Communication:*   The market must be an integrated whole, not segmented by limitations of information. In actuality there are cases in which an individual i is in communication with j, and j with k, but where i and k are not themselves able to make direct contact. Real-world markets have informational imperfections, as we can see by the efforts made to overcome them: the use of classified newspaper advertising to communicate supply–demand offers, specialized "middlemen" (such as real-estate brokers) through whom buyers and sellers can reach one another, and organized exchanges (such as the New York Stock Exchange) which aim to bring all relevant offers into a single combined marketplace.

2. *Instantaneous Equilibrium:*   A market can be viewed as a mechanism, taking as input all potential traders' supply and demand functions, and yielding as output the equilibrium or "market-clearing" price at which purchases and sales are all to be executed. A perfect market would instantaneously digest the inputs and proclaim the correct market-clearing price. But in the real world a farmer bringing vegetables to a city produce market, for example, may by cleverness or chance realize a sale at a price higher than the (unknown) true equilibrium. Or, unluckily, the farmer may accept a price lower than might have been obtained. Thus, in real-world markets there is some "trading at false prices." (One of the functions of *speculation* is to minimize such accidental fluctuations of price that lead to false trading, since speculators enter the market so as to buy when they perceive that the price is accidentally too low and to sell when price is accidentally too high.)

3. *Costless Transactions:*   Markets that are perfect would also be costless. In the real world, market "middlemen" such as wholesalers and retailers, brokers, dealers, and jobbers exist, and obviously must be paid for their services. While these middlemen may improve the perfection of the market in other respects, the fees and payments they receive constitute a burden on the process of exchange. Transaction taxes, in which *government* collects "middleman" payments (possibly reflecting actual services to taxpayers, but possibly not), are another important factor. (The Stamp Act of 1765 imposed a transaction tax that played an important role in American history.)

Chapter 8
COST OF
EXCHANGE
AND THE ROLE
OF MONEY

234

An interesting series of economic experiments on the functioning of markets has been conducted by Vernon L. Smith.[5] One question studied was the following: Given that real-world market situations, whether arising naturally or in artificially constructed experiments, can never fully meet the theoretical conditions of "perfect markets," how far can the conditions diverge from "perfection" and still achieve the same essential *results*? For example, if traders are not in perfect communication, or if "trading at false prices" may occur, to what extent is it the case that equilibrium is nevertheless attained quite quickly and at a price–quantity outcome close to the theoretical ideal?

EXAMPLE 8.2
EXPERIMENTS IN
PERFECT AND
IMPERFECT
MARKETS

In a typical experiment, Smith provided each subject with information as to demand price (the maximum unit price he or she should be willing to bid), if buying, or as to supply price (the minimum he or she should be willing to accept), if selling. With different subjects having different demand prices and supply prices, demand and supply curves were brought into implicit existence (though not visible as such to any single participant). So the observers knew the true equilibrium price, although the subjects did not. Under the experimental conditions, any buyer (or seller) could at any time make a bid (or offer) which, if accepted by a seller (or buyer), became a binding contract. The process was public, so that the terms of any deals consummated became known to as-yet-uncommitted traders.

In the experimental situations almost all contracts agreed upon were near the "true" (but unknown) equilibrium price, except possibly for the first few transactions in any series. When an initial divergence occurred, convergence toward the "true" price was very rapid. While not literally all transactions took place at the equilibrium price, even toward the end of a market sequence, the model of perfect markets nevertheless provided a high degree of approximation of actual transaction prices. Furthermore, the *quantities* exchanged were also very close to the theoretical ideal. In short, substantially all the potential advantages of trade (in the form of Consumer Surplus and Producer Surplus) were in fact achieved despite the experimental departure from ideal conditions.

Results such as these suggest that the economist's perfect-market model is "robust," in the sense of having a high degree of predictive reliability even though the exact conditions for its validity are not fully met. A very similar situation in physics is the model of a "perfect gas" that leads to the prediction known as Boyle's Law. No actual gas can meet the requirements of a "perfect gas," and yet Boyle's Law is a very reliable predictive equation in physics.

[5] V. L. Smith, "An Experimental Study of Competitive Market Behavior," *Journal of Political Economy*, v. 70 (April 1962); "Effects of Market Organization of Competitive Equilibrium," *Quarterly Journal of Economics*, v. 78 (May 1964); "Experimental Auction Markets and the Walrasian Hypothesis," *Journal of Political Economy*, v. 73 (Aug. 1965).

CONCLUSION: Absence of costs of exchange is one element of the concept of *perfect markets*, the other elements being perfect communication and instantaneous equilibrium. While transaction costs considered alone are an element of imperfection, such costs are ordinarily incurred in order to reduce other imperfections—for example, when someone selling a house is willing to pay a commission to a real-estate broker for establishing communication with potential homebuyers. *Perfect competition* involves perfect markets together with "price-taking behavior" of buyers and sellers, which is normally a consequence of the existence of large numbers of traders on both sides of the market.

8.C

TRANSACTION COSTS AND MARKET EQUILIBRIUM

In the discussion that follows, markets will be assumed perfect *except* for the existence of transaction or exchange costs. This amounts to assuming that middlemen function so effectively as to totally eliminate the other two types of market imperfection—informational segmentation, and false trading at non-equilibrium prices. But of course these efficient middleman services must be compensated by fees or charges upon transactions. Costs of exchange have, we shall see, important consequences for the scope of trading and for the degree of specialization in production and consumption.

EXAMPLE 8.3
COSTS OF
TRADING ON THE
NEW YORK STOCK
EXCHANGE

An organized exchange like the New York Stock Exchange goes a considerable way toward the ideal of a perfect market. The key feature of an organized exchange is the guarantee of the transaction, i.e., of the quality of merchandise delivered, of payment arrangements, etc., by the exchange authorities themselves. As a result the buyer can forego personal inspection of the merchandise, and the seller need not be concerned with the credit standing or the character of the buyer. In the case of the New York Stock Exchange, the buyer does not have to worry about whether the stock certificates acquired are counterfeit, nor need the seller fear that the buyer may be making payment with a bad check.

However, there are costs of dealing on the New York Stock Exchange. These fall into two main categories: (1) commission charges, and (2) bid–ask price spread. The *commission charges* are the explicit fees paid to brokers by buyers and sellers. These charges are quoted separately from the amounts paid or received for the securities themselves. The *bid–ask spread* is a less obvious portion of the cost of transacting. At any instant of time the market price of a stock like General Motors to a seller, the "bid price," is less than the "ask price" that a buyer of GM stock would have to pay. The difference goes mainly to the Exchange's "specialist" in General Motors stock who plays the role of making a continuous market in (standing ready always to buy or sell) that security. Specialists, like retail or wholesale merchants, must on the average buy for less (the bid price) than they sell for (the ask price) if they are to remain in business. (The customer's *broker*, in contrast with the specialist, is normally a pure intermediary who does not buy or sell on his own account.)

A study by Harold Demsetz[6] indicated that in 1965 the bid–ask spread on the New York Stock Exchange comprised about 40% and explicit commission charges about 60% of total transaction cost, on the average. The two together amounted to about 1.3% of the value of the securities exchanged. The study also found that the bid–ask spread is normally much lower for frequently-traded than for infrequently-traded securities. This is reasonable if we regard the Exchange's specialist as a merchant who must hold an ''inventory'' of securities in order always to stand ready to sell. On average the specialist's funds must be tied up longer, and therefore also at greater risk of price fluctuation, in the case of a ''slow-moving'' commodity like an infrequently-traded stock. Commission charges also proved to be relatively lower for bigger transactions, which is easily understandable in terms of a saving in communications and recording costs.

[6]H. Demsetz, ''The Cost of Transacting,'' *Quarterly Journal of Economics*, v. 82 (Feb. 1968).

Costs of exchange are generally a function of: (1) the volume of goods traded; (2) the number of distinct transactions per unit of time; (3) the number of parties involved in a transaction; and (4) the number of distinct commodities per transaction. In the next sections we will be dealing only with two-party, two-commodity trades, ruling out the third and fourth elements above. (Some comments upon costs of multi-party and multi-commodity trading will be made in later sections.) For simplicity, we will deal below with special cases that isolate each of the two sources of exchange cost to be considered here. Specifically, the implications of *transaction costs strictly proportional to volume* will be studied first; afterward, *costs dependent solely on the number of separate transactions* will be taken up.

We have already noted in Chapter 2 (see Figure 2.4) certain consequences of a particular type of proportional transaction cost—a uniform tax on sales. If an excise tax of $1 per unit were levied upon purchases of a commodity X, then the *gross price* P_x^+ paid by buyers would necessarily be $1 per unit greater than the *net price* P_x^- received by sellers. Figure 8.2 here is equivalent to the earlier diagram. It indicates that, as compared with a no-tax situation with price P_x^* and quantity X^*, after imposition of the tax the quantity exchanged would be only X'. As for price, the gross price P_x^+ paid by buyers will always be higher than, but the net price P_x^- received by sellers will be lower than, the no-tax equilibrium price P_x^*. The shaded area in the diagram, equal to $X'(P_x^+ - P_x^-)$, represents the tax collections.

But a more generalized interpretation of the diagram is possible. We can think of it as representing the effects of *any* proportional transaction cost, not just a tax. The *price gap* $G = P_x^+ - P_x^-$ is the rate charged by middlemen (e.g., the ''bid–ask spread'' of Example 8.3 above) to effectuate the exchange of a unit of

Chapter 8
COST OF
EXCHANGE
AND THE ROLE
OF MONEY

Figure 8.2

Proportional Transaction Costs. A proportional transaction charge in the amount of G per unit of commodity X exchanged means that, in equilibrium, there must be a price gap of this amount between the price paid by demanders (P_x^+) and the price received by suppliers (P_x^-). The quantity exchanged is X', and the shaded area represents the aggregate transaction costs paid by traders.

X. The shaded area is then the aggregate amount received by middlemen for their services in this market.

Let us now consider the situation from the viewpoint of an individual trader. In Figure 8.3 a price-taking trader in a world of *costless* exchange could, starting from an endowment combination E, attain any position along the solid market line KL. The market opportunity set would be the entire triangle OKL, the shaded area plus the dotted areas. The slope of the market line is $-P_x/P_y$, or simply $-P_x$ since, as usual, we interpret Y as a numeraire (representing "all other goods") with price $P_y \equiv 1$. The dashed line-segments show the impact of a proportional trading charge. If the individual tries to buy X by moving *southeast* from E (note direction of the arrows) along the line-segment EL', there is a steeper slope because P_x^+ is greater than P_x. And if the person tries to sell X by moving *northwest* along EK', he or she receives only the lower price P_x^- reflected in the flat slope of EK'. The existence of transaction costs narrows the individual's opportunity set, from the triangle OKL that would be relevant under costless exchange to the quadrilateral $OK'EL'$ bounded by the dashed line-segments (shaded area in the diagram).

Transaction costs obviously lessen the gains from trade. If individuals have both productive and exchange opportunities, any costs of trading tend to reduce the benefit from (and therefore the extent of) specialization in production. In the limiting case transaction costs may lead individuals to choose *autarky*

Chapter 8
COST OF
EXCHANGE
AND THE ROLE
OF MONEY

238

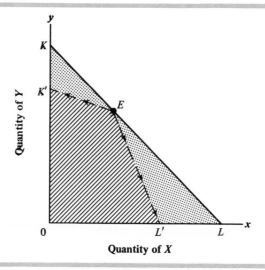

Figure 8.3

Individual Trading Opportunity: Costless versus Costly Exchange. An individual with trading opportunities and initial endowment *E* would have, under costless exchange, a market opportunity set consisting of the entire triangle *OKL*. But if there is a proportional transaction charge, the person would face a steeper budget line as buyer of *X* (line-segment *EL'*) or a flatter budget line as seller of *X* (line-segment *EK'*). The market opportunity set is therefore reduced to the shaded area.

productive–consumptive solutions, in which self-sufficiency is preferred to engaging in trade.

The two panels of Figure 8.4 illustrate autarky solutions under costless and costly exchange respectively. In each case, starting from an endowment point *E*, the individual's autarky optimum is the "Robinson Crusoe solution" *R**, where the Production-Possibility Curve *QQ* is just tangent to indifference curve U_0. At this point, as we know from equation (7.5), $MRS_C = MRS_T$; the Marginal Rate of Substitution in Consumption (the absolute slope of his indifference curve) is just equal to the Marginal Rate of Transformation (absolute slope of *QQ*).

Under *costless* exchange as pictured in Panel (a), it is only in the very special case shown in the diagram, where the market price ratio P_x/P_y is just equal to this common value of MRS_C and MRS_T, that there will be no way for the individual to gain from exchange. If the market price ratio (absolute slope of the market line) tilts away in either direction from this common value, as it almost always will, the productive optimum and consumptive optimum for the individual diverge (as in Figure 7.6). Such a divergence means that the individual can participate in and benefit from trade.

Under *costly* exchange, autarky becomes a much more likely possibility. In Panel (b) the Crusoe solution is *R** as before. *R** on *QQ* is obviously preferable to any other point in the shaded quadrilateral *OK'R*L'* that shows the lessened market opportunities. Autarky now may be best for the individual in a much wider class of cases. Considerable tilting of the slopes of *R*K'* and *R*L'* (upward or downward

Chapter 8
COST OF
EXCHANGE
AND THE ROLE
OF MONEY

239

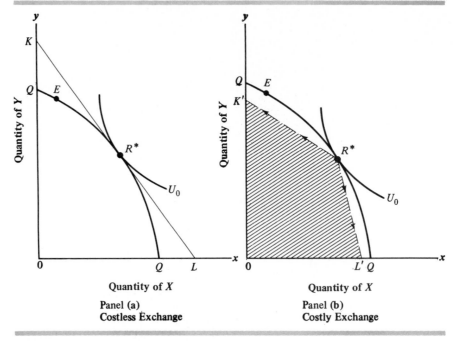

Figure 8.4

Production and Exchange Opportunities: Autarky Solutions. Under costless exchange in Panel (a), autarky will be preferred by the individual only if the price ratio P_x/P_y is exactly such that the market line *KL* passes through the mutual tangency of *QQ* and U_0 at the Robinson Crusoe solution *R**. Under costly exchange in Panel (b), in contrast, *R** might remain preferred over a considerable range of values for the gross price P_x^+ and net price P_x^-.

shifts of buying and selling prices) could take place and still leave the *R** position best for the individual.

Whether or not autarky solutions will be preferred under costly exchange depends upon the buying and selling prices P_x^+ and P_x^- and of course also upon the shapes of the individual's productive opportunities and preferences. In Figure 8.5 the two dotted areas show the increments to the individual's overall opportunity set still provided by the possibility of trading (even though a transaction charge is being levied). Consider the dotted area at the upper left. *A* is the point where the Production-Possibility Curve *QQ* has the same slope as (is tangent to) the dashed market line-segment whose flatter slope represents the lower selling price P_x^-. Hence, in attempting to move northwest (acquire *Y* by giving up *X*) beyond *A* the individual does better along *AK'* (selling *X* for *Y* in the market) than along *QQ* (converting *X* into *Y* via productive transformation). A corresponding argument applies, of course, for the dotted area at the lower right bounded by the steeper line-segment *BL'* whose slope represents the higher buying price P_x^+.

Now if the preference map is, as shown in Figure 8.5, such that the Crusoe tangency *R* falls between* A *and* B, autarky is preferred. The high buying price

Chapter 8
COST OF
EXCHANGE
AND THE ROLE
OF MONEY

240

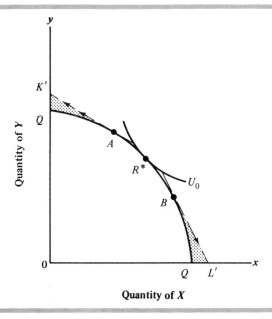

Figure 8.5
Opportunity Set with Transaction Costs: Autarky Solution. The gross price P_x^+ determines the slope of the line-segment BL' tangent to the Production-Possibility Curve QQ at point B, thus adding the lower-right dotted area as a portion of the individual's overall opportunity set. Similarly, the net price P_x^- determines the slope of the line-segment AK' tangent to QQ at point A, which adds the upper-left dotted area to the overall opportunities. Nevertheless, here the autarky solution R^* remains preferred, since R^* lies between A and B.

P_x^+ and the low selling price P_x^- then *straddle* the common value of $MRS_C = MRS_T$ at the autarky point. On the other hand, if the shape of the preference map and/or transformation locus QQ are such that R^* falls outside the range AB along QQ, the individual will engage in market trade as a net buyer or seller. Specifically, suppose that the R^* tangency falls northwest of A along QQ as in Figure 8.6. But in this range the individual can do better (can attain a higher indifference curve) along the market line-segment AK' than along AQ. The *productive* optimum Q^* would then be at the point A and the person would sell X for Y to attain a *consumptive* optimum C^* along AK'.

Thus, the condition for the individual to become a net seller of X (specializing in production of X), despite the existence of a price gap G due to proportional transaction costs, is that *the low net price P_x^- must exceed* the common value of $MRS_C = MRS_T$ at the autarky point. Again, a corresponding argument will apply to the opposite case of specialization in production of Y: this will occur only if the high gross price P_x^+ *is less than* the common value of $MRS_C = MRS_T$ at R^*.

Let us now make the connection between the individual's optimizing decision and market equilibrium. We saw in Section 7.D that in *costless* exchange there is a unique autarky price P_x^o at which the individual's net transaction demand

Chapter 8
COST OF
EXCHANGE
AND THE ROLE
OF MONEY

241

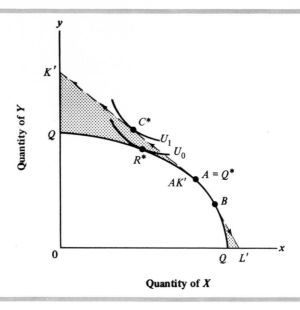

Figure 8.6

Opportunity Set with Transaction Costs: Specialization Solution. Here R^* does not lie between the tangency points A and B on QQ. The productive optimum Q^* is at point A (the individual specializes in production of good X). The consumptive optimum C^* lies to the northwest along AK', indicating that the individual sells some of the produced X (at the low selling price $P_{\bar{x}}$) to obtain the desired consumption quantity of Y.

x^t, i.e., the difference between gross (consumptive) demand x and total (productive) supply x^q, will be zero. Below this price the individual will be a positive net demander; above, a positive net supplier. Panel (a) of Figure 8.7 represents this situation. The underlying picture is exactly that portrayed in Figure 7.7 (the superscript t having been deleted). Furthermore, under conditions of costless exchange we see in Panel (b) that the aggregate market supply and market demand curves—the horizontal summations of the individual transaction supply and transaction demand curves—must intersect at an equilibrium representing a positive volume of transactions ($X^* > 0$). The only exception would be if, by some unbelievable coincidence, every individual in the market had exactly the same autarky price P_x^o.

With proportional costs of transacting, the individual and overall market situations are represented in Figure 8.8. In Panel (a) the autarky price P_x^o for any individual is the common value of $MRS_C = MRS_T$ at his Crusoe solution R^*. If the low *net* price $P_{\bar{x}}$ exceeds P_x^o, the individual will be a supplier to the market as shown by the dashed curve labelled $s(P_{\bar{x}})$. Similarly, this person will be a net demander only if the high *gross* price P_x^+ is lower than P_x^o, as shown by the solid curve labelled $d(P_x^+)$. Thus, it is the *inner pair* of curves that directly show the individual's market behavior. It is convenient, however, also to show the (solid) supply curve in terms of the gross price, $s(P_x^+)$ and the (dashed) demand curve in

Chapter 8
COST OF
EXCHANGE
AND THE ROLE
OF MONEY

242

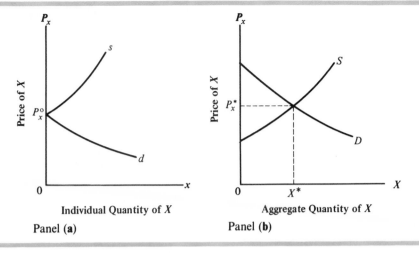

Figure 8.7

Supply and Demand, Costless Exchange. In Panel (a), s represents the transaction supply curve and d the transaction demand curve (denoted s^t and d^t in Figure 7.7) under costless exchange. At prices above the autarky price P_x^o, this individual will supply a positive quantity of X to the market; below P_x^o, a positive quantity will be demanded. In Panel (b), S and D are the aggregate market-wide transaction supply and demand curves whose intersection determines the equilibrium price P_x^* and quantity exchanged X^*.

terms of the net price, $d(P_x^-)$. Each of these differs from its partner by the constant vertical distance G—the price gap.

Summing over all the individuals, we have the corresponding pairs of aggregate market supply and demand curves shown in Panel (b). Now we can see why it was convenient to draw the curves in terms of both gross and net prices. For, the solution that determines the gross or buying price P_x^+ will be at the intersection of $S(P_x^+)$ and $D(P_x^+)$, the two solid curves. This intersection will be at the same market quantity X' as the intersection of the two dashed curves $S(P_x^-)$ and $D(P_x^-)$ that determines the net or selling price P_x^-. The two prices are related by the fixed gap G that was assumed to represent the fee charged in equilibrium by middlemen.

What would happen if the bid–ask spread, the size of the gap G, were to increase? In Panel (a) of Figure 8.8 the *inner pair* of curves would remain unchanged, since they directly represent individual behavior in terms of the relevant (gross or net) prices. But the outer pair of curves would be pushed further outward as G rises. Since the equilibrium solution determined in Panel (b) necessarily involves an intersection with one or the other of the outer curves, *the consequence of higher transaction costs is a fall in the volume of transactions.*

CONCLUSION: Proportional transaction costs create a gap between buying price and selling price. The higher the transaction charges, the more likely that individuals will choose autarky solutions, and the smaller the aggregate volume of market trading.

Chapter 8
COST OF
EXCHANGE
AND THE ROLE
OF MONEY

243

Figure 8.8

Supply and Demand, Proportional Exchange Cost. In Panel (a), for a given individual the inner pair of curves represent the transaction supply as a function of the *net* selling price P_x^- (where this exceeds the autarky price P_x^o) and the transaction demand as a function of the *gross* buying price P_x^+ (where this is less than the autarky price). The upper solid curve shows supply as related to the gross price, and the lower dashed curve shows demand as related to the net price. Panel (b) pictures the market-wide aggregates of these four curves. The equilibrium quantity X' is found at the intersection of either the two (solid) curves defined in terms of the gross prices or the two (dashed) curves defined in terms of the net prices; the equilibrium gross and net prices are determined accordingly.

EXAMPLE 8.4
URBAN–FARM
FOOD COST
DIFFERENTIALS

In the absence of transaction costs, there would be no reason for a specialist in the *production* of commodity X to be a particularly heavy consumer of X. The tailor would not have an unusually ample wardrobe, the candlestick-maker would not substitute his product for electric lights in his home, and the Detroit assembly-line worker would have no special inducement to drive a car rather than use public transit. It follows that where we *do* observe a producer heavily consuming his or her own product, transaction costs are likely to be an important factor.

Urban and farm consumption expenditures for 1960–61 were studied by F. Y. Lee and K. E. Phillips. As can be seen in the table below, farmers spend relatively more on "Food prepared at home," urban-dwellers relatively more on "Food prepared away from home." There seems little reason to doubt that transaction costs impose a greater degree of autarky upon farmers, making it more advantageous for them to consume home-prepared food. Farmers must, on the average, travel a longer distance to non-home sources of food such as restaurants. And upon getting there, they will to some degree be consuming at relatively high prices (after adding on middleman charges of all descriptions) products very similar to those available back home on the farm without payment of transaction charges.

Of course, transaction costs may not be the *sole* explanation of the divergence visible in the table. It may be that farmers simply have a greater comparative preference for home-prepared food (if not, they might not have chosen farming as an occupation). Perhaps more important, in the period studied farm families on the average were poorer than urban families. Since "Food prepared away from home" is a relatively superior good (income elasticity greater than unity), the income difference may also provide a partial explanation.

Percent of Total Consumption Expenditures

EXPENDITURE	NORTHEAST		WEST	
	URBAN	FARM	URBAN	FARM
Food prepared at home	21.0%	31.0%	18.9%	27.5%
Food prepared away from home	4.8	3.0	4.9	2.9

Source: F. Y. Lee and K. E. Phillips, "Differences in Consumption Patterns of Farm and Non-Farm Households in the United States," *American Journal of Agricultural Economics,* v. 53 (Nov. 1971), p. 575.

With a sufficiently large transaction cost G, there would be no exchange whatsoever in the entire market. Under costless trading, total absence of market transactions could occur only with a fantastic coincidence of all the individuals' autarky prices P_x^o. But given that trading costs exist, markets can easily disappear or become non-viable. In poorer economies active trading occurs in products like used containers and cigarettes by the unit (rather than by the pack)—markets not seen in wealthier countries. The market for used clothes is one that has substantially disappeared in recent years in the United States; it has become cheaper to throw used clothes away than to pay a middleman to resell them.

A per-unit tax on transactions, we have seen, is a special case of proportional trading costs. The point just made therefore corresponds with the well-known result that a tax can become so large as to be *prohibitive*. "The power to tax is the power to destroy."

The model of proportional exchange costs discussed above is a simplification. But it does explain a number of important aspects of the process of exchange observed in the world: among them, the normal gap between buying and selling prices, and the viability or non-viability of markets as transaction costs rise or fall. But one crucial aspect of exchange has not been explained: the holding of *inventories* (stocks of goods) for purposes of trading. All the models so far studied in this book have taken the form of continuous *flows*—of production, consumption, and

*8.C.2
Lump-Sum
Transaction
Costs

* The section between the asterisk and the symbol ■ may contain somewhat more difficult or advanced material.

exchange—over time. In such models, at least in the simple versions dealt with to this point, there was no need for *stocks* of commodities to be held by anyone. But in real life people do not transact continuously; we go to market at discrete separated moments of time. Over the intervals between transactions, traders must accumulate and decumulate inventories of goods purchased or to be sold.

In this section, the role of the elements of cost associated with the discreteness of transactions will be highlighted. Let us make the extreme assumption that costs of exchange take only the form of a fixed lump-sum *charge per transaction*. This obviously provides a strong incentive for the trader to minimize the number of transactions engaged in per unit of time. On the other hand, the less frequent the transactions the larger the inventories needed to bridge over the intervals between successive trips to market. The cost of holding inventories must be balanced against the cost of frequent trading.

Suppose the lump-sum charge is a fixed amount F, incurred for each transaction. The individual trader's decision problem may be interpreted as the choice of an *optimal trading interval* θ. Figure 8.9 shows a possible inventory history for an individual with constant production and consumption flows of a commodity X, making discrete trades at a time-interval of θ. There is a self-supplied productive flow at the rate x^q. At discrete intervals θ, 2θ, 3θ, etc., the individual purchases a quantity χ (not a flow, but a stock magnitude) of commodity X. This makes it possible to maintain a level consumption flow of $x^c = x^q + (\chi/\theta)$ continuously. For example, if $x^q = 10$ units per day, χ is 140 units, and $\theta = 7$ days, a consumption rate of $10 + \frac{140}{7} = 30$ units per day can be maintained.

Figure 8.9

Inventory History for an Individual. The individual has a self-supplied continuous production flow x^q while maintaining a continuous consumption flow x^c, the difference being made up by discrete market purchases at time-intervals θ. At each multiple of θ, inventory falls to zero and a new stock quantity χ is purchased to re-commence the cycle.

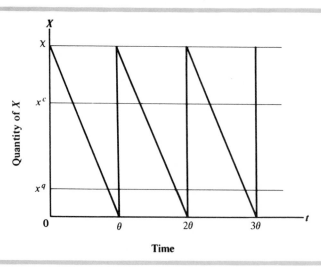

Chapter 8
COST OF
EXCHANGE
AND THE ROLE
OF MONEY

246

As a net purchaser of X, this person would have to be a net seller of the "other" commodity Y; a similar diagram, showing regular accumulation rather than decumulation of inventory between trades, could be constructed to portray the inventory history for commodity Y.

Now let us consider the individual's decision as to *autarky*, i.e., as to the desirability of engaging in trade at all. Figure 8.10 shows a situation where autarky is preferred; the "Robinson Crusoe solution" R^*, at the tangency of the Production-Possibility Curve QQ and the indifference curve U_1, is the best position attainable. In the lump-sum transaction cost model, it is important to appreciate that there are two distinguishable disadvantages of trading. The first is *inventory holding costs*. In the diagram these have the effect of contracting the production possibilities of X and Y from the solid QQ curve to the dashed $\hat{Q}\hat{Q}$ curve; resources devoted to maintaining inventories cannot be applied to production. The second disadvantage is, of course, the *lump-sum trading charges* themselves—the explicit fees F paid at each transaction. In the diagram, the average fee incurred per unit of time is represented by the vertical distance $\hat{Q}^* - N^*$. This distance is equal to F/θ, paid out in units of Y. The key point to appreciate is

Figure 8.10

Autarky and Lump-Sum Transaction Costs. An autarky solution can be attained at R^* on the (solid) Production-Possibility Curve QQ. But if trading is engaged in, inventories must be held, reducing the effective production possibilities to the (dashed) $\hat{Q}\hat{Q}$. Also, lump-sum transaction charges F must be paid, representing a cost of F/θ per unit of time—represented by the vertical distance $\hat{Q}^*N^*$. The best the individual can do via trading is to move along the market line NN. In this diagram the autarky solution R^* (on indifference curve U_1) is preferred to the best position C^* (on U_0) that can be attained through trading.

that the individual in this model must, short of choosing the autarky solution, trade along the market line NN, parallel to but below the market line MM that is tangent to $\hat{Q}\hat{Q}$. The line NN represents the *effective* trading opportunities, the combinations of X and Y achievable in the market after payout of the average lump-sum charges F/θ per unit of time.

Autarky is of course not inevitable. Lowered costs of holding inventories would decrease the gap between QQ and $\hat{Q}\hat{Q}$; lowered transaction charges would decrease the gap between MM and NN. Either of these forces would tend to make the trading solution (the tangency C^* with the highest indifference curve attained along the market line NN) relatively more attractive in comparison with the autarky solution R^*. For the trading solution to be superior, C^* would of course have to lie on a higher indifference curve than R^*.

Even with trading costs held constant, the outcome as to autarky or trading will depend upon the market price P_x. Returning to Figure 8.10, as P_x falls the absolute slope of MM and NN will decrease. The tangency of MM with $\hat{Q}\hat{Q}$ (the point $\hat{Q}^*$) will rotate along $\hat{Q}\hat{Q}$ to the northwest, enlarging the trading opportunity set toward the southeast of the diagram. Eventually, a price may be reached at which the trading optimum C^* along NN will be preferred to R^*—the individual will enter the market as a net demander of X. Similarly, at a sufficiently high price P_x the person may enter the market as a net supplier of X.

Translating this information into a supply–demand representation, Figure 8.11 is the analog (for lump-sum transaction charges) of Panel (a) of Figure 8.8 that applied to proportional transaction costs. But here there is no divergence between the buying price and selling price; in this case, middlemen are reimbursed

Figure 8.11

Individual Net Supply and Demand, Lump-Sum Transaction Cost. Market price must diverge from the autarky price P_x^0 by a certain discrete amount before the individual will enter the market as a supplier or a demander. If the price divergence is just great enough, the individual will offer or demand a minimal discrete quantity—represented by the point J where the supply curve begins and the point H where the demand curve begins.

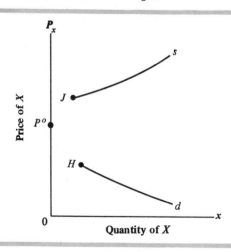

Chapter 8
COST OF
EXCHANGE
AND THE ROLE
OF MONEY

248

by lump-sum transaction payments F, not by a price gap G. As before, for each individual there is an autarky price P_x^o represented by the common slope $MRS_C = MRS_T$ at his Crusoe solution R^*. There will now be a *range* of prices around the autarky price for which it will not pay the individual to undergo both the inventory holding costs and the lump-sum transaction charges of entering the market. But as the market price P_x increasingly diverges from P_x^o, consumptive combinations that are attainable only by trading become increasingly attractive. For a sufficiently wide divergence, it will pay to incur the average trading fee F/θ and the inventory costs associated with market exchanges.

Another interesting feature of Figure 8.11 is that the supply and demand curves do not go all the way to the vertical axis, but are shown as beginning at the respective points J and H in the interior of the diagram. There must be a certain minimal discrete divergence of P_x upward or downward of the autarky price P_x^o before it pays to trade at all—and when trade does begin to pay, there will also be a discrete minimal quantity offered or demanded. (Verification of this point is left as a challenge to the more advanced student.)

The individual transaction supply and demand curves can as usual be aggregated, in analogy with Panel (b) of Figure 8.8, into market-wide supply and demand curves. Again, in contrast with the situation under costless exchange where the market-wide curves necessarily intersected in the interior so that positive trading takes place (unless all the different individuals' autarky prices are identical), for lump-sum transaction costs as for proportional transaction costs there is a serious possibility that the market-wide curves do not intersect. If so, the market disappears; there is no price at which any buyer-seller pair of traders are willing to incur the transaction charges and associated inventory costs of market dealings in preference to autarky solutions.

CONCLUSION: Lump-sum transaction costs do not create a price gap. But they dictate that exchanges take place at discrete intervals, so that inventories must be held. Transaction charges plus inventory costs due to trading make individual autarky solutions more likely, reduce the aggregate volume of market trade, and may even totally destroy the market. ∎

8.D

THE ROLE OF MONEY

Money is a device that reduces the cost of market trading. But it does not, and in the nature of the case cannot, *reduce the cost of physical transfers*—which are, as described in Section 8.A, essentially an aspect of production. As to transportation, for example, geographical dispersion of producers and consumers will dictate shipping costs that would have to be incurred even in a perfectly functioning command economy. Money can do nothing to reduce these shipping costs. And similarly, imperfect synchronization of production and consumption will dictate

Chapter 8
COST OF
EXCHANGE
AND THE ROLE
OF MONEY

249

the presence of commodity inventories at various places along the manufacturer-wholesaler-retailer-consumer chain. Again, money cannot eliminate this category of expense.

What money does is to reduce trading costs proper, the cost of integrating individual activities through the process of voluntary exchange. Money thus tends to counter the tendency toward autarky so as to promote a more efficient division of labor. It does so by serving the two key functions of *medium of exchange* and *temporary store of value*. These functions can be best visualized if we consider three social regimes in logical succession: (1) pure command economy, with no trading whatsoever but only dictated physical commodity transfers; (2) barter economy, with trading but without any monetary commodity; and (3) money economy.

Money as medium of exchange:

To fix ideas, suppose that there are N commodities, each produced by a single individual. In the absence of any transfer or trading costs, imagine that all N persons would be willing to consume positive quantities of all N goods. Thus, there is specialization in production but diversity in consumption—the normal situation.

Under a pure command regime, let us suppose the dictator is perfectly efficient and benevolent. In this economy there is no resource "wastage" due to costs of *trading*, i.e., no bidding, negotiating, contracting, etc. Even so, pure costs of *transfer* such as transportation expense may rule out some of the $N(N-1)$ possible commodity movements as uneconomic. Suppose that oranges are produced in California, and lobsters in Maine. Lobsters might be so expensive to ship that, from the viewpoint of overall economic efficiency, the dictator correctly decides that Californians would have to do without them. But if oranges are not very costly to ship, the dictator might still find it feasible and efficient to command that California oranges be sent to Maine.

Now suppose that a revolution displaces the dictator, substituting a regime of barter trade. In this regime, we will suppose, *only two-party trade is feasible*. (In actuality, multi-party transactions can and do take place, but they seem to be exceedingly costly to negotiate and enforce and are therefore relatively rare.) Then, and this is the crucial point, instead of the $N(N-1)$ possible *one-directional commodity movements* that were available to the dictator in a command economy, under bilateral barter only $N(N-1)/2$ possible *two-way channels of exchange* are possible. If shipment of Maine lobsters to California is barred by the high costs of physical transfer (transportation cost), then the two-way channel is blocked. The California oranges cannot go to Maine either, since the lobstermen cannot provide appropriate compensation. As compared with an ideal command economy (perfectly efficient and benevolent dictator), not only is there wastage of resources due to the necessity of negotiating trades but also an inferior allocation of production and consumption due to a higher degree of autarky.

We can now see how the invention of a universal *medium of exchange* improves matters. The medium of exchange can be one of the original N goods or it

Chapter 8
COST OF
EXCHANGE
AND THE ROLE
OF MONEY

250

can be an artificial $(N + 1)$th commodity like paper money. In either case, the effect is *to make multilateral trading indirectly possible through a bilateral accounting device*.

Suppose, to begin with, that one of the N initial commodities is chosen as medium of exchange. In the prisoner-of-war situation of Example 4.1, *cigarettes* served this function. But in keeping with modern economic history, we will speak of *gold* as medium of exchange. Then all the other commodities are no longer traded for one another, but only for gold. This involves a saving, in that there is a drastic reduction in the number of markets that must be provided.

For the moment, let us assume there are no markets blocked under barter by the high real turnover costs in one direction (e.g., by the cost of shipping Maine lobsters to California). In general, the number of two-way trading channels required is $N(N - 1)/2$. Then if there are five goods (four ordinary consumption goods A, B, C, D, plus gold G), Figure 8.12 pictures the 5(4)/2 or *ten* trading channels. But if all other commodities are traded only for gold, *four* channels or markets will suffice. In general, the market system of a money (gold) economy would be required to generate prices and to execute exchanges for only $N - 1$ types of transactions. As compared with barter, there will be a considerable reduction of the costs of finding trading partners and negotiating, recording, and enforcing trades.

Figure 8.12

Trading Channels—Five Goods. With five commodities, under two-way barter exchange there would have to be *ten* channels of trade or markets. If commodity G is instead the sole "medium of exchange," only *four* markets would be needed.

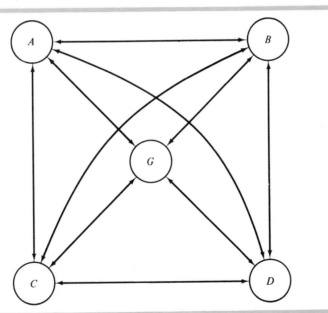

Chapter 8
COST OF
EXCHANGE
AND THE ROLE
OF MONEY

251

But this direct saving has less overall importance than the *indirect* gain due to the greater degree of productive specialization made possible. Consider the lobster-orange example once again. With gold as medium of exchange, the Maine lobsters will still not go to California; the physical transfer costs remain excessive. But the California oranges can now go to Maine! For, the Maine lobstermen can pay for oranges in gold that they obtain by selling lobsters to other, non-Californian customers. Thus, gold makes possible triangular or still more complex turnovers, without requiring anything beyond bilateralism in trading.

There is, however, one element of cost likely to be greater in a gold economy than in a barter economy: There will be greatly increased handling and shipping back and forth of *gold*, the monetary commodity itself. Clearing arrangements, one aspect of banking, will arise to reduce these costs. Also, gold as medium of exchange can be replaced by an artificial commodity (e.g., paper money) for which the shipping and handling costs are less. Ultimately the money economy tends to move toward a non-physical, purely abstract medium of exchange, *banking deposits*, to minimize handling costs of money.

Money as temporary store of value:

So far we have considered money only as medium of exchange, an intermediating commodity in transactions. A mere intermediating commodity could exist as a pure flow—a good produced and consumed at a constant rate over time. The only difference between it and other flow goods would be that it works somewhat harder, entering into multiple transactions on the way from production to consumption. Thus, a single cigarette in the P.O.W. camp example might pass through many hands, helping to mediate many transactions, before eventually being smoked as a consumer good. But we generally think of money not as a flow good but as a stock. A butcher and baker, in trading with one another, produce and consume flows of meat and bread. But over any time period, each will begin and end with a *stock* holding of money. As temporary store of value ("abode of purchasing power"), inventories of money bridge time gaps between receipts and payments. By carrying an inventory of money a baker can obtain meat today, even though out of bread for sale until tomorrow.

We saw above that, even in a pure command regime where no voluntary exchange occurs, imperfect synchronization of the processes of production, transportation, and consumption will lead to the existence of inventories of all types of goods as they are passed along the interpersonal transfer chain. The unique feature of a *monetary inventory* is that it is held to facilitate the process whereby goods are transferred by the specific mode of market exchange.

Consider once again the revolution that overthrows the dictator of a pure command economy, substituting a regime of barter exchange. Now *trading inventories* come into existence. Let three individuals a, b, c be sole specialized producers of commodities A, B, and C, respectively. Imagine that to meet consumption preferences the desired pattern of trade is triangular: Commodity A is to flow from a to b, commodity B from b to c, and commodity C from c to a. If multilateral trading is ruled out, we have here the famous "double coincidence" problem

Chapter 8
COST OF
EXCHANGE
AND THE ROLE
OF MONEY

252

of barter. Consider individual b, who wants commodity A from individual a but produces nothing that the latter wants from him. Although b can provide commodity B to individual c, the latter produces nothing that b desires.

Under triangular barter, this dilemma could be resolved by having some or all individuals hold inventories of the third commodity, i.e., the one they neither produce nor consume. With a great many individuals and a great number of commodities, barter exchange requires an enormous extent and variety of such holdings. Essentially all the people involved would have to carry trading inventories of numerous commodities they neither produce nor wish to consume. They must accept goods in exchange for commodities they do produce, in order to have something available for exchange (when opportunity permits) for commodities they wish to consume.

Rather than hold a multiplicity of different trading inventories, it is obviously efficient for all traders to agree to accept in exchange some single "store of value" commodity. It should be a commodity both cheap to produce and cheap to store, and preferably one that is not eroded (as were cigarettes in the P.O.W. example) by consumption. These criteria will enter into the selection of gold (or some alternative commodity) as the monetary medium. Again, there will be a natural tendency to move toward a money having the form of a purely abstract artificial commodity like banking deposits, almost costless to produce and to store, and not needed for consumption.

CONCLUSION: The invention of money reduces the costs of market trading, not the costs of physical transfers which would be required in any economic system employing a division of labor. With a money serving as *medium of exchange,* all other goods may be traded for amounts of the single monetary commodity. This reduces the number of two-way market channels required, and makes triangular or even more circuitous trade patterns viable that would be excessively costly or impossible under barter. Where inventories of goods must be carried for trading purposes, this is done most economically by holding the single monetary commodity—which then serves also as *temporary store of value.*

An interesting network of exchanges among primitive peoples in the East Indies was analyzed by the anthropologist M. Sahlins.[7] A puzzling problem was described by Sahlins. The Busama, who serve as middlemen between the Tami Islanders and certain southern villages, allegedly acquire bowls worth 10 to 12 shillings from Tami Island which they then carry to the south and exchange one-for-one against pots worth only 8 shillings!

The supposed explanation is that, while pots and bowls are desired throughout the region, the Busama are producers of taro which is wanted only by the southern villagers. The latter can only pay in pots. As these are

EXAMPLE 8.5
BARTER IN THE
EAST INDIES

[7]Marshall Sahlins, *Stone Age Economics* (Chicago: Aldine-Atherton, Inc., 1972), Chap. 6.

in excess of the Busama's own requirements, the Busama carry the excess pots to Tami and exchange them against bowls as the only product there available. The quantity of bowls thus acquired being again in excess of the Busama's own needs, some are carried back down to the southern villages to be traded along with taro once again for pots.

COMMENT: It is clearly not rational for the Busama to carry bowls from Tami—where they are, according to the report, *more* highly valued than pots (10 to 12 shillings against 8)—to southern villages where bowls are relatively *less* highly valued (one against one). Indeed, the logic of the situation strongly suggests that the relative values have been misreported. Surely the pots are relatively less highly valued where they are plentiful, at their origin in the south, and the bowls relatively less highly valued at their origin on Tami Island. Only if this is the case does the two-way shipping traffic of the Busama become understandable. The Busama must accept pots from the southern villagers, their only customers for taro, but nothing forces the Busama to carry bowls from north to south at a loss.

Another point to note is that since this is a situation of barter exchanges, the cited shilling values may lack any real meaning. Since shillings are not actually employed everywhere in the region as a medium of exchange, price quotations may be reported that do not reflect the actual terms in which trades are taking place. Thus, a pot may be "worth" 8 shillings somewhere, but not necessarily on Tami Island, if shillings are not actually exchanged for pots there.

SUMMARY OF CHAPTER 8

This chapter examines the process of exchange and, in particular, costs and imperfections of the trading process and the consequent invention of money as a device for minimizing these costs and imperfections. The costs associated with *trading* must not be confused with costs due simply to interpersonal physical *transfers* of commodities. The latter would persist in any economic system (even one of total command socialism) so long as individuals specialize in production.

"Perfect competition" is an idealized situation in which price-taking individuals interact in perfect markets. Perfect markets in turn involve perfect communication among buyers and sellers, instantaneous equilibrium (so that no trading takes place at "false prices"), and costless transactions. Actual markets can at best approximate these ideal conditions.

Chapter 8
COST OF EXCHANGE AND THE ROLE OF MONEY

Costs of trading are, most importantly, a function of the volume of goods exchanged and the number of distinct transactions that have to be made per unit of time. The former can be isolated by assuming transaction costs proportional to the quantity of goods changing hands, the latter by assuming costs incurred as a fixed lump-sum each time a transaction takes place.

Proportional transaction costs are similar, from the traders' point of view, to excise taxes. In equilibrium the gross price P_x^+ paid by buyers will exceed the net price P_x^- received by sellers, by the amount of the unit transaction expense.

And of course the volume of goods exchanged will be less than in a hypothetical world free of transaction costs. *Lump-sum* transaction costs provide an incentive to minimize the number of distinct transactions. In consequence, inventories of goods purchased and sold must be held between trading dates. Both types of transaction costs diminish the extent of specialization in production, and make autarky solutions more likely.

Money is a device that reduces the cost of trading. As *medium of exchange* the existence of money lessens the number of different two-way channels of exchange that must be provided (in comparison with barter). This lowers the costs of collecting information, keeping records, and shipping goods to settle transactions. As *store of value,* money economizes on inventories that would have to be carried for trading purposes under barter. As a result of these cost savings, the institution of money makes possible a higher degree of specialization in production.

QUESTIONS FOR CHAPTER 8

Mainly for Review

*R1. How can there be "price-taking" behavior if supply curves and demand curves are not really horizontal?

R2. What are perfect markets? What is perfect competition?

*R3. Can autarky occur in costless exchange? Why is autarky more likely, the higher the transaction costs? Do you think the increasing burdens of payroll taxes (income tax, Social Security tax) and sales taxes in recent decades have anything to do with the "do-it-yourself" trend observed in such areas of activity as furniture construction and repair, car maintenance, dressmaking, etc.?

R4. Some markets are illegal (markets for babies, for narcotic drugs, for government favors, and so on). Law enforcement that is short of being *totally* effective can be regarded as imposing a transaction cost upon participants. In terms of this chapter's analysis, what effects would you anticipate from increased law-enforcement effort against the narcotics traffic? Would the volume of transactions be affected? What about the gross price paid by buyers in comparison with the net price received by sellers?

R5. Illustrate how sufficiently heavy *proportional* transaction costs might make a market non-viable. Do the same for *lump-sum* transaction costs.

*R6. Since the existence of markets necessarily involves some burden of transaction costs, wouldn't a command economy dispensing with markets always be more efficient? Explain.

R7. Distinguish between transfer costs and exchange costs. How would you class transportation of goods between producer and consumer? What about the costs of negotiating a contract? Enforcing a contract?

Chapter 8
COST OF
EXCHANGE
AND THE ROLE
OF MONEY

* The answers to asterisked questions appear at the end of the book.

*T1. Give examples of markets that have existed historically, but do not now exist. Can you explain their disappearance?

T2. According to the economist K. E. Boulding, a tariff can be regarded as a "negative railroad"—whereas a railroad *connects* trading communities, a tariff *separates* them. Is the analogy valid?

*T3. How can integration of individuals' productive and consumptive choices be achieved *without* the use of markets? Can it be achieved with markets, but without the use of money?

*T4. Flowers provide bees with nectar, while bees facilitate the pollination of flowers. Is this exchange?

T5. Fresh fruits are cheaper at farm roadstands than in city markets. Does the price difference reflect transfer costs or exchange costs, or are there elements of each?

T6. Give examples of exchange costs that are reduced by the existence of money as a *medium of exchange*. Of money as a *store of value*.

*T7. If *rationing* is introduced, money is no longer fully effective as a medium of exchange. What types of additional exchange costs emerge in a world where ration coupons and cash are *both* required in order to effectuate a transaction?

*T8. According to elementary textbooks, a commodity selected to serve as money should be portable, divisible, storable, generally recognizable, and homogeneous. In terms of the discussion in this chapter, why are these desirable qualities? Can you think of other desirable qualities? [*Hint:* Think of cigarettes serving as money in a prisoner-of-war camp.]

T9. Suppose a gasoline tax is imposed, taking the form of a fixed number of cents per gallon (the same for regular and for premium gas), and assume that the supply curves for regular and premium gas are both horizontal. Consider the following arguments. (1) While we'd expect the quantity demanded of both premium and regular gasoline to fall after the tax is imposed, there should be a *relatively smaller* effect for the premium quality—since a fixed number of cents is a smaller *proportionate* tax for the premium gas. (2) On the contrary, we'd expect a *relatively bigger* effect for the premium quality—because premium gasoline is more of a "luxury" good, and the regular gasoline more of a "necessity" good. Is one or the other of these arguments totally wrong, or is it a matter of which of two valid arguments is the stronger? Analyze each argument separately, and explain.

PART FOUR
The Firm
and
The Industry

9.A   FIRMS AND THE CIRCULAR FLOW OF ECONOMIC ACTIVITY, 260

9.B   WHY FIRMS? THE ROLE OF THE ENTREPRENEUR, 262

9.C   THE GOAL OF THE FIRM AS OPTIMIZING AGENT, 265

9.D   PRODUCTION FUNCTION AND COST FUNCTION, 270
      9.D.1   From Production Function to Cost Function—Single Variable Factor, 271
    *9.D.2   From Production Function to Cost Function—Several Variable Factors, 278

9.E   OPTIMUM OF THE COMPETITIVE FIRM—SHORT RUN AND LONG RUN, 288

Examples
    9.1   THE EFFECTIVENESS OF MANAGEMENT, 263
    9.2   NON-PROFIT GOALS AND ''TECHNOSTRUCTURE ORIENTATION,'' 266
    9.3   SAVINGS AND LOAN ASSOCIATIONS—STOCK VERSUS MUTUAL, 267
    9.4   COTTON IRRIGATION EXPERIMENT, 273
    9.5   MISSOURI CORN, 280
    9.6   PIGS, 282
    9.7   LOAD DISPATCHING: ELECTRICAL ENGINEERS AS ECONOMISTS, 286
    9.8   ELECTRICITY: SHORT-RUN AND LONG-RUN COSTS, 297

THE BUSINESS FIRM

9

Core Chapter

In Part Two of this book, the consuming *individual* or *household* held the center of attention. In Part Three, attention shifted to the interaction of individuals through the *market*. We will be concentrating in Part Four upon the *business firm*, and upon the aggregate of firms in a given market that we call the *industry*. This chapter is devoted specifically to the firm. Chapter 10 following will develop the relationships between the competitive (price-taking) firm and the industry; later chapters will be devoted to firms and industries under conditions other than perfect competition.

9.A

FIRMS AND THE CIRCULAR FLOW OF ECONOMIC ACTIVITY

Referring back to Figure 1.1, in that diagram one of the two poles of the circular flow of economic activity is the class of economic agents we call individuals—natural persons, or groupings of such persons into households. Economic analysis usually takes the existence of natural persons as a given fact determined "outside" the economic system (see Section 2.A.2 above). But actually, the size of the human population does respond to economic incentives, as has been recognized since the time of Malthus.[1] Economic conditions influence birth rates and death rates, as well as immigration and emigration movements. And the clustering of individuals into families and households is also in part a response to economic circumstances; the marriage rate rises, for example, when business conditions are favorable (see also Example 4.3).[2] But in this text the existing numbers and types of individuals or households will generally be taken as fixed elements of the economic situation. Individuals or households constitute the *demand side* of the "product market," the market for consumption goods and services discussed in previous chapters. And they also constitute the *supply side* of the "factor market," the market for resources employed in production. (The factor market will be the object of attention in Part Five of the text.)

The other pole of economic activity is the business firm. The firm, as an artificial entity created in response to economic incentives, is clearly a subject for economic attention. For our purposes, the emphasis will be upon firms as the crucial *productive* agents of society,[3] engaged in the conversion of resources into final goods.[4] Thus, firms constitute the supply side of the product market and the demand side of the factor market.

The invention of *money*, as discussed in the chapter preceding, facilitates the process of exchange and consequent specialization in production. The diagram of the circular flow of economic activity, Figure 1.1, shows two opposed circuits: a "real" flow of productive services from individuals to firms and then of consumptive goods from firms to individuals, balanced by a "financial" flow of expenditures from individuals to firms (purchase of goods) and then from firms back to individuals (payment for resource services). Even in the absence of a money commodity, resource-supplying individuals could hardly be compensated *directly* out of the physical output of firms. Workers in a candy shop would not want to take their wages in bonbons. So firms would have to suffer the inconvenience of barter in converting their products into the various consumption goods desired by resource-suppliers in payment for their services. Under barter conditions firms would therefore tend to be much less specialized, themselves producing a diversity of commodities of interest to their resource-suppliers. In contrast, if a monetary medium of exchange exists, firms need only provide *indirect* (monetary or financial) compensation to resource-suppliers. As this can be done regardless of the physical nature of the firm's own output, firms can specialize to whatever extent is

[1]T. R. Malthus (1766–1834), English clergyman and economist. Malthus maintained that population would always tend to expand to the limits of subsistence. His views had an important influence upon Charles Darwin's thinking that culminated in the theory of biological evolution.

[2]Following the tendency of economics to overflow conventional boundaries in finding applications for our analytical tools (see Section 1.A.2), there has been a recent flowering of exciting economic investigations in which such topics as population size, family formation, and education of children are subjected to analysis using the tools of economics.

[3]Of course, households also engage in production. Indeed, in primitive societies there is *only* household production; the institution we call the firm is absent. In modern economies the firm is the characteristic unit for organizing production.

[4]As was indicated above, our analysis of the productive process will be simplified by excluding complications connected with the existence of partially finished or "intermediate" goods.

productively advantageous. Conversely, existence of a medium of exchange permits any individual to supply productive resources to whatever firm can use them most effectively; he or she need not be a consumer of the good produced by that firm.

9.B

WHY FIRMS? THE ROLE OF THE ENTREPRENEUR

But we could have productive specialization without firms. Why does a special kind of economic agent, apart from natural individuals, emerge for this purpose? The key to the answer is two-fold: (1) Production opportunities are commonly *multi-personal*, and (2) exchange through the market is, as discussed in the chapter preceding, not a costless process—despite the existence of money.

The productive transformation opportunities examined to this point belonged only to single individuals. In Figure 7.6, for example, a typical individual had a productive opportunity set bounded by the curve QQ that shows the alternative combinations of commodities X and Y the person can produce as a "Robinson Crusoe" apart from the existence of a market. The consequences of opening up a market in which the individual can trade X for Y, or vice versa, were analyzed in Chapters 7 and 8. It was implicitly assumed there that the emergence of the individual from isolation *did not affect the productive opportunity set itself*. But it is a fact of the greatest practical importance that the possibilities of multi-person or "team" production enormously expand output potentialities. The advantages of the division of labor lie not only in specialization in terms of *products* (shoemaker, butcher, baker) but also in the specialization of *tasks* in the joint production of a given end-product (clerk, assembly-line worker, inspector, foreman, etc.). Indeed, our modern economy could not exist without such specialization of tasks.

But the mere fact that attractive productive opportunities are multi-personal, requiring integration of the skills and resources of a number of distinct individuals, does not suffice to explain the institution of the business firm. For, even without forming a firm, it would in principle be possible to combine resources owned by many different persons via a *multilateral contract* among all the individuals concerned. In creating a motion picture, the producer, director, writer, stars, supporting actors, stagehands, cameramen, electricians, and so forth—not to mention suppliers of costumes, film, sets, and utilities—might all get together and agree upon a contract that would state for each party what types and quantities of resources each would contribute, at stated times, to the productive process. The contract must also specify, of course, each party's financial reward in the form of the division of output achieved. Such contractual arrangements are relatively rare because of the high costs of negotiating and (what is extremely important) *enforcing* multilateral contracts. The business firm provides a way of reaping the advantages of team production without going beyond *bilateral* contracting. Each resource-owner need not deal separately with every other participant in the productive process but instead only with a single artificial entity—the firm itself.

In actuality, however, the "firm" is an abstraction. People can really deal only with other persons. Therefore some person or group, called the "management," must be authorized to deal in the name of the abstract firm. The management may simply be the *owner or owners* of the firm, the residual claimants to the firm's profits or losses after meeting contractual obligations. But here again, especially where relatively large-scale productive operations are involved, a division of labor tends to come into existence. Management itself becomes a specialized kind of employed resource. The function of the manager is to make contractual agreements with other resource-suppliers and also to enforce or monitor performance of these contracts.

Using "pre-delinquent" boys in a youth home as experimental subjects, the psychologist E. L. Phillips[5] conducted experiments to evaluate the effectiveness of payment systems for the performance of various tasks. Task completion was "reinforced" by points awarded, which could be converted into desired commodities or privileges. One of the experiments involved bathroom cleaning chores.

EXAMPLE 9.1
EFFECTIVENESS OF
MANAGEMENT

The youths were assigned sixteen specific tasks to do in cleaning the bathroom. Among the experimental set-ups examined were the "group" condition and the "manager" condition. In the "group" condition, responsibility was collective. All boys received the same reward or fine, depending upon the overall group performance. In the "manager" condition, there was a weekly auction in points for the right to be responsible for the collective performance. The auction winner as manager could assign every boy to tasks, and then distribute rewards or fines based upon his judgment of the work performed. The manager himself was rewarded or fined in accordance with the overall level of achievement.

Results under the "group" condition typically showed completion of about six of the sixteen tasks. Under the "manager" condition, in contrast, about fourteen of the sixteen tasks were usually completed.

COMMENT: Under the "group" condition each boy failing to complete any task suffered only a portion of the *overall* penalty (which was assessed upon *every* boy in the group). So the incentive to work rather than shirk was weak in the absence of a manager fully responsible for achievement. (The question of how to arrange for efficient *collective action* will be discussed in more detail in Part Six below, as a problem of "political economy.")

[5]E. L. Phillips, "Achievement Place: Token Reinforcement Procedures in a Home-Style Rehabilitation Setting for 'Pre-Delinquent' Boys," *Journal of Applied Behavior Analysis*, v. 1 (Fall 1968).

A manager who is not personally the owner of the firm must of course then be monitored by someone else—ultimately, by the owner or owners themselves. Hence, an inescapable decision-making aspect attaches to firm ownership; this combined function is traditionally called *entrepreneurship*. While the institution of the firm emerges in order to achieve certain economies in transacting among resource-suppliers, the execution and enforcement of the contract *among the owners* (if there are more than one) that creates the firm, and of the contract *between the owners and the manager* (if those two functions are not combined), both pose considerable difficulties.

A variety of devices have arisen to overcome these problems. With regard to the contract among owners that creates the firm, the legal invention of the *corporate form* has greatly eased matters. By engaging in business as a corporation, large groups of people can combine their resources to exploit even very big and very risky multi-person productive opportunities. The key features of the corporation are *limited liability* and *transferable shares*. Legal and contractual obligations of the corporation, as a fictional person, cannot be brought home to the individual owner's personal account. Such a person's ownership shares may become valueless (at worst), but individual finances are otherwise safe. And an individual who is dissatisfied with the policies and procedures adopted by the other owners, or by the manager on behalf of the owners, has the option of selling out his or her shares. In consequence, the corporation is enabled to acquire and commit large amounts of resources to exploit productive opportunities, far beyond what would be achievable by a partnership without the advantages of limited liability and transferability of ownership interests. With regard to the contract between owners and management, devices like profit-sharing and stock options have emerged with the aim of linking managers' interests more closely with those of the shareholders, thus minimizing the need for detailed owner monitoring of managerial performance.

One interesting question is: Which classes of resource-suppliers tend to become the *entrepreneurs* or owners of the firm, whose compensation comes from residual profit and loss rather than fixed payment terms under contract of hire with the firm? In farming, the landowner may be the entrepreneur, hiring labor at a fixed contractual wage. Or, the working farmer (supplier of labor input) may be the entrepreneur instead, the land being leased at a fixed rental payment. There are also mixed ''share cropping'' cases, where the supplier of land and the supplier of labor share the uncertainty of residual profit and loss. In small industrial firms, *management* tends to be combined with ownership, thus avoiding the difficult problem of contracting and monitoring between the two. The owner of such a small firm will, quite commonly, also supply some labor and some of the capital required. In large industrial enterprises, on the other hand, under the corporate form the owners of the firm (stockholders) are typically only providers of capital—generalized purchasing power allowing the firm to carry on its operations. Other inputs are typically hired, including management, labor, and even capital provided at fixed contractual interest (through debt instruments such as corporate bonds).

THE GOAL OF THE FIRM AS
OPTIMIZING AGENT

Individuals maximize utility, but what do firms maximize? In the traditional formulation the firm is said to maximize *profit*, which is the difference between *revenue* and *cost*.

Revenue consists of the receipts of the firm from sales, i.e., price times quantity sold. *Cost* is a somewhat more elusive concept. The ultimate economic cost of any activity is to be interpreted as the alternative *opportunities foregone*. The firm, in order to attract the resources or "factors" necessary to engage in production, must pay resource-owners amounts sufficient to induce them to sacrifice their best alternatives, whether these alternatives be employment elsewhere, or leisure. The payments required are, of course, the going market prices for the services of the factors of production. So *cost can be regarded as the sum, taken over all resources employed, of the factor prices times factor quantities*.

There is one tricky feature here. The owner is, as defined above, the *residual* claimant to the firm's earnings. Payment for any factor services supplied by the owner himself or herself will not ordinarily be made by explicit contract but will be mixed with the residual claim. "Profit" in the legal or accounting sense fails to distinguish these two economically distinct categories. If a small merchant works long hours in his own store, his accountant will calculate a "profit" that is likely to amount to little more than a normal wage payment for the merchant's labor services. In the case of a large corporation, "profit" as reported to the Internal Revenue Service will be confounded with a normal interest return upon the funds committed by share-owners to the firm. *Economic* or "pure" profit is arrived at by deducting the normal factor return on owner inputs, sometimes called the "normal" profit, from this accounting profit. The *value in alternative uses* of all the resources employed in production (whether explicitly hired and paid for, or only implicitly hired and not separately paid for because they are provided by the owner himself) constitutes "economic" cost. *Economic profit is thus the difference between accounting profit and normal profit, and also the difference between revenue and economic cost*. In this book, unless otherwise indicated, the word "profit" will always be used in the sense of *economic* profit.

According to the classical formulation, the aim of the firm as a decision-making agent is to maximize (economic) profit. This view has not gone unchallenged, however. Some observers maintain that the behavior of large modern corporations cannot be explained in terms of the profit-maximizing hypothesis. In such corporations the *separation of ownership and control* may be carried to an extreme degree. Where no single shareowner accounts for more than a minuscule fraction of the shares outstanding, management may (it is contended) be in a position to run things without significant monitoring by nominal owners.

Of course, there are limits. If the shareholders were literally powerless, management could do whatever it wished, even dissipate the value of the firm by

Chapter 9
THE BUSINESS
FIRM

means of enormous executive salaries and expense accounts. But no management is ever given a license to steal. Shareholders as owners have judicial recourse; they can sue for damages if they believe that management has violated the contract with the owners. Such lawsuits frequently do take place, indicating that at least some owners are actually monitoring performance of management. Perhaps a more important check is the presence of competing groups anxious to take over the managerial function. Suppose a self-serving or inefficient management is in control of a corporation. Then the reduced earnings now and in prospect make the value of the corporate shares lower than they would otherwise be. An alternative management group can then try to purchase shares, at their current cheap prices, with the hope of obtaining enough for control. Or they may instead try to win the proxy votes of existing shareholders and thus overturn the current management.

The challenge to the profit-maximizing hypothesis need not, however, postulate a literally all-powerful management. The critics might admit that management aims to achieve at least a certain minimal level of (accounting) profit, enough to placate the shareholders and avoid legal sanctions. But beyond this level, the contention is, management pursues its own goals rather than those of owners. Because of the takeover threat in the background, management's goals may take a somewhat more subtle form than crude monetary emoluments. They may involve power and growth ("empire-building"), advertising or charitable outlays to enhance a favorable "corporate image" (really a management image), amenities like luxurious offices and attractive secretaries, and the pursuit of stability so as to achieve a world without risk of unpleasant surprises.

That forces like those just described are actually operative can hardly be doubted. But are they significant enough, restrained as they are by the ever-present takeover threat from outside contenders for managerial positions, to make the profit-maximization hypothesis unworkable? That is a question for empirical investigation. So far at least, there is no convincing evidence for a general formulation of the goal of the business firm that competes successfully with the classical conception of the profit-maximizing firm.

EXAMPLE 9.2
NON-PROFIT
GOALS AND
"TECHNO-
STRUCTURE
ORIENTATION"

J. K. Galbraith has given wide dissemination to the idea that the management-dominated modern American corporation does not aim to maximize profit. Among the possible competing goals satisfying management desires rather than stockholder interests, he lays particular stress upon (1) *growth of sales* and (2) *stability*.[6] In Galbraith's view, those firms he calls "technostructure-oriented" are best able to achieve these goals through devices like advertising and defense contracts.

Harold Demsetz[7] attempted to test these hypotheses by converting them into quantifiable form. Demsetz used a variety of statistical criteria to interpret Galbraith's concept of "technostructure orientation," so as to be able to

[6] J. K. Galbraith, *The New Industrial State* (Boston: Houghton Mifflin, 1967), pp. 171, 199, 210, 309–10.
[7] H. Demsetz, "Where is the New Industrial State?" *Economic Inquiry*, v. 12 (March 1974).

distinguish those firms that could be expected to adhere (on Galbraith's theory) to non-profit goals more than others. The measures of "technostructure orientation" employed by Demsetz included advertising intensity, capital intensity, and proportion of defense contracts.

With regard to sales growth as an alternative to profit-maximization, the statistical evidence was examined to see whether firms with high indexes of "technostructure orientation" tended to have high sales growth *relative to* profit rates. Had this in fact occurred, it would suggest that profit had been sacrificed for sales growth (i.e., the interests of owners for the benefit of managers) by these "technostructure-oriented" firms. But no visible effect was found in the data, except that (contradicting the tested hypothesis) high advertising intensity was found to be associated with relatively *low* sales growth relative to profit rate.

With regard to Galbraith's second stated goal, a number of alternative measures of *stability* were considered by Demsetz. But in no case was there any indication that firms with high "technostructure orientation" sacrificed profits for stability in such a way as to be distinguishable from firms of low "technostructure orientation."

The book is not yet closed on the issue of conflict between manager and owner. It may well be that, with more precise specification, classes of firms will be detected that can successfully be analyzed in terms of pursuit of non-profit goals. Among the possibilities that come to mind are *monopoly* firms and *regulated* firms, both to be discussed in Chapter 11. And the example following may be suggestive.

Alfred Nicols compared the performance of savings and loan associations organized as *corporations* owned by stockholders ("stock" associations) with those organized as *cooperatives* owned by depositors ("mutual" associations). While J. K. Galbraith (see previous example) had emphasized the separation of ownership and control in the modern corporation, this separation is carried to a far more extreme degree in the savings and loan "mutuals." It may be difficult to overturn management by takeover or proxy fight in a corporation, but legal provisions make it essentially impossible to do so in a "mutual" savings and loan association.

Nicols argued that managers of mutuals, practically free of owner-depositor control, would find ways of diverting association income to their own advantage. While Galbraith had maintained that a main management goal would be *growth* as an alternative to profit, Nicols' position is in sharp contrast. The diversion of association income to managers must mean that mutuals have less to offer their depositors. Hence income diversion to management, he argues, is necessarily in *conflict* with rapid growth.

The legislation of most states effectively bars stock associations, thus providing a competitive shield for the mutuals. But in California, where legislation has permitted competition between mutual and stock associations, the

EXAMPLE 9.3
SAVINGS AND
LOAN
ASSOCIATIONS—
STOCK VERSUS
MUTUAL

latter have indeed grown so as to sharply increase their percentage of the market at the expense of the mutuals. The table below provides comparative performance indicators for three classes of institutions: non-California institutions (overwhelmingly mutuals), California mutuals under federal charter, and California stock associations. Note that the indicators for California mutuals generally fall between those of the California stock associations and the non-California institutions; Nicols attributes this to the competitive pressure of California stock associations forcing more efficient performance upon the California mutuals.

Performance Indicators—Mutual and Stock Associations, 1963

INDICATOR	U.S. NON-CALIFORNIA	CALIFORNIA FEDERAL MUTUALS	CALIFORNIA STOCK
$\dfrac{\text{Gross operating income} - \text{expenses}}{\text{Average assets}}$	4.31%	4.95%	5.18%
$\dfrac{\text{``Dividends''}}{\text{Average saving capital}}$	4.04	4.72	4.78
$\dfrac{\text{New Loans}}{\text{Average Assets}}$	21.2	34.9	45.1

Source: Alfred Nicols, "Stock versus Mutual Savings and Loan Associations: Some Evidence of Differences in Behavior," *American Economic Review,* v. 57 (May 1967), p. 342.

These data suggest better performance by the stock associations, whether measured in terms of association net income (gross operating income minus expenses), or in terms of interest paid out to depositors (called "dividends" in savings and loan jargon), or in terms of growth (new loans divided by average assets). The "mutual" form thus does appear to permit managers to pursue goals in conflict with those of the owner-depositors.

In the analysis here, following the classical model it will be assumed that the firm aims to maximize profit—the difference between revenue and cost—in its output decision. More specifically, this chapter deals with the competitive or "price-taking" firm. The market price P is regarded as, for all practical purposes, independent of the firm's level of output. As the discussion in Section B of the previous chapter indicated, this cannot be literally true if the Law of Demand holds, but the price-taking assumption may still be a usable approximation of reality. Then Total Revenue or simply revenue R, which is by definition equal to the product of price P times quantity q (that is, $R \equiv Pq$) can be plotted in the upper panel of Figure 9.1 as a ray through the origin. Since price P is constant, revenue is zero when output q is zero, and out of the origin R increases proportionately with q. (The Total Revenue line in the upper panel of Figure 9.1 is a special case of the more general Total Revenue function discussed in Section 2.B and pictured in the upper panel of Figure 2.8.) The vertical axis in the upper panel

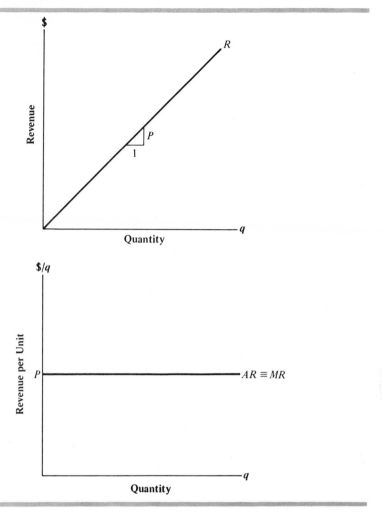

Figure 9.1
The Revenue Function of the Price-Taking Firm. If price *P* is constant, the Total Revenue function *R* in the upper diagram is a straight line (of slope *P*). This constant slope implies a horizontal Marginal Revenue curve *MR* of height *P* in the lower diagram. And Average Revenue *AR* coincides with *MR*, since *AR* is definitionally equal to the constant price *P*.

is scaled in dollars, the unit in which revenue is measured.[8] The lower panel of Figure 9.1 represents the corresponding average and marginal functions. In this case the average and marginal functions take a particularly simple form: to wit, Average Revenue *AR* and Marginal Revenue *MR* are coinciding horizontal lines.

---

[8]Since a rationale for the use of *money* has been provided in the preceding chapter, henceforth in the text it will be assumed that goods and services are valued in terms of money as "numeraire."

The relations that logically must hold among total, average, and marginal magnitudes were expounded in Section 2.B: (1) A *marginal* function corresponds to the rate of increase along a total function, and (2) an *average* function is simply the total function divided by the argument or choice variable. Marginal Revenue *MR* was formally defined in equation (2.6) as:[9]

$$(9.1) \qquad MR \equiv \lim_{(\text{as } \Delta q \to 0)} \frac{\Delta R}{\Delta q}$$

We will use the notation $\Delta R/\Delta q$, on the understanding that we are dealing with small increments Δ. Geometrically, *MR* corresponds to the *slope* along the Total Revenue curve in the upper panel of Figure 9.1; this slope is a constant, equal to the market price *P*. That is, any unit increase of *q* will yield an increment of revenue equal to the constant price *P* received for that unit. The Marginal Revenue *MR* is therefore plotted in the lower panel as a horizontal line of height *P*. In terms of dimensionality, note that the vertical axis of the lower diagram is scaled in units of $/q$, the dimensions of price.

Average Revenue *AR* is defined as R/q. But since $R \equiv Pq$ by definition, it is also definitionally true that $AR \equiv P \equiv R/q$. In this case, price *P* being taken as constant, the Average Revenue curve *AR* in the lower diagram must also be a horizontal line at the level of *P*. Thus, for a price-taking firm the *AR* and *MR* curves coincide in the form of a horizontal line at the level *P*.[10]

Having dealt with revenue *R*, the next step is to provide a similar representation for cost *C*. But the derivation of the cost function involves a more complex analysis, which is taken up in the section following.

9.D

PRODUCTION FUNCTION AND COST FUNCTION

Cost was expressed above as the sum, taken over all resources employed, of the factor prices times the factor quantities. This is the amount, in dollars, required to hire a combination of *inputs*. But the revenue function of Figure 9.1 is a relation between the firm's receipts and its *output*. Since it is the firm's output decision that concerns us here (the input or factor-employment decision will be taken up in Chapter 14), what we need (in order to balance against the revenue function) is the firm's *cost function*: the connection between cost incurred and output produced by the firm. The linking relationship, which allows us to translate from the cost of the firm's inputs to the cost of its outputs, is called *the production function*. The production function shows, as a matter of technology, how output produced depends upon the amounts of input factors employed.

[9]*Mathematical Footnote:* This definition is equivalent to the calculus derivative: $MR \equiv dR/dq$.

[10]Recall also Proposition 2.2c of Section 2.B: When an average magnitude is neither rising nor falling, the marginal magnitude must be equal to it.

In this text, we will deal only with simplified production functions that involve a single output commodity Q. Then a firm's production function can be written in the algebraic form:

(9.2) $q = \Psi (a,b,c, \ldots)$

This equation says that specified amounts $a,b,c, \ldots$ of the different factors or resources $A,B,C, \ldots$ yield quantity q of output commodity Q. One important special case is a production function in which there is only a *single variable factor*, that is, where the quantities of all but one of the factors used by the firm are held fixed. For this special case, the firm's cost function will be derived in Section 9.D.1; the generalized derivation for the case of multiple variable factors follows in Section 9.D.2.

If A is the single variable factor, the production function reduces to the form:

(9.2′) $q = \psi(a)$

The quantities of the fixed factors $B, C, \ldots$ no longer appear in equation (9.2′) as arguments of the production function. But of course they still have an effect; the amounts of the fixed factors enter into the *shape* of the $\psi(a)$ function that shows how much Q can be obtained per unit of A.

There is a famous technological relation between variable factor input on the one hand, and output quantities on the other. This relation is known as the *Law of Diminishing Returns*. Sometimes, to emphasize the fact that the relation applies where one factor varies in amount *relative* to others, it is called also the *Law of Varying Factor Proportions*.

THE LAW OF DIMINISHING RETURNS: If one factor (or group of factors) is increased while another factor (or group of factors) is held fixed, output or Total Product q will at first tend to rise. But, eventually at least, a point will be reached where the rate of increase, the Marginal Product[11] $mp_a \equiv \Delta q/\Delta a$ associated with increments of the variable factor, begins to fall; this is the point of diminishing marginal returns. With further increases of the variable factor, the Average Product $ap_a \equiv q/a$ will also eventually begin to fall; this is the point of diminishing average returns. As the amount of factor A employed rises still more, A may become actually counterproductive, reducing the Total Product q. This is the point of diminishing total returns to factor A.

The Law of Diminishing Returns is illustrated in Figure 9.2. The upper panel shows the Total Product curve tp_a relating output quantity q and factor input

---

[11]*Mathematical Footnote:* Formally, the Marginal Product is (like all marginal concepts) defined as a limit: $mp_a \equiv \lim\limits_{\Delta a \to 0} \dfrac{\Delta q}{\Delta a} \equiv \dfrac{dq}{da}$. (Henceforth in the text, note of the translation of marginal concepts into derivative notation will not be taken except where there may be a danger of misunderstanding.)

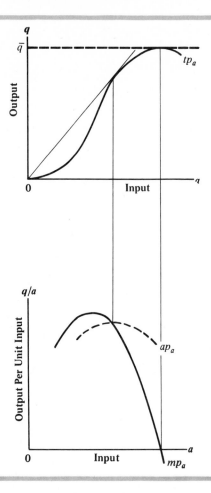

Figure 9.2

The Law of Diminishing Returns. The upper panel shows the Total Product function tp_a or $q = \psi(a)$; the lower panel shows the corresponding Average Product function ap_a or q/a and Marginal Product function mp_a or $\Delta q / \Delta a$. For the production function pictured here, diminishing *marginal* returns to employment of factor A set in first (the mp_a curve reaches its peak), then diminishing *average* returns set in (the ap_a curve reaches its peak), and finally diminishing *total* returns set in (the tp_a curve reaches its peak, at the maximum producible output $\bar{q}$).

a. The lower diagram shows the corresponding average function (the Average Product curve ap_a representing q/a as the factor input *a* varies) and marginal function (the Marginal Product curve mp_a showing $\Delta q / \Delta a$ as a function of factor input *a*). The relations among the total, average, and marginal magnitudes here are of course consistent with the general laws developed in Section 2.B. As Total Product tp_a is rising or horizontal or falling, Marginal Product mp_a is correspondingly positive or zero or negative (Propositions 2.1a, 2.1b, 2.1c). And the Marginal Product curve mp_a lies above the Average Product curve ap_a when the latter is rising, intersects it when ap_a is horizontal, and lies below it when ap_a is falling (Propositions 2.2a, 2.2b, 2.2c).

The Law of Diminishing Returns is a physical law, taken as an "outside" fact or premise by economists; it is not a proposition of economic science. But the commonsense of the Law is understandable in economic terms. There will, in general, tend to be (at any level of output) some most effective *proportion* among the several factors. When we increase the quantity of factor A from a very low level (say, from zero) with other factor quantities held fixed, we are likely to be getting closer to the most effective proportion of factors. Hence, Total Product is likely to be increasing rapidly. Then the Marginal Product of factor A will be high (and may even be increasing over a certain range). When we reach this most effective proportion and push beyond to further augment the quantity of the variable factor A, Total Product will still tend to increase, but at a slower and decreasing rate (smaller and declining Marginal Product of factor A). For, while the additional units of factor A are useful, input proportions are increasingly diverging from optimal. Eventually indeed, we may so swamp our productive process with factor A that additional quantities of it actually interfere with production (*negative* Marginal Product of factor A).

In 1960 A. Marani and Y. Fuchs conducted a cotton irrigation experiment in Israel. On April 3 "Pima 32" variety cotton was planted. All plots received 50 mm of water immediately after planting, but none thereafter until July 4. On that date plots were irrigated with varying quantities of water. The following table shows the results at harvest.

EXAMPLE 9.4
COTTON
IRRIGATION
EXPERIMENT

Irrigation Treatment and Yield

WATER APPLIED JULY 4 (MM)	GROWTH IN HEIGHT AFTER JULY 4 (CM)	COTTONSEED YIELD (G/M^2)	LINT YIELD (G/M^2)
0	1	58	19
100	8	99	31
150	22	136	42
200	33	131	40

Source: A. Marani and Y. Fuchs, "Effect of Amount of Water Applied as a Single Irrigation on Cotton Grown under Dryland Conditions," *Agronomy Journal*, v. 56 (May/June 1964), p. 282.

In this case there are two outputs of interest: cottonseed and lint. However, the Total Product curves are quite similar for each. The lack of observations at the intermediate 50 mm level unfortunately leaves some doubt as to the shapes of the Total Product curves in the early ranges. But for both products it is evident that over the range from 150 mm to 200 mm of irrigation water there are diminishing *total* returns, i.e., Marginal Product is negative. (The plants do actually grow higher at 200 mm than at 150 mm, but the seed and lint yields are both less.) The Average Product of irrigation water, in terms of both cottonseed and lint, appears to be declining throughout the range of application. Thus, diminishing average returns seem to hold from the start. But the Marginal Product appears to be highest in the interval between 100 and 150 mm of irrigation water, so that diminishing *marginal* returns begin somewhere in this range.

We now proceed to derive the cost function of the firm, for this case of a single variable factor, from a production function like that illustrated in Figure 9.2.

The firm is best thought of as *hiring* the factors of production, that is, the firm buys the *services* of the factors rather than the factors themselves. The "hire-prices" of factors $A,B, \ldots$ will be symbolized as $h_a, h_b, \ldots$. We will assume in this chapter that the firm is a "price-taker" with regard to these factor-market prices of inputs as well as with regard to the product-market price P of the output commodity. Therefore, all the hire-prices are taken as known constants.

In general, the firm's cost for any given combination of inputs is:

(9.3) $\qquad C \equiv h_a a + h_b b + h_c c + \ldots$

In our special case where all the factors except A are held "fixed," cost can be divided into a fixed component F and a variable component V, and can be expressed as:

(9.3′) $\qquad C \equiv F + V \equiv F + h_a a$

Here $h_a a$, the expenditure on factor A, corresponds to the "variable cost" V.

The only additional step required is to transform (9.3′) into a function of output q rather than of input a. To do this, we need to "invert" the production-function equation (9.2′) so as to express a in terms of q for substitution in equation (9.3′). For example, if (9.2′) had the specific algebraic form $q = \sqrt{a}$, the "inverted" relation is $a = q^2$, so that (9.3′) could be written as $C = F + h_a q^2$. More generally, the "inverted" production function can be expressed algebraically as:

(9.4) $\qquad a = \phi(q)$

Then the cost function, for a single variable factor A, is:

(9.5) $\qquad C \equiv F + h_a \phi(q)$

This relation between cost and output is completely determined upon insertion of the fixed cost F and the hire-price h_a.

The geometrical interpretation of the process of translating cost from input units to output units is illustrated in Figure 9.3. The shape of the Total Cost curve

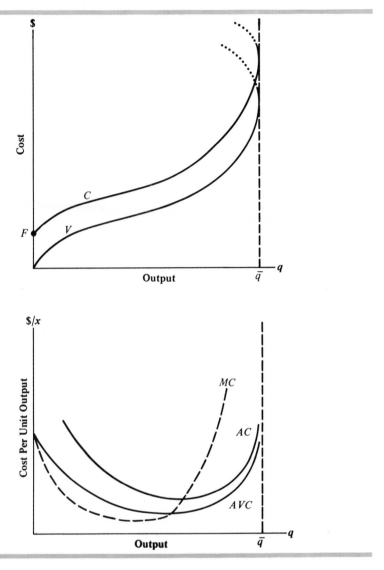

Figure 9.3

The Firm's Cost Function. In the upper diagram, F is the level of fixed cost incurred independently of output. Total Cost rises with output, first possibly at a decreasing rate but ultimately at an increasing rate—until the maximum producible quantity $\bar{q}$ is attained. The curve V showing Total *Variable* Cost lies below the curve C by the fixed amount F. (The dotted upper branches of the C and V curves, curving back from $\bar{q}$, are not economically relevant.) In the lower panel, the curves showing Marginal Cost $MC \equiv \Delta C/\Delta q$ and Average Cost $AC \equiv C/q$ are derived in the usual way from the Total Cost curve. The curve of Average Variable Cost $AVC \equiv V/q$ is similarly derived from the Total Variable Cost curve. The MC curve cuts first through the low point of AVC and then through the low point of AC, both from below.

C in the upper panel suggests the shape of the tp_a curve in the upper panel of Figure 9.2, rotated 180° and flipped over. And in particular, the dashed *vertical* bound on the right represents the same maximum producible output $\bar{q}$ indicated by the dashed *horizontal* bound in the upper panel of the earlier diagram. (The dotted upper branch of the Total Cost curve in Figure 9.3, above the point of contact with the vertical bound, is economically irrelevant—the firm would not produce a given output at greater cost if it can produce the same output at lower cost—but has been retained here to point up the derivation from the earlier tp_a curve.) Starting from the level of fixed cost F incurred independently of any output, the economically relevant portion of the Total Cost curve C rises throughout as output increases, possibly first at a decreasing but ultimately at an increasing rate. It is also of interest to show the curve of Total Variable Cost V, which evidently must lie always below the C curve by a fixed vertical distance equal to F.

For any level of output q, the slopes along the Total Cost curve C and along the Total Variable Cost curve V are identical, since the curves are vertically parallel. Marginal Cost $MC \equiv \Delta C/\Delta q$, which is by definition the slope along C, is therefore independent of the fixed cost F. MC in the lower panel is shown as first positive but decreasing (corresponding to the range where C and V are rising at a decreasing rate) and then positive and increasing (corresponding to the range where C and V are rising at an increasing rate).

Comparing the lower panels of Figures 9.2 and 9.3, the geometry reveals that here also there is an "inverted" relationship. The logical connection between the marginal curves can be expressed in terms of the definitions of Marginal Cost MC and Marginal Product mp:

$$(9.6) \qquad MC \equiv \frac{\Delta C}{\Delta q} \equiv \frac{h_a \Delta a}{\Delta q} \equiv \frac{h_a}{\Delta q/\Delta a} \equiv \frac{h_a}{mp_a}$$

Since the hire-price h_a is assumed constant, Marginal Cost moves inversely to Marginal Product. In particular, *rising* Marginal Cost corresponds to *diminishing* Marginal Product (diminishing marginal returns to employing factor A).

A corresponding inverse relationship holds between Average Product ap_a and Average *Variable* Cost $AVC \equiv V/q$:

$$(9.7) \qquad AVC \equiv \frac{V}{q} \equiv \frac{h_a a}{q} \equiv \frac{h_a}{q/a} \equiv \frac{h_a}{ap_a}$$

Because of the presence of the fixed cost term F, a slightly more complicated relation connects Average Cost AC and Average Product ap_a:

$$(9.8) \qquad AC \equiv \frac{C}{a} \equiv \frac{F + h_a a}{q} \equiv \frac{F}{q} + \frac{h_a}{ap_a}$$

Turning to the association between Total Cost in the upper panel and Average Cost in the lower panel of Figure 9.3, Average Cost or C/q corresponds to the slope of the line that could be drawn in the upper panel from the origin to the point on the Total Cost curve at that q. At $q = 0$, Average Cost must be infinite, as can be seen directly from the definition C/q, or geometrically from the ever-steepening slope of the line from the origin to the C curve as q approaches zero. The AC curve has a falling region so long as MC lies below it (Proposition 2.2a) and later a rising region where MC lies above it (Proposition 2.2b). It then follows that AC reaches a minimum (is neither rising nor falling) at the point where MC equals AC (Proposition 2.2c). Or, we may say, the MC curve cuts through the low point of the AC curve (from below). It is left as a challenge for the student to derive the curve of Average Variable Cost AVC in the lower panel from V in the upper panel, and to explain the relation between the MC and AVC curves. (In particular, why does MC also cut AVC from below, and do so before it cuts through AC?)

As a numerical example illustrating these ideas, suppose that the production function (9.2′) takes the specific form:

$$q = 2\sqrt{a}$$

Note that in this case there is no finite upper bound $\bar{q}$ on Total Product, the amount of Q that can be produced as A increases. Put another way, the point of diminishing *total* returns is never reached. The "inverted" function (9.4) can be written as:

$$a = q^2/4$$

If we let the hire-price $h_a = 4$ and the fixed cost $F = 50$, equation (9.5) for Total Cost C becomes:

$$C = F + V = 50 + h_a a = 50 + 4q^2/4 = 50 + q^2$$

So the function showing the cost of producing various levels of output has been derived from the firm's production function, the data on hire-price h_a, and the amount of fixed cost F.

Let us also verify the correspondences between the *average* magnitudes stated in equations (9.7) and (9.8). Variable Cost V in our example is simply $V = q^2$. Then Average Variable Cost can be found directly from the definition of an average magnitude as $AVC = V/q = q$. Now, since Total Product is $q = 2\sqrt{a}$, Average Product is $q/a = 2/\sqrt{a}$. So we can confirm the last of the string of identities (9.7) by verifying that:

$$AVC \equiv \frac{h_a}{ap_a} = \frac{4}{2/\sqrt{a}} = 2\sqrt{a} = q$$

Similarly, Average Cost can be found directly as $AC \equiv C/q = 50/q + q$. Verifying the last equality in (9.8), we have once again:

$$AC \equiv \frac{F}{q} + \frac{h_a}{ap_a} = \frac{50}{q} + \frac{4}{2/\sqrt{a}} = \frac{50}{q} + q$$

*9.D.2

*From
Production
Function to
Cost Function
—Several
Variable
Factors*

Where, as in the preceding Section 9.D.1, certain of the factors are held fixed in quantity, the output decision involved is called "short run" (as will be described more fully in Section 9.E below). Thus, the cost function derived above and pictured in Figure 9.3 is a *short-run cost function* of the firm. But when, as in the case to be considered now, the input quantities of all factors can vary, the *long-run cost function* is obtained. Actually, there are a variety of intermediate "runs" between short and long, depending on the range of factors considered to be variable. The discussion here deals with just *two* variable factors *A* and *B*; there may or may not be still other factors held fixed.

The firm's choice as to the hiring of factors is in some ways analogous to the consumer's decision as to the purchase of consumption goods. Just as consumption goods can be regarded as generating *utility*, so factors as inputs generate *product*. The relation between inputs and output is the production function of the firm. Specifically here, the production function can be written:

(9.9) $q = \Psi(a,b)$

Diagrammatically, the production function is the "output hill" of Figure 9.4 which shows output quantity *q* as a function of input quantities *a* and *b*. Section 3.D contained a discussion of the difficulty or impossibility of quantifying "cardinal" utility for scaling the vertical axis of the utility hill (shown in Figure 3.3). Here, however, there is no such problem. The quantity of the output commodity *Q* provides a natural "cardinal" scale for the vertical axis of a three-dimensional production function (output hill) like Figure 9.4. Still, the convenience of working in just two dimensions is such that we will often make use of the "contour map" instead of the output hill, as illustrated here in Figure 9.5. But we can always attach some definite numerical output quantity index *q* to each contour or *isoquant* of the contour map; we are not restricted, as we were in the case of utility, to merely "ordinal" comparisons of higher and lower.[12]

There are two essential aspects of the multi-factor production function: (1) The effect of changes in *relative factor proportions*, and (2) the effect of changes in *scale* (i.e., of proportionate increases or decreases in all factors simultaneously).

With regard to *relative* factor proportions, the Law of Diminishing Returns

---

*The section between the asterisk and the symbol ■ may contain somewhat more difficult or advanced material.

[12]The sharp-eyed reader will have detected one difference between the utility hill as pictured in Figure 3.3 and the output hill of Figure 9.4. In the utility diagram the hill had positive height over the horizontal (*x* and *y*) axes away from the origin—whereas in the output diagram, the hill slopes down to zero all along the horizontal (*a* and *b*) axes. The interpretation is that in Figure 3.3 neither of the two commodities was assumed to be "essential" in utility terms—some satisfaction can be gained, say, from good *Y* even when none of *X* is being consumed. On the other hand, in Figure 9.4 both factors are assumed "essential" to production—if either *a* or *b* is zero, then output *q* will be zero. This difference between the two diagrams is not, however, at all intrinsic to the logic of either situation. We could imagine consumptive commodities that are "essential" for deriving any utility at all—air to breathe may be an instance. And there could be factors of production which are not "essential"—for example, fertilizer may contribute to agricultural output, but the absence of fertilizer need not dictate that crop yield must be zero. So it would be possible to have a utility hill looking like Figure 9.4, or an output hill looking like Figure 3.3.

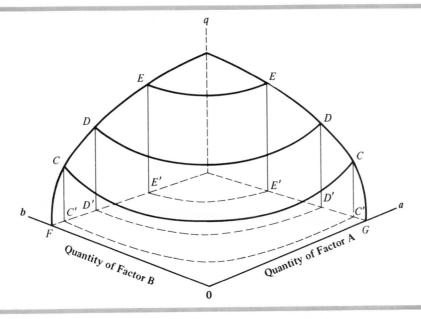

q

E E

D D

C C

E' E'

b C' D' D' C' a

F G

Quantity of Factor B   Quantity of Factor A

0

Figure 9.4

Output as a Function of Two Inputs. Output q, measured vertically, is shown as a function of the input quantities a and b. CC, DD, and EE are contours of equal height (output) along the three-dimensional surface. The curves $C'C'$, $D'D'$, and $E'E'$ are the projections of these contours in the base plane.

continues to hold (as a postulated technological fact) in the two-factor case. Consider Figure 9.6. Here, along the surface of the output hill are sketched several curves showing the change in output quantity q as one input varies with the other input held constant. These can be regarded as *Total Product curves*, analogous to the tp_a curve defined for a single variable factor A in the previous section. But there are now Total Product curves for each of the two factors A and B—tp_a and tp_b. Indeed, for each factor there is an infinite family of such curves, since in general both tp_a and tp_b will depend also upon the specific magnitude at which the *other* factor is held constant. The Total Product curves for factor A are given labels like $tp_a(b = b_0)$ and $tp_a(b = b_1)$. Each such curve shows the variation of Total Product q with changes in the input quantity of factor A, factor B held constant—in the one case at $b = b_0$ and in the other at $b = b_1$. And a set of tp_b curves can correspondingly be defined. It is possible, of course, to associate with any of the Total Product curves of Figure 9.6 an Average Product curve and Marginal Product[13] curve as in the lower panel of Figure 9.2.

In Figure 9.7 the two families of Total Product curves are shown suggestively on (q, a) and on (q, b) axes, respectively. Each single curve has a form

[13]*Mathematical Footnote:* With two or more variable factors, the Marginal Product of any single factor such as A becomes a *partial* derivative:

$$mp_a \equiv \lim_{\Delta a \to 0} \frac{\Psi(a + \Delta a, b) - \Psi(a,b)}{\Delta a} \equiv \frac{\partial q}{\partial a}$$

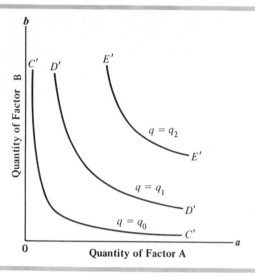

Figure 9.5

Isoquants of Output. The projections $C'C'$, $D'D'$, and $E'E'$ in the base plane of Figure 9.4 are shown here as isoquants (curves of equal output) in a contour map, without the overlying vertical dimension. Each isoquant is associated with a definite quantity of output (q_0, q_1, or q_2).

similar to the tp_a curve of Figure 9.2, as dictated by the Law of Diminishing Returns. In Panel (a) the entire tp_a curve is shown as shifting upward as quantities of the other factor B rise from b_0 to b_1 to b_2, and similarly for the other factor in Panel (b). Such an upward shift must occur, if the "other" factor is productive.

With regard to changes in *scale*, the shape of the output hill in Figure 9.4 shows that a kind of diminishing returns *may* prevail even where both factors increase proportionately. We will assume here that, eventually at least, *diminishing returns to scale* also apply. (That is, when all inputs are increased in the same proportion, output rises in a lesser proportion.) However, constant or even increasing returns to scale would not be a contradiction of the Law of Diminishing Returns as defined for *varying factor proportions*. Total Product curves can have the normal diminishing-returns shape even on an output hill with constant or increasing returns to scale.

EXAMPLE 9.5
MISSOURI CORN

An agricultural experiment in Missouri reported by J. Ambrosius examined the response of corn yield X (bushels per acre) to variation in two inputs A and B (*number of plants* per acre and *pounds of nitrogen* per acre). Reading horizontally across any single row, the table shows selected points on the Total Product curve tp_a for plants per acre—with b, nitrogen input per acre, held constant along the row. Reading vertically down any column, points are shown on the tp_b curve for nitrogen input b—holding fixed the number of plants per acre, a. The entire tp_a curve tends to shift upward as b increases, and the tp_b curve tends to shift upward as a increases.

Bushels of Corn Per Acre (q)

POUNDS OF NITROGEN PER ACRE (B)	NUMBER OF PLANTS PER ACRE (A)				
	9,000	12,000	15,000	18,000	21,000
0	50.6	54.2	53.5	48.5	39.2
50	78.7	85.9	88.8	87.5	81.9
100	94.4	105.3	111.9	114.2	112.2
150	97.8	112.4	122.6	128.6	130.3
200	88.9	107.1	121.0	130.6	135.9

Source: John Ambrosius, "The Effects of Experimental Size upon Optimum Rates of Nitrogen and Stand for Corn in Missouri" (1964), quoted in J. P. Doll, V. J. Rhodes, and J. G. West, *Economics of Agricultural Production, Markets, and Policy* (Homewood, Ill.: Richard D. Irwin, Inc., 1968), p. 89.

It is also possible to see that diminishing returns apply here even to *proportionate variation* in both factors together. For example, a doubling of both inputs from the combination $a_0 = 9,000$, $b_0 = 50$ to the combination $a_1 = 18,000$, $b_1 = 100$ raises output from 78.7 only to 114.2.

Figure 9.6

Total Product Functions. Here Total Product curves are drawn along an output hill like that of Figure 9.4. The Total Product curves for factor A, designated tp_a, hold constant the amount of the other factor B. However, the heights of the tp_a curves depend upon the specific constant values assumed for b in each case, and similarly the tp_b curves depend on the values assumed for a.

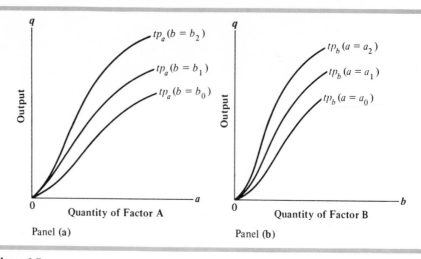

Figure 9.7

Families of Total Product Curves. Here tp_a curves like those drawn along the output hill of Figure 9.6 are shown on q,a axes in Panel (a); the tp_b curves are similarly shown on q,b axes in Panel (b).

The "Missouri Corn" example suggests a possible rationale for diminishing returns to scale (i.e., to proportionate variation of factors). Nitrogen and number of plants as inputs were varied, but there exists at least one other factor—the number of acres—which was still held constant. Since in the real world it will not generally be possible to vary literally *all* inputs, we are always in practice dealing still with changes in *relative* factor proportions. The very definition of the firm suggests that some input, to which the label "entrepreneurship" is sometimes applied, remains constant throughout. Even abstracting from this element, certain unchanging aspects of our planet (the gravitational constant or the distribution of minerals, for example) may enter into productive processes. So even though all *marketable* inputs are varied in proportion, the condition wherein some inputs are physically "fixed" is, in some degree, ultimately inescapable.

EXAMPLE 9.6
PIGS

The agricultural economist E. O. Heady[14] reported an experiment which involved varying the amounts of corn (high in carbohydrate content) and soybean oilmeal (high in protein content) fed to young pigs. The experiment was conducted on 302 pigs, carried from a weaning weight of 34 pounds to a market weight of around 250 pounds. Observations on weight gain were used to estimate output as a function of these two inputs.

It was found that rather different production functions were appropriate for different weight ranges, as the effects of inputs of carbohydrate versus protein upon weight gained tended to be different for younger (smaller) ver-

[14]E. O. Heady, "An Econometric Investigation of the Technology of Agricultural Production Functions," *Econometrica*, v. 25 (April 1957).

sus older (larger) pigs. The results obtained (rounded off) were as follows, where G indicates weight gain, P is input of soybean oilmeal (protein), and C is input of corn (carbohydrate)—all measured in pounds per pig.

$G = 1.60 \, P^{.30}C^{.53}$,   for the weight interval 34–75 pounds
$G = .71 \, P^{.14}C^{.77}$,   "   "   "   "   75–150 pounds
$G = .46 \, P^{.09}C^{.86}$,   "   "   "   "   150–250 pounds

The exponents of P and C in the different functions indicate, as is reasonable, that weight gain in young pigs responds relatively more to protein input while weight gain in older pigs responds more to carbohydrates.

COMMENT: It can be shown mathematically that, in functions of this form, there would be increasing returns to scale (more than proportionate effect upon output for proportionate variation of both inputs) if the *sum* of the exponents exceeds unity. Constant returns to scale hold if the sum of exponents exactly equals unity, and decreasing returns to scale if the sum falls short of unity. Evidently, all three production functions here show decreasing returns to scale.

Figure 9.8 illustrates how the two aspects of the multi-factor production function—the effect of changes in relative factor proportions, and the effect of changes of scale—are involved in the derivation of the cost function.

With respect to the first aspect, the Scale Expansion Path (SEP) connects all the points on the contour map of Figure 9.5 that satisfy an optimal choice of relative factor proportions at a given set of factor prices h_a and h_b. In Figure 9.8 are shown, in addition to the contour map or isoquants of *output*, parallel straight lines called "iso-cost lines" or isoquants of *cost*. Each such straight line represents the equation:

$$(9.10) \qquad C = h_a a + h_b b$$

Any single iso-cost line represents combinations of factor quantities a and b such that cost C (total expenditure on hiring factors) is held constant, at given hire-prices h_a and h_b. All the iso-cost lines have slope $-h_a/h_b$, equal to the negative of the factor price ratio.[15] It will be geometrically evident that, moving along a given iso-cost line in Figure 9.8, the best attainable position is found where the cost isoquant is just tangent to the highest attainable output isoquant.[16] When we

[15]For any single iso-cost line with given C, the vertical intercept in Figure 9.8 equals C/h_b (the number of units of B purchasable when $a = 0$); correspondingly, the horizontal intercept is C/h_a. The slope is given by the ratio of the vertical to the horizontal intercept, with negative sign, and of course C cancels out. [Compare equation (4.2) of Chapter 4.]

[16]Note the analogy with the optimum of the consumer that was pictured in Figure 4.1. There the consumer was maximizing utility by choice of consumption quantities x and y, at a specified level of income $I = P_x x + P_y y$. Here the firm maximizes output by choice of factor employments a and b, at a specified level of cost $C = h_a a + h_b b$.

Figure 9.8

Scale Expansion Path. Along any iso-cost line, the tangency with an output isoquant represents the largest output attainable at that cost. Each such tangency shows the best factor proportions for that level of cost and output. The Scale Expansion Path SEP connects all these tangency positions.

consider different levels of cost, the changing magnitude of C will generate the entire family of iso-cost lines as shown in the diagram. The Scale Expansion Path SEP connects all the points of tangency along the individual iso-cost lines, and thus represents the solutions to the problem of best factor proportions for all levels of cost.

Let us now consider this factor-proportion decision analytically. Assuming diminishing marginal productivity for each of the two factors, at any level of cost the firm will be at an (interior) optimum when the Factor Balance Equation (9.11) holds:[17]

[17] *Mathematical Footnote:* We can use again "the method of Lagrangian multipliers" (see Mathematical Footnote 5 of Chapter 4), to maximize output $q = \Psi(a,b)$ subject to a given level of cost $C = h_a a + h_b b$.

$$\underset{(a,b,\lambda)}{\text{Max } L} = q - \lambda(h_a a + h_b b - C)$$

The first-order conditions are:

$$\frac{\partial q}{\partial a} - \lambda h_a = 0 \qquad\qquad \frac{\partial q}{\partial b} - \lambda h_b = 0 \qquad\qquad h_a a + h_b b - C = 0$$

The first two conditions can be written as:

$$\lambda = \frac{\partial q/\partial a}{h_a} = \frac{\partial q/\partial b}{h_b}$$

So these first-order conditions correspond to the Factor Balance Equation (9.11). With more than one variable factor, however, diminishing Marginal Product ($\partial^2 q/\partial a^2 < 0$, $\partial^2 q/\partial b^2 < 0$) does not guaran-

(9.11) $\quad \dfrac{mp_a}{h_a} = \dfrac{mp_b}{h_b} \qquad$ Factor Balance Equation

That is, at any given scale the relative factor employments are optimal when the Marginal Products *per dollar* spent are equal for each variable factor employed.[18]

MRS_Q, the Marginal Rate of Substitution in Production between factors A and B with regard to product Q, is defined as the amount of factor B which can be substituted for a small reduction of factor A in such a way as to hold output q constant. Geometrically, this can be interpreted as the absolute slope at any particular point along an output isoquant. Thus:

$$MRS_Q \equiv - \left. \frac{\Delta b}{\Delta a} \right|_q.$$

(For the analogous concept of the Marginal Rate of Substitution in Consumption, MRS_C, representing the absolute slope of the consumer's indifference curve, see Section 4.A.2.) And the *Marginal Rate of Substitution in Exchange* between the two factors, MRS_E, is the absolute slope of the iso-cost line. So the tangency condition of Figure 9.8 representing optimal factor balance also can be written as:

(9.11′) $\quad MRS_Q = MRS_E$

That (9.11) and (9.11′) represent the same relationship (see also the discussion of equation [4.4] in Chapter 4) follows from the identities:

$$MRS_E \equiv \frac{h_a}{h_b} \quad \text{and} \quad MRS_Q \equiv \frac{mp_a}{mp_b}$$

The equivalence of MRS_E with a price ratio is familiar by now. The equivalence of MRS_Q, the absolute slope along the cost isoquant, with the ratio of marginal products[19] may be illustrated by a simple example. MRS_Q is, for small changes, the

---

tee that the *second-order* conditions for a maximum are met. (Compare the analogous statement about diminishing Marginal *Utility* in footnote 12 of Chapter 4.) An additional required condition is:

$$\frac{\partial^2 q}{\partial a^2} \frac{\partial^2 q}{\partial b^2} > \left(\frac{\partial^2 q}{\partial a\, \partial b} \right)^2.$$

[18] If D is some third factor *not* actually being employed ($d = 0$) at current factor prices, its Marginal Product per dollar is related by an *inequality* condition to the others:

$$\frac{mp_a(a > 0)}{h_a} = \frac{mp_b(b > 0)}{h_b} > \frac{mp_d(d > 0)}{h_d}$$

For the optimal employment of D to be zero, its Marginal Product per dollar must be less than that of other factors, even for the very first unit of D.

[19] *Mathematical Footnote:* Along any output isoquant, q is constant. Thus:

$$dq = \frac{\partial q}{\partial a}\, da + \frac{\partial q}{\partial b}\, db = 0$$

Then

$$-\frac{db}{da} = \frac{\partial q/\partial a}{\partial q/\partial b} \quad \text{or} \quad MRS_Q = \frac{mp_a}{mp_b}$$

additional number of units Δb of factor B required to maintain output intact (i.e., to get back to the same output isoquant) after a unit reduction $\Delta a = 1$ in employment of factor A. If $mp_a = 10$ and $mp_b = 5$ and if we are dealing with small changes (so that the marginal products are approximately constant), it follows that 2 units of B will be required to make up for 1 of A. That is, $2 = {}^{10}/_5$ is the MRS_Q, which here and generally must numerically equal the ratio mp_a/mp_b.

Finally, the Factor Balance Equation (9.11) is related to Marginal Cost MC in the following way:

$$(9.12) \qquad MC = \frac{h_a}{mp_a} = \frac{h_b}{mp_b}$$

This is of course a generalization of equation (9.6), which expressed MC as the ratio of hire-price to the Marginal Product of a *single* variable factor. The interpretation of (9.12) is that, at the correct factor proportions dictated by the Factor Balance Equation, it is no more and no less costly to expand output by hiring a small increment of factor A than of factor B (or any mixture of the two).[20] The Marginal Cost of expanding output by hiring more of A is the same as the MC of doing so by hiring more B.

Equation (9.12) represents a principle of very broad significance. It says essentially that if there are two (or more) ways of achieving some end, and if we have found an optimal balance of the two, then on the margin (that is, for small changes) we can increase achievement further in either of the two ways, with equal effectiveness. (If one way *were* clearly better than the other, we could not have already been at an optimal balance between the two.) Among the many possible applications of this idea is the division of output of a firm between two of its *plants*. In such a case, supposing there are diminishing marginal returns (increasing Marginal Cost) in each plant, and that we have an interior solution so that both plants are actually producing, the optimal solution is to equate Marginal Cost in the two. Then an *additional* unit of output can be produced, equally effectively, in either of the two plants.

EXAMPLE 9.7 LOAD DISPATCHING: ELECTRICAL ENGINEERS AS ECONOMISTS	Electricity is typically generated by companies that operate a number of separate producing plants, with a transmission network providing connections to consumers as well as ties among the generating plants. Since electricity companies are (with rare exceptions) required to meet instantaneously the demands placed upon them by consumers, the operating problem at any moment of time is to assign output most economically among the generating

[20] *Mathematical Footnote:* First, $dq = (\partial q/\partial a)da + (\partial q/\partial b)db$. Since $C = h_a a + h_b b$, $dC = h_a \, da + h_b \, db$. So:

$$MC \equiv \frac{dC}{dq} = \frac{h_a \, da + h_b \, db}{(\partial q/\partial a) \, da + (\partial q/\partial b) \, db}$$

Since $h_a/(\partial q/\partial a) = h_b/(\partial q/\partial b)$ from the Factor Balance Equation, it follows algebraically that:

$$MC = \frac{h_a}{\partial q/\partial a} = \frac{h_b}{\partial q/\partial b}$$

plants. The required total output varies widely within the day, and even from moment to moment, and so the problem is ever-present and of great practical importance.

Fred M. Westfield[21] investigated the operating practices of a leading American electric utility. He discovered that this company employs a dispatcher to actually "assign the load" from moment to moment among the different plants. The dispatcher is guided by a Station-Loading Sliderule that shows what the economist would regard as the Marginal Cost function of each plant. By mechanically manipulating his Sliderule, the dispatcher automatically equates Marginal Cost for all plants in operation in such a way as to meet the total generation requirement. For some older plants, Marginal Cost is high throughout. These plants are operated at non-zero levels only in peak-demand periods.

The company's method of division of output, and the Sliderule itself, were developed by engineers lacking the slightest acquaintance with economic theory. The company's engineers thus independently "discovered" Marginal Cost analysis—a striking intellectual achievement, though one that knowledge of intermediate economic theory would have made unnecessary.

[21]F. M. Westfield, "Marginal Analysis, Multi-Plant Firms, and Business Practice: An Example," *Quarterly Journal of Economics*, v. 69 (May 1955).

The relation between cost and *scale* of output can also be visualized in Figure 9.8. In that diagram the iso-cost lines $C°$, C', C'' are equally spaced moving out of the origin, so as to represent proportionate increases in cost. Whether there is more than, less than, or exactly proportionate increases in output at these levels of cost will be indicated by the numerical values associated with the $q°$, q', q'' curves at the respective tangency points along the Scale Expansion Path. Suppose the three cost levels of C are $100, $200, and $300, while the associated three output levels of q are 50, 150, and 200 units. Then there are increasing returns to scale in the region between $q = 50$ and $q = 150$ (the output triples, while the cost only doubles), but decreasing returns to scale between $q = 150$ and $q = 200$ (output increases by ⅓, while cost increases by ½).

The only step remaining is to re-plot the C and the q magnitudes associated with each point of the Scale Expansion Path SEP on q,C axes, in the form of a Total Cost function—as in the upper panel of Figure 9.3. (If no factors are being held fixed, there will not be any positive F intercept on the vertical axis. Or, we could say, Total Cost and Total Variable Cost will coincide.) From the curve of Total Cost, the Average Cost and Marginal Cost curves as represented in the lower panel of Figure 9.3 can be derived in the usual way.

The inverse relation between Total Cost and Total Product, or between Marginal Cost and Marginal Product, will continue to hold even with several variable factors. For example, diminishing Marginal Product is associated with rising Marginal Cost. But in the case of multiple factors, movement along the Marginal Product curves for *all* the variable factors would be involved. The important consequence is that Marginal Product for any factor tends not to decline so fast when several factors are permitted to vary, in comparison with the case where output can be raised only by adding to the quantity of that single variable factor. Correspondingly, Marginal Cost *MC* does not rise so fast when several factors are variable. (This point will come up again in the discussion of short-run versus long-run in Section E below.) ∎

OPTIMUM OF THE COMPETITIVE FIRM— SHORT RUN AND LONG RUN

According to the classical goal, the firm aims to maximize profit. Such maximization, like all behavior, is subject to constraints. In this case, the constraint is the relation between *revenue* received and *costs* incurred as larger or smaller outputs are contemplated.

For the case of the *competitive* or "price-taking" firm dealt with here, the revenue function was derived and pictured in Figure 9.1 above. And, on the assumption that the firm is also a "price-taker" with regard to the hire-prices of factors, the cost function was derived and pictured in Figure 9.3. Putting the two together as in Figure 9.9 here provides all the elements needed for the profit-maximization decision.

Profit is Revenue minus Cost. In symbols, $\Pi \equiv R - C$. In the upper diagram, the profit-maximizing output $q*$ is the level of q such that the positive vertical difference between the R and the C curves is greatest. The maximum level of profit, $\Pi*$, is shown as the bold line-segment in the diagram. It is geometrically evident that this maximum difference occurs where the Total Cost curve C is parallel to (has the same slope as) the Total Revenue curve R. (The parallelism is suggested by the dashed tangent drawn along the C curve at $q = q*$.) This provides the key to the connection between the solution in "total" units as shown in the upper panel and the solution in "average-marginal" units below. Since the *slopes* along the "total" curves correspond to the *heights* of the "marginal" curves, the optimum output $q*$ is illustrated in the lower diagram as the point where Marginal Revenue (a horizontal line here, equal to the fixed price P) and Marginal Cost intersect.

In terms of economic logic, if a unit increment of output will increase revenue more than it does cost ($MR > MC$) then the increment should be produced; we are not yet at the profit-maximizing output. If $MR < MC$, on the other hand, the last unit caused a decrease in profit so that output has been pushed beyond the optimum. For profit to be a maximum, then, the condition $MC = MR$ must hold. And since we are dealing with competitive (price-taking) firms for which $MR \equiv AR \equiv P$, this condition takes on the specific form:

(9.13) $MC = MR \equiv P$ Maximum-Profit Condition, Competitive Firm

Figure 9.9

Optimum of the Competitive Firm. In the upper diagram, at the optimal output $q*$ the vertical difference between the Total Revenue curve R and the Total Cost curve C is greatest. At $q*$ the slopes along R and C are equal so that, in the lower diagram, the Marginal Revenue curve MR and the Marginal Cost curve MC intersect at that output. $\Pi*$ is the amount of the maximized profit, shown by the bold vertical line-segment in the upper diagram and the shaded rectangle below. P_V, the height of the minimum of the Average Variable Cost curve AVC, is the "shut-down price" below which zero output would be produced.

The economic logic also tells us something further. We have just seen that if $MR > MC$ the firm should expand output, and if $MR < MC$ it should contract. This suggests that $MC = MR$ is an optimum *only if the* MC *curve cuts the* MR *curve from below*. Note that in the lower panel of Figure 9.9 there are *two* intersections of the MC curve with the horizontal MR curve. But at the left-hand intersection, *MC cuts MR from above*. By means of economic logic we see that it pays to go beyond the left-hand intersection into the range of output where $MR > MC$, until the right-hand intersection is reached[22] where *MC cuts MR from below*.[23]

PROPOSITION: The profit-maximizing output for the firm is that for which Marginal Cost equals Marginal Revenue, provided that the *MC* curve cuts the *MR* curve from below.

The *size* of the economic profit, at the profit-maximizing output q^*, is represented in the upper panel of Figure 9.9 as the bold vertical line-segment Π^* between the Total Revenue and the Total Cost curves. In terms of average-marginal units of measurement, we can think of profit as equal to $(AR - AC)q$. That is, profit equals the difference between *Average* Revenue and *Average* Cost, multiplied by the number of units of output. So in Panel (b), maximum profit is shown as the shaded rectangle whose area is $(P - AC)q^*$.

Table 9.1 illustrates a hypothetical set of revenue and cost data for a competitive profit-maximizing firm. Price is constant at $P = 60$, so that the Total Revenue column (R) is given simply by $R = 60q$. The specific cost function assumed is $C = 128 + 69q - 14q^2 + q^3$. This formula was used to compute the Total Cost column C. If plotted, the Total Revenue and Total Cost functions would have the general shapes pictured in the upper panel of Figure 9.9, and the average and marginal functions would resemble those in the lower panel.

Three different Marginal Cost columns are shown in the table. The first, MC_1, is the "poorer approximation" discussed in Section 2.B. Let $C(q)$ be Total Cost at a particular level of output q, and $C(q + 1)$ be Total Cost at a unit greater level of output. Then, according to MC_1, the difference $C(q + 1) - C(q)$ is the Marginal Cost *at* $(q + 1)$. The "better approximation" discussed in Chapter 2, tabulated as MC_2 here, calls this same cost difference the Marginal Cost *at* $(q + \frac{1}{2})$. To find MC_2 for integer values of q, simple interpolation is used; these interpolated numbers are shown in parentheses in the MC_2 column of the table. The precise Marginal Cost, finally, is tabulated as MC; this was determined by calculus techniques which yielded the equation $MC = 69 - 28q + 3q^2$.[24] As can

---

[22]The left-hand intersection of *MC* and *MR* in the lower panel corresponds to the output in the upper diagram where the vertical difference is greatest between a *higher* Total Cost curve C and a *lower* Total Revenue curve R. This is a *minimum*-profit (or maximum-loss) output.

[23]*Mathematical Footnote:* We are maximizing $\Pi = R - C$ with respect to q. Differentiating and setting equal to zero, we have as the *first-order* condition for a maximum: $dR/dq = dC/dq$, or $MR = MC$. The *second-order* condition for a maximum is that $d^2\Pi/dq^2 < 0$, or $d^2R/dq^2 < d^2C/dq^2$. This says that MR must be falling relative to MC, i.e., that MC must be cutting MR from below to have a maximum of Π.

[24]*Mathematical Footnote:* $C = 128 + 69q - 14q^2 + q^3$. Then $MC \equiv dC/dq = 69 - 28q + 3q^2$.

Table 9.1

Hypothetical Revenue and Cost Functions—Competitive Firm

$$P = 60, \text{ or } R = 60q$$
$$C = q^3 - 14q^2 + 69q + 128$$

q	P	R	C	MC_1	MC_2	MC	AC	V	AVC
0	60	0	128	—		69	∞	0	—
					56				
1	60	60	184	56	(45)	44	184	56	56
					34				
2	60	120	218	34	(26)	25	109	90	45
					18				
3	60	180	236	18	(13)	12	78.7	108	36
					8				
4	60	240	244	8	(6)	5	61	116	29
					4				
5	60	300	248	4	(5)	4	49.6	120	24
					6				
6	60	360	254	6	(10)	9	42.3	126	21
					14				
7	60	420	268	14	(21)	20	38.3	140	20
					28				
8	60	480	296	28	(38)	37	37	168	21
					48				
9	60	540	344	48	(61)	60	38.2	216	24
					74				
10	60	600	418	74		89	41.8	290	29

be seen, MC_2 is indeed a much better approximation than MC_1 to the true Marginal Cost MC.

Since $P = 60$, the condition $MC = P$ leads to the profit-maximizing solution $q^* = 9$. (Using MC_2 and interpolating would yield a close approximation, but note that use of MC_1 and interpolating would lead to a substantial error.) At $q^* = 9$, Total Revenue $R = 540$ and Total Cost $C = 344$; hence profit $\Pi^* = 196.$[25]

The last two columns of Table 9.1 show *Total Variable Cost* $V \equiv C - F$ and Average Variable Cost $AVC \equiv V/q$. The fixed cost F here is equal to 128, and the curve V is everywhere lower than the curve C by this amount. $AVC \equiv V/q$ is less than Average Cost $AC \equiv (F + V)/q$ by the amount F/q. As q increases, this difference diminishes—as indicated numerically in the table and geometrically by the vertical convergence of AVC and AC as we move to the right in the lower diagram. Conversely, of course, the divergence between AVC and AC is greatest for small q at the left; indeed, at $q = 0$, AC is infinite.[26]

[25]There is also a false solution (where MC cuts MR *from above*) at $q = \frac{1}{3}$. At this output, Revenue $= P(\frac{1}{3}) = 20$, and Cost can be computed as equaling (approximately) 149.48. Here a loss is being incurred. (Mathematically, at the false solution the *second-order* condition for a maximum is violated—see footnote 23 above.)

[26]*Mathematical Footnote:* What about Average Variable Cost? At $q = 0$, $AVC = 0/0$ is indeterminate. But applying L'Hôpital's Rule, it can be seen that AVC approaches a finite limit as q approaches zero. This limit is the Marginal Cost MC at $q = 0$. So MC and AVC coincide at $q = 0$. (In effect, the Marginal Cost of the very first infinitesimal unit is also the Average Variable Cost at that output.)

In terms of the geometrical discussion above, it was stated that the MC curve cuts through the low points of both AVC and AC. As shown numerically in the table, the true $MC = AVC = 20$ when $q = 7$; hence this is the minimum of AVC. The table indicates that $MC = AC = 37$ at $q = 8$; this is the minimum of the Average Cost AC.[27]

The maximum-profit condition for the competitive firm is, according to equation (9.13), $MC = MR \equiv P$ (assuming MC cuts MR from below). There is a supplementary condition, however, that runs in terms of the concept of Variable Cost. If the Total Revenue R does not even cover the Total Variable Cost V, then the firm is losing by producing any output at all. Even though the fixed cost F runs on, the firm would do better incurring that fixed expense rather than generating output whose sales value falls short of the variable cost incurred. Hence we have:

(9.14) $R > V$ or equivalently $P > AVC$

                                             Condition for Non-Zero Output

In geometrical terms, the optimal output $q*$ is given by the intersection of MC with the horizontal $MR = P$, as in the lower panel of Figure 9.9, but only if P is greater than a certain minimum "shut-down" price P_V. This minimum is at the level defined by the intersection of the MC and AVC curves, i.e., the shut-down price P_V is the low point or minimum of the Average Variable Cost function. If the actual price P is less than P_V, the optimal output for the firm is simply zero.

PROPOSITION: If market price P is less than the minimum attainable Average Variable Cost AVC, a competitive firm will not produce at all.

But at zero output, and consequently zero revenue, if the fixed cost F runs on then the firm must be incurring a loss. And if $AVC < P < AC$, even though here it pays the firm to produce, still a loss is being suffered. How can a firm stay in business at a loss? The explanation of this possibility runs in terms of the economist's distinction between *short-run* and *long-run* solutions for the firm.

"In the short run some costs are fixed; in the long run they become variable." This is the fundamental difference between long run and short run. The distinction between "long run" and "short run" is not a simple dichotomy, however. The longer the run contemplated, the greater the range of costs that are variable rather than fixed.

Consider a manufacturing firm. Toward the variable end of the fixed/variable cost spectrum are the expenses of input elements like electric power, supplies of materials, and ordinary labor services. Over toward the fixed end are costs associated with ownership or leasing of real estate and machinery. Suppose circumstances (e.g., an interruption of supplies, or breakdown of equipment) call for a very short, say an hour's, reduction of output. Some electric power would be

[27]*Mathematical Footnote:* To find the minimum of AVC, differentiate $AVC = q^2 + 14q + 69$ and set equal to zero. The solution is $q = 7$. To find the minimum of AC, differentiate $AC = q^2 - 14q + 69 + (128/q)$. A cubic equation is obtained, but the only root in the relevant range is $q = 8$.

saved in the slowdown, and somewhat less materials would be used, but little else could or would be changed in the way of cost. If output were cut back over a period as long as a day, some labor might also be laid off. Over a period like a month a large fraction of the labor force might be furloughed (their wages would become a variable cost), and perhaps some leased equipment (e.g., trucks) would be dispensed with. Finally, for a permanent reduction in output the firm will sell off machinery and scale down real-estate commitments.

For simplicity, in the discussion that follows we shall treat the long–short distinction as if it were a dichotomy. The "long run" will mean that *all* costs are variable; the "short run," that some costs are fixed. The relations between *total* short-run and long-run costs, under this assumption, are shown in the upper panel of Figure 9.10. The single Long-Run Total Cost curve $LRTC$ goes through the origin; since there are no fixed costs, if $q = 0$ then $LRTC = 0$. The $LRTC$ function shows the *lowest cost* of producing any given level of output. Why the lowest cost? Because, with all costs variable, for any output q the firm is free to choose the best (most economical) mix and proportion of all resources employed.

Three different Short-Run Total Cost functions are shown in the diagram. First, $SRTC_1$ represents a low level of fixed cost F_1, adapted for a relatively small rate of output. The adaptation is optimal for the rate of output q_1 at which $SRTC_1$ is tangent to $LRTC$; this is optimal because at q_1, $SRTC_1 = LRTC$, and the latter is the *lowest* cost possible of producing output q_1. Along $SRTC_1$ the fixed costs are small, which is fine if output is to be at a low rate. On the other hand, if actual production should become greater than initially contemplated, $SRTC_1$ rises steeply—increments of output beyond q_1 rapidly become very costly. $SRTC_2$ is an adaptation that is optimal for a middling rate of output, q_2 in the diagram. The fixed cost F_2 is at a sufficiently high level to make larger output rates cheaper along $SRTC_2$ than they were along $SRTC_1$; on the other hand, should it turn out that only small output is desired, it would have been better to be operating along $SRTC_1$. Finally, $SRTC_3$ represents a level of fixed cost F_3 that is optimal for the relatively large output rate q_3. It represents the best of the three situations for high output, but the worst if it should turn out that only a small output is wanted.

A common confusion runs somewhat as follows: "The short run is distinguished from the long run in that certain factors are fixed in the short period but variable in the long. Since short-run costs of expanding output involve increases in only *some* of the resources or factors, while long-run costs may involve increases in *all*, short-run costs must be less than long-run costs. Isn't it cheaper to increase output by expanding only variable cost than by expanding both variable and fixed cost?" Expressed this way, the fallacy is evident. The firm would rationally accept an increase in its fixed cost, in its long-run decision, precisely because doing so is *less costly* (involves a more economical mix or proportion of the various factors) than trying to expand output by increasing variable cost alone.

Let us now translate from the total units in the upper panel of Figure 9.10 to average-marginal units in the lower panel. Since $SRTC_1$ lies always above $LRTC$ except at the tangency point q_1 it follows that the corresponding Short-Run Average Cost curve $SRAC_1$ will lie always above the Long-Run Average Cost curve

Figure 9.10

Short-Run and Long-Run Cost Functions. In the upper diagram, *LRTC* is the Long-Run Total Cost function showing the cost of producing any output q when all factors are allowed to vary. The Short-Run Total Cost curve $SRTC_1$ applies when the fixed factor is held constant at a level appropriate for small-scale production (q_1); similarly, $SRTC_2$ and $SRTC_3$ are associated with the higher levels of fixed cost appropriate for medium-scale production (q_2) and for large-scale production (q_3). The corresponding average and marginal curves are shown in the lower diagram. At output q_1, $SRAC_1 = LRAC$ (a tangency) and $SRMC_1 = LRMC$ (an intersection), and similarly for output levels q_2 and q_3. At any output, the Total Cost curves and the Average Cost curves are *never* higher in the long run than the short run. However, over certain ranges Short-Run Marginal Cost may lie below *LRMC*.

$LRAC$ except at q_1.[28] A similar argument applies for the other short-run and long-run curves. The upshot is that the Long-Run Average Cost curve $LRAC$ has the same "lower envelope" property relative to the Short-Run Average Cost curves that $LRTC$ has relative to the Short-Run Total Cost curves.

There is a famous conundrum reflected in the shapes of the various $SRAC$ curves relative to the $LRAC$ curve in the lower panel. Note that while the point of contact of the middle curve $SRAC_2$ with $LRAC$ is at the minimum of the $SRAC_2$ curve itself, this is *not* true for the other two $SRAC$ curves. For $SRAC_1$, the point of contact with $LRAC$ is along the downward slope, and so the minimum of the $SRAC_1$ curve lies to the right of (at a greater output than) the tangency point q_1. For $SRAC_3$ the situation is reversed, and the minimum of $SRAC_3$ is to the left of q_3. This seems puzzling, as suggested by the question: "The point of tangency is a low-cost point. Hence shouldn't the points of tangency coincide with the low-cost points (minima) along the various $SRAC$ curves?"

Exploratory curve-bending will show that it is geometrically impossible to draw an $LRAC$ curve through the *minima* of the $SRAC$ curves, and still have it lie everywhere *below* these curves. For $LRAC$, what we really want to know is the lowest unit cost of producing any given level of output, i.e., the "lower envelope" of the $SRAC$ curves. A point on this envelope is *not generally the lowest-cost output for any given level of fixed cost*, i.e., a minimum along any specific $SRAC$ curve.

Consider now the short-run and long-run *Marginal* Costs. At the tangencies of the $SRTC$ and $LRTC$ curves in the upper panel of Figure 9.10 not only the *levels* but also the *slopes* of the curves in contact are equal. But the marginal function is always the slope of the corresponding total function. It follows that at output q_1, the short run $SRMC_1$ equals the long run $LRMC$; at q_2, $SRMC_2 = LRMC$; and at q_3, $SRMC_3 = LRMC$. This leads to the relation among the various short-run and the long-run marginal curves shown in the lower panel. Note that $LRMC$ has a generally less steep slope than the Short-Run Marginal Cost curves. This feature will play a role in the distinction between the short-run versus long-run *supply functions of the firm*, to be discussed in the chapter following.

There is one difficulty with the concept of "fixed" costs that has been pushed into the background, but now ought to be faced. Common sense tells us that, for an hour's shutdown of output, a firm will not sell off its buildings and machinery with the intention of buying them back when output picks up again. But is this consistent with our analytical models? Why should a firm continue to incur any needless "fixed" costs not dictated by immediate production requirements? Why not sell off the buildings if not needed today? It is sometimes said that "fixity" is the result of previous contractual arrangements, for example, a mortgage on an owned building or a long-term lease on a rented one. But mort-

Chapter 9
THE BUSINESS
FIRM

[28] $SRTC_1 > LRTC$ implies $SRTC_1/q > LRTC/q$. But $SRTC_1/q$ is simply $SRAC_1$ and $LRTC/q$ is simply $LRAC$, so $SRTC_1 > LRTC$ evidently implies $SRAC_1 > LRAC$. At the point of contact itself, at output q_1, the equality $SRTC_1 = LRTC$ implies the equality $SRAC_1 = LRAC$.

gages and leases on an excessive scale can always be renegotiated; any losses incurred in the process are attributable to past errors of judgment, and are in no way costs of current production.

The explanation of "fixity" is connected in part with the feature of the real world discussed at length in the previous chapter—the fact that exchange transactions are not costless. The costs of negotiating and executing complex contracts are what make absurd the idea of sale and repurchase of factory buildings for an hour's production shut-down. But there is an additional element also involved: the *specialization of resources to the firm*.

Many different types of resources may have a degree of specialization to the firm. Machinery can be made to order, buildings partitioned or remodeled, and labor can incur specific training of little or no use to other employers. The presence of such specialized resources imports a degree of *irreversibility* into the firm's employment decision. If the firm used only unspecialized factors it could indeed, subject to the limitations of transaction costs, purchase or sell off resources as required (or enter into or cancel leases) so as to preclude any significant "fixity" as output expands or contracts. Thus temporary increases or decreases in output can, to the extent permitted by transaction costs, be responded to with "appropriate" resource combinations, i.e., along the long-run cost curves. But highly specialized assets owned by the firm will be of little use to other firms and thus have little or no resale value. Hence, the firm will not be inclined to dispose of such assets to meet a reduction of output evaluated as temporary in nature. Nor will the firm very readily acquire more of such a resource merely to achieve a temporary increase in production. Even if such specialized resources are *leased* rather than *owned* (specialized labor may be placed in this category), the cost of cancellation of the lease will tend to be high. The owner of such a resource will, before tailoring it to the needs of the firm and thereby reducing its marketability elsewhere, surely have protected himself by insisting upon steep penalties in the event of cancellation.

In the absence of transaction costs, and if only unspecialized resources were employed in production, *there would then be only a single cost function*—the distinction between "long run" and "short run" would be meaningless. Continuing to neglect transaction costs, but admitting that specialized resources permit firms to produce more cheaply, there are two modes of response to a decline in demand (which a competitive firm would observe as a fall in product price P). (1) The "short-run" response, appropriate for a *temporary* decline in price and so in output, holds the firm's specialized resources fixed and continues to count their cost as a cost of doing business. Thus, "a loss may be incurred in the short run" (AC may exceed P), meaning that it is rational for the firm to accept a temporary loss rather than dispose of a specialized factor that would shortly have to be reacquired. (2) The "long-run" response, appropriate for a *permanent* decline in output, is to dispose of specialized resources no longer needed for projected future production. Hence their cost is no longer "fixed," though in general not all the expenses incurred can be recovered in disposing of them. Whatever accounting loss is incurred in the disposition of specialized factors is a "sunk" cost. It is the consequence of a past error of judgment, but not a relevant cost for any current decision.

Corresponding considerations apply to an *increase* in demand (for a competitive firm, a *rise* in market price P). If regarded as temporary, it will not pay the firm to incur the cost of specializing additional resources, since the expense of doing so will not be fully recovered when the time comes to dispose of them. To the extent that the demand change is regarded as permanent, however, it will become increasingly attractive for the firm to incur additional "fixed" (specializing) costs that make it possible to produce large rates of output cheaply.

CONCLUSION: Factors may be held fixed in the face of a temporary demand fluctuation, in order to avoid round-trip transaction costs associated with purchase and re-sale (or sale and re-purchase), and also to save the costs of specializing factors to the firm. When this occurs, the firm is making a *short-run* response to the fluctuation in demand. A *long-run* response, in which all factors are varied in amount, will be made if the demand change is regarded as permanent.

There have been a good many studies by econometricians and by engineers of the *long-run* costs of electricity production. The general conclusion has been that economies of scale exist, i.e., that in the region of historical experience the Long-Run Average Cost curve *LRAC* has been a declining function of output.[29] Thus, electric power firms appear to characteristically choose levels of capacity (i.e., of "fixed" plant) so as to operate to the left of the minimum of the *LRAC* curve in the diagram of Figure 9.10. This means, in particular, that Long-Run Marginal Cost *LRMC* is less than *LRAC*.

The main technological source of economies of scale is in power *generation*; almost without exception, the larger the generating plant capacity, the cheaper the power output. The main counterbalancing force is the cost of power *transmission*. The more that power generation is concentrated in a single plant of huge capacity, the higher are the transmission losses in carrying power to geographically dispersed customers.

With regard to *short-run* costs, the picture is quite different. A power system must provide for enormous variation in usage even within short periods like a single day; since electricity is non-storable, in peak hours far more power must be produced and delivered than in off-peak quiet hours. Of course, it would be absurd to expect the firm to respond by adjusting "fixed" capacity up and down within the day. And in any case, since these demand fluctuations are obviously temporary, the firm would not want to do so. Hence we would expect to find contractions and expansions of short-run output associated with *SRMC* and *SRAC* curves like $SRAC_1$ and $SRMC_1$ in

EXAMPLE 9.8
ELECTRICITY:
SHORT-RUN AND
LONG-RUN COSTS

---

[29] A review of recent studies is contained in D. Huettner, *Plant Size, Technological Change, and Investment Requirements* (New York: Praeger Publishers, 1974), especially pp. 29–39.

Figure 9.10. In particular, with capacity held fixed, *rising* average and marginal costs should be encountered, at least at the high outputs required for meeting peak demands.

Technologically, there are two main reasons for rising short-run costs in the range of larger outputs. (1) Pieces of electrical equipment generally have a rated "capacity." This is not an absolute limit; capacity can be temporarily exceeded. But if this is done there are corresponding losses from overheating, risk of breakdown, etc. (2) Any power system has plants, and generating units within plants, of differing "technical efficiency" (output/fuel ratio). Rationality dictates that the most efficient equipment will typically be run continuously to carry the "base load." Only as required by demand will increasingly less efficient units be started up, so that average costs rise. (The less "efficient" units may simply be obsolescent equipment close to replacement, but not necessarily. It pays an electrical system to keep some units with relatively poor fuel efficiency, provided that they possess otherwise desirable properties such as low capital costs, rapid start-up, etc.)

Our "Load Dispatching" example 9.7 showed that integrated power systems do take account of the rising *SRMC* curves of generating plants. If plant *SRMC* curves were not rising, there would be no need for dispatching; all the load would always be assigned to the single most efficient plant!

In the circular flow of economic activity, business firms constitute the main *productive* agents of society, engaging in the conversion of resource services into consumption goods. Firms face consumers as suppliers of goods in the product markets, and face resource-owners as demanders of resource services in the factor markets.

In principle all production could be arranged even in the absence of firms, via multilateral contracts among all the resource-owners involved. But the costs of negotiating and enforcing multilateral contracts may make it advantageous to set up a firm, as an artificial entity which can contract *bilaterally* with each separate resource-supplier. The owners of firms (entrepreneurs) are those who take ultimate responsibility, by agreeing to receive only those residual rewards that remain after making contractually agreed payments to other resource-suppliers. In their own self-interest, the owners must monitor performance of these contracts, either directly or indirectly through a hired manager.

Standard economic theory postulates that the business firm can be said to maximize economic *profit*—the difference between revenues and economic costs. Economic costs include not only explicit contractual payments made to hire resources, but also implicit charges to cover the use of those resources self-supplied to the firm by owners, valued at their best alternative employments. To maximize profit, the firm chooses that output at which the excess of revenue over cost is greatest.

For a competitive ("price-taking") firm in the product market, Total Revenue R is simply proportionate to product price P (perceived as constant) as well as to output q. The constant product price itself is equal to both Average Revenue AR and Marginal Revenue MR.

The derivation of the cost function is more complex; it involves the technological relation between inputs and outputs (the production function) as well as the given factor hire-prices h (assuming that the firm is also a "price-taker" in the factor markets). The cost function reflects the operation of the Law of Diminishing Returns in the employment of factors.

If there is only a single variable factor A, marginal and average returns to that factor may rise over a limited range but must eventually diminish. Correspondingly, the firm must eventually face rising Marginal Cost, rising Average Variable Cost, and rising Average Cost in producing output. The relations between these cost variables and the factor Marginal Product and Average Product functions are:

$$MC \equiv \frac{h_a}{mp_a} \, , \quad AVC \equiv \frac{h_a}{ap_a} \, , \quad \text{and } AC \equiv \frac{F}{q} + \frac{h_a}{ap_a}$$

With several variable factors, we can distinguish the effects of varying *factor proportions* and of varying *scale*. At any scale of output, the best factor proportions (for an interior solution involving two factors A and B) are determined by the Factor Balance Equation:

$$\frac{mp_a}{h_a} = \frac{mp_b}{h_b}$$

The relation between Marginal Cost for any scale of output and the two Marginal Products is then:

$$MC = \frac{h_a}{mp_a} = \frac{h_b}{mp_b}$$

It follows that, if optimal factor proportions are attained, Marginal Cost is the same whether output is increased by expanding employment of A or of B (or any mixture of the two). Once again, diminishing Marginal Product for each factor implies rising Marginal Cost of output.

The output level that maximizes profit, for the competitive firm facing constant product price P, is given by:

$$MC = MR \equiv P$$

This is subject to the provisos that: (1) MC must cut MR from below, and (2) Revenue must exceed Total Variable Cost (or equivalently $P > AVC$) so that it does not pay the firm to shut down and not produce at all.

To remain in business in the long run, however, the firm must cover *all* its costs ($P > AC$). But here we are referring to the *long-run* cost function. For producing any level of output, the Long-Run Total Costs can never exceed Short-Run

Total Costs (and similarly the Long-Run Average Costs are never greater than the Short-Run Average Costs). This raises the problem of how it can be rational to respond to a demand change by moving along a short-run cost function, rather than by "unfixing" the fixed factors so as to produce the new output in the cheapest way along the long-run cost function. The answer is that, for permanent demand changes, it *will* be rational always to "unfix" the fixed factors. Short-run responses, which hold some factors fixed, are appropriate for demand changes expected to be only *temporary*. The amount of a fixed factor is not continually varied up or down with temporary demand changes because of transaction costs, together with the fact that such a factor may have been specialized to the firm so as to have comparatively little value in alternative uses.

QUESTIONS FOR CHAPTER 9

Mainly for Review

R1. Why is most productive activity carried out by firms, rather than simply by individuals who contract mutually with one another?

R2. Partnership firms are generally small and are generally managed directly by their owners. Why? How does the corporate form facilitate the organization of larger enterprises?

*R3. What is meant by economic profit? Is profit maximization an appropriate goal for owners? For managers? What tends to happen if owners are not themselves managers?

R4. What would be the effect upon the firm's decisions of a 50 percent tax upon *economic* profit?

*R5. Draw a typical Total Product curve tp_a for a factor of production A. Compare the implications for the Average Product and Marginal Product curves if tp_a has a positive or has a zero intercept on the output axis. Compare the implications if tp_a is increasing at an increasing rate in the initial portion of the curve or if tp_a is increasing at a decreasing rate from the very beginning.

R6. As the quantity of factor A increases, explain why the point of diminishing *marginal* returns is reached first, then the point of diminishing *average* returns, and finally the point of diminishing *total* returns.

*R7. When will a firm respond to changes in economic conditions by a "short-run" adjustment? When by a "long-run" adjustment?

R8. Why is it that a Long-Run Average Cost curve *LRAC* cannot be drawn with both of these properties: (a) It shows the lowest cost at which any given output can be produced (i.e., it is a "lower envelope" of the Short-Run Average Cost curves); and (b) it shows the lowest-cost output at any given level of the fixed factor (i.e., it goes through the minimum points of all the *SRAC* curves)? Which of the two conditions is the correct one?

*T1. Do firms tend to "specialize" or to "diversify" in the employment of factors? Explain why *convex* output isoquants are consistent with observation. What would be observed if output isoquants were *concave* to the origin?

*T2. In railroading, about two-thirds of costs are said to be "fixed" and only one-third "variable." If so, *AVC* is approximately one-third of *AC*. It would therefore always be financially advantageous for railroads, it has been argued, to take on *additional* traffic even at rates lower than Average Cost. Is this argument valid? Explain.

*T3. Why will a firm ever keep *any* factors fixed in the face of changing economic conditions? What determines which classes of factors are held fixed, and which varied?

T4. Compare the effect upon the firm's decisions of (a) a tax of $1 per unit upon output versus (b) a license fee of $200 payable each year regardless of output.

T5. Is the firm's Total Cost curve necessarily rising, or can it have a falling range? Is the firm's Average Cost curve necessarily U-shaped, or can it be rising throughout (or falling throughout)? What of the Average Variable Cost curve? For each allowable shape of the *AC* and *AVC* curves, show the implied shape of the Marginal Cost curve *MC*.

T6. Consider the problem of dividing output most economically between two plants (as in electricity load dispatching). If the Marginal Cost curves are rising, when will one of the plants not be operated? What can be said if the Marginal Cost curves are falling?

*T7. What is wrong with the following reasoning on the part of a factory manager:

> My plant is working steadily at its most efficient output. Nevertheless, I could always meet a short-run surge in demand simply by running the machines a little faster and deferring maintenance. So in the short run my Marginal Cost is practically zero.

T8. Electric utilities commonly keep their most modern and efficient generating equipment, characterized by low ratio of fuel input to power output, working around the clock. Older equipment still on hand is used only to meet periods of higher load. What does this imply about the shape of the Short-Run Marginal Cost curve for generation of electricity? Why doesn't the firm *always* use only the most modern equipment?

*T9. An urban rapid-transit line runs crowded trains (200 passengers per car) at rush hours, but very empty trains (ten passengers per car) at off hours. A management consultant makes the following argument:

> The cost of running a car for one trip on this line is about $50 regardless of the number of passengers. So the per-passenger cost is about 25 cents at rush hour but rises to $5 per passenger in off hours. Consequently, we had better discourage off-hour business.

Is there a fallacy in the consultant's argument? "Commutation tickets" sold by some transit systems (reduced-price, multiple-ride tickets) are predominantly used in rush hours. Are such tickets a good idea?

10.A FROM FIRM SUPPLY TO MARKET SUPPLY: THE SHORT RUN, 304

10.B LONG-RUN AND SHORT-RUN SUPPLY, 308

10.C DETERMINANTS OF THE INDUSTRY'S SUPPLY FUNCTION, 313

10.D FIRM SURVIVAL AND THE ''ZERO-PROFIT THEOREM,'' 318

10.E AN APPLICATION OF SUPPLY AND DEMAND: MANAGING A ''SHORTAGE,'' 321

Examples
    10.1 COTTON SPINDLES, 310
    10.2 PRECLUSIVE BUYING OF WOLFRAM, 312
    10.3 ECONOMIES OF SCALE AND THE SURVIVOR PRINCIPLE—MEDICAL PRACTICE, 319
    10.4 TWO SAN FRANCISCO HOUSING CRISES, 321
    10.5 REPRESSED INFLATION IN POSTWAR GERMANY, 324

10

COMPETITIVE SUPPLY, AND EQUILIBRIUM IN THE PRODUCT MARKET

Core Chapter

This chapter moves on from the behavior of the single firm as a decision-making agent (an optimization problem) to the supply side of the product market as a whole. Competitive (price-taking) behavior on the part of firms leads to a *supply function* in which the outputs of the firms, and therefore the aggregate output of the industry, respond to changes in the market price of the product. Putting this supply function together with the consumers' *demand function* developed in Part Two, we will have all the elements needed to solve the problem of equilibrium in the product market.

10.A

FROM FIRM SUPPLY TO MARKET SUPPLY: THE SHORT RUN

The competitive firm's maximum-profit condition, equation (9.13), is $MC = P$, product price P being taken as constant by the firm. This determines output q at any given level of P. The *supply function* for a competitive firm shows how, meeting this condition, output q responds to changes in price P. The firm's short-run reaction is also subject to the qualification expressed in inequality (9.14):

when market price is less than P_V—the minimum level of Average Variable Cost AVC—the optimal output for the firm is simply zero. Thus, the competitive firm's short-run supply function s_f may have a discontinuity as illustrated by the broken bold curve of Figure 10.1. First s_f runs along the vertical axis, from the origin up to the price P_V, indicating that at any price lower than P_V zero output will be supplied. The supply curve then skips to the right (dotted line) and thereafter follows the rising branch of MC above the point K. The discontinuity is associated with a minimum positive output q_V; as P rises from zero, at the level P_V the firm's output response jumps suddenly from $q = 0$ to $q = q_V$.[1]

Aggregating over all firms producing a particular good, the economy-wide supply curve for that good is obtained. This aggregation is analogous to that of Section 4.D. There, the quantities *demanded* by the separate *individuals* at any given price were summed to obtain the economy-wide or market demand at that price; doing this for all prices led to the overall market demand curve. Here, the quantities *supplied* by the separate *firms* at any given price are summed to obtain the market supply at that price; doing this for all possible prices, we have the overall market supply function. As a result of specialization in production, however, a given good is produced only by a limited subset of firms in the economy—a subset that is called the *industry* associated with that good. So the

Figure 10.1
Competitive Firm's Supply Function—Short Run. At product prices less than P_V, the minimum level of Average Variable Cost AVC, the quantity supplied is zero (the firm's supply curve s_f runs along the vertical axis). Above this price, s_f runs along the Marginal Cost curve.

Output Quantity

Chapter 10
COMPETITIVE
SUPPLY, AND
EQUILIBRIUM
IN THE
PRODUCT
MARKET

[1]*Question for the Student:* Why do we say that the supply function "may" have such a discontinuity? (*Hint:* Is it logically necessary for the curve of Average Variable Cost, AVC, to have an initial falling range?)

aggregate of the firm supply curves for a particular product becomes the *industry supply curve*.

There are two complications to consider, however. First, the number of firms in an industry is not fixed but is itself responsive to price. If an outside firm sees a way of earning a profit in an industry, it will enter; if an inside firm faces the prospect of losses, it will exit. The aggregation of individual firms' supply curves to obtain an industry supply curve must therefore take account of a larger number of firms at high prices, a smaller number at low prices. Entry and exit of firms are considered *long-run* adaptations to changes in demand, to be discussed in the section following. Here we are discussing *short-run* adaptations and will assume that the number of firms is fixed.

The second complication is that each competitive firm was assumed in Chapter 9 to be a price-taker not only with regard to product price but also with regard to factor prices. But when the *industry as a whole* expands or contracts output in response to changes in product price P, there may well be an impact upon the prices of some or all of the resources used in production.

The effect of this consideration is shown in Figure 10.2. Let us suppose that an initial level of product price P' is associated with an industry aggregate output Q'; this price and quantity therefore determine one point on the industry supply curve S. At this initial price each firm has a Marginal Cost curve, like MC in Figure 10.1, which (for prices $P > P_V$) shows the supply reaction of the firm to changes in price. It might then be thought that the effect of a product price increase from P' to P'' can simply be found by moving along the curve denoted $\Sigma s_f'$ in Figure 10.2—the simple horizontal summation of the firm's supply curves—to the output level $\hat{Q}$. But, if the collective expansion of industry output affects factor prices, the industry *as a whole* cannot expand output along $\Sigma s_f'$. Normally, the consequence of increased output would be a *rise* in the prices of factors used by the industry; this would entail an *upward shift* of all the firms' Marginal Cost curves and, therefore, of their supply functions. The upshot is that with a product price rise from P' to P'', the new quantity supplied by the industry will not be $\hat{Q}$ along $\Sigma s_f'$ in Figure 10.2. The correct quantity Q'' lies along a somewhat higher summation curve $\Sigma s_f''$, which reflects the *firms'* upward-shifted MC curves at the higher level of *industry* output. The true supply curve, the dashed curve S in Figure 10.2, will therefore tend to be steeper than would be inferred from looking at the separate firms' MC curves. Put another way, an observer who failed to take this factor-price effect into account would be led to predict too big a supply response of the industry to variations in product price P.

Chapter 10
COMPETITIVE
SUPPLY, AND
EQUILIBRIUM
IN THE
PRODUCT
MARKET

CONCLUSION: The short-run supply curve of a competitive firm is identical to its MC curve (above the minimum of its AVC curve). The short-run supply curve of a competitive industry is the horizontal sum of the firms' supply curves, adjusted for the factor-price effect upon firms' MC curves as the industry output expands or contracts. The factor-price effect normally operates to reduce the magnitude of the supply response to changes in demand, that is, it steepens the industry supply curve.

P

Price

P''

P'

S

$\Sigma s_f''$

$\Sigma s_f'$

0 $Q'\ Q''$ $\hat{Q}$ Q

Industry Quantity

Figure 10.2

Industry Supply Function (Factor-Price Effect). At price P' the industry produces the quantity Q', as one point on the industry supply curve S. When actual industry output is Q', the aggregate of the supply curves *visualized by the separate firms* is $\Sigma s_f'$. But as industry output expands, in response to a product price increase to P'', factor prices tend to be driven up. This raises costs to the firms, forcing their separate supply curves upward so that the aggregate is represented by a curve like $\Sigma s_f''$. Thus, the effective industry supply curve tends to be steeper (less elastic) than the aggregate of firms' supply curves.

It is desirable to have a measure of responsiveness of quantity supplied to price, analogous to the corresponding demand measures discussed in Chapter 5. The most obvious measure of supply responsiveness would be $\Delta Q/\Delta P$, the ratio of the change in quantity per unit change in price along the supply function. But, as explained in Chapter 5, such a ratio has the disadvantage of being affected by changes of conventional units of measurement. Different values for the measure of responsiveness would be obtained if the unit of quantity were pounds instead of tons, or if price were quoted in dollars instead of in cents.

The *elasticity* concept eliminates this difficulty by expressing changes of quantity and price in terms of proportionate rather than arithmetic variation. In this case, we are interested in proportionate response of quantity supplied to proportionate change in price. This concept is called the "elasticity of supply."

DEFINITION: The elasticity of supply κ is the proportional change in the quantity supplied, $\Delta Q/Q$, divided by the proportional change in price, $\Delta P/P$.

For consistency with the treatment of elasticity of demand in Chapter 5, Sections B and C, a symbol like κ_x would more explicitly signify the elasticity of

Chapter 10
COMPETITIVE
SUPPLY, AND
EQUILIBRIUM
IN THE
PRODUCT
MARKET

307

supply of commodity X in response to changes in P_x. *Cross*-elasticity of supply (response of supply of commodity X to changes in the price of any other commodity Y) could be symbolized as κ_{xy}. *Income* elasticity of supply could be defined as well.[2] But attention will be limited here to the direct price elasticity symbolized simply as κ.

$$(10.1) \qquad \kappa \equiv \frac{\Delta Q/Q}{\Delta P/P} \equiv \frac{\Delta Q}{\Delta P} \cdot \frac{P}{Q}$$

To distinguish different commodities, appropriate subscripts would of course be used.

Aside from eliminating undesired effects due to shifts in conventional units of measurement, the elasticity concept permits *inter-commodity* comparisons of the degree of supply responsiveness to price. We can meaningfully say that the supply of some commodity X is more sensitive to price (X has greater elasticity of supply) than some other commodity Y. The elasticity concept also allows price-responsiveness comparisons despite wide variations in *scale*, for example, between a firm's supply function and an industry's supply function. The relation between the firm supply curves and the industry supply curve derived in the previous section, i.e., the relation between the shapes of the Σs_f curves and the S curve in Figure 10.2, can be expressed as follows:

PROPOSITION: The short-run elasticity of supply of the industry is normally *less* than the separate short-run elasticities of supply of its component firms (because of the factor-price shifts that take place with industry-wide changes of output).

10.B

LONG-RUN AND SHORT-RUN SUPPLY

The supply curve of the firm discussed in Section 10.A and pictured in Figure 10.1 is a *short-run* supply function. The *MC* curve involved is a particular *Short-Run* Marginal Cost curve *SRMC* (like the ones in the lower panel of Figure 9.10), that is always associated with a given quantity of a "fixed" factor. As explained in Section 9.E, a factor may be held "fixed" in quantity when the firm is responding to price changes regarded as temporary. The short-run supply curve S of the industry is derived by aggregating these short-run supply curves of the separate firms (with due allowance, of course, for the factor-price effect discussed above).

What if a fall in price were to take place that is regarded as *permanent*? Then the firm has clearly made a mistake in past over-expansion of the "fixed" factor. Its past planning decision that equated *Long-Run* Marginal Cost *LRMC* to

Chapter 10
COMPETITIVE
SUPPLY, AND
EQUILIBRIUM
IN THE
PRODUCT
MARKET

308

[2]The *cross-elasticity* of supply would be relevant for two goods related in production, e.g., wool and mutton. The *income elasticity* of supply might be significant if, for example, higher individual incomes led to a withdrawal of labor from the industry. (In this case, the income elasticity would be *negative*.)

anticipated price P was based upon an over-optimistic evaluation of the price prospects. It now wishes to contract the scale of the "fixed" factor back to the level associated with the condition $LRMC = P$, using the more realistic value of P.[3] In the opposite case, of course, an *increase* in price regarded as permanent would be reacted to by an output adjustment setting $LRMC = P$ via an increase in the scale of the fixed factor.

The competitive firm's long-run supply function Ls_f is pictured as the broken bold curve in Figure 10.3. It has a branch along the vertical axis up to the level of P_C, the low point of the $LRAC$ curve, but above that is represented by the firm's $LRMC$ function. Suppose that a firm is initially in optimal short-run and long-run adjustment to a given level of price P°. In Figure 10.3, we see that at output q° both $SRMC$ and $LRMC$ are equal to P°. Now imagine that price suddenly jumps to P'. If the price change is regarded as *temporary* by the firm, the correct reaction will be to set $SRMC = P'$ at output level q'_s; if regarded as *permanent*, the correct

Figure 10.3

Firm's Long-Run Supply Function. The firm's long-run supply function Ls_f runs along the vertical axis (zero quantity supplied) up to P_C, the minimum level of the Long-Run Average Cost curve $LRAC$. Above this price, the supply function is represented by the curve of Long-Run Marginal Cost $LRMC$.

Output Quantity

Chapter 10
COMPETITIVE
SUPPLY, AND
EQUILIBRIUM
IN THE
PRODUCT
MARKET

309

[3]How *rapidly* it pays to move from the over-expanded to the correct level of the fixed factor depends upon a number of features, including the durability and the resale value of the "excessive" fixed equipment specialized to the firm. If resale value is relatively high, the firm may sell off the excess equipment and move to the correct scale almost immediately. But if resale value is very low, it may pay the firm to retain the equipment until it wears out, rather than dispose of an asset of positive productivity for almost nothing. Note that it may or may not take a long period of *calendar* time to make a "long-run" scale adjustment.

reaction is to set $LRMC = P'$ at output level q'_L. Of course, there will be various degrees rather than a strict dichotomy between "temporary" and "permanent" price changes. In addition, firms may differ in their estimates of the permanence of price fluctuations. In consequence, over any period of time we would expect to observe some *mixture* of "short-run" and "long-run" responses by firms to price changes.

EXAMPLE 10.1
COTTON
SPINDLES[4]

Cotton spinning in the United States is generally regarded as a good approximation of a competitive industry. There are two main geographical concentrations of the industry, in New England and in the South. The table below shows, for each region, the average variation (by calendar quarters over the period 1945–59) in "spindle hours." Spindles as fixed equipment are of course an essential element of spinning, so that spindle hours can be regarded as measuring output. "Changes in Hours per Spindle" may be interpreted as an index of the firms' "short-run" adjustment to the price changes taking place quarter by quarter. "Changes in Active Spindles" represents a "long-run" adjustment—variation in the amount of fixed equipment.

Changes in Cotton Spinning, per Quarter (1945–1959)

AREA	CHANGE IN HOURS PER SPINDLE	CHANGE IN NUMBER OF ACTIVE SPINDLES
Southern States	90.5%	9.2%
New England	76.5	21.8

Source: U.S. Census data cited in G. J. Stigler, *The Theory of Price,* 3rd ed. (New York: Macmillan, 1966), p. 144.

Evidently, the quarterly price changes in this period were predominantly interpreted by firms as temporary, since only to a small extent did they lead to changes in the quantities of "fixed" equipment.

The difference between the two regions appears to be due to the fact that the industry, while relatively static in the South, was definitely declining in New England. In periods of low prices, the higher-cost New England firms were more likely to make long-run adjustments, gradually disposing of their fixed spindle equipment.

[4] Discussion based upon G. J. Stigler, *The Theory of Price,* 3rd ed. (New York: Macmillan, 1966), pp. 143–44.

The *industry* long-run supply curve, like the industry short-run supply curve, is based upon the horizontal summation of the firm supply curves. As before, allowance must be made for the impact of industry-wide expansions or contractions upon factor prices, the effect of which will be as already pictured in Figure 10.2. For both short-run and long-run supply, this factor-price variation makes the industry supply curve less elastic than the separate firms' supply curves.

There is one new element that operates in the long run: *entry and exit of firms*. In long-run equilibrium, for every firm that remains in the industry, price must cover Average Cost: $P \geqq LRAC$. Or, we may say, *profit* must be non-negative. Profits are the excess of revenue (market value of output) over costs (market value of input). If this excess is negative, in the long run the resources will be freed to move to higher-valued uses elsewhere. As this applies to entrepreneurial resources as well, those firms that cannot make a profit at any achievable level of output will eventually exit or cease to exist (the entrepreneur will move to a new industry or will shift to non-entrepreneurial employments). And if a new firm (whether newly organized, or already in existence but outside the industry) can earn a profit within the industry, it will eventually enter.

Summarizing, a given price change leads to a larger supply reaction when firms in the industry adjust along *LRMC* (i.e., when they interpret the price change as permanent) than when they adjust only along *SRMC* (i.e., when they interpret the price change as temporary). And the entry of firms into, or exit from, the industry works in the same direction. A high price leads in the long run not only to a larger quantity response along existing firms' *LRMC* curves, but also to an increase in the *number* of firms; a low price leads in the long run not only to output reductions along *LRMC* curves, but to a contraction in the *number* of firms.

PROPOSITION: Supply response to price changes will be greater in the long run than in the short run. Or, we may say, long-run supply elasticity is greater than short-run.

The effect of "length of run" upon market supply–demand equilibrium is pictured in Figure 10.4. The initial equilibrium situation is represented by price $P°$ and $Q°$ along demand curve DD. Now suppose that demand shifts upward to $D'D'$. The vertical curve labelled IS is what is sometimes called the "immediate run" supply function. It is supposed to represent a period so momentary that production has no time to respond at all. In these circumstances the entire brunt of the equilibrating adjustment must fall upon price, which is determined by the intersection of supply curve IS with the demand curve $D'D'$ at the level P_I. In the period of time allowing short-run adjustments, firms will react by varying output along their *SRMC* curves. These responses, properly aggregated, are represented by the industry's short-run supply curve SS. In the new short-run equilibrium, price P_S is higher than the initial $P°$ but lower than the immediate-run price P_I. Finally, in the long run a greater supply reaction is elicited, so that price declines further to the level P_L—still higher, however, than $P°$ (if the industry long-run supply curve LS has any positive slope).

CONCLUSION: In progressing from immediate-run to short-run to long-run modes of industry response to changes in demand, the impact upon price is moderated while the impact upon quantity produced and exchanged becomes greater.

Chapter 10
COMPETITIVE
SUPPLY, AND
EQUILIBRIUM
IN THE
PRODUCT
MARKET

311

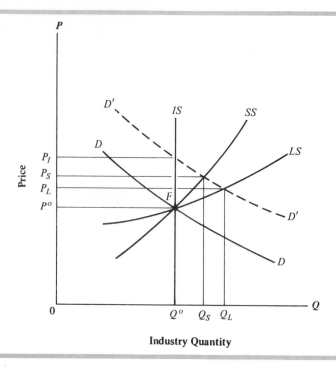

Industry Quantity

Figure 10.4

Market Response to Change in Demand. Starting from an equilibrium at point *F* (price *P°* and Output *Q°*), the demand curve shifts upward from *DD* to *D'D'*. In the "immediate run" it is supposed that quantity *Q°* cannot be changed at all (vertical supply curve *IS*); the entire impact is therefore upon price, which rises to *P_I*. In the "short run" (that is, if firms can vary output but evaluate the demand change as temporary), the sloping supply curve *SS* is relevant; there is now an increase in aggregate quantity produced to *Q_s* and therefore a lessened impact on price (*P_s*). In the "long run" (if firms evaluate the demand change as permanent), *LS* becomes the relevant supply curve; the change in quantity is greatest (*Q_L*), and the change in price is least (*P_L*).

EXAMPLE 10.2
PRECLUSIVE
BUYING OF
WOLFRAM[5]

A striking example of the responsiveness of supply to price changes resulted from the Allied powers' "preclusive buying" program in World War II. In this program the U.S. and Great Britain attempted to cut off the flow of strategic materials from neutral countries to the Axis powers, by prior purchase in the open market.

Wolfram is an ore of tungsten, a vital alloying metal for steel. It is produced in Spain and Portugal, countries that were both neutral in the war and potential suppliers to the Axis. In August of 1940, before the commencement of preclusive buying, the market price of wolfram in Portugal and Spain was $1,144 per ton. Since the Allies were trying to buy up literally

[5]Discussion based on D. I. Gordon and R. Dangerfield, *The Hidden Weapon* (New York: Harper & Brothers, 1947), pp. 105–16.

all the wolfram that would otherwise have gone to Germany and Italy, the price was rapidly driven to unprecedented high levels. By October of 1941 it had reached $20,000 per ton. Portugal reacted by controlling the price and allotting the wolfram supply (in a presumably "equitable" manner) between the Axis and the Allies. Spain, however, chose to let the market process operate unhindered (to the advantage of the Spanish wolfram miners).

The program "succeeded" in the sense that Germany eventually (in July of 1943) quit bidding for Spanish wolfram, making do with substitutes for tungsten alloy. But before this occurred, wolfram production in Spain had increased to ten times its pre-war level. It seemed at times to Allied purchasing agents that every man, woman, and child in the country must be back in the hills digging wolfram. In undertaking the program, the long-run supply elasticity of wolfram production had been seriously underestimated.

DETERMINANTS OF THE INDUSTRY'S SUPPLY FUNCTION

It is useful to classify the determinants of the industry supply function into: (1) elements that are *internal* to the separate firms of the industry; (2) elements that are *external* to the separate firms (but still "internal" to the industry as a whole); and (3) elements associated with entry of firms into, or exit of firms from the industry.

The first determinant of supply, reflecting elements *internal* to the firms, is the variation of cost of production as a function of each firm's *own* output. An "economy of scale" is said to exist when larger output is associated with lower Average Cost; a "diseconomy of scale," when larger output entails higher Average Cost. In the short run, as shown by the shape of the firm's supply function s_f in Figure 10.1, *diseconomies* of scale are dominant—everywhere beyond the minimum output level q_V. This is due fundamentally to the Law of Diminishing Returns studied in the previous chapter. In particular, if one or more factors are held constant in amount, then beyond a certain point increasing inputs of the other factors will be required per unit of added output; diminishing Marginal Product of these variable factors implies rising Marginal Cost of production. The Law of Diminishing Returns is applicable in the short run, since in the short run one or more of the factors are being held "fixed." Hence the *internal diseconomies* of scale dictate rising short-run supply functions for the firms in an industry.

Matters are not so clear in the long run. Figure 10.3 shows that the *LRMC* curve is *less steep* than the *SRMC* curve; i.e., the individual firm's long-run supply function Ls_f is *more elastic* than its short-run supply function s_f. Indeed, it is sometimes contended that if literally *all* factors were variable in the long run, the Law of Diminishing Returns would not be operative. The firm could choose the best factor proportions, and then increase or decrease all factors together as re-

Chapter 10
COMPETITIVE
SUPPLY, AND
EQUILIBRIUM
IN THE
PRODUCT
MARKET

313

quired to produce more output or less. One would then expect to find a *horizontal* Long-Run Average Cost curve *LRAC*, in which case the Long-Run Marginal Cost curve *LRMC* would coincide with *LRAC* (Proposition 2.2c). We need not concern ourselves with this hypothetical issue, as to whether in the "longest of all runs" (with all factors variable) the *LRAC* would be horizontal. For, as discussed in the preceding chapter, it is not really possible for the firm to vary literally all factors. Some inputs to production take forms that are not readily duplicable, for example, the entrepreneurship that characterizes an individual firm, or certain immutable facts of the world.[6] Realistically speaking, even in the long run the Law of Diminishing Returns will apply, so that a range of internal diseconomies will eventually be reached. Thus the competitive firm's Ls_f curve, while more elastic than its short-run supply curve s_f, will still be a rising function of output.

Even granting that a region of internal diseconomies will *eventually* be reached, for sufficiently great output, it still remains possible that this "eventual" condition will not be encountered until the firm's output is too large to be consistent with the survival of competition. If economies of scale dominate through the relevant range, one firm with very large output can always produce more cheaply than its smaller competitors, and will drive them out of business. This is the condition called "natural monopoly," to be discussed in Chapter 11.

The second important determinant of industry supply consists of elements *external* to the separate firms, but nevertheless "internal to the industry." We have already encountered one such influence, illustrated in Figure 10.2—the effect of industry output upon prices of resources used by the industry. No single firm's output decision, in a competitive industry, has other than a negligible effect upon factor prices. But when the industry *as a whole* expands, the prices of factors heavily employed in that industry tend to be driven up. The factor-price effect is thus normally an *external diseconomy* of scale. As shown in Figure 10.2, it makes the supply curve of the industry less elastic than the simple horizontal sum of the separate firms' supply functions. (This is the normal situation. But we will see in Chapter 15 that the supply curve of a factor may be *negatively* sloped, in which case an increase in demand will tend to lower its equilibrium price. This would be an *external economy* of scale.)

External economies and diseconomies can be divided into two categories: "pecuniary" and "technological." In both cases, the externality exists because changes in the *output of the industry* affect the *cost functions of its component firms*. For a "pecuniary" economy or diseconomy, the interaction between industry output and firm cost function comes about solely through changes in the market prices of inputs. For a "technological" economy or diseconomy, on the other hand, industry output directly affects firms' physical possibilities of production— the firms' production functions. The factor-price effect just discussed is an external *pecuniary diseconomy*. As we have seen, pecuniary external effects upon cost functions are normally (though not necessarily always) diseconomies. Technological external effects, on the other hand, can equally well be economies or diseconomies.

Chapter 10
COMPETITIVE
SUPPLY, AND
EQUILIBRIUM
IN THE
PRODUCT
MARKET

314

[6]A traditional example is the following: Would it be possible, by duplicating all the components of the Paris Metro (subway), to double its output? The answer is no, unless we can also duplicate Paris.

As an example of a *technological external economy*, consider firms in the business of farming on marshy soil. In order for farmer A to produce, he must drain his land. But pumping water out of his marshy soil will necessarily help to drain the lands of his neighboring competitors $B, C, D, \ldots$. These latter find that their lands, being less marshy than before, now produce better (Average Cost and Marginal Cost are lower). Similarly, any drainage efforts by his neighbors $B, C, D, \ldots$ will help to shift AC and MC downward for farmer A. If all try to expand output together, all engaging in more drainage, the situation is as pictured in Figure 10.5. The original industry price-quantity equilibrium is at P', Q'. With a rise in price to P'', the $\Sigma s_f'$ curve (the simple aggregation of the firms' s_f' curves) would indicate industry output $\hat{Q}$. But with the externality shifting the firms' MC curves downward, the curve $\Sigma s_f''$ becomes relevant so that the new equilibrium will be at $Q'' > \hat{Q}$. The industry supply curve S is thus more elastic than the separate supply curves of its component firms. It will be apparent that the effect is the reverse of that pictured in Figure 10.2 earlier.

Now consider a *technological external diseconomy*. We can still use an example of neighboring farming firms. But suppose now that the farm lands are too dry rather than too wet. Each farmer must irrigate, pumping water up from underground wells. Doing so drains water away from neighbors' wells, thus *increasing* their Average Cost and Marginal Cost. Here the picture corresponds to

Figure 10.5

Industry Supply Function (External Economy). The picture here is the reverse of Figure 10.2. There, the "external diseconomy" of *rising* hire-prices of inputs, as industry output expands, raised firms' costs and so tended to steepen the industry supply curve. Here an "external economy"—*falling* costs of production incurred by firms as industry output expands—tends to flatten the industry supply curve.

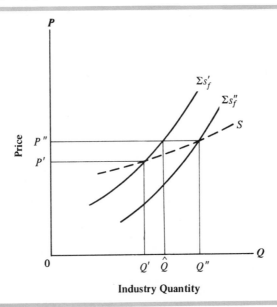

Chapter 10
COMPETITIVE
SUPPLY, AND
EQUILIBRIUM
IN THE
PRODUCT
MARKET

315

Figure 10.2. Note that the diagrams do not of themselves indicate whether the *source* of the externality is pecuniary or technological. Indeed, as a matter of *positive* analysis—for example, predicting the industry's response to price changes—it does not matter whether the "external" effect upon industry supply stems from pecuniary considerations (rising or falling factor prices as industry output expands) or from technological considerations (favorable or unfavorable impacts upon production functions of the separate firms as industry output expands). The only thing that is finally relevant is the ultimate shape of the industry supply function. The distinction between pecuniary and technological externalities is important for *normative* analysis, where we might (for example) be asking whether taxing or subsidizing the industry would be wise social policy.[7]

Is it possible for a favorable externality, an external economy reducing costs of the separate firms as industry output expands, to be so powerful as to make the industry supply curve slope downwards? That is, can the *external economies* be so great as to override the inevitable *internal diseconomies* of scale? The answer is yes. A possible instance is pictured in Figure 10.6 (which represents a more ex-

Figure 10.6

Negatively Sloped Supply Function Due to External Economies. As demand shifts upward from D' to D'', temporarily raising price, firms begin to respond along their individual supply curves whose summation is indicated by the $\Sigma s_f'$ curve through the original price-quantity equilibrium point F. But here the increased industry output sharply reduces firms' costs of production (there is a technological or pecuniary external economy), shifting the summation of the firm's supply curves downward to $\Sigma s_f''$. The new equilibrium point G represents larger quantity at lower price. Thus, the industry's supply curve S is negatively sloped.

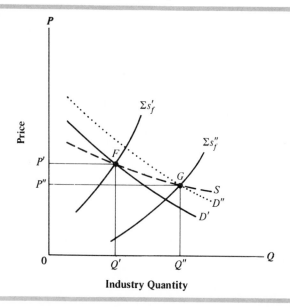

Chapter 10
COMPETITIVE
SUPPLY, AND
EQUILIBRIUM
IN THE
PRODUCT
MARKET

[7]A normative analysis involving the pecuniary vs. technological distinction appears in Chapter 17, under the heading "Welfare Economics."

treme version of the external-economy situation pictured in the preceding Figure 10.5). Starting from an initial equilibrium at F, we can imagine that demand shifts from D' upward to D''. At first (in the "immediate run") there must be an upward movement of price, and so firms begin to expand output along their individual supply curves whose summation is $\Sigma s'_f$. But the resulting increase of industry output sharply reduces firms' costs of production, via a technological or pecuniary external economy. Firms find they can produce more profitably than before, even after the rise in industry output has brought price back down to its old level. Point G shows the ultimate result: in response to an upward shift of demand, equilibrium quantity is larger and price lower. Thus, the industry supply curve has negative slope. At this equilibrium, however, the *firm* supply curves must still be positively sloped; we know that, for an optimum, the firm's Marginal Cost curve MC must cut the horizontal $MR \equiv P$ from below (see Figure 10.1). What has happened is that, at the new equilibrium, the summation curve $\Sigma s''_f$ is so much *lower* than the previous $\Sigma s'_f$, while remaining positively sloped, that equilibrium price is less at the greater output.

The third important determinant that affects the shape of the industry supply curve is entry and exit of firms. This is a long-run phenomenon. Any firm now *inside* the industry that finds market price P to be lower than the price P_C (representing the minimum level of its Long-Run Average Cost $LRAC$ in Figure 10.3) will—if it evaluates this situation as permanent—leave the industry. Any firm now *outside* the industry that can anticipate producing with a Long-Run Average Cost function whose minimum is less than the market price of the industry's product can and therefore will profitably enter.

Exit and entry make industry supply curves more elastic: the industry response to changes in price, upward or downward, will be greater than if only output adjustments by existing firms were allowed for. After an upward demand shift, if an outside firm by entry can produce an increment of industry output more cheaply than existing firms can by expansion, entry will take place—and the reverse in case of a downward demand shift. Indeed, if there were an indefinitely large number of essentially identical firms standing ready to enter or leave, an industry's supply curve would be effectively horizontal (infinitely elastic).[8] But this is an unlikely situation. We must suppose that some firms have a degree of cost advantage in one industry, other firms in other industries. Therefore, if demand increases so as to induce an increment of industry output, we can expect that the new firms that enter characteristically have somewhat *higher* average costs of production than those firms already in the industry. This need not mean that the new firms are more "inefficient"; it may only be that their alternatives elsewhere are relatively more attractive.

CONCLUSION: In a competitive industry, the *internal* determinants (effects of firms' own outputs upon costs) tend to be diseconomies—making the industry supply curve more upward-sloping (more inelastic),

Chapter 10
COMPETITIVE
SUPPLY, AND
EQUILIBRIUM
IN THE
PRODUCT
MARKET

[8]*Qualification:* For this to hold, there must also be no external economies or diseconomies, as discussed above.

though less so in the long run than in the short run. The *external pecuniary* effects of industry output upon firms' cost functions, which work through changes in factor hire-prices, also are normally diseconomies. But *external technological* effects upon cost functions, which work through changes in production functions, can be either economies or diseconomies. *Exit and entry* of firms, a long-run phenomenon, tend to make the industry supply curve more elastic, increasing the quantity response to an upward or downward shift of demand.

FIRM SURVIVAL AND THE "ZERO-PROFIT THEOREM"

Under competitive conditions there is always pressure on economic profit. Wherever profit exists, output tends to expand so that product prices move downward (lowering firms' revenue functions) while resource prices tend to move upward (raising firms' cost functions). Profit is thus squeezed from above and from below.

Returning to Figure 10.4, suppose that starting from a position of supply-demand equilibrium at price P° and industry output Q°, an unanticipated increase in demand from DD to $D'D'$ takes place. As we saw in Section 10.B, in the *immediate run* the full impact is on product price, which shifts upward to P_I; every firm in the industry will then (momentarily) be receiving increased profit. Moving from the immediate period to the *short run*, the firms in the industry will increase output. The consequence will not only be a fall of product price to P_S, a partial return toward the previous equilibrium price P°, but also a tendency for *factor prices* to rise in response to the industry's expansion of output. Firms will still be predominantly better off at price P_S than at the previous equilibrium P° (though it is conceivable that a few who are especially vulnerable to factor-price increases might actually end up worse off). The opportunity of earning an economic profit—revenues greater than economic costs—leads in the *long run* to still further expansion of firm output and also to the entry of new firms. Product price therefore moves still further back downward to P_L. Also, the additional industry output expansion tends to force factor-input prices upward still more.

Where does this process end? Entry stops (long-run equilibrium is attained) when no firm still outside the industry can see its way to earning a profit within. It follows that the "marginal firm," the one just on the borderline of entering or leaving the industry, can earn only negligibly more within the industry than outside. Thus, its *economic* profit (excess of revenues over the best alternative foregone) in the industry is essentially zero.

Does it follow that the "infra-marginal" firms, i.e., firms whose lower costs in the industry (or poorer alternatives elsewhere) permit them to remain in the industry even at lower prices than P_L, are earning positive economic profits in long-run equilibrium? No, because if they were there would still be upward pres-

Chapter 10
COMPETITIVE
SUPPLY, AND
EQUILIBRIUM
IN THE
PRODUCT
MARKET

318

sure on *factor* prices. The reasoning goes as follows. If an "infra-marginal" firm is earning positive economic profit, it must be that its Average Costs are lower than those of the marginal firm. Some special resource employed by the infra-marginal firm must be responsible for its unusually low cost of production. *All firms in the industry will be bidding for the right to employ that special resource*, and in the long run its hire-price must be driven upward so as to eliminate the profit.

A clear case occurs in mining. Suppose the demand for copper rises, and the long-run equilibrium price for copper is higher than before. New firms will have entered to develop copper ore bodies previously too lean to work. If the marginal firm working a very thin ore just breaks even, it might be thought that an infra-marginal firm exploiting a richer ore body should be making a handsome profit. And indeed it may, in the short run. But in the long run all firms in the industry will be bidding for the right to work the richer ore. Consequently, the owner of the resource, i.e., the owner of the richer body of ore, will be able to renegotiate the contract with the user firm so as to recapture any extra profit earned.

What if the firm is itself the legal owner of the richer ore body? Here is where the distinction between *economic profit* and *accounting profit* (see Section 9.C) becomes essential. The accounting profit attributed to the firm controlling a rich ore body may indeed be high. But in principle, that firm could cease its operations and lease or sell the ore body to another firm. It should therefore charge itself, as an *economic cost* of its mining operations, the highest bid an outsider would make for the right to exploit its ore. In this way, its *economic profit* as a mining firm also becomes zero in long-run equilibrium.

PROPOSITION: In the long run, economic profit for any firm in a competitive industry is zero.

Of course, in an ever-changing world the "long run" may never actually arrive. Something almost always happens to change the conditions of long-run equilibrium before that state is achieved. But the *tendency* toward zero economic profit, due to downward pressure on product price and upward pressure on factor prices, is an important aspect of competitive industries.

The continuing pressure upon firm survival provides a source of information about *efficient scale* of production for firms in a competitive industry. Those firms having chosen inappropriately small or inappropriately large levels of "fixed" factors will have high Average Costs of production. In the long run, if they are to survive in the industry, such firms must shift to a more appropriate scale. "The survivor principle"[9] uses observed changes in the proportions of industry output accounted for by firms of different sizes as evidence concerning typical cost functions in the industry.

EXAMPLE 10.3
ECONOMIES OF
SCALE AND THE
SURVIVOR
PRINCIPLE—
MEDICAL
PRACTICE

[9]See G. J. Stigler, "The Economies of Scale," *Journal of Law & Economics*, v. 1 (Oct. 1958).

The survivor principle was applied to medical practice by H. E. Frech III and P. Ginsberg. They compared the market shares of physicians engaged in solo versus joint practice for the years 1965 and 1969. As can be seen from the table, the share accounted for by solo- and two-physician practices declined, whereas all larger-sized groups gained in market share between 1965 and 1969. There is a suggestion in the data that moderately-sized groups (3–6 physicians) as well as rather large groups (26 or more physicians) may both have constituted efficient sizes in this period.

Market Share by Group Size, Medical Practice

GROUP SIZE	1965	1969	RATIO (1969/1965)
1–2	84.69%	78.25%	0.92
3	3.12	4.39	1.41
4	2.33	3.13	1.34
5	1.33	1.87	1.41
6	0.87	1.38	1.59
7	0.73	0.77	1.06
8–15	2.76	3.43	1.24
16–25	1.54	1.66	1.08
26–49	0.75	1.78	2.37
50–99	0.58	1.22	2.10
100+	1.31	2.12	1.62
Total	100.0	100.0	

Source: H. E. Frech III and P. Ginsberg, "Optimal Scale in Medical Practice: A Survivor Analysis," *Journal of Business*, v. 47 (Jan. 1974), p. 30.

The data in the table can be interpreted quite differently, however, depending upon whether a static or dynamic viewpoint is adopted. From the former point of view, even in 1969 the great bulk of the market was accounted for by surviving single- or two-physician groups. This strongly suggests that small size must indeed be the most efficient in medical practice. On the other hand, it is precisely this size that is declining, relative to all others. So it appears that, *on the margin*, firms of moderate and large size are the most profitable. New entrants find it advantageous to form groups of moderate or large size, while exiting forms come disproportionately from the small 1–2 physician class.

A reasonable interpretation of the data is that at any point of time there is an efficient *mixture* in an industry, of firms varying over a spectrum of sizes. Even though the small 1–2 physician class may on the whole be most efficient in medical practice, there may still at the present moment be relatively *too many* in this size class. So we observe proportions shifting in favor of the larger groups.

AN APPLICATION OF SUPPLY AND
DEMAND: MANAGING A "SHORTAGE"

In a world of change, the conditions determining supply and demand—preferences, productivity, and resources—are continually varying. In consequence, equilibrium or "market-clearing" prices are also ever-changing. Some of this variation does not seem to generate serious complaint. People are not disturbed that department-store sales take place after Christmas (i.e., that consumers must pay higher prices in their pre-Christmas shopping). Nor does the fact that vegetables are cheaper after harvest, or cheaper at farm roadstands than in big-city markets, seem to raise controversy. But shifts in supply or demand are sometimes both unexpected and dramatic, drastically affecting the established relations among groups in the community. In such circumstances political pressures may arise for government interventions designed to prevent or to cancel out some or all of the price effects of the shift to a new market-clearing solution.

Interferences with market equilibrium were studied in Section 2.A as an illustration of the use of supply-demand analysis; in Section 7.E their consequences were evaluated employing the concepts of Consumer Surplus and Producer Surplus. Our purpose here is to analyze the repercussions of government market interventions upon short-run and long-run supply-demand responses.

Interventions designed to prevent price from adjusting to an increase in demand, or to a decrease in supply, tend to create a "shortage."[10] The standard use of the word "shortage" in economics refers not to physical scarcity, but to a supply–demand imbalance at the existing price. This does indeed seem to correspond with popular terminology. People speak of "shortages" when goods become not just expensive but *unavailable*, partially or completely, in the market. Thus, faced with a supply or demand shift dictating a higher equilibrium price, consumers are bound to lose out one way or the other—either from the higher price if the market adjustment proceeds unimpeded, or from the "shortages" consequent upon interventions that succeed in maintaining a lower price.

In the 1906 earthquake and fire, the city of San Francisco lost more than half its housing facilities in three short days. Nevertheless, the first post-disaster issue of the *San Francisco Chronicle* had no report of a "housing shortage"! Indeed, the newspaper's classified advertisements carried 64 offers of houses or apartments for rent and only 5 ads for apartments or houses wanted. Of course, prices of accommodations rose sharply.

EXAMPLE 10.4
TWO SAN
FRANCISCO
HOUSING CRISES[11]

[11]Discussion based on M. Friedman and G. J. Stigler, "Roofs or Ceilings?" The Foundation for Economic Education (Irvington-on-Hudson, New York, Sept. 1946).

[10]In the opposite case, where interventions prevent adaptation to decreased demand or to increased supply, commodity "surpluses" are generated.

In contrast, in 1946 San Francisco was gripped by the national postwar "housing shortage." In the first five days of 1946 newspapers carried only 4 ads offering houses or apartments for rent, but around 150 ads by persons wanting to rent houses or apartments. The explanation is that in 1906 the catastrophic reduction in the housing stock led to a price adjustment in the form of a sharp rise in rents to a new equilibrium level. But in 1946, rents "frozen" below the market-clearing price left an excess of quantity demanded over quantity supplied.

COMMENT: In the physical sense, housing supply relative to population was clearly much more scarce after the 1906 earthquake and fire than in 1946. The 1946 "shortage" was an outgrowth of the general price freeze aimed at controlling inflation during and after World War II. Actually, housing supply had not decreased at all in the wartime period. But rising money incomes, the return of war veterans, and a high rate of family formation led to an upward shift in demand for housing. With rents frozen, a "shortage" ensued.

We shall not be concerned here with the normative question of how a shortage "should" be managed, but only with the positive consequences of alternative ways of coping with it. It is important to distinguish between short-run and long-run consequences. Figure 10.7 illustrates a "ceiling," holding price at its previous equilibrium $P°$ after demand has shifted upward from D to D'. The *perceived* shortage is the magnitude H in the diagram—the demand-supply gap at price $P°$. In the unimpeded market process, price would jump in the first instance to the immediate-run level P_I, as previously discussed, but would eventually come down to the long-run equilibrium at P_L. The market would eliminate the shortage, in the short run primarily by a high price choking off demand, but in the long run increasingly via an augmentation of supply. At the price P_L in Figure 10.7, the interval ΔD is the long-run *reduction* in demand quantity while ΔS is the long-run *increment* of supply.

With a price ceiling, in the immediate run the effect is often said to be "purely distributive." The same supply remains on the market; a ceiling price at $P°$ means only that producers fail to make a "windfall" gain (the shaded area in the diagram) at the expense of consumers. But a price ceiling that remains effective for a longer period increasingly forecloses the operation of forces that would have provided additional supply.

Chapter 10
COMPETITIVE
SUPPLY, AND
EQUILIBRIUM
IN THE
PRODUCT
MARKET

The assertion that the immediate-run effect of a price ceiling is purely distributive between consumers and producers is also somewhat of an oversimplification. In the absence of a ceiling, price would rise in the immediate run to P_I, and the supply on hand $Q°$ would go to those consumers willing to pay at least as much as P_I. But at the low ceiling price $P°$ there will be an *enlarged potential demand*—the amount $\hat{Q}$. It may be, in consequence of whatever commodity allocation scheme is adopted, that some relatively low-valued demands (for which consumers are willing to pay little above $P°$) are actually satisfied while some

Industry Quantity

Figure 10.7

Effect of a Shortage. An upward shift of demand in an uncontrolled market, from D to D', is met in the "immediate run" by an increase only in price (from P^o to P^I). Producers benefit from a temporary "windfall" gain (shaded area) at the expense of consumers. Ultimately, an increase in supply is induced so that in long-run equilibrium price comes back down part-way to P_L. If a "ceiling" is enforced at the initial price P^o, both supply and demand adjustments are blocked. H is the perceived "shortage" at the ceiling price. In uncontrolled long-run equilibrium, ΔD of the shortage amount would be the demand quantity choked off by the higher price, while ΔS would be the supply increment provided.

high-valued demands (for which consumers would be willing to pay more than P_I) are not. Thus some consumers may benefit at the expense of others.

Some consequences of blocking the price rise that would adapt supply to demand are not visible in the supply and demand functions themselves. Unable to raise price openly, firms may divert energies and resources to subterfuges. They may eliminate discounts or seasonal sales, reduce quality or variety or convenience of their offerings, or concentrate production in product lines that happen to have received a better break from the price-control authorities. Supplies may be attracted into uncontrolled foreign markets that were previously unremunerative, leaving even less available for domestic consumers. And of course black markets may arise, providing a wider scope for elements of the population specializing in illegal activity. In extreme cases, the cumulative effect may be a breakdown of legitimate trade.

General price inflation, such as has been experienced in much of the world during the decade of the 1970s, is a topic in *macro*economics. But in an attempt to remedy or perhaps only to mask the inflationary process, governments may be led

Chapter 10
COMPETITIVE
SUPPLY, AND
EQUILIBRIUM
IN THE
PRODUCT
MARKET

323

to impose price ceilings or "freezes" in some or all markets. Then, prices over greater or lesser reaches of the economy will no longer be free to reconcile supply and demand. While the initiating source of the disequilibrium lies in the realm of macroeconomics, the imbalances in particular markets can be analyzed by using the tools of *micro*economics. In this connection, we can learn much that is useful from a previous great inflationary episode—that associated with World War II and its aftermath.

EXAMPLE 10.5
REPRESSED
INFLATION IN
POSTWAR
GERMANY[12]

Germany, like most of the belligerent countries in World War II, had financed her war effort by inflationary expansion of money and credit. Simultaneously, price freezes were employed to prevent this expansion from being reflected in market prices. By 1945, wartime finance had increased liquid funds in the hands of the public around tenfold, while prices were still largely at the levels frozen by the Nazi government back in 1936. And, of course, Germany faced not only the "normal" aftermath of a war that saw her cities and industry smashed by bombing, but also the special problems of a defeated nation—divided, occupied, and subjected to punitive reparations.

In the early postwar years, the Occupation authorities directing the German economy maintained the wartime price freeze. (This was not a special attempt to punish Germany, but represented the "conventional wisdom" of the period; very much the same policies were pursued by the Western occupying powers in their own domestic economic programs.) But the levels of German prices were so drastically out of line with supply-demand reality that over most of the economy production for legal sale could take place only at a financial loss. Industrial production in the first half of 1948 was only 45% of 1938, despite a larger population. The black market was, surprisingly, estimated to account for only 10% of transactions. This figure is extremely low because in Germany the term "black market" was given a very narrow definition: to wit, outright trading of goods for cash at illegal prices (a practice professionally engaged in by a specialized class of disreputable individuals). In contrast, *everybody* engaged without moral taint in a form of transaction known as "bilateral exchange" or "compensation trade." This trade took place at entirely legal prices in money, with one catch: No one could acquire goods or services for money alone. In addition to the money price, the purchaser had to provide "compensation" in real goods and services. Estimates are that one-third to one-half of all transactions took this form. Even the Occupation authorities engaged in it; the noon meal provided to German employees of the Occupation administration (at legal prices, of course) was often the chief attraction of such employment. Thus, the "legal" monetary transaction was a fig-leaf. What was actually taking place was the *de facto* elimination of money as medium of exchange—regression to the inefficiencies of barter (as discussed in Section 8.D).

The longstanding price freeze meant that relative prices were more or less seriously out of line, but the overwhelming fact was that almost *all* money

[12]Discussion based on J. Hirshleifer, *Disaster and Recovery: A Historical Survey*, The Rand Corporation, RM–3079–PR (April 1963), pp. 83–112.

prices were too low. The Erhard policy of June 1948 was correspondingly double-barreled: (1) a drastic currency reform, exchanging new marks for old, cut down the money supply by a factor of about ten; and (2) price controls were removed. The effect was dramatic. According to one observer: "It was as if money and markets had been invented afresh as reliable media of the division of labor."[13] The German postwar economic miracle was under way.

[13]H. Mendershausen, "Prices, Money and the Distribution of Goods in Postwar Germany," *American Economic Review*, v. 39 (June 1949), p. 646.

The German example suggests that a *general* shortage of goods relative to money, i.e., an inflationary situation repressed by price controls, can to some degree be coped with by reduction of liquid funds in the hands of the public. In the extreme situation of Germany, this took the form of actually calling in the old currency and replacing it with smaller amounts of the new. More normally, funds in the hands of the public could be reduced by fiscal and monetary policies—by raising taxes, increasing bank reserve requirements, selling bonds to the public, etc.—as discussed in courses in macroeconomics.

Even for specific shortages in narrower sectors, it remains true that a general reduction of purchasing power will tend to mitigate the upward pressure on price. But more sharply focused measures would have a more concentrated effect. In place of a ceiling, a specific *tax* might be levied upon consumption of the commodity. As discussed in Section 2.A.3, a tax introduces a gap between the *gross* price P^+ paid by buyers and the *net* price P^- received by sellers. In Figure 10.8, a tax has been imposed that brings the *net* demand back from D' to the same D that it was initially. The result, as indicated, is that the price P_I along the immediate-run supply curve is the same as the gross price P^+ paid by buyers; similarly, the price P^- received by sellers is the initial price P°. The consequences of such a tax are: (1) The shortage is eliminated; supply and demand are in balance at the specified gross and net prices. (2) There is no "windfall" benefit *to sellers*. Buyers will lose, but the windfall amount (the shaded area in the diagram) goes to the government instead. (3) The limited supply available in the immediate run is allocated only to consumers with highest demand prices—those willing to pay at least P_I. (4) But there is no tendency for supply to increase, in the short run or the long run. Thus, the supply side of the normal economic response to the upward shift of demand from D to D' has been cancelled out. This last is the great weakness of "managing" a shortage through a tax.

It would be possible, by a tax somewhat smaller than that just described, to achieve an intermediate result. Suppose as before that demand shifts upward from an initial D to D'. Now let a tax be imposed that brings the *net* demand down only to the dashed curve labelled D^- in Figure 10.9. The long-run equilibrium is at output Q', some expansion from Q° having taken place. The gross price to buyers is P^+, and the net price to sellers P^-. Had such a tax been combined with imposition of a price ceiling at the level of P^+, the net price would have been high

Chapter 10
COMPETITIVE
SUPPLY, AND
EQUILIBRIUM
IN THE
PRODUCT
MARKET

325

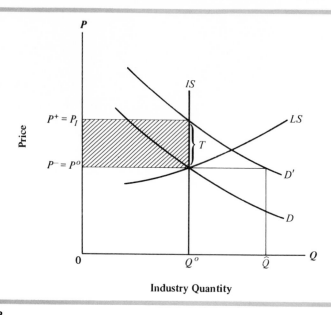

Industry Quantity

Figure 10.8

Tax versus Shortage, 1. As in Figure 10.7, here also demand initially shifts upward from D to D'; in the "immediate run," equilibrium price would increase from P' to P_I. Imposition of a per-unit tax in the amount T (equal to the upward shift of the demand curve) dictates that the gross price paid by consumers (P^+) will equal the new equilibrium price P_I while the net price received by producers (P^-) remains at the old equilibrium level P^o. The consequence is that there is no shortage; the increase in demand is entirely choked off by the higher gross price (the "windfall gain" goes to the government). But the supply response that would have taken place in the longer run is also completely blocked.

enough to elicit a partial long-run supply increment $Q' - Q^o$, while still lopping off the "immediate-run" tendency of price to go still higher. (However, the market would be in disequilibrium during the immediate-run period, since only a price as high as P_I can reconcile supply and demand in the very short run.)

Another line of attack upon a shortage would be through *rationing*. Effective demand for a particular good could be controlled by the requirement that the consumer possess a valid ration ticket for each unit consumed. Rationing was discussed in Section 6.B above. We saw there that ration allotments can be regarded as a secondary type of "income constraint" upon the consumption of individuals. Since *both* money and ration coupons must be on hand to acquire consumable goods, the effect of rationing is to reduce the legal market demand for the rationed good.

Rationing can therefore reduce pressure upon a price ceiling. Or, rationing may be imposed *instead* of a price ceiling. Under rationing, only the portion of demand validated by coupons can legally enter the market. In Figure 10.7, therefore, imposition of rationing may bring the effective demand curve back down from D' to the original D once more, so that the market can clear at the original price P^o. Sufficiently severe rationing can entirely eliminate the shortage—the dif-

Chapter 10
COMPETITIVE
SUPPLY, AND
EQUILIBRIUM
IN THE
PRODUCT
MARKET

326

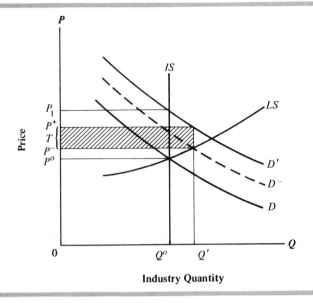

Figure 10.9

Tax versus Shortage, II. With an initial demand increase from *D* to *D'* as in Figure 10.8, here the tax *T* imposed is somewhat smaller. Some partial supply response takes place in the long run, since the net price received by producers *(P⁻)* is greater than the previous equilibrium level *P°*. Consumers pay a higher gross price *(P⁺)*, but not so high as to entirely choke off increased consumption. Again, in the absence of a price ceiling there is no shortage. The shaded area represents the tax receipts of the government.

ference between quantity demanded and quantity supplied at a price ceiling. But without an increase of price to suppliers, *there will still be no supply response* to the original rise in demand. And, in contrast with a tax, rationing will involve an additional loss of Consumer Surplus unless the coupons are "ideally" assigned to those with highest demand prices for the good (see Section 7.E.2).

This last objection would be eliminated if the ration coupons were legally *salable*. In that case, apart from transaction costs, the coupons would be purchased by those most willing to buy the good. The initial assignment of ration tickets is then irrelevant, except insofar as it involves a redistribution of income. In effect, part of Consumer Surplus is transferred from buyers of the good to those coupon-holders who choose to sell their ration entitlements. As a practical matter, it should be noted that ration tickets may be surreptitiously transferred even where sale is not legal. Also, a black market in the rationed good may come into existence whether or not coupons are salable; either way, there remains a motive to engage in unrationed transactions.

CONCLUSION: Attempts to protect consumers from the effects of a *price* increase tend to deflect the *quantity* response that suppliers would otherwise be induced to provide. And since supply is increasingly elastic in the long run, this disadvantage increases over time.

Chapter 10
COMPETITIVE
SUPPLY, AND
EQUILIBRIUM
IN THE
PRODUCT
MARKET

327

The supply curve of the firm may have a discontinuity. For the short-run supply curve s_f, zero quantity will be offered at any price lower than P_V (the low point of the curve of Average Variable Cost AVC); above that price, s_f is identical with the Marginal Cost curve MC. For the long-run supply curve Ls_f, the minimum price for non-zero output is P_C, the low point on the Average Cost curve AC; above that price, Ls_f is identical with the Long-Run Marginal Cost curve $LRMC$.

In moving from firm supply to industry supply, at each price the quantities offered by all firms are added (horizontal summation). However, it is necessary to take into account not only the "internal" effects upon firms' costs of production (impacts on cost due to variation in each firm's own output) but also the "external" effects upon firms' costs due to changes in industry-wide output. The extent of entry into or exit from the industry as demand shifts up or down must also be considered.

The "external" effects are rather complex to analyze. External *economies* reduce firms' costs as industry output rises; external *diseconomies* do the opposite. The external effects may be "pecuniary" (impact of industry-wide output changes upon hire-prices of factors) or "technological" (impact upon firms' production functions). Pecuniary external effects are normally *diseconomies*, since increases in industry output generally drive up the hire-prices of factors used in that industry; the result is to make the industry supply curve less elastic. But technological external effects can go either way. It is even possible for *external economies* to override the inevitable *internal diseconomies* of scale, so as to bring about a negatively sloped industry supply curve.

In the "immediate run," quantity produced by the industry is considered to be invariant (the *IS* supply curve is absolutely inelastic). The entire impact of any demand shift is therefore reflected by change in price. Allowing short-run adjustment of firms' outputs leads to the industry *SS* supply curve, along which positive elasticity is normal; the change in price following a demand shift is therefore moderated by a quantity response. In the long run, the industry supply curve *LS* is even more elastic. This is due to the "internal" fact that *LRMC* curves slope less steeply upward than *SRMC* curves, and also to the entry of new firms in response to price increases (or exit of old firms in response to price decreases).

Under competitive conditions there is always pressure on firms' profits. If profit exists, output expansions on the part of the industry tend to reduce product price (pressure from above) and to raise factor prices (pressure from below). In long-run equilibrium the *marginal* firm must be making zero economic profit, thus precluding either entry or exit. But even *infra-marginal* firms also achieve only zero profit in the long run. Since different firms in the industry can compete for any input responsible for the low costs leading to positive profit, in the long run that factor will command a hire-price capturing the entire benefit for its owner.

If demand shifts upward, the imposition of a price freeze creates a shortage—an excess of quantity demanded over quantity supplied. Consumers gain by not having to pay a higher price, but the supply response that would have occurred in the long run is blocked. This is a source of loss to producers and consumers

Chapter 10
COMPETITIVE
SUPPLY, AND
EQUILIBRIUM
IN THE
PRODUCT
MARKET

328

together. There are also losses and difficulties due to the need for non-price methods of coping with the imbalance between demand and supply at the artificially low price. Tax and/or rationing schemes that limit demand can be imposed, thereby tending to eliminate the shortage. When the rise in price that would otherwise have gone to sellers is deflected, however, the long-run supply response remains blocked.

QUESTIONS FOR CHAPTER 10

Mainly for Review

*R1. At any rate of output, the industry *long-run* supply curve tends to be less steep than the *short-run* supply curve. Is it also necessarily more elastic? Explain.

*R2. "In the long run, a firm could always produce twice as much simply by doubling the amount of every factor employed. So, in the long run there must be constant returns to scale." Evaluate.

 R3. Does elasticity of supply for an industry tend to be great or small if the firms' Marginal Cost curves are sharply upward-sloping? What is the effect on elasticity of supply if higher industry output markedly drives up the prices of factors employed in the industry?

*R4. If there are N identical firms and no "external" effects on factor prices, is the *industry* supply curve more or less steep than the *firm* supply curve? More or less elastic?

 R5. Explain the distinction between "internal" and "external" economies or diseconomies.

*R6. In long-run equilibrium, why does the marginal firm (the highest-cost firm in the industry) earn zero economic profit? Why do infra-marginal firms earn zero economic profit?

 R7. Consider an industry with a downward-sloping supply curve. Starting from an initial equilibrium, will a decline in demand lead to a rise or a fall in price? To a rise or a fall in output? Explain.

For Further Thought and Discussion

*T1. "In a competitive industry, for any firm there may be internal economies of scale over a certain range. But each firm must be actually operating in the region where internal *diseconomies* of scale dominate over the economies of scale." True or false? Explain.

 T2. Under what circumstances would you expect a rise in demand for an industry's product to be met primarily by a "short-run" output response on the part of existing firms? By a "long-run" response on the part of existing firms? By entry of new firms?

*The answers to asterisked questions appear at the end of the book.

Chapter 10
COMPETITIVE
SUPPLY, AND
EQUILIBRIUM
IN THE
PRODUCT
MARKET

T3. Which of the following is a "pecuniary" effect, which a "technological" effect? Which is "internal" to the firm, which "external" to the firm (but internal to the industry)?

a. As the number of films produced rises, stars' salaries go up.
b. As fishing intensifies, each fisherman finds fish scarcer.
c. As new shops open, existing shops find customers scarcer.
d. Steel mills along a river use the water for cooling—but the greater the use, the warmer the water gets.

*T4. If at a certain equilibrium price every firm in the industry is earning zero economic profit, doesn't that imply that a fall in market price would mean that no firms at all could continue to survive? Explain.

T5. A number of techniques are available to cope with increased scarcity and higher world prices of petroleum. Analyze the following in terms of supply–demand responses in the short run and long run:

a. Price freeze and "rationing by queue" (waiting in line for gasoline).
b. Price freeze and rationing by coupon (non-salable).
c. Rationing by coupon (non-salable) without a price freeze.
d. A tax on all petroleum used.
e. A tariff on *imports* of petroleum.

*T6. In policy (c) above (rationing by coupon without a price freeze), suppose consumers were permitted to sell ration coupons to one another. Would this tend to elicit more supply? Would the limited supplies be reallocated to those with higher demand prices? Explain the consequences in terms of the concept of Consumer Surplus.

T7. Suppose that, after a decline in demand for a product, a *floor* is placed under its market price. Then the problem arises of managing a "surplus." What are the disadvantages of a price floor? Would the disadvantages tend to increase over time, as in the case of managing a shortage, or would the disadvantages tend to evaporate over time in the "surplus" case? Would black markets tend to develop?

*T8. Under recent petroleum regulation in the United States, a price freeze was placed on "old oil"—defined, roughly speaking, as petroleum from existing wells. The justification was that producers had to be offered more to induce them to drill new wells, but the output from existing wells would be forthcoming even at low prices. Is this argument correct?

T9. In the longer run, the presence or even the threat of price freezes may induce firms to integrate vertically (to merge with "upstream" supplier firms or with "downstream" customer firms). Explain why.

11.A MONOPOLY AND NON-PROFIT GOALS, 333

11.B MONOPOLY PROFIT-MAXIMIZING OPTIMUM, 334
    11.B.1 Price–Quantity Solution, 334
    11.B.2 Monopolist versus Competitive Solution, 338
    11.B.3 An Application: Author versus Publisher, 342

11.C MONOPOLY AND ECONOMIC EFFICIENCY, 344

11.D REGULATION OF MONOPOLY, 348

11.E MONOPOLISTIC PRICE DISCRIMINATION, 350
    11.E.1 Market Segmentation, 351
    11.E.2 Multi-Part Pricing, 352
    11.E.3 Perfect Discrimination, 355

11.F CARTELS, 357

Examples
    11.1 COMPETITION AND COSTS OF TRADING, 341
    11.2 GAS AND ELECTRIC UTILITIES, 342
    11.3 ECONOMISTS AS AUTHORS, 344
    11.4 MONOPOLY EFFICIENCY LOSS, 346
    11.5 AGRICULTURAL MARKETING ORDERS, 358
    11.6 THE OPEC, 359

11

MONOPOLY AND THE QUESTION OF ECONOMIC EFFICIENCY

Core Chapter

Perfect competition is one model of the market structure of an industry; monopoly is another model. Traditionally, market structure has been associated with the number of firms active in the industry. A monopoly is said to exist when the industry contains only a single firm. If that firm is able to drive out competitors because its costs of production are lower, the situation is termed "natural monopoly." Not all monopolies are "natural," however. One other important source of monopoly is exclusive privilege granted by government, as in the case of a franchised public utility or a legal patent. At the other extreme from monopoly is the large-numbers or "competitive" case. Actually, the number of firms is economically significant only as a clue to behavior. In the large-numbers situation, what is essential is *price-taking behavior*: each firm has so negligible an effect upon price that it acts as if price were independent of its own output decision. (But, as we shall see below under Cartels [Section 11.F], large numbers of firms can sometimes behave like a collective monopolist.) In the case of a single firm, or a small number of firms in an industry, price-taking is not plausible behavior, as the impact of each firm's output decision upon the price of the product is too large to be disregarded.

Where more than one but still only a very few firms survive in an industry, the market structure is called "oligopoly"—competition among the few. Under oligopoly each single firm's output decision noticeably affects the demand conditions faced by *other* firms, which can be expected to respond. As a result there is *conscious interaction* among firms, a condition that leads to "strategic" rather than price-taking behavior, as will be explored in Chapter 13. Another important market structure is "monopolistic competition." Here each firm in an industrial grouping produces a unique product and thus has some degree of monopoly power over a subset of customers that constitute a clientele for its particular output. Chapter 12, "Product as a Variable," covers monopolistic competition in Section 12.B. The present chapter considers only the cases of: (1) a single-firm monopolist and (2) a cartel of firms acting collectively as a monopoly.

MONOPOLY AND NON-PROFIT GOALS

Do monopolists seek profit more than or less than competitive firms do? Demagogic orators often suggest that monopolists are exceptionally ruthless in their search for profit. On the other hand, there is some reason to believe that a monopoly firm, sheltered from competition, would be inclined to give more weight to *non-profit* goals (as discussed in Chapter 9). For a competitive firm, we know there is always a problem of survival (Section 10.D). Since competitive downward pressure on product prices and upward pressure on input prices are continually forcing profits toward zero, in pure competition no firm can have much leeway for indulging non-profit goals. Monopolistic firms, in contrast, may have some safety margin for freedom of choice among goals.

Among possible non-profit goals of a monopolistic firm are empire-building for ambitious managers (or, alternatively, an easy life for unambitious ones), support of charitable institutions, favors to friends and relatives, and exercise of discrimination against unpopular demographic groups. Some of these activities might be intended to generate favorable public notice, with others better left unpublicized.

However, the argument that *monopoly* is especially able to pursue such non-profit goals is by no means clear-cut. Owners of a monopolistic firm are likely to put just as much pressure upon managers to maximize profit as would owners of a competitive firm. Consider a monopoly organized as a corporation with tradable shares. The value of those shares depends upon the firm's present and future profits. If a monopoly earns less than it otherwise could, the loss will be borne by share-holders—who can be expected to complain, in extreme cases to sue in the courts, or to support an alternative management group that is threatening to take over the firm.[1] It seems likely that non-profit goals, creditable or discreditable, will be significant mainly for those firms—whether monopolists or not—whose

[1]If *owners* are unwilling to accept a reduction of profits to achieve non-profit goals, does that mean that empire-building, nepotism, group prejudice, and the like will in fact not occur? Such a conclusion is unwarranted. It may be that suppliers of resource services will accept a lower hire-price in order to achieve such goals. A manager might serve at lower pay if able to hire relatives, for example. Or men might work for less if women employees are (or, perhaps, are not) also employed, or vice versa.

Chapter 11
MONOPOLY
AND THE
QUESTION OF
ECONOMIC
EFFICIENCY

managements are protected both against competition in the product market and against threats to their managerial positions. One such instance has already been described: "non-profit" savings and loan associations (Example 9.3). In this chapter, however, we will assume that profit-maximization remains the operative goal, even for monopolistic firms.

11.B

MONOPOLY PROFIT-MAXIMIZING OPTIMUM

11.B.1
Price-Quantity Solution

Figure 11.1 displays the basic price-quantity optimum for the monopolistic firm. As in Figure 9.9 for the competitive firm, the upper panel here shows the solution in terms of the Total Cost function C and Total Revenue function R. And the lower panel shows the solution in terms of AC, AR, MC, and MR (the corresponding average and marginal functions of output Q).[2] The bold line-segment labelled Π^* in the upper panel is the maximized profit—the excess of Revenue over Cost at the optimal output Q^*. At this optimal output the R and C curves are farthest apart, so that their slopes must be parallel as suggested by the dashed tangent lines drawn at the points R^* and C^*. Consequently, in the lower panel the Marginal Revenue MR (representing the slope of the Total Revenue function) and the Marginal Cost MC (representing the slope of the Total Cost function) intersect at this same output Q^*. The maximized profit Π^* is represented in the lower panel by the shaded rectangle, whose base is the optimum quantity Q^* and whose height is $P^* - AC \equiv AR - AC$. Since Average Revenue AR is R^*/Q^* and Average Cost AC is C^*/Q^*, the shaded area can be written as $Q^*[(R^* - C^*)/Q^*] = R^* - C^*$, demonstrating the equivalence of the representations of profit in the two panels.

The cost function of the monopoly firm in Figure 11.1 is derived exactly as already described in Chapter 9. The difference between the competitive and monopoly solutions lies on the revenue side. For the competitive firm of Figure 9.1, the constancy of price P led to a Total Revenue curve R taking the form of a ray out of the origin. But for the monopolistic firm, price P is a falling function of output—as the single firm is facing the demand curve of the entire industry. The consequence is that the Total Revenue curve R in the upper panel of Figure 11.1 is concave downward, like the cross-section of a mountain.

Geometrically, we know that Marginal Revenue MR is the slope along the Total Revenue curve R. Along the concave-downward R function, slope decreases algebraically throughout (from a high positive magnitude at small Q, to zero slope at the point where R reaches a maximum, and then to increasingly negative slope as the R curve turns downward). The MR curve in the lower panel is correspondingly first positive, then zero, then negative; it decreases along its entire length. The demand curve, we know, is the Average Revenue curve AR, since

Chapter 11
MONOPOLY
AND THE
QUESTION OF
ECONOMIC
EFFICIENCY

---

[2]The capital letter Q has previously been used to signify *industry* output. Since the monopolist is a single-firm industry, Q can be used to denote the output of a monopolist firm.

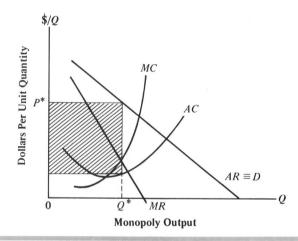

Figure 11.1

Monopoly Profit-Maximizing Solution. Maximum profit Π^* occurs at output Q^*, where the vertical difference between the Total Revenue curve R and the Total Cost curve C in the upper panel is greatest. At this output the R and C curves are parallel (note dashed tangent lines). In the lower panel, it follows that the curves of Marginal Revenue MR and Marginal Cost MC intersect at output Q^*. Profit in the lower panel is represented by the shaded area, equal to Q^* times the difference between price P^* and Average Cost AC^* at that output: $Q^*(P^* - AC)$.

Chapter 11
MONOPOLY
AND THE
QUESTION OF
ECONOMIC
EFFICIENCY

price P is Average Revenue R/Q. As the monopolist by definition faces a downward-sloping demand curve, AR also declines throughout.

In the lower panel MR always lies below AR, i.e., Marginal Revenue is less than Average Revenue. This follows from the logical relations between average and marginal magnitudes discussed in Section 2.B. Proposition 2.2a there states: *When the average magnitude is falling, the marginal magnitude must lie below it.*

WARNING: It is important not to confuse the *price* charged for the last unit sold with the *Marginal Revenue MR*. Note the two shaded areas in Figure 11.2. As sales increase from Q to $Q + 1$ units, the demand curve D shows that price must fall slightly from P' to P''. We can think of P'' as the price received for the last unit, represented by the thin tall rectangle of width unity and height P''. But to see the full effect on Revenue of a unit increase in quantity, it is necessary to remember that price has fallen from P' to P'' *on all the other units* sold. The effect of this price reduction is represented by the flat thin rectangle of width Q and height $P' - P''$.

There are, therefore, two elements entering into Marginal Revenue. First is the positive price P received for the last unit. Second is the price reduction on all the other units, which could have been sold at higher prices. Marginal Revenue can be expressed as the algebraic sum of these two elements:[3]

Figure 11.2

Marginal Price versus Marginal Revenue. Marginal *price*, the price of the last unit sold, corresponds in revenue terms to the area of the tall shaded rectangle of unit base and height P''. To calculate *Marginal Revenue* we must deduct from this amount the thin wide rectangle of height $P' - P'' \equiv \Delta P$ and width Q. This rectangle corresponds to the loss of receipts due to lowering the price on units that could have been sold at P'.

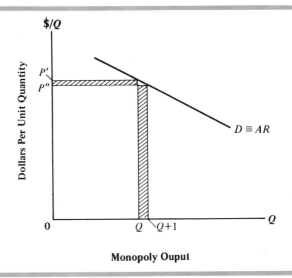

Monopoly Ouput

Chapter 11
MONOPOLY
AND THE
QUESTION OF
ECONOMIC
EFFICIENCY

336

[3]According to this definition, P in the first term on the right of equation (11.1) corresponds to the price of the last unit sold (the *lower* price P'' in Figure 11.2). But Q in the second term corresponds to the smaller quantity Q in the diagram associated with the *higher* price P'. The equation therefore ignores the slight difference between P' and P'', which is strictly justified only if Marginal Revenue is defined as the *limit* of the ratio $\Delta R/\Delta Q$ for small changes ΔQ. This limit is the true Marginal Revenue (corresponding to the calculus derivative dR/dQ).

$$\text{(11.1)} \qquad MR \equiv P + Q \, \frac{\Delta P}{\Delta Q}$$

Since $\Delta P/\Delta Q$, the slope along the demand curve, is negative for a monopolist it follows that the second term has negative sign. Then Marginal Revenue MR must be less than Average Revenue $AR \equiv P$.

The cost function for the monopolistic firm, as shown in terms of total magnitudes in the upper panel of Figure 11.1 and in terms of average and marginal magnitudes in the lower panel, has essentially the same appearance as for the competitive firm. Of course, the monopolistic firm may be of relatively large size, so that the horizontal scale would then be correspondingly large. In connection with this, there is one difference of substance. The competitive firm was assumed to be a price-taker not only with respect to the product market but also with respect to *factor prices*. In consequence, the competitive firm's cost function does not allow for any effects on factor prices; only after turning to the supply function of the competitive industry (in the discussion of Section 10.A) was the factor-price effect encountered. But the single monopolistic supplier is itself an entire industry. Hence, any factor-price effect would be displayed *within* the cost function of the monopolist firm. As will be recalled from Chapter 10, an increase in industry output will normally tend to push factor prices upward. Hence the factor-price effect makes the monopolist firm's cost functions—total, average, and marginal—all tend to rise more sharply as output increases.

Formally, the monopolist's optimizing problem can be expressed as:

$$\text{(11.2)} \qquad \text{Max } \Pi = R(Q) - C(Q) = P(Q)Q - C(Q)$$

Here the parenthesis notation (Q) is to call attention to the fact that the R, C, and P variables are all functions of output Q. (In the solution for the competitive firm, price P was *not* a function of firm output.) As usual, the condition of optimality (maximum of profit or minimum of loss) is the equality of Marginal Cost and Marginal Revenue:[4]

$$\text{(11.3)} \qquad MC = MR \equiv P + Q \, \frac{\Delta P}{\Delta Q}$$

Maximum-Profit Condition, Monopolist Firm

As in Section 9.E, there is again the technical qualification that the MC curve must cut the MR curve *from below* to have a profit maximum. If MC cuts MR *from above*, profit is a *minimum* (or loss a maximum) at that output.[5]

[4]*Mathematical Footnote:* Taking derivatives of profit Π as defined in (11.2), and setting equal to zero:

$$\frac{d\Pi}{dQ} = \frac{dR}{dQ} - \frac{dC}{dQ} = P + Q \, \frac{dP}{dQ} - \frac{dC}{dQ} = 0$$

Marginal Revenue dR/dQ is $P + Q(dP/dQ)$, and Marginal Cost is of course dC/dQ. The equality of MC and MR is the first-order condition for a maximum of Π.

[5]*Mathematical Footnote:* The second-order condition for a maximum of Π is $d^2R/dQ^2 < d^2C/dQ^2$. That is, MR must be falling relative to MC, i.e., MC must cut MR from below.

Chapter 11
MONOPOLY
AND THE
QUESTION OF
ECONOMIC
EFFICIENCY

The maximum-profit condition of equation (11.3) is evidently a generalization of the condition (9.10) that applied to the competitive firm. For the latter as price-taker, the ratio $\Delta P/\Delta Q$ is zero so that (11.3) reduces simply to $MC = MR \equiv P$.

The (price) elasticity of demand was defined in equation (5.3). In terms of the notation of this chapter, the elasticity of demand is:

$$\textbf{(11.4)} \qquad \eta \equiv \frac{\Delta Q/Q}{\Delta P/P} \equiv \frac{\Delta Q}{\Delta P} \cdot \frac{P}{Q}$$

(Recall that η ordinarily has a negative sign.) We can use (11.3) and (11.4) to obtain an important expression connecting Marginal Revenue MR and price elasticity η. First, equation (11.4) can be rewritten:

$$\frac{\Delta Q}{\Delta P} \equiv \eta \frac{Q}{P} \quad \text{or} \quad \frac{\Delta P}{\Delta Q} \equiv \frac{1}{\eta} \frac{P}{Q}$$

Substituting for $\Delta P/\Delta Q$ on the righthand side of (11.3), we have:

$$MR \equiv P + Q \left(\frac{1}{\eta} \frac{P}{Q} \right) \equiv P + \frac{P}{\eta}$$

This is usually written in the form:

$$\textbf{(11.5)} \qquad MR \equiv P \left(1 + \frac{1}{\eta} \right) \quad \text{or} \quad MR \equiv P \left(1 - \frac{1}{|\eta|} \right)$$

Again, since elasticity η is ordinarily negative, $MR < P \equiv AR$.

We saw also in Section 5.B that elastic demand (η greater than unity in absolute value) corresponded to increasing consumer expenditure on a good as its price P falls (and quantity purchased Q rises). Consumer expenditure is, of course, the opposite side of the same coin as *Revenue* to the firm. So elastic demand corresponds to the region where Total Revenue R is an increasing function of output Q in the upper panel of Figure 11.1, or equivalently to the region of positive Marginal Revenue MR in the lower panel. Inelastic demand corresponds to the region of falling Total Revenue in the upper panel or negative Marginal Revenue in the lower panel. Since Marginal Cost MC is surely positive, the condition $MC = MR$ dictates that the monopolist optimum must be in the region where the Total Revenue curve is rising so that $MR > 0$, i.e., in the range of *elastic* demand.

11.B.2
Monopolist versus Competitive Solution

Table 11.1 illustrates a hypothetical set of revenue and cost data for a monopolist firm. The cost data are exactly the same as those employed for a hypothetical competitive firm in Table 9.1. But on the revenue side, the monopolist's demand function is assumed here to be $P = 132 - 8Q$; price is a declining function of output. The equation has been so chosen that if the monopolist *were* following the

Table 11.1

Revenue and Cost Functions—Monopolist Firm

$$P = 132 - 8Q, \text{ or } R = 132Q - 8Q^2$$
$$C = Q^3 - 14Q^2 + 69Q + 128$$

Q	P	R	MR$_1$	MR$_2$	MR	C	MC	η
0	132	0	—		132	128	69	$-\infty$
				124				
1	124	124	124	(116)	116	184	44	-15.5
				108				
2	116	232	108	(100)	100	218	25	-7.25
				92				
3	108	324	92	(84)	84	236	12	-4.5
				76				
4	100	400	76	(68)	68	244	5	-3.125
				60				
5	92	460	60	(52)	52	248	4	-2.3
				44				
6	84	504	44	(36)	36	254	9	-1.75
				28				
7	76	532	28	(20)	20	268	20	-1.36
				12				
8	68	544	12	(4)	4	296	37	-1.06
				-4				
9	60	540	-4	(-12)	-12	344	60	$-.83$
				-20				
10	52	520	-20		-28	418	89	$-.65$

competitive optimality rule $MC = P$ [equation (9.13)] he would be led to the same numerical output ($Q = 9$) as in Table 9.1. For although the demand curve here is a declining function of Q, the numbers have been so contrived that, at $Q = 9$, Marginal Cost MC and price P are both equal to 60.

The monopolist, therefore, has it in his power to behave like a competitive firm. But, in the interests of profit-maximization he will set $MC = MR < P$ [equation (11.3)]. In the table here, three approximations for Marginal Revenue are shown. The first, MR_1, is the "poorer approximation" as discussed in Section 2.B. Here the revenue difference $R_{Q+1} - R_Q$ is considered the Marginal Revenue *at* $(Q + 1)$. MR_2 is the "better approximation" of Chapter 2, where this same difference is taken as the Marginal Revenue *at* $(Q + \frac{1}{2})$. In this column, the numbers in parentheses have been interpolated to show MR_2 at integer values of Q. The *true* Marginal Revenue MR (the perfect approximation) is given in the third column. This can be attained by calculus techniques, which show that if the demand function is $P = 132 - 8Q$ then Marginal Revenue is $MR = 132 - 16Q$.[6] As can be seen from the table, the "better approximation" MR_2 is in this case precisely correct. (This will always be true for a quadratic revenue function.)

It is easy to prove the following, without using calculus.

PROPOSITION: Given any *linear* demand curve $P = A - BQ$, the true corresponding Marginal Revenue function is $MR = A - 2BQ$. Geometri-

[6]*Mathematical Footnote:* If $P = 132 - 8Q$, then $R \equiv PQ = 132Q - 8Q^2$. Differentiating: $MR \equiv dR/dQ = 132 - 16Q$.

Chapter 11
MONOPOLY
AND THE
QUESTION OF
ECONOMIC
EFFICIENCY

cally, starting at the same vertical intercept on the P-axis, the MR curve falls twice as fast as the AR curve. *Proof:* From equation (11.3), $MR = P + Q(\Delta P/\Delta Q)$. Now $\Delta P/\Delta Q$ is by definition the slope of the demand curve, a constant for a linear demand curve. Given the demand equation $P = A - BQ$, this slope is equal to $-B$. Substituting on the righthand side of (11.3): $MR = (A - BQ) + Q(-B)$ or $MR = A - 2BQ$.

COROLLARY: The MR curve bisects the horizontal distance between the vertical axis and the demand curve, if the latter is a straight line.

As for the Marginal Cost MC, only the "true" figures are taken over from Table 9.1. The condition $MC = MR$ is met at $Q = 7$, which is the monopolist's profit-maximizing output. The corresponding profit-maximizing price (or Average Revenue) is $P = 76$. Total Revenue is $R = 532$ and Total Cost $C = 268$, so that the maximized profit is $\Pi^* = 264$.

It was argued above that the monopolist's solution must lie in the elastic range of demand, i.e., where $|\eta| > 1$. The last column of Table 11.1 shows the elasticity at the various levels of output. The computation was based on the relation $\eta \equiv P/(MR - P)$, derived by solving equation (11.5) above for η. Note that had the monopolist been following the competitive rule so as to choose $Q = 9$, the solution would have been in the inelastic range from the viewpoint of industry demand.

We thus see that it is quite possible for a *competitive* price-quantity equilibrium, but not for a monopolist's price-quantity optimum, to be in the inelastic range of demand. More specifically, suppose that the demand curve here, $P = 132 - 8Q$, were the true industry demand curve for a competitive industry with 1000 identical firms. For simplicity, assume that Q is measured in thousands whereas the competitive-firm cost data shown in Table 9.1 are a function of q measured in units. Then at the price $P = 60$, the aggregate demand quantity would be $Q = 9$ thousands, whereas at the firm output $q = 9$ we know that Marginal Cost $MC = 60$. So the 1000 firms will supply 9000 units in the aggregate, clearing the market at $P = 60$. But this is in the inelastic range of demand. The competitive industry as a whole is actually receiving less revenue by producing more output—in addition, of course, to incurring positive costs of production on the extra output.

Chapter 11
MONOPOLY
AND THE
QUESTION OF
ECONOMIC
EFFICIENCY

340

PROPOSITION: The monopoly output solution occurs where $MC = MR < P$. Since competitive firms produce to where $MC = P$, a monopolized industry achieves higher price and produces smaller output than would a competitive industry.

What might be called "monopoly power" is indicated by the divergence between Marginal Revenue MR (equal to Marginal Cost MC) and price P. From equation (11.5), we see that the difference between MR and P is greater the *smaller* (in absolute value) is the price elasticity η. In the extreme, for a price-taking firm the elasticity of demand is infinite and the difference between P and MR disappears—there is no monopoly power. Monopoly power tends to increase as the number of firms diminishes, since smaller numbers make price-taking behavior less plausible.

Apart from the number of firms in an industry, the underlying elasticity of consumers' demand for the product (the elasticity of the *industry* demand curve) will also be highly relevant. If in a particular industry the demand happens to be highly elastic to begin with, even a single-firm monopolist will have little *monopoly power* (will be unable to profitably raise price P much above Marginal Cost MC).

What determines the elasticity of consumers' demand for a product? One important determinant mentioned in Section 5.G was the "necessity vs. luxury" distinction. As price falls, consumers are effectively enriched. If the good is strongly superior (a "luxury" good), the *income effect of the price change* will reinforce the pure *substitution effect* that leads to increased purchases. Thus, luxuries tend to have elastic demands. It then follows that a monopolist tends to have greater monopoly power—ability to raise price—if the commodity is a necessity. The second major determinant emphasized in Chapter 5, and probably much the more important, is *closeness of substitutes*. If a good substitute for a commodity is available, a price increase will lead to a large loss of sales; demand tends to be elastic, and monopoly power is necessarily small.

Chapter 11
MONOPOLY
AND THE
QUESTION OF
ECONOMIC
EFFICIENCY

EXAMPLE 11.2
GAS AND
ELECTRIC
UTILITIES

Public utility corporations are generally granted exclusive (monopoly) rights to serve a particular locality. Among such public utilities are companies providing gas and electricity. But in some areas these two commodities are provided by the *same* company, while in other communities the services are separately supplied. Since gas and electricity as alternative sources of energy are close *substitutes* over a considerable range of uses (see Example 5.2), a company providing only one of those commodities faces an effectively more elastic demand (has less monopoly power). Such a company would always be seriously concerned about shift of business to the other energy source if it were to raise its price.

Bruce M. Owen made a comparative study of prices and outputs of combined versus separated gas and electricity services.[8] He found that private companies supplying combined gas and electric services charged, other things equal, on average about 6% more for electricity while providing about 15% less output in comparison with companies supplying only electricity. (On the other hand, there seemed to be no significant effect of combined versus separated service upon gas prices. Perhaps gas may have relatively elastic demand for reasons apart from availability of electricity as a substitute.)

COMMENT: Privately owned public utility corporations are almost always *regulated* (as will be discussed in Section D following); the prices they charge must be approved by a government agency. The evidence above of seeming ability to exploit monopoly power suggests that regulation may have been ineffective, at least to some degree.

[8]Bruce M. Owen, "Monopoly Pricing in Combined Gas and Electric Utilities," *The Antitrust Bulletin*, v. 15 (Winter 1970).

11.B.3
An Application: Author versus Publisher

In the publishing industry, it is common practice for authors' royalties to take the form of a simple percentage of sales receipts. The question arises: Is there any difference between the incentives of author and publisher as to how high a price should be set on a book?

Since there is only one seller of any single text, monopoly theory is applicable. Suppose that the author receives as royalty just 10% of Total Revenue R. Denote his royalty as $R_a = .1R$. Writing the net revenue to the publisher as R_p, it must be that $R_p = .9R$. This problem is most simply analyzed in "total" units, by an extension of the geometry in the upper panel of Figure 11.1. In Figure 11.3 the Total Revenue R received from customers is divided between the dashed R_p (nine-tenths the height of R) and the dotted R_a (one-tenth the height of R). The publisher would prefer the output Q_p^* such that the *slopes* along R_p and along the Total Cost curve C are equal; his profit Π_p^* at that output is indicated by the height of the upper bold line-segment. The lower solid line-segment drawn along the same vertical, between R_a and the horizontal axis, indicates the corresponding royalty to the author.

Chapter 11
MONOPOLY
AND THE
QUESTION OF
ECONOMIC
EFFICIENCY

342

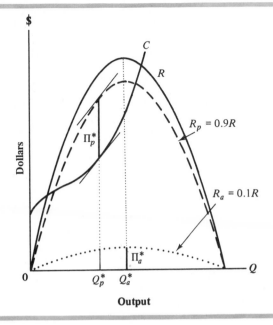

Figure 11.3

Author versus Publisher. Of the receipts from sales indicated by the Total Revenue curve R, 10% go to the author (R_a curve) and 90% to the publisher (R_p curve). Since the author bears no costs of production, from his point of view the optimal output is Q_a^* at the maximum of the R_a curve (where his income is Π_a^*). The publisher's maximum profit Π_p^* occurs at output Q_p^*, where the R_p curve has the greatest vertical divergence over the Total Cost curve C. The publisher will prefer a smaller output (will want to set a higher price) than the author.

It will be evident from the geometry that this is *not* the preferred output from the point of view of the author. *Since the latter incurs no cost of production*, from his point of view the optimum output Q_a^* is simply that which maximizes R_a. (We can think of this as the output where the horizontal slope of R_a equals the horizontal slope of a Total Cost curve that is, from the author's viewpoint, zero everywhere). Since $R_a = .1R$, the author wants to set a price that will simply maximize sales (Revenue R), without regard to cost. The author's "ideal" royalty in the diagram is shown by the bold line-segment Π_a^*; it will be evident that the corresponding profit to the publisher will be less than ideal from the latter's point of view. The upshot of the analysis is that *it is in the interests of the publisher to set a higher price (implying a smaller number of books sold) than the author would rationally prefer.*

In the publishing industry authors do not normally have the power to fix price, which is the sole domain of the publisher. However, it might be advantageous for an author to make a deal accepting a smaller royalty percentage in return for the publisher setting a lower price for his book.

Chapter 11
MONOPOLY
AND THE
QUESTION OF
ECONOMIC
EFFICIENCY

343

11.C

MONOPOLY AND ECONOMIC EFFICIENCY

Monopoly, we have just seen, leads to higher price and lower output as compared with competitive supply. Is this a good or a bad thing? Obviously, while high price is bad for the customers it is good for the monopolist. The possibility of making valid statements concerning the impartial or *social* desirability of alternative economic states of affairs will be discussed under the heading of "Welfare Economics" in Part Six below. However, recall the Fundamental Theorem of Exchange—*trade is mutually beneficial*. We can use the concepts of Consumer Surplus and Producer Surplus developed in Chapter 7 to show that monopoly can be regarded as a *hindrance to trade*. As such, it leads to an "efficiency loss," apart from the transfers associated with high monopoly price.[10]

Figure 11.4 illustrates the interpretation of monopoly as a hindrance to trade. Assume that there are no economies or diseconomies of scale tending to shift the cost function downward or upward for a single producer in comparison with an aggregate of small competitive suppliers. Then the Marginal Cost curve MC of the monopolist is essentially the same as the competitive supply function S of Figure 10.2. (The factor-price effect, if any, due to expanding industry supply is already incorporated in the shape of the monopolist's MC curve.) The monopoly solution is at quantity Q_m (the quantity level at which $MC = MR$) and price P_m (the height of the demand curve at quantity Q_m). The hypothetical competitive solution would be at quantity Q_c and price P_c (the intersection of the demand curve D and supply curve S).

Chapter 11
MONOPOLY
AND THE
QUESTION OF
ECONOMIC
EFFICIENCY

344

[10]However, we cannot therefore conclude that monopoly "should" be abolished. (Any more than we could conclude in Section 7.E that taxes, as the cause of losses in Consumer Surplus and Producer Surplus, "should" therefore be abolished.) There may be other considerations to be balanced against the efficiency loss.

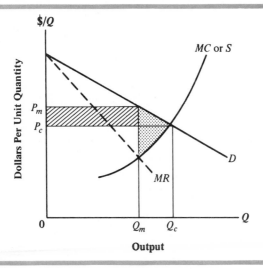

Figure 11.4

Monopoly and Efficiency Loss. If there are no *productive* losses or gains from organization of the industry into a single large firm versus competing small firms, the supply curve S of the competitive industry is identical with the Marginal Cost curve MC of the monopolist. The competitive equilibrium would occur at price P_c and quantity Q_c; the monopoly optimum at the higher price P_m and smaller quantity Q_m. In comparison with the competitive outcome, the shaded area is a transfer from consumers to the monopolist supplier (equal to the price difference times the quantity still produced). The upper dotted area is the loss of Consumer Surplus due to the reduction in quantity traded (inability of consumers to buy the amount $Q_c - Q_m$ at the old price P_c). The lower dotted area is the analogous loss in Producer Surplus on the amount $Q_c - Q_m$, since Marginal Cost would have been less than price P_c in that range.

The hindrance to trade can be analyzed on the analog of Figure 7.12 that showed the effect of a tax on transactions. The rectangular shaded area $(P_m - P_c)Q_m$ is the buyers' loss of Consumer Surplus due to the higher monopoly price on the quantity Q_m. As the monopolist seller derives an exactly equal benefit, this is a "transfer" that does not enter into efficiency calculations. The upper roughly triangular (dotted) area is the deadweight loss in Consumer Surplus for units that *would have been* produced and purchased at the price P_c but are not purchased at the higher price P_m. The lower dotted area is the corresponding deadweight loss in Producer Surplus. The monopolist could have produced these additional units at the successive marginal costs indicated along the MC curve, which are less than the price P_c that could have been received for each unit had the quantity Q_c been supplied. Of course, the monopolist chose not to provide so large a quantity because by cutting output a higher profit was obtained.

Thus, for the monopolist the net advantage of the monopoly over the competitive solution is the shaded area (a transfer) less the lower dotted area (a deadweight loss). As for the consumers, the upper dotted area represents their deadweight loss, and, in addition, they are on the losing side of the transfer. The transfer cancels out; the *efficiency loss* is measured by the two dotted areas alone.

Chapter 11
MONOPOLY
AND THE
QUESTION OF
ECONOMIC
EFFICIENCY

345

CONCLUSION: In comparison with the competitive outcome, monopoly involves a transfer from consumers to suppliers. But the efficiency loss consists solely of the reductions in Consumer Surplus and Producer Surplus that are due to the lessened volume of trade.

EXAMPLE 11.4
MONOPOLY
EFFICIENCY LOSS

A. C. Harberger[11] estimated the aggregate magnitude of the efficiency loss due to monopoly in the United States, for the period 1924–28. He was able to do so only by making a number of heroic assumptions, in particular, that Marginal Cost MC was constant for all industries, and that the price elasticity of demand was *unity* everywhere. Identifying monopolized industries on the basis of high average profit rate on assets, he obtained a surprisingly low estimate of the loss: only around 0.1% of national income.

Harberger's results were criticized by G. J. Stigler[12] on several grounds, among them: (1) A rational monopolist will always produce in the range where elasticity is *greater* than unity (as we have just seen in Section 11.B); (2) reported profit rates for monopolists may omit monopoly returns in the form of disguised "cost" items such as patent royalties and executive salaries; and (3) for monopoly firms, "intangible" items may become counted among assets, so as to reduce the reported profit as a percentage of assets.

A number of later studies examined different sets of data, allowing in various ways for Stigler's objections. D. R. Kamerschen[13] studied the period 1956–61, making rather strong assumptions toward the opposite extreme from Harberger. For example, he included royalties, intangibles, and advertising expenditures with the monopoly returns. He obtained demand-elasticity estimates by industry, averaging around (minus) 2 or 3. On this basis Kamerschen concluded that the annual welfare loss due to monopoly is around 6% of national income. Still later, D. A. Worcester, Jr.,[14] studied the period 1965–69, using *firm* rather than *industry* data for added precision. Taking account of the Stigler objections in a variety of ways, and using an overall elasticity figure of (minus) 2, he still obtained low "maximum defensible" estimates of the welfare loss due to monopoly, in the range of 0.5% of national income.

COMMENT: As this very condensed report suggests, we have here an as-yet-unresolved economic controversy, involving issues both of theory and of statistical data. Even if the low estimates prove correct, it would be wrong to infer automatically that anti-monopoly activities of government should be suspended. Perhaps the low monopoly losses are to be attributed to the success of those very activities.

[11]A. C. Harberger, "Monopoly and Resource Allocation," *American Economic Review*, v. 54 (May 1954).

[12]G. J. Stigler, "The Statistics of Monopoly and Merger," *Journal of Political Economy*, v. 64 (Feb. 1956).

[13]D. R. Kamerschen, "An Estimation of the 'Welfare Losses' from Monopoly in the American Economy," *Western Economic Journal*, v. 4 (Summer 1966).

[14]D. A. Worcester, Jr., "New Estimates of the Welfare Loss to Monopoly, United States: 1956–1969," *Southern Economic Journal*, v. 40 (Oct. 1973).

There is, however, a possible *additional* source of efficiency loss not considered in the preceding analysis: whatever sacrifice of resources is involved in acquiring or defending the monopoly position itself. How much would a potential monopolist be willing to pay to win and retain such a privilege? Evidently, any amount short of the net monopoly gain. In Figure 11.4, the amount would be the excess of the shaded rectangular area (representing the transfer gain to the monopolist of an industry) over the lower dotted triangle (representing loss of Producer Surplus when the industry reduces output). If instead of a single claimant there were competing contenders all struggling for the monopoly position, each would have to discount this possible net gain in accordance with his estimate of his chances of success in the contest—but in the aggregate, the costs that *all* the contenders together would be willing to incur probably remain comparable to the monopoly gain.[15]

The degree to which costs incurred to gain a monopoly position are *efficiency losses* depends, however, on the way in which the contest takes place. Suppose a government authority simply auctioned off a monopoly privilege. (Something like this now occurs for the right to supply cable television service; communities generally grant an exclusive francise to whichever cable company makes the most attractive bid.) In an ideal auction, where the expenses incurred by losing bidders are negligible and the cost to the winning bidder is simply the amount bid, the contest would represent a mere transfer—in this case from the monopolist (ultimately, from the consumers of the monopolized product) to the government. There is no *additional* efficiency loss due to the contest for monopoly position. But to the extent that an auction involves real costs (for example, if contestants hire economists to advise on how high to bid), resources will be diverted from alternative employments and the striving for monopoly privilege will itself cause an efficiency loss.

Since economists are not too expensive (alternative employments are not that valuable), this efficiency loss might not seem large. But consider other forms of struggle for monopoly position. One that comes immediately to mind is violence. Chicago-style gang wars were attempts to gain monopoly over crime—evidently, a highly costly process to all concerned. Less picturesque, entirely lawful, but still often quite costly are contests in which prizes are awarded at the discretion of a government authority. The Federal Communications Commission is in a position to award television channels, the Patent Office grants patents, the Civil Aeronautics Board awards airline routes, and so on. Here the proceedings typically involve extremely expensive documentary submissions, often leading to burdensome litigation, and perhaps very large costs incurred to bring political or other pressures to bear upon the awarding agency.[16]

One final thought is that these *costs of achieving monopoly rights* are not

[15]Estimates of the expenses incurred to achieve monopoly positions in a number of industries are provided in R. A. Posner, "The Social Costs of Monopoly and Regulation," *Journal of Political Economy*, v. 83 (August 1975).

[16]What if the prize were given instead simply to the contestant offering the highest bribe? This is like an auction, so that (to a first approximation, at least) there would be no efficiency loss. Only a transfer is involved, in this case going to the private purse of the corrupt official rather than to the government

Chapter 11
MONOPOLY
AND THE
QUESTION OF
ECONOMIC
EFFICIENCY

347

essentially different from those involved in acquiring or defending any form of rights in our society. Rights to property, rights to sue in court, and even "civil" rights like freedom of speech can often only be gained or exercised at considerable cost.

11.D

REGULATION OF MONOPOLY

Between the two extremes of *laissez-faire* toleration of monopoly on the one hand, and "trust-busting" on the other, lies a third possibility—regulation of monopoly. Regulation is almost universal for privately-owned public utilities providing power, water, gas, and telephone service, all generally considered to be "natural monopolies." But not all regulation is of monopolized industries, and not all monopolized industries are regulated. The positive factors leading governments to choose one economic policy or another will be studied in Part Six. Here our purpose is only to illustrate some aspects of the typical outcome under regulation.

The usual regulatory goal is that monopoly revenue should be allowed to cover only costs plus a *normal profit*, i.e., an amount necessary to attract and retain the resources employed in the industry. But the "normal" profit to the owners of a firm is (as explained in Section 9.C) the economic or opportunity cost of the resources provided by them. Hence regulatory policy can be interpreted as aiming at zero *economic profit* for the firm.

Figure 11.5 repeats the comparison of the monopoly solution (Q_m and P_m) and the competitive solution (Q_c and P_c) of Figure 11.4, and adds the regulatory solution (Q_r and P_r) as interpreted above. As can be seen, the regulatory zero-economic-profit condition is equivalent to setting a price and output such that $AC = AR$. Note that whereas the laissez-faire monopoly solution had "too small" output and "too high" price in comparison with the competitive outcome ($Q_m < Q_c$ and $P_m > P_c$), in this diagram the regulatory correction "overshoots" the competitive outcome ($Q_r > Q_c$ and $P_r < P_c$).

A striking feature of Figure 11.5 is that, in the range of output greater than Q_c, Marginal Cost MC exceeds demand price (marginal "willingness to pay"). Thus there is an efficiency loss from "too great" a regulated output, as represented by the dotted area in Figure 11.5. This, plus the small cross-hatched triangle, represents *negative* Producer Surplus due to the excessive output. On the other hand, the cross-hatched area is also a region of positive Consumer Surplus. So the triangle cancels out, leaving the dotted area as the *net* efficiency loss. (Consumers receive also a transfer gain represented by the shaded rectangle.)

Regulation is, as has been indicated, the policy often chosen by government for dealing with "natural" monopolies. One type of natural monopoly is characterized by an Average Cost curve AC that is falling throughout the relevant range.

Chapter 11
MONOPOLY
AND THE
QUESTION OF
ECONOMIC
EFFICIENCY

348

treasury. Note that illegal or immoral methods may involve an efficiency loss (gang war) or may not (bribery), just as legal and moral methods may or may not. (This may perhaps suggest that efficiency ought not be the *sole* criterion for social judgments.)

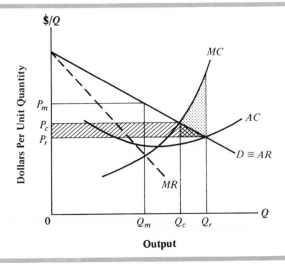

Figure 11.5

Regulation of Monopoly (Increasing Cost). The regulatory solution, fixing price so that the firm achieves zero economic profit, is the price-output combination P_r, Q_r where the AC and AR curves intersect. If this occurs in the range where Average Cost AC is rising, regulated output Q_r will be even greater than the competitive equilibrium output Q_c. In comparison with the competitive solution, the shaded rectangle is a transfer from suppliers to consumers. The dotted area is an efficiency loss due to *excessive* output.

If all potential firms in an industry had the same cost function, with AC declining throughout, any single firm able to achieve an output lead over the others would be able to produce more cheaply. Since the cost advantage grows as the output lead increases, the ultimate outcome is likely to be a single surviving firm.

This situation is pictured in Figure 11.6. Since AC is falling in the diagram, Marginal Cost MC lies always below it (Proposition 2.2a). Note that in Figure 11.6 the regulatory solution (Q_r and P_r) lies *between* the monopoly solution (Q_m and P_m) and the competitive solution (Q_c and P_c). It follows that in this type of regulated natural monopoly, there is still "too small" output and "too high" a price. The dotted region shows the efficiency loss due to "too small" a regulated output.[17]

An implication of this analysis is that regulated firms should be rather less interested than unregulated firms in making technological advances so as to reduce Average Cost, or in heading off cost increases from any source. Indeed, if regula-

---

[17]There is a paradox here. At the competitive solution, since $MC = P$ and $MC < AC$, then $AC > P$. So at the competitive outcome Average Cost exceeds price; the firm suffers a financial loss. It might therefore seem that the competitive solution could hardly serve as standard of efficiency. Nevertheless, the competitive solution remains the efficient one in the situation of Figure 11.6, as may be seen from the following argument. At the regulatory solution, $AC = P$, and there would be no financial loss. Now, given that output is at the regulatory level Q_r, is it or is it not efficient to expand production further to Q_c? Clearly it is, since in the region between Q_r and Q_c the demand price is always greater than the Marginal Cost. The resulting price drop, leading to the result $AC > P$, is a pure "transfer" that is not relevant for calculations of efficiency.

Chapter 11
MONOPOLY
AND THE
QUESTION OF
ECONOMIC
EFFICIENCY

349

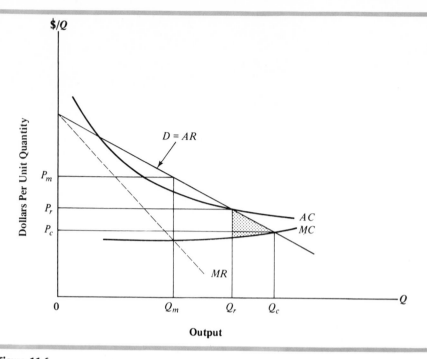

$/Q

Dollars Per Unit Quantity

D = AR

P_m

P_r

P_c

AC

MC

MR

0   Q_m Q_r Q_c Q

Output

Figure 11.6

Regulation of Monopoly (Decreasing Cost). Here the regulatory solution P_r, Q_r at the intersection of the AC and AR curves (zero economic profit) occurs in the range where Average Cost is falling. In this "natural monopoly" situation the regulated output Q_r, though greater than the profit-maximizing monopoly output Q_m, is still less than the ideally efficient output Q_c where MC = P. In comparison with the efficient outcome, the dotted areas represent losses of Consumer Surplus and Producer Surplus due to insufficient output.

tion were perfectly effective in maintaining the condition $AC = P_r$, the firm would have no incentive at all to hold costs down. Any cost increase would be immediately reflected in higher prices, maintaining the "normal" profit of the firm. However, there is always a regulatory lag. If costs rise or fall, it will be some time before the regulatory commission gets around to adjusting prices. Consequently, the cost-reducing incentive, while somewhat attenuated, is not completely eliminated for regulated monopolies.

11.E

MONOPOLISTIC PRICE DISCRIMINATION

A monopoly firm is a "price-maker" rather than "price-taker." But up to now it has been assumed that the monopolist offers all customers a single price—at which they are free to choose desired quantities. In certain circumstances, however, a monopolist may be able to engage in more complex price-making. By offering different terms to different purchasers, it would be possible to divide the market (*market segmentation*). Or, for any given purchaser, the monopolist might be able to impose a price schedule of greater or lesser complexity (*multi-part pricing*). In the limiting case a different price can be charged to each consumer for each successive infinitesimal unit purchased; this is called *perfect discrimination*.

In the most elementary segmentation scheme, the monopolist divides the market into two and quotes a different simple price to customers in each portion. Apart from questions of legality, this can only be achieved by the monopolist when the two segments are effectively *insulated* one from another. If they are not insulated, customers in the low-price sector of the market would be able to reap an immediate windfall gain by resale to the high-price sector—and the whole scheme would necessarily break down.[18]

The underlying logic of the market-segmentation solution is perhaps easier to grasp than the geometrical representation. Denote the separate demand or Average Revenue functions of the two segments as $ar_1(q_1)$ and $ar_2(q_2)$. (The parentheses indicate that ar_1 is a function of q_1 and ar_2 of q_2.) There are, of course, corresponding Marginal Revenue functions $mr_1(q_1)$ and $mr_2(q_2)$. The monopolist's Marginal Cost function can be expressed as $MC(Q)$, where $Q = q_1 + q_2$.

Now, at any level of output Q, whenever $mr_1 = mr_2$ the monopolist would want to reallocate units from the sector with lower to the sector with higher Marginal Revenue. Consequently, one optimality condition is $mr_1 = mr_2$. Also, he would want to produce more units of output so long as, and only so long as, $MC < mr_1 = mr_2$. Putting these conditions together, we have:

(11.6) $MC(Q) = mr_1(q_1) = mr_2(q_2)$ (where $Q = q_1 + q_2$)

Market-Segmentation Optimality Condition[19]

The geometrical construction appears in Figure 11.7. The key device is the curve labelled Σmr, the *horizontal* sum of mr_1 and mr_2. The intersection of the firm's Marginal Cost curve MC with Σmr at the point W establishes optimal output $Q = q_1 + q_2$. The separation into q_1 and q_2 is determined by picking off the lengths $ST(= q_1)$ and $TW(= SU = q_2)$ along the horizontal $STUW$. The final step is the determination of the segment prices P_1 and P_2; these are simply the prices associated with the respective quantities q_1 and q_2 along the segment demand curves ar_1 and ar_2.

From equation (11.5), and knowing that $mr_1 = mr_2$, we see that:

(11.7) $P_1 \left(1 + \dfrac{1}{\eta_1}\right) = P_2 \left(1 + \dfrac{1}{\eta_2}\right)$

Chapter 11
MONOPOLY
AND THE
QUESTION OF
ECONOMIC
EFFICIENCY

---

[18]However, the insulation of the two segments need not be *total*. The monopolist could accept some "leakage" and still remain ahead.

[19]The technical qualification earlier, that MC must cut MR from *below*, here takes the form: MC must cut the horizontal sum of the *mr* curves (see Figure 11.7) from below.

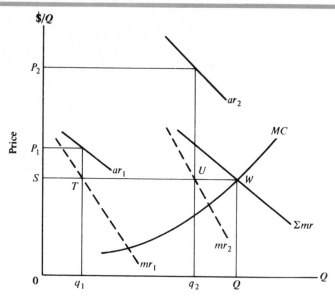

Firm Output and Segment Sales Quantities

Figure 11.7

Market Segmentation. The market is divided into segments 1 and 2, whose independent demand curves are ar_1 and ar_2. The profit-maximizing solution for the firm is to produce where $MC = mr_1 = mr_2$. Geometrically, the optimal output Q is at the intersection of Marginal Cost MC with the Σmr curve representing the horizontal sum of the separate Marginal Revenue curves mr_1 and mr_2. Of this total output the amount q_1 (which equals ST) is sold to the first sector at price P_1, while q_2 (SU, which equals TW) is sold to the second sector at price P_2.

It follows that if, for example, $|\eta_1| > |\eta_2|$ (demand in segment 1 is the more elastic), then $[1 + (1/\eta_1)] > [1 + (1/\eta_2)]$, so that $P_1 < P_2$. Thus, *the segment with more elastic demand receives the lower price.*

This feature explains the phenomenon called "dumping abroad," i.e., selling to foreigners at a price lower than the price a monopolist charges in his domestic market. Suppose a firm has a considerable degree of monopoly power in its own national market. But in the international market the suppliers of all nations compete, and so demand tends to be much more elastic. (More precisely, since any single national supplier may be a relatively small element in the international market, the elasticity of demand there as *perceived* by such a single seller tends to be relatively great.) A monopolist able to insulate foreign and domestic markets (for example, by inducing the government to set a tariff or ban upon imports) generally finds it profitable to charge a lower price abroad than at home.

11.E.2

Multi-Part Pricing

A second type of monopolistic price discrimination, a multi-part pricing scheme, is illustrated in Figure 11.8. It involves the monopolist's presenting a single price *schedule* to each separate consumer, such that a relatively high price P_1 is charged for initial units up to some given limit B, and a lower price P_2 for additional units

$\$/Q$

Initial Block
Price

P_1

Second Block
Price

Price

$P_2 = P^*$

d

q_1

q_2

0

B

q^*

q

Block Sales Quantities

Figure 11.8

Two-Part Pricing. Here P^* is assumed to be the profit-maximizing simple price for a monopolist. If d is the demand curve of a typical consumer, the illustration shows that the monopolist can do even better by charging a higher price P_1 on an initial block quantity B, and $P_2 = P^*$ thereafter. This two-part pricing scheme allows the monopolist to capture the portion of Consumer Surplus represented by the rectangle lying within the shaded area. (The diagram is strictly correct only if the consumer's purchases in the second block are not affected by higher outlays for the first block. Ordinarily, the income effect would bring about a reduction of second-block sales, so the monopolist engaging in two-part pricing could not do quite so well as shown.)

taken thereafter. The basic intent of such a scheme is to capture for the seller a portion of the Consumer Surplus (see Section 7.E) that would otherwise have gone to buyers.

In Figure 11.8, the monopolist is facing the individual demand curve d of one typical consumer. The cost function cannot be shown in this diagram, but we may assume that the intersection of MC and MR as pictured in the lower panel of Figure 11.1 leads to the determination of an optimal *simple* monopoly price P^*. At this price the consumer would choose the quantity q^*. Simple pricing would leave the shaded area under the demand curve as Consumer Surplus.[20] A two-part pricing scheme might specify an initial higher P_1 up to the limit B, and the lower $P_2 = P^*$ thereafter as indicated in the diagram. Suppose we can assume that the same total quantity $q_1 + q_2 = q^*$ will still be purchased by the individual as under simple monopoly. The consumer would buy $q_1 = B$ units at the price P_1, and $q_2 = q^* - B$ units at the price P_2. Then the revenue received by the seller would obviously be greater than under simple pricing, by the area $(P_1 - P^*)q_1$ of the rectangle shown as cutting into the Consumer Surplus.

This is, however, somewhat of an idealized situation. The monopolist would ordinarily not be able to do quite so well as pictured. First of all, the adverse

Chapter 11
MONOPOLY
AND THE
QUESTION OF
ECONOMIC
EFFICIENCY

[20]This area is normally a slight exaggeration of the true Consumer Surplus, as explained in Section 7.E.3. See also the next footnote.

"income effect" (Section 4.C) of paying the higher price P_1 for the first B units would *tend to reduce the consumer's demand for additional units*. The ordinary demand curve d is constructed on the hypothesis of simple uniform pricing; only in the case of goods for which the income effect is zero (the income elasticity of demand is zero) will the curve remain the same when multi-part pricing is employed to extract more revenue from the consumer.[21] Consequently, the monopolist must consider, as a partial offset to the advantage gained from selling the first B units at the high price P_1, that there will be a reduction in the overall number of units that can be sold.

Another, generally more important, qualification stems from *differences among consumers*. The monopolist would ideally like to offer differing price schedules to different customers. But legal restrictions, or perhaps the cost of making such distinctions among customers, may dictate a common price schedule in which P_1, P_2, and B are the same for all purchasers. Then there are likely to be a number of buyers in the situation of Figure 11.9. For these customers B is so large that the initial price P_1 becomes a simple price for them: they will not purchase any additional units at all at the lower price P_2 quoted for units beyond B. (In effect, a kind of market-segmentation price discrimination is being put into

Figure 11.9

Unsuccessful Two-Part Pricing. Here we see a two-part pricing scheme inappropriate for this particular consumer. No sales are actually made at the second block price, so in effect a simple price P_1 is being charged.

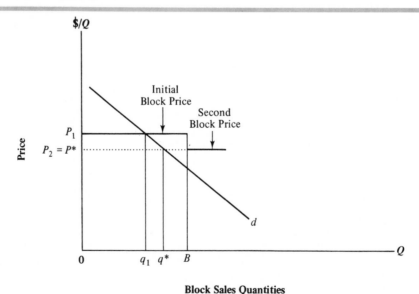

Block Sales Quantities

Chapter 11
MONOPOLY
AND THE
QUESTION OF
ECONOMIC
EFFICIENCY

[21]The "income effect" is the reason why the true Consumer Surplus is normally less than the shaded area in Figure 11.8. Only when the income effect is zero will the shaded area be the precise measure of Consumer Surplus.

effect against such a customer.) While it is conceivable that the monopolist derives increased profit from the buyer shown in the diagram, as a result of the higher effective price, this would generally not be the case. (Recall that $P_2 = P^*$ was the profit-maximizing simple price, so that for a typical consumer any further increase in price would mean *less* profit to the firm.) So if it is not feasible to offer different schedules to different customers, the gains from multi-part pricing will be much less.

The two qualifications here considered are reinforcing, tending to reduce the advantage of multi-part pricing to the monopolist. In addition, of course, the *transaction cost* of more complex pricing schemes will be greater. Not only will more detailed metering and recording of sales be required, but it will be necessary to control "leakage" of units from low-price to high-price buyers. Thus, it is not always evident that the monopolist will find such discrimination advantageous.

At first sight, it may appear that discrimination via multi-part pricing is very common. Electric and water utilities, for example, normally charge on a "declining-block" basis. There is an initial high price for the first block consumed in any period, and a lower price thereafter. Utility price schedules may often have four or five parts (blocks), and also, possibly, some segmentation of different classes of customers. Printers and furniture-movers also commonly have declining-block pricing arrangements. Indeed, wherever "quantity discounts" are encountered multi-price discrimination may be suspected.

However, the suspicion is not conclusive; the pricing scheme may be due not to discrimination but to the costs incurred in serving different classes of customers. In the case of electric utilities, for example, there may be a recurrent "fixed" cost of providing the consumer's connection to the main cable, a cost that is essentially independent of the number of kilowatt-hours consumed. Similarly, for printing jobs there is normally a "fixed" cost per transaction (e.g., the cost of setting up the type for a printing order) and a variable cost representing the actual run of the press. Ideally, then, bills should have a fixed and a variable component. For a variety of reasons, it may be more convenient to express the recurring fixed component as a premium price on the first few units taken. Thus, the question of the actual prevalence of discriminatory multi-part pricing versus "cost-justified" quantity discounts remains subject to some controversy.

11.E.3

Perfect Discrimination

Chapter 11
MONOPOLY
AND THE
QUESTION OF
ECONOMIC
EFFICIENCY

Finally, we can now go to the logical extreme of *perfect* discrimination. This of course is not a practical possibility, but is illuminating to analyze. It combines the *interpersonal* discrimination of market segmentation and the *intrapersonal* discrimination of multi-part pricing. In addition, these processes are imagined as carried to their limits. Each separate consumer is charged according to an individually tailored price schedule, which specifies a different amount to be paid for each successive infinitesimal unit he purchases.

In Figure 11.10 we see a four-part pricing schedule, an extension of the two-part schedule pictured in Figure 11.8. As in the previous analysis, we make the simplifying assumption of zero income effect (zero income elasticity of demand) for the commodity. Then the quantities taken at the lower prices are unaf-

Figure 11.10

Four-Part Pricing. In contrast with the two block prices in the preceding diagrams, here there are four blocks. The block sizes and prices, in the case illustrated, leave only the shaded areas as Consumer Surplus.

fected by the higher amounts paid out (in accordance with the specifics of the price schedule being enforced) for earlier units. As can be seen, the effect of the multi-part schedule is to transfer great portions of the Consumer Surplus to the seller; in Figure 11.10, only the small shaded areas remain as Consumer Surplus to the buyer.

When this process is carried to the limit, with different prices for each successive infinitesimal unit, *all* the Consumer Surplus will have been transferred from the buyer to the seller. Consequently, the buyer receives essentially zero advantage from trade. (Presumably, the buyer can be allowed to retain some tiny benefit, to rule out a shift to an autarky solution.) By repeating this process with every separate consumer, the perfectly discriminating monopolist absorbs essentially all the achievable mutual advantage of trade.

Despite the seeming "inequity" of this totally unbalanced distribution of the benefits from trade, the remarkable thing about the perfect-discrimination solution is that it is *efficient*—there are no deadweight losses! For the last infinitesimal unit purchased by each consumer, the monopolist will charge an amount equal to Marginal Cost. Since each buyer's marginal willingness to pay (demand price) is thus equal to the seller's Marginal Cost of production, there is no social gain available from increasing or decreasing output. So the perfectly discriminating monopolist cannot be said to produce "too little" or "too much" from the point of view of economic efficiency.

Chapter 11
MONOPOLY
AND THE
QUESTION OF
ECONOMIC
EFFICIENCY

356

A cartel may be defined as a group of independent firms attempting, via collusive agreement, to behave as a collective monopoly. Each firm in a cartel agrees to produce less than it would under unrestrained competition, the overall effect being to drive the price up so that all in the group will benefit.

Cartels have an Achilles heel. However desirable the arrangement is to the firms as a group, for any single one of them it pays to "chisel" on the agreement. Consider a firm in a cartelized industry that would otherwise have been perfectly competitive.[22] Figure 11.11 illustrates such a situation. At the price $P°$ that would rule in perfect competition, $d°$ is the familiar horizontal demand curve *as viewed by* the competitive firm. Assuming that Average Variable Cost is covered, the firm would produce output $q°$ where Marginal Cost $MC = P°$. If a cartel is organized with the objective of raising prices, industry output Q must somehow be cut back—for example, by fixing production quotas for each firm. Suppose that this firm is assigned an output quota q', and furthermore that the cartel is success-

Figure 11.11

Incentive to Chisel Under a Cartel. If the competitive equilibrium price is $P°$, this price-taking firm would produce output $q°$ (at the intersection of its *MC* curve with its perceived horizontal demand curve $d°$). If a cartel is organized, it can drive up price only by forcing its members to cut back production. If this firm's assigned production quota were q', and the cartel succeeded in driving price up to P', the firm's potential gain from chiselling (increase in profit due to exceeding its quota) would be the shaded area. Note that, at the high price P', the firm would find it profitable to produce output q'', *greater* than its competitive output $q°$.

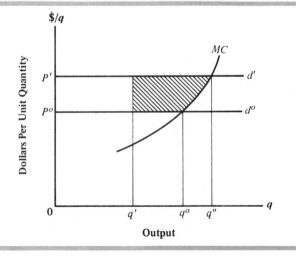

Chapter 11
MONOPOLY
AND THE
QUESTION OF
ECONOMIC
EFFICIENCY

[22]Collusive behavior in market structures that would otherwise be less than perfectly competitive (e.g., oligopoly) will be studied in the chapters following.

ful in pushing prices up to P'. The incentive to chisel is evident. The new demand curve *as viewed by* the firm (a tiny slice of the industry demand curve) is d' — effectively horizontal, just like the $d°$ curve before cartelization. This means that by charging an infinitesimally lower price, any single firm can get as much business as desired, taking away sales from others. Even at the old competitive price $P°$, the firm was motivated to produce $q°$, more than the quota amount q'. (Cartel production quotas must of course be less than competitive firm outputs, or the price could not rise from $P°$ to P'.) But once the cartel has raised price, the incentive to secretly chisel so as to achieve greater sales is that much greater. At the price P' the firm would want to set output q'' in the diagram. The potential profit increment available to a chiseller, assuming all the other firms are faithfully abiding by the cartel agreement so that price does not fall, is indicated by the shaded area in the diagram.

CONCLUSION: Cartels can only raise prices by cutting firm outputs. But at the higher prices, member firms are motivated to produce even more than at competitive equilibrium. So the more successful the cartel, the greater the incentive to chisel.

Cartels, therefore, require enforcement devices. The power of the state may do the trick; the law may treat the cartel agreement as a legally enforceable contract. This has indeed been the situation in a number of European countries. Some jurisdictions take a neutral position: the cartel agreement is not unlawful, but the power of the state will not enforce it. Finally, as typically has been the case in the United States, the law may be actively hostile to cartels as "conspiracies in restraint of trade." In such a situation, control of chiselling would require enforcement devices that are *both effective and secret*—an unlikely combination when any detected chiseller can threaten to complain to the authorities.

Collusive agreements alleged to be in restraint of trade are prosecuted in the United States mainly by the Anti-Trust Division of the Department of Justice and by the Federal Trade Commission. (In addition, it is possible for individuals or firms to sue for damages suffered as victims of such agreements.) But it is a curious paradox that, in parallel with this activity, other branches of the United States government are themselves active in the organization and enforcement of cartel agreements. A number of agricultural products, for example, are sold subject to governmentally-sponsored "marketing orders" designed to limit production and sales.

EXAMPLE 11.5
AGRICULTURAL
MARKETING
ORDERS

On the basis of legislation of the Federal government, and of some states as well, the growers of certain agricultural products may draw up an agreement to limit supply and assign marketing quotas. If two-thirds of the growers (by number or by volume) vote for such an agreement the Secretary of Agriculture is authorized to make it binding upon *all* growers.

Quantities produced beyond the marketing quotas are "dumped" abroad, used in special government programs outside normal trade channels (e.g., school lunches), or simply destroyed. In effect, the cartel (representing the growers as an aggregate) buys up excess production in order to limit supplies and drive up price in the ''primary'' market. However, this means that each individual producer has an incentive to produce more and more. In addition, the higher the cartelized price, the more growers of *other* commodities tend to shift over to the cartelized product. Consequently, we would expect to see over time an increasing percentage of the cartelized crops having to be diverted away from ''primary'' markets. This is illustrated in the following table.

Percentage of Annual Supply Diverted from Primary Markets
under Federal Marketing Orders

CROP	1960–64 AVG.	1965–68 AVG.
California Raisins	28.2	39.6
California-Arizona Lemons	55.2	62.5
California Almonds	15.0	21.2
California-Oregon-Washington Walnuts	0.8	7.5
Oregon-Washington Filberts	21.8	27.5
California Dates (Deglet Noor)	21.4	28.2

Source: John A. Jamison, ''Marketing Orders and Public Policy for the Fruit and Vegetable Industries,'' *Food Research Studies in Agricultural Economics, Trade, and Development,* v. 10, no. 3 (1971), p. 347.

Of course, there can hardly be anyone in the world unfamiliar with the most successful cartel in history—the Organization of Petroleum Exporting Countries (OPEC).

EXAMPLE 11.6
THE OPEC

Before 1960 the international oil companies (especially seven or eight ''majors'' such as Royal Dutch Shell and Standard Oil of New Jersey) dominated the world petroleum market. These companies, while often accused of acting as a cartel, cannot have diverged far from competitive behavior— judging (in retrospect) from the low prices formerly ruling. Indeed, it was the attempt of the majors to cut oil prices further that led the exporting governments to form the Organization of Petroleum Exporting Countries in 1960. (The U.S. State Department, in what must have been an all-time low point for intelligent foreign economic policy, actively encouraged formation of the OPEC, with the misguided aim of helping these ''underdeveloped'' countries.) The exporting governments, with increasing effectiveness over the years, have gained control over production and have appropriated the great bulk of the revenues. (The private companies still operating in those countries now receive what amount only to fees for current services rendered in production and marketing.)

While the OPEC kept oil prices from falling in 1960, lack of unity among the exporting nations allowed prices to remain stable for some time thereafter. But in solidarity with the attack of Egypt and Syria upon Israel in late 1973, the Arab countries dominating OPEC decided to use oil as an economic weapon. The effect upon prices was dramatic. On January 1, 1973, the sale price of Saudi Arabian crude oil had been $2.12 per barrel. Most of this amount, in fact $1.52, was already being taken by the Saudi Arabian government, leaving only some $.60 per barrel to cover the private companies' costs of operation and return on investment. By a year later, price had been raised to $7.61 per barrel. Practically all of the increase went into government take, which now amounted to $7.01 per barrel.[23] By January 1, 1975 the Saudi Arabian government take had risen to $10.12 per barrel, and the price to around $10.50. Other OPEC nations conformed to this price schedule, though the details varied from country to country in accordance with local circumstances. Still, it is evident that the price increase went in its entirety into the coffers of the exporting governments. (It is a tribute to economic gullibility that the Shah of Iran, the King of Saudi Arabia, and other oil potentates succeeded in convincing a large part of Western public opinion that it was the wicked oil companies rather than the OPEC member countries who were responsible for the higher prices!)

Not surprisingly, the drastic price increases had an impact upon consumption. In 1974 use of oil was down from 1973 by 14% in Holland and Belgium, by 10% in West Germany and Spain, by 3.5% in the U.S., and by 2% in Japan and Italy.[24] These percentages are more impressive when it is appreciated that demand had previously been on a sharp upward trend—growing at the rate of 4% per year in the United States, for example.

The problem for the OPEC was and is to hold production down despite its member countries' incentives to "chisel." Each separate exporting nation can gain by expanding its output so long as the others are holding back. In fact, in the period from 1974 to late 1978 most of the member countries were probably not holding back but were instead producing all-out. The cartel was viable in that period because a few major producers, notably Saudi Arabia and Kuwait, were willing to cut back production (or maintain it at a relatively low level). Nevertheless, in this period OPEC's power may have been weakening. While the official selling price of Saudi Arabian light oil rose from $10.84 per barrel at the beginning of 1974 to $13.34 five years later (an increase of about 24%), in this same period the U.S. dollar was depreciating rapidly. In fact, in terms of the GNP deflator the dollar's purchasing power fell by around 38% over the same period. Thus, by January 1, 1979 the real price of OPEC crude oil was substantially down from its peak.

However, a new chapter began with the revolution that displaced the Shah of Iran. During the period of turmoil in late 1978, oil exports from Iran fell almost to zero. Production revived somewhat under the new government that took over in January 1979, but a policy of drastically reduced exports was

[23]Data on prices from *International Economic Report of the President*, Feb. 1974 (Washington: U.S. Government Printing Office), pp. 110–11.

[24]Data on consumption from "OPEC Tries To Tackle a World Oil Surplus," *Business Week* (March 17, 1975), p. 20.

decided upon. The consequence was an upward leap in petroleum prices, which rose even above the official OPEC quotations. In the first half of 1979 the OPEC member governments had difficulty agreeng upon how high they should go. As of June 1979, a "split-level" price arrangement was adopted: Saudi Arabia raised its official price to $18 per barrel (32% above the beginning of the year), while the other countries agreed to a ceiling of $23.50 (76% above the beginning of the year).[25] Saudi Arabia can, if it expands production, force market prices down to the level it prefers, but the policy chosen by its rulers is subject to important political as well as financial considerations.

[25]*The Oil and Gas Journal* (July 2, 1979), p. 60.

With a small number of firms in an industry, *price-taking* behavior is unlikely. Each firm will be aware of the effects of its own output decision upon market price. The extreme case, where only a single firm is viable in an industry ("natural monopoly"), occurs where one firm can always produce more cheaply than (and so drive out) any larger number. But monopolies may also be the result of exclusive government privileges or franchises.

Monopolists, like ordinary firms, are assumed to be profit-maximizers. Profit is maximized by setting output (or price) such that:

$$MC = MR$$

For the monopolist firm, in contrast with the price-taking firm, Marginal Revenue MR is less than price P. The relation between these two variables involves the demand elasticity η:

$$MR \equiv P(1 + 1/\eta).$$

"Monopoly power" may be measured by the divergence between $MC = MR$ and price P; it tends to decrease with the number of firms in the industry, and with the consumers' elasticity of demand for the product. Thus, monopoly power tends to be greater for necessity goods and for goods without close substitutes.

Monopoly output is smaller than output would be if the industry had a competitive structure. There is an efficiency loss (reduction in Consumer Surplus and Producer Surplus) due to the smaller volume of production and exchange, and also a pure transfer from consumers to the monopolist seller. There may also be an additional efficiency loss, of a different type, if resources are expended in the struggle to gain and maintain a monopoly position.

Monopolies, and in particular franchised public utilities, are often subjected to regulation. The goal of regulation is commonly to insure that the monopolist

Chapter 11
MONOPOLY
AND THE
QUESTION OF
ECONOMIC
EFFICIENCY

receives only enough revenue to attract and retain the resources employed in the industry, i.e., receives only a "normal" profit and no *economic* profit. Then Average Revenue and Average Cost must be equal. If the monopolist's Average Cost curve is rising, the intersection of *AC* and *AR* "overshoots" the competitive equilibrium; there will be an efficiency loss due to *excessive* production in this industry. On the other hand, if *AC* is in its falling range (natural monopoly), the regulated solution lies between the monopolist's profit-maximizing output and the competitive outcome.

By engaging in price discrimination, a monopolist can acquire still more revenue from given consumer demands (can capture more of what would have been Consumer Surplus). Under *market segmentation*, the monopolist would set overall Marginal Cost of production equal to the Marginal Revenue in each segment. It follows from the equation relating *P*, *MR*, and elasticity η that higher prices will be charged in segments with less elastic demands. *Multi-part pricing*—an alternative form of price discrimination—captures some of Consumer Surplus via a declining-block price schedule. This type of discrimination is most effective if an individualized schedule can be offered to each consumer. *Perfect* discrimination is a limiting case in which each consumer is charged the maximum he or she would be willing to pay for each unit—so that no Consumer Surplus at all remains. Surprisingly, perhaps, there is no efficiency loss under perfect discrimination.

Cartels are associations of smaller firms able to act collectively like a monopolist. Since a higher price can only be achieved if production is cut back, output quotas typically have to be imposed on members of a cartel. Each member is therefore motivated to "chisel" (produce beyond quota). As a result, cartels have historically been fragile except where supported by government power.

QUESTIONS FOR CHAPTER 11

Mainly for Review

*R1. Why will a monopolist's profit-maximizing rate of output always be in the region of elastic demand?

R2. Why is monopoly power over price smaller as elasticity of demand increases?

*R3. "Monopoly is a bad thing for consumers, but a good thing for producers. So, on balance, we can't be sure that monopoly is responsible for any loss in economic efficiency." Analyze.

R4. A competitive industry may have its equilibrium in the range of inelastic demand. Then the industry would receive less revenue than if its output were smaller. Does it follow that such a competitive industry is producing "too much" of the good in terms of efficient use of resources?

Chapter 11
MONOPOLY
AND THE
QUESTION OF
ECONOMIC
EFFICIENCY

*The answers to asterisked questions appear at the end of the book.

*R5. Monopoly firms are accused of pursuing "non-profit goals" to a greater degree than competitive firms. Why might a monopolist be any less interested in profit than a competitor?

*R6. Compare the profit-maximizing conditions for simple monopoly, for market-segmentation monopoly, and for perfect-discrimination monopoly. Why is only the last of these said to be *efficient*?

*R7. In making efficiency comparisons between a monopolized and a competitive industry, the Marginal Cost function of the monopolist was said to correspond to the supply function of the competitive industry. Explain why.

R8. When will zero-profit regulation of a monopoly lead to too high a price from an efficiency point of view? Too low a price?

R9. Show how behavior of its own members may threaten the survival of a cartel. Show how behavior of outsiders may threaten it.

For Further Thought and Discussion

*T1. Is there a contradiction between the assertions that: (1) the oil industry is an effective monopoly (cartel) and (2) higher prices for petroleum products will do little to discourage demand?

T2. Is it better (more efficient) to have a monopolized industry, or no industry at all?

*T3. In comparison with a simple monopolist, does a perfectly discriminating monopolist *possibly* or *necessarily* produce more output? Does a market-segmentation monopolist? A multi-part pricing monopolist?

*T4. Price discrimination tends to be more common in the sale of services (e.g., discrimination by income for medical services, by age for air transportation services) than in the sale of manufactured goods. Explain.

*T5. Movie theaters often offer price discounts to the young. Is there likely to be a "leakage" problem in this form of market segmentation?

*T6. Observers have noted that pornographic movie-theaters seem to discriminate against single patrons (a discount price is offered to couples). Can you explain this?

T7. Doctors often charge poorer customers lower fees for medical services. They usually explain this as a charitable gesture. Might another explanation be offered?

T8. It has been alleged that sellers' cartels are more effective in dealing with *government* as a buyer because of the existence of public records of all transactions in which government engages. Explain. How might the contention be tested?

T9. Historically, governments have sometimes auctioned off the right to monopolize a commodity (the *gabelle*, or salt monopoly of pre-Revolutionary France, was an example). Show diagrammatically the maximum amount the government might expect to acquire by auctioning off a monopoly. Is this likely to generate more or less income for the government than the most lucrative excise tax the government might impose?

Chapter 11
MONOPOLY
AND THE
QUESTION OF
ECONOMIC
EFFICIENCY

363

*T10. If an organization like the Mafia effectively monopolized illegal activity, would you expect to observe less crime than under competitive free entry into this "industry"?

T11. The text stated that a "natural" monopoly might result from firms in an industry all having declining Average Cost curves AC. Are there other possible causes of natural monopoly, i.e., of a situation where only one firm is viable in an industry?

12.A OPTIMAL PRODUCT ASSORTMENT—MONOPOLY, 367

12.B MONOPOLISTIC COMPETITION, 371

12.C EQUILIBRIUM QUALITY LEVEL—COMPETITIVE INDUSTRY, 376

12.D EQUILIBRIUM QUALITY LEVEL—MONOPOLY VERSUS COMPETITION, 381

12.E AN APPLICATION: SUPPRESSION OF INVENTIONS, 382

Examples
      12.1   PRICE AND QUALITY: MOVIE THEATERS, 380
      12.2   MONOPOLY AND QUALITY: BASEBALL, 381

12

PRODUCT AS A VARIABLE

Supplementary Chapter

Up to this point, the nature of the commodities or goods produced by firms and industries has been taken to be fixed. We considered that a firm producing wheat or electricity or haircuts could vary the *amount* of output, and sometimes (if it has a degree of monopoly power) also the *price*—but not the characteristics that constitute the good itself. In actuality, these characteristics can, to a degree, be selected by the firm. A number of possible strains or varieties of wheat could be grown, haircuts come in different styles, and even electricity can be generated with different voltages or number of cycles. Furthermore, the "new theory of consumption" (Section 6.C) indicates that consumers are not really interested in the physical commodities as such. Rather, consumer preferences should be thought of as attaching to the utility-relevant attributes or characteristics represented by or contained in the commodities. Market goods are desired only because and insofar as they constitute convenient packages of attributes.

Firms therefore have another dimension of choice available for their profit-maximizing decisions. Aside from the possibility of quoting alternative prices for any given product, or varying the quantity of product offered, firms can alter the nature or attribute content of the commodities they produce.

In this chapter, two main types of situations will be investigated. In the first, consumers' tastes and desires for a particular product are assumed to be distributed over a range of some quantifiable characteristic such as size, color, or weight.

Some people like small cars, others prefer big ones.[1] The market response to this situation will typically be to offer an assortment to consumers. This will be called the problem of *variety*; we will be examining the forces determining the equilibrium nature and extent of the assortment produced and sold. Section 12.A will cover the variety or product assortment decision of a monopolistic supplier. Afterward, Section 12.B takes up the market structure known as "monopolistic competition"—where each firm offers consumers its own unique product, but there may be many closely competing firms.[2] The remainder of the chapter considers a second type of situation, called the problem of *quality*. Here consumers do not have diverging preferences. Instead, it is supposed that all consumers agree on the desirability of some objective quality attribute (e.g., strength or durability) contained, to greater or lesser degree, in the products offered for sale. But higher quality will, in general, involve higher cost of production. The problem is the determination of the equilibrium level or levels of quality offered in the market.

12.A

OPTIMAL PRODUCT ASSORTMENT—MONOPOLY

Before bringing in the element of competition, let us consider how a monopolist would solve the problem of variety—the profit-maximizing assortment of products to be offered on the market. Products may of course vary in an indefinitely large number of ways, but for simplicity we consider a single dimension of variation. In the case of an item of clothing, we might think in terms of the assortment of *sizes* to be offered. Alternatively, the assortment of *colors* might be a relevant consideration.

A locational metaphor or analogy will help to visualize the problem. With clothing *size* as the attribute, we can think metaphorically of consumption preferences as distributed over a line-segment as in Figure 12.1 (linear attribute preference). For example, a consumer looking for a small-sized product can be regarded as located toward the left, one desiring a large size toward the right. In such a situation we would normally expect to find greater density toward the middle; as indicated in Figure 12.1, desires for extreme sizes are less common than demand for intermediate sizes. However, it will be easier, and sufficient for our purposes, to imagine that preferences are *uniformly* distributed over the range. Apart from uniformity, one other analytically convenient change will be made from the picture given by Figure 12.1: we will assume that the varying product characteristic

---

[1]For some commodities, one or more of the preference-determining characteristics may not be objectively quantifiable. Toothpaste may have a sweet or spicy taste, clothing may be in mod or conservative style, an automobile may or may not have a sporty design. We deal here only with attributes that *can* be objectively scaled.

[2]Under monopolistic competition, we will assume that each firm specializes by producing only a single type of product. Variety is offered to consumers by the market as a whole, rather than by any single firm. This of course will not always or even usually be the case, but it provides a simple starting point for analysis.

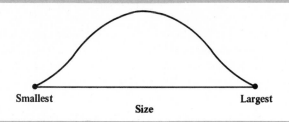

Smallest   Largest
                  Size

Figure 12.1

Distribution of Linear Attribute Preferences. Differing consumer preferences for an attribute like size of goods can be pictured as a distribution over a line-segment. Ordinarily, more consumers will be found toward the middle than toward the ends (intermediate sizes will be more popular than extreme sizes).

or attribute does not have a lower limit and upper limit but instead can be described by a ring, as in Figure 12.2. *Color* might be such a characteristic. If as many prefer red as yellow as green, and so on, consumers can be thought of as distributed uniformly around the color circle of Figure 12.2.

In this locational metaphor, the attribute variety (color) preferred by a particular consumer can be regarded as a *consumption locale*, i.e., the geographical location of the consumer's residence on the ring. Similarly, any given variety actually produced and offered in the market can be regarded as a *production locale*. In general, the consumer will have to pay some transport cost to cover shipment of the good from the nearest production point. This cost is the locational analog of the satisfaction loss involved in the imperfect matching of consumer preferences with the available products on the market.

Figure 12.2

Ring of Circular Attribute Preferences. An attribute like color may be described as a circle, rather than as a line-segment with end-points. (It is assumed that consumer preferences are uniformly distributed around the ring.)

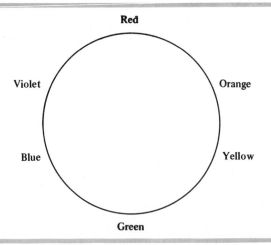

Red

Violet   Orange

Blue   Yellow

Green

Using the ring metaphor, the first problem for the monopolist is to determine *how many* varieties to produce, i.e., the number of distinct production locales to establish around the ring. Having done so, it will then be necessary to decide *how much* to produce at each production point, and what *prices* to charge for the outputs. There is an advantage to be gained by increasing the number of production locales (of ''plants''), since this will reduce transport costs and therefore increase the amount of consumers' expenditures that the monopolist is able to capture as revenue. What prevents carrying this process to the limit (a separate plant for each consumer) is *economies of scale*. Over some range, at least, Average Cost per plant will ordinarily be a decreasing function of plant output. So the monopolist must balance savings in production costs against savings in transport costs, i.e., against the gains achievable by closer matching of product assortment to consumer desires.

For simplicity again, assume that the monopolist's cost of production is *identical* at all possible locations around the ring. Then, given a uniform distribution of consumers, the producing plants (whatever their number may be) should be spaced evenly around the ring to minimize the transport costs of delivery to consumption locales. And, it also follows from the symmetry of the situation that the price at the factory (the ''f.o.b. price'') will be identical at each producing plant. Each consumer, of course, must pay this f.o.b. price *plus* the unit transport cost from the nearest plant.

Looking first at the demand side, note in Figure 12.3 the limiting highest aggregate consumer demand function D_∞. This represents the ideal case in which there are an infinite number of production locales around the ring. As consumers

Figure 12.3

Aggregate Demand as Related to Number of Producing Plants. $D_1, D_2, \ldots, D_\infty$ show the aggregate effective demand, as viewed by a monopolist seller, for increasing numbers of plants (production locales) spaced evenly around the ring of Figure 12.2. Effective demand increases with the number of plants (since there is less wastage in transport costs), but at a decreasing rate.

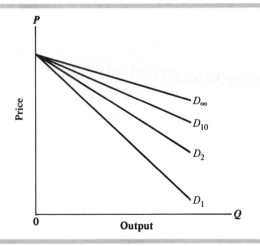

then incur no transport costs, their desires for product become wholly reflected in the effective demand curve faced by the monopolist. At the opposite extreme is the curve labelled D_1, which shows effective demand with just a single productive plant (placed at any arbitrary point on the ring). Here the worst-off consumer must pay for shipment halfway around the ring; the *average* transport cost corresponds to a quarter-circle of circumference about the ring. Any amounts expended to cover transport costs leave that much less of the consumers' outlays as receipts to the seller, hence whenever Q is positive D_1 must lie below D_∞. The curve D_2 represents the effective demand faced by a monopolist with two plants, so that the average consumer is separated by an eighth-circle from the nearest production locale. The D_{10} curve in the diagram shows the effective demand with 10 plants. Note that the curve of effective demand shifts upward, *but at a decreasing rate*, as the number of plants is increased, i.e., as the assortment offered more closely approximates the distribution of consumer preferences.

To arrive at the monopolist's solution, we also need the cost function for output. This is conveniently illustrated under the special assumption that plant production costs are linear. Thus for the nth plant, $C_n = A + Bq_n$. Here A is the Fixed Cost of each plant, and B the Marginal Cost. Then if there are N identical plants, the overall Total Cost will be symbolized here as $TC_N = \Sigma_{m=1}^N C_n$. Thus $TC_N = \Sigma_{m=1}^N (A + Bq_n) = NA + BQ$, where $Q \equiv \Sigma_{m=1}^N q_n$ is the monopolist's overall output of product. For a range of possible numbers of plants N, the overall Total Cost functions TC_N are shown by the dashed lines $TC_1, TC_2, \ldots$ in Figure 12.4. Because of the existence of the fixed cost A *per plant,* the Total Cost of producing any aggregate output Q rises with *number* of plants N.

The Total Revenue functions corresponding to different numbers of plants are also shown in Figure 12.4. TR_1 is the Total Revenue curve corresponding to the effective demand curve D_1 of the previous diagram; TR_2 similarly corresponds to D_2, etc.

For any given number of plants N, the monopolist chooses the f.o.b. price P_m and the associated quantity Q by using the familiar condition $MC = MR$ so as to maximize profit—the vertical distance between the appropriate pair of TR_N and TC_N curves (compare the upper panel of Figure 11.1). For different numbers of plants N, the various possible profits are indicated by the vertical bold line-segments in Figure 12.4. As may be seen, there will normally be a range in which profit increases as N rises. In this range the gain from better matching of product to consumer desires (i.e., from the fact that consumers are willing to pay more when they avoid the metaphorical "transport costs"), evidencing itself by upward shifts of the TR curve, is greater than the increased cost due to the larger number of production locales. But the gains from increasing N tend to taper off, as indicated in Figure 12.3. Meanwhile the costs tend to rise steadily as N grows, because of the necessity of incurring another fixed-cost element A each time a new plant is added. There will, consequently, be an optimum number of plants. In Figure 12.4, the largest profit Π^* (greatest of the bold vertical line-segments) is achieved at $N = 4$; having exactly four production locales represents the best compromise between production costs and transport costs.

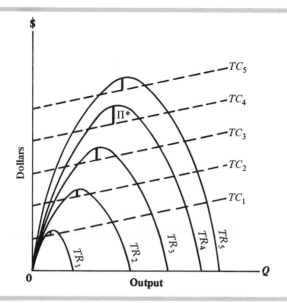

Figure 12.4

Monopoly Total Revenue and Total Costs, as Related to Number of Plants. The aggregate Total Revenue curves TR_1, TR_2, . . . represent the same data as shown by the aggregate demand curves (curves of Average Revenue) D_1, D_2, . . . of the previous diagram. As number of plants N rises, Total Revenue TR_N also rises *but at a decreasing rate*. The Total Cost curves TC_1, TC_2, . . . show the aggregate cost of producing any output Q with 1, 2, . . . plants. Under the assumption of an identical linear cost function for each plant, TC_N shifts upward by a constant amount as N rises (since an additional fixed cost is incurred each time a new plant is brought into production). The bold vertical segments show the highest achievable profit for each N; the greatest of these is the profit maximum Π^*, which occurs here at $N = 4$.

MONOPOLISTIC COMPETITION

The monopoly solution of the previous section provides the needed background for analyzing the market structure known as *monopolistic competition*. This market structure combines the following characteristics: (1) competition among plants, now treated as independent *firms*; (2) free entry; and (3) heterogeneous products among firms. The first two characteristics represent the competitive aspects of monopolistic competition. The monopolistic aspect is represented by the third element, the uniqueness of the firm's product offered to the market. This uniqueness corresponds metaphorically to a degree of *geographical* monopoly. Each firm will have a "clientele" consisting of those consumers located closer to it than to any other firm around the ring of preference.

It will be convenient first to provide a reinterpretation of the monopoly solution in terms of an average-marginal diagram as in Figure 12.5. In a monopoly

$/q

Dollars Per Unit Quantity

P_m

B ———————————————————— MC

D_∞

D_N

MR_N

$D_n \equiv \dfrac{D_N}{N}$

$MR_n \equiv \dfrac{MR_N}{N}$

$0 \qquad q_n^* \qquad\qquad\qquad Q_N^* \qquad\qquad$ —q, Q

Plant Output and Aggregate Output

Figure 12.5

Monopoly Solutions, Aggregate and Plant. For a given number of plants N, the monopolist's effective *aggregate* demand curve is D_N. And $D_n \equiv D_N/N$ is the pro-rata *plant* demand curve. MR_N and $MR_n \equiv MR_N/N$ are the associated Marginal Revenue curves. Under the linear cost assumption, the constant Marginal Cost is shown by a horizontal MC curve at the level B. The profit-maximizing *aggregate* output is Q_N^* (where $MC = MR_N$), and *plant* output is q_n^* (where $MC = MR_n$). Of course, $Q_N^* \equiv Nq_n^*$. For either the plant or the firm solution, the same profit-maximizing price P_m is found along the associated demand curve.

with N identical plants, the effective aggregate demand (Average Revenue) is D_N, a curve some distance below the "ideal" D_∞. Marginal Revenue is MR_N. Now consider the *pro-rata shares* of D_N and MR_N attributable to any single plant, $D_n \equiv D_N/N$ and $MR_n \equiv MR_N/N$. Geometrically, these are found simply by dividing the respective aggregate curves horizontally by N. If $N = 4$, the pro-rata plant curves D_n and MR_n will simply represent one-fourth the quantities along the aggregate curves D_N and MR_N, respectively. The profit-maximizing solutions for aggregate *firm* output Q_N^* and for *plant* output $q_n^* \equiv Q_N^*/N$ can be seen by inspection of Figure 12.5. The *plant* output q_n^* is determined by the intersection of MC with MR_n. (Under the linear cost assumption $C_n = A + Bq_n$, the Marginal Cost curve MC is horizontal at the level B.) The aggregate *firm* output Q_N^* is found at the intersection of MC with MR_N. The monopoly price, P_m, may be found equally well along the aggregate demand curve D_N (at quantity Q_N^*), or along the plant pro-rata demand curve D_n (at quantity q_n^*). Of course, $Q_N^* = Nq_n^*$.

We now shift gears, in order to introduce the element of *competition*. Imagine that each *plant* of the monopolist becomes a separate small *firm*. For the moment, we will assume there is some definite number N of such firms, that all of them have identical cost functions, and that they have distributed themselves evenly around the preference ring of Figure 12.2. Then the monopolist's *aggregate* demand curve of Figure 12.5 can be regarded as the *industry* demand curve, since from the consumers' point of view the transport costs incurred are the same regardless of whether shipment is from a monopoly plant or an independent firm. The pro-rata demand curve $D_n (\equiv D_N/N)$ in Figure 12.6 is therefore also the same as the correspondingly labelled curve in the previous diagram; it now indicates, at every price, the share of the industry output that can be sold by each of the *firms*. At the intersection of MC and MR_n, we see once again what the profit-maximizing monopoly plant output q_n^* would be.

But the key point is that, once the plant has become an independent firm, the monopoly plant output will *not* be the solution arrived at. The reason is that, *for a plant that is an autonomous firm, the perceived demand function* d_n *becomes more elastic (flatter) than the* D_n *curve that represents the monopoly plant's pro-rata share of the overall demand curve.* The curve d_n is more elastic than D_n because, by lowering price relative to its neighbors, each firm figures that it can win customers away from them—whereas the monopoly plant's demand curve D_n was based on the premise that the *same* (f.o.b.) price P_m will be charged by all N plants. (It is not in the interest of the monopolist, of course, to have his plants cutting price at one another's expense.) Corresponding to the *more elastic* firm demand curve d_n in Figure 12.6 is a *higher* perceived Marginal Revenue curve

Figure 12.6

Monopoly Plant versus Monopolistic-Competition Firm, at Monopoly Solution. The solution for the monopoly plant, where $MC = MR_n$ at output q_n^* and associated monopoly price P_m, is the same as in the previous diagram. But once the monopoly plant becomes an independent firm, at the price P_m the *perceived* demand curve would be d_n. This is more elastic than the pro-rata demand curve D_n, since the firm can win customers from its neighbors if it lowers its price relative to theirs. Under monopolistic competition the firm will therefore attempt to achieve the solution where Marginal Cost MC cuts the curve mr_n, the latter being the Marginal Revenue curve associated with the perceived d_n demand curve. At this attempted solution, firm output would be q_n' and price P'.

mr_n.[3] The firm in Figure 12.6 will therefore be competitively motivated to attain the larger output q'_n where $mr_n = MC$. Doing so implies setting a lower price $P' < P_m$ for its particular variety of product.

Figure 12.6 suggests that the output of a monopolistic-competition firm will surely be larger than the per-plant output of an ordinary monopolist. But we are not yet entitled to draw that conclusion. The reason is that the seeming firm solution in Figure 12.6, with output q'_n sold at the price P' along demand curve d_n, is not possible as an *overall equilibrium* of the industry. With a fixed number N of producing locations (whether plants of a monopolist, or competing firms), the sales achievable per location at any given price can be no greater than those represented by the pro-rata demand curve $D_n = D_N/N$. Each firm's flatter demand curve d_n is an illusion (akin to the illusion of the seemingly horizontal demand curve faced by the firm in pure competition). Any single firm can hope to cut price so as to expand output along d_n. But the symmetry of the situation, with N identical firms, dictates that in equilibrium *they must all end up choosing the same price*. They each cut price, hoping to sell output q'_n at price P'. But the result of their collective action is that output expands less than expected, along the steeper pro-rata demand curve D_n in the diagram.

The overall equilibrium must therefore represent a point on the pro-rata demand curve D_n, like S in Figure 12.7. Each firm produces quantity q''_n, and the associated price is P''. Once again the firm *perceives* a flatter demand curve d_n, but the d_n pictured in Figure 12.7 is such that the firm's desired price-output combination P'', q''_n (determined by the intersection of MC with mr_n) lies along the pro-rata demand curve. Thus, the solution on the firm level is now in balance with the overall consumer demand for the industry's production. At this solution each firm's output is clearly greater (and price to consumers lower) in comparison with the monopoly pro-rata solution P_m, q^*_n.

We are not yet at the full or *long-run* equilibrium for monopolistic competition, however. Possible changes in the *number* of firms in the market (associated with the condition of free entry) must also be taken into account. Depending upon the level of the fixed cost per firm, the short-run equilibrium shown in Figure 12.7 might either be a profitable one for firms in the industry (inducing entry) or an unprofitable one (dictating exit). Let us assume that the short-run equilibrium is profitable, with price P'' greater than the representative firm's level of Average Cost AC_n at the production rate q_n. As entry of new firms occurs, both the true pro-rata demand curve $D_n = D_N/N$ and the illustory d_n as viewed by an existing firm will *shift inward* toward the vertical axis.[4] The long-run solution is as shown in Figure 12.8 for the representative firm. Here, in addition to the conditions

---

[3]This will be evident from the geometry, recalling (from the "Corollary" of Section 11.B.2) that the Marginal Revenue curve bisects the horizontal distance from the axis to a linear demand curve. Or, consider the definition $MR \equiv P + Q(\Delta P/\Delta Q)$, where the ratio $\Delta P/\Delta Q$ represents the slope of the demand curve. For a given (P, Q) combination, the smaller the slope in absolute value (the flatter the demand curve), the smaller in absolute magnitude is the second term in the definition of MR. But this second term is of negative sign. So the flatter the slope of the demand curve, the greater is Marginal Revenue.

[4]This shift is due to dividing the aggregate demand curve D_N horizontally by a larger N. There is a countervailing factor, however, since a larger N is associated with a more perfect matching of con-

$/q

Dollars Per Unit Quantity

P_m
P''

B

d_n

MC

mr_n D_n

S

MR_n

0 q_n^* q_n'' q

Plant or Firm Output

Figure 12.7

Monopoly Plant versus Monopolistic-Competition Firm, at Monopolistic-Competition Equilibrium. With N firms, price P'' and per-firm output q_n'' represent a monopolistic-competition equilibrium (point S in the diagram). Each firm is maximizing profit since $MC = mr_n$, where mr_n is the Marginal Revenue associated with the *perceived* (flatter) firm demand curve d_n. And this outcome is consistent with overall equilibrium of the industry as a whole, since the combination of output q_n'' and price P'' constitutes a point on the pro-rata demand curve D_n. Price is lower and output greater than in the monopoly case.

satisfied in the previous diagram, that $MC = mr_n$ and that the firm's price-output combination be consistent with the pro-rata demand curve D_n, we have a *zero-profit solution*. This is represented in the diagram by the tangency at point L of the firm's demand curve d_n with its Average Cost curve AC_n, at output q_n''' and price P'''.

CONCLUSION: In comparison with multi-plant monopoly, under monopolistic competition aggregate output will be greater and hence product price lower. And in long-run equilibrium zero economic profit will be earned. But there may or may not be a larger number of producing locales. Thus, while consumers benefit from a lower price, they may or may not find a better assortment of varieties of product available under monopolistic competition as compared with monopoly.

---

sumer desires, so that the aggregate curve D_N itself shifts upward as N rises (as shown in Figure 12.3). So both the numerator and the denominator of the ratio D_N/N (which defines the pro-rata demand curve D_n) rise as N increases. However, the numerator tends not to rise as fast as the denominator. If we go from two to three firms there is a 50% increase in N, but not in general such an enormous improvement in the matching of production locales to consumer preferences as to warrant a 50% increase in quantity demanded at any given price. So, despite this countervailing factor, the D_n curve (and therefore also the d_n curve) must, at least eventually, shift inward as N rises.

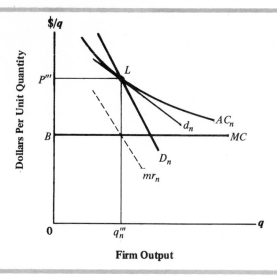

Figure 12.8

Long-Run Equilibrium, Representative Firm in Monopolistic Competition. For long-run equilibrium in monopolistic competition, the short-run equilibrium conditions of the previous diagram continue to hold: $MC = mr_n$, and the representative firm's price-output combination constitutes an achievable point on the true pro-rata demand curve D_n. The additional long-run condition is that entry or exit takes place until the representative firm is earning zero profit (price equals Average Cost). All these conditions are met at point L in the diagram, where the representative firm's output is q_n''' and price is P'''.

12.C

EQUILIBRIUM QUALITY LEVEL—COMPETITIVE INDUSTRY

In the remainder of this chapter quite a different type of product variation will be considered. It will now be assumed that there is some single attribute or characteristic that *all* consumers want to obtain from the product purchased in the market. It is no longer a matter of some customers preferring yellow clothing and others red, or big men wanting big sizes and small men small sizes. Instead we here assume that in the purchase of light bulbs, for example, all buyers agree that light output in lumens is the sole desired feature. In the purchase of gasoline, transportation mileage may be the desired feature. In such cases the amount of the desired attribute obtainable per unit of the physical commodity may be considered the *quality* of the product. Of course, quality will generally be multi-dimensional. Gasoline may be valued for attributes like rapid acceleration and easy starting as well as for cruising mileage. The color or shape or size of light bulbs may be important to consumers in addition to sheer light output. In the interests of simplicity, however, we will deal here only with a one-dimensional quality index.

Many different questions might be asked about quality equilibrium. One is: Will a monopolist tend to produce a higher-quality or lower-quality product than a competitive industry? This topic will be considered in Sections D and E below. The issue to be considered here is: Will a competitive industry tend to settle on a single grade of quality of product, or will a quality assortment be produced? And if the latter, will it be the case (as might seem plausible) that poorer people would tend to buy a lower-quality product?

There is one key idea to be kept in mind: Only superficially are consumers and producers dealing in quantities of *product* Q (e.g., gasoline); more fundamentally, consumers are demanding and firms are supplying quantities of *attribute* K (e.g., mileage). Thus we are concerned here with conditions of equilibrium in the *market for the quality attribute* (mileage).

Assume to begin with a fixed number N of competitive firms. Each separate firm will, it is assumed, choose a quality grade z_n as well as an output rate q_n for its physical product. Then, the firm's *output of the attribute* k_n will simply be:

(12.1) $k_n \equiv z_n q_n$

For example, a firm producing $q_n = 1,000,000$ gallons of gasoline per day, with quality grade $z_n = 20$ miles per gallon, is effectively producing $k_n = 20,000,000$ units per day of "mileage" for sale to consumers.

Since it is the attribute that they are really concerned with, the underlying demand function of the consumers shows the aggregate quantity of *attribute* they demand, K_d, as a function of the *"price of attribute"* P_k that is implicit in the prices charged by the various firms for their physical products. On the assumption that consumers are always fully informed as to quality, the price P_n of the nth firm's physical product will depend strictly upon its attribute content:

(12.2) $P_n \equiv z_n P_k$

If one gasoline yields 10% greater mileage per gallon than another, its price must be just 10% higher.

The equilibrium *price of attribute* P_k is determined by the overall supply and demand of attribute. The supply quantity K_s, to be balanced against the demand quantity of K_d as a function of price P_k, is simply the sum of the separate firms' outputs of attribute:

(12.3) $K_s \equiv \Sigma_{n=1}^{N} k_n$

The firm's decision problem, as a competitive price-taker in the market for attribute, is to choose the profit-maximizing combination of z_n and q_n. A possible situation is illustrated in Figure 12.9. Suppose an initial quality $z_n = z^\circ$ were set by the firm. The associated Average Cost and Marginal Cost functions, indicated by the solid curves $AC(z^\circ)$ and $MC(z^\circ)$, lead to the optimal attribute output k_n°. Knowing k_n and z_n, the required physical output of commodity is then given, from equation (12.1), as $q_n = k_n/z_n$.

Figure 12.9

Uniform Optimal Quality Level. The horizontal scale represents amounts of attribute $k_n \equiv z_n q_n$ produced by the nth firm, where q_n is the firm's output of the commodity and z_n the quality grade (attribute content per unit of commodity produced). The ruling market price for attribute, P_k, is shown by the firm's horizontal demand curve d. In the situation pictured quality z' is always more profitable than z°, because $AC(z')$ lies always below $AC(z^\circ)$. Any desired output of attribute can be produced more cheaply at quality grade z' than at z° (where z' might represent either higher or lower quality than z°).

But attribute output of k_n° is optimal only given the initial choice of quality $z_n = z^\circ$. What would happen if other quality grades were considered? It might be that a 20% increase in quality grade z_n (miles per gallon) would only raise cost by 10% per unit of physical commodity (gallons of gasoline). This would imply that the cost *per unit of attribute* (mileage) has fallen. Geometrically, this would be reflected in Figure 12.9 by a downward displacement of MC and AC, as suggested by the dashed curves $AC(z')$ and $MC(z')$ in the diagram. With $z_n = z'$, the optimal output of attribute is k_n'.

What is the *best* z_n to choose? If for some choice of z_n such as z' in Figure 12.9, $AC(z')$ were *uniformly lower* than the Average Cost curve associated with any other z_n, then clearly z' is the profit-maximizing quality grade.

In general, however, things may not be quite so simple. It might be the case that, as illustrated in Figure 12.10, some quality grades are better at low production levels ($z_n = z^\circ$ in the diagram), some at middling output levels ($z_n = z'$), and still others at high production levels ($z_n = z''$). Then the optimal choice of quality will vary with optimal firm output, which will itself be a function of the market price P_k. At a very high price, for example, the firm will want to produce large amounts of attribute for the market, which can best be done by choosing quality grade $z_n = z''$ in the diagram. But at lower prices, a different level of production and consequently a different choice of z_n may be dictated.

When we take into account the possible variation of cost functions as among

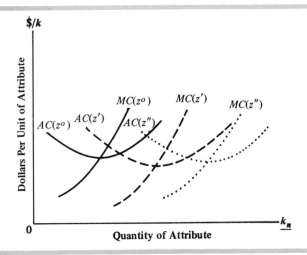

Figure 12.10
Optimal Quality Varying with Output. Here the optimal quality grade associated with the firm's lowest-cost way of generating attribute varies with the scale of output. Since the firm will always want to set its Marginal Cost of producing attribute equal to the price of attribute P_k, the optimal quality changes as P_k varies.

non-identical firms, we see that there is no presumption that competitive firms will all choose the same quality level. In the case of a mining industry producing ore for sale, for example, some firms will be exploiting richer and others leaner deposits. Each firm will market an ore whose richness (mineral content per ton) represents its quality level z_n. But, assuming informed purchasers, the prices offered for ores of different mineral content will be such as to reflect (after due allowance for any special chemical or physical features that might affect extraction cost, storage requirements, etc.) a single underlying price P_k for the mineral contained.

We have already in effect answered the question posed above, as to willingness of consumers to pay for differences in quality grades. If all buyers are interested only in the attribute content (mileage) of the commodity produced (gasoline), and all are fully informed, then in equilibrium all will be paying the same going market price P_k for the attribute. Neglecting special features like costs of extraction or storage, each firm's product must sell at a price representing simply its attribute content. At these equilibrium prices, every consumer will be *indifferent* as to buying higher-quality or lower-quality goods (obtaining the same mileage with fewer gallons of high-quality but expensive gasoline or with more gallons of low-quality but cheap gasoline). And in particular, there is no reason to expect poorer consumers to buy goods of lower quality than richer consumers.

CONCLUSION: Each firm will, at its optimal level of output, choose the quality grade minimizing its Average Cost of producing attribute. The chosen quality may vary with output, and between different firms, so an assortment of qualities will normally be offered by firms. But, with fully informed consumers, the equilibrium price of any firm's output will be proportional to its attribute content; at these prices, all consumers will be indifferent as among the outputs of any of the firms.

EXAMPLE 12.1
PRICE AND
QUALITY: MOVIE
THEATERS

R. D. Lamson studied the effect of a number of objective quality attributes upon the prices charged for movie admissions in a large metropolitan area over the period 1961–64.[5] As suggested by the preceding analysis, there was considerable variation in quality attributes of different theaters.

For 1961, the adult evening admission price P (in cents) was estimated from the data by the equation:

$$P = 4.13 + 31.46 \log_{10} U + 5.77L + 8.21T - 7.68D$$

$$- 1.13F + 27.09S + .81R$$

The symbols used on the right-hand side represent the explanatory (quality) variables:

U: average percentage of unused seating capacity per showing
L: theater location (1 if suburban, 0 if city center)
T: theater age (1 if less than 10 years since construction or major renovation, 0 otherwise)
D: type of theater (1 if outdoor, 0 if indoor)
F: parking (1 if provided, 0 otherwise)
S: screening policy (1 if first-run, 0 otherwise)
R: average film rental (cents per ticket charged by distributor)

The results are generally in the directions anticipated. For example, other things equal, newer (or renovated) theaters charged on the average 8.21¢ more per admission; first-run houses charged 27.09¢ more; each penny per ticket paid for film rental (a measure of *film* quality or, at least, film popularity) was associated with a 0.81¢ increment to admission price; etc. The one paradoxical component of the equation is parking provision, associated with a 1.13¢ *reduction* in price. This might possibly be due to an inter-correlation of parking availability (a positive quality element) with remote or low-rental location (an unfavorable element) not captured in the crude index L.

One rather important element is the role of U, unused capacity. This can be regarded as a measure of quality of movie seating—*uncrowdedness*. The equation shows that a 10% increase in unused seating capacity (e.g., from 20% to 22%) is associated with a 1.3¢ increase in admission price. It is of interest to note that since *quality* in the form of uncrowdedness U automatically rises when *quantity* of sales fall off in response to a rise in admission price, the true (quality-constant) elasticity of demand for movie admissions must be greater than that implicit in these data.

[5]R. D. Lamson, "Measured Productivity and Price Change: Some Empirical Evidence on Service Industry Bias, Motion Picture Theaters," *Journal of Political Economy*, v. 78 (March/April 1970).

EQUILIBRIUM QUALITY LEVEL—MONOPOLY VERSUS COMPETITION

The question to be considered here is: Will a monopolist producer tend to offer a lower quality level to consumers than would a competitive industry? Since a monopolist produces a lesser *quantity* of product than a competitive industry (see Section 11.B), by analogy one might anticipate a lower *quality* of product as well. But, as it turns out, this superficial analogy is mistaken.

The essential feature at work can be seen in terms of the simplest case of a uniformly best quality level, as illustrated for a competitive firm in Figure 12.9 above. Clearly, if Average Cost is lowest with quality $z = z'$ for *all* outputs of attribute k, then *that same quality grade would be selected by a monopolist as well as by a competitive firm*.

A somewhat more complicated situation is shown by the cost picture of Figure 12.10, where the quality grade representing lowest Average Cost of producing attribute k varies at different outputs. Since we would expect the attribute output of a monopolist to be large (in comparison with the output of a *single* firm if the industry in question had a competitive market structure), the monopolist would tend to choose a quality permitting low-cost production at large firm output. But there seems to be no general reason to presume that this quality grade is necessarily higher or lower than the most profitable quality level for small outputs.[6]

H. G. Demmert, in a study of the economics of professional team sports,[7] examined as one topic the determinants of the ''quality'' choices made by the owners of the various major league baseball clubs. An owner can most obviously upgrade quality by hiring more skilled players, coaches, and so forth. In this case, ''output'' is produced by two teams meeting in a contest. Hence a natural quality measure is how well a particular team fares in its games relative to other league members.

Using a sample of 282 observations on 16 major league baseball teams over the period 1951–1969, two determinants were found to be important. First, teams in more populous areas were, on the average, of higher quality. This seems reasonable, since fans generally prefer winning teams and a greater population base can better afford to ''buy'' this objective. Spe-

EXAMPLE 12.2
MONOPOLY AND
QUALITY:
BASEBALL

[7]H. G. Demmert, *The Economics of Professional Team Sports* (Lexington, Mass.: D. C. Heath & Co., 1973), especially p. 71.

[6]Conceivably, at small outputs it might be most economical to use hand labor, and at large outputs machinery. Hand labor may often produce work of higher quality than machinery, but this is by no means a universal phenomenon.

cifically, a population difference of 5,000,000 was found to be associated with a difference of .018 in the team's win ratio.

More closely relevant to the discussion of this section, it was found that teams with major league baseball competitors (where more than one team was franchised in a given population area) were of poorer quality than teams with monopoly positions in their area. Specifically, it was found (other things held equal) that the existence of a competitor was associated with a *decrease* of .034 in the win ratio.

At least for this peculiar good, then, a monopolist tended to produce a product of higher quality than a firm facing a competitor or competitors in its market area.

12.E

AN APPLICATION: SUPPRESSION OF INVENTIONS

Monopolists are sometimes accused of suppressing inventions. Let us interpret the term "invention" as a discovery permitting production of a higher-quality product at given cost, or a given-quality product at lower cost.[8] Then it can be shown, under the key assumption that buyers are fully informed as to the quality improvement, that suppression is *never* rational.

Take the instance of a monopolist of gasoline, where consumers are interested only in the quality attribute yield (mileage). The monopolist discovers a way, let us say, of doubling the mileage per gallon of product, without any additional cost of production. We can see immediately that, in terms of a cost function like that in Figure 12.9, the Average Cost of producing mileage will be halved at all output levels if the new invention is adopted. Then, regardless of whether the monopolist decides to produce more output or less, it would surely be absurd to suppress such an invention.

The assumption of *full knowledge* on the part of consumers is, however, a strong one. If the invention really improves product quality but the consumers do not believe it, they would not (at least not initially) be willing to pay any more for the higher-mileage gasoline. Under the reasonable assumption that it costs somewhat more per gallon to produce gasoline of doubled mileage yield, the monopolist's incentive to introduce the innovation would be impaired. In this case, however, we should really consider the *cost of informing consumers* as part of the economic cost of the invention. It is not really "suppression" when an invention, even though a genuine improvement of quality, cannot be put on the market except at a cost too great (including the cost of spreading the information) in comparison with the benefit received.

[8]Obviously, there is no problem in explaining the "suppression" of discoveries that lead to production of a *lower*-quality product at the same cost, or a constant-quality product at *higher* cost!

Another possible motivation for suppression emerges in a case where the invention *would destroy the monopoly*. Consider a monopolist of the only currently exploitable aluminum ore—bauxite. Conceivably, this monopolist might come into possession of a cheap process for extracting aluminum from alumina. The latter, one of the most plentiful components of the earth's crust, could not effectively be monopolized. But even here, the monopolist can in principle do better by using than suppressing the invention. The monopoly *of the information* as to how to reduce alumina is more valuable than the previous monopoly of bauxite. The monopolist could patent and license the new process, or alternatively use it while keeping the key steps a secret.[9]

It is of some interest to work through the monopolist's solution for a cost-reducing invention, to see the implications for *output of attribute K* (mileage) versus *output of product Q* (gasoline).

Let us return to the simple assumption that the invention doubles the quality (mileage per gallon) of the product without any added cost of production. Then the situation may be pictured as in Figure 12.11, a diagram in "Total" units with attribute quantity k (mileage) on the horizontal axis. The original Total Cost curve

Figure 12.11

A Quality-Improving (Cost-Reducing) Invention, Attribute Units. In the case pictured, a monopolist is considering adoption of an innovation that costlessly doubles the quality (attribute content) of the product. Since the horizontal axis represents amount of attribute k, the original Total Cost curve $C°$ shifts to C'—attribute quantity is doubled at each level of cost. Fully-informed consumers are interested only in amount of attribute, and so in terms of attribute the Total Revenue function R is unchanged. The monopolist will necessarily achieve a higher profit by adopting rather than suppressing such an invention. In the situation pictured, the increased profit is Π'; consumers also benefit, since greater output is produced to be sold at a lower price.

Quantity of Attribute (Mileage)

[9]In practice, however, there might be difficulties either with patenting or with maintaining secrecy. Thus, a rational motivation for suppression might persist in the case of an invention tending to destroy one's own monopoly.

is $C°$. At any given cost of producing the commodity (gasoline), the invention doubles the mileage output k. This shifts the Total Cost curve in mileage units to the position C'—a horizontal doubling (stretching) to the right. The key assumption, that consumers are fully informed, means that the *Total Revenue curve in terms of attribute* k *remains unchanged*. Consumers have no interest in gasoline as such; whether quality is high or low, they can determine and pay for only what concerns them—the mileage content.

In Figure 12.11 the profit-maximizing levels of attribute output are $k°$ for the pre-invention situation and k' for the post-invention situation. The pre-invention profit $\Pi°$ is the bold line-segment indicating the greatest vertical difference between the Total Revenue curve R and the original Total Cost curve $C°$. The necessarily larger post-invention profit Π' similarly represents the greatest vertical difference $R - C'$. The diagram illustrates a "normal" case in which output of attribute increases $(k' > k°)$ but by less than a doubling $(k' < 2k°)$. This means that consumers benefit from having more attribute k (mileage), while the firm saves some cost by having to produce less physical output q (gallons of gasoline).

If the Total Revenue curve were rising almost linearly, however (i.e., if Marginal Revenue MR were almost constant), it might conceivably happen that output of attribute k *more* than doubles. The stretching of the Total Cost curve from $C°$ to C' may have the effect of lowering Marginal Cost MC in the relevant range. If throughout the doubling interval MC remains lower while MR is nearly unchanged, the profit-maximizing output of attribute k will be more than twice the pre-invention amount.

Paradoxically, it is logically possible for the output of attribute at the post-invention solution to fall $(k' < k°)$. In this case, while the invention will not have been suppressed, the consumers are nevertheless worse off! How this might happen is more clearly visible in Figure 12.12, which is an Average-Marginal diagram. On the horizontal axis we see attribute quantity k as before, while the vertical axis is in units of dollars/k. Corresponding to the Total Revenue curve of the preceding diagram is the monopoly firm's negatively sloped demand curve D_k for the attribute. The quality-improving invention is equivalent to a reduction in Average Cost of producing any amount of attribute—the new AC' curve (dashed) is therefore everywhere lower than the original $AC°$ curve (solid). But, as the diagram illustrates, there may be a range in which the Marginal Cost MC' associated with the new technology is *higher* than the original $MC°$. If, as shown here, the intersection of Marginal Cost with Marginal Revenue occurs in this range, the firm's profit-maximizing output of attribute will be smaller $(k' < k°)$. This implies that monopoly price must be higher, and consumers must be worse off!

CONCLUSION: Monopoly cannot validly be accused of *suppressing* inventions (given the assumption of fully informed buyers). But it remains open to the accusation of possibly using inventions in such a way that consumers may derive no benefit therefrom, or may even be made worse off.

Figure 12.12

A Quality-Improving (Cost-Reducing) Invention Adverse to Consumers. Here the diagram is in Average-Marginal units. A quality-improving invention is equivalent to a reduction in the Average Cost of producing the quality attribute k, and so the new AC' curve lies everywhere below the original $AC°$ curve. Nevertheless, as shown here, there may be range in which the new Marginal Cost MC' is *higher* than the original $MC°$. As a result, the new $MC' = MR$ intersection may determine a profit-maximizing attribute output k' that is *smaller* than the original output k'. If so, consumers will be worse off for the invention.

SUMMARY OF CHAPTER 12

In previous chapters a firm could vary only the *amount* of output produced and possibly (if it has monopoly power) also the *price*. In this chapter it is assumed that any firm is also in a position to change the characteristics that define its own product. Under this general heading, two main topics are considered: the problem of *variety*, and the problem of *quality*.

The problem of *variety* arises when consumer preferences are distributed over a range of some characteristic (size, color, weight) of the commodity. Then the greater the number of different varieties produced, the less the average consumer's dissatisfaction from having to choose a good with characteristics less close to what he or she desires. A locational metaphor permits us to think of "closeness" of preference in geographical terms.

Under certain simplifying assumptions, the profit-maximizing solution for a monopolist was obtained in terms of number of varieties offered consumers (number of geographically distributed production locales or plants), together with the price and production at each plant. The market structure known as *monopolis-*

tic competition is defined by independent producers (each plant becomes a separate firm) and free entry constituting the competitive elements, plus a monopoly element provided by a degree of product differentiation—analogous to the firm having a locational monopoly over those consumers closer to it than to other producers. In comparison with ordinary monopoly, the industry under monopolistic competition produces greater aggregate output at lower price, but may or may not provide consumers with more variety to choose from.

The problem of *quality*, in its simplest form, assumes unanimity of consumer preference for larger amounts of some underlying attribute contained in the physical goods produced. Demand and supply ultimately determine an equilibrium price and quantity *of attribute*. Each firm will produce that quality grade (amount of attribute per unit of commodity) which minimizes its Average Cost of producing attribute. In general, because of differing production conditions, firms' outputs will be of differing quality grades. But there is no reason to expect a monopolist's output to be of higher or lower quality than a competitive industry's average quality grade. If consumers are fully informed, they will be paying only for attribute content of the goods purchased, at the going equilibrium price for attribute. It follows that the price of each firm's product must be simply proportional to its attribute content, so that in equilibrium consumers are indifferent as to buying higher-quality or lower-quality products.

When consumers are fully informed, a rational monopolist would never suppress an invention that *increases quality*, since such an invention is equivalent to one that *reduces cost* (of producing the underlying attribute desired by consumers). By adopting the invention, the monopolist necessarily increases profit. The consumers usually gain as well, from increased output of attribute. It is, however, logically possible for the monopolist's profit-maximizing output of attribute to fall, in which case the consumers would be worse off after adoption of the invention.

QUESTIONS FOR CHAPTER 12

Mainly for Review

*R1. If consumers are distributed among different locations, is it true that the greater the number of distinct producing plants the larger will be aggregate demand for the product? How is this argument analogous to one concerning the number of distinct *varieties* offered consumers?

*R2. What stops the monopolist from offering an infinite number of varieties? Under what circumstances will only a single variety be produced?

R3. How does monopolistic competition differ from pure competition? From pure monopoly?

R4. In monopolistic competition, why is the firm's "perceived" demand curve flatter than the "true" demand curve (as in Figure 12.6)?

R5. Why is the firm's "illusory" demand curve in monopolistic competition analogous to the horizontal demand curve faced by the firm in pure competition?

*The answers to asterisked questions appear at the end of the book.

*R6. If a monopolist normally produces less *quantity* of product than a competitive industry would, why is it not correct to presume that the monopolist would normally also offer a product of lower *quality*?

*R7. Would a monopolist ever suppress an invention that would reduce the cost of producing its given product? Would it ever suppress an invention that would raise the quality of product at its given cost? Will consumers in either case be necessarily better off if the invention is adopted?

For Further Thought and Discussion

*T1. Is there reason to expect monopolistic competition (rather than pure competition) to emerge when the desired commodity is really a single "quality" attribute contained in the marketed good? Explain.

T2. Would the price-quantity equilibrium under monopolistic competition tend to lie between that achieved under pure monopoly on the one hand, and pure competition on the other hand? Explain.

*T3. Could a quality-improving invention in a competitive industry ever be adverse to the consumers' interests?

*T4. It is sometimes argued that only relatively high-quality products can "bear the cost" of shipment to distant locations. Thus, California oranges shipped to New York are (on the average) better quality than those consumed by Californians at home. Does this follow from the analysis in this chapter? [*Hint:* Does it cost much more to ship high-quality oranges than low-quality ones?]

*T5. In seeming contradiction to the statement in the preceding question about California versus New York oranges, for lobsters it is said that one can never get top quality except by going oneself to the New England shore. Can this be explained?

*T6. Would imposition of a fixed per-unit tax (e.g., ten cents per gallon of gasoline) tend to increase or decrease the equilibrium *quality* of gasoline (miles per gallon) offered on the market?

T7. A says: "A monopolist will produce a product of higher quality, since cut-throat competition must lead to a decline in quality." B says: "A monopolist produces a smaller *quantity* of product than would a competitive industry, and by the same logic will also produce a product of lesser quality." Is either correct, or are they both wrong?

*T8. Poor people seem to purchase articles of lower quality than do rich people. Can this be explained in terms of the analysis in the text?

13.A OLIGOPOLY AND STRATEGIC BEHAVIOR, 389

13.B HOMOGENEOUS PRODUCTS, 391

13.C HETEROGENEOUS PRODUCTS, 396

    13.C.1 The "Kinked" Demand Curve—A Partial Solution? 396

   *13.C.2 Optimum Conditions Under Homogeneous and Heterogeneous Oligopoly, 400

    13.C.3 Variation of Product, 402

13.D OLIGOPOLY AND COLLUSION, 405

Examples

    13.1 PREDATORY PRICE-CUTTING, 395

    13.2 OLIGOPOLY AND PRICE RIGIDITY, 398

13

OLIGOPOLY

Supplementary Chapter

Oligopoly is competition among the few. But, as explained in Chapter 11, mere number of firms in an industry does not conclusively determine how the market functions. While large numbers normally lead to competitive (price-taking) behavior, under certain circumstances the firms may act as a collective monopolist (cartel). Conversely, a single firm in an industry normally behaves as a monopolist (price-maker), but in certain circumstances may be unable to achieve monopoly profit. In the case of oligopoly, a variety of outcomes are possible *depending upon the degree to which the firms act either as rivals or as cooperators.*

OLIGOPOLY AND STRATEGIC BEHAVIOR

A "strategic" situation arises when a number of economic agents, with at least partially conflicting interests, are mutually conscious of the interactions of their decisions. In a strategic situation the concept of *optimizing*, choosing a "best" outcome, can become somewhat hazy. What is best for A to do may depend upon B's choice, and B in turn must make a decision in the light of options open to A. Thus, there is room for conscious *cooperation* or *conflict*. Strategic behavior may involve promises, threats, or other types of communications among the parties. The timing of decisions, each individual's state of information, and the enforceability of agreements may all be important elements in the final outcome. These topics are studied in the "theory of games," a relatively new field of mathematics stimulated in large part by the economic problem of oligopoly.

In all market situations there are elements of conflict and elements of parallelism or mutuality of interests—among sellers as a group, among buyers as a group, and between buyers and sellers. The sellers always have a common group interest in keeping prices high, but within the group there is a conflict of interest as to which suppliers are to obtain larger fractions of profitable sales. The buyers have a common interest in keeping prices low, but there is a conflict of interest as to which ones will be able to make purchases at a desirably low price. Between sellers as a group and buyers as a group there is of course conflict of interest over the price to be set, but the two still have a strong shared interest in having exchange take place (the mutual advantage of trade).

How conflict and mutuality of interests can be mixed together is exemplified by an important type of social interaction situation studied in the theory of games: "The Prisoners' Dilemma." Suppose the police have apprehended two men, accomplices in a crime, but have rather poor evidence against them. In fact, in the absence of a confession from one or both, the authorities will be able to convict them only of a minor infraction carrying a mild penalty. With a confession, on the other hand, conviction on a major count is guaranteed. Keeping the prisoners out of communication with one another, the district attorney offers to let either of them off for turning state's evidence—provided that he confesses, but the other does not! And, in that case, severe punishment will be meted out to the one who does not confess.

The choice situation is summarized in Table 13.1. Along the left margin we see the possible strategies of prisoner A: *Confess* versus *Don't confess*. Across the top are the same choices for prisoner B. Within each cell of the table, at the lower left is the penalty (months of imprisonment) to be imposed on prisoner A, depending upon his choice of strategy as well as upon B's choice. Similarly, at the upper right in each cell we see the corresponding outcome for B. (Since imprisonment outcomes are bad, they have minus signs attached.)

The prisoners evidently have a *mutual* interest, in that both gain from both choosing "Don't confess" so as to incur only a mild penalty (1 month imprisonment). But, looking at the table from the point of view of A's *selfish* interest, note that he is better off choosing "Confess" regardless of what B does! And B is in exactly the same situation. So, the table suggests, both will confess and both suffer 24 months' imprisonment. In the language of game theory, the strategy-pair "Confess, Confess" is called the *Nash*[1] *solution* for this game. It is an equilibrium, since, once the strategy-pair is arrived at, neither party has any motive to change his choice. Put another way, each is doing the best he can, given the decision of the other. In this example, either criminal who changes from "Confess" to "Don't confess" will suffer 36 months imprisonment instead of 24.

[1]J. F. Nash, contemporary American mathematician.

Table 13.1
The Prisoners' Dilemma

		B'S CHOICE OF STRATEGY	
		Confess	Don't Confess
A'S CHOICE OF STRATEGY	Confess	-24 B -24 A	-36 B 0 A
	Don't Confess	0 B. -36 A	-1 B -1 A

There is evidently a very close parallel here with the "chiselling" problem discussed in the context of *cartels* in Chapter 11, Section F. Firms there could mutually gain from cooperating (restraining output), but separately each was motivated to increase output—regardless of how others behaved.

It would be premature to conclude, however, that the non-cooperative "Nash solution" will necessarily be the outcome in oligopoly. There may be ways of escaping the Prisoners' Dilemma, particularly when the parties know one another's identity and are likely to have a continuing relationship. Under oligopoly—competition among a few—these conditions are often met. As a result, a number of different outcomes become possible under oligopoly, as will be discussed in the sections following.

To avoid needless complications, our discussion will be simplified by assuming (except where otherwise specified) that: (1) there are exactly *two* selling firms, so that oligopoly becomes the special case called "duopoly"; (2) the firms are identical, except possibly in degree of strategic skill or aggressiveness; (3) production is carried on at zero cost (i.e., the Total Cost, Average Cost, and Marginal Cost functions are all zero throughout).

The analysis differs depending upon whether the product is considered *homogeneous* or *heterogeneous*. In the homogeneous case the duopolists produce exactly the same product; hence, even a slightly lower price on the part of one can deprive the other one of *all* sales. Consequently, no price differential between the two firms can exist in homogeneous oligopoly equilibrium. In the heterogeneous case the products differ to some degree, with the result that a firm raising its price may still generally retain *some* of its customers. Hence, in heterogeneous oligopoly a price differential may persist.

13.B

HOMOGENEOUS PRODUCTS

A pure competitor is always a price-taker; his choice variable is *quantity* of output. A monopolist is usually regarded as deciding upon *price*, letting quantity be determined in the market. Sometimes, however, it is convenient to think of the monopolist as choosing *quantity* and letting the market process determine the price at which that quantity can be sold. Since the result is the same point on the industry demand curve in either case, it makes no difference whether we think of a monopolist as choosing the most profitable price or the most profitable quantity. But in the oligopoly case, whether price or quantity is the decision variable turns out to be important for the *interaction* of the parties. Consequently, the final result may be affected.

Let us first take *quantity* as the decision variable. Table 13.2 categorizes a number of different oligopoly (duopoly) "solutions."[2] The table was constructed on the hypothesis that the overall *industry* demand curve is expressed by the equation $P = 100 - Q$, where the industry output Q is the sum of the two firm outputs: $Q \equiv q_1 + q_2$. (Zero production cost is assumed.)

Table 13.2
Duopoly Solutions, with Industry Demand Curve $P = 100 - (q_1 + q_2)$

	q_1	q_2	Q	P	Π_1	Π_2
Symmetrical						
Collusive	25	25	50	50	1250	1250
Cournot	33⅓	33⅓	66⅔	33⅓	1111⅑	1111⅑
Competitive	50	50	100	0	0	0
Asymmetrical						
Pre-emptive	50	25	75	25	1250	625
Threat	50	0	50	50	2500	0

The first solution shown in the table is the Collusive outcome. Here the two firms act together as a collective monopolist or cartel, sharing the gain equally. A collective monopolist would want to set Marginal Revenue MR equal to Marginal Cost MC, both defined for the industry as a whole. Since production costs are assumed zero throughout, $MC = 0$ for each firm and therefore $MC = 0$ for the industry as well. Marginal Revenue for the industry is readily obtained from the demand curve for the industry, using the Proposition (obtained in Section 11.B.2) describing Marginal Revenue when the demand curve is *linear*: If $P = A - BQ$, then $MR = A - 2BQ$. In this case the industry demand equation has the linear form $P = 100 - Q$, so that industry Marginal Revenue is $MR = 100 - 2Q$. Since Marginal Cost MC is zero, the monopoly-optimum condition $MR = MC$ becomes $100 - 2Q = 0$, so that $Q = 50$ is the profit-maximizing industry output. Then $P = 50$ is the associated price along the demand curve for the industry. Total Revenue $R \equiv PQ$ is 2500 which, in the absence of any costs, is also the total profit Π. With equal division, each firm's profit under the Collusive solution will be $\Pi_1 = \Pi_2 = 1250$.

Skipping to the third outcome in the table, note that this is called the Competitive solution. It is what would come about if each firm were so ignorant of the effect of its own output upon price P as to behave like a price-taker. That is, the firms are both assumed to be adopting the decision rule $MC = P$, an erroneous

[2]A somewhat similar table appears in M. Shubik, "Information, Duopoly and Competitive Markets: A Sensitivity Analysis," *Kyklos*, v. 26 (1973), p. 748.

policy in this case since the correct rule is always $MC = MR$, and here $MR < P$. (The Competitive solution is therefore a highly implausible outcome if there really are only two firms; it becomes a more realistic possibility, the larger the number of firms.) Since $MC = 0$, acting as price-takers the firms would each be willing to produce indefinitely large amounts for any price P greater than zero. The consequence, of course, is that the competitive equilibrium price can only be $P = 0$. Combined output is then 100, as dictated by the demand equation, but revenue and profits are zero.

Of particular interest is the "Cournot[3] solution" on the second line of Table 13.2, lying between the Collusive and the Competitive outcomes. In the Cournot solution the firm recognizes that varying its own output will affect price, but it does not take into account any *interdependence between its output decision and the other firm's output decision*. The assumptions underlying the Cournot solution correspond therefore to the Nash equilibrium in game theory: each decision maker is doing the best he can *given* the decision of the other. (This outcome is accordingly sometimes known as the Nash-Cournot solution.) Then for any output level q_1 that might be chosen by the first firm, there will be some unique optimal output choice q_2 for the second firm. In effect, firm 2 becomes a monopolist over the demand not satisfied by the first firm's output q_1 already on the market. Specifically, the demand equation for firm 2 becomes $P = (100 - q_1) - q_2$, with q_1 regarded as constant. This is still a linear demand equation, so for firm 2 the Marginal Revenue is $MR_2 = (100 - q_1) - 2q_2$. For example, if $q_1 = 10$ the condition $MR = MC$ for firm 2 leads to the equation $90 - 2q_2 = 0$, so that firm 2's output would be $q_2 = 45$. Plotting the q_2 chosen by firm 2 as a function of the given output of firm 1 leads to a "Reaction Curve" RC_2 like that shown in Figure 13.1. Since the firms are symmetrically situated, by a corresponding process a Reaction Curve RC_1 can be developed for firm 1. The curves are *mutually consistent only at the point of intersection*, which is therefore declared to be the equilibrium. At the solution point the outputs are $q_1 = q_2 = 33\frac{1}{3}$, intermediate between the Collusive and the Competitive solutions.[4] Thus the Cournot solution may be regarded as representing a kind of imperfect collusion technique.

By postulating different types of reaction functions, a range of alternative solutions can be arrived at. There are many other possible classes of reaction functions. Among the more interesting are those associated with the *asymmetrical* outcomes in the lower portion of Table 13.2, outcomes which become possible when one firm is notably more aggressive than the other. (In the table, the first firm is always assumed to be the more aggressive.)

The *Pre-emptive* solution occurs when firm 1 picks an output level and proclaims that it will not modify that decision regardless of the other firm's behavior. If the proclamation is believed, the best that the second firm can do is to behave as

[3]Antoine Augustin Cournot (1801–77), French mathematician and economist.

[4]To verify that $33\frac{1}{3}$ is indeed the equilibrium, we can proceed as follows: If firm 1 sets $q_1 = 33\frac{1}{3}$, the demand equation for firm 2 is $P = 66\frac{2}{3} - q_2$. The associated Marginal Revenue is $MR_2 = 66\frac{2}{3} - 2q_2$. Setting $MR = MC = 0$, we obtain $q_2 = 33\frac{1}{3}$. Reversing the process, we see that under the assumed reaction conditions both firms are satisfied to set output at $33\frac{1}{3}$.

q_2

Output of Second Firm

q_2^*

RC_1

RC_2

q_1

0

q_1^*

Output of First Firm

Figure 13.1

Duopoly Reaction Curves. Given any output q_2 of the second firm, the first firm can determine its profit-maximizing output q_1—in which it makes use of its monopoly power over the *remainder* of the market. Considering all possible levels of q_2, a Reaction Curve RC_1 for the first firm is thereby defined. Similar reasoning (based on taking q_1 as given) leads to the construction of RC_2, the Reaction Curve of the second firm. The intersection of the two Reaction Curves is a Nash equilibrium, since each firm is then at its optimum *given* the decision of the other.

a Cournot reactor. The first firm can then optimize by setting $q_1 = 50$, in which case it achieves as much profit for itself as under the symmetrical Collusive solution. Firm 2 then monopolizes the remainder of the market, setting $q_2 = 25$, and reaping half the profit of the other firm.[5] Here RC_1, if drawn in a diagram like Figure 13.1, would simply be a vertical line at $q_1 = 50$—while RC_2 would remain the same Cournot type of Reaction Curve as before. Again, the equilibrium would be at the intersection of RC_1 and RC_2.

The *Threat* solution is a still stronger asymmetrical outcome. Suppose firm 1 proclaims that if the other firm enters the market at all, it (the first firm) will produce enough to drive price P down to zero. If this proclamation is believed, the second firm will see no way to make a profit in the market. Hence it might as well

[5] This solution may be verified as follows. Firm 1, the aggressor, knows that firm 2 will behave as a Cournot reactor, i.e., that firm 2 will choose output q_2 to satisfy the equation $MR_2 = (100 - q_1) - 2q_2 = 0$. So $q_2 = (100 - q_1)/2$, and this is known to firm 1. Substituting in the industry demand curve:

$$P = 100 - Q = 100 - q_2 - q_1 = 100 - \frac{100 - q_1}{2} - q_1 = 50 - \frac{q_1}{2}$$

This becomes the overall demand curve facing firm 1, and is again linear. Then $MR = 50 - q_1$, and $MR_1 = MC_1 = 0$ leads to $q_1 = 50$. For firm 2, the condition $MR_2 = MC_2 = 0$ becomes $MR_2 = 50 - 2q_2 = 0$, so that $q_2 = 25$. The total industry output is $Q = 50 + 25 = 75$, and market price is $P = 25$.

stay out. (A very small side-payment from the first firm may be postulated to provide a positive inducement for the second to stay out.) In the Threat solution, the first firm does as well as if it itself had the *sole* monopoly of the industry. Viewed in terms of Reaction Curves, the postulated conditions would lead to RC_1 and RC_2 curves of the same general shapes as in Figure 13.1, but *intersecting along the horizontal axis* so that the equilibrium level of q_2 is zero. (It is left for the student to justify this assertion.)

What would happen if *both* firms attempted to act as aggressors? Each would make his threat, only to be defied by the other. Actual execution of the threats would then force the situation into the symmetrical Competitive outcome of the upper part of the table.

Now suppose that *price* rather than output is the decision variable of the firms. The key point here is that, given homogeneity of product, the firm quoting a lower price will (however small the differential) attract *all* the customers. Then the Cournot solution becomes impossible, or, rather, it coalesces with the Competitive solution. *Given* any fixed price quoted by firm 2, the first firm will do best if it just barely undercuts it. But firm 2 will do the same for any fixed price quoted by firm 1. So there can be no stable outcome short of $P = 0$, the Competitive solution.

The asymmetrical Pre-emptive solution also must disappear if price is the decision variable. It does no good for firm 1 to announce that it will quote some fixed price regardless of what firm 2 does, because again firm 2 will then just barely undercut and reap all the profit. On the other hand, the asymmetrical Threat solution is still valid. Here firm 1 announces that, if firm 2 attempts to do any business at all while charging a positive price, firm 1 will quote a price of zero and so drive its competitor out. If this threat is believed, firm 2 might as well stay out of business completely. Firm 1 gains all the profit—as on the bottom line of Table 13.2.[6]

The Threat solution of Table 13.2, but with price rather than output as the decision variable, corresponds to what is known as "predatory" price-cutting. A single firm sufficiently well-equipped with resources and ruthlessness might always stand ready to undertake a price war to drive out any competitors. Having achieved this reputation, the predator firm would not need to execute its threat often. Occasional punishment meted out to foolish interlopers would suffice to deter all others from entering.

The leading instance cited of a predatory price-cutter firm is John D. Rockefeller's old Standard Oil Company—dissolved in 1911 as a result of a landmark anti-trust decision. Standard Oil had achieved, before that date, a substantial degree of monopoly in oil refining through merger and acquisitions. Common opinion, as illustrated in historical writing about the period, is that these mergers and acquisitions were mainly secured under threat of predatory price-cutting.

EXAMPLE 13.1
PREDATORY
PRICE-CUTTING

[6]The student will find it interesting to plot these solutions in terms of the firms' Reaction Curves, but with the *prices* charged by the two firms on the two axes.

A study by John S. McGee demonstrated, surprisingly, that the tale is a myth.[7] Standard Oil rarely if ever started costly price wars to achieve its monopoly. Rather, its practice was to buy out competitors on relatively handsome terms, made possible by the prospect of higher monopoly profits achievable by the withdrawal of competition.

[7]J. S. McGee, "Predatory Price Cutting: The Standard Oil (N.J.) Case," *Journal of Law and Economics*, v. 1 (Oct. 1958).

13.C

HETEROGENEOUS PRODUCTS

In the previous Section we saw that, depending upon the degree of rivalry among the sellers, there are a number of solution concepts for oligopoly with a single or *homogeneous* product. All the different solutions had one condition in common: the firms' identical products must sell in the market at a single common price. But when oligopolists produce differing or *heterogeneous* products, the situation to be considered here, the prices will in general *not* be identical. However, the same underlying forces remain operative. There is on the one hand an incentive for the sellers to cooperate so as to achieve a collusive monopoly outcome, but on the other hand a temptation for each to benefit at the expense of the others (as in the Prisoners' Dilemma) by aggressive or rivalrous behavior. One further consequence of eliminating the requirement that the products of the different firms sell at identical prices is that it will no longer matter whether price or quantity is the decision variable of the interacting firms.

13.C.1
The "Kinked" Demand Curve – A Partial Solution?

One idea relating to equilibrium under heterogeneous oligopoly has been the subject of considerable controversy. After an equilibrium pattern of prices and outputs for the different firms is once achieved, it has been alleged, the demand curve for any single oligopolist has a "kink" at the point of equilibrium. Figure 13.2 pictures the situation of a single oligopolist firm in a position to choose output q_1 (or price P_1) after an initial price for its product has been established at P^*. The argument goes as follows. Suppose one oligopolist, firm 1, attempts to sell more by cutting its price P_1. Then all other firms will respond by *meeting* the price cut, so that firm 1 will reap only a relatively small increase in sales. In other words, in the region below the initial equilibrium price P^* the demand curve D_1 as seen by firm 1 will be steep. What if firm 1 attempted to raise price? Then, assertedly, competing oligopolists would *not* meet the price increase, so that firm 1 suffers a relatively large decline in sales. In other words, in the region above the initial equilibrium price P^* the demand curve as seen by firm 1 is relatively flat. Note

$/q

Dollars Per Unit Quantity

P*

MC₁

D₁

MR₁

q₁

0   q₁*

Firm Output

Figure 13.2

Kinked Demand Curve—Heterogeneous Oligopoly. For oligopolists producing heterogeneous (non-identical) products, it is supposed that an initial equilibrium exists where the pictured firm produces output q_1^* at price $P_1 = P^*$. If the firm were to cut its price, the other oligopolists meet the price reduction so that the price-cutter's sales gain is small; if the firm raises price, the others do not follow the increase and the sales loss is large. These assumptions define a *kink* in the firm's demand curve D_1 which is associated with a *vertical gap* in the curve of Marginal Revenue MR_1. The profit-maximizing condition $MC_1 = MR_1$ is therefore met at the initial equilibrium. The equilibrium price P^* will be relatively stable, since demand and cost conditions can shift somewhat without affecting the fact that the MC_1 curve cuts through the vertical gap of the MR_1 curve.

that this argument makes sense only in the heterogeneous case, since only then can any price difference persist.[8]

This hypothesis is not a complete theory. It says nothing about how the original ruling price P^* was arrived at. But there is nevertheless an interesting implication: *the equilibrium prices arrived at by oligopolistic sellers should be relatively stable over time.*

This hypothesis is based upon the relation between the *marginal* curves in Figure 13.2. Note that the kink in the demand or Average Revenue curve D_1 for firm 1 becomes a *vertical displacement* in the Marginal Revenue curve MR_1. It is simple to verify this geometrically in the special case where the two branches of the demand curve are linear. We know (from the "Corollary" in Section 11.B.2) that for any linear demand curve the Marginal Revenue curve must bisect the horizontal distance to the vertical axis. With two separate linear branches of the

[8]*Query for the student:* Assume, under *homogeneous* oligopoly, that a single firm finds that competitors meet its price cuts but do not meet its price increases. Would the firm's demand curve here also be "kinked"? What would the shape of the demand curve be above the initial equilibrium price P^*? Below P^*?

demand curve, there must then be a vertical break or jump in the MR_1 curve as shown.

For the price-quantity situation (P^*, q_1'') to be an equilibrium, it must be the case that Marginal Cost equals Marginal Revenue for firm 1 at q_1^*. Of course, a similar condition must hold for the other oligopolists. Then, as illustrated for firm 1 in the diagram, the MC_1 curve must *cut through* the vertical jump of MR_1. The tendency toward price stability stems from this feature. Suppose some disturbance brought about a moderate change in the cost function of oligopolist 1. Its MC_1 curve would accordingly move up or down. But this could occur, to some extent, *without* affecting the fact that the intersection of MC_1 with MR_1 occurs in the vertical break of the latter, in which case optimal price and output remain unchanged for this firm. Even if the disturbance affected other firms as well, their behavior also might not be affected, leaving the equilibrium unchanged. Alternatively, suppose that a force operated to increase or decrease *demand* for firm 1's output. But so long as other firms continued to respond to firm 1's price changes in the way specified (meeting and following price decreases, but not following price increases), a demand-curve kink would remain at the initial price $P_1 = P^*$. The entire D_1 curve could shift, to the right or the left, but retaining the kink at the same height P^*. The vertical break of the MR_1 curve would then move correspondingly to the right or left, in association with the kink-point of the D_1 curve. Again, it will be evident geometrically that moderate shifts of MR_1 to the right or left are likely to preserve the property that the Marginal Cost curve MC_1 cuts through the vertical jump of MR_1. Where this holds, price $P_1 = P^*$ quoted by firm 1 will remain unchanged, but output q_1^* will increase or decrease in accordance with the direction of shift of the Marginal Revenue function.

The competing oligopolists' behavior, on this hypothesis, is *strongly rivalrous*. One might therefore wonder how the initial equilibrium, which suggests a degree of cooperation, could have come about. One possible explanation: the firms might have agreed on a collusive initial solution which is to be *enforced by* punitive behavior against any single firm that departs from the agreement. In short, cooperation and conflict are not entirely mutually exclusive, but are often found to be intertwined in observed patterns of behavior.[9]

EXAMPLE 13.2
OLIGOPOLY AND
PRICE RIGIDITY

Under the hypothesis of the kinked oligopolist-firm demand curve, demand and cost conditions can vary (to some extent) without affecting the equilibrium prices charged by firms. For a simple monopolist, on the other hand, any shift of the Marginal Cost or the Marginal Revenue curves should lead to a new optimizing price. Consequently, an implication of the kinked-demand hypothesis is that oligopoly prices should be relatively rigid.

This implication was tested by G. J. Stigler. The data in the following table are typical of his findings. As can be seen, there is a strong indication that oligopoly prices are *less* rigid than monopoly prices. This is certainly true in terms of the *number* of monthly price changes, and tends to be

[9] This is a topic that will take on importance when *government* is studied in Chapter 18.

confirmed by the *quantitative* measure of price change represented by the "coefficient of variation" (the standard deviation of monthly prices divided by their mean).

Price Flexibility (June 1929–May 1937)

	NO. OF FIRMS IN INDUSTRY	NO. OF MONTHLY PRICE CHANGES	COEFFICIENT OF VARIATION OF PRICES
Oligopolies			
Bananas	2	46	16
Grain-Binder	2	5	3
Plows	6	25	6
Tires	8	36	9
Monopolies			
Aluminum	1	2	6
Nickel	1	0	0

Source: G. J. Stigler, "The Kinky Oligopoly Demand Curve and Rigid Prices," *Journal of Political Economy,* v. 55 (1947), p. 443.

One possible objection to Stigler's test is that *inter-industry comparisons* of price changes cannot be made with very much confidence. Customs and conditions of conducting business vary from one industry to another, and it may have just so happened that the "monopolized" sectors in the table would have had relatively rigid prices regardless of number of firms. Another objection is that what is statistically reported as a *single* industry is often mere convention. Had aluminum and nickel been placed together in a single "non-ferrous metals" category, they would have been classed as an oligopoly rather than as two separate monopolies.

A study by Julian L. Simon[10] employed data that were less vulnerable to these objections. He studied prices quoted for business-magazine advertising, where the magazines had been classified into groups by the Standard Rate and Data Service (SRDS). Since all the groups fell into the business-magazine category, there was relative uniformity in conditions and methods of price quotation. And since the group classification by SRDS was undertaken for the convenience of customers (advertisers), it presumably represented an economically meaningful rather than a merely conventional categorization.

The numbers of magazines in the 148 groupings on which data were provided varied from 1 to 29. A magazine without competitors in its grouping could then be considered a monopolist. The data for two different periods, 1955–61 and 1961–64, both suggested that the monopoly groups had *more* rigid prices than the oligopoly groups. Simon's test thus confirmed Stigler's previous negative conclusion as to the kinked-demand hypothesis. (However, the *quantitative* differences found by Simon were by no means as great as those reported by Stigler.)

[10]J. L. Simon, "A Further Test of the Kinky Oligopoly Demand Curve," *American Economic Review,* v. 59 (Dec. 1969).

* **13.C.2**
Optimum Conditions Under Homogeneous and Heterogeneous Oligopoly

In the discussion following, a number of the different profit-maximizing solutions for the firm under oligopoly (more particularly, under *duopoly* since, for simplicity, only the two-firm case will be considered here) are examined. The intention is to bring out analogies and divergences between the homogeneous-product and heterogeneous-product situations, and also to make more precise exactly how the different solution concepts (Collusive, Cournot, Competitive) affect the outcome. This objective requires us to look rather closely at the profit-maximizing equations, that is, at the particular special form of the general profit-maximizing condition $MC = MR$ in each of the situations described. (Only the *symmetrical* solution concepts in the upper portion of Table 13.2 are considered here; quantity is taken as the decision variable throughout, but recall that in the heterogeneous case it makes no difference whether decisions are made in terms of price or quantity.)

1. Collusive (monopoly) solution:[11]

HOMOGENEOUS PRODUCTS $\qquad$ HETEROGENEOUS PRODUCTS

$$\begin{cases} MC_1(q_1) \\ MC_2(q_2) \end{cases} = MR(q_1 + q_2) \qquad \begin{cases} MC_1(q_1) = MR_1(q_1,q_2) \equiv \dfrac{\Delta R_1}{\Delta q_1} + \dfrac{\Delta R_2}{\Delta q_1} \\ MC_2(q_2) = MR_2(q_1,q_2) \equiv \dfrac{\Delta R_1}{\Delta q_2} + \dfrac{\Delta R_2}{\Delta q_2} \end{cases}$$

[11]*Mathematical Footnote:* In the homogeneous case, the Collusive solution maximizes $\Pi = \Pi_1 + \Pi_2 = PQ - C_1 - C_2$. The first-order conditions are:

$$\frac{\partial \Pi}{\partial q_1} = P + Q\frac{\partial P}{\partial q_1} - \frac{dC_1}{dq_1} = 0$$

$$\frac{\partial \Pi}{\partial q_2} = P + Q\frac{\partial P}{\partial q_2} - \frac{dC_2}{dq_2} = 0$$

But $\partial P/\partial q_1 \equiv \partial P/\partial q_2$, so $P + Q(\partial P/\partial q_1) = P + Q(\partial P/\partial q_2) \equiv MR$. Thus the conditions reduce to $MC_1 = MC_2 = MR$ as stated in the text.

In the heterogeneous case, the problem is to maximize $\Pi = P_1q_1 + P_2q_2 - C_1 - C_2$. The first-order conditions are:

* The section between the asterisk and the symbol ■ may contain somewhat more difficult or advanced material.

In these equations it is important to take note of the parentheses, which indicate the variables entering into or affecting the respective Marginal Cost functions MC or Marginal Revenue functions MR. Starting with the *homogeneous* case, we see that the firms' Marginal Costs $MC_1(q_1)$ and $MC_2(q_2)$ depend only on their own outputs. But the Marginal Revenue $MR(q_1 + q_2)$ for the colluding pair depends upon the *sum* of the two outputs. The profit-maximizing collusive solution sets each firm's Marginal Cost equal to this combined Marginal Revenue.

In the *Collusive heterogeneous* case, we can no longer sum q_1 and q_2. Since the firms produce different products, units are not commensurable. But the price consumers will pay for each firm's product will still depend upon *both* outputs q_1 and q_2. The price P_1 of the first firm's product will of course be a declining function of q_1, because of the Law of Demand. And it will also decrease as q_2 increases, since for consumers the two commodities are close substitutes (they are highly similar, though not identical). Analogous statements apply of course to P_2. The Marginal Revenue relevant for each firm's output decision therefore has two elements—the effect of the output change upon its *own receipts* and the effect upon the *receipts of the other colluding firm*. Specifically, the first firm would set $MC_1(q_1)$ equal to $MR_1(q_1,q_2)$, the latter being the sum of two terms: $\Delta R_1/\Delta q_1$ is the marginal addition to its *own receipts* in response to an increase of output Δq_1, while $\Delta R_2/\Delta q_1$ is the marginal change in the *other firm's receipts* following upon the first firm's output increase Δq_1. (*Query for the student:* Is the first term necessarily positive, necessarily negative, or might it have either sign? What about the second term?) A corresponding argument holds for the output decision of the second firm.

2. Cournot solution:[12]

$\qquad$ HOMOGENEOUS PRODUCTS $\qquad\qquad$ HETEROGENEOUS PRODUCTS

$$\begin{cases} MC_1(q_1) = MR_1(q_1 + \hat{q}_2) \\[2ex] MC_2(q_2) = MR_2(\hat{q}_1 + q_2) \end{cases} \qquad \begin{cases} MC_1(q_1) = MR_1(q_1,\hat{q}_2) \equiv \dfrac{\Delta R_1}{\Delta q_1} \\[2ex] MC_2(q_2) = MR_2(\hat{q}_1,q_2) \equiv \dfrac{\Delta R_2}{\Delta q_2} \end{cases}$$

$$\frac{\partial \Pi}{\partial q_1} = P_1 + q_1 \frac{\partial P_1}{\partial q_1} + q_2 \frac{\partial P_2}{\partial q_1} - \frac{dC_1}{dq_1} = 0$$

$$\frac{\partial \Pi}{\partial q_2} = P_2 + q_1 \frac{\partial P_1}{\partial q_2} + q_2 \frac{\partial P_2}{\partial q_2} - \frac{dC_2}{dq_2} = 0$$

These are the conditions stated, in somewhat different notation, in the text.

[12]*Mathematical Footnote:* In contrast with the Collusive solution, here the firms maximize separately *without* attention to any interaction. In the homogeneous case, this leads to the conditions:

$$\frac{d\Pi_1}{dq_1} = P + q_1 \frac{\partial P}{\partial q_1} - \frac{dC_1}{dq_1} = 0$$

$$\frac{d\Pi_2}{dq_2} = P + q_2 \frac{\partial P}{\partial q_2} - \frac{dC_2}{dq_2} = 0$$

And in the heterogeneous case, the conditions are:

$$\frac{d\Pi_1}{dq_1} = P_1 + q_1 \frac{\partial P_1}{\partial q_1} - \frac{dC_1}{dq_1} = 0$$

In the Cournot solutions, each firm chooses output by setting its own Marginal Cost equal to its *own* Marginal Revenue—not concerning itself with the effect upon profitability of the other firm. Also, each firm calculates its own Marginal Revenue on the (erroneous) supposition that the other firm will not revise its output in response. (The supposed fixed output of the other firm is indicated in each case by the superimposed caret, as in $\hat{q}_1$ or $\hat{q}_2$.) In the homogeneous case, once again Marginal Revenue of each firm is a function of the simple *sum* of the outputs, whereas in the heterogeneous case it is a more complex function of the two outputs as separate arguments.

3. Competitive solution:

HOMOGENEOUS PRODUCTS	HETEROGENEOUS PRODUCTS

$$\begin{cases} MC(q_1) = P(q_1 + \bar{q}_2) \\ MC(q_2) = P(\bar{q}_1 + q_2) \end{cases} \qquad \begin{cases} MC(q_1) = P_1(q_1, \bar{q}_2) \\ MC(q_2) = P_2(\bar{q}_1, q_2) \end{cases}$$

The Competitive solution is like the Cournot solution in that the other firm's output is erroneously supposed fixed (indicated by the superposed bar as in $\bar{q}_1$ and $\bar{q}_2$). But in the Competitive solution each firm acts as a price-taker with respect to its own output. Thus the firm sets its Marginal Cost MC_1 or MC_2 equal to price P along the demand curve (for the homogeneous case), rather than equal to Marginal Revenue MR_1 or MR_2, respectively. The heterogeneous case again differs only in that price along the demand curve for either product is not a function simply of the *sum* of the two outputs, but of the two quantities as separate arguments. ■

13.C.3

Variation of Product

In heterogeneous oligopoly, there is another dimension of behavior for the firm to consider: the specification of the product itself. One oligopolist can compete with others not only by raising or lowering price, but also by varying the nature of the commodity placed on the market.

Product variation was studied in the preceding chapter under a number of market structures: monopoly, pure competition, and monopolistic competition. Two main types of product variation were considered: (1) product *variety* (i.e., the degree to which the range of products offered in the market coincides with the range of subjective consumer preferences), and (2) product *quality* (i.e., the degree to which an objective quality attribute, desired by all consumers, is contained in the market commodity).

The topic of product *quality* under oligopoly will not be considered here. But we will deal with one model of oligopolistic product *variety* that has received considerable attention. This model employs a *linear* locational metaphor like that of Figure 12.1 to represent the range of consumer preferences. Specifically, in

$$\frac{d\Pi_2}{dq_2} = P_2 + q_2 \frac{\partial P_2}{\partial q_2} - \frac{dC_2}{dq_2} = 0$$

These correspond to the conditions stated (in different notation) in the text.

Figure 13.3 the consumers are supposed to be *uniformly* distributed[13] along a line-segment scaled from 0 to 1, with midpoint $M = \frac{1}{2}$. There is a constant unit transport cost t from the producing location to the consumer. If P is the f.o.b. price at the producing location R, the solid lines show what the delivered price $P + ts$ would be at any distance s from point R; the dashed lines show the delivered prices if the production locale is at the midpoint M.

A curious solution to this problem has been proposed by H. Hotelling.[14] Assume that there are just two firms (duopoly), with identical costs of producing and delivering the commodity. Now suppose that consumers everywhere along the line-segment want exactly one unit of the commodity, and are willing to pay any price for it. That is, their demands are absolutely inelastic. Let one of the two firms be located at R in Figure 13.3, and the other at M. Then the firm at M has a larger share of the market. Comparing the dashed and solid lines, we see that location at M leads to lower delivered price for all consumers located to the left of M and also for some consumers located to the right—those nearer to M than to R. The firm at R would thus clearly have an incentive to move toward the midpoint M. (The firm

Figure 13.3

Delivered Price. If P is the f.o.b. price, t is the unit transportation cost, and s the distance from a production point, the delivered price from that point to any consumer location is $P + ts$. The solid lines in the diagram show the delivered prices from a production locale at R; the dashed lines show the delivered prices from a production locale at the midpoint M.

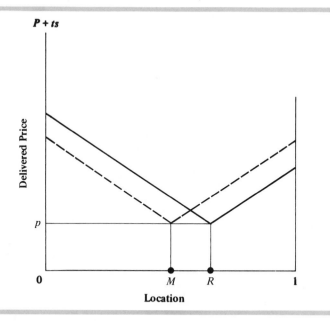

[13]In contrast, Figure 12.1 pictured a bell-shaped distribution, in which consumer locations were more common toward the middle than at the ends (i.e., more consumers preferred intermediate product types than extreme product types).

[14]H. Hotelling, "Stability in Competition," *Economic Journal*, v. 39 (March 1929).

Chapter 13
OLIGOPOLY

403

at M might seem also to have an incentive to move farther toward R, but it would thereby leave itself vulnerable to the other firm skipping over it and relocating to *its* left.) The conclusion is that in equilibrium the duopolists would locate back-to-back, an infinitesimal distance apart at either side of the midpoint M. In that way each is closer to that half of the market which serves as its "clientele."

Interpreting the locational metaphor in terms of product *variety*, the equilibrium here has both firms supplying nearly identical products of middling character. Essentially no variety is offered to consumers at all. As an interesting extension, Hotelling and others have commented that similar forces not only make different companies' toothpastes and refrigerators very much alike but tend to make the Republican and Democratic political platforms converge toward a centrist position, to induce the Catholics and Protestants to minimize their theological differences, and so forth.

In the Hotelling equilibrium, it is clear that *not enough* variety is offered consumers. Putting it in locational terms, avoidable waste of resources is incurred in transporting the good to consumers from distant production points. When both firms are located at M the average distance between consumers and the nearest production locale is ¼. If the two firms were to spread apart and ideally locate at the quartile points, the average distance would be reduced to ⅛ instead. Thus, by offering more differentiated products the two firms could better satisfy the range of consumer preferences without incurring additional cost. In terms of Table 13.2, the Hotelling result is analogous to a Cournot solution; each firm reacts (with respect to location as a decision variable) on the presumption that the other firm's decision will remain fixed.

The assumption of absolutely inelastic demand is of course highly unreasonable. Indeed, if this were the case the duopolists' Collusive solution (raise price indefinitely high) would yield *infinite* revenue and profit, regardless of location. Once we allow for elasticity of consumer demand, the duopolists would be pulled away from the midpoint locations. In Figure 13.3, suppose there are initially two firms located back-to-back at M—the firm just to the right having as "clientele" all those to the right of M, while the one just to the left takes the remainder. Suppose the righthand firm were to shift location toward position R. Since it could then reduce price to most of its old clientele, and in particular to everyone remaining to the right of R, it could sell more product to them—while losing to the other firm only a small fraction of its old clientele (those located in the neighborhood of M). As the other firm would behave similarly, under this more reasonable demand assumption some variety would after all be offered to consumers. However, the degree of variety remains less than efficient; the firms are not motivated to move away from one another as far as the ideal quartile locations.

Another oddity of the Hotelling model is that the whole argument collapses when numbers increase beyond two. A third oligopolist would want to locate an infinitesimal distance on one or the other side of the initial duo. But then one of the firms would be boxed in between two others, leaving it without clientele. This firm would then surely "jump" to the outside, to be followed by the one now left in the middle, and so on in an unending musical-chairs situation. So with more than two firms there cannot be a Cournot-Hotelling equilibrium.

More reasonable results may be obtained using the locational metaphor of consumers distributed uniformly *around a ring* (see Figure 12.2) rather than along a line-segment. Even if faced with absolutely inelastic demands, two firms following Cournot behavior would then not necessarily be located back-to-back; they could equally well place themselves at any arbitrary pair of points around the circle—since, no matter what the locations may be, each will have half the customers as its clientele. Assuming instead a degree of demand elasticity, as is certainly appropriate, Cournot behavior in the ring model would lead to an efficient result; for any arbitrary location of one firm, the other would place itself 180° away around the circle. This would of course minimize transport cost. The ring model also generalizes easily to any number of firms, which are motivated to spread themselves evenly around the circle. Of course, whether the ring metaphor or the line-segment metaphor is more appropriate depends upon the nature of the variable in question.[15]

OLIGOPOLY AND COLLUSION

The intricacies of strategic models of oligopoly are intellectually challenging, but the results seem unsatisfyingly inconclusive. Another approach[16] has been to assume away all strategic games, and simply treat oligopoly situations as *imperfect collusive arrangements* (i.e., imperfect cartels as described in Section 11.F). Since there is a joint advantage of collusion, all firms under this approach agree upon that aim. However, they all also recognize that each cannot be restrained from "chiselling" (see Figure 11.11) except through a policing mechanism. That is, the assumption is that anyone who can cheat, will. Given that there are costs of trickery on the one hand, and of detection on the other hand, there will be some equilibrium amount of slippage from the Collusive solution that represents the ideal for the sellers (though not, of course, for consumers). Thus, the parties involved will agree upon forming a cartel with some kind of policing scheme, in the anticipation that it will be tolerably (though imperfectly) effective.

While models of imperfect oligopolistic collusion are not yet reduced to textbook form, it is possible to derive a number of qualitative implications for real-world behavior. First and most obviously, the fewer the firms involved, the easier it is for them to police one another. And, hence, the more effective the cartel. Second and almost equally obvious, secret price cuts are more likely to be offered to large than to small buyers. To increase business 10% by a chiselling deal with a single customer is one thing; to try to get the same increase of business

---

[15]In terms of politics, for example, it is sometimes argued that a ring is a better picture than a line-segment. It has been noted that supporters of extreme-left parties are often psychologically very similar to those on the extreme right—the extremes may have more in common with one another than either has with moderate positions.

[16]Proposed in G. Stigler, "A Theory of Oligopoly," *Journal of Political Economy*, v. 72 (February 1964).

from ten small customers is stretching secrecy too far. Third, enforcement of collusion should be much easier where the product is homogeneous. Otherwise, price cuts can take the hard-to-penetrate guise of better quality. (Even where the physical commodity is homogeneous, there may be an element of heterogeneity in aspects of the transaction such as credit terms or delivery date.) Fourth, the more unstable the conditions of the industry, the harder it will be to negotiate and enforce agreement on industry adaptation to ever-changing circumstances of supply and demand.

<table>
<tr><td>

SUMMARY
OF CHAPTER
13

</td><td>

Oligopoly is *competition among a small number* of firms in an industry. With small numbers, all the decision-makers are likely to be conscious of the interdependence of their choices: what is best for each to do depends upon what the others are doing. Behavior in such contexts is called *strategic*. Strategic behavior is a topic studied in the mathematical *theory of games*. Depending upon the degree of rivalry versus cooperation, there are a number of different equilibrium or solution concepts possible for games in general, and for oligopoly in particular.

"The Prisoners' Dilemma" typifies social interactions in which there are potential gains from cooperation, and yet it is in the private interest of each party to behave selfishly—so that, in what is called the *Nash solution*, all lose. But where the parties know one another's identity and may be engaging in repeated interactions or plays of the game, as is often the case under oligopoly, they may be able to achieve a cooperative outcome.

Oligopoly may be *homogeneous* (all the firms produce exactly the same product) or *heterogeneous* (the firms produce distinct, though similar commodities). In the former case, no price difference between the firms can persist in equilibrium.

Under homogeneous oligopoly, and assuming for simplicity just two firms (duopoly), first consider that *quantity* of output is the decision variable. If the two firms behave symmetrically, at one extreme they may *collude* to attain the monopoly outcome—while at the other extreme they may act as *competitive* price-takers. But if each firm simply reacts optimally to what is perceived as a fixed output decision of the other, the "Cournot" equilibrium (a special case of the Nash solution) is attained, intermediate between the Collusive and Competitive outcomes. The key idea is that each firm chooses the best monopoly output for the *remainder* of the market, after subtracting the other firm's given production. If *asymmetrical* behavior is allowed, the more aggressive firm may be able to gain more profit by forcing the other to an inferior position—in the limit, driving the other out entirely.

Considering instead that *price* is the decision variable, and that the firms behave symmetrically, then given each firm's choice of price the optimal reaction for the other firm is to just barely undercut it. Then the Cournot outcome reduces to the Competitive one. Possibilities remain, however, for profitable symmetrical *collusion* on price, or for asymmetrical gain to a more aggressive firm.

In *heterogeneous* oligopoly, in contrast, a price difference between the firms may persist. Apart from this, the analysis of the symmetrical and asymmetrical

</td></tr>
</table>

outcomes is much the same. (Here it no longer matters whether price or quantity is the decision variable, and the Cournot solution remains intermediate between the Collusive and Competitive outcomes.)

For oligopoly producing heterogeneous products, one particular type of assumed strategic interaction leads to a "kinked" demand curve for any single firm. If the other producers will meet any price cut, the firm's demand curve below the current price will be steep (inelastic); if the others will not meet any price increase, above the current price the firm's demand curve will be flat (elastic). The effect is to discourage price changes. This theory does not explain how the equilibrium price was originally arrived at, but suggests that once equilibrium is attained price will be rather stable.

A new element arising in heterogeneous oligopoly is the problem of product variety. One much-discussed model concludes that an oligopolistic industry would provide *too little* variety to consumers; this result depends, however, upon doubtful features of the model.

Another approach to oligopoly interprets the problem as one of an imperfect enforcement of collusion. Forces bearing upon the likelihood of successful collusion have been suggested, but no model of this situation is as yet widely accepted.

As can be seen from the wide range of solution concepts, the theory of oligopoly is one of the most unsettled (and therefore one of the most exciting) areas of analytical economics.

QUESTIONS FOR CHAPTER 13

Mainly for Review

R1. What is strategic behavior? Why are suppliers more likely to engage in strategic behavior when there are only a few of them in the market? What if there is only one supplier (monopoly)?

*R2. What is the "Prisoners' Dilemma"? Do the participants in this game have an unexploited mutual gain from trade, and if so, why?

*R3. Distinguish oligopoly from monopolistic competition.

*R4. Justify the statement in the text that the Cournot oligopoly outcome is a special case of the Nash solution in the theory of games.

R5. Explain the Cournot solution to the duopoly problem.

R6. Diagram the Reaction Curves for the asymmetrical "Pre-emptive" and "Threat" cases of Table 13.2 (letting output be the decision variable).

*R7. Why does a "kinked" demand curve tend to lead to rigid prices? How might a kinked demand curve for a single oligopolist result from the behavior of others designed to enforce a collusive agreement?

For Further Thought and Discussion

T1. It seems somewhat strange that different duopoly solutions are obtained depending upon whether price or quantity is the decision variable.

*The answers to asterisked questions appear at the end of the book.

Which outcomes are different, and why?

*T2. Under the assumptions of the Cournot model, each duopolist *incorrectly* imagines that the other's output is a fixed constant. Over time, however, each would surely learn that this assumption about the other's behavior is incorrect. What would then be likely to happen?

*T3. Can a kinked demand curve arise under *homogeneous* duopoly? If so, what would be its shape?

T4. In recent anti-trust cases, the courts appear to believe that small numbers almost inevitably imply cartel-like collusion. Is this inference justified?

*T5. Some economists have argued that "predatory price cutting" to enforce the Threat solution will almost never be observed. The reason given is that the symmetrical Collusive solution is typically better for both parties. Is this necessarily correct? Is it ever correct? Under what circumstances will predatory price cutting be likely to emerge, if ever?

*T6. Show how the "curious" Hotelling back-to-back solution for product variation under duopoly is modified if consumers are uniformly distributed about a ring rather than along a line-segment. What if demand is not absolutely inelastic? If there are more than two oligopolists?

PART FIVE

Factor Markets, Distribution, and Intertemporal Analysis

14.A FIRM'S DEMAND FOR A SINGLE VARIABLE FACTOR, 413

14.B FIRM'S DEMAND FOR SEVERAL VARIABLE FACTORS, 419
  14.B.1 Factor Employment Conditions, 420
  14.B.2 Shifts in Factor Prices—Substitution and Scale Effects, 422
  14.B.3 Firm's Demand for Factors, 426

14.C INDUSTRY DEMAND FOR FACTORS, 428

14.D MONOPSONY IN THE FACTOR MARKET, 432
  14.D.1 Monopsony Solution, 432
  *14.D.2 General and Special Optimality Conditions, 435

14.E AN APPLICATION: MINIMUM-WAGE LAWS, 436

Examples
  14.1 FACTOR PRICES AND OCEAN SHIPPING, 423
  14.2 MONOPSONY IN PROFESSIONAL BASEBALL, 434
  14.3 MINIMUM-WAGE LEGISLATION, 439

14

THE DEMAND
FOR FACTORS
OF PRODUCTION

Core Chapter

In the circular flow of economic activity pictured in Figure 1.1, consumers represent the demand side and firms represent the supply side of *the product market* (the upper portion of the diagram). In previous chapters we studied the determinants of individuals' demands for and firms' supplies of consumer goods and services like shoes or haircuts. Now we will turn to the *factor market*, the lower portion of the circular flow diagram. In this chapter we will examine the demand side of the market for factors of production—the decisions of firms and industries concerning the employment of land, labor, or other productive services. In the chapter following we will look at the supply side of the factor market, the choices of resource-owners as to the terms on which they offer their land, labor, or other productive services for employment.

In the equilibrium of the factor market, *market structure* (degree of competition) continues to play an important role. Indeed, we must take account of market structures not only in the factor market itself but also in the associated product market or markets. A company may be a monopolist of a product like aluminum, and still be only one among many employers (and therefore be a competitive or "price-taking" buyer) of a productive service like secretarial help in a large city. Conversely, a textile firm may face a highly competitive world market for its product and still be a ''price-making'' or *monopsonist*[1] employer of labor in a small town.

Unfortunately, having to take account of *combinations* of product-market structure and factor-market structure makes the analysis in this chapter relatively intricate. To help organize thought, the alternative market-structure combinations to be considered in the chapter are shown in Table 14.1. Across the top margin we see the two extreme market-structure possibilities for the product market: the firm as competitive seller or price-taker is represented by the first column, and as monopolist or price-maker by the second column.[2] On the left margin are the analogous extreme cases for the factor market: the firm as competitive or price-taking employer of productive services in the upper row, and as monopsonist or price-making employer in the lower row. (These market-structure combinations refer only to the *demand side* of the factor market, however; the possibility of monopoly on the *supply side* of the factor market is a topic taken up in Chapter 15 following.)

Table 14.1
Firm's Optimality Conditions for Employment and Production

| FACTOR MARKET STRUCTURE | PRODUCT MARKET STRUCTURE | |
	Price-taker	Monopolist
Price-taker	$\begin{cases} h_a \equiv mfc_a = mrp_a \equiv vmp_a \\ MC = MR \equiv P \end{cases}$	$\begin{cases} h_a \equiv mfc_a = mrp_a \\ MC = MR \end{cases}$
Monopsonist	$\begin{cases} mfc_a = mrp_a \equiv vmp_a \\ MC = MR \equiv P \end{cases}$	$\begin{cases} mfc_a = mrp_a \\ MC = MR \end{cases}$

The paired equations in the body of Table 14.1 will be explained and derived in this chapter. They represent the conditions that characterize the combined profit-maximizing decisions of a firm with respect to the employment of factors and with respect to the production of output—for each of the four possible market-structure combinations considered.

FIRM'S DEMAND FOR A SINGLE VARIABLE FACTOR

To start with the simplest case, we assume (in this Section A only) that the firm holds the quantities of all factors but one *fixed*. (Thus, this analysis concerns the ''short-run'' as discussed in Section 9.E.) So we will be dealing with relations

---

[1]A monopolist is a sole *seller* in a market; a monopsonist is a sole *buyer*.

[2]Firms might also be oligopolists or monopolistic competitors in their respective product markets, as discussed in Chapters 12 and 13, but only the polar cases of pure competition and pure monopoly will be covered here.

between output quantity q of a single product Q and input quantity a of a single *variable* factor A. In function form this can be expressed as:

(14.1) $q = \psi(a)$

This single-factor production function was discussed in Chapter 9 (see equation [9.2']) and pictured in Figure 9.2. The form of the function, of course, reflects the operation of the Law of Diminishing Returns.

In Sections A, B, and C of this chapter we will be dealing with a *price-taking* firm in the factor market (upper row of Table 14.1). For such a firm, whether monopolist or competitor in the product market, the *cost* of hiring factor A is represented by a constant hire-price h_a per unit of A.[3] In Figure 14.1, a horizontal line drawn at the level of the constant hire-price h_a can be regarded as the *factor supply curve* s_a to the firm. (The horizontality of s_a corresponds to the assumption that the firm is too small a demander to noticeably affect factor price.) Denoting the total expenditure on (the total cost of hiring) factor A as $C_a \equiv h_a a$, where a is the quantity of factor A employed by the firm, this supply curve can be

Figure 14.1

Optimal Factor Employment, Price-Taking Firm in Both Factor Market and Product Market. The horizontal line at the level of the going hire-price h_a for factor A is the curve of Average Factor Cost (afc_a) and of Marginal Factor Cost (mfc_a) to the price-taking firm, and is also its factor supply curve s_a. If the firm is a price-taker in the product market as well, the Value of the Marginal Product (vmp_a) curve and the Marginal Revenue Product (mrp_a) curve coincide. The firm's demand curve d_a for factor A is then the downward-sloping branch of the $vmp_a \equiv mrp_a$ curve.

Quantity of Factor A

[3]In some cases a firm may be able either to *hire* or to *buy* a factor. Thus, a business may be able to rent office space or to buy a building for that purpose. Later on we will find it useful to distinguish the hire-price h_a of factor A from the price P_a of the factor itself—of the *source* of the productive services used by the firm. But in this chapter we will deal only with the hire-price h_a, the price of the factor's services.

interpreted as a curve of *Average Factor Cost* $(afc_a \equiv C_a/a)$. And, since the price per unit is constant, it is also a curve of *Marginal Factor Cost* $(mfc_a \equiv \Delta C_a/\Delta a)$. Note the analogy: For a price-taking firm in the product market the given product price P defines the firm's horizontal *product demand curve,* as pictured in the lower panel of Figure 9.1; similarly, for a price-taking firm in the factor market, the given hire-price h_a defines the horizontal *factor supply curve* to the firm pictured in Figure 14.1.

To determine its optimal (profit-maximizing) employment of factor A, the firm must balance the *returns* from hiring A against the hire-price h_a. Two elements are involved in calculating these returns: (1) the *physical productivity* of A as an input to production, and (2) the *revenue* gained from the units of commodity produced.

In successively choosing whether or not to hire one more unit of factor it is evident that, so far as physical productivity is concerned, only *Marginal* Product will be relevant to the firm's decision. However great the contribution to *Total* Product may have been for earlier units of factor, only the incremental yield from an additional unit will be considered in hiring that last unit. Thus, the Marginal Product mp_a curve, as in the lower panel of Figure 9.2, pictures the physical productivity element.

In dealing with the revenue element, by similar reasoning it is only the *Marginal* Revenue that is relevant. But where the firm is a price-taker not only in the factor market but also in the product market (the market-structure combination in the upper-left cell of Table 14.1), the increment to revenue from sale of one more unit of product is simply the given product price P. Valuing the factor's physical productivity at this price P leads to the concept called *Value of the Marginal Product* of factor A.

DEFINITION: Value of the Marginal Product vmp_a equals product price P
   times physical Marginal Product mp_a.

(14.2) $vmp_a \equiv P(mp_a)$

Since P is assumed constant, the curve showing vmp_a in Figure 14.1 will have the same graphical shape as the mp_a curve in the lower panel of Figure 9.2. The only difference, due to the multiplication by a constant P, is the change of the vertical scale—from output per unit of input (q/a) in Figure 9.2 to dollars of revenue per unit of input $(\$/a)$ in Figure 14.1.

Turning to the employment decision, if the Value of the Marginal Product vmp_a exceeds the price h_a of factor A, it will surely pay the firm to employ an additional unit of A. Thus, the optimum condition for employment of factor A by a price-taking firm can be expressed as:

(14.3) $vmp_a = h_a$

It so happens that this equality is satisfied at the two different employment levels a' and a^* in Figure 14.1. However, a subsidiary condition for an optimum is that the vmp_a curve be *falling* relative to the horizontal $afc_a \equiv mfc_a$ curve,[4] and this holds only at a^* in the diagram.[5] In terms of economic logic, to employ only a' units of A would be to forego the profitable range where the returns from successively hiring additional units of factor (vmp_a) exceed the costs thereof ($h_a \equiv mfc_a$).

Now suppose that the firm employing factor A, while still a price-taker in the *factor market*, is no longer a price-taker (now has monopoly power) in the *product market*. Here we are dealing with the market-structure combination at the upper right of Table 14.1, the corresponding picture being Figure 14.2. In this situation the firm's returns from increased factor employment will be adversely affected by the falling tendency of price P as more output is produced. For a monopolist firm, the return on the margin from the employment of an additional unit of factor A is not the *value* of the physical Marginal Product but the *revenue increment* achievable by sale of that Marginal Product. This leads to the concept known as *Marginal Revenue Product* of factor A, denoted mrp_a:

(14.4) $mrp_a \equiv MR(mp_a)$

DEFINITION: Marginal Revenue Product mrp_a equals Marginal Revenue MR times physical Marginal Product mp_a.

Returning to the competitive (price-taker) firm in the product market (Figure 14.1), product price P is perceived as constant—in which case (as we know from Section 9.D) Marginal Revenue MR identically equals price P. It follows immediately that, *for a competitive firm in the product market the* vmp_a *and the* mrp_a *curves*—as defined in equations (14.2) and (14.4) respectively—*are identical*. This was indicated by the labelling $vmp_a \equiv mrp_a$ in Figure 14.1. For a firm with monopoly power in the product market, on the other hand, Marginal Revenue MR and product price P are both decreasing functions of output. And the MR curve falls faster than the demand or Average Revenue curve—as shown, for example, in the lower panel of Figure 11.1. So, *for a monopoly firm, the* mrp_a *curve must lie below and fall faster than the* vmp_a *curve*, as in Figure 14.2. The optimal

---

[4]This condition corresponds to the technical qualification (in Section 9.D) that the output optimum for the firm occurs at $MC = MR$ *provided that the* MC *curve cuts* MR *from below*. Here the optimum occurs when vmp_a cuts mfc_a *from above*.

[5]*Mathematical Footnote:* The firm chooses the amount of A to maximize profit $\Pi = R - C = Pq - h_a a - F$ (where F stands for fixed costs representing expenditures on factors other than A). Differentiating Π and setting the derivative equal to zero, we have as *first-order* condition:

$$P\,\frac{dq}{da} = h_a \quad \text{or} \quad P(mp_a) \equiv vmp_a = h_a$$

thus verifying (14.3). Taking the second derivative of Π, the *second-order* condition for a maximum is

$$P\,\frac{d^2q}{da^2} < 0 \quad \text{or simply} \quad \frac{d^2q}{da^2} < 0$$

This means that Marginal Product mp_a (and so the curve vmp_a) must be *falling* to have a profit maximum.

Figure 14.2

Optimal Factor Employment, Monopolist in Product Market. The firm pictured here (like the firm in Figure 14.1) is a price-taker or competitive purchaser in the factor market, as indicated by the horizontal supply curve s_a at the level of the going hire-price h_a for factor A. But here the firm has monopoly power in the product market. The consequent divergence between price P and Marginal Revenue MR is reflected in the divergence between the vmp_a (Value of the Marginal Product) and mrp_a (Marginal Revenue Product) curves. The firm's optimum is at the intersection of s_a and mrp_a, leading to employment $a*$ of factor A. The downward-sloping branch of the mrp_a curve is also the firm's demand curve for factor A.

factor employment $a*$ for the firm with monopoly power in the product market is determined in this diagram as the intersection of the mrp_a curve with the horizontal factor-supply curve $afc_a \equiv mfc_a$ at the level h_a.[6] It follows that, in the situation of Figure 14.2, the firm's demand curve d_a for factor A is given by the mrp_a curve rather than the vmp_a curve.

Since for the competitive firm in the factor market vmp_a and mrp_a are identical, equation (14.3) can be superseded by the following more general Factor Employment Condition that holds for *both* monopolist and pure competitor in the product market:

[6]*Mathematical Footnote:* The firm is maximizing $\Pi = R - C = Pq - h_a a - F$ as before, but now recognizes that P is a decreasing function of output q—and so, indirectly, of input a. Differentiating and setting equal to zero, the first-order condition is:

$$P \frac{dq}{da} + q \frac{dP}{dq} \frac{dq}{da} = h_a \quad \text{or} \quad \left(P + q \frac{dP}{dq}\right) \frac{dq}{da} = h_a$$

The element in parentheses on the left is Marginal Revenue, as defined in equation (11.2). So the condition can be expressed as:

$$MR(mp_a) \equiv mrp_a = h_a$$

$$(14.5) \qquad mrp_a = h_a \qquad \begin{array}{l} \text{Factor Employment Condition,} \\ \text{Price-Taking Firm} \\ \text{in Factor Market} \end{array}$$

Again, we have as a technical qualification that the mrp_a curve must cut the horizontal factor-supply curve from *above*.[7] This implies that the demand curve d_a is the *downward-sloping* branch of the mrp_a curve.

Summarizing in terms of Table 14.1, we have now gone through the two upper-row cases associated with the firm as price-taker in the factor market. Note that in each cell of the table two lines of equations, connected by a brace, are shown. Starting with the upper-row righthand column (for a factor-market price-taker but product-market monopolist), the upper-line equation is $h_a \equiv mfc_a = mrp_a$. The *identity* between h_a and mfc_a reflects the straight-line factor supply curve pictured in both Figures 14.1 and 14.2. The *equality* of h_a (or mfc_a) with mrp_a is the Factor Employment Condition of equation (14.5). Moving to the upper-left cell of Table 14.1 (for a price-taker in both product market and factor market), the only change is the *additional* identity $mrp_a \equiv vmp_a$, corresponding to the coalescing of these two curves in Figure 14.1.

As for the lower-line equations in the upper-row cells of Table 14.1, these represent the *output* optimality conditions that were discussed in Chapters 9 and 11. For the monopolist in the product market (upper-right cell), $MC = MR$ is the familiar profit-maximization condition of equation (11.3). For the product-market price-taker (upper-left cell) this condition continues to hold with the additional identity $MR \equiv P$ as in equation (9.13).

The separate treatments of the firm's *output* decision in Chapter 9 and 11 (for the competitive and monopolist firm, respectively) and of the *factor-employment* decision here might suggest that these are two distinct choices. But, given the production function (14.1), the two decisions are inextricably connected. Having made the factor-employment decision, output is determined; there is no further degree of freedom for the firm to choose a level of output. And, so long as we are dealing with a *single* variable factor, the converse is also true. Choosing output necessarily determines factor employment.[8] Thus, the output solutions of Chapters 9 and 11 and the factor-employment solutions in the present chapter are but different aspects of the firm's single optimizing productive choice.

The equivalence of the output decision and the factor-employment decision follows almost immediately from the identity (9.12) showing the logically necessary connections between Marginal Cost MC and the Marginal Product mp_a for a single variable factor A, which will be repeated here:

Chapter 14

THE DEMAND
FOR FACTORS
OF
PRODUCTION

418

[7]*Mathematical Footnote:* The second derivative of Π can be written as $d(mrp_a)/da$, which must be negative to satisfy the second-order condition for a maximum. So the mrp_a curve must be falling relative to the horizontal factor-supply curve s_a.

[8]With several variable factors, however, the determination of output still leaves a range of freedom for selection of the best resource combination to produce that output. This topic is taken up in Section 14.B.

(14.6) $\quad MC \equiv \dfrac{h_a}{mp_a}$

Dividing both sides by Marginal Revenue MR, we have:

(14.7) $\quad \dfrac{MC}{MR} \equiv \dfrac{h_a}{MR(mp_a)} \equiv \dfrac{h_a}{mrp_a}$

So satisfaction of the Factor Employment Condition (14.5), $h_a = mrp_a$, directly implies $MC = MR$, which is the general Maximum-Profit condition of equation (11.3). The converse also holds, of course. Also, for a price-taking firm in the product market, for which $MR \equiv P$, equation (14.7) takes the special form:

(14.7′) $\quad \dfrac{MC}{P} \equiv \dfrac{h_a}{P(mp_a)} \equiv \dfrac{h_a}{vmp_a}$

Here $h_a = vmp_a$ (equation [14.3]) immediately implies $MC = P$ (the competitive Maximum-Profit condition [9.13]), and conversely.

CONCLUSION: For any given hire-price h_a, the Factor Employment Condition (14.5) specifies the amount of A employed by the firm. As h_a varies up or down, the optimal employment of A is that for which $mrp_a = h_a$ (in the downward-sloping range of the mrp_a curve). The curve of Marginal Revenue Product mrp_a, for any factor-price-taking firm employing a single variable factor A, is (in its downward-sloping range) the firm's demand curve for A.[9] In Figure 14.1, for a competitor firm in the product market, the factor demand curve d_a coincides with the curve of $vmp_a \equiv mrp_a$. In Figure 14.2, for a monopolist in the product market, the factor demand curve d_a coincides with mrp_a (and *not* with vmp_a).

FIRM'S DEMAND FOR SEVERAL VARIABLE FACTORS

The employment decision for a single variable factor, other factors held fixed, corresponds to the firm's output decision in the "short run" (see Section 9.E). In the general or "long run" case all factors are variable. For simplicity here, how-

[9]A technical qualification: Strictly speaking, this holds only for that portion of the downward-sloping range where the total expenditure $C_a \equiv h_a a$ on the variable factor A is less than Total Revenue R. (The analogy is with the proviso in Section 10.A that the Marginal Cost curve MC is the firm's *supply curve of product* only over the range where price P exceeds Average Variable Cost AVC.)

ever, the exposition deals with just *two* variable factors, A and B. The production function, as pictured for example in Figure 9.4, can be expressed as:

$$(14.8) \qquad q = \psi(a,b)$$

Continuing to assume that the firm is a price-taker (not a monopsonist in either factor market), it now faces two given hire-prices—h_a and h_b. We know from Chapter 9 that, in terms of relative factor proportions, the firm will always seek to satisfy the Factor Balance Equation (9.11), which will be rewritten here:

$$(14.9) \qquad \frac{mp_a}{h_a} = \frac{mp_b}{h_b}$$

As explained in Chapter 9, meeting this condition corresponds to the firm's remaining on the Scale Expansion Path (SEP) of Figure 9.8.

We also know from Chapter 9 that, provided the Factor Balance Equation is met, Marginal Cost MC can be written as (from equation [9.12]):

$$(14.10) \qquad MC = \frac{h_a}{mp_a} = \frac{h_b}{mp_b}$$

Dividing through by Marginal Revenue MR, we have as a generalization of equation (14.7) to the multi-factor case:

$$(14.11) \qquad \frac{MC}{MR} = \frac{h_a}{mrp_a} = \frac{h_b}{mrp_b}$$

Then satisfaction of the Maximum-Profit Condition $MC = MR$ implies the joint Factor Employment Conditions:

$$(14.12) \qquad \begin{cases} mrp_a = h_a \\ mrp_b = h_b \end{cases} \qquad \begin{array}{l} \text{Factor Employment Conditions,} \\ \text{Price-Taking Firm} \\ \text{in Factor Markets} \end{array}$$

Thus, the scale of factor employments is correct if (for each factor actually employed) Marginal Revenue Product equals factor hire-price. For a firm with no monopoly power in the product market, $MR \equiv P$. For such a firm, therefore, equations (14.11) and (14.12) could be written in terms of Value of the Marginal Product vmp (price times Marginal Product) instead of mrp (Marginal Revenue times Marginal Product). The equations in their present general form, however, hold whether the firm is a monopolist or a competitor in the product market.

Equations (14.12) are of course a direct generalization of the single-factor employment condition of equation (14.5). But there is one important complication in the multi-factor case: the Marginal Product mp_a and therefore the Marginal Revenue Product mrp_a may depend not only upon the amount of factor A but also upon the associated employment of the other factor B—and similarly, of course, mp_b and mrp_b may depend upon the amount of factor A.[10]

Two factors are said to be *complementary* if increased employment of one raises the Marginal Product of the other. Complementarity represents a kind of harmonious or mutually helpful interaction of factors: executives and secretaries, ships and sailors, land and fertilizer are examples of complementary pairs. In the absence of such an interaction, where increased employment of one factor has no effect upon the marginal productivity of the other, the two are said to be *independent*. Handcraftsmen and mass-production machines might be an example. If a firm simultaneously produces high-quality hand products and low-quality machine products, it may be that the handcraftsmen work entirely apart from the machines so that there is no interaction one way or the other between them.

If increased employment of one factor actually *reduces* the Marginal Product of the other, the negative interaction is called *anti-complementarity*.[11] Classes of inputs that are close substitutes one for another tend to be anti-complementary. An increase in employment of A necessarily reduces its *own* Marginal Product mp_a (in the economically relevant range where the Law of Diminishing Marginal Returns applies). But if resource A is a close substitute for B, increased employment of A might also reduce mp_b. Examples might be male versus female labor, large machines versus small machines, or one brand of fertilizer versus another.[12]

A complementary interaction between two factors A and B is illustrated in Figure 14.3. The family of Marginal Product curves mp_a shown in Panel (a), and the family of mp_b curves shown in Panel (b), may be regarded as derived from the corresponding families of *Total* Product curves tp_a and tp_b in the two panels of Figure 9.7. (The shapes of the marginal curves are related to the total curves in the usual way, as illustrated by the upper and lower panels of Figure 9.2.) The crucial point is that the mp_a curves shift *upward* as the associated amount of factor B

---

[10]*Mathematical Footnote:* If $q = \psi(a,b)$, the Marginal Products or partial derivatives $\partial q/\partial a$ and $\partial q/\partial b$ will in general both be functions of a and b. Geometrically, in Figure 9.6 we see that the slope along the Total Product curves tp_a in the a-direction ($\partial q/\partial a$) varies not only as a increases, but also from one curve to the next as b increases. And similarly of course for the slope along the tp_b curves ($\partial q/\partial b$).

[11]*Mathematical Footnote:* The presence or absence of complementarity corresponds to the sign of the second cross-derivative of the production function. In the normal *complementary* case, $\partial(\partial q/\partial a)/\partial b \equiv \partial^2 q/\partial a \partial b$ is positive. *Independence* corresponds to a zero cross-derivative, and *anti-complementarity* to a negative cross-derivative.

[12]Anti-complementarity should be distinguished from what might be called *interference*, where the two factors actually hamper one another. In a situation such that sex differences are distracting, hiring more females might actually reduce output and therefore reduce the *Total* Product of the male employees—and vice versa if more male workers are employed. In the anti-complementary cases to be considered here, however, employing more of one factor A leads to a fall in the *Marginal* Product of B ($\Delta q/\Delta b$) but not to a reduction in the *Total* Product q. Jointly employing interfering factors may be irrational, but employment of anti-complementary factors is not at all absurd.

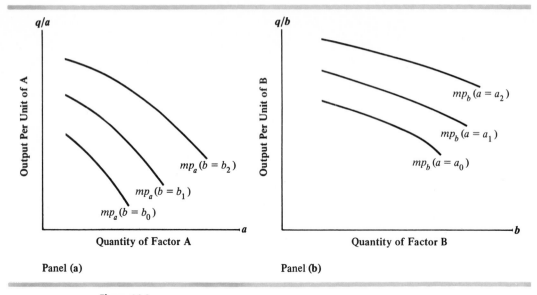

Panel (a)   **Panel (b)**

Figure 14.3

Families of Marginal Product Curves—Complementary Factors. The family of Marginal Product curves mp_a in Panel (a) is derived from the corresponding family of Total Product curves tp_a in Panel (a) of Figure 9.7. The mp_b curves in Panel (b) correspond similarly to the tp_b curves in Panel (b) of Figure 9.7. In the illustrated range here, the curves have negative slope (the Marginal Product of each factor is a decreasing function of its own quantity). But the curves shift upward as the quantity of the *other* factor increases (the Marginal Product of each factor is an increasing function of the quantity of the other input). This illustrates the normal case of complementarity.

increases from b_0 to b_1 to b_2; similarly, the mp_b curves move higher as A rises from a_0 to a_1 to a_2.

14.B.2

Shifts in Factor Prices— Substitution and Scale Effects

We saw in Section 4.C that a change in the price of a consumer good had a *substitution effect* and an *income effect* upon purchases. Analogously here, a change in the price of a factor has a *substitution effect* and a *scale effect* upon factor employment. The substitution effect follows from the change in factor proportions due to the shift in *relative* factor prices h_a/h_b; the scale effect follows from the effect on optimal output due to the implied change in Marginal Cost MC.

The substitution effect is illustrated in Figure 14.4. Here the initial position $Q°$ represents a typical point on the Scale Expansion Path SEP° (see Figure 9.8), at a tangency of a cost isoquant $C°$ and an output isoquant $q°$. A fall in h_a, the price of factor A, necessarily lowers (flattens) the absolute slope h_a/h_b of the cost isoquants. The dashed C' is that member of the family of flatter cost isoquants that is tangent to the initial output isoquant (at position Q'). The new Scale Expansion Path SEP' will therefore be displaced to the right, as indicated in the diagram. *There will be a shift of optimal factor proportions toward the relatively cheapened factor A.*

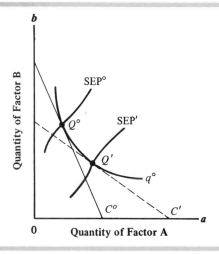

Figure 14.4

Factor Substitution Effect. At initial hire-prices h_a^o and h_b^o, a Scale Expansion Path (SEP°) connects all points of tangency between isoquants of cost C and isoquants of output q. That is, all points where the slope $\Delta b/\Delta a$ along isoquants like q^o equals the slope $-h_a^o/h_b^o$ along cost lines like C^o. If h_a falls to h_a', the new isoquants of cost have flatter slope, like C'. The changed price ratio h_a'/h_b^o determines a new Scale Expansion Path SEP'. From an initial position Q^o, the *factor substitution effect* is the increased employment of A due to moving to a new tangency at Q'—where the original output isoquant q is just attained along a cost line C' whose slope represents the new hire-price ratio.

Newly constructed ships used by Japanese, continental European, and British shippers during the years 1952–55 were examined by W. Y. Oi in order to compare the relative factor proportions employed. In ocean shipping the important factors of production may be divided into: (a) "capital" (amortization of construction expenses, plus ship maintenance), (b) fuel, and (c) labor (wages plus subsistence at sea). In the period studied, fuel prices were very similar for all shippers. So the essential element was the capital cost versus labor cost comparison. Labor costs were relatively cheapest for the Japanese shippers and most expensive for the continental Europeans, with the British in between.

One consequence of relatively high labor cost (or, equivalently, relatively low capital cost) is the employment of ships with a high designed speed. Faster ships are costlier to construct and maintain, but permit a saving of labor time per voyage. The following table indicates that, as anticipated, the Japanese chose ships with lowest and the continental Europeans with highest designed speed.

EXAMPLE 14.1
FACTOR PRICES
AND OCEAN
SHIPPING

The scale effect is somewhat trickier to illustrate geometrically. Figure 14.5 shows the effect of a fall in h_a alone (from h_a^o to h_a') upon a typical initial cost isoquant. Evidently there is an outward rotation of the cost isoquant, from the position C^o to C''. The new tangency will necessarily be on a higher output isoquant q''. Thus, *at any given cost* it will be optimal for the firm to produce more output after a cheapening of a factor. Or, put another way, any given output can be produced at a lower Total Cost than before.

Figures 14.4 and 14.5 together show that if *output* is held constant after hire-price h_a falls, cost will be less—while if *cost* is held constant, output will be greater. But no general conclusion is warranted as to whether cost will in fact be

Figure 14.5

Cheapening of Factor *A*. As in the previous diagram, Q' is the factor combination attained upon shifting from an initial combination Q^o in response to a fall in hire-price h_a. As between Q^o and Q', output q is held constant. This diagram shows also the new position Q'' reached if Cost C is held constant instead of output q. The points Q' and Q'' are both on the new Scale Expansion Path SEP'.

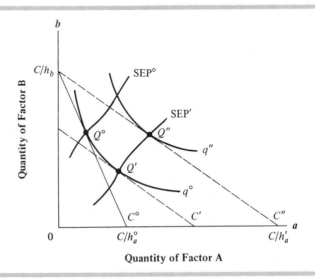

lower or output greater at the new optimum position. It might have seemed plausible to expect that a fall in factor price would surely lead to an expansion of the optimum scale of output, but this does *not* necessarily follow. It is true that the Total Cost curve falls with a cheapening of any factor. But the optimal output is determined by the relation between *Marginal* Cost and *Marginal* Revenue ($MC = MR$), i.e., between the *slopes* of the Total Cost and Total Revenue curves. Panel (a) in Figure 14.6 shows a normal situation in which the lowering of the Total Cost curve from TC° to TC' does lead to an expansion of optimal output from q° to q' (note the location of the profit magnitudes Π° and Π'). Panel (b) shows the more surprising case in which the lowering from TC° to TC' is combined with a *steepening* of the slope (thus increasing the MC) in the relevant region, so that the new optimal output q' is less than q°.

In this latter case, A is called a "regressive factor." It is not difficult to give an economic interpretation of the seemingly paradoxical result, however. Think of A as a factor particularly specialized to and useful for small-scale production, for example, skilled craftsmen. If the price of skilled craftsmen falls, it may pay a

Figure 14.6

Scale Effect. A fall in the hire-price h_a of any factor employed necessarily reduces the Total Cost of producing any level of output q, so in both panels here the new TC' curve lies everywhere below the original TC° curve. But profit $\Pi = TR - TC$ is greatest where Marginal Revenue (slope along the TR curve) equals Marginal Cost (slope along the TC curve). In the "normal case" shown in Panel (a), the TC' curve is not only lower than the TC° curve at each output but also flatter—so Marginal Cost has also fallen everywhere. Then the new optimal output q' is greater than the previous q°. But in the "regressive case" of Panel (b), the TC' curve is lower but (over a portion of its range) *steeper* rather than flatter than TC°. In this range Marginal Cost is greater than before, and so the new optimal output q' is less than q°. In both cases, the new profit Π' is necessarily greater than the original profit Π°.

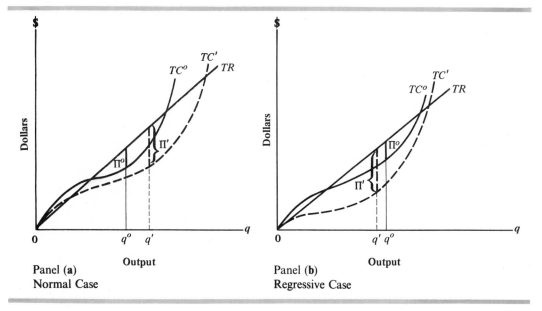

Panel (a)
Normal Case

Panel (b)
Regressive Case

firm to shift away from a large-scale mass production technique so as to earn more profit with smaller output—by making better use of the now cheaply available craft skills.

CONCLUSION: A change in factor price leads to a substitution effect and a scale effect upon factor employment and firm output. The substitution effect is *always* in the normal direction: relatively more of the now relatively cheaper factor will be used. The scale effect of a fall in factor price is normally to increase output, and of a rise in factor price to decrease output. But in the case of a "regressive" factor, the scale effect is reversed; cheapening of a factor *may* lead to smaller output.

14.B.3

Firm's Demand for Factors

In the single-factor situation, the firm's demand curve for the variable factor was given by its Marginal Revenue Product curve mrp.[13] In the multi-factor analysis, the firm's demand curve for any of the variable factors still depends upon the Marginal Revenue Product of that factor. However, it is necessary now to take account of the interaction among the factor Marginal Products associated with the concept of complementarity.

In deriving the demand curve for either of two variable factors, for example factor A, we will suppose that the firm is at an initial position where the Factor Employment Conditions in equations (14.12) are all met. In Figure 14.7, point G is supposed to represent such a position. At the initial hire-price h_a^o, employment of factor A is the amount a^o such that $mrp_a(b = b^o) = h_a^o$. (The expression on the lefthand side represents the Marginal Revenue Product for A as measured along the particular mrp_a curve associated with the amount b^o of factor B.) It is understood that, correspondingly, employment $b = b^o$ of the other factor B is also such that $mrp_b(a = a^o) = h_b^o$.

Now let the hire-price h_a fall from h_a^o to the level h_a'. If the quantity of the other factor B remained unchanged, the firm would find it advantageous to employ $a = \hat{a}$ units of factor A since, at that level of employment, $mrp_a(b = b^o) = h_a'$. But now we must allow for the complementarity effects. Suppose that factors A and B are actually complementary. Analysis of the interaction proceeds as follows. Let price h_a^o fall to h_a', leading to an initial employment expansion from a^o to $\hat{a}$ as just indicated. But this is not the full adjustment. The condition $mrp_b = h_b$ for the *other* factor B is now violated—since the increased employment of A will, assuming complementarity, have shifted the entire mrp_b curve upward. A corresponding diagram for factor B would show that such an upward shift dictates more employment of factor B as well. When the secondary adjustment of factor B's employment is made, mrp_a will now in turn shift upward, and so on. This reciprocal interaction must have a limit, however. That is, there must be some increased employment of *both* factors such that the pair of equations (14.12) are restored. The restored equalities can be expressed more explicitly as:

Chapter 14

THE DEMAND

FOR FACTORS

OF

PRODUCTION

426

---

[13]More precisely, by a portion of the downward-sloping branch of the mrp curve, as explained in Section 14.A.

Figure 14.7
Firm's Demand Curve for Factor A. At the initial hire-price h_a it is supposed that the Factor Employment Conditions (14.12) are met by employments $a = a°$ and $b = b°$. Thus $mrp_a(b = b°)$ equals h_a^o at G—providing one point along the firm's demand curve for factor A. If the hire-price of A falls to h_a', increased employment of A in the amount $\hat{a}$ would be indicated by a movement along $mrp_a(b = b°)$. But this movement throws the employment condition for factor B out of equality, if there is any complementarity (or anti-complementarity) between A and B. Restoring the equality for factor B will then (regardless of whether the interaction is complementary or anti-complementary) raise the Marginal Product of factor A. The conditions in equation (14.12) can only be re-established at a point like K, where h_a' is set equal to $mrp_a(b=b')$—with b' representing the adjusted amount of the *other* factor. The firm's demand curve d_a for factor A is therefore flatter than the general slope of the mrp_a curves, wherever there is a complementary (or anti-complementary) interaction between the factors.

$$\begin{cases} mrp_a(b = b') = h_a' \\ mrp_b(a = a') = h_b^o \end{cases}$$

Note that the hire-price of B is still at its original level; only the price of factor A has changed.

The upshot is that the firm's demand curve for factor A is related in a somewhat more complex way to the mrp_a curves than in the case where A was the only variable factor. In Figure 14.7 the demand curve goes through points like G (showing employment of $a°$ at price h_a^o) and K (showing employment of a' at price h_a').

CONCLUSION: Given normal complementarity between factors, the demand curve for any factor is flatter (more elastic) than the Marginal Revenue Product curves. One implication is that employment of a variable factor tends to be more sensitive to price change in the *long run*, when the amounts of the "fixed" factors can be varied.

If the factors are *independent* rather than *complementary* in production, however, the interaction effect disappears. Given an initial adjustment from a° to $\hat{a}$ along the mrp_a curve in response to a fall in price from h_a° to h_a', the condition $mrp_b = h_b$ for the *other* factor B is in no way disturbed. The initial adjustment is then the full adjustment. The initial mrp_a curve remains the firm's demand curve for factor A, as in the case of a single variable factor. Putting it more generally: In the case of productive *independence* between factors, each factor's family of mrp curves coalesces into a single mrp curve that is not affected by the employment of the other factor.

What about "anti-complementary" factors? Intuition might suggest that if the firm's demand curve for factor A is *flatter* than the mrp_a curves in the complementary case and is *the same* as the (unique) mrp_a curve in the intermediate independent case, then it should be *steeper* than the mrp_a curves in the anti-complementary case. *This is incorrect!* In the anti-complementary as in the normal complementary case, the firm's demand curve for factor is *flatter* than the mrp curves as illustrated in Figure 14.7. The student can verify this, making use of equations (14.12) in parallel with the argument used for the case of complementarity. (*Hint:* After the initial adjustment from a° to $\hat{a}$, do the mrp_b curves shift up or down? What is the direction of the secondary effect upon the employment of B? How does that secondary effect further react upon the mrp_a curves?)[14]

INDUSTRY DEMAND FOR FACTORS

In proceeding from the *firm's* demand to the *industry's* demand for a factor of production, we can begin with the simple case of a single variable factor, as studied in Section 14.A.

First, consider the demand of a *monopolized* industry (i.e., an industry composed of a single seller in the product market) for a factor A. Evidently, the industry demand will be identical with the demand of the monopolist firm itself. The demand curve d_a of Figure 14.2 then becomes without further change the factor demand curve of the monopolized industry. (Where more than one factor is considered to be variable, it is the demand curve d_a of Figure 14.7 that is relevant.)

If the industry consists of a large number of *competitive* producers in the product market, however, there is a complication. The two panels of Figure 14.8

[14]A direct implication is that there cannot be a "Giffen factor"—that is, a factor whose demand curve has positive rather than negative slope. (Compare the discussion of possible "Giffen consumption goods" in Chapters 4 and 5.) We know that, in the range of relevant economic interest, Marginal Product must be declining (the Law of Diminishing Marginal Returns), which implies that the curve of Marginal Revenue Product must have negative slope. But the demand curve d_a is, if anything, even flatter than the mrp_a curves; there is no possibility of its becoming so steep as to eventually "curl back" like the curve pictured in Panel (b) of Figure 4.12.

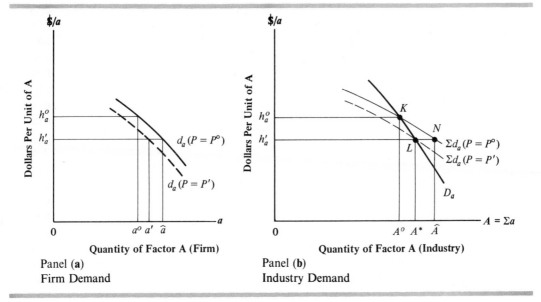

Panel (a)
Firm Demand

Panel (b)
Industry Demand

Figure 14.8

Demand for Factor—Competitive Firm and Industry, Product-Price Effect. Panel (a) pictures a firm's demand for factor A; Panel (b) pictures industry demand. At an initial factor hire-price h_a^o, position K in Panel (b) represents a point on the industry demand curve for A associated with a product price P^o. This product price is regarded as fixed by the firm, as indicated by the associated (solid) firm demand curve $d_a(P = P^o)$ in Panel (a). In Panel (b) the solid curve $\Sigma d_a(P = P^o)$ is the horizontal summation of these firm demand curves. When factor price falls to h_a, the firm aims to expand production from a^o to $\hat{a}$—the corresponding industry-wide summations in Panel (b) being A^o and $\hat{A}$. But as employment of A expands, industry-wide output Q also tends to rise, driving down product price to some level P'. Thus the firm's demand curve will fall to a position like the (dashed) curve $d_a(P = P')$ in Panel (a); the dashed summation curve in Panel (b) will move similarly. The consequence is that the new point on the industry factor demand curve in Panel (b) will be L. Thus, the product-price effect tends to make the industry demand curve for a factor relatively inelastic.

show the situation of a typical firm and then that of the competitive industry as a whole. Suppose an initial equilibrium exists at factor price $h_a = h_a$ and product price $P = P^o$. The firm's demand curve, derived from its curve of Marginal Revenue Product mrp_a (in this competitive case, identical with the firm's Value of Marginal Product vmp_a), is shown in Panel (a) as the curve labelled $d_a(P = P^o)$. Along the $d_a(P = P^o)$ curve, a^o is the indicated employment of factor A. For the industry as a whole, we can sum these firm demand curves horizontally so as to obtain the curve labelled $\Sigma d_a(P = P^o)$. At the initial factor price h_a^o, this horizontal summation curve shows industry employment $A^o = \Sigma a^o$ of the factor (at point K).

Now let factor price fall to h_a'. In Panel (a) the firm will first move along the initial demand curve, $d_a(P = P^o)$, to employment level $\hat{a}$ of factor A. The corresponding industry-wide movement in Panel (b) would be to the aggregate employment level $\hat{A}$ (point N). But this is not the full solution. The increased employment of factor A will entail increased firm output q.[15] Correspondingly, the industry as a whole will expand its aggregate output Q. Given a normally downward-sloping consumers' demand curve for good Q, the rise in output will necessitate a fall in product price P. And since $vmp_a \equiv P(mp_a)$, each firm will observe a downward shift of the overall position of its d_a curve taking place.

After taking the product-price effect into account, the factor demands of the firm and industry at the new factor price h_a' are illustrated by the dashed curves in the two panels of Figure 14.8. Here *product* price P has fallen to the level P'. The firm operates along the lower (dashed) factor demand curve labelled $d_a(P = P')$ to employ a' units of factor A. The industry correspondingly employs A' units in the aggregate, at point L on the horizontal summation curve $\Sigma d_a(P = P')$. The precise amount that product price must fall is determined, of course, by the elasticity of the consumers' demand for the increased output of Q. The true industry demand curve for factor A is illustrated in Panel (b) by the bold curve D_a that cuts through points K and L on the two different horizontal-summation curves.

Parallel to the product-price effect is the effect of increased industry output upon the prices of *other* factors. As employment of A expands in response to a fall in its hire-price h_a, in the normal complementarity case the industry will be attempting also to increase use of other factors $B, C, \ldots$ But the consequence on the industry level will be that hire-prices $h_b, h_c, \ldots$ will tend to *rise*; employment of these cooperating factors will then not increase as much as would otherwise have been the case. Then the demand for factor A will not benefit as much from complementarity as the picture in Figure 14.7 (which, for a given firm, assumed that hire-prices $h_b, h_c, \ldots$ were not affected by increased employment of A) might suggest. The complementary-factor-price effect therefore reinforces the product-price effect in tending to make industry demand D_a for factor A steeper (less elastic).

However, this is not the only possible outcome. One countervailing consideration not yet taken into account is that, given a reduction in the hire-price of factor A, production becomes more profitable so that *new firms will tend to enter* the industry. Therefore, in Panel (b) of Figure 14.8 the *number* of firms over which the summation is taken in the lower (dashed) summation curve $\Sigma d_a(P = P')$ will tend to exceed the number of firms relevant for the (solid) summation curve $\Sigma d_a(P = P°)$. The effect of entry (or of exit, if a rise rather than a fall in h_a were to take place) considered alone would tend to make the dashed summation curve in Panel (b) of the diagram lie *above* rather than below the solid summation curve.

Weighing the counterbalancing considerations, in general we cannot say which way the final result will go. If the product-price effect is very big (if consumer demand for the industry's product is quite inelastic, so that P falls sharply when industry output rises) then the entry-exit effect tends to be small—few new firms will be induced to enter. Then the D_a curve will tend to be steeper than the

[15] This is a necessary consequence if A is the only variable factor. With several variable factors, factor A might conceivably be "regressive" (as explained in Section 14.B.3), in which case output would not expand. The "regressive" case will henceforth be set aside, however.

summation curves, Σd_a, as pictured in Figure 14.8. But if the product-price effect is small (if consumer demand for Q is quite elastic so that P falls very little), the fall in h_a will bring about a sharp rise in profits. This will tend to induce considerable new entry, and thus to lead to the reverse of the situation pictured in the diagram—the D_a curve would be flatter than the summation curves. With several variable factors, the analog of a big product-price effect would be a big complementary-factor-price effect—if the supply curves of the cooperating factors are highly inelastic, h_b, h_c, . . . will tend to rise sharply. As in the case of the product-price effect, a big factor-price effect tends to reduce the entry incentive for new firms.

CONCLUSION: The industry's demand curve for a factor A tends to be steeper (less elastic) than the horizontal-summation curves that represent the aggregate of firms' factor demand curves for A: (i) when the consumers' demand curve for the industry's product is highly inelastic (strong product-price effect), and (ii) when the supply curves of other factors B, C, . . . complementary to A are highly inelastic (strong factor-price effect). If consumer demands and cooperating-factor supplies are highly elastic, on the other hand, the product-price effect and factor-price effect will be weak, inducing a strong entry-exit effect tending to make the industry's demand curve for factor A highly elastic.

In summary, we can say that demand for a factor is a *derived* demand. Firms and industries will employ factors only insofar as their employment contributes to the production of *goods* valued by consumers. The elements underlying demand for a particular factor fall under two headings: physical marginal productivity, and value of the goods produced. These are in turn governed by more fundamental forces: (1) Physical marginal productivity of a particular factor A is determined by the laws of technology as a function of the amount of A employed. But productivity is also affected by the amounts employed of *other* factors that are complements or substitutes of A in production. (2) The values placed by consumers, upon the goods to whose production factor A contributes, depend upon the demand-determining conditions studied in Part II: tastes, consumer incomes, etc. An additional element affecting factor demand is *market structure in the product market*. Specifically, we have seen that a monopolized industry will demand less of a factor than a competitive industry would.

Another question of importance concerns the determinants not of the *level* of factor demand but of its *elasticity*, i.e., its responsiveness to changes in factor price. Demand for factor A will be more elastic: (1) the more elastic are the consumer demands for the goods produced by A; (2) the slower and less powerful is the operation of the Law of Diminishing Returns as employment of A increases. Allowing for multiple variable factors, we can add that demand for A will be more elastic: (3) the closer are the substitutes available for factor A, and (4) the more elastic is the *supply* of factors complementary to A in production.

We can think of there being two main avenues of adjustment to a change in the hire-price of some factor A: input substitution, and output substitution. As h_a rises, each firm and industry employing factor A tends to substitute other factors for A, as limited by the production function and by the tendency of the hire-prices of these other factors to rise in response. But even if no input substitution were possible, over the economy as a whole consumers would change their consumption patterns, consuming more of other products and less of products making heavy use of the now-more-expensive factor A.

14.D

MONOPSONY IN THE FACTOR MARKET

The analysis thus far in the current chapter, while allowing for either competition or monopoly in the *product* market, has assumed that firms are price-takers in the *factor* market—so we have covered only the upper-row cells of Table 14.1. In this Section we turn to the analysis of a single buyer or "monopsonist" on the demand side of the factor market. Thus, we are now dealing with the cells shown in the lower row of Table 14.1.

14.D.1

Monopsony Solution

The situation of such a monopsonist is illustrated in Figure 14.9. The worth of incremental units of factor A to the firm is indicated, as before, by the curve of Marginal Revenue Product mrp_a. But the monopsonist firm recognizes that the factor supply curve which it faces is upward-sloping (rather than effectively horizontal as in Figures 14.1 and 14.2). The firm is so large an employer of factor A that its own decisions to hire more or fewer units drive the price h_a up or down.

Recall that $C_a \equiv h_a a$ is the total expenditure of the firm in hiring factor A. With regard to C_a as a total, the supply curve s_a is a curve of Average Factor Cost afc_a, since $h_a \equiv C_a/a$ is the average amount that must be paid to hire any specified number of units of factor A. The *additional* expense incurred by the firm in hiring an incremental unit of factor A is its Marginal Factor Cost $mfc_a \equiv \Delta C_a/\Delta a$.

When the supply curve s_a, or equivalently the Average Factor Cost afc_a, is horizontal (as in Figures 14.1 and 14.2) the curve of Marginal Factor Cost mfc_a coincides with it at the level of the given market hire-price h_a. But here the afc_a curve is a rising function of factor quantity. Therefore the mfc_a curve must lie above it (Proposition 2.2b).

More explicitly, the increment of expense due to hiring an additional unit of factor is the sum of two elements: h_a is the payment to the additional unit of factor itself, and $a\Delta h_a$ is the expense due to the increased price paid to all units previously employed. Thus:

$$(14.13) \qquad mfc_a \equiv \frac{\Delta C_a}{\Delta a} \equiv h_a + a\,\frac{\Delta h_a}{\Delta a}$$

Figure 14.9
Monopsony in the Factor Market. The rising supply curve of A to the firm, s_a, is also a curve of Average Factor Cost afc_a. The curve of Marginal Factor Cost mfc_a will then lie above afc_a, as shown here. The optimum factor employment for the firm is $a*$, where the mfc_a and mrp_a curves intersect (point M). The associated hire-price h_a^* is the price along the s_a curve at this level of employment.

Here the rising supply curve means that $\Delta h_a / \Delta a$ is positive in sign, thus verifying that $mfc_a > h_a \equiv afc_a$.

For any factor A, the monopsonist firm maximizes profit by equalizing the marginal benefit and the marginal expense of hiring A. Thus:

(14.14) $\qquad mrp_a = mfc_a \qquad$ Factor Employment Condition, Monopsony Firm

In Figure 14.9, this equality is found at employment level $a*$. The firm will then pay the factor price h_a^* required to elicit this quantity of factor, as indicated by the height of the supply curve s_a at $a = a*$. Note that h_a^* lies *below* the intersection of mrp_a and mfc_a at point M in the diagram.

The analogy between the monopsonist solution in the factor market and the monopolist solution in the product market will not have escaped the reader. Geometrically, the *factor-market monopsony* picture of Figure 14.9 is a kind of inverted analog of the *product-market monopoly* pictured in Figure 11.4. For monopoly in the product market, Marginal Revenue MR lies below and falls faster than Average Revenue AR; for monopsony in the factor market, Marginal Factor Cost mfc lies above and rises faster than Average Factor Cost afc.

EXAMPLE 14.2
MONOPSONY IN
PROFESSIONAL
BASEBALL

The leading (and perhaps the only important) example of labor-market monopsony exists in the realm of professional sports. Here a legal quirk, perhaps based upon the idea that sports are play (a "pastime") rather than a business, has permitted the organization of buyers' cartels with respect to employment of players. The most important cartel instrument is the "reserve clause," which makes the player the exclusive property of the team that first signs him up, or to which he is "traded" thereafter. Should a player refuse to accept the wage offer of the team whose property he is, he cannot play for any other team in the cartel.

Gerald W. Scully investigated the effect of the reserve clause in major league baseball. He anticipated that the buyers' cartel would cause a divergence between Marginal Revenue Product *mrp* and wage (see Figure 14.9).

But first, differences in player *quality* (i.e., in *mrp*) had to be allowed for. Using 1968 and 1969 data, Scully estimated the "gross" *mrp* in terms of the player's effect on gate receipts and broadcast revenues. Deducting related expenses, and in particular player development costs, led to estimates of "net" *mrp* for players of different qualities. Since substantial player development costs, on the order of $300,000, are incurred before it is known how successful the athlete will be, it sometimes happens that net *mrp* turns out to be negative. On the average, however, in a competitive situation wages should be equal to net *mrp*. If the actual structure is one of monopsony, on the other hand, wages on the average would fall short of net *mrp*.

The table below shows some of Scully's results. For batters and pitchers falling into different quality groups, net *mrp* and average salary are compared. While for "mediocre" players salary is above net *mrp*—and indeed, the latter is actually negative—for "average" and "star" players, net *mrp* far exceeds salary. Thus, on balance there is considerable evidence of monopsony power.

Quality versus Pay of Baseball Players

	QUALITY GROUP	NET *mrp*	SALARY
Hitters	Mediocre	$-30,000	$17,200
	Average	128,300	29,100
	Star	319,000	52,100
Pitchers	Mediocre	-10,600	15,700
	Average	159,600	33,000
	Star	405,300	66,800

Source: G. W. Scully, "Pay and Performance in Major League Baseball," *American Economic Review*, v. 64 (Dec. 1974), p. 928.

COMMENT: Contrary to common opinion among fans and sports writers, star players are not "overpaid." In fact, they receive far less than their economic worth. Since the time of Scully's study, however, the "reserve clause" in professional sports has been substantially weakened. And in consequence, as would be expected, stars' salaries have tended to rise.

Let us now return to Table 14.1. Since a product-market price-taker can be regarded as a special case of a product-market monopolist (the special case where MR and AR coincide), and since a factor-market price-taker is similarly a special case of a factor-market monopsonist (the special case where mfc and afc coincide), the equations shown for the Monopolist-Monopsonist combination in the lower-right cell of the table can be considered the *general* results that apply in all cases. These general results are $mfc_a = mrp_a$ as the Factor Employment Condition (upper-line equation) and $MC = MR$ as the Optimal Output Condition (lower-line equation).

Assuming price-taking behavior in the *product* market, we are dealing with the two cells of the left-hand column of Table 14.1. Here the identity $MR \equiv P$ is applicable for the output condition so we have $MC = MR \equiv P$. And corresponding to this is the identity $mrp_a \equiv vmp_a$ applicable for the employment condition so that $mfc_a = mrp_a \equiv vmp_a$.

Consider now price-taking behavior in the *factor* market. Now we are dealing with the two cells of the upper row of the table. Here the identity $h_a \equiv mfc_a$ becomes applicable for the employment condition—so that $h_a \equiv mfc_a = mrp_a$ holds. There should, strictly speaking, be a corresponding special identity holding for the output condition in this factor-market price-taker case (the two cells of the upper row). Showing this identity requires us to define a new concept, which might be called Cost of the Marginal Unit (CMU):

$$(14.15) \qquad CMU \equiv \frac{afc_a}{mp_a}$$

The Cost of the Marginal Unit is in general distinct from the more familiar concept of Marginal Cost, which is defined as:

$$(14.16) \qquad MC \equiv \frac{mfc_a}{mp_a}$$

Since $afc_a \equiv h_a$ by definition, we see that CMU counts only the hire-price h_a in costing the amount of factor needed to generate a marginal unit of output. The Marginal Cost MC, in contrast, counts not only the direct cost of purchasing the inputs for the marginal unit of output but allows also for any increase in hire-price h_a that raises the cost of producing the earlier or *infra*-marginal units of output. This is precisely the distinction between mfc_a and afc_a. Thus in the monopsonist case (lower row of Table 14.1) where $mfc_a > afc_a$, then $MC > CMU$. But in the upper row of Table 14.1 the firm is a factor-market price-taker. Thus, in the upper row, $afc_a \equiv mfc_a$ so that $CMU \equiv MC$.[16] Then the optimal output condition could be written $CMU \equiv MC = MR$ in the upper row of Table 14.1.

[16] Algebraically, the following identities hold for Marginal Cost MC:

$$MC \equiv \frac{\Delta C}{\Delta q} \equiv \frac{\Delta C_a}{\Delta q} \equiv \frac{\Delta C_a}{\Delta a} \frac{\Delta a}{\Delta q} \equiv \frac{mfc_a}{mp_a}$$

* The section between the asterisk and the symbol ■ may contain somewhat more difficult or advanced material.

For a single variable factor, it is elementary to verify that satisfaction of the Factor Employment Condition necessarily implies the Optimal Output Condition, and vice versa. We can do this for the Monopolist-Monopsonist case in the lower-right corner of Table 14.1 (which, being most general, includes all the others). Using the definitions $MC \equiv mfc_a/mp_a$ and $mrp_a \equiv MR(mp_a)$, the Factor Employment Condition $mfc_a = mrp_a$ in the lower-right cell can be written:

$$MC(mp_a) = MR(mp_a)$$

Cancelling out mp_a, we have immediately the general Optimal Output Condition $MC = MR$.[17] ∎

14.E

AN APPLICATION: MINIMUM-WAGE LAWS

Two economic models are in contention for explaining or predicting the consequences of minimum-wage legislation. For the *competitive-market model*, the effects of price floors or ceilings are as previously discussed in Section 2.A. The alternative *monopsony-market model* is based on the analysis of the preceding section 14.D.

The competitive model is illustrated in Figure 14.10. The commodity is a certain grade or class of labor L, whose hire-price is the wage rate w. A competitive equilibrium exists at wage w_c and employment L_c. Now a legal minimum wage is imposed, at a level higher than w_c.[18] At wage $w°$ the labor offered on the market is the quantity L_s but the labor demanded is only L_d. The perceived *unemployment gap* at the legal wage is the quantity BC or $L_s - L_d$. However, the *disemployment effect* actually due to the wage floor is the somewhat lesser quantity FE or $L_c - L_d$. Analysts using the competitive-market model would clearly pre-

---

This justifies the definition in equation (14.16). But MC can also be written:

$$MC \equiv \frac{\Delta C_a}{\Delta q} \equiv \frac{\Delta(h_a a)}{\Delta q} \equiv \frac{h_a \Delta a + a \Delta h_a}{\Delta q} \equiv h_a \frac{\Delta a}{\Delta q} + a \frac{\Delta h_a}{\Delta q}$$

The first term on the righthand side here is afc_a/mp_a, and thus represents the Cost of the Marginal Unit CMU. The second term shows the monopsony effect. For a monopsonist in the factor market, $MC > CMU$. In contrast, since for a factor-market price-taker $\Delta h_a = 0$, in the upper row of the table we have $MC \equiv CMU$.

[17] If there is more than one variable factor, by a natural generalization of equation (14.14) we will have for the Factor Employment Conditions (compare also [14.12]):

$$\begin{cases} mrp_a = mfc_a \\ mrp_b = mfc_b \end{cases}$$

Since $MC \equiv \dfrac{mfc_a}{mp_a} \equiv \dfrac{mfc_b}{mp_b}$ and $MR \equiv \dfrac{mrp_a}{mp_b} \equiv \dfrac{mrp_b}{mp_b}$, $MC = MR$ follows immediately.

[18] A legal minimum wage *lower* than w_c would clearly be without effect.

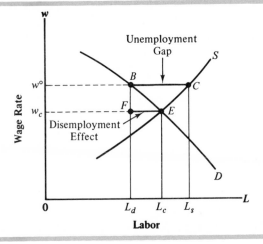

Figure 14.10

Minimum Wage, Competitive Model. The competitive equilibrium at point E is associated with wage w_c and employment L_c. If a wage floor or minimum wage were imposed at the level $w°$, employment would fall to L_d. The quantity FE is the "disemployment effect." At the higher wage there would be L_s units of labor seeking employment, so the perceived "unemployment gap" would be the larger quantity BC.

dict some degree of *disemployment* and a larger degree of *unemployment*, as a result of imposition of a minimum wage higher than the pre-existing market equilibrium wage.

The monopsony model leads to rather different implications, illustrated in Figure 14.11. The pre-existing situation has employment L_m (at the intersection of the *mrp* and *mfc* curves); the wage $w_m < mrp$ is determined along the labor supply curve S. With the introduction of an effective minimum-wage law, *the market supply curve is replaced by a horizontal line at the level of the imposed minimum wage* (in the range where the market supply curve S lies below the level of the minimum wage). That is, the monopsonist employer is *forced to be a price-taker* at the minimum wage, wherever the market supply conditions would otherwise have permitted establishing a monopsony hire-price lower than the legally imposed floor.

Three classes of possibilities are illustrated in Figure 14.11. First, suppose that the minimum wage is only a little higher than w_m, for example w' in the diagram. Then the *effective* supply curve to the firm is horizontal at the level w' until the S curve is reached at point N. In this range the Marginal Factor Cost *mfc* also equals w'. If the firm could actually hire as many units as desired at wage w', it would employ the quantity associated with point G, where $w' = mrp$. But this is not possible. Beyond point N, the effective supply curve of labor to the firm rejoins the original S curve; the laborers are not willing to supply more than L' units at wage w'. It follows also that, beyond employment L', the effective Marginal Factor Cost leaps upward discontinuously to rejoin the original *mfc* curve (at point U). Since the *mrp* curve in the diagram passes through this vertical discon-

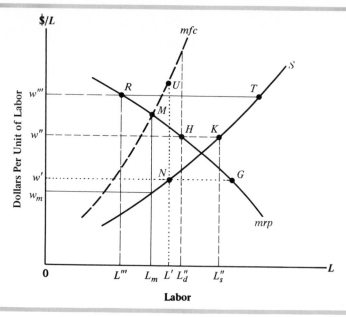

Figure 14.11

Minimum Wage, Monopsony Model. Under monopsony, the optimality condition $mfc = mrp$ determines the wage w_m at employment L_m. At a relatively low imposed minimum wage w', the optimality condition is satisfied at employment L'—both wage and employment rise slightly. At an intermediate imposed wage w'', the optimal employment is L_d''. Here there is a considerable increase in both wage and employment; nevertheless, a perceived "unemployment gap" HK arises, since at wage w'' the offered employment has increased to L_s. At the high imposed minimum wage w''' the wage has risen even further, but now employment falls (to L''')—as in the competitive model of the previous diagram.

tinuity of the *mfc* curve, the firm will find it optimal to employ L' workers at wage w'. Note that, relative to L_m, the minimum-wage law here has *increased* employment! Nor is there any perceived unemployment at the legally imposed wage.

Now consider a somewhat higher minimum wage, w'' in Figure 14.11. At this wage the firm would again be forced to be a price-taker, and would not want to employ more than L_d'' units (at point H), using the condition $w'' = mrp$. This employment is also greater than the L_m of the unregulated monopsony solution; no *disemployment* takes place. However, at wage w'' some *unemployment* will be perceived. At the w'' wage the offered labor supply would be L_s'', which is more than the firm wants to hire. The resulting unemployment gap is indicated by the distance HK in the diagram.

Finally, w''' represents a still higher minimum wage, higher than the level at which the *mrp* and *mfc* curves intersect. Here the effective employment would be reduced to L'''. Thus, a minimum wage as high as w''' would lead to the same qualitative implications as in the competitive-market model. With this high wage there would be some *disemployment* as compared with L_m, and a large *unemployment* gap represented by the distance RT in the diagram.

CONCLUSION: The competitive-market model unambiguously implies both disemployment (less L employed) and unemployment (a supply-demand gap) as a result of any imposed minimum wage higher than the unregulated equilibrium. The monopsony-market model has three possible outcomes: (1) At a relatively low minimum wage w', employment *increases* and there is no perceived unemployment. (2) At an intermediate minimum wage w'', employment increases but there is also some unemployment. (3) At a relatively high minimum wage w''', there is both disemployment and considerable unemployment.

Which of these models is the more relevant? That is an empirical question which has been investigated by a number of economists.

In determining the effects of minimum-wage legislation upon wages and employment, it is essential to appreciate that labor is not homogeneous. There is a spectrum of labor skill and quality. At the moment of imposition of a new or increased legal minimum wage, some workers will already be earning more than the imposed minimum and others less. Under any market model, minimum-wage laws will have quite different impacts upon high-wage and low-wage workers.

Using the *competitive* model, low-skilled (low-wage) workers would be affected as in Figure 14.10. Their wage rates would rise, but some workers would find themselves disemployed. For higher-skilled workers, in contrast, the equilibrium wage level is likely to be already above the imposed minimum wage—so no direct impact is to be expected. If the *monopsony* model of Figure 14.11 were valid, on the other hand, a more complex set of observations would be anticipated: (a) For very low-skilled workers the imposed minimum wage would be effectively at a high level, like w''' in Figure 14.11—so higher wages but lesser employment would be expected. (b) For medium-skilled workers, the w'' picture might be appropriate—*both* wage rate and employment might increase. (c) For quite high-skilled workers, the imposed minimum wage would be relatively low, even lower than w' in Figure 14.11—little or no direct effect on wages or employment would be anticipated.

An early study by A. F. Hinrichs[19] classified plants in the seamless hosiery industry by wage group. It was found that, after imposition of the 25-cent minimum wage in October 1938, low-wage plants had a relatively greater loss in employment (and a relatively greater rise in average hourly earnings) than high-wage plants. Indeed, despite generally improving business conditions, the lowest-wage plants suffered an *absolute* loss in employment. A more extensive study by J. M. Peterson[20] confirmed Hinrichs' results as to the seamless hosiery industry, and showed a similar picture for Southern

EXAMPLE 14.3
MINIMUM-WAGE
LEGISLATION

[19] A. F. Hinrichs, "Effects of the 25-Cent Minimum Wage on Employment in the Seamless Hosiery Industry," *Journal of the American Statistical Association*, v. 35 (March 1940).

[20] J. M. Peterson, "Employment Effects of Minimum Wages, 1938–50," *Journal of Political Economy*, v. 65 (Oct. 1957).

sawmills and for men's cotton garments, over several steps of minimum-wage increases between 1938 and 1950. The pattern was consistent, in that in each case low-wage plants lost relatively more in employment while paying a relatively greater wage increment. In addition, Peterson showed a relative loss in employment position for low-wage versus high-wage *cities*, and a *regional* tendency of industry to shift away from the low-wage South. The regional effect was emphasized in a study by M. R. Colberg,[21] who examined the impact of the 1957 $1.00 minimum-wage law upon high-wage and low-wage *counties* in Florida. The law was found to have caused a relative decrease in employment in low-wage counties.

A number of recent studies have directed attention specifically to low-wage *workers*, and particularly to the effects of minimum-wage laws on *teenagers*. In general, teenagers are relatively lacking in the skills and experience necessary to earn high wages. Hence a large fraction of them are likely to be in the position where a uniform legal minimum wage is higher than their equilibrium market wage. Under the competitive model, in consequence, a relatively large disemployment effect upon teenagers would be anticipated. A study by Y. Brozen[22] found that successive increases in the legal minimum wage were indeed reflected by rises in the teenage unemployment rate. But as productivity and inflation progressed over time, the equilibrium wage for teenagers tended to "catch up" with the legally fixed minimum so as to erode the disemployment effect, until the next round of minimum-wage legislation began the cycle over again.

A sophisticated statistical regression analysis over the period 1954–1968 by T. G. Moore allowed not only for the *level* of the minimum wage but also for *coverage* of the labor force (since, over time, not only level but coverage has tended to increase). A portion of Moore's results are shown in the following table.

Effect of Minimum Wage upon Younger Age-Group Unemployment

| | DETERMINING VARIABLES | |
UNEMPLOYMENT RATE OF:	EMPLOYED WORKERS COVERED BY MINIMUM WAGE (%)	MINIMUM WAGE AS PROPORTION OF HOURLY EARNINGS
Nonwhites, 16–19	.2549	1.75927
Whites, 16–19	.077	.58461
Males, 16–19	.080	.61649
Females, 16–19	.171	.73988
Males, 20–24	−.063	.05346

Source: T. G. Moore, "The Effect of Minimum Wages on Teenage Unemployment Rates," *Journal of Political Economy,* v. 79 (July/Aug. 1971), p. 901.

[21]M. R. Colberg, "Minimum Wage Effects on Florida's Economic Development," *Journal of Law and Economics,* v. 3 (Oct. 1960).

[22]Y. Brozen, "The Effect of Statutory Minimum Wage Increases on Teen-Age Unemployment," *Journal of Law & Economics,* v. 12 (April 1969).

The data in the table may be interpreted as follows, using the first row as an example. The unemployment rate of Nonwhites aged 16–19: (1) increased .2549% for each percent rise in the *coverage* of the minimum-wage law. And (2) increased 1.75927% for each percent increase in the *ratio* of the legal minimum wage to the average hourly earnings of production workers in private nonagricultural employment. Note that males aged 20–24, above the teenage category, were *not* substantially affected by the minimum-wage legislation (bottom row).

COMMENT: All these studies provide solid confirmation for the predictions of the competitive model of Figure 14.10. The monopsony model of Figure 14.11, being consistent with a variety of outcomes, is not conclusively refuted by these results. However, none of the studies show any hint of the *favorable* effect of a minimum-wage law on employment of some middle-quality workers that would be anticipated on the basis of the monopsony model.

Regardless of economic impact, it appears that minimum-wage legislation must have satisfied some criteria of *political* effectiveness to have become so important a feature of the economic situation. The supposed "beneficiaries"—those directly impacted low-wage workers previously receiving less than the minimum wage (largely teenagers and "minorities")—have mixed incentives with regard to such legislation. While many of the directly impacted group will indeed receive a wage increase, a good proportion are likely to find themselves disemployed. The most significant political pressure for higher minimum wages seems to come not from the "beneficiaries" but from organized labor, in particular the AFL–CIO. Few of the relatively high-paid workers represented by the AFL–CIO are in the directly impacted group that would otherwise be receiving less than the minimum wage. For such skilled high-wage workers an increased minimum wage may, however, represent an indirect kind of benefit. A higher minimum wage raises the cost of unskilled relative to skilled workers. The consequence is to induce firms to employ fewer of the unskilled workers, raising relative demand for the skilled workers represented by the AFL–CIO. (*Query for the student:* An imposed minimum wage making low-skilled labor more expensive would clearly raise *relative* demand for high-skilled workers, but can we be sure that actual overall demand for high-skilled labor would rise? Does the answer depend upon the presence or absence of complementarity between high-skilled and low-skilled workers?)

This chapter deals with the demand for factors of production on the part of the firm, and on the part of the industry. A key theme is that the optimal *output* decision (studied in Chapter 9 for the competitive firm, and in Chapter 11 for a monopoly firm) and the *factor employment* decision considered here are logically

SUMMARY OF CHAPTER 14

interconnected rather than independent choices. The Factor Employment Conditions that the firm must satisfy to maximize profit depend also upon *market structure* both in the product market (whether the firm is a price-taker or a monopolist for output) and in the factor market (whether the firm is a price-taker or a monopsonist for input).

A factor-market price-taker (non-monopsonist) firm will employ a single variable factor A until its hire-price h_a equals its Marginal Revenue Product mrp_a, defined as Marginal Revenue (MR) times Marginal Product of factor A (mp_a):

$$h_a = mrp \equiv MR(mp_a)$$

If it is also a product-market price-taker (non-monopolist), the firm's Marginal Revenue Product becomes identical to Value of the Marginal Product vmp_a, defined as price P times Marginal Product mp_a. Then the condition for optimal employment of factor A becomes:

$$h_a = mrp_a \equiv vmp_a \equiv P(mp_a)$$

The firm's demand curve for a single variable factor A is simply the downward-sloping branch of the mrp_a curve. From the definition of Marginal Revenue Product, it is evident that factor demand depends upon the physical productivity of the factor (mp_a) and the value to the firm of the output produced (MR).

If there are several variable factors, productive interdependencies among them must also be taken into account. With just two factors A and B, the Factor Employment Conditions are a natural generalization of the single-factor condition above:

$$\begin{cases} h_a = mrp_a \\ h_b = mrp_b \end{cases}$$

The productive interdependence between A and B is called *complementary* if an increase in employment of either raises the Marginal Product of the other, and *anti-complementary* if the reverse holds. Complementarity is the normal case. (If there is no interdependence, the factors are called *independent* in production.) Any productive interdependence, whether complementary or anti-complementary, tends to make the firm's demand curve for either factor relatively elastic.

As factor prices shift, there will be both a *substitution effect* and a *scale effect* upon factor employment. The substitution effect, considered alone, dictates increased employment of the relatively cheapened factor and decreased employment of the other. For a fall in a hire-price h_a, the scale effect (due to increased firm output) will normally increase employment of the cheapened factor A further. (But a "regressive" case is possible, in which cheapening of a factor leads to a reduction in the optimal output.)

The competitive *industry's* demand for a factor is, to a first approximation, the summation of the member firms' demands. But there are several complications. As h_a falls, the industry will expand employment of A, which will normally tend to raise aggregate output Q. Then product price will tend to fall. This *product-price effect*, by lowering the value of the output, tends to make the industry demand curve for factor A more inelastic than the firms' demands. If there are several variable factors, there will be also a *complementary-factor-price effect*. As h_a falls and employment of A expands, the increased demand for factors complementary to A will raise their prices. These increases in the prices of complementary factors will reinforce the product-price effect, tending to make industry demand more inelastic. On the other hand, reductions in any hire-price will make production in the industry more profitable (and the reverse for increases in hire-prices). So, as a countervailing consideration, there will be an *entry-exit effect* tending to make the industry demand for a factor relatively more elastic than individual firms' demands.

If the firm is a *monopsonist* purchaser of factor A, its Marginal Factor Cost mfc_a for A will exceed the hire-price or Average Factor Cost $h_a \equiv afc_a$ of A:

$$mfc_a \equiv h_a + a \; \frac{\Delta h_a}{\Delta a}$$

The optimal employment condition is:

$$mfc_a = mrp_a$$

Just as the curve of Marginal Revenue MR lies below and falls faster than the product demand curve (AR curve), the curve of Marginal Factor Cost mfc_a lies above and rises faster than the factor supply curve (afc_a curve). The monopsonist firm therefore employs less of the factor than would a factor-market price-taker firm.

One important application of alternative market-structure models is to the analysis of minimum-wage laws. The competitive model unambiguously predicts that, whenever an imposed minimum wage actually represents an increase over the market equilibrium wage, reduced employment will result. Under a monopsony model, however, the results will differ depending upon how high the imposed minimum wage is in comparison with the previous market monopsony wage. And, in particular, the monopsony model predicts a range over which an imposed wage increase would actually *raise* employment. Empirical investigations, however, have failed to turn up any hint of such an outcome. It seems that, at least for wage levels where the imposed minimum wage is effective, the competitive factor-market model is applicable.

Demand for a factor A tends to be *greater*: (1) where the employers are product-market competitors rather than monopolists, and are factor-market price-takers rather than monopsonists; (2) where the physical Marginal Product mp_a is high; and (3) where the output produced by employing A is highly valued by consumers. Demand for A tends to be *more elastic*: (1) the more elastic is the consumers' demand for the output; (2) the less powerfully the Law of Diminishing Returns operates as employment of A increases; (3) the greater the normal productive interdependence (complementarity) between A and other factors; (4) the more elastic is the supply of these complementary factors; and (5) the greater the exit-entry effect as the hire-price h_a changes.

QUESTIONS FOR CHAPTER 14

Mainly for Review

R1. Distinguish the *productivity* and the *revenue* considerations entering into a firm's demand for a factor.

*R2. Does the curve of Marginal Revenue Product for factor A, mrp_a, necessarily lie below (to the left of) the curve of Value of the Marginal Product, vmp_a? Explain. Which is the firm's demand curve for factor A?

R3. Why is $mrp_a = h_a$ the Factor Employment Condition for a price-taking firm in the *factor* market? What if the firm is not a price-taker in the *product* market? Is this condition sufficient, or are there other subsidiary conditions that must be met?

*R4. Is it ever rational to employ so much of a factor as to be in the region of diminishing marginal returns? In the region of diminishing average returns? In the region of diminishing total returns?

*R5. With two factors A and B, explain why the conditions $mrp_a = h_a$ and $mrp_b = h_b$ lead not only to the choice of optimal factor proportions but also to the optimal *scale* of output.

*R6. With two factors of production, is the slope of the output isoquant equal (in absolute value) to the ratio of the Marginal Products? Explain. Interpret the absolute slope of the *cost* isoquant as a ratio.

R7. Explain why, if two factors are complementary, the demand curve for either is flatter than its *mrp* curve. What if the two are anti-complementary?

*R8. Is the factor demand curve of a competitive industry necessarily less elastic than the summation of the demand curves of the separate firms present in the industry at a particular moment?

*R9. True or false? Explain in each case. The economy-wide demand curve for factor A will be more elastic:

   a. The more elastic the consumer demand for goods in the production of which A is employed.
   b. The weaker the operation of the Law of Diminishing Returns as employment of A is varied.
   c. The more elastic is the *supply* of factors complementary to A.

R10. In the competitive minimum-wage model of Figure 14.10, why is the "unemployment gap" bigger than the "disemployment effect"?

R11. Show how, upon imposition of a minimum-wage law, the monopsony model might predict *increased* employment. Given an initial dispersion of wage rates (high-skilled, mid-skilled, and low-skilled workers) under

*The answers to asterisked questions appear at the end of the book.

this model, which groups would tend to find employment decreasing and which increasing? Compare the predictions with the competitive model.

*T1. Are there examples in this text providing empirical support for the Laws of Diminishing Marginal and Average Returns? Would you expect to find any exceptions?

*T2. Can a demand curve for factor *A* be derived if the employer of *A* is a *monopsonist*? That is, is there a relation that shows the quantity employed as a function of price? Why or why not?

T3. With regard to Table 14.1, the monopolist-monopsonist Factor Employment Condition $mfc_a = mrp_a$ is said to be the "most general." Show that this condition also covers the case of a firm that is a price-taker in both product and factor markets.

*T4. Why might a firm at a given moment hire positive amounts of two factors that are anti-complementary? Would it ever simultaneously hire "interfering" factors?

T5. Would you expect, typically, that combinations of different classes of labor (like skilled versus unskilled) are more or less likely to be complementary—in comparison with combinations of labor and machines?

T6. Assuming that labor organizations were interested only in the selfish gains of their members, would you expect them to oppose immigration?

*T7. Historically, wages in the United States have been high relative to wages elsewhere. Does this chapter shed light on this phenomenon? Explain.

*T8. Would you expect technological progress to raise wage rates, on the average?

T9. A minimum wage law raises firms' *relative* demand for skilled labor versus unskilled. Would it tend to raise the *absolute* demand for skilled labor, if skilled and unskilled are complementary? If they are anti-complementary? How does your answer bear upon the attitudes of trade unions toward minimum wage laws?

15.A THE OPTIMUM OF THE RESOURCE-OWNER, 447

15.B AN APPLICATION: THE "NEGATIVE INCOME TAX" PROPOSAL, 454

15.C RESOURCE SUPPLY TO THE MARKET, AND FACTOR-MARKET EQUILIBRIUM, 460

15.D MONOPOLIES AND CARTELS IN FACTOR SUPPLY, 465
    *15.D.1 Optimum of the Monopolist Resource-Owner, 465
     15.D.2 Resource Cartels, 468

15.E THE "FUNCTIONAL" DISTRIBUTION OF INCOME, 471
     15.E.1 The Problem of Classification, 471
     15.E.2 An Application: Investment in Human Capital, 472
     15.E.3 Capital versus Income—Sources and Services—The Rate of Interest, 474

15.F ECONOMIC RENT AND PRODUCER SURPLUS, 477

15.G CAPITAL INTERTEMPORAL CHOICE, AND THE CIRCULAR FLOW, 480

Examples
     15.1   RETIREMENT DECISIONS, 453
     15.2   NEGATIVE INCOME TAX EXPERIMENT, 458
     15.3   ANIMAL LABOR SUPPLY, 461
     15.4   BRACEROS AND THE SUPPLY OF "STOOP LABOR," 461
     15.5   THE BLACK DEATH, 464
     15.6   UNIONIZATION AND HOTEL WORKERS, 469
     15.7   BARBERS, 470
     15.8   TOBACCO ALLOTMENTS, 471
     15.9   RETURNS TO MEDICAL EDUCATION, 473
     15.10 CAPITAL IN THE SLAVE-OWNING SOUTH, 475
     15.11 ECONOMIC RENT AND THE MILITARY DRAFT, 479

FACTOR SUPPLY, FACTOR-MARKET EQUILIBRIUM, AND INCOME DISTRIBUTION

Core Chapter

In this chapter, our analysis of *the supply side of the factor market* will complete the circular flow of economic activity first pictured in Figure 1.1. Factor supplies derive ultimately from the choices of resource-owners between two categories of employments: (1) service to others for hire-payment (*market uses*), versus (2) self-employment (non-market or *reservation uses*). These choices are discussed in the first two sections of the chapter. In Sections C and D, factor demand (studied in Chapter 14) will be brought together with this treatment of factor supply so as to arrive at *equilibrium* in the market for factors. The *distribution of income*, that is, the division of the national product among various categories and classes of resource-owners, is the next subject covered. This leads finally into the topic of "capital," or more generally, the intertemporal choice process that generates changes in resource supplies over time.

15.A

THE OPTIMUM OF THE RESOURCE-OWNER

In the analysis of consumption and demand in Chapter 4, the individual was supposed to be already in possession of a given income I out of which he could purchase desired consumption goods. But, of course, this income does not come out of thin air. *Income consists of earnings received from the employment of resources (factors) owned.* Thus the consumer, viewed from another aspect, is the resource-owner.

In the resource-owning role, as in the consumptive role, everyone has a decision problem. It is necessary to decide how much to supply on the market, as against the alternative of reserving some or all of one's owned resources for non-market use. For concreteness, let us think of labor capacity as the owned resource. Then the decision problem is to choose *between labor income and "leisure."* [1]

Figure 15.1 shows an individual's preference map in terms of indifference curves between *income I* (which stands here as a proxy for the consumption goods purchasable out of income) and *leisure R* (i.e., reservation uses of one's time). The arrows showing preference directions indicate that income and leisure are both "goods" rather than "bads." Before any exchange takes place, the individual at *endowment* position E has $R^{\dagger}$ units of leisure (24 hours per day, let us say) and $I^{\dagger}$ units of endowed non-labor income (from property earnings, perhaps). The diagram is bounded both on the right and on the left. The bound on the right at $R^{\dagger}$

Figure 15.1

Optimum of the Resource-Owner. The resource-owner's preferences, as indicated by indifference curves $U_0, U_1, U_2, \ldots$, show that Income I and reservation uses (or "leisure") R are both goods. At endowment position E the person has $R^{\dagger}$ of leisure and possibly some initial income $I^{\dagger}$ as well. The slope of the budget line EK indicates the terms (the hire-price or wage) at which the individual can obtain income by sacrificing leisure uses of the resource. The tangency point $G*$ is the resource-owner's optimum position.

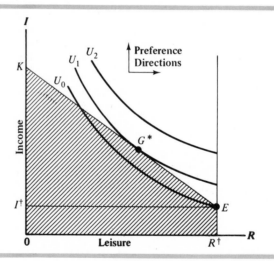

Chapter 15
FACTOR
SUPPLY,
FACTOR-
MARKET
EQUILIBRIUM,
AND INCOME
DISTRIBUTION

448

[1] "Leisure" perhaps suggests a mere lazing away of one's time. But the term as used here may include productive activities, so long as these are outside the market context. An obvious and enormously important example is homemaking, an activity which involves productive services that would be extremely costly to procure on the market.

says that, no matter what, the individual cannot "buy" more than 24 hours of leisure per day; the bound on the left at zero says that the individual cannot sell more than 24 hours of labor per day.

The opportunity set is the shaded area lying below the budget line EK. Starting from E, as an hour of labor is sold (as an hour of leisure is sacrificed), the person receives in exchange the hourly wage rate h_L, where h_L is the "hire-price" of labor. If the individual is a price-taker with respect to the wage rate, the budget line has constant slope $\Delta I / \Delta R = -h_L$.[2] The wage rate h_L can be regarded, equivalently, as the price of an hour of *labor* or of an hour of *leisure*.

The individual's *resource-employment optimum* (balance between market and reservation uses of labor-time resource) is at the tangency position G^* in Figure 15.1. The logic is entirely parallel to that used in finding the *consumptive optimum* in Chapter 4, Section A (compare Figure 4.1). That is, G^* is the point on the highest indifference curve attainable within the opportunity set.

Let us now look more formally at the determination of the resource-employment optimum. First, the equation of the budget line is:

(15.1) $\quad h_L R + I = h_L R^{\dagger} + I^{\dagger}$

This equation tells us that the value of the individual's endowment, shown on the right hand side as non-labor income $I^{\dagger}$ plus the market value $h_L R^{\dagger}$ of endowed time, must equal achieved income I plus the market value $h_L R$ of the leisure that the person in effect "purchases" (by not working). Alternatively, this same relation can be formulated in terms of *labor or working hours L* rather than leisure hours R, where by definition $L \equiv R^{\dagger} - R$. Then (15.1) can be rewritten:

(15.1') $\quad I^{\dagger} + h_L L = I$

In this form, the budget equation says that the person's achieved income I is composed of endowed or property income $I^{\dagger}$ plus labor earnings $h_L L$.

Analytically, the tangency condition can be expressed as a Substitution Equivalence Equation (like that in Section 4.A) between two Marginal Rates of Substitution:

(15.2) $\quad MRS_R = MRS_E \equiv h_L$

This equation, in exactly the same form as equation (4.4), says: At a tangency optimum the *Marginal Rate of Substitution in Resource Supply* (i.e., the ratio $\left. \dfrac{\Delta I}{\Delta R} \right|_U$ representing the amount of additional income ΔI for which the individual is just *willing* to sacrifice another unit of leisure ΔR) must be equal to the *Marginal Rate of Substitution in Exchange* between income and leisure (i.e., the ratio $\left. \dfrac{\Delta I}{\Delta R} \right|_E$

Chapter 15
FACTOR
SUPPLY,
FACTOR-
MARKET
EQUILIBRIUM,
AND INCOME
DISTRIBUTION

[2]More explicitly, the slope of the budget line might be expressed as $-h_L/P_I$, where P_I is the "price" of a unit of income. But P_I is by definition unity, since income is measured in units of "numeraire" (in this case, dollars).

representing the income increment h_L which the market *permits* him to acquire in exchange for another hour of leisure). MRS_R is the absolute value of the indifference-curve slope in Figure 15.1; following the argument of Section 4.A, MRS_R can also be interpreted as the ratio of the *Marginal Utilities* of leisure and income—$MRS_R \equiv MU_R/MU_I$. And MRS_E is the absolute slope of the budget line, or in this case simply the wage rate h_L. So (15.2) can equivalently be written:[3]

$$(15.2') \qquad \frac{MU_R}{MU_I} = h_L$$

As in Chapter 4, *convexity* of the indifference curves here is justified by the observation of "diversification" between income and leisure. (People normally work somewhere between zero and 24 hours per day.) Of course, an individual very well endowed with property income (very large $I^\dagger$) might choose not to work at all. In terms of the geometry, such a "corner solution" would be preferred if the indifference curve U_0 in Figure 15.1 were steeper than the budget line EK at the endowment position E.[4]

Continuing to pursue the analogy with the consumptive optimum of Chapter 4, let us now consider what happens: (1) when endowed (non-labor) income $I^\dagger$ varies, and (2) when the hire-price (wage) h_L changes.

Variation of income is illustrated in Figure 15.2, where the budget line takes successively higher positions from $E^\circ K^\circ$ to $E'K'$ to $E''K''$. Both income I and leisure R are, it is reasonable to assume, "normal" (or "superior") goods. That is, an upward shift of the budget line due to a rise in endowed non-labor income $I^\dagger$ would be expected to lead to choice of increased consumptive income I *and* increased leisure R. The consequence is a positively-sloped *Income Expansion Path* (IEP). The individual takes only part of the benefit of any increment of endowed

---

[3]*Mathematical Footnote:* Using the method of Lagrangian multipliers, the optimization problem of the resource-owner can be expressed as:

$$\underset{(I,R,\lambda)}{\text{Max }} L = U(I,R) - \lambda(h_L R + I - h_L R^\dagger - I^\dagger)$$

Then:

$$\frac{\partial L}{\partial I} = \frac{\partial U}{\partial I} - \lambda = 0$$

$$\frac{\partial L}{\partial R} = \frac{\partial U}{\partial R} - \lambda h_L = 0$$

$$\frac{\partial L}{\partial \lambda} = -(h_L R + I - h_L R^\dagger - I^\dagger) = 0$$

Chapter 15
FACTOR
SUPPLY,
FACTOR-
MARKET
EQUILIBRIUM,
AND INCOME
DISTRIBUTION

450

Eliminating λ in the first two equations:

$$\frac{\partial U/\partial R}{\partial U/\partial I} = h_L$$

This is the form of (15.2').

The form (15.2) follows directly from the equivalences:

$$-\left.\frac{dI}{dR}\right|_U \equiv \frac{\partial U/\partial R}{\partial U/\partial I} \equiv MRS_R \quad \text{and} \quad -\left.\frac{dI}{dR}\right|_E \equiv h_L \equiv MRS_E.$$

[4]The analytical condition for this corner solution is that at $R = R^\dagger$, $MRS_R > MRS_E$.

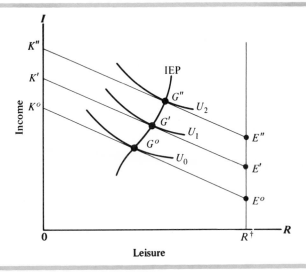

Figure 15.2

Income Expansion Path. As endowed income $I^\dagger$ rises, with the hire-price (wage) held constant, the budget line shifts upward parallel to itself. If I and R are both normal (superior) goods, the successive resource-employment optimum positions $G^\circ, G', G'', \ldots$ show that more income *and* more leisure will be chosen. Thus, the Income Expansion Path (IEP) has positive slope.

income in the form of consumption goods; the remainder of the gain is taken in the form of increased leisure.

Figure 15.3 shows the consequence of variation in h_L, the wage rate or "price of leisure." As the wage rate rises, the budget line rotates around the endowment position E so as to become increasingly steep. The *Price Expansion Path* (PEP) goes through all the tangency-optimum positions along these steepening budget lines $EK^\circ, EK', EK'', \ldots$. For relatively low wage rates the negative slope of PEP indicates that more labor L will be offered (i.e., less leisure R "purchased") as the wage rises. But for sufficiently high wage rates, it is quite possible for PEP to enter a range of positive slope (in the diagram, the range above point G') where a higher wage will lead to a *lesser* quantity of labor offered.

This seemingly puzzling situation is due to the interaction of the *income effect* and the *substitution effect* of the change in h_L. As explained in Section 4.C, when the substitution effect alone of a price change is considered (i.e., when real income is held constant) a *rise* in price must lead to a *fall* in quantity purchased. In this case, an increase in the wage rate h_L means a rise in the price of leisure and so less leisure will be "purchased." And since choice of a smaller amount of leisure means that labor supplied must be larger, the pure *substitution effect* dictates that the higher the wage h_L the greater the hours worked L.

But an increase in wage is not a pure substitution phenomenon. As the individual here is a *seller of labor*, he is effectively enriched by any increase in the wage rate. And since leisure is a normal good, the income or enrichment effect considered in isolation would lead to *greater* "purchases" of leisure as the wage

Chapter 15
FACTOR
SUPPLY,
FACTOR-
MARKET
EQUILIBRIUM,
AND INCOME
DISTRIBUTION

451

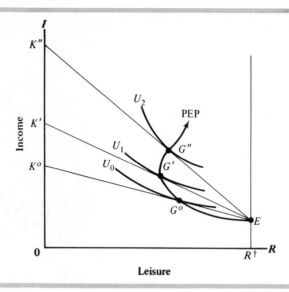

Figure 15.3

Price Expansion Path. As the wage or hire-price h_L increases, the slope of the budget line rotates clockwise around E. In an initial range where the wage rate is still low, increases in h_L will lead to choice of more income but less leisure (that is, more labor will be offered). Thus, the Price Expansion Path (PEP) has negative slope. A range *may* be reached where further increases in h_L lead to less labor being offered—the PEP curve may "bend backward," taking on a positive slope for sufficiently high h_L.

rises. Thus, the income and substitution effects of a wage change normally act in opposite directions. This contrasts with the situation in the theory of consumption, where, for a "normal" superior good, the substitution effect and the income effect of a price change are *reinforcing*.

Not only does the income effect act in opposition to the substitution effect in the labor-supply decision, but the *magnitude* of the income effect is relatively large. The reason is the contrast between "diversification in consumption" and "specialization in production." Since the consumer generally buys a wide variety of products, a rise in the price of any single commodity is not likely to impoverish him or her substantially. But in terms of factor-supply, there is one single price that will be *very* important for the resource-owner, namely, the wage of the particular type of labor service in which the individual specializes. Changes in this wage will typically represent a very considerable shift in real income.

Despite the potential importance of the income effect, *the substitution effect must nevertheless dominate the labor-supply decision at very low wage rates*. This may be seen as follows. Since the indifference-curve slope is negative at the endowment position E, there is some wage rate so low (corresponding to this slope) that it would elicit from the person a zero offer of labor.[5] If we consider wage

Chapter 15
FACTOR
SUPPLY,
FACTOR-
MARKET
EQUILIBRIUM,
AND INCOME
DISTRIBUTION

[5]As would, of course, any still lower wage.

rates only slightly above this, any income or enrichment effect must be very small. The magnitude of enrichment due to a wage increase is on the order of $L(\Delta h_L)$, where Δh_L is the wage increment and L is the hours worked. If L is close to zero hours, the person cannot be *substantially* enriched by a wage-rate change. It is only in the upper regions of the PEP curve that enough hours are worked to make the enrichment $L(\Delta h_L)$ substantial, in which case it might overcome the substitution effect so as to cause the PEP curve to enter a range of reversed slope as shown in Figure 15.3.

CONCLUSION: In the resource-employment decision, the income and substitution effects of changes in hire-price h_L normally work in opposite
directions. The substitution effect must dominate (more employment
will be chosen as h_L rises) at low hire-prices; the income effect may
dominate, however, for sufficiently high h_L.

EXAMPLE 15.1
RETIREMENT
DECISIONS

In recent years, the labor force participation of the elderly has declined markedly. Of white males aged 65 and over, 46.5% participated in the labor force in 1948 but only 22.5% in 1974. For non-white males, the decline was from 50.3% to 21.7%.[6] A study by Michael J. Boskin[7] sought to explain this development by evaluating a number of the forces bearing upon the decisions of white married males who were aged 61–65 in 1968 whether or not to retire.

The statistical evidence for the period 1968–1972 indicated that, other things equal, an increase of $1000 in annual income from assets (equivalent to an upward shift of the endowment point E in Figure 15.2) *increased* the probability of retirement by 15%. As anticipated, for the observed sample leisure turned out to be a normal (superior) good. An increase of $1000 in net earnings (equivalent to a clockwise rotation of the budget line in Figure 15.3) *reduced* the probability of retirement by about 60%. Thus, in these data it appears that the substitution effect of wage increases heavily outweighed the income effect.

Boskin was particularly concerned to investigate the effect of social-security benefits upon retirement decisions. He found that a $1000 increase in these benefits more than doubled the probability of retirement. Since increased social-security payments act like increased income from assets to shift the endowment point E upward as in Figure 15.2, the question is why the social-security effect is so much bigger. There are a number of possible explanations, some of the more important of which are connected with the fact that (subject to a complicated statutory formula) *receiving social-security payments limits the income that an individual is legally permitted to receive from working*. During the period in question, any income from employment earned by social-security recipients fell into four ranges: (1) a

[6]From *Manpower Report of the President, 1975.*

[7]Michael J. Boskin, "Social Security and Retirement Decisions," *Economic Inquiry*, v. 15 (Jan. 1977).

certain exempt level of working income that the recipient could retain without penalty; (2) above the exemption, a certain range where earned income was in effect taxed 50% (by a corresponding reduction in social-security benefits); (3) above the 50% bracket, another bracket where earned income was taxed 100%; (4) and above the 100% bracket, a final range where income earned could again be fully retained (since no social-security benefits remain). The key point is that an increase in social-security benefits, if not linked to an increase in the exemption level, would for many people be largely taxed away *unless* they chose to retire (or at any rate, chose to work considerably less than before). Since receipt of increased social-security benefits depended heavily upon the individual's not working, such an increase had a powerful tendency to promote retirement.

15.B

AN APPLICATION: THE "NEGATIVE INCOME TAX" PROPOSAL

Existing relief or "welfare" arrangements for support of the unemployed have a strongly adverse effect upon the incentive to work. The Negative Income Tax proposal is an attempt to overcome this adverse effect.

With some oversimplification, the current welfare-relief arrangement may be pictured as in Figure 15.4. The individual here is assumed to have no property income, and so the endowment position E lies along the horizontal axis at $R = R^\dagger$ (24 hours of leisure per day). The pre-tax wage rate at which the person could work is reflected in the slope of the solid budget line EK; in the absence of taxes or a welfare system, the tangency optimum would lie along EK. But in actuality income and social security taxes would have to be paid on labor earnings, so that the effective or post-tax budget line is the dashed EK'.[8] Along EK', the employment optimum is indicated by the tangency with indifference curve U_0 at G^*.

Now suppose that the welfare system provides a level of *minimal income maintenance* represented by the horizontal line MM'. This means that, should earnings from employment be less than the amount $OM = EM'$, they will be supplemented to bring income I up to that level. Persons who attain G^* by working would therefore receive a cash payment bringing them up to position G' on MM'. But if leisure is always a good, the position M' on indifference curve U_2, attainable without working at all, is clearly preferred to G' on indifference curve U_1. Subject to the proviso that income and leisure are both *goods* (preference di-

Chapter 15
FACTOR
SUPPLY,
FACTOR-
MARKET
EQUILIBRIUM,
AND INCOME
DISTRIBUTION

454

[8]The diagram assumes that taxes on income are a simple proportion of earnings. Ideally, we should allow for exemptions, progressivity, and other complex features of the tax structure. But doing so is not essential for our purposes.

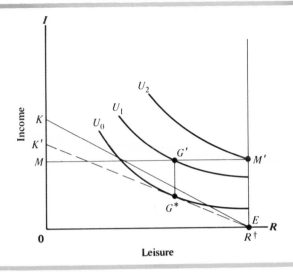

Figure 15.4

Employment versus Welfare, I. For a person with endowment E, initial non-labor income $I^\dagger$ is zero. In the absence of taxes, EK would be the budget line. Assuming a simple proportional income tax, the effective after-tax (dashed) budget line EK' leads to a resource-employment optimum at G^*. Welfare arrangements guaranteeing income M would provide a cash supplement so as to bring the individual up from G^* to G'. But if leisure is always a good, the person will prefer the point M' where income M is received without any work at all.

rections are north and east), no one will work at all if the employment optimum G^* along EK' lies below MM'.[9]

Furthermore, even for some individuals whose employment optimum G^* would otherwise lie *well above* MM', the no-work position M' available under welfare may still be preferable. In Figure 15.5 indifference curve U_1 through M' represents a higher level of satisfaction than can be achieved at the employment optimum G^*. Even though G^* would generate more spendable income I than the amount received under the dole, the increased leisure at point M' may be valued more highly by the individual.

The Negative Income Tax (NIT), as an alternative to the existing welfare system, is pictured in Figure 15.6. We see once again the pre-tax (solid) budget line EK and the after-tax (dashed) budget line EK' of the previous diagram, with an employment optimum G^* that is inferior (in the eyes of the individual) to the unemployment position at M' attainable under the welfare system. The NIT alternative is based upon the following considerations: (1) The income maintenance level MM' is still guaranteed, whether or not the individual works. (2) A

Chapter 15
FACTOR
SUPPLY,
FACTOR-
MARKET
EQUILIBRIUM,
AND INCOME
DISTRIBUTION

[9]Welfare administrators sometimes attempt to require that those capable of working do so. But, *de facto*, effective control is very limited. An unwilling worker can easily arrange to be discharged by his employer.

Figure 15.5

Employment versus Welfare, II. Here, in the absence of welfare-relief the individual would attain position G^* along his after-tax budget line EK', earning more than the guaranteed welfare level M. Nevertheless, the person's tastes are such that position M' (yielding income M without working) would be chosen under a welfare system in preference to G^*.

"breakeven level" of income is established, represented by the horizontal line BB' in the diagram, that is *higher* than MM'. (3) Above the breakeven level, the individual is a payer of (positive) taxes; below, the individual is a recipient of (negative) taxes.

The effect is to make a different NIT budget line, represented in Figure 15.6 by the dotted line $M'K''$, relevant for the individual's employment decision. $M'K''$ incorporates the effect of positive or negative taxes. It intersects the horizontal breakeven line BB' at the point B'' which also lies on the pre-tax (solid) budget line EK. A person who supplied so much labor as to exactly attain the position B'' would neither pay taxes nor receive any supplementary income. Beyond B'', the person would be a net payer of taxes,[10] but short of B'' would be a net recipient of income supplement.[11] In the case illustrated in the diagram, the individual chooses the position G^{**}, offering $L = R^\dagger - R'$ hours of labor. Pre-tax earnings are $R'H$ in the diagram, and the income supplement is HG^{**}. The person is working (at least some hours) under the NIT, and there is to that extent a social gain over the welfare system that led him or her to prefer total unemployment.

Defenders of NIT point to the psychologically corrosive effect of welfare-induced unemployment upon the worker's sense of independence and self-esteem.

Chapter 15
FACTOR
SUPPLY,
FACTOR-
MARKET
EQUILIBRIUM,
AND INCOME
DISTRIBUTION

456

[10]That is, the pre-tax budget line EK is *higher* than the NIT budget line $M'K''$ in this range.
[11]That is, in this range EK is lower than $M'K''$.

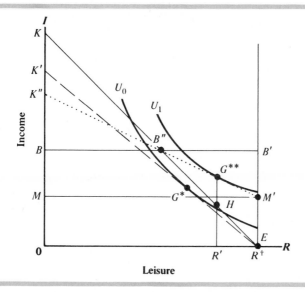

Figure 15.6

NIT versus Welfare, I. The Negative Income Tax (NIT), as an alternative to welfare, again guarantees an income level M. There is a breakeven level of income, however, such that earned incomes below the line BB' receive supplementation (negative taxation) while those above BB' pay positive taxes. If EK (solid) is the pre-tax budget line, and EK' (dashed) the usual after-tax budget line, under NIT the effective after-tax budget line becomes $M'K''$ (dotted). Here NIT has a "favorable" effect: an individual who would have chosen G^* in the absence of either welfare or NIT, and who would have shifted to M' (choosing complete unemployment) under welfare, is now motivated to choose G^{**}—he or she is induced not to totally abandon employment.

Opponents, on the other hand, argue that the NIT may itself constitute a source of psychological corrosion for a *much larger* number of workers who will now be receiving "unearned" income supplements from government, even though remaining (to some extent, at any rate) employed. Furthermore, the higher *marginal* tax rate under NIT (flatter slope of $M'K''$ as compared with EK' in Figure 15.6) is likely to induce working individuals to choose a lesser *degree* of employment.

    Both of these adverse effects are illustrated in Figure 15.7. This diagram again compares the welfare after-tax budget line EK' (dashed) with the NIT after-tax budget line $M'K''$ (dotted). (The *pre-tax* budget line EK of the previous diagram is not needed here, and so has been omitted.) But the individual's preferences and opportunities are now such that under the welfare system the preferred position along EK' is at G^* on indifference curve U_0; he or she does not accept relief, but on the contrary shows relatively great willingness to work. Along $M'K''$, however, the preferred position is G^{**} on indifference curve U_1. As is evident, under NIT the individual will work far fewer hours, and furthermore has been induced to abandon a position of sturdy tax-paying independence at G^* in favor of a socially dependent role below the breakeven income level BB'.

Chapter 15
FACTOR
SUPPLY,
FACTOR-
MARKET
EQUILIBRIUM,
AND INCOME
DISTRIBUTION

457

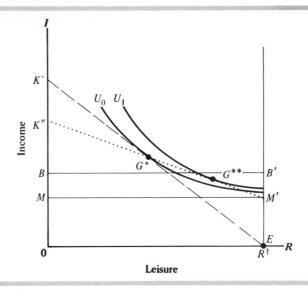

Figure 15.7

NIT versus Welfare, II. In contrast with the previous diagram, this illustrates that an individual under the welfare system who would have chosen G^* along EK', in preference to unemployment at M', may be induced under NIT to work considerably less (at position G^{**}). Further, the individual shifts from being a positive taxpayer at G^* to becoming a social dependent (recipient of negative taxes) at G^{**}.

It is even possible that an individual who would have chosen employment under the welfare-relief system could turn to unemployment under the NIT. Such a situation is illustrated in Figure 15.8. The analysis (showing that G^* along EK' would have been preferred to the welfare-unemployment position M', but that unemployment at M' is superior to any other attainable position along the NIT budget line $M'K''$) is left to the student as an exercise.

Whether the NIT proposal is on balance a desirable one depends, at least in part, upon the frequency with which the various types of situations described in these diagrams will be encountered. A number of experiments have been conducted to cast light upon this question.

EXAMPLE 15.2
NEGATIVE
INCOME TAX
EXPERIMENT

The Federal Office of Economic Opportunity initiated an extensive experiment in 1967 aimed at estimating the effect of the Negative Income Tax (NIT) upon work incentives. Subject families in four cities in New Jersey and Pennsylvania were assigned to one of eight experimental NIT programs or to a control group.

One of the important considerations in evaluating the statistical results was that acceptance of assignment to an NIT program was voluntary; a fam-

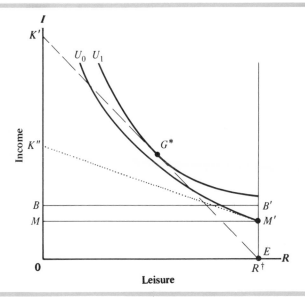

Figure 15.8

NIT versus Welfare, III. This illustrates an even more extreme possible adverse result of NIT. An individual who would have worked rather than remain unemployed under welfare (choosing G^* along budget line EK' over M') now finds unemployment at M' preferable along the NIT budget line $M'K''$.

ily could not be compelled to participate. A family that refused participation remained subject to ordinary taxation and also eligible for welfare-relief. (Note that the family in Figure 15.8 would have chosen *not* to participate.) Had the program been introduced nationally, however, it would presumably have entirely replaced ordinary taxation and relief. As would be expected, participation in the program tended to increase the *higher* the guaranteed income offered under NIT and the *lower* the tax rate. (In our diagrams, the higher the point M' and the steeper the slope of the line $M'K''$.)

A study by John F. Cogan[12] found, among those families choosing to participate, a rather substantial work disincentive effect: an average reduction of 5–7 labor hours per week. The reduced level of employment would also be associated with a heavy increase in required transfer payments under NIT. Thus, this experiment suggests that the possible favorable effects of NIT upon employment incentives and taxpayer burdens (as in Figure 15.6) may be outweighed by the negative possibilities (pictured in Figures 15.7 and 15.8).

[12]John F. Cogan, *Negative Income Taxation and Labor Supply: New Evidence from the New Jersey–Pennsylvania Experiment*, The Rand Corp., R–2155–HEW (Feb. 1978).

RESOURCE SUPPLY TO THE MARKET,
AND FACTOR-MARKET EQUILIBRIUM

The data represented by a person's Price Expansion Path PEP of Figure 15.3 could be plotted in a separate diagram on R, h_L axes as his or her "demand curve for leisure R." It is more usual, however, to present the data on L, h_L axes as the individual's *supply curve for labor L* (where by definition $L \equiv R^{\dagger} - R$ as before).

Figure 15.9 shows such an individual supply curve s_L. The hire-prices h_L^o, h_L', and h_L'' in Figure 15.9 correspond respectively to the slopes of the budget lines EK^o, EK', and EK'' in Figure 15.3. The lower range in which the PEP curve of the earlier diagram is moving westward corresponds to the range of prices below h_L in which the supply curve s_L has normal positive slope—where an increased wage elicits increased offers of labor hours. Above this range, however, the PEP curve shown in Figure 15.3 is moving eastward. This means that, once wage rates are above h_L', a further wage augmentation will lead to a decreased labor offer; should that occur, the labor-supply curve is said to be "backward-bending" in the range above h_L'. Recall from the discussion of Figure 15.3, however, that while at low wage rates the PEP curve *must* move westward (the substitution effect outweighs the income effect), it may or may not be the case that PEP eventually curves back eastward (the income effect may or may not ever outweigh the substitution effect). Correspondingly, a "backward-bending" supply curve as in Figure 15.9 is a strong possibility, but not a necessity.

Figure 15.9

Backward-Bending Supply Curve of Labor. The supply curve of labor shown here, s_L, has normal positive slope for wage rates up to h_L but "bends backward" above that wage.

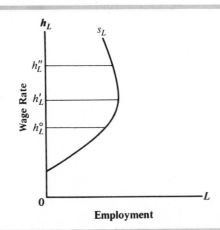

Chapter 15
FACTOR
SUPPLY,
FACTOR-
MARKET
EQUILIBRIUM,
AND INCOME
DISTRIBUTION

460

A study by R. C. Battalio and J. H. Kagel[13] examined the labor-supply behavior of rats under simulated working conditions. The rats had to press a lever in order to obtain a food reward (sucrose solution). The "wage" was varied by increasing the number of presses required to obtain a fixed quantity of reward.

EXAMPLE 15.3
ANIMAL LABOR
SUPPLY

The rats' responses typically generated a backward-bending supply curve (as in Figure 15.9). In one experiment with 16% sucrose solution as reward, the increasing-supply range applied as the wage rose from a low of one reward per 320 presses up to a high of one reward per 20 presses. A further wage increase, however, requiring only 10 presses per reward, brought about reduced supply. In another experiment, with a richer reward (64% glucose solution), the backward-bending range set in earlier (at 20 presses per reward).

[13]R. C. Battalio and John H. Kagel, "Labor Supply Behavior of Animal Workers: Towards an Experimental Analysis," in V. L. Smith, ed., *Research in Experimental Economics*, v. 1 (JAI Press, Inc., 1979).

When individual supply curves are aggregated (summed horizontally), the overall factor-market supply curve S_L is obtained as in Figure 15.10. The aggregate S_L is likely to have a normal positive slope even if some of the component individual supply curves have backward-bending ranges, since the various individuals' h'_L points as in Figure 15.9 will differ. But it is possible that even the aggregate supply curve may be found to be backward-bending at high wage rates.

In considering the possibility of backward-bending supply, one important qualification must be kept in mind. While supply of labor *to the market as a whole* (as against the alternative of unemployment or leisure) may quite easily be backward-bending above a certain wage level, supply of labor *to a limited sector or a particular type of employment* is most unlikely to be backward-bending. The reason is that there are many more alternatives. As the wage rises in a particular sector, individuals are attracted not only from leisure but from employment in any of a larger number of other areas or activities. Thus, the supply of labor to a limited sector is always *much more elastic* than the supply of labor as a whole.

From 1953 to 1964 the supply of agricultural workers in the United States was supplemented by foreign contract workers primarily from Mexico, who were known as "braceros." When domestic political pressures arose to abolish the program allowing this importation, employers of braceros contended that it would not be possible to find American workers willing to do the "stoop labor" in the fields. Presumably, the contention was that higher wages would make Americans no more and perhaps even less willing to provide the required amounts of this form of labor (the supply curve of

EXAMPLE 15.4
BRACEROS AND
THE SUPPLY OF
"STOOP LABOR"

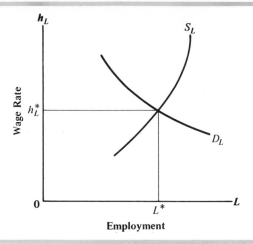

Figure 15.10

Equilibrium in the Factor Market. The intersection of the aggregate demand curve for labor D_L and the aggregate supply curve of labor S_L determines the equilibrium wage rate h_L^* and the level of market employment L^*.

American "stoop labor" was supposedly vertical or even backward-bending).

Despite these arguments, the bracero program was in fact terminated in 1965. Growers did, as it turned out, find it possible to attract American labor—though at a much higher wage. A study by Donald E. Wise[14] indicated that, for two California crops (winter melons and strawberries), the labor-supply elasticity was quite high: in the range from 2.7 to 3.4. For California winter melons, the results of abolition of the bracero program included: a 67% increase in wage rate, a 262% increase in employment of American workers (but a 22% reduction in *total* employment, since braceros were no longer used), and a 23% reduction of output.

[14]Donald E. Wise, "The Effect of the Bracero on Agricultural Production in California," *Economic Inquiry*, v. 12 (Dec. 1974).

Market equilibrium under conditions of competition is of course determined by the intersection (as shown in Figure 15.10) of the aggregate supply curve just discussed and the aggregate demand curve derived in the previous chapter. Changes in equilibrium price and quantity, as always, come about as a result of shifts in supply or demand functions, or both.

In terms of the discussion of determinants of factor demand in Section 14.C, we know that the forces that may shift *demand* functions for factors include:

1. *Technological change:* Technical progress tends to shift Marginal Product (*mp*) upward, and hence to raise the curve of $mrp \equiv MR(mp)$ that determines firms' demand for factors.[15]

2. *Demand for final products:* Similarly, an increase in the demand for some product, leading to a rise in its price and associated Marginal Revenue, raises the demand for any factor used in its production.

3. *Supply of cooperating or competing factors:* As the Marginal Products of different factors are interrelated (as discussed in Section 14.B), the demand for any one will be affected by changes in the availability of other factors that can complement it or substitute for it. In particular, an increase in the *supply* of one of a pair of complementary factors will raise the *demand* for the other.

Some of the important influences operating to shift *factor supply* functions are:

1. *Wealth:* Higher endowed wealth increases resource-owners' ability to "purchase" *reservation uses* of owned factors, and hence tends to diminish the supply offered on the market.

2. *Social trends and legal context:* Social and legal forces may at times encourage, at other times discourage, market availability of factors. In some societies women may be secluded from employment except for domestic activity. In other communities there have been severe restrictions upon the permitted market uses of land or other resources.

3. *Investment and accumulation:* In recent centuries in the Western world, stocks of produced resources ("capital goods") have accumulated enormously over time. Each generation has so arranged its affairs as to leave its successor generation better endowed with these man-made resources. (The process of intertemporal choice leading to this result will be considered in Chapter 16.)

4. *Demography:* The growth of the human stock has paralleled the accumulation of goods over time. (Of course, human beings are also a kind of "produced resource," though generated in response to somewhat different motivations.) The aggregate size of the human population and its detailed age-sex composition obviously affect the supply of labor available to the market.

---

[15]It is possible (though perhaps not very likely) for technical progress to have a favorable effect on Average Product *ap* while reducing Marginal Product *mp* (for some or all factors) in the relevant range. Since factor demand is related to the *Marginal* Product, such a change would, at least in the neighborhood of the previous equilibrium, tend to shift the factor demand curve *downward*.

Chapter 15
FACTOR
SUPPLY,
FACTOR-
MARKET
EQUILIBRIUM,
AND INCOME
DISTRIBUTION

463

EXAMPLE 15.5
THE BLACK
DEATH[16]
The Black Death (1348–50) is generally believed to have wiped out between a quarter and a third of the population of Western Europe. Later recurrences of plague in 1360–61, 1369, and 1374 may each have killed perhaps 5% of the populations remaining. There was a drastic reduction in labor supply, with an immediate effect on wages: "The increase due to the plague is 32% for the threshing of wheat, 38% for barley, 111% for oats in the eastern counties. In the middle counties the percentages of rise are 40, 69, 111; in the south, 33, 38, 75; in the west, 26, 41, 44; in the north, 32, 43, and 100."[17]

The English government responded to this shock with what we would now call a "wage freeze," eventually formalized as the Statute of Laborers (1351). This decree not only froze wages but forbade idleness and required reasonable prices for necessities. Another ordinance in the same year prohibited emigration. Efforts were made for some years to enforce these regulations, though a similar Statute of Laborers in France seems to have been largely a dead letter.

Despite governmental interventions and the inherent rigidities of the feudal-manorial system, the economic logic of the situation (the increased scarcity of labor relative to other resources and, in particular, relative to land) dictated a rise in wages and in per-capita incomes of the laboring classes. This is evidenced by innumerable reports of individuals stepping up to fill vacant higher places in the manorial economy, by records of remissions and recontracts of feudal dues owed the lords, as well as by loud complaints against unwontedly lavish living by the lower orders. (For example, a Statute of Dress of 1363 forbade the lower classes to imitate upper-class attire.)

COMMENT: The feudal system was about as far removed from the economists' competitive model as can be imagined. Feudal economic relationships are in principle dictated solely by custom and status. Nevertheless, competitive forces could not be denied. The system could not withstand the pressure of such a drastic and sudden change in factor availabilities as represented by the Black Death; hence the complaints about flight of labor, vagrancy, "wasting," etc., and calls upon the government to cancel the market concessions granted to the upstart tenants. A concerted governmental attempt early in the reign of Richard II to reverse the clock and enforce feudal dues and status relationships led to the Peasants' Revolt of 1381, which came within a hair of overturning the monarchy. Among the peasants' demands were the abolition of serfdom, of feudal dues and services, of governmental monopolies, and of restrictions on buying and selling. In short, the peasants anticipated Adam Smith; they wanted *laissez faire* so that market-place revisions of economic status could proceed in their favor.

[16]Discussion based upon J. Hirshleifer, "Disaster and Recovery: The Black Death in Western Europe," The Rand Corporation Memorandum RM–4700–TAB (Feb. 1966).

[17]H. Robbins, "A Comparison of the Effects of the Black Death on the Economic Organization of France and England," *Journal of Political Economy*, v. 36 (Aug. 1928), p. 463.

Monopoly on the *demand* side of factor markets—monopsony—was studied in Section 14.D. Monopoly on the *supply* side of the factor market is the subject here.

As every firm's product is in some respects unique, every firm has *some* degree of monopoly power on the supply side of the product market. Similarly for resources: every resource has some degree of uniqueness and therefore every resource-owner has *some* monopoly power on the supply side of the factor market. But if a sufficient range of close substitutes is available, the competitive model, which postulates price-taking behavior of market participants, will nevertheless be a satisfactory approximation of reality. Ownership of resources is, in actuality, very widely diffused in modern economies of the Western world. Hence *monopoly* power over resource supply is likely to be significant only in very unusual cases. (Motion picture stars and athletic champions are possible examples.) On the other hand, more or less successful *cartels* of resource-suppliers (e.g., trade unions) are very common.

The formal solution for the resource-monopolist is very simple in the special case where the owner has no reservation uses for the factor. Then the monopolist will merely seek to maximize "Total Revenue" or, we shall say, *Total Factor Income (TFI)*. TFI is equal to the factor earnings $h_L L$ from the owner's given quantum $R^\dagger$ of resources. This maximization *may* dictate holding some units of the resource off the market, not for reservation uses (as, by assumption, there are none) but simply in the interests of obtaining a higher price through monopoly power. Figure 15.11 illustrates such a situation, in terms of a "total" function in the upper panel, and "average-marginal" functions in the lower. The monopolist's earnings-maximizing employment L^* occurs at the maximum of the *TFI* curve in the upper panel; the lower panel shows, equivalently, how L^* is determined at the point where *Marginal Factor Income* $MFI \equiv \Delta I/\Delta L$ falls to zero. The wage set by the monopolist will be h_L^*, the height of the factor demand curve D_L at $L = L^*$; this equals the slope of the dotted line in the upper panel. Since $h_L \equiv TFI/L$, the factor demand curve can be identified with the *Average Factor Income* function *(AFI)*.

If, on the other hand, the curve of Total Factor Income *TFI* is rising throughout the relevant range where $L \leq R^\dagger$ (equivalent to a factor demand curve that is *elastic* throughout), the resource-monopolist without reservation uses will *not* find it advantageous to hold any units off the market. In that case *MFI* remains greater than zero at $L = R^\dagger$, where all of the resource available is employed.

If there are *reservation* uses of the factor, however, the monopolist would

*15.D.1
*Optimum of
the Monopolist
Resource-Owner*

Chapter 15
FACTOR
SUPPLY,
FACTOR-
MARKET
EQUILIBRIUM,
AND INCOME
DISTRIBUTION

---

* The section between the asterisk and the symbol ■ may contain somewhat more difficult or advanced material.

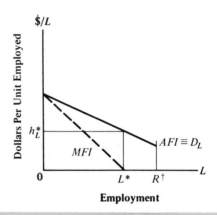

Figure 15.11

Factor Monopoly—No Reservation Uses. In the upper panel, the curve of Total Factor Income *TFI* represents total earnings of a monopolist seller of a resource service. In the lower panel, the corresponding curve of Average Factor Income *AFI* is also the market demand curve D_L for the factor. The dashed line is the associated Marginal Factor Income *MFI*. At employment *L**, *TFI* is at its peak while *MFI* is zero. *L** will be the preferred employment offer of a factor monopolist with no alternative uses of the resource.

Chapter 15
FACTOR
SUPPLY,
FACTOR-
MARKET
EQUILIBRIUM,
AND INCOME
DISTRIBUTION

466

have to balance these uses against increased factor earnings in the market. The decision may be illustrated in terms of the preference diagram of Figure 15.12. This differs from Figure 15.1 in that the shaded opportunity set is now bounded by a concave curve rather than a straight line. The concave "budget curve" represents the fact that the wage h_L is *not* constant, but rather is a decreasing function of employment $L \equiv R^\dagger - R$. The monopolist's optimum position is of course at the indifference-curve tangency *G**; the reservation quantity is *R**, and the corresponding employment quantity is *L**.

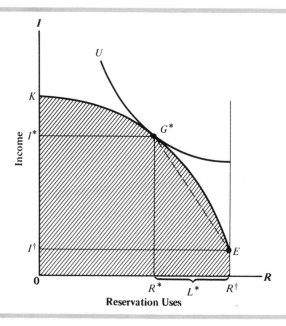

Figure 15.12

Factor Monopolist with Reservation Uses, I. On R,I axes a factor monopolist will have a "budget curve" EK bounding the shaded market opportunity set. If there are alternative uses for the resource, the monopolist's preferences can be expressed by indifference curves of standard shape. In the diagram, the monopoly optimum is at G^*, the tangency of EK with the highest attainable indifference curve U. Retained reservation uses are R^*; offered employment is $L^* \equiv R^\dagger - R^*$. The slope of the dashed line EG^* represents the market wage for the offered level of employment. EK can also be regarded as a Total Factor Income curve as L increases to the left, the factor income being the *excess* of the income I attained along EK over the endowed income $I^\dagger$.

This solution is translated to a price-quantity diagram on L, h_L axes in Figure 15.13. The Marginal Factor Income $MFI \equiv \Delta I/\Delta L$ for any employment level L corresponds to the absolute slope $-\Delta I/\Delta R$ (since $\Delta L = -\Delta R$) of the concave budget curve in Figure 15.12. This is the "Marginal Revenue" in income units of sacrificing an hour of leisure. What corresponds to "Marginal Cost" for the factor-monopolist is the *marginal value of the reservation uses*, which is nothing but the Marginal Rate of Substitution MRS_R between income and the reservation uses of the resource, as analyzed in Section 15.A. As indicated there, MRS_R corresponds to the absolute indiffence-curve slope $\left.\dfrac{\Delta I}{\Delta R}\right|_U$. The rising curve MRS_R in Figure 15.13 shows increasing "Marginal Cost" of accepting income in place of leisure. So the tangency at G^* in Figure 15.12 (equality of the budget-curve slope and indifference-curve slope) corresponds to the intersection of MFI and MRS_R in Figure 15.13. The monopoly optimum wage h_L^* in Figure 15.13, corresponding to the Average Factor Income $AFI \equiv (I^* - I^\dagger)/L^*$, is shown by the absolute slope of the dashed EG^* in Figure 15.12.

Chapter 15
FACTOR
SUPPLY,
FACTOR-
MARKET
EQUILIBRIUM,
AND INCOME
DISTRIBUTION

467

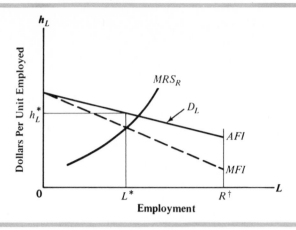

Figure 15.13

Factor Monopolist with Reservation Uses, II. The curves of Average Factor Income *AFI* (the demand curve D_L for the factor) and of Marginal Factor Income *MFI* are derived from the budget curve *EK* o)f the previous diagram. The curve MRS_R, representing the Marginal Rate of Substitution in Resource Supply, plays the role of Marginal Cost. The intersection of *MFI* and MRS_R determines the factor monopolist's optimum level of employment, with h_L^* the associated price along the demand curve.

CONCLUSION: The monopolist supplier of a resource, like the monopolist supplier of a product, will set Marginal Revenue equal to Marginal Cost. In the factor market, Marginal Revenue corresponds to Marginal Factor Income *MFI*. Marginal Cost corresponds to MRS_R, the owner's Marginal Rate of Substitution between income and reservation uses of the resource. If there are no reservation uses, MRS_R will be everywhere zero. Even so, the monopolist factor-supplier may still hold some units of the factor off the market, if *MFI* falls to zero before the marketed quantity exhausts the owned supply. ∎

15.D.2

Resource Cartels

Chapter 15
FACTOR
SUPPLY,
FACTOR-
MARKET
EQUILIBRIUM,
AND INCOME
DISTRIBUTION

468

Trade unions of employees are often accused of being labor monopolies. Technically, they are *cartels*, associations or coalitions of resource-suppliers. Their members have little or no monopoly power individually, but as a collective group they may be able to influence the ruling price-quantity outcome of the market process.

As was explained in Section 11.F, cartels have an Achilles heel. Given that the other members are loyally abiding by the agreement, it pays any single member to "chisel" by undercutting the standard terms. All cartels therefore require enforcement devices, most commonly achieved through use of government power. In the case of trade unions in the United States, an election is normally held under the terms of the National Labor Relations Act to determine "collective-bargaining representation." Whichever union wins a majority of the vote cast in the final round becomes the exclusive bargaining agent for *all* workers in the collective-bargaining unit.[18] ("No union" is also one of the options.) When a collective-bargaining agent has been officially certified, individual bargaining is prohibited—thus ruling out, or at any rate minimizing, the possibility of the worker "chiselling" by accepting less than the standard pay for the given work or offering more work at the standard pay.

EXAMPLE 15.6
UNIONIZATION
AND HOTEL
WORKERS[19]

Before 1929, there was very little unionization of hotel workers. In the two decades after 1929, the Hotel and Restaurant Employees and Bartenders International Union was able to organize in a number of cities. As may be seen in the following table, wage rates rose somewhat faster in the unionized cities.

Average Hourly Earnings of Hotel Employees (1929 = 100)

	1929	1935	1939	1948
Weighted mean index, 19 union cities[a]	100	81	88.4	188
Weighted mean index, 12 non-union cities[b]	100	76	80	168
Ratio (union/non-union)	1.0	1.06	1.10	1.12

Source: Joseph Scherer, "Collective Bargaining in Service Industries: A Study of the Year-Round Hotels," Ph.D. dissertation, University of Chicago, 1951.

[a]More than 35% of hotel workers organized in 1948.

[b]Less than 10% of hotel workers organized in 1948.

After adjustment of the data to eliminate regional wage effects (since unionized cities tended to be northern and non-unionized cities southern), the ratio of union to non-union wage indexes was found to be 1.06. That is, wages in the union cities grew about 6% more, in the course of twenty years, as compared with non-union cities.

Note, however, that the union versus non-union differential is small in comparison with the overall wage swings over the twenty years covered by the table.

[19]Discussion based on H. Gregg Lewis, *Unionism and Relative Wages in the United States* (Chicago: University of Chicago Press, 1963), p. 58.

Since different interests must be reconciled in collective decisions, the determination of the market policy of any cartel creates internal political conflict. In the case of trade unions, elaborate internal machinery often exists to solve this "problem of collective action."[20]

But trade unions are by no means the only cartels effective in resource supply. Professional associations, such as the American Medical Association (see

Chapter 15
FACTOR
SUPPLY,
FACTOR-
MARKET
EQUILIBRIUM,
AND INCOME
DISTRIBUTION

[18]The administrative-legal process that determines just what is the appropriate "bargaining unit" may be quite crucial for the final outcome of the election.

[20]The topic of "collective action" will be considered more fully in Chapter 18.

Example 15.9, "Returns to Medical Education," below) are frequently charged with cartel-like behavior. In general, loosely organized resource-supply cartels find it easier to achieve their ends by *restricting entry to the trade* than by trying to gain agreement on prices. Entry is relatively visible, where price-chiselling may be secret. A sufficiently tight lid on supply, through control of entry, will inevitably force up the market price even though market behavior remains competitive for those actually in the trade. In a supply-demand equilibrium like that of Figure 15.10, entry control may have shifted the supply curve S_L so far to the left as (essentially) to achieve a monopoly-like price-quantity outcome.

EXAMPLE 15.7
BARBERS

In 1962, a study by Simon Rottenberg[21] showed that 47 of the old 48 states had laws licensing barbers. The main impetus for the legislation was lobbying by barbering associations. Educational requirements for securing a barber's license are an important barrier to entry. The Illinois law, for example, requires (among other things) 1872 study hours in a recognized barber school as well as passing an examination covering topics related to the theory and practice of barber science and art. These include anatomy and physiology, hygiene and sanitation, barber history and law, pharmacology, electricity and light, and even haircutting, shaving, etc. Apprenticeship rules may be an even more important restriction on entry: A minimum apprenticeship of 2¼ years must be served, and no shop may employ more than one apprentice for each registered barber. The barber associations also oppose licensing reciprocity among states (for then students would acquire licenses in the less restrictive jurisdictions).

While the barbering associations have also pressed for minimum price-fixing, only fourteen states had such laws.

COMMENT: Non-legal methods were at one time a significant deterrent to price "chisellers." A disproportionately large number of unexplained fires used to occur, from time to time, on the premises of price-cutting barbers.

[21]Simon Rottenberg, "The Economics of Occupational Licensing," in H. Gregg Lewis *et al.*, *Aspects of Labor Economics* (Princeton, N.J.: Princeton University Press, 1962).

One notable exception to tight control over occupational entry is the legal profession. A very large increase in the capacity of law schools and in their throughput of students into the profession has occurred in the United States recently, without apparent objection on the part of those in the trade. This exception is, however, understandable and in a sense "proves the rule." Each additional barber or doctor or accountant competes with his fellows and takes business away from them. But the legal process is such that each additional practitioner, by adding to the number of lawsuits, presentments, hearings, trials, pleadings, appeals, writs, demurrers, briefs, rebuttals, rejoinders, etc., makes *more* business for his colleagues.[22]

Of course, cartels may be effective over non-labor resources as well.

Chapter 15
FACTOR
SUPPLY,
FACTOR-
MARKET
EQUILIBRIUM,
AND INCOME
DISTRIBUTION

[22]Old folk saying: "When will a lawyer be poor? When he's the only lawyer in town."

EXAMPLE 15.8
TOBACCO
ALLOTMENTS

Under the market order[23] regulating the supply of tobacco, certain specific acres of farmland carry "allotments" permitting tobacco to be grown thereon. Anyone may grow tobacco, but must compete with all other growers to buy or rent some "allotted" acres on which to do so. Thus, the government-sponsored cartel works in behalf of owners of the resource of "allotted" land, not in behalf of growers as such. One study has estimated the *premium* paid by growers for land with an allotment (over rental paid for equivalent land without allotment) as between $962 and $2500 per acre (for land suitable for growing flue-cured tobacco in North Carolina and Virginia counties in the period 1954–57).[24] A later study[25] estimated that the premium had risen to $3281 per acre in 1962 for allotted land in eastern North Carolina.

[23]See also Example 11.5, "Agricultural Marketing Orders."

[24]F. H. Maier, J. L. Hedrick, and W. L. Givson, Jr., "The Sale Value of Flue-Cured Tobacco Allotments," Agricultural Experiment Station, Virginia Polytechnic Institute, Technical Bulletin No. 148 (April 1960), p. 40.

[25]James A. Seagraves, "Capitalized Values of Tobacco Allotments and the Rate of Return to Allotment Owners," *American Journal of Agricultural Economics*, v. 51 (May 1969).

15.E

THE "FUNCTIONAL" DISTRIBUTION OF INCOME

15.E.1
The Problem of Classification

Factors of production have traditionally been classified under the headings of *labor*, *land*, and *capital*. These were thought to correspond to three categories of "functional" factor returns, namely: *wages* to labor, *rent* to land, and *interest* to capital. In the emerging period of economic thought, most particularly in England in the late eighteenth and early nineteenth centuries, this categorization had political and sociological relevance. The three factor groupings corresponded to major social classes of the time. Land was mainly owned by the aristocracy, capital (material assets other than land) by the rising bourgeoisie, while the working classes could be regarded as owning their labor power. Even sociologically speaking, this classification was never very useful for societies (like America) lacking a feudally-based aristocracy; with changes in economic circumstances it hardly remains interesting today.[26] And in any case, the claim that these three factors are "functionally" distinct in economic terms is analytically indefensible.

LAND VERSUS CAPITAL: *Land* is traditionally defined as the "natural and inexhaustible productive powers of the soil," i.e., its native fertility, mineral content,

[26]Ditch-diggers and corporate presidents both appear within the category of "labor," while the category of "land-owners" includes impoverished southern blacks together with the descendants of John Jacob Astor.

Chapter 15
FACTOR
SUPPLY,
FACTOR-
MARKET
EQUILIBRIUM,
AND INCOME
DISTRIBUTION

topographical features, and location. *Capital* in contrast with land is thought of as "produced means of production." Thus, capital is supposed to consist of man-made resources (e.g., buildings or machines), created and accumulated by human forethoughted sacrifice of present consumption for future production. But the distinction collapses once it is realized that the actual powers of the soil are as much a human creation as any building or machine. Human effort went into the discovery of the vast new lands of America, and, for that matter, into the draining of marshes and clearing of wasteland in the Old World. Nor can the fertility of land be maintained except by continuing human effort and sacrifice. Most important of all, the original *source* of any productive power is only of historical, not of economic or functional, significance.

It is sometimes claimed that a useful distinction between land and capital can be made in terms of supply curves. Supposedly, the supply of land is absolutely fixed by nature (a vertical supply curve) while the supply of man-made resources is responsive to price (a positively-sloping curve). But more land *will* be provided at a price (if necessary, reclaimed from the ocean), while existing land will be permitted to erode away if the reward for maintaining it is insufficient. Furthermore, as long as there are any reservation uses of land, its supply *to the market* will not in general be fixed (independent of price).[27]

LABOR VERSUS CAPITAL: Nor is it possible in the last analysis to distinguish between *labor power* (the source of human services) and capital. In modern society a worker does not sell raw labor power, but rather his or her trained and educated capacity to apply effort. Training is part of the worker's capital ("human capital"), just as a tool a worker owns is a part of that person's capital. There is no functional difference between the worker's sacrificing time and effort to acquire training (to improve labor skills) on the one hand, or purchasing a set of tools on the other.[28]

15.E.2

An Application: Investment in Human Capital

There is an interesting interaction between the returns from investment in human capital and the income-versus-leisure choice (the resource-employment decision) discussed in Section 15.A.

Figure 15.14 shows a situation in which an individual is *indifferent* between two situations G^* and D^* on indifference curve U. The endowment E, consisting of $R^\dagger$ of labor capacity and $I^\dagger$ of property income, lies on budget line EK. At the resource-employment optimum G^* the person has labor earnings equal to G^*G', making the total income I_G. But now suppose there is another alternative—adding to "human capital" by investing in education. Let us assume it is necessary to give up all of endowed property income $I^\dagger$ (sacrifice all non-human capital) to

Chapter 15
FACTOR
SUPPLY,
FACTOR-
MARKET
EQUILIBRIUM,
AND INCOME
DISTRIBUTION

472

[27]The supply curve of land to *all* uses (including reservation uses) will indeed be a vertical line independent of price. But this is true for any resource, including labor. (If "leisure" is counted as a use of labor, the supply of labor is necessarily the entire quantum in existence.) Meaningful supply curves always refer to quantities offered for *market* use, excluding reservation uses.

[28]There remain, of course, important differences between human capital and material capital. For one thing, training is less subject than material property to confiscation. (It is said that the emphasis of the Jews upon education is based upon the "portability" of this form of capital.) On the other hand, human capital perishes instantly with the death of its possessor, and can only with difficulty be transferred to others.

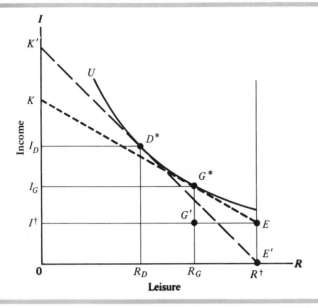

Figure 15.14

Returns to Education. The individual here is just indifferent between making or not making an investment in education. With endowment at *E*, the initial budget line *EK* permits attainment of position *G** on indifference curve *U*. Incurring a cost of education, represented by the vertical distance *EE'*, raises the market wage, allowing the person to move instead along the steeper budget line *E'K'*. But the tangency optimum *D** along *E'K"* is located on the same indifference curve *U*. Comparison of *D** with *G** indicates that the individual making the educational investment will thereafter choose less leisure and correspondingly higher market income.

acquire this training; the effective position after this sacrifice therefore becomes *E'* on the horizontal axis. But as a result of the education this worker now earns a higher wage, so that the new budget line *E'K'* is steeper than *EK*.

Although position *D** is by hypothesis indifferent to *G**, the income I_D achieved at *D** is much greater than (while the leisure R_D is less than) at *G**. The circumstances faced by the educated person, after having invested so heavily in acquiring human capital, lead him or her to select a resource-employment optimum with relatively little leisure R_D and relatively high achieved income I_D. Those who become educated should rationally work harder ever after!

The professional medical associations, in particular the AMA, have been accused of functioning as an entry-restricting cartel. Evidence has been brought forward showing that, *in terms of income achieved*, there seems to be an "excess" return to investment in medical education. That is, medical education seems to be more profitable than is normal for investment in material capital, suggesting that there may be a cartel at work effectively limiting entry into this profitable form of training.

EXAMPLE 15.9
RETURNS TO
MEDICAL
EDUCATION

473

C. M. Lindsay has contended, however, that this comparison in terms of additional income achieved fails to allow properly for the *lesser leisure* typically associated with the resource-employment decisions made after human-capital investments, and after medical training in particular. A true comparison should adjust for this lesser leisure.

In the table, the "unadjusted" MD returns represent the seeming excess value of medical education ($24,376) in comparison with college graduates generally. This measures the net balance of additional income achieved, deducting the cost of medical training, but *without* any offset for additional working hours of MDs. There are two ways of allowing for the difference in working hours: adjusting college-graduate hours worked *up*, or adjusting MD hours worked *down*. (The true comparison must lie between the results of these two alternative adjustments.)

Reportedly, MDs worked 62 hours per week on the average. For the sake of comparison, alternative assumptions of a 40- and a 45-hour average workweek were used for college graduates. If college graduates are working 45 hours per week, the table shows that a differential or excess net return to medical education persists, the true number lying somewhere between the alternative adjusted excess-return figures of $10,830 and $1,950. On the 40-hour assumption, however, the two adjustments average out very close to zero. So if college graduates generally are working close to 40 hours per week, there is no evidence of an excess return to medical education *once the MDs' loss of leisure is properly taken into account*.

Excess Returns to Medical Education

	40-HOUR WEEK	45-HOUR WEEK
Unadjusted MD excess returns	$24,376	$24,376
Adjusted by raising college graduate hours (to 62)	4,660	10,830
Adjusted by lowering MD hours	−4,580	1,950

Source: C. M. Lindsay, "Real Returns to Medical Education," *Journal of Human Resources,* v. 8 (Summer 1973), p. 338. An interest rate of 10% was used to represent the "normal" return from which the "excess" was calculated. (The original source shows the computation in terms of interest rates of both 5% and 10%).

COMMENT: The 62-hour figure for MDs may be suspect, however. Doctors (like others) are apt to report themselves as working harder than they really are. If doctors do not in fact work as many as 62 hours per week, the evidence here would tend to support the hypothesis of an excess (cartel-like) return to medical education.

15.E.3
Capital versus Income – Sources and Services – The Rate of Interest

The key to understanding the nature of "capital" lies not in the distinction between capital and land or labor, but in the *contrast between capital and income*. This contrast rests upon the difference between a source of productive services and the productive services themselves. The human being is the source of labor services, but the labor service proper is the "man-hour" (or other such unit representing the employment of a worker over some defined period of time). Similarly, land is a source of productive services, but the service itself is measured in units like acre-years. And again, it is necessary to distinguish buildings and machines (both sources) from the services of building and machines.

Sources and their services may both be traded in markets. There is a price for an acre of land, and a price for a year's use of an acre of land (the latter being the hire-price or rental). There is a price for a building, and a rental for use of the building over some period of time. In a non-slave economy, in contrast, the *sources* of labor services (the human beings themselves) may not be sold, though labor still can be hired for a periodic wage (the hire-price per man-hour). The "factor prices" discussed in this and previous chapters have been the *hire or rental prices of the productive services*, the "wage rates" per unit of time for the use of the resources—not the prices of the resources themselves.

The sources of factor services constitute an individual's or a nation's "capital." Land is capital, machines and buildings are capital, and the human being's training, strength, and skill, as sources of labor power, are capital.

The following table, based on a study by Louis Rose, summarizes the value of various categories of property (capital) in the 15 states where slaves were emancipated by President Lincoln's proclamation. Slave values varied of course with age and other characteristics; the mean was $933. Emancipation constituted an enormous loss to the slave-owners but this was balanced by a corresponding gain to the slaves in the form of the transferred ownership of their own persons. (Indeed, since free labor is certainly more productive, the economic value of the gain to the former slaves must have exceeded the loss to the slave-owners.)

EXAMPLE 15.10
CAPITAL IN THE
SLAVE-OWNING
SOUTH

Wealth Data, 15 Southern States, 1860 (millions of dollars)

Value of real estate and personal property	$8644
Value of land in farms	2550
Value of implements and machinery in use	104
Value of livestock	515
Value of slaves emancipated	3685

Source: L. Rose, "Capital Losses of Southern Slaveholders Due to Emancipation," *Western Economic Journal*, v. 3 (Fall 1964), pp. 43, 49.

COMMENT: A complete tabulation of the capital of the South would also have to include the labor-power value of the *free* population.

Two important senses of the word "capital" must be carefully distinguished: *real-capital* versus *capital-value*. Real-capital refers to the sources themselves: buildings, land, labor power, etc. Capital-value is the market valuation of these sources. (To avoid the ambiguity of the word "capital" standing alone, it is good practice always to specify whether it is real-capital or capital-value that is meant.) There are two corresponding senses of the word "income." The services of land generate a flow of *real-income* (e.g., bushels of wheat per year). But if the prefix "real" is omitted, the word "income" standing alone is commonly understood to be in value terms. Thus, an acre of land yields a rental income (dollars per year) to the owner, corresponding to the dollar value of the real-income in bushels per year actually produced.

Consider the Factor Employment Condition of the previous chapter, equation (14.5): $h_a = mrp_a \equiv MR(mp_a)$. Here the physical Marginal Product mp_a is the real-income produced in units of the good Q, so the dimensionality of mp_a might be bushels per acre per year. The dimensionality of Marginal Revenue MR is dollars/Q (dollars per bushel) so Marginal Revenue Product mrp_a is in units of dollars per acre per year. On the left hand side of the equation, the hire-price or "wage" of land is of course also in units of dollars per acre per year.

If a resource as source of productive services is itself a marketable asset, there will be a market-determined ratio between the *annual value of the service* and the *market value of the source*, i.e., ratio between the income and the capital-value. This ratio, the proportionate yield on the capital-value of the source, corresponds to the *rate of interest* earned from ownership of the resource. Suppose an acre of land is valued at $1000 and generates real-income (has a Marginal Product) of 50 bushels of wheat per year. If the price of wheat is $2 per bushel, the income is $100 per year. Then the rate of interest r earned upon the investment in land is $100/$1000 or 10% per annum. More generally, for any asset:

$$(15.3) \qquad \text{Rate of interest } r \equiv \frac{\text{Annual income}}{\text{Value of asset}}$$

In performing this calculation, however, it is important to account for all aspects, both positive and negative, of "income." For example, suppose the asset *depreciates* in value during the year because of wear-and-tear or obsolescence. Then the loss due to the depreciation during the year must be taken into account as an offset in calculating the "net" income from the source. If we symbolize as V the value of any source of income, as ΔV the positive or negative change in this value (appreciation or depreciation) during the year, and as z the "cash-flow" generated during the year, equation (15.3) defining the annual rate of interest r can be written more explicitly as:

$$(15.3') \qquad r \equiv \frac{z + \Delta V}{V}$$

Chapter 15
FACTOR
SUPPLY,
FACTOR-
MARKET
EQUILIBRIUM,
AND INCOME
DISTRIBUTION

476

With income properly accounted for, there is a fundamental proposition that governs the relation between income and capital-value:

PROPOSITION: The proportionate yield (rate of interest earned) on all assets tends to come into equality.

If the yield on asset T were lower than on another asset S, holders of T would be trying to sell out in order to buy S instead. This would drive down the price P_T (capital-value) of T and drive up the price P_S (capital-value) of S. As may be seen from equation (15.3), as the dollar value of source T falls its percent yield must rise, while as the dollar value of source S rises its percent yield must fall. In this way the incentives of individuals to achieve the maximum returns on their asset-holdings tend to bring the rate of interest earned on all assets into equality.

Taking this point into account together with equation (15.3′) leads to an important implication: assets whose values are expected to *depreciate* during a given time-period should yield relatively large cash-flows z; assets whose values are expected to *appreciate* may be attractive despite small cash-flows. As an example, a land speculator may pay a steep price for a city lot, even though intending to hold it vacant for a year or more. Here there would be no positive cash-flow at all, and indeed very likely a substantial negative cash-flow when taxes are taken into account. But the decision may be proved to be correct, *if* the value of the site appreciates enough to surpass the earnings that could have been achieved via alternative investments.

We can now see more clearly into the relation between interest and the traditional "functional" categories—such as rent as return to land and wages as return to labor. Since rent is the hire-price of land, *annual rent* on land will (in equilibrium) be equal to *the interest yield on the capital-value* of the land. In a slave economy, annual wages as the hire-price of labor would tend to equal the interest yield on the capital-value of the slave. And even in a free economy, the additional income due to investment in training would, allowing for loss of leisure, tend to equal the interest yield on the cost of acquiring that training (see Example 15.9, "Returns to Medical Education").

In equation (15.3), dollars/year of net income from the services of any factor A must equal the hire-price h_a. Dollar value of the source, the price of factor A itself, can be denoted as P_A. For any factor A, then, in equilibrium:

(15.4) $h_a = rP_A$

CONCLUSION: Interest is not the return to a particular factor called "capital". Rather, any factor income represents the interest yield on the *capital-value* of the corresponding resource. Or put another way: The interest rate is, for any factor, the ratio between the hire-price of the factor and the value of the *source* of the factor services.

15.F

ECONOMIC RENT AND PRODUCER
SURPLUS

A portion of the income earned by any factor may constitute what is sometimes called "economic rent," to wit, that part of the return to the factor in excess of the minimum amount required to induce it into employment.

Consider Figure 15.15. Here, for some factor service A, the supply curve S_a is vertical; i.e., there are no reservation uses. It follows that the entire income

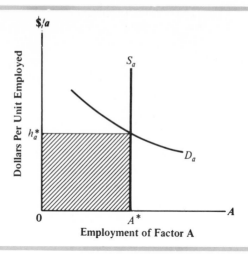

Figure 15.15

Economic Rent, I. If the supply curve S_a of factor A is vertical, the entire market receipts to suppliers (the rectangle whose height is the hire-price h_a^* and whose base is employment A^*) is "economic rent"—an excess over the minimum payment required to call the units of the factor into market employment.

payment for the hire of that resource, the shaded rectangle in the diagram, is an "excess" payment and therefore constitutes economic rent. For, the vertical supply curve shows that the quantity A^* would be forthcoming even at an infinitesimal wage. With an upward-sloping factor supply curve as in Figure 15.16, however, the region of "excess" payment is the shaded area lying above S_a but below the market price h_a^*. Here not all of factor income is economic rent, because of the existence of reservation uses (compare the upward-sloping MRS_R curve of Figure 15.13).

Economic rent as pictured in Figure 15.16 looks very similar to the representation of *Producer Surplus* in Figure 7.10. And indeed, economic rent is the analog of Producer Surplus. Producer Surplus measures a selling individual's net gain from trade *in the product market*; economic rent measures the net gain from trade *in the factor market*. That is, from market employment (as opposed to non-market or reservation uses) of the resources the person owns.

Economic rent is a rather slippery category, one that must be handled with care. Its magnitude depends upon the range of alternatives being considered. If we are thinking of supply of a resource to *all* market employments (as against the alternative of non-market or reservation uses), the economic rent is likely to be large. But if we speak of supply to some narrower range of activity, the economic rent received by the resource-owner is only the excess over the *next-best* market or non-market employment—which is likely to be much smaller. Diagramatically, in Figure 15.16 the supply curve S_a to a narrow range of activity is likely to be much more elastic than the supply curve to a wider category of activities, and so the shaded area is likely to be smaller.

Chapter 15
FACTOR
SUPPLY,
FACTOR-
MARKET
EQUILIBRIUM,
AND INCOME
DISTRIBUTION

478

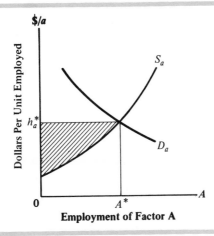

$/a

Dollars Per Unit Employed

S_a

h_a^*

D_a

0   A^* A

Employment of Factor A

Figure 15.16

Economic Rent, II. If S_a is upward-sloping, economic rent is the area lying above the supply curve but below the market equilibrium hire-price h_a^*.

Until recently, a sizeable portion of the human resources employed by the Department of Defense was acquired by conscription. Wages to enlistees were low, and military requirements were met by supplementing volunteers with draftees.

In 1967 Walter Oi[29] analyzed the losses in economic rents that would be suffered, given a continuation of conscription, by suppliers of labor services to the armed forces. For a desired intake of 472,000 recruits annually, it was estimated that the yearly recruitment at the then-current starting wage of $2500 per year would be composed of 263,000 "true" volunteers, 153,700 "reluctant" volunteers (individuals induced to volunteer only to gain some advantages over being drafted), and 55,300 draftees.

The draft as a "tax" on economic rent affects all three of these groups. The true volunteers are those already willing to serve at the $2500 rate. But if military salaries were to be raised enough to eliminate any need for reluctant volunteers or draftees, the true volunteers would also receive more pay. Under the most favorable assumption as to the elasticity of voluntary supply to the armed forces, Oi estimated that to attract the required numbers the annual wage would have to be $5900. (Under what he regarded as a more realistic supply-elasticity assumption, the wage would have to be $7450.) The loss of this benefit (the economic rent that a true volunteer would otherwise have received) is therefore $3400 per true volunteer per year.

The reluctant volunteers, it is reasonable to assume, had better market opportunities than the true volunteers. As a result of enlistment at the $2500

[29]W. Y. Oi, "The Economic Cost of the Draft," *American Economic Review*, v. 57 (May 1967), pp. 39–62.

EXAMPLE 15.11
ECONOMIC RENT
AND THE
MILITARY DRAFT

rather than $5900 wage they were estimated to lose on average $918 per year from foregoing these market opportunities, leaving $2482 as their average loss in economic rent (where $918 + $2482 = $3400). For the draftees, individuals who had to be compelled to serve, market opportunities were presumably better still. Oi estimated the loss to them as $3165 per year in foregone market opportunities and only $235 per year in economic rent. (These estimates for reluctant volunteers and draftees are minimal figures, which would be appropriate only if individuals drafted or induced to volunteer were those with the poorest alternative non-military employments.)[30]

[30]This is the analog of the "ideal" assignment of ration tickets, described in Section 7.E.2, that minimizes the loss of Consumer Surplus under rationing.

15.G

CAPITAL, INTERTEMPORAL CHOICE, AND THE CIRCULAR FLOW

We have now taken account of the individual in two decision-making aspects, as *consumer* and as *resource-owner*. But there remains at any moment of time a third dimension of choice: *between consumption and increased resource-ownership*. Each person not only has to make decisions as to how to employ currently-owned resources and how to consume income, but also whether and to what extent to refrain from consuming now (to save) so as to provide for the future. Having chosen to save, the individual has funds available for increasing his or her resource-ownership. This might be done by purchasing already-existing sources of factor services (land, machines, buildings, etc.) from someone else. Over the economy as a whole, of course, such transactions cancel out as there must be a seller for each buyer. But a firm or an individual might also physically *produce* a social increment of real-capital by manufacturing new resources not previously in existence, or, for that matter, by "manufacturing" new human capital through undergoing training. *Saving* is the process of refraining from consumption; the process of actually building new real-capital is called *investment*.

From the individual's point of view, today's consumption-versus-saving decision can be reinterpreted as an intertemporal choice between *present* consumption and *future* consumption. By not consuming today and saving instead, the person builds up a stock of owned resources so as to augment future income—convertible into consumption at later dates. Eventually, in retirement perhaps, the person is likely to "dis-save" by gradually disposing of owned resources (real-capital) to provide for consumption in old age. (He or she may, however, plan to leave a legacy to descendants, thereby participating by proxy in consumption activities beyond death.) We are thus led to the topic of *intertemporal* choice, which will constitute the subject of Chapter 16.

The familiar picture in Figure 1.1 of the circular flow of economic activity can now be made a degree more realistic by separating consumption and saving

Chapter 15
FACTOR
SUPPLY,
FACTOR-
MARKET
EQUILIBRIUM,
AND INCOME
DISTRIBUTION

480

flows, as in Figure 15.17. We now imagine that there are two types of firms: those producing *consumption goods* and those producing real-capital or *investment goods* (buildings, land, machines, etc.). In the upper portion of the diagram (the product market) the two types of products are purchased by the consumers' consumption expenditures and savings expenditures, respectively. In the lower part of the diagram (the factor market), resource-owning individuals supply factor-services to the employing firms. A decision to save rather than consume will involve the acquisition of an augmented stock of resources, permitting an individual at some later date to supply a larger quantity of productive services and thereby earn more future income.[31]

Figure 15.17
The Circular Flow: Consumption and Investment.

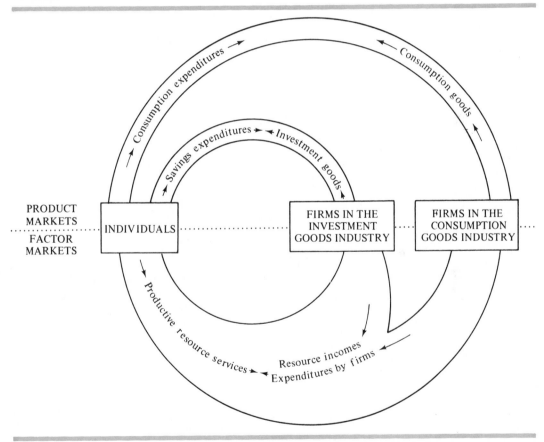

[31]The implicit assumption underlying the diagram is that all resources are *owned* by individuals and *rented* to firms for productive employment. In actuality firms themselves may legally *own* as well as hire resources. But resource-ownership on the part of firms can be regarded merely as a convenient fiction, since ultimately all firms are themselves owned by individuals.

Just as individuals face the product markets as demanders of consumer goods, they face the factor markets as suppliers of resource services. Their receipts from provision of factor services become their incomes available for spending on consumer goods.

The services of owned resources can be sold on the market, or else retained for reservation (leisure) uses. The individual can be regarded as having preferences for alternative combinations of income I and reservation uses R_a of any factor A. At the resource-owner's optimum, the Marginal Rate of Substitution in Resource Supply MRS_R (the marginal value of reservation uses) will be equal to the factor hire-price h_a. As endowed income (income from other sources) rises, an Income Expansion Path IEP will be traced out. Assuming that R_a and I are both normal goods, the IEP will have positive slope—showing that as income rises more reservation uses will be chosen (less of the factor will be supplied). As hire-price h_a varies, a Price Expansion Path PEP will be traced out. In decisions as to factor supply, the income and substitution effects normally work in opposite directions. At very low hire-prices (in the neighborhood of the all-leisure corner solution) the substitution effect must dominate, so that PEP has normal negative slope. But for sufficiently high h_a the income effect may dominate, so that the PEP "bends backward."

Corresponding to the possible backward-bending range of PEP would be a hire-price h_a' above which the supply curve of resource A to the market also bends backward (less is offered as the hire-price rises). However, even if there should be a range where the overall supply curve *to the entire market* (as against the alternative of leisure) bends backward, the supply of resource *to any limited sector or particular activity* is almost certain to have the standard positive slope—since there are so many other alternatives to draw supply from as h_a rises.

Market equilibrium for any factor A under conditions of competition is of course determined by the intersection of an overall demand curve and an overall supply curve. Factor demand tends to rise with technological progress (raising Marginal Product), with higher consumer demand for final products, and with increased supply of cooperating factors. On the supply side, greater wealth in the form of stocks of human and non-human resources increases overall factor availability, but at the same time tends to decrease the fraction provided to the market—since suppliers can afford to "purchase" more reservation uses of their resources.

Chapter 15
FACTOR
SUPPLY,
FACTOR-
MARKET
EQUILIBRIUM,
AND INCOME
DISTRIBUTION

A monopolist owner of a factor would in effect have a "budget curve" rather than a budget line in the indifference-curve diagram. This can be translated into a curve showing Total Factor Income TFI as a function of the amount of resource supplied. The corresponding curves of Average Factor Income AFI (an Average Revenue or demand curve) and Marginal Factor Income MFI (a Marginal Revenue curve) are declining functions of the amount supplied. The relevant Marginal Cost for such a monopolist would be the Marginal Rate of Substitution in Resource Supply, MRS_R, representing the marginal value of reservation uses. The factor-monopolist would offer the market an amount such that $MRS_R = MFI$ (akin to a product-monopolist setting $MC = MR$). In the absence of reservation uses, the factor-monopolist would have MRS_R of zero and so would simply maximize Total Factor Income TFI (would set $MFI = 0$).

Trade unions and other forms of resource cartels represent attempts on the part of smaller suppliers to act together as a collective monopolist. As in the case of product-market cartels, there are strong incentives to "chisel"—which, for the most part, can be effectively countered only by government support of the cartel.

A traditional classification divides factors of production into the categories of *land* (resources provided by Nature), *capital* (resources provided by human sacrifice and forethought), and *labor* (the human resource itself). This classification is not logically defensible: elements provided by Nature and elements provided by human effort enter into all three of the usual categories.

A more valid distinction is that between the *sources* of productive services (which can be regarded as "real-capital," whether in the form of land or machines or human beings) and the *services* themselves. The services are sold in the factor markets for *hire-prices*. If the sources themselves can be sold, a logical relation must hold between the price of the source and the hire-price of its services. The *interest rate r* is defined as the ratio between the annual net income of any asset and the value of the asset itself, or in particular between the hire-price and the purchase price of any factor.

The excess return paid to any factor, over and above the amount necessary to call it into the service considered, is *economic rent*. Economic rent is the analog, in factor-market units, of what was called Producer Surplus in Chapter 7. Economic rent is smaller the narrower the range of uses considered: even if economic rent in all market uses taken together (as against the alternative of non-market uses) is large, the economic rent in the best market use (as against the second-best use) may be quite small.

At any moment of time the individual must make choices among consumption goods (the decision problem of the consumer), and as to the employment of resources (the decision problem of the resource-owner). A third decision problem is between consumption and increased resource-ownership, via saving and investment. This is in effect a choice between present consumption and future consumption.

QUESTIONS FOR CHAPTER 15

Mainly for Review

R1. Explain, in terms of income and substitution effects, how a "backward-bending" supply curve of a resource service can come about.

*R2. If leisure were an inferior good, would a backward-bending supply curve of labor be possible?

*R3. Why *must* the substitution effect dominate the income effect at very low wage rates?

Chapter 15
FACTOR
SUPPLY,
FACTOR-
MARKET
EQUILIBRIUM,
AND INCOME
DISTRIBUTION

*The answers to asterisked questions appear at the end of the book.

*R4. Is the supply curve of a resource to a particular employment likely to be more or less elastic than the supply to all market uses? Why?

R5. In what way does the market opportunity set of a factor-monopolist differ from that of a competitive supplier of factor services? How will the optimum of the resource-owner be affected?

*R6. An individual who invests heavily in developing labor skills will afterward earn a higher wage. But he or she is then likely to work more hours than otherwise would have been the case. Explain why.

R7. Explain the traditional "functional" classification of factors of production.

*R8. How can land and labor power be thought of as capital?

*R9. What is the relationship between the hire-price of a factor and the purchase price of that factor?

R10. What causes the rate of return on all assets to tend toward equality?

*R11. What is economic rent? What is its relation to Producer Surplus?

R12. Show that an individual who would have chosen employment under a welfare-relief system *might* prefer to remain unemployed if there is a Negative Income Tax.

For Further Thought and Discussion

T1. What would be the effect upon the budget line and the resource-employment optimum of a *progressive* income tax on labor earnings? Of a time-and-a-half rule for overtime work?

*T2. Apart from leisure as a reservation use of labor, what other resources are likely to have nonmarket reservation uses yielding utility to their owners?

T3. Diagram a situation in which a resource-owner chooses a "corner solution" so as to devote all of his resource to reservation uses. Does this necessarily imply that income *I* must be a "bad" or a "neuter" commodity at the solution point? Diagram a situation in which the resource-owner's optimum is such that no reservation uses *R* are retained. Does this imply that *R* must be a "bad" or a "neuter" commodity at the solution point? Explain.

*T4. With the advent of the women's liberation movement, there is reason to believe that women's preferences may be changing so as to make reservation uses of their time less attractive than before, in comparison with market employment. What effect would such a taste change have upon the supply curve of female labor? Upon the relative market wages of male and female workers?

*T5. In modern times, real wealth and real wage rates have steadily increased throughout the western world. But average working hours in market employment have steadily fallen. Would the pure "income effect" (due to rising per-capita wealth) tend to lead to reduced market employment? Would the pure "substitution effect" (due to the relative price shift represented by the rising wage rate) tend to have this effect? Comment upon the relative importance of the two in the light of the evidence.

Chapter 15
FACTOR
SUPPLY,
FACTOR-
MARKET
EQUILIBRIUM,
AND INCOME
DISTRIBUTION

484

*T6. Consider the situation of a slave who has no market opportunity set for disposition of his labor power. Suppose the master simply provided a fixed "income" I (in the form of consumption rations) to the slave. What would be the optimum I,R position from the point of view of the slave? What position would the master prefer? How is the divergence likely to be resolved? Might it be in the interests of the master to free his slave and pay him wages? Might it not?

T7. Suppose that entry into a particular field of employment for a resource like labor or land is restricted by the requirement to obtain a special license, but that the license is traded in the market. Assuming a fixed number of licenses, use supply–demand analysis to determine the equilibrium price of a license. How is the market demand curve for licenses derived from the demand curve and supply curve for the resource service?

T8. In some nations, higher income taxes are imposed upon "unearned" as opposed to "earned" income (i.e., higher taxes upon income from property as opposed to income from labor services). What are the likely effects upon investment in human capital in comparison to investment in physical capital? On the other hand, it has been maintained that most income taxes are biased against labor income by failing to allow any deductions for *depreciation* of the worker's labor power over time. What would be the consequence of allowing such deductions?

*T9. According to the "single tax" movement, a tax on land is likely to be particularly effective. (Allegedly, the supply curve of land is vertical, and so its availability to society will not be affected no matter how heavy is the tax on land.) If a land tax is levied upon *market uses* of the resource (income tax), would the market availability of land be affected? If the tax were levied instead upon *ownership* of the resource (wealth tax), would the market availability of land be affected? Then make an analogous comparison, in terms of the market availability of labor, of an *income* tax upon labor earnings versus a *wealth* tax upon labor capacity. (The latter is a so-called "facultative" tax, a fixed sum proportioned to a person's *ability* to earn rather than to his actual market earnings.)

*T10. Following up Question T7 in Chapter 14, what *supply-side* considerations may help explain the relatively high wages received by U.S. workers?

T11. Over a century ago Karl Marx, in what is known as the "immiserization hypothesis," predicted that workers' wages and incomes in the advanced industrial countries would tend to fall—thus bringing on a socialist revolution. This prediction has failed. Some defenders of Marx have argued that the reason for the failure of the prediction is that in the meantime capitalism has adopted "socialistic" reforms. Among these might perhaps be classed minimum-wage laws, the forty-hour week, welfare relief for the unemployed, and laws encouraging trade unions and collective bargaining. What effects would you expect each of these reforms to have upon wage rates? Upon workers' incomes?

*T12. Wage rates are high in New York City, compared to the rest of the U.S. But so is the cost of living. Explain why this pattern exists.

16.A CONSUMPTION AND PRODUCTION OVER TIME, 488
    16.A.1 Borrowing–Lending Equilibrium, 488
    16.A.2 Saving–Investment Equilibrium, 492

16.B INVESTMENT DECISIONS AND THE PRESENT-VALUE RULE, 497
    16.B.1 The Separation Theorem, 497
    16.B.2 The Present-Value Rule for Investment Decision, 498
    16.B.3 Multi-Period Analysis, 499

16.C RISK AND THE INTEREST RATE, 502

16.D REAL INTEREST AND MONEY INTEREST, 507

16.E DETERMINANTS OF INTEREST RATES, 510

Examples
    16.1 SOCIAL SECURITY, SAVING, AND NATIONAL INCOME, 496
    16.2 PRESENT VALUES OF LIFETIME EARNINGS FOR HOLDERS OF BACHELOR'S DEGREES, 501
    16.3 PRESENT VALUES OF THE FEATHER RIVER PROJECT, 502
    16.4 PROFESSORS AND PUBLICATIONS, 503
    16.5 RISK PREMIUMS, 505
    16.6 FIRE YOURS, HIRE OURS!, 506
    16.7 REAL AND MONEY RATES OF INTEREST, 509
    16.8 INTEREST AND THE GOLD RUSH, 512

16

INTERTEMPORAL CHOICE: SAVING, INVESTMENT, AND INTEREST

Supplementary Chapter

At the end of the preceding chapter we saw that individuals have to make choices not only (1) as to purchase of current consumption goods out of income and (2) as to the supply of resource services to the market so as to generate income, but also (3) between current consumption and the acquisition of *additional* amounts of resources or "real-capital." This last is commonly described as the choice between consumption and *saving* or *investment*. "Saving" means refraining from consumption, while "investment" indicates the actual formation of new resources (increasing the quantity of real-capital). For an isolated Robinson Crusoe, the two must necessarily be equal: by saving some of this year's corn, Robinson has automatically invested so as to create real-capital in the form of a stock of seed (that will provide him with more of next year's corn). In an exchange economy, however, those who save and those who invest do not have to be the same individuals. Nevertheless, as we shall see, the market works to bring the aggregate of saving and the aggregate of investment in the economy into equality.

In this chapter we will emphasize, as the motive underlying the choices between consumption on the one hand and saving or investment on the other, desires on the part of individuals to *achieve a preferred intertemporal balance of consumption* between present and future. An individual may buy or build a house to provide future shelter; a farmer may hold back corn from current use to plant seed for next year's crop; and a business firm may maintain or replace its machinery and equipment in order to provide for productive capacity in coming years. In each case capital assets are being acquired, at the sacrifice of current consumption, as a way of providing for future income and consumption.

Section 16.A shows how individuals' intertemporal productive and consumptive decisions interact to determine equilibrium levels of borrowing and lending and of saving and investment, and the equilibrium market rate of interest. Section 16.B considers the criteria used by business firms or by government agencies in making investment decisions. The very important bearing of *risk* for observed market rates of interest is examined in Section 16.C, and the distinction between *real* interest and *money* interest is covered in Section 16.D. The concluding section reviews the underlying forces determining rates of interest in different economies and different historical periods.

16.A

CONSUMPTION AND PRODUCTION OVER TIME

In Part Two of this book it was assumed that the individual could choose among a number of goods $X, Y, Z, \ldots$ so as to find a preferred consumption basket. In dealing with intertemporal choice in this chapter, the simplification will be adopted of collapsing all these different consumption goods into a single consumptive commodity C. However, consumption will be differentiated by date. Specifically, individuals will be regarded as making choices among goods defined as *this year's consumption C_0, consumption one time-period in the future C_1, consumption two time-periods from now C_2,* etc. Here the subscript 0 represents "now," and the other numbered subscripts are time-units (years) from the present period. For utmost simplicity, however, in this section only two-period models will be analyzed: choice between *this year's consumption C_0* and *next year's consumption C_1*. As in the case of ordinary consumption choices, the optimum position for an individual will depend upon his or her preferences and opportunities. And the equilibrium in the market, determining the relative prices of claims or entitlements to current consumption C_0 and future consumption C_1, will integrate and balance the separate choices of all the individuals in the economy.

16.A.1
Borrowing–
Lending
Equilibrium

In the light of the above, we can see that the problems of individual decision and overall market equilibrium over time are in principle no different from the corresponding problems for ordinary consumption commodities X and Y within a single period of time. And specifically, on the level of the individual, the intertemporal optimization that is pictured in Figure 16.1 looks almost exactly like the "optimum of the consumer" shown originally in Figure 4.1. In Figure 16.1 here we once again have an individual's *preference map* (indifference curves U', U'', U''', $\ldots$), and a consumption *opportunity set* bounded on the northeast by a *budget line KL*. The optimum of the consumer will again be at a tangency like situation of an "heir with great expectations," as in Charles Dickens' novel, i.e., someone poor today but with rich prospects for the future.

What is the rate of exchange at which the market will permit the trading of current consumption entitlements C_0 against future entitlements C_1 (by lending or borrowing)? This rate corresponds geometrically to the slope of the budget line. Let the price of C_0-claims be symbolized as P_0 and the price of C_1-claims be P_1. Then the ratio at which the two claims can be exchanged, $\Delta c_1/\Delta c_0$, equals $-P_0/P_1$. (The minus sign is needed, since Δc_1 and Δc_0 have opposite signs—one must be given up to obtain the other.) We will usually be assuming that current claims C_0 serve as the "numeraire" or basis of pricing, so that $P_0 \equiv 1$. If we interpret this as saying that the price of a current real claim C_0 is by definition a dollar, the slope of the budget line becomes simply $-1/P_1$ in numeraire or dollar units.

In the special terminology of intertemporal exchange, the concept of "the rate of interest" r is introduced. Specifically, we shall define the annual rate of interest r here as the *premium* on the relative value of current consumption claims units over one-year-in-the-future consumption claims. Looking at it the other way, $1 + r$ consumption claims units of future claims C_1 is what the market will return for each unit of current claims C_0 sacrificed (by being lent out). Thus:

$$(16.1) \qquad P_1(1 + r) \equiv P_0 \equiv 1$$

It is also useful to keep in mind the logically equivalent expressions:

$$(16.1') \qquad P_1 \equiv \frac{1}{1 + r}$$

$$(16.1'') \qquad r \equiv \frac{P_0}{P_1} - 1$$

Consequently, the slope of the budget line in Figure 16.1 can also be written as $-(1 + r)$.

One other point of great importance concerns the nature of the constraint fixing the distance of the budget line from the origin, and thereby determining the magnitude of the individual's consumption opportunities. In the previous analysis of consumption in a single period (in Section 4.A), it was the individual's *income* I that constrained choices according to equation (4.1), $P_x x + P_y y = I$. This equation was employed as a simplification in Chapter 4, while admitting the known fact that people often spend less than their current income on consumption (they may save) or more than their income on consumption (they may borrow). We are now in a position to correct this flaw in the preceding analysis. It is not *income I* that limits the individual's consumption choices over time but rather endowed *wealth* $W_0^{\dagger}$.

DEFINITION: Endowed wealth $W_0^{\dagger}$ is the market value today of an individual's intertemporal endowment of present and future claims.

Chapter 16
INTEMPORAL
CHOICE:
SAVING,
INVESTMENT,
AND INTEREST

490

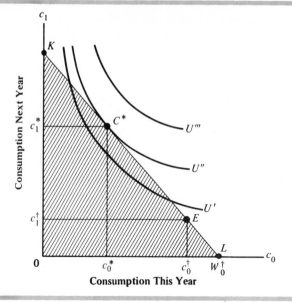

Figure 16.1

Intertemporal Consumptive Optimum. The individual's intertemporal choice problem, between consumption this year C_0 and consumption next year C_1, has the same elements as the simple problem of consumer choice: preference map (indifference curves U', U'', U'''), endowment position (E), budget line (KL), and optimum position C^*. The individual here chooses to lend the amount $c_0^\dagger - c_0^*$ of current claims, receiving in repayment the amount $c_1^* - c_1^\dagger$ of future claims. $W_0^\dagger$ is the endowed wealth measured in units of current claims C_0.

C^*—representing a "consumption basket" that takes the form of an intertemporal income stream consisting of the amounts c_0^* of current consumption and c_1^* of future consumption.

A special terminology is employed for the analysis of intertemporal choice, however, and we need to translate this familiar solution into that terminology. First, note that in Figure 16.1 the budget line KL goes through an intertemporal *endowment* position E (compare the analysis of Chapter 7, Section C) representing given entitlements $c_0^\dagger$ and $c_1^\dagger$ of anticipated current and future income available to the individual before entering into exchange.[1] When the individual moves northwest along the budget line from endowment position E, he or she is said to be "lending," i.e., sacrificing some units of current consumption C_0 in exchange for claims to future consumption C_1. Should the person move southeast, obtaining more C_0 at the expense of C_1, he or she is said to be "borrowing." The individual pictured in Figure 16.1 chooses to be a lender in the amount of $c_0^\dagger - c_0^*$, the anticipated repayment next year being $c_1^* - c_1^\dagger$. Had endowment position E been to the northwest of the intertemporal optimum C^* along the budget line, on the other hand, the individual would have been a borrower. The latter case is the traditional

[1] In this analysis, *uncertainty* is ruled out. Thus, anticipations as to the future are sure to be realized.

Using the conventional "price" terminology, endowed wealth would be expressed in terms of the values of the endowment elements $(c_0^\dagger, c_1^\dagger)$ as follows:

$$(16.2) \qquad W_0^\dagger \equiv P_0 c_0^\dagger + P_1 c_1^\dagger$$

And in terms of the alternative "interest" terminology, since $P_0 \equiv 1$ and $P_1 \equiv 1/(1 + r)$, endowed wealth is:

$$(16.2') \qquad W_0^\dagger \equiv c_0^\dagger + \frac{c_1^\dagger}{1 + r}$$

Geometrically, if $P_0 \equiv 1$ then the endowed wealth is the horizontal intercept of the budget line KL. Note that the subscript 0 is attached to the symbol for wealth. The reason is that wealth signifies a *present* market value, a worth *today* (in numeraire or C_0-units) of the specified endowment combination or time-stream.

The constraint itself, the budget line KL of Figure 16.1, can similarly be expressed in two ways:

$$(16.3) \qquad P_0 c_0 + P_1 c_1 = W_0^\dagger$$

$$(16.3') \qquad c_0 + \frac{c_1}{1 + r} = W_0^\dagger$$

The intertemporal borrowing–lending equilibrium in terms of commodities C_0 and C_1 is entirely analogous to the market equilibrium involving commodities X and Y discussed in Section 7.C. By imagining different prices P_1 (or interest rates r) determining different budget lines through each individual's endowment position E, a Price Expansion Path can be derived for each individual as in Figure 7.3. And these can then be translated into supply and demand curves for the separate individuals, and for the market as a whole, as in Figures 7.4 and 7.5. The successive steps in the development will not be recapitulated here. However, the final result is pictured in Figure 16.2, which corresponds to Panel (a) of Figure 7.5. On the horizontal axis here are measured aggregate amounts of market borrowing or lending. The L^t curve is the market supply of lending, the summation over individuals of the "transaction quantities" of C_0 offered at each interest rate r. (For any single individual, this will be the excess of endowment quantity $c_0^\dagger$ over desired consumption or full-demand quantity c_0 at that interest rate.) B^t represents the market demand for borrowing, the aggregate transaction quantity of C_0 demanded at any r by those whose current endowments fall short of desired consumption at that interest rate. Thus, the L^t curve represents the aggregate responses (desired transactions at different market interest rates) of individuals like the net lender pictured in Figure 16.1, and the B^t curve the responses of borrowers, i.e., of persons for whom the endowment position E lies to the northwest rather than to the southeast of the preferred intertemporal optimum position $C*$.[2]

---

[2]It should be realized, however, that for a sufficiently high rate of interest someone previously a borrower might shift over and become a lender, while for a sufficiently low rate of interest someone previously a lender might become a borrower.

Chapter 16
INTEMPORAL
CHOICE:
SAVING,
INVESTMENT,
AND INTEREST

491

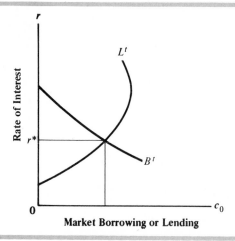

Figure 16.2

Intertemporal Borrowing–Lending Equilibrium. The L^t curve shows the aggregate supply of current claims offered for lending at each interest rate r; the B^t curve shows the aggregate demand for borrowing at each r. The intersection determines the equilibrium amount borrowed and lent, and the equilibrium interest rate r^*.

On the vertical axis of the borrowing–lending diagram it is usual to put the interest rate r, so that the supply–demand intersection determines the equilibrium rate of interest r^*. The height of the rate of interest is an indication of the *relative value* of current versus future consumption claims. More precisely, as is evident from the relation $r \equiv P_0/P_1 - 1$ of equation (16.1″), r is the *premium* component in the relative value of C_0 to C_1—the amount by which the price ratio P_0/P_1 of current over future consumption entitlements exceeds unity.

The analysis so far has been of a pure borrowing–lending equilibrium. The lending that corresponds to *saving* (refraining from consumption) on the part of some persons in the economy is exactly balanced by the borrowing or *dis-saving* of others. So no actual new formation of real-capital (no *investment*) is taking place. The pure borrowing–lending model corresponds, therefore, to what was called ''pure exchange'' in Section 7.C. The formation of real-capital, in contrast, falls under the heading of *production*. More specifically, it represents *intertemporal productive transformation*, as when current corn is transformed into future corn by the physical planting of seed. Consequently, the discussion of real investment in the section following corresponds to the model of productive transformation analyzed under the heading of ''Exchange and Production'' in Section 7.D.

16.A.2

Saving – Investment Equilibrium

Figure 16.3, analogous to Panel (a) of Figure 7.6, shows the intertemporal productive-consumptive situation of a Robinson Crusoe isolated from all trade. Starting from an intertemporal endowment combination $E = (c_0^\dagger, c_1^\dagger)$, Robinson's productive transformation opportunities are indicated by his Production-Possibility Curve QQ. The QQ curve is the locus of possible productive combinations (q_0, q_1) of this year's corn q_0 and next year's corn q_1. Since the endowment combination is

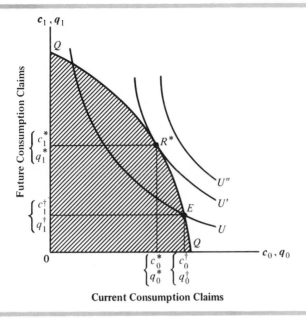

c_1, q_1

Future Consumption Claims

Q

$\left\{\begin{array}{c} c_1^* \\ q_1^* \end{array}\right.$

R^*

U''

U'

$\left\{\begin{array}{c} c_1^\dagger \\ q_1^\dagger \end{array}\right.$

E

U

Q

0

$\left\{\begin{array}{c} c_0^* \\ q_0^* \end{array}\right.$ $\left\{\begin{array}{c} c_0^\dagger \\ q_0^\dagger \end{array}\right.$

c_0, q_0

Current Consumption Claims

Figure 16.3

Intertemporal Productive–Consumptive Optimum, Robinson Crusoe. A Robinson Crusoe has no intertemporal *exchange* (borrowing–lending) opportunities, but can engage in *productive* transformations between consumption this year and consumption next year. QQ is the Production-Possibility Curve through the endowment position E. The Crusoe optimum is at R*, where QQ is tangent to the highest attainable indifference curve. This is an "autarky" solution: the amounts produced $(q_0^* q_1^*)$ equal, respectively, the amounts consumed $(c_0^* c_1^*)$.

one point on the curve, we can also write $E = (q_0^\dagger, q_1^\dagger)$. The concave shape of QQ represents a kind of diminishing returns in intertemporal transformation. For example, doubling the consumptive sacrifice of this year's corn (input of seed) will not generally double the return (output of next year's corn). Evidently, the optimum position for Robinson is the tangency point R^* in the diagram. This is a joint productive-consumptive optimum: $R^* = (c_0^*, c_1^*) = (q_0^*, q_1^*)$.

We can now interpret the Crusoe or "autarky" solution in terms of the special terminology of intertemporal choice. Robinson's *saving* (refraining from consumption) is, as before, the horizontal distance $c_0^\dagger - c_0^*$. But here no lending occurs, as there is no other person with whom an exchange of current for future consumption claims can take place. Rather, Robinson's saving is used solely for physical *investment* (planting seed): $c_0^\dagger - c_0^* = q_0^\dagger - q_0^*$. The yield in terms of future corn is shown in the diagram by the vertical distance $q_1^* - q_1^\dagger = c_1^* - c_1^\dagger$. For an isolated Robinson Crusoe, therefore, plantings of seed (investing) exactly equal non-consumption of current corn (saving).

Once there is a possibility of exchange with other persons, the saving-investment equality need no longer apply for any single person separately. Figure 16.4 pictures an individual possessing *both* productive opportunities and market

Chapter 16
INTEMPORAL
CHOICE:
SAVING,
INVESTMENT,
AND INTEREST

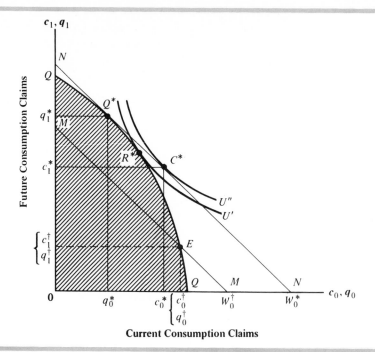

Figure 16.4

Intertemporal Productive–Consumptive Optimum with Exchange. The individual here has intertemporal productive opportunities (shown by the Production-Possibility Curve QQ) as well as exchange opportunities indicated by the market lines like *MM* and *NN* of slope $-P_0/P_1 \equiv -(1 + r)$. The productive optimum Q^* involves physical investment in the amount $q_0^\dagger - q_0^*$. The consumptive optimum C^* indicates that only the amount $c_0^\dagger - c_0^*$ is provided by this individual's own saving; the remainder of his investment is financed by borrowing in the market.

opportunities, as in Panel (b) of Figure 7.6. The productive opportunities are represented, as before, by the Production-Possibility Curve QQ. The market opportunities can be represented by straight market lines of slope $-P_0/P_1 \equiv -(1 + r)$ through attainable points on QQ. Each market line is associated with a particular magnitude of attained wealth according to the equation:

$$(16.4) \qquad W_0 = q_0 + \frac{q_1}{1 + r}$$

Chapter 16
INTEMPORAL
CHOICE:
SAVING,
INVESTMENT,
AND INTEREST

494

One such line, *MM*, shows the possibilities for market exchange from the endowment position E—the associated wealth being $W_0^\dagger$ as before. But it is obviously superior for the individual here first to attain a productive optimum at Q^*, where QQ is tangent to the *highest* attainable market line *NN*. This line *NN* is associated with the maximum attainable level of wealth, W_0^*.

$$(16.5) \qquad W_0^* = q_0^* + \frac{q_1^*}{1 + r}$$

much he or she was willing to self-finance (save). If so, the productive and co[n]sumptive decisions would not be entirely separated. Take the extreme case of a[n] isolated Robinson Crusoe, where costs of transacting are infinite so that there ar[e] no market opportunities at all. For Robinson Crusoe, the productive and consump[-]tive decisions must be identical; *all* his physical investment must be self-financed and so his preferred time-pattern of consumption will surely affect his scale o[f] investment.

If the conditions underlying the Separation Theorem can be regarded as ap[-]proximately applicable, there is a very important practical implication. Suppose that one individual (the "principal") were to delegate productive decisions to another (the "agent"). *The agent would not have to know anything about the personal time-preferences of the principal. If the agent maximizes attained wealth* W_0^*, which is an objective market magnitude, this suffices to assure that the princi-pal is made as well off as possible.

Even more important, an agent could work simultaneously for a number of *different* principals with diverging time-preferences. These principals might be in a position to advantageously combine their productive opportunities by forming a *firm* or corporation (see Chapter 9), agreeing first upon some fractional division of ownership. Then the agent's maximizing the wealth of the corporation suffices to maximize the wealth increments going to each and every one of the owners, re-gardless of divergences in their intertemporal consumption desires. So the types of investments a firm could advantageously undertake need not take into account whether the owners are "heirs with great expectations," or forethoughted savers, or any mixture thereof.[5]

16.B.2
The Present-Value Rule for Investment Decision

Suppose that a "project," i.e., an investment (or disinvestment) opportunity, is under consideration for adoption. What is the appropriate *Investment Decision Rule*?

A project can be regarded, in the simple two-period model so far assumed, as characterized by a sequence of dated "cash flows" or "payments"—income increments (or income decrements) here denoted z_0 and z_1. If z_0 is negative and z_1 is positive, present income is being sacrificed for future income and we have an *investment* project. If z_0 is positive and z_1 negative, it would be a *disinvestment* project.

No matter what the pattern of positive or negative elements, the *Present Value* V_0 of a project is defined as:

$$(16.7) \qquad V_0 \equiv z_0 + \frac{z_1}{1 + r}$$

Comparison with the definition of wealth in equation (16.4) shows that Present Value can be regarded as a *wealth increment* (to the decision-making unit) as-sociated with adoption of the project in question. *If* the Separation Theorem is

[5]When the Separation Theorem is *inapplicable*, there is said to be a "clientele effect" in the decisions of the firm. We would expect principals of different tastes to sort themselves out, becoming owners of different types of firms, each of which could cater to the particular time-preferences of its owners.

Having made the productive decision maximizing wealth, the person can *then* en-gage in market exchange along NN, attaining a consumptive optimum at C^* far superior to what could have been achieved by isolated production. The attained wealth W_0^* becomes the effective *constraint* or budget line for his consumptive optimization decision:

$$(16.6) \qquad c_0 + \frac{c_1}{1 + r} = W_0^*$$

In terms of the special intertemporal terminology, the individual pictured in Figure 16.4 is engaging in physical *investment* (planting of seed corn) to the extent of the horizontal distance $q_0^\dagger - q_0^*$. But his *saving* is a lesser amount, indicated by the horizontal distance $c_0^\dagger - c_0^*$. Here the individual is saving a portion of his endowed current income, but not enough to fully "finance" the investment. It follows that some other members of the society must be saving enough to make up the deficiency, i.e., to provide the remainder of the needed seed corn for the individual of Figure 16.4 to plant. *In the aggregate,* saving (e.g., refraining from current consumption to provide seed corn) must equal investment (e.g., physical sacrifice of current consumption via the planting of seed corn). The condition of market equilibrium is precisely that this equality must hold.

Market equilibrium is shown in Figure 16.5, which corresponds to the inter-section of the transaction supply and demand curves in Figure 7.8 earlier. On the

Figure 16.5

Intertemporal Productive–Consumptive Equilibrium. The aggregate supply of current claims C_0 saved, at each interest rate r, is indicated by the S_s curve; the D_I curve shows the aggregate claims demanded, at each r, for purposes of investment. The intersection determines the equilibrium amount of aggregate saving and investment and the interest rate r^*.

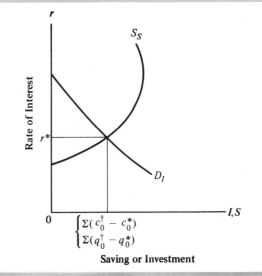

Saving or Investment

Chapter 16
INTEMPORAL
CHOICE:
SAVING,
INVESTMENT,
AND INTEREST

495

[C]hapter 16
[IN]TIPORAL
[CHOIC]E:
[SAVING]S,
[INVEST]MENT,
[AND IN]TEREST

horizontal axis are represented aggregate saving and investment quantities. The curve S_S shows the overall "supply of saving," i.e., the sum of the individual $c_0^\dagger - c_0^*$ magnitudes. The curve D_I shows correspondingly the overall "demand for investment," i.e., the sum of the individual $q_0^\dagger - q_0^*$ magnitudes. The supply of saving and the demand for investment are both functions of the interest rate $r \equiv P_0/P_1 - 1$. The derivation of these curves, proceeding from the individual optimization diagram to individual supply and demand curves and then to market-wide aggregates, follows Section 7.D in all essentials and so is omitted here.

CONCLUSION: In pure exchange, at any given interest rate r each individual will borrow or lend so as to achieve a preferred intertemporal pattern of consumption. At the equilibrium interest rate r^*, the supply of lendings and the demand for borrowings balance out. If intertemporal productive transformation (investment) opportunities exist, at any given interest rate each individual with such opportunities will choose the scale of investment maximizing wealth—planning also to borrow or lend, as required, to achieve a preferred time-pattern of consumption. At the equilibrium interest rate r^*, the aggregate supply of saving balances the aggregate demand for investment.

EXAMPLE 16.1
SOCIAL SECURITY,
SAVING, AND
NATIONAL
INCOME

Before the Social Security program came into effect, individuals generally provided for income to be received in their retirement years by saving out of income earned in their productive working years. This saving might have taken the form of holdings of bank deposits, annuities, stocks and bonds, or of productive assets like real estate. No matter what form such saving took, it served to finance economy-wide real investments that increased the real-capital of the nation.

Upon introduction of Social Security, however, retirement income was guaranteed to beneficiaries—reducing their need to save during their working years. Also, Social Security taxes on earnings reduced the funds in individuals' hands available for saving. Thus, aggregate *private* saving would be expected to decline as a result of the Social Security program. On the other hand, the federal government was receiving huge inflows of Social Security contributions. Had the government adopted a policy of "funding" these contributions, the cash inflows would have been used to purchase stocks and bonds, real estate, etc. (Indeed, this is precisely what insurance companies do with premiums paid in under their private "social security" programs for individuals who purchase retirement annuities.) Then the collective saving of the Social Security Administration would have balanced the reduction in saving of contributors.

However, the decision was made *not* to fund Social Security by creating and holding reserves sufficient to generate required future outlays. Instead, Social Security tax revenues were used to support the general expenses of government. Some economists have contended that, in consequence, there has been a severe adverse effect upon aggregate saving in the economy (and

therefore also upon aggregate real investment). Martin Feldstein[3] has estimated that the Social Security program has reduced overall private saving 38%—without, as just explained, providing any compensating increase in collective or government saving. As a result, the nation's real investment has been considerably diminished. The lower scale of investment over the years means that the nation's stock of real-capital is substantially smaller than it would otherwise have been. And since real-capital contributes to production (raises the Average Product of labor and other resources), total and per-capita national income have also been affected. Feldstein estimates that, by 1972, the Social Security program had led to a startling reduction in GNP—of between 11% and 15%.

[3]Martin Feldstein, "Social Security, Induced Retirement, and Aggregate Capital Accumulation," *Journal of Political Economy*, v. 82 (Sept./Oct. 1974).

The analysis of consumption and production patterns over time is widely regarded as constituting one of the more difficult branches of economic theory. On the other hand, this is also a branch of economics that is of intense and immediate concern for practical men of affairs. Decision-makers in government and business continually face such choices as: What investment projects to adopt? How to finance the set of chosen projects? Over what time frame to pay out the benefits? In this section and the one following, the theoretical results just derived will be applied to certain aspects of the investment decision problem arising in the world of affairs.

An essential feature of productive–consumptive optimization as pictured in Figure 16.4 is the fact that *the productive optimum position is entirely independent of the individual's preferences*. No matter how the indifference curves may shift around, the productive optimum Q^* is unchanged. Note, by way of contrast, that the *consumptive* optimum C^* surely will be affected if the indifference curves shift so as to change relative preferences for present versus future consumption. But the location of Q^* depends only on the Production-Possibility Curve QQ and the slope of the market lines. This independence, called the *Separation Theorem*, follows from the assumption of perfect and costless markets (see Chapter 8). Suppose that market transactions were instead costly, that an individual could only borrow at much higher rate of interest than that at which he or she could lend.[4] The amo that such a person would physically invest, the choice of Q^* on the Produc Possibility Curve, could then depend in part upon preferences, i.e., upo

[4]This difference might be due to "proportional transaction costs" as discussed in Secti

applicable, wealth-maximization is the object of all productive decisions. Then positive wealth increments are unambiguously desirable and negative wealth increments undesirable. These considerations lead to:

PRESENT-VALUE RULE #1:   Adopt any project for which Present Value V_0 is positive; reject any project for which Present Value V_0 is negative. (Note that this rule has the same form for investment and disinvestment projects.)

There are possibilities of complications where projects are *interdependent*. Conceivably, adoption of any one project might change the z_0, z_1 sequence associated with another. The obvious implication for these cases is to adopt that *set* of projects whose combined payment stream has maximum Present Value. We shall not go through all the interdependence possibilities here, but rather state the rule that applies when projects or combinations of projects are *mutually exclusive*:[6]

PRESENT-VALUE RULE #2:   If two projects (or combinations of projects) are mutually exclusive, adopt that which has the higher Present Value V_0.

The discussion to this point has been limited to consumption and investment choices over two dates: "now" (time-0) and "one year from now" (time-1). But the same general principles apply to more complex multitemporal decisions. We can think of individuals as attempting to attain preferred consumption combinations over any number of dates from "now" to an "economic horizon" at some future date T. Thus, the ultimate objects of choice are consumption sequences c_0, $c_1, c_2, \ldots, c_T$. In proceeding from an endowed sequence $c_0^\dagger, c_1^\dagger, \ldots, c_T^\dagger$ to his preferred consumption sequence, the individual will be making a variety of intertemporal productive transformations and market exchanges. But as before, if the Separation Theorem is applicable, determination of the productive optimum $Q^* = (q_0^*, q_1^*, q_2^*, \ldots, q_T^*)$ can be guided solely by the goal of *wealth-maximization* independent of preferences. Thus, the Present-Value Rule continues to apply. However, we must generalize the concept of Present Value to a multiperiod form.

In terms of market equilibrium, the interaction of individuals' supplies and demands today for consumption claims at different dates will determine prices $P_0, P_1, P_2, \ldots, P_T$.[7] We can fix $P_0 \equiv 1$, letting current income claims (current dollars) continue to serve as "numeraire." The equilibrium prices ruling at different dates will depend, of course, upon the transactions resulting from the interaction of all the separate individuals' time-endowments, productive opportunities, and time-preferences.

---

[6] Any list of alternative projects, interdependent or not, can be grouped into mutually exclusive combinations. Thus, three projects A, B, C can be sorted into the eight mutually exclusive combinations 0, A, B, C, AB, AC, BC, and ABC (where 0 represents adopting *no* project at all).

[7] It is important to note that while the claims represent rights to income at different dates, the prices are those quoted in the trading that takes place now. P_1 is the price *today* of a claim to income (dollar) payable one year in the future, P_2 is the price *today* of a dollar payable two years in the future, etc.

Chapter 16
INTEMPORAL
CHOICE:
SAVING,
INVESTMENT,
AND INTEREST

In translating from *prices* to *interest rates*, there are two different formulations in common use.

Consider the successive one-year price ratios P_1/P_0, P_2/P_1, . . . , P_T/P_{T-1}. These can be used to define the successive one-year "forward" interest rates r_1, r_2, . . . , r_T on the left side of the Table of Interest-Rate Equivalents below. Here r_1 is the rate appropriate in exchanging or "discounting" time-1 claims into their present or time-0 equivalents, r_2 the rate for discounting time-2 claims into time-1 equivalents, etc.

Alternatively, we can consider the ratios P_1/P_0, P_2/P_0, . . . , P_T/P_0—defined so that P_0 appears in all the denominators. These can be used, as on the right side of the table, to define the "long-term" interest rates R_1, R_2, . . . , R_T. These rates are appropriate for discounting the claims of any date *directly* into current (time-0) equivalents.

Table of Interest-Rate Equivalents

$$\frac{P_1}{P_0} = \frac{1}{1 + r_1} \qquad\qquad \frac{P_1}{P_0} = \frac{1}{1 + R_1}$$

$$\frac{P_2}{P_1} = \frac{1}{1 + r_2} \qquad\qquad \frac{P_2}{P_0} = \frac{1}{(1 + R_2)^2}$$

$$\cdots \qquad\qquad\qquad \cdots$$

$$\frac{P_T}{P_{T-1}} = \frac{1}{1 + r_T} \qquad\qquad \frac{P_T}{P_0} = \frac{1}{(1 + R_T)^T}$$

The Present Value of a multi-period sequence of income increments (or decrements) can be correspondingly expressed in two different forms:

$$\textbf{(16.8)} \qquad V_0 \equiv z_0 + \frac{z_1}{1 + R_1} + \frac{z_2}{(1 + R_2)^2} + \cdots + \frac{z_T}{(1 + R_T)^T}$$

$$\textbf{(16.9)} \qquad V_0 \equiv z_0 + \frac{z_1}{1 + r_1} + \frac{z_2}{(1 + r_2)(1 + r_1)}$$

$$+ \cdots + \frac{z_T}{(1 + r_T)\ldots(1 + r_2)(1 + r_1)}$$

For some purposes the first formulation is the more convenient, for other purposes the second. There is no ultimate difference between them. The "long term" rate R_t applicable for discounting claims dated t years from now is obviously a kind of average of the forward rates r_1, r_2, . . . , r_t between now and that date.

While there are important economic forces leading to systematic patterns in the "term structure" of the r_t or R_t interest rates, in most practical investment-decision applications it is customary to assume that the currently applicable rate will maintain itself into the future. Of course, if the r_t are all equal to some common value r then all the R_t will also be equal to r, so that the two formulations of (16.8) and (16.9) become identical in the form:

Chapter 16
INTEMPORAL
CHOICE:
SAVING,
INVESTMENT,
AND INTEREST

500

$$(16.10) \qquad V_0 \equiv z_0 + \frac{z_1}{1+r} + \frac{z_2}{(1+r)^2} + \cdots + \frac{z_T}{(1+r)^T}$$

Let us now modify equation (16.10), which defines the Present Value V_0 of a project at some constant intertemporal interest rate r, in the following ways. First, assume that the "economic horizon" T is infinite. Second, suppose that returns on the project begin at time-1 so that there is no current payment element z_0. And third, assume that the future receipts $z_1, z_2, \ldots$ extending out to infinity remain at some constant level z. Then (16.10) reduces to the simple form:[8]

$$(16.10') \qquad V_0 \equiv \frac{z}{r} \quad \text{or} \quad r \equiv \frac{z}{V_0}$$

Compare these with equation (15.3) of the previous chapter. We can now see why the interest rate r entered into the relation between annual income from a source of productive services and the value of the source itself. Our derivation has shown how the rate of interest r can be interpreted in two different ways: (1) as the *time-premium*, the extra market value of an earlier over a later-dated claim and (2) as the relation that must hold in equilibrium between an *income flow* z in comparison with the *value of its source* V_0. We sometimes say that V_0 in equation (16.10') is the "capitalized" value of the annual income z, or that z is the annual yield of V_0 as "principal sum." These statements are all correct, under the special assumptions that led to the expression of (16.10) in the special form (16.10').

A study by A. Razin and J. D. Campbell[9] calculated Present Values of lifetime earnings for holders of bachelor's degrees in various fields. National Science Foundation 1968 data on yearly incomes of scientific manpower were used. The authors assumed that earnings begin in the 5th year after admission to college, and terminate in the 44th year, so that equation (16.10) was applied in the special form:

EXAMPLE 16.2
PRESENT VALUES
OF LIFETIME
EARNINGS FOR
HOLDERS OF
BACHELOR'S
DEGREES

[9]Assaf Razin and James D. Campbell, "Internal Allocation of University Resources," *Western Economic Journal*, v. 10 (Sept. 1972), esp. p. 315.

[8]The derivation proceeds from (16.10), under the special assumptions above, as follows:

$$V_0 = z \left[\frac{1}{1+r} + \frac{1}{(1+r)^2} + \cdots \right]$$

Let $1/(1+r)$ be denoted as k. Then:

$$V_0 = z(1 + k + k^2 + \cdots) - z = \frac{z}{1-k} - z$$

But

$$1 - k = 1 - \frac{1}{1+r} = \frac{r}{1+r}$$

So

$$V_0 = z \left(\frac{1+r}{r} \right) - z = \frac{z}{r}$$

Chapter 16
INTEMPORAL
CHOICE:
SAVING,
INVESTMENT,
AND INTEREST

501

$$V_0 = \frac{z_5}{(1 + r)^5} + \frac{z_6}{(1 + r)^6} + \dots + \frac{z_{44}}{(1 + r)^{44}}$$

Calculating in terms of an interest rate $r = 3\%$, the table indicates some of the results obtained. (The relatively favorable position of the economics degree is consistent with the salary standing of economics instructors reported in Example 1.2.)

Present Values of Earnings for Bachelor's Degrees

Mathematics	$342,068
Economics	339,482
Computer Sciences	306,733
Political Science	300,000
Physics	282,758
Psychology	262,127
Agricultural Science	225,118
Biological Science	215,691
Sociology	213,590

COMMENT: In interpreting these calculations, it must not be assumed that the numbers shown represent the *net* or overall Present Value of going to college and receiving the degree. Only the benefits, the earnings received by holders of the degree, have been shown. The cost side of the picture, which would allow for college-related outlays (tuition, living expenses, books, etc.) and also for earnings foregone by students during the four college years, has not been taken into account.

16.C

RISK AND THE INTEREST RATE

The numerical interest rate r employed in calculating equation (16.10) usually has a very substantial effect upon the Present Value obtained. This is especially the case when the annual payments z_t, whether negative (representing costs) or positive (representing benefits or receipts), extend to a relatively distant time-horizon T.

EXAMPLE 16.3
PRESENT VALUES
OF THE FEATHER
RIVER PROJECT

The Feather River Project is an enormous undertaking of the State of California, designed to convey water from a dam and reservoir in the northern part of the state to numerous delivery points in the central and southern portions. The table that follows shows the results of an independent assessment (made prior to construction) of the prospective costs and receipts of the project and of the net balance of the two, all calculated in terms of present values. Three alternative routes then under consideration were evaluated.

The present-value calculation considered two alternative interest rates, 2.7% and 5%.

While all the Present Values were negative, the higher 5% interest rate was associated with relatively lower present values of both costs and receipts. Since the cost sequence is a series of positive payments at each date, and the receipts sequence also a series of positive elements, the larger the r the smaller the discounted sum for each, as may be seen from equation (16.10). But the table shows that the impact of a higher r upon receipts is greater than upon costs. The reason is that costs are typically incurred *earlier* in time than receipts are received, so that a rise in the discount factor $(1 + r)$ operates more powerfully to reduce the latter. It often happens that a project will show a favorable balance of receipts over costs when *undiscounted*, i.e., when calculated in terms of $r = 0$ in the discounting equation. *The higher the* r, *the less attractive the project* is a reliable general rule.

Present Values of the Feather River Project (millions of dollars)

INTEREST RATE	COSTS	RECEIPTS	NET PRESENT VALUE	NET PRESENT VALUE, ADJUSTED*
2.7%				
Route 1	$1,241	$1,079	$−162	$− 97
Route 8A	1,123	1,012	−111	− 46
Route 10A	1,029	919	−110	− 46
5%				
Route 1	1,035	515	−520	−502
Route 8A	860	445	−415	−397
Route 10A	799	409	−391	−372

Source: J. C. DeHaven and J. Hirshleifer, "Feather River Water for Southern California," *Land Economics*, v. 33 (Aug. 1957), p. 201. (Some technical footnotes omitted.)

*Adjustment credits an allowance for flood-control benefit and salvage value.

COMMENT: The Feather River Project was adopted, despite the showing of negative net Present Value. Thus, the investment decision rule of this chapter was violated. Indeed, the route adopted was that which had the *most unfavorable* receipts-cost balance. (Reasons why this might have occurred are suggested in the analysis of the political process in Chapter 18.)

The next example also illustrates the powerful effect of interest rates upon Present Values.

Professors in general, and economics professors in particular, devote a considerable portion of their time to research. The output of successful research usually takes the form of articles published in scholarly journals. Publications lead to professional recognition and so tend to raise the lifetime earnings of their authors.

EXAMPLE 16.4
PROFESSORS AND
PUBLICATIONS

H. P. Tuckman and J. Leahey[10] conducted a study estimating the worth to authors of a published article. Their results indicate that a *first* article by an Assistant Professor is associated with an increase of $12,340 in Present Value of lifetime earnings, calculated at an interest rate of 5%. At a higher 10% interest rate, the future earnings gains are discounted more heavily, however, leading to a lower Present Value estimate of $7,074.

The Present Values of lifetime income increments due to articles published by Associate and Full Professors were generally lower than for Assistant Professors, the main explanation being the fact that the higher-rank professors are nearer retirement age. Another interesting point observed was the operation of the Law of Diminishing Returns. At the lower $r = 5\%$, the Present Value of a marginal article published by an Assistant Professor steadily declined from $12,340 for the first article, to $4,310 for the fifth article, down to only $1,544 for the thirtieth published article!

[10]Howard P. Tuckman and Jack Leahey, "How Much Is an Article Worth?" *Journal of Political Economy*, v. 83 (Oct. 1975).

An interest rate of $r = 3\%$ was used in one of the studies reported above; a second employed two alternative rates, 2.7% and 5%; and the third used 5% and 10%. Can all these be correct? How do we determine the correct rate to use?

Interest rates may vary for a number of reasons. First, they change historically, so that decisions involving Present Values calculated in 1950 or 1960 were subject to a different r than were 1970 decisions. And even at a specific moment of time, as we saw above, there is a "term structure" of interest rates—differing rates can be relevant for discounting near-future cash flows versus far-future cash flows. On December 27, 1978, for example, U.S. Treasury issues (bonds and notes) of different maturities were selling at prices representing different net interest yields to purchasers. As of that date, issues maturing in the nearer future (1979 and 1980) were typically yielding from 10.0% to 10.5%; issues maturing in the medium future (1982 and 1983) were yielding from 9.2% to 9.5%; while distant future maturities (beyond 2000) were yielding around 8.8%.

The major reason for a variety of interest rates existing at a moment of time, however, is the element of *risk*. Even if maturity and all other elements of the transaction are the same, bonds of foreign governments or of municipalities or of private corporations are generally considered riskier than U.S. Treasury issues— and so can only be sold at prices generating a higher risk-compensating interest yield to their holders. Similarly, a potential borrower will find that a bank or other lending institution may offer a variety of interest rates—a higher rate for an unsecured loan than for a loan secured by a mortgage or other collateral or guarantees.

Two rather different aspects of risk should be distinguished:

(a) *Default risk*: Some transactions, like a bank loan or a bond issue, represent an explicit promise of performance by the borrower (promise to pay interest and to repay principal). If these promises are not fully carried out, the borrower has to some degree defaulted. Suppose a bank makes a one-year $1000 loan to an individual at a contractual (promised) interest rate of 10%, and imagine that the

Chapter 16
INTEMPORAL
CHOICE:
SAVING,
INVESTMENT,
AND INTEREST

504

bank has 99% confidence in the borrower's performance but believes there is a 1% chance of a complete default on both principal and interest. Then the "expected" or average interest yield in probabilistic terms for the bank is not 10% but only 8.9%.[11] It is the 8.9% that approximates the "true" interest rate; 10% is the "nominal" interest rate, containing an adjustment or premium for default risk.

(b) *Variability Risk*: Some financial instruments, like equity shares of corporate stock, do not have any explicit promise of performance. The returns to the lender or investor, in the form of dividends or other cash payments, may vary considerably up or down from some average value the investor may expect to receive; this is variability risk. In general, there is an aversion to variability risk. As between two securities with the same average yield, the typical investor will prefer the one with lesser variability, the one more nearly approaching a fully certain yield. It follows that securities whose returns are highly uncertain will sell at prices yielding their holders *greater* average yields—the difference being the adjustment or premium for the greater variability risk.

A study by R. G. Ibbotson and R. A. Sinquefield[12] examined the actual yields obtained over the period 1926–1974 by investors holding a number of different classes of financial instruments. Since U.S. Treasury Bonds can be assumed free of default risk, the excess of experienced yields on comparable corporate bonds over yields on Treasury issues provides an estimate of the *default risk* on corporate bonds. And the excess of experienced yields on common stocks over Treasury Bonds provides an estimate of the *variability risk* of stocks. Some of their results are summarized in the table.

EXAMPLE 16.5
RISK PREMIUMS

Rates of Return and Risk Premiums

	GEOMETRIC MEAN ANNUAL RATE OF RETURN	DEFAULT RISK PREMIUM	VARIABILITY RISK PREMIUM
Long-term Government Bonds	3.2%	—	—
Long-term Corporate Bonds	3.6%	.3%	—
Common stocks	8.5%	—	6.1%

The long-term corporate bond rate less the estimated default-risk premium approximates the long-term government (riskless) rate, as does the common-stock yield less the estimated variability-risk premium. (The inexactness of the approximations is due to technical adjustments made in working with the data.)

[12]Roger G. Ibbotson and Rex A. Sinquefield, "Stocks, Bonds, Bills, and Inflation: Year-by-Year Historical Returns (1927–1974)," *Journal of Business*, v. 49 (Jan. 1976), esp. p. 40.

---

[11]The bank anticipates receiving $1100 at the end of the year if all goes well (99% probability), but otherwise receiving nothing. Its "expected" or average net interest return is .99($1100) + .01($0) − $1000, or $89, which is a rate of yield of 8.9% on the $1000 principal amount.

The problem of choosing an interest rate, for calculating Present Value via equation (16.10), may arise in either *normative* or *positive* analysis (see Section 1.A.3). From the *positive* point of view, we may ask: "What interest rates are economic decision-makers actually employing in their investment decisions?" From a *normative* point of view, we could be asking: "What interest rate ought a decision-maker employ in accepting or rejecting an investment project?"

Example 16.2 represents positive analysis. Here the economists are acting as scientific observers; in choosing a discount rate r they are making an assumption as to how heavily college students (explicitly or implicitly) discount anticipated future earnings in deciding whether or not to earn a college degree. Example 16.4 on the worth of a published article, and Example 16.5 on the realized rates of return observed in the financial markets, similarly constitute positive analyses. In these terms it seems that the 3% discount rate employed in Example 16.2 is on the low side. The decision to invest time and resources in obtaining a bachelor's degree is obviously a highly risky one; a rational investor would demand a very substantial variability-risk premium before doing so. In contrast, Example 16.4 studies a considerably less risky decision (whether or not to invest in producing a single publishable article), and uses a considerably higher range of interest rates (5% and 10%).

Example 16.3 is on a rather different footing, representing a *normative* analysis. The economists there were concerned with the question: Should the Feather River Project have been built? When governmental decisions are involved, as was the case here, questions of collective choice arise that are better left for discussion in Part Six following. However, normative analyses can be conducted on behalf of private agencies as well. A firm might find itself in a position where the Present Value of a more or less risky project is positive (indicating that the project should be adopted) at a low interest rate but negative (indicating that the project should be rejected) at a high interest rate. What is the appropriate rate to use? In general, the correct rate (the one that would lead to the correct decision in terms of maximizing private wealth) would be the rate explicitly or implicitly used by the market in evaluating investments of comparable risk. How can the firm actually determine that r? By hiring a consulting economist, of course.

EXAMPLE 16.6
FIRE YOURS, HIRE
OURS!

Errors in economic reasoning involving time often stem from an elementary fallacy: failure to appreciate that a dollar in the distant future is worth less today (has lower Present Value) than a dollar in the relatively near future. The following is an extract from a letter to Consumers Union (the well-known consumer advice organization).

Dear Editor:

I have just read your "Economics for consumers: Notes to home buyers" in the April 1972 issue. As it happens, I am in charge of job placement for the fledgling economists trained here at _____ University. Putting these two together, I can say in short: FIRE YOURS, HIRE OURS.

Your consumer economist compares the same appliances, available at $675 from a store but at $450 through the builder. The store's financing arrangement is a 2-year contract at 15% interest. The builder's is a mortgage add-on, 27-year contract at 7¾%. Your economist assures CU's readers that the store offers the better deal! He arrives at this conclusion by adding up all the interest payments and tacking them onto the purchase price—making the totals $785 for the store deal and $1075 for the builder deal. One's mind reels at the enormity of the error here, flying as it does in the face of both formal economics and common sense. Formally speaking, it suffices to point out that a dollar payment deferred 27 years has a present worth of only 13 cents (at 7¾% interest, a reasonable current rate). Payments at different dates cannot be aggregated meaningfully without allowing for the time value of money.

Returning to common sense, I don't suppose many of your readers could really have been fooled into thinking that it's better to buy at $675 than at $450, or better to pay 15% than 7¾% interest.

Sincerely,
Professor X

REAL INTEREST AND MONEY INTEREST

What we have been referring to as the rate of interest so far in this chapter is more specifically known as the *real* rate of interest. Following the usual practice in price theory, we have looked behind the "veil of money" so as to gain an understanding of how the concept of interest is related to the rate of market exchange between current real consumption claims and future real consumption claims. Returning for simplicity to a two-date model (time-0 and time-1), the real rate of interest is the proportionate market premium on current real claims C_0 relative to real claims C_1 to be received one year in the future. Denoting quantities exchanged in markets as Δc_0 and Δc_1, and dropping minus signs for the sake of convenience (i.e., dealing in terms of absolute values), the exchange ratio between present and future real claims can be expressed as:

$$(16.11) \qquad \frac{\Delta c_1}{\Delta c_0} = 1 + r$$

But, in common parlance, "the rate of interest" is ordinarily understood to be associated with the lending and borrowing of *money*. The *money rate of interest*, which can be symbolized as r', need not in general be exactly equal to the real rate of interest r. The money rate of interest is the premium on *current money* m_0 relative to *future money* m_1. That is, if current money is exchanged in the loan

Chapter 16
INTEMPORAL
CHOICE:
SAVING,
INVESTMENT,
AND INTEREST

markets against future money in the amounts Δm_0 and Δm_1, the exchange ratio (in absolute terms) defines the *money* rate of interest in the expression:

$$(16.12) \qquad \frac{\Delta m_1}{\Delta m_0} = 1 + r'$$

What is the relation between the real rate of interest r and the money rate of interest r'? This is connected with movements of the "price level," that is, with changes in the prices (in contemporaneous *money* units) of *real* goods. At time-0, money is traded for real goods in the exchange ratio $\Delta m_0/\Delta c_0$. At time-1, the ratio is $\Delta m_1/\Delta c_1$. These exchange ratios (in absolute values) define the current and future money *price levels* P_0^m and P_1^m:

$$(16.13) \qquad P_0^m = \frac{\Delta m_0}{\Delta c_0} \quad \text{and} \quad P_1^m = \frac{\Delta m_1}{\Delta c_1}$$

These imply:

$$\frac{\Delta m_1}{\Delta m_0} = \frac{P_1^m (\Delta c_1)}{P_0^m (\Delta c_0)}$$

Finally, this can be rewritten, using equations (16.11) and (16.12):

$$(16.14) \qquad 1 + r' = (1 + r) \frac{P_1^m}{P_0^m}$$

In terms of economic logic, equation (16.14) is readily understandable. The left hand side, $1 + r'$, is what a lender receives in future money in return for giving up one unit of current money. The amount so received must depend, in part, upon the *real* future return $1 + r$ per unit of current *real* claims sacrificed. But money may rise or fall in value relative to the underlying real claims. Hence, the rate of money interest r' must be sufficiently high to make up for any increase in the price level that makes future real claims more expensive relative to future money.

It is convenient to express the ratio of money price levels, P_1^m/P_0^m, as $1 + a$, where a is the *anticipated rate of price-level inflation*. Then:

$$(16.15) \qquad 1 + r' = (1 + r)(1 + a)$$

Chapter 16
INTEMPORAL
CHOICE:
SAVING,
INVESTMENT,
AND INTEREST

or

$$(16.16) \qquad r' = r + a + ra$$

This says that the money rate of interest equals the real rate of interest plus the anticipated rate of price inflation, plus the cross-product of the latter two. When r and a remain in their usual range of percentage points, the cross-product term can to a fair approximation be ignored. With *compound* interest, the shorter the period of compounding the more correct it is to drop the cross-product. For continuously-compounded interest, the cross-product drops out entirely and we have exactly:

(16.17) $r' = r + a$

It is in this simple form (16.17) that the relation between real and money interest is usually expressed.[13]

PROPOSITION: The money rate of interest equals the real rate of interest plus the anticipated rate of price inflation.

William E. Gibson[14] examined the effects of inflationary expectations upon the "nominal" (money) rates of interest paid on U.S. Treasury securities in the period 1962 to 1970. In all such studies, the practical problem is to find a measure of "inflationary anticipations," which are not a directly visible magnitude. The measure used by Gibson was derived from a semi-annual survey of economists conducted by Joseph Livingston, a nationally syndicated financial columnist.

Using this information as an estimate of anticipations a, and the recorded interest rates as the measure of the money rate r', Gibson estimated statistically an equation in the form:

$r' = H + Ka$

Here H and K were the parameters of the line of best fit to the observed data. On the assumption that the *real* rate of interest r was constant over this period, comparison with equation (16.17) above shows that the fitted

EXAMPLE 16.7
REAL AND
MONEY RATES OF
INTEREST

[14]William E. Gibson, "Interest Rates and Inflationary Expectations: New Evidence," *American Economic Review*, v. 62 (Dec. 1972).

---

[13]*Mathematical Footnote:* If i is any annual interest rate, a dollar will grow in value to $1 + i$ dollars at the end of one year. With quarterly compounding of interest, the terminal value will be $\left(1 + \dfrac{i}{4}\right)^4$; with any compounding frequency of f per year, it will be $\left(1 + \dfrac{i}{f}\right)^f$ For continuous compounding, we let f approach infinity. Then $\lim_{f \to \infty}\left(1 + \dfrac{i}{f}\right)^f \equiv \lim_{h \to \infty}[(1 + \dfrac{i}{h})^h]^i$ where $h \equiv f/i$. But the limit within the brackets is e, the base of the natural logarithms. The terminal value of a dollar continuously compounded at interest rate i, at the end of a year, is then e^i. The terminal value of Z dollars at the end of T years is Ze^{iT}.

Expressed in terms of continuously-compounded rates, equation (16.14) becomes:

$e^{r'} = e^r e^a$

Taking logarithms, (16.17) follows directly.

Chapter 16
INTEMPORAL
CHOICE:
SAVING,
INVESTMENT,
AND INTEREST

509

parameter H is an estimate of the real rate r. Also, the fitted parameter K should be simply equal to unity.

The statistical evidence varied somewhat according to the type of security considered. But the H figures obtained suggested a *real* rate of interest between 2% and 3% (much lower than the nominal interest rates in this period, of course). And the K estimates were not far from unity (for example, .9300 for 3-month Treasury bills, .8959 for 3-year to 5-year Treasury notes).

One interesting point is that the K estimates were closer to unity in the latter than in the earlier portion of the period. The suggestion is that the general public was gradually "learning" to adjust its investments to the prospect of continuing inflation.

Equation (16.17) is connected with important issues of *macro*economic policy. Suppose the government desires, for reasons that do not concern us here, to reduce the money interest rate r'. One thing the government can do is to increase the aggregate money balances in the economy (for example, by paying its bills with newly printed money). In the short run, as the aggregate amount of current money m_0 rises, this does tend to lower the money rate of interest. For, if people have more m_0 in their hands they are more inclined to make market exchanges Δm_0 of current money against future money, i.e., they are more inclined to *lend* money for future return. As we can see in equation (16.12), when the denominator Δm_0 on the lefthand side rises then r' on the righthand side falls. However, there is an important after-effect to consider. When government increases the aggregate of current money m_0, equation (16.13) tells us that the current money price-level P_0^m also tends to rise ("more money chasing the same amount of goods"). It *may* happen that this process tends to generate public anticipations of further future price inflation. People may think that if the government has found it convenient to print more money forcing up the current price-level P_0^m, they will find it convenient to do so again in the future. Should these anticipations become general, *a* rises in equation (16.17), so that the money rate of interest r' must rise. Hence, a successful attempt to lower r' *in the short run* may only serve to raise it higher *in the long run*.

16.E

DETERMINANTS OF INTEREST RATES

Chapter 16
INTEMPORAL
CHOICE:
SAVING,
INVESTMENT,
AND INTEREST

510

What are the underlying forces tending to cause interest rates to be high in some countries and low in others, high in some historical periods and low in others? In line with the analysis here, the determinants of *real* interest rates may be classified under the headings of: (1) time-preference, (2) time-endowment, and (3) time-productivity. Given these determinants of *real* interest, the *money* interest rate is accounted for by incorporating the anticipations of price-level inflation as shown by equation (16.17). And in fact, countries with established patterns of ongoing price inflation do have correspondingly high money rates of interest (as can be observed in the United States today).

1. TIME-PREFERENCE: The higher the general pattern of preference in a community for *current* as against *future* consumption, the steeper the indifference curves on c_0, c_1 axes (as in Figure 16.1) tend to be. The market price ratio $P_0/P_1 \equiv 1 + r$ (the absolute slope of the market lines) must to a greater or lesser extent reflect this, so that *high time-preference causes high interest*. Low time-preference is associated with personal characteristics such as forethoughtedness, strong family ties, willingness to defer enjoyment, etc. The later years of the Roman Empire were characterized by a decline in such "Puritanical" attitudes, and interest rates were accordingly high. A similar shift in values appears to be taking place in the Western world today, which might help explain the recent tendency of Western interest rates to rise.

2. TIME-ENDOWMENT: As we have seen, an "heir with great expectations," whose personal income-endowment lies mainly in the future, tends to be a borrower. In Figure 16.1 the endowment position E for such an heir would lie toward the northwest, in the region where the indifference curves are steep. If an entire society were in the situation of expecting future income to be much greater than current income, the interest rate (reflecting the absolute slope of the market lines) would correspondingly tend to be high. A notable example is a community struck by a disaster. It is usually the case that a catastrophe damages goods relatively close to consumption more drastically than it impairs the basic productive powers of the economy. A drought or a hurricane, for example, will commonly destroy growing crops to a greater degree than long-term productive fundamentals such as fertility of the land, capacity and training of the population, etc. It follows that present or near-future income-endowments are affected more seriously than far-future endowments, so that interest rates tend to rise when disaster strikes.

3. TIME-PRODUCTIVITY: Higher time-productivity of investment is represented by greater ratios $\Delta q_1/\Delta q_0$, i.e., steeper absolute slopes of individuals' intertemporal Production-Possibility Curves QQ in Figure 16.4. If this pattern is typical of a community, the market interest rate must to a greater or lesser extent reflect it. Thus interest rates have tended to be high in newer and more productive communities, e.g., higher in America than in England, and higher in California than in Massachusetts. Also, technological change works somewhat like new settlement of territory in making available improved opportunities for investment. Thus, interest rates tend to be higher in technologically progressive than in more static countries and eras.

Finally, a very important consideration is the *degree of isolation* of a community. There may be a very special or idiosyncratic situation as to time-preference, time-endowment, or time-productivity in a small local area. Nevertheless, unless that region is isolated from commerce the interest rates there cannot diverge too far from the more normal rates representing the typical picture in the outside world. The process of exchange will lead to a flow of investments and

Chapter 16
INTEMPORAL
CHOICE:
SAVING,
INVESTMENT,
AND INTEREST

511

loans (in the form of money and real claims) from the low-interest area to the high-interest area of any integrated market. The differences historically observed between interest rates in England and America, or between Massachusetts and California, have therefore been much smaller than would have been the case had the communities in question been isolated from one another.

EXAMPLE 16.8
INTEREST AND
THE GOLD RUSH[15]

Gold was struck in California in 1848, and the gold rush was on. The gold miners (and most other Californians as well) typically thought of themselves as having little current endowed income, but as prospectively very rich. Thus, they were in a situation comparable to that of "heirs with great expectations," and would be expected to be borrowers.

However, until the completion of the first transcontinental railroad in 1869, California was largely isolated from the rest of the world. Hence, Californians for the most part could only borrow from one another. Consequently, the interest rate during the period of the gold rush was generally very high, 24% per annum being a typical figure. This was far higher than the rate then ruling in the East. In the decade following the completion of the transcontinental railroad, it became much more feasible to transfer real resources in the form of loans from the East, and the interest rate in California dropped to around 6%.

[15] See Irving Fisher, *The Theory of Interest* (New York: The Macmillan Company, 1930; reprinted [Augustus M. Kelley] 1955), Chap. 18.

SUMMARY
OF CHAPTER
16

Individuals' decisions as to saving or investment are based upon their preferences and their opportunities regarding intertemporal consumption. *Saving* is consuming less than income; *investing* is a productive operation that actually transforms potential current consumption into future income. These decisions interact in the market to determine the price ratio between current and future claims, P_0/P_1. This ratio is also defined as $1 + r$, where r is the rate of interest representing the market premium of current claims over one-year future claims.

In a world of pure exchange, without intertemporal productive opportunities, each individual would choose a preferred intertemporal pattern of consumption subject to a fixed wealth constraint. Saving by some (lending) would necessarily be balanced by the dis-saving of others (borrowing). The intersection of the aggregate supply curve of lending and the aggregate demand curve for borrowing would determine the equilibrium interest rate and the amount of borrowing and lending. Where there are productive opportunities, however, individuals would choose a wealth-maximizing *productive optimum* solution, determining their level of investment, together with a utility-maximizing *consumptive optimum* solution determining their level of saving. In the market as a whole, the intersection of the aggregate supply curve of saving and the aggregate demand curve for investment would determine the equilibrium rate of interest and the amount of saving and investment.

Chapter 16
INTEMPORAL
CHOICE:
SAVING,
INVESTMENT,
AND INTEREST

512

If markets for intertemporal claims are perfect, the Separation Theorem holds. As the productive decision then involves maximizing an objective market quantity, wealth, the task can more easily be delegated to an agent. This feature facilitates the formation of firms. If managers exploit productive opportunities so as to maximize wealth of the firm, they will also be maximizing wealth for all the owners individually.

A project or set of projects that is wealth-increasing has a positive Present Value V_0. In the simple two-period case, in terms of cash-flow payments z_0 and z_1, Present Value is defined as:

$$V_0 \equiv z_0 + \frac{z_1}{1 + r}$$

Any project with positive Present Value should be adopted; any project with negative Present Value should be rejected. The equation defining Present Value can be generalized to the multi-period case, making use of the anticipated stream of payments $z_0, z_1, \ldots, z_T$ and the sequential forward interest rates $r_1, \ldots, r_T$. If the interest rate is expected to be constant at the level r over time, the generalization takes the simple form:

$$V_0 \equiv z_0 + \frac{z_1}{1 + r} + \ldots + \frac{z_T}{(1 + r)^T}$$

An important issue in many empirical studies or practical choice situations is the selection of an appropriate interest rate r for the Present Value calculation. The major problem is to allow properly for risk. Securities promising fixed payments (e.g., bonds) are subject to *default risk*; securities with uncertain returns varying around some expected average level (e.g., stocks) are subject to *variability risk*. For any type of investment, market opinions as to risk attach an appropriate risk-premium to the promised or expected return that the decision-maker should take account of in calculating Present Value.

The *real* interest rate r is the premium commanded in the market by current real claims over future real claims. The *money* interest rate r' is the premium of current monetary claims over future monetary claims. The latter premium is affected by the anticipated rate of price-level inflation, a, so that:

$$r' = r + a$$

Someone who borrows money, in order to repay in money, must offer the lender an additional monetary return to cover the increase in the money price of real claims anticipated by the time of repayment.

The determinants of the real interest rate r in a community include: the individuals' patterns of *time-preference* (more urgent desires for current goods raise interest rates), *time-endowment* (anticipations of increased future income raise interest rates), and *time-productivity* (remunerative investment opportunities raise interest rates). And since the observed interest rate in a community is normally the monetary rate r', *anticipations of inflation* will also raise quoted interest rates.

Chapter 16
INTEMPORAL
CHOICE:
SAVING,
INVESTMENT,
AND INTEREST

513

Mainly for Review

R1. Explain the analogy between the intertemporal optimum of the consumer (choice between current consumption C_0 and future consumption C_1) and the optimum of the consumer at a moment of time (choice between consumption of commodity X and commodity Y). What determines the shape of the intertemporal market opportunity set?

*R2. Which is correct: (a) The annual rate of interest is the ratio P_0/P_1 of the price of a current consumption claim over the price of a consumption claim dated one year in the future; (b) The annual rate of interest is the *premium* on the value of current relative to one-year future claims, as given by the expression $(P_0/P_1) - 1$? Explain.

R3. What is *wealth*? How is it related to current and future *incomes*?

*R4. In a pure-exchange situation, at market equilibrium the total of borrowing equals the total of lending. What can be said about saving and investment?

*R5. In a productive situation, at market equilibrium the total of saving equals the total of investment. What can be said about borrowing and lending?

R6. What is the Separation Theorem? What is its importance? What would tend to happen if it were not applicable?

*R7. What is the Present Value Rule? Will this rule always lead decision-makers to correct choices of projects when the Separation Theorem holds? What if the Separation Theorem does not hold?

*R8. For a particular project M, the time sequence of payments is $z_0 = -100$, $z_1 = 125$. Is this an investment or a disinvestment? What is its Present Value V_0 when the interest rate r is 10%? At $r = 20$%? At $r = 30$%? What is the highest rate of interest at which the project should be adopted?

*R9. The table here shows alternative payments sequences for two *interdependent* projects M and N. The columns headed "Alone" show the payments associated with each if it were adopted *separately*. The other columns show the payments associated with each if the other were *also* to be adopted. If the interest rate r were 20% and you were required to adopt no more than one project, which (if any) should be adopted? If you could adopt both together, would you want to do so?

PROJECT	ALONE		WITH THE OTHER PROJECT	
	z_0	z_1	z_0	z_1
M	-100	125	-95	110
N	-50	90	-60	95

Chapter 16
INTEMPORAL
CHOICE:
SAVING,
INVESTMENT,
AND INTEREST

R10. Explain the relation between the rate of interest r as defined in the equation $r = (P_0/P_1) - 1$ and as defined in the equation $r = z/V_0$.

*The answers to asterisked questions appear at the end of the book.

R11. What is the *money* rate of interest, and how is it related to the *real* rate of interest?

T1. In a two-period preference diagram, illustrate plausible endowment positions in the following cases. Indicate whether each person is likely to be a borrower or a lender.

   a. A young man with an elderly, wealthy, loving uncle in Australia.

   b. A farm-owner whose crop has been destroyed by hurricane.

   c. A sugar-*beet* farmer who has just learned that this year's sugar-*cane* crop has been destroyed by hurricane.

   d. A 35-year-old star baseball player.

*T2. "Saving need not equal investment for any single individual, but the two must be equal for the market as a whole." Is this necessarily true in equilibrium? Would it be true in a disequilibrium situation, as might result from a floor or ceiling upon interest rates?

*T3. In a newly settled country, resources are likely to have great potential but are as yet undeveloped. Would you expect the real interest rate to be high or low? Comparing situations in which the new country is or is not in close contact with the rest of the world, in which situation will the interest rate be higher? In which will more investment take place? Explain.

*T4. One country is "stagnant" (i.e., little investment and little economic growth are taking place) because productive opportunities yielding a good return on investment are lacking. Another "stagnant" country has excellent investment opportunities, but little investment because time-preferences are very high. Which country would tend to have a high, and which a low, real interest rate? Explain.

T5. Money interest rates have been on a sharply rising trend over the past thirty years throughout the world. Which of the following might provide part of the explanation, and analyze:

   a. Higher rates of time-preference (changes in tastes).

   b. Higher rates of time-productivity (changes in investment opportunities).

   c. Lower ratios of current to anticipated future incomes (increased relative scarcity of current endowments).

   d. Higher rates of inflation (changes in anticipations as to monetary policies of governments).

*T6. Are negative rates of interest impossible? If not impossible, why are they rarely observed?

T7. "Annual income twenty pounds, annual expenditure nineteen nineteen six, result happiness. Annual income twenty pounds, annual expenditure twenty pounds ought and six, result misery" —Mr. Micawber in Dickens' *David Copperfield.* Is this sound economics? Analyze.

PART SIX
Political Economy

17.A GOALS OF ECONOMIC POLICY, 521
    17.A.1 Efficiency versus Equity, 521
    17.A.2 Utilitarianism, 524

17.B THE THEOREM OF THE INVISIBLE HAND, 526

17.C WHAT CAN GO WRONG? ALMOST EVERYTHING!, 529
    17.C.1 Monopoly, 529
    17.C.2 Disequilibrium, 530
    17.C.3 Externalities and Coase's Theorem, 532
    17.C.4 Public Goods, 539
    17.C.5 Appropriative Activity, 543

17.D THE PROBLEM OF EQUALITY, 544
    17.D.1 An Application: Rawls' Concept of "Justice," 544
    17.D.2 Equality and Pareto-Optimality, 545
    17.D.3 Equality as a Public Good, 546

17.E WELFARE ECONOMICS—CONCLUSION, 547

Examples
    17.1 HEALTH COSTS OF NUCLEAR POWER VERSUS COAL POWER, 533
    17.2 THE APPLES AND THE BEES, 536
    17.3 WATER LAW, 538

WELFARE ECONOMICS: THE THEORY OF ECONOMIC POLICY

17

Supplementary Chapter

The discipline of economics was originally called "political economy," a title reflecting the concern of early economic thinkers with *normative* questions of public policy. By way of contrast, in this book the main emphasis has been upon economics as a *positive* science. The intent has been to analyze and explain the determinants of individual optimizing behavior and of market equilibrium in a world of scarcity. We have not been concerned so far either to attack or defend the morality of such behavior, or to favor or oppose reforms of the market system. In the present chapter, however, some of the great problems of *normative* political economy will be considered: the choice between efficiency and equity, the possible justifications for governmental interventions aimed at correcting the functioning of markets, and the distribution of wealth. As was mentioned in Chapter 1, in laying the foundations of modern economics in *The Wealth of Nations*, Adam Smith was motivated largely by a desire to recommend very definite economic policies. (Or perhaps we should say *non*-policies since, for the most part, he urged *laissez faire*.) And economists to this day remain active in criticism of or in defense of alternative plans, programs, institutions, or legislation designed to cope with social problems. The title "welfare economics" is currently given to study of the theoretical underpinnings of economic policy.

The first section of the chapter considers the *goals* of policy. Section 17.B reviews what might be called Adam Smith's "Theorem of the Invisible Hand," which asserts a kind of optimality of the laissez-faire economy. Following this, in Section 17.C we take up the flies in the ointment, the various reasons that have been adduced to explain why Smith's theorem fails (or why it is, perhaps, irrelevant whether it fails or not). Section 17.D considers the ever-challenging issue of economic equality.

GOALS OF ECONOMIC POLICY

Economic theorists have concentrated attention almost entirely upon only two of the many possible goals of policy: (1) efficiency, and (2) distributive equity. Roughly speaking, these two criteria represent the *size* of the economic pie and the *distribution* of slices among the possible claimants.

To begin with, suppose that an individual's well-being can be summarized simply by the amount of income I available for consumption. Then, as between two persons John and Karl constituting a community, the alternative social allocations of income might be represented on I^j, I^k axes as in Figure 17.1. The shaded area shows the set of I^j, I^k combinations potentially available to this two-person community, i.e., the "social opportunity set," as a result of the social processes governing the production of goods and the assignment of income claims to individuals.

17.A.1
Efficiency
versus Equity

Figure 17.1
Social Allocations of Income. The shaded region is the social opportunity set, showing the attainable combinations of income for John (I^j) and income for Karl (I^k); its boundary is the Social Opportunity Frontier II'. The aggregate income is maximized at I^*, where II' is just tangent to a line of slope -1 (line NN).

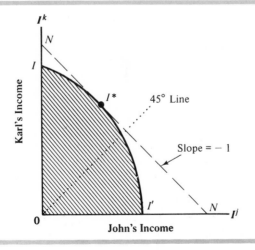

Chapter 17
WELFARE
ECONOMICS:
THE THEORY OF
ECONOMIC
POLICY

The curve II' that bounds the social opportunity set on the northeast, the Social Opportunity Frontier, might have any of a variety of shapes. As drawn, it is concave to the origin suggesting that a greater *aggregate* social income $I^T \equiv I^j + I^k$ could be attained toward the middle of II' rather than at the corners. This might be plausibly justified as follows. At the lower right corner John is totally dominant; I^j is as high as it can be, while Karl receives literally nothing—$I^k = 0$. But then Karl will surely exit from the community (by death or emigration), in which case his productive powers will no longer be available to augment the aggregate social product I^T. If production is a cooperative process, providing Karl with some incentive in the way of income I^k will, up to a point at least, make the aggregate I^T larger than it would otherwise be. In a different terminology, the social mechanism that generates and distributes income is not a ''constant-sum game.'' If Karl is induced to produce more as a result of receiving more, John will not lose the entire amount that Karl gains.

Let us now consider *efficiency* as a goal of social policy. It might seem natural to define efficiency, in Figure 17.1, as achieving the largest *sum* of income I^T. Geometrically, this maximum is reached at $I*$ in Figure 17.1. $I*$ is the point of contact of II' with the dashed line NN, the highest attainable line of slope -1 in the diagram (aggregate income I^T being constant along any such line). But this is not the way the economist defines efficiency. For, treating $I*$ as some kind of social maximum involves a hidden assumption—that it would be acceptable to deprive John of one dollar if Karl thereby gets two dollars, or to deprive Karl of a smaller amount if John can thereby get a larger amount. Instead, the economist uses a somewhat weaker concept of efficiency. Any particular income distribution I^j, I^k is called efficient if it corresponds to a point on the Social Opportunity Frontier II' rather than in the interior of the shaded region.[1]

We know, however, that money income, or even ''real'' income, is not an adequate index of an individual's well-being. First of all, a person may derive satisfaction from *reservation uses* of resources (e.g., leisure) as an alternative to maximizing market income. Second, how the individual *spends* income over the many different consumption goods will clearly affect his or her achieved level of satisfaction. Perhaps most important, markets might be imperfect or even non-existent, as in a feudal or a communist society. In such an environment, ''income'' defined as the market earnings from owned resources would be a defective or even entirely meaningless measure of well-being.

We can get around this problem by using the familiar concept of *utility U* as index of the degree of satisfaction. Figure 17.2 shows the social opportunity set in terms of achievable utilities U^j and U^k of the two individuals. Utility, we saw in Chapter 3, is regarded as only an *ordinal* magnitude. An individual is assumed to

Chapter 17
WELFARE
ECONOMICS:
THE THEORY OF
ECONOMIC
POLICY

522

[1] It might be asked, why not have the parties go initially to $I*$ and then *redistribute* the maximized aggregate income I^T along NN on any basis agreed between them? Moving along the dashed line NN, a point could always be found that is superior for both parties (yields higher income for each) as compared with any point along II' away from $I*$. But such redistribution is not possible, by the definition of II' as the Social Opportunity Frontier. (If it were possible, the dashed line NN would *be* the frontier.) Presumably, the costs of redistribution or the inability of the parties to agree on how to go about it dictate a ''concave'' curvature of II' as the Social Opportunity Frontier.

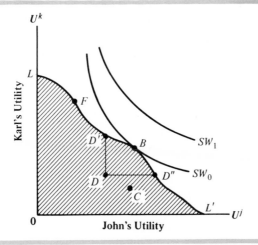

Figure 17.2

Social Allocations of Utility. Since utility has no unique cardinal scaling, in utility units only the *ordinal* properties of the Social Opportunity Frontier *LL'* are relevant—in particular, the negative slope along *LL'*. This slope indicates that John cannot be made better off without making Karl worse off, and vice versa. SW_0 and SW_1 are hypothetical indifference contours of social well-being or "welfare," which would be maximized at point *B*. But if comparisons can be made only in terms of the Pareto criterion, no such contours exist. All that can be said is that distributions to the northeast of any point like *D* (those in the shaded region *DD'BD"*) are preferred to *D*. The Social Opportunity Frontier *LL'* is the set of Pareto-efficient distributions; Pareto comparisons cannot be made between points on *LL'*.

be able to distinguish a more preferred from a less preferred outcome, but not the utility difference between them. Also, utility is *incommensurable* between individuals. For both these reasons we cannot meaningfully speak of aggregate utility $(U^j + U^k)$, and so cannot maximize any such aggregate. Also, the Social Opportunity Frontier in terms of utilities (*LL'* in Figure 17.2) has no meaningful shape apart from the *ordinal* property represented by its negative slope. This negative slope tells us only that one party cannot be made somewhat better off without making the other somewhat worse off.

DEFINITION: An allocation of goods in an economy is said to be "Pareto-preferred,"[2] in comparison with another, if all parties concerned are *at least* as well off and one or more of the parties is actually better off.

Consider the allocation *D* in the interior of the social opportunity set of Figure 17.2. Comparing *D'* with *D*, Karl is better off and John is no worse off, so *D'* is Pareto-preferred to *D*. At *D"* John is better off and Karl is no worse off, so the allocation *D"* is also Pareto-preferred to *D*. And for any point *between* *D'* and

Chapter 17
WELFARE
ECONOMICS:
THE THEORY OF
ECONOMIC
POLICY

[2] Vilfredo Pareto (1848–1923), Italian economist and sociologist (mentioned in Section 3.D above).

D'' along the boundary LL', *both* parties are better off so that any such point is Pareto-preferred to D.

Generalizing this reasoning, for any point like D in the interior of the social opportunity set there will be points on the frontier LL' that are Pareto-preferred to it. But comparing any two allocations along the boundary LL' itself, the utility gain to one party will necessarily be associated with a utility loss to the other. Hence, for no point on the frontier will there be any other allocation Pareto-preferred to it.

The set of boundary points, the Social Opportunity Frontier, is called the set of *Pareto-optimal* allocations. Any of these points can be said to "maximize the size of the economic pie," in the weak sense represented by the absence of any allocation Pareto-preferred to it. And so *in utility terms, the efficient set of income allocations is the Pareto-optimal set.*

What about the goal of distributive equity? Here we lack any principle with as compelling appeal as Pareto-optimality.[3] *Equality* as a goal receives a great deal of support, but because of non-cardinality and incommensurability the "equality of utilities" is meaningless. In practice, something like *equality of incomes* is often taken as an important goal. (This question is considered further in Section 17.D.) Another issue is whether the initial distribution, the *status quo,* has any presumptive standing as an equitable ranking. It is said that "possession is nine points of the law." That is, under our legal system the *status quo* is generally enforced unless there is some special reason to the contrary. But from a sufficiently abstract point of view, there is perhaps no sound justification for attaching even such tentative validity to the *status quo.*

One tradition in welfare economics "solves" the social optimality problem by imagining a special kind of interpersonal utility measure summarized in a so-called *social welfare function.* In Figure 17.2 we might lay down indifference contours of interpersonal utility or "welfare" (SW_0 and SW_1 in the diagram) and declare that the social optimum of perfect bliss occurs at point B where the boundary LL' touches the highest attainable welfare-indifference contour. The "only" difficulty is the absence of any agreement as to what the content of such a social welfare function might be!

Turning to somewhat deeper issues, the narrowness of the two criteria traditionally recognized by economists has been the object of some criticism. The philosophy underlying welfare economics is called *utilitarianism.*[4] The main themes of utilitarianism may be summarized in the two-fold assertion: (1) Social policies, rules, and institutions are to be judged solely in terms of their *consequences*; and (2) the only relevant consequences are the degrees of satisfaction of the *wants of individuals* ("pleasures and pains").

The first assertion represents a kind of social pragmatism. For utilitarians, all social practices or arrangements (e.g., monarchy or voting or the market or capital

Chapter 17
WELFARE
ECONOMICS:
THE THEORY OF
ECONOMIC
POLICY

524

---

[3]Not everyone would agree that Pareto-optimality is a very compelling principle. (See below.)

[4]The similarity between the words "utility" and "utilitarianism" is not accidental. Both are due to Jeremy Bentham.

punishment or the family or the nation) are merely means or instruments. They should not be adopted or rejected because they agree or disagree with the word of the Bible, or with natural law, or with the dictates of ethical principles, or with historical tradition or timeless custom. Instead, the only criterion is: Do they give rise to desirable social outcomes? Where others might say "The ends do not justify the means," the utilitarian replies: "What can justify means except the ends attained?"

The second assertion represents a radical individualism. Policies may or may not serve the purposes of God, may or may not advance science and learning, may or may not promote the survival of the race or nation or the gene pool; none of this is relevant for the utilitarian. What counts is whether the results comport with the desires of individuals. President John F. Kennedy once declared, "Ask not what your country can do for you, ask what you can do for your country!" To which a utilitarian might reply, "Why have a country except for what it can do for you?"

A somewhat separate question turns on the issue of *hedonism*. Are the "goods" entering into the utilitarian calculus of social well-being limited exclusively to individuals' sensate satisfactions, as the hedonists would have it? What about "higher wants," for example benevolent desires to help others? The economic utilitarians generally answer this question by saying that it is the satisfaction of factually observable wants, whether sensate or "higher," that should govern policy. On this approach, benevolent desires are counted as well as hedonistic ones, but of course only to the extent that they are actually present—as measured, for example, by individuals' willingness to sacrifice sensate for higher goals. Unfortunately, in the world as we know it there are also "lower wants," for example malevolent urges to punish or dominate others. What legitimate weight to attach to such wants remains a problem for utilitarians.

Upon departing from utilitarian premises, *both* efficiency and equity as goals lose much of their force. Non-utilitarians might make any of the following arguments.

1. Social policy should be directed not at giving individuals what they *want,* but what they *ought to have*. As the great moralists and our sacred texts have told us, as observation of others and candid self-examination reveal, and as history demonstrates, most of what people want most of the time they would be better off not getting. Efficiency is a goal for raising pigs, not for the social life of a community of people. Even the "equity" goal means little more than fair division among pigs at the trough.

2. Even admitting that an efficient and equitable distribution of satisfactions of individual wants might to some extent be a legitimate social goal, it is absurd to assert that this is the only relevant goal. Liberty, justice, order, community—all express goals of policy that transcend the satisfaction of individual wants.

3. More important than the social allocation of *outcomes* (the attainment of goals) is the question of the *means* by which these social outcomes are achieved. It is far better to have an allocation of goods and services that

Chapter 17
WELFARE
ECONOMICS:
THE THEORY OF
ECONOMIC
POLICY

525

is both inefficient and inequitable, but arrived at in a spirit of voluntary cooperation under law, than a perfectly ideal allocation established by dictatorial decree or political trickery.

4. Recognition of the social provenance of individual "wants" exposes the emptiness of utilitarian criteria. What individuals desire is very largely a result of their social conditioning. Much more important than the *want-satisfaction* process is the *want-creation* process. The main goal of policy should be to affect the formation of the proper wants.

No resolution of these difficult philosophical questions can be provided here. It is clear that utilitarianism can be criticized from many different points of view: dictatorial or democratic, radical or conservative, ethical or cynical. In any case economics is the science of the *instrumental,* of the choice of proper means for given ends. However defective utilitarian ends may be, they do carry a great deal of force in modern value systems and therefore must be reckoned with in the analysis of economic policy.

Most of the debates among economists—over monetarism vs. fiscalism, minimum wages or price controls, depletion allowances or import quotas—are carried on within utilitarian ground rules. But for a second class of issues, e.g., racial discrimination, capital punishment and abortion, the proper extent and scope of government activities, individual liberty versus civic order, questions are raised that go beyond the utilitarian. The progress of economic science, the development of more accurate data and more fruitful and rigorous theories, can be expected to go far toward resolving the former class of disagreements. But if one economist prefers Maoism and another capitalism, or one prefers to exterminate and the other to tolerate an inconvenient minority group, the fundamental sources of contention are almost surely divergences in ethical values not capturable within the utilitarian framework. Such divergences will not be eliminated by advances in scientific economics.

17.B

THE THEOREM OF THE INVISIBLE HAND

Chapter 17
WELFARE
ECONOMICS:
THE THEORY OF
ECONOMIC
POLICY

526

Adam Smith asserted that the invisible hand of self-interest "frequently" leads men to effectually promote the interests of society. Economists in modern times have refined this idea into a more precise theorem that can be worded as follows: *Given a number of ideal conditions, optimizing behavior on the part of individuals and firms under pure competition leads to an efficient (Pareto-optimal) social outcome.* In this section we shall go through the meaning of this "Theorem of the Invisible Hand." The ideal conditions, and the consequences of their separate or combined violation, are discussed further in Section 17.C. But note that the theorem relates solely to the social goal of *efficiency*. The question of distributive *equity* will be considered further in Section 17.D.

A formal demonstration of the Theorem of the Invisible Hand requires rather high-level mathematics, and will not be attempted here. Intuitively, however, we can see that efficiency for the economy as a whole requires: (1) efficiency as among consumers (in the allocation of consumption goods), (2) efficiency as among resource-owners (in the provision of resources for productive uses), and (3) efficiency as among firms (in the conversion of resources into consumable goods). What will be shown here (as a reminder of previous results, rather than as anything really new) is that *all three of these conditions are met in competitive equilibrium.*

To isolate the question of *efficiency among consumers,* we can return to the analysis of Section 7.B. Equation (7.1) can be repeated, in slightly changed notation, here:

(17.1) $$MRSC_{XY}^j = \frac{P_x}{P_y} = MRSC_{XY}^k$$

This says that, for any pair of individuals John and Karl, as a condition of competitive equilibrium each person's *Marginal Rate of Substitution in Consumption,* here denoted $MRSC_{XY}$ (the absolute slope $-\left.\frac{\Delta y}{\Delta x}\right|_U$ along his indifference curve between commodities X and Y), must equal the price ratio P_x/P_y (the absolute slope of the budget line). In this discussion, it will be convenient once again to pierce the veil of money and think in terms of real commodities only. One of the consumption goods, in particular Y, can be chosen as the "numeraire" or basis of pricing. Then P_y is necessarily unity (the price of Y, in units of Y, must be 1) so that P_x/P_y reduces to P_x. With this understood, the condition of efficiency among consumers can be expressed more simply as:

(17.1′) $$MRSC_{XY}^j = P_x = MRSC_{XY}^k \qquad \text{Efficiency among Consumers}$$

It is the equality $MRSC_{XY}^j = MRSC_{XY}^k$ that represents the condition of efficiency. Its meaning is that, on the margin, John is just as willing as Karl to sacrifice a unit of Y (in order to obtain more X). Inequality between these Marginal Rates of Substitution would imply inefficiency, since then the two parties could mutually benefit from trade. (The one more willing to give up Y in exchange for X would do so, receiving in payment some X from the one more anxious to acquire Y.) A benevolent and omniscient dictator might directly impose such an equality between $MRSC_{XY}^j$ and $MRSC_{XY}^k$ without the aid of any market system. In a regime of competitive markets, however, the equality emerges from the self-regarding actions of each trader in setting his own $MRSC_{XY}$ equal to the market exchange rate between X and Y, i.e., to the price P_x. Thus, the market price P_x *mediates* the efficient equality of the individuals' Marginal Rates of Substitution in Consumption.

For *efficiency among resource-owners,* an exactly corresponding argument leads to the condition that can be expressed as:

Chapter 17
WELFARE
ECONOMICS:
THE THEORY OF
ECONOMIC
POLICY

527

(17.2) $MRSR_{AI}^j = h_a = MRSR_{AI}^k$ Efficiency among Resource-Owners

This equation follows, again with slightly changed notation, from equation (15.2). As described in Section 15.A, each owner of a resource A sets $MRSR_{AI}$, the *Marginal Rate of Substitution between reservation uses of A and market income I,* equal to the hire-price h_a of factor A. Geometrically, the equality is between the absolute slope $-\dfrac{\Delta I}{\Delta R_a}\bigg|_U$ of the indifference curve (between income I and "leisure" or reservation uses R_a) and the absolute slope h_a of the budget line. Since Y is the numeraire commodity in which real income is measured, $MRSR_{AI}$ is equivalent to $MRSR_{AY}$, that is, to the Marginal Rate of Substitution between reservation uses of A and consumption of the numeraire commodity Y. Again, the individuals' separate Marginal Rates of Substitution are not equated directly, as might be done by a dictator. Rather, in a regime of competitive markets the separate optimizations are mediated and brought into efficient equality by the hire-price h_a of factor A.

With regard to *efficiency among firms,* think of production as the process of converting resource A into good X. We know from Section 14.A that the competitive (price-taking) firm sets vmp_a, the Value of the Marginal Product of factor A, equal to the hire-price h_a. Specifically, equation (14.3) implies that for any two price-taking firms f and g:

(17.3) $vmp_a^f = h_a = vmp_a^g$ Efficiency among Firms

That this is an efficiency condition is immediately evident. If the equality did not hold, on the margin one firm could convert a unit of resource A into greater product value than the other. Furthermore, since by definition $vmp_a \equiv P_x(mp_a)$, and since P_x will be the same as among all firms in a given market, the inequality would have to be between the physical Marginal Products mp_a^f and mp_a^g. It would then be socially more efficient to shift some units of resource A away from the firm with lower mp_a and to the firm with higher mp_a. Once again, the efficient equality condition is not imposed by dictation but rather emerges from the mediating role of competitive price.

An alternative version of the efficiency condition as among firms takes the familiar form:

(17.3') $MC_x^f = P_x = MC_x^g$

This condition differs from (17.3) only in being expressed in units of output X rather than units of input A.[5]

Formally speaking, these results should be generalized to deal with any

---

[5] The equivalence of the two formulations follows immediately from the identity (14.6):

$$MC_x \equiv \frac{h_a}{mp_a}$$

Since $vmp_x \equiv P_x(mp_a)$, simple algebra converts (17.3') into the form (17.3).

Chapter 17
WELFARE
ECONOMICS:
THE THEORY OF
ECONOMIC
POLICY

528

numbers of individuals, of firms, of products, and of resources. But the generalization would merely be a complication; the essence of the efficiency conditions is epitomized in what has already been set down.

WHAT CAN GO WRONG? ALMOST EVERYTHING!

The trouble is, the Theorem of the Invisible Hand is too good to be true! There are many ways in which things can go wrong. Indeed, a large portion of modern economic analysis has taken the form of exploration of conditions leading to failure of the theorem.

The most obvious real-world feature limiting the applicability of the Theorem of the Invisible Hand is *monopoly*. Monopoly can and does exist, to some degree at least, on both sides of the various product and factor markets in the economy. Firms might be monopolist sellers of product or monopsonist employers of resources, while individuals might be monopolist sellers of resources or monopsonist buyers of products. And it is not necessarily monopoly or monopsony in the strict sense that lead to failure of the theorem. Any non-price-taking behavior, whether due to cartels, oligopoly, or any of the situations analyzed in Chapters 11 through 13, implies violation of the efficiency conditions of the previous section.

17.C.1
Monopoly

An important policy distinction has been made between *natural* and *contrived* monopoly. In "natural" monopoly, productive economies such as the advantage of large scale make it possible for one firm to produce more cheaply than can a larger number. Public utilities (electricity, telephone, gas, etc.) are commonly believed to fit into this category. Traditional policy with regard to natural monopoly has been to retain the single large firm but to prevent monopolistic exploitation through a regulatory process (see Section 11.D). "Contrived" monopoly is said to arise when the economies of scale are not a dominant feature; certain other circumstances have somehow blunted competitive forces. Here the traditional "trust-busting" policy has attempted to break up monopolistic concentrations. Despite this supposed dedication to competition, however, government policy has in many ways tended to support the monopolization, or at any rate the cartelization, of sectors of the economy.[6]

Given either natural or contrived monopoly, the Invisible Hand does not induce behavior that serves the interests of others, at least not to the optimal degree. The profit-maximizing monopoly firm is motivated to set $MC_x = MR_x$ rather than $MC_x = P_x$ (see Section 11.B.2), thus violating the condition in equation (17.3'). Since $MR_x < P_x$, the monopolist ordinarily produces "too little" output of X. In terms of factor units, it is equation (17.3) that is violated. As shown in Section 14.A, the profit-maximizing factor-employment condition for the

Chapter 17
WELFARE
ECONOMICS:
THE THEORY OF
ECONOMIC
POLICY

[6]See, for instance, Examples 11.5 ("Agricultural Marketing Orders") or 15.7 ("Barbers").

firm is $mrp_a \equiv MR_x(mp_a) = h_a$ whereas the efficiency condition (17.3) is $vmp_a \equiv P_x(mp_a) = h_a$. Then $MR_x < P_x$ implies $mrp_a < vmp_a$. So also "too little" of factor A will be hired by the monopolist firm.

By corresponding arguments it can be shown that a monopsonist employer of a factor, or a monopolist supplier of a factor, or even a monopsonist consumer of a product (should that case ever arise) will all violate one or more of the efficiency conditions of the preceding section.

CONCLUSION: Under both monopoly and monopsony there is "too little" market exchange. And in consequence, there will also be "too little" productive specialization and "too little" market employment of factors.

In effect, monopoly deprives society of some of the mutual benefits of trade. Although the economic agent possessing monopoly power derives advantages therefrom, in principle it would be possible to improve matters by achieving a Pareto-preferred solution. If price-taking behavior were substituted for monopolistic exploitation, the gain would be great enough to permit compensating the monopolist while still leaving something over for the rest of society.[7]

In the case of monopoly or monopsony, failure to achieve efficiency is due to non-price-taking behavior on the part of economic agents. But violations of the efficiency conditions may remain even if all agents are price-takers.

One extremely important source of difficulty is *market disequilibrium*. In Section 17.B great emphasis was placed upon the mediating role of prices in bringing the separate optimizing decisions of individuals and firms into accord. But what if the currently quoted price is not the right one for clearing a market? It is true that there will then surely be corrective forces at work tending to restore equilibrium (as explained in Section 2.A). But given a world in which the determining conditions are ever-changing, the chances are that prices will always be some distance from and scarcely ever at their equilibrium values. Disequilibrium is therefore the prevalent state of affairs.

Since prices will sometimes be too high and at other times too low, it might be thought that the effects of disequilibrium would tend more or less to cancel out over the economy. That, however, is not the case. Prices that diverge from equilibrium levels, whether too high or too low, tend to *reduce* quantities exchanged in markets and therefore limit the economy's ability to derive the advantages of specialization in production. Like monopoly, disequilibrium wipes out some of the potential gains from trade.

This is easy to see in Figure 17.3, which pictures a market with normally sloping supply and demand curves. The price P^+ is too high to equate supply and demand. At that price the effective quantity exchanged Q^+ is the *lesser* of the supply and demand quantities, in this case, the demand quantity. It is true that at

Chapter 17
WELFARE
ECONOMICS:
THE THEORY OF
ECONOMIC
POLICY

[7] These gains and losses were discussed in terms of the concepts of Consumer Surplus and Producer Surplus in Section 11.C (see especially Figure 11.4).

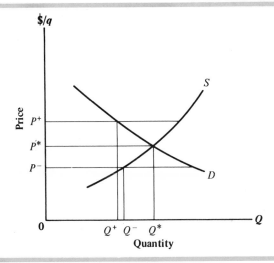

Figure 17.3

Disequilibrium. At the equilibrium, price is P^* and quantity exchanged Q^*. If the ruling price were at the high disequilibrium level P^+, the associated quantity exchanged would be Q^+; at the low disequilibrium price P^- the quantity would be Q^-. Whether price is above or below equilibrium, the quantity exchanged is always *less* than the equilibrium amount—since trade requires both willing buyers and willing sellers.

the high price P^+ there are unsatisfied sellers, but they cannot find customers. ("It takes two to tango.") The price P^- on the other hand is too low to clear the market, but again here it is the *lesser* (offered) quantity Q^- that governs; there are now unsatisfied buyers, but they cannot find willing suppliers. While price is in the one case above and in the other case below the equilibrium P^*, in both situations the quantity exchanged is *less* than the equilibrium Q^*.[8]

CONCLUSION: Disequilibrium, like monopoly, leads to non-Pareto-optimal outcomes because of reduced volumes of trade.

Disequilibrium in one or more particular markets may have significant *macroeconomic* consequences. The incomes that consumers have available for spending on goods do not come out of the air; they derive from earnings received as resource-owners. A market disequilibrium, reducing the scale of production in one or more markets, must adversely affect individuals' real incomes. Factor suppliers will have to select less remunerative alternative employments or less desired reservation uses of the resources they own. The reduction in real incomes will in turn affect consumers' demand functions for goods, in accordance with the "Engel curve" analysis in Section 4.B.1. Thus, disequilibrium in *one* market will tend to reduce demand (to shift demand curves to the left) *in all other* markets. A

[8] The consequent efficiency loss can be analyzed in terms of Consumer and Producer Surplus, in the same way as the losses due to the *artificial* government-imposed disequilibria (price ceilings or price floors) that were studied under the heading of "Hindrances to Trade" in Section 7.E.2.

Chapter 17
WELFARE
ECONOMICS:
THE THEORY OF
ECONOMIC
POLICY

second-order adjustment in these other markets will then carry the process further. A self-reinforcing process may thus ensue in which an initial disequilibrium has a multiplied negative effect upon resource employment and real incomes. Some macroeconomic theories, starting from an assumed disequilibrium in the labor market, place this "multiplier" process in a central role as explaining fluctuations in overall business activity.

"Externalities" are said to arise when the decisions of some economic agents—whether in production, in consumption, or in exchange—affect the interests of other economic agents in a way *not* setting up legally recognized rights of compensation or redress. But this definition is too broad for present purposes. Each individual person is affected by the infinitely varied actions of other people all over the globe that may tend to raise or lower the prices of commodities he or she either consumes or produces. We here rule out these merely "pecuniary" externalities that affect other people only through movements in market prices. Rather, we will be concerned with the *direct* externalities, whose impact upon other parties operates not through price shifts but immediately upon technological opportunities or preference functions.

Consider the problem of *pollution*. A firm using river water, let us say, discharges the effluent back to the river after degrading its quality. The upstream use may adversely affect the operations of another firm downstream; for example, the polluted river water may no longer be productively usable downstream, at least not without further input of resources for purification. Or residential consumers downstream may suffer a loss of consumptive satisfaction (utility) from having to use lower-quality water for drinking and other domestic purposes.

A related problem is called *congestion*. Congestion may be regarded as a special case of pollution, in which the operations of one economic agent (firm or individual) adversely affect other economic agents *engaged in the same industry or activity*. Thus, each additional driver crowds the highways for other drivers; each additional radio broadcasting station impairs reception of other stations' signals; each additional well-pumper reduces water levels in neighbors' wells.

But a direct externality may also be beneficial. An upstream user's activities may actually improve the quality of river water, from the point of view of some or all downstream users. What might be called a "beneficial congestion" externality occurs, for example, in drainage of marshy soils. Each farmer's attempt to drain his own land lowers water levels and therefore improves the productivity of neighboring lands.

A harmful externality, which might or might not be of congestion type, is pictured in Figure 17.4. We can suppose that a competitive (price-taking) firm f produces commodity X, aiming to maximize profit by setting perceived Marginal Cost MC^f equal to price P_x at output x_f^*. But as amount produced x_f increases, there is a non-perceived direct externality imposed on some other firm g, which we may call the Marginal Externality ME^g. The true social Marginal Cost MC at any output x_f is the vertical sum $MC^f + ME^g$. The output x_f^{**} at which true MC equals price P_x, the efficient output, is evidently less than x_f^*. (But if the externality were beneficial, the efficient output x_f^{**} would be greater than x_f^*.)

Chapter 17
WELFARE
ECONOMICS:
THE THEORY OF
ECONOMIC
POLICY

532

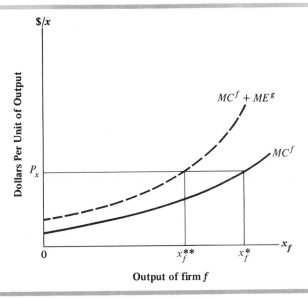

Figure 17.4

Harmful Externality. The competitive firm f is motivated to produce output x_f^*, where its perceived Marginal Cost MC^f equals price P_x. But, counting also the Marginal Externality imposed on another firm g, the true social Marginal Cost is the vertical summation $MC^f + ME^g$ (dashed curve); the efficient output would be x_f^{**}.

A great deal of concern has been expressed about the health consequences of nuclear power. In judging these, a comparison with the health consequences of electricity generation from alternative sources (predominantly from coal) is highly relevant.

A study by L. B. Lave and L. C. Freeburg[9] provided a coal versus nuclear comparison, taking into account the entire fuel cycle from exploration through extraction, transportation, refining, generation, and recovery. It turned out that, so far as the occupational health effects were concerned (effects upon workers in the industry), the mining phase was the main consideration in each case. The costs of mine accidents and chronic diseases were estimated at around 2.4¢ per thousand kilowatt-hours (thousand KWH) of energy produced by nuclear power—but at around 32¢ per thousand KWH, over 13 times as great, for coal. (If these *occupational* health hazards are reflected in higher wages, as discussed in Example 6.2 under "The Value of Safety," the associated costs would not be *externalities*—they would be paid for and thus taken into account by producers. On the other hand, to the extent that occupational health costs are borne by others, as in the case of the federal program to help coal-miners suffering from "black-

EXAMPLE 17.1
HEALTH COSTS OF
NUCLEAR POWER
VERSUS COAL
POWER

[9] Lester B. Lave and Linnea C. Freeburg, "Health Effects of Electricity Generation from Coal, Oil and Nuclear Fuel," *Nuclear Safety*, v. 14 (Sept.–Oct. 1973).

lung disease," an externality is being imposed on the rest of the community.)

A much more uncertain part of the analysis examined the health effects upon the outside public, which are undoubted externalities. Several elements had to be left out of the comparison for lack of generally agreed data, among them the risk of nuclear accidents, the chance of terrorist hijacking of nuclear materials, and the long-term environmental effects of coal and nuclear waste disposal. Setting these aside, the public health costs were mainly the result of chronic low-intensity radiation exposure in the case of nuclear, and pollution with combustion waste products in the case of coal. For nuclear power, the estimated public health costs were within the range of .0003 to .03¢ per thousand KWH; note that even the upper limit is small relative to the already small occupational health costs. For coal, on the other hand, the estimated range for public health costs was 10¢ to $5.00 per thousand KWH—15,000 times as great as nuclear at the upper limit, and 30,000 times as great at the lower limit! These results suggest, therefore, that some of the concern about the health hazards of nuclear power might better be redirected toward the very large health externalities associated with coal power.

COMMENT: Unfortunately, as often occurs in analysis of practical decision problems, the unknown or "unquantifiable" elements are likely to be very large here. The accident record at nuclear plants has on the whole been excellent, and accidental nuclear detonation is considered close to impossible. But, as the 1979 Three Mile Island incident in Pennsylvania indicated, the potential consequences should a major accident occur are truly enormous. It is more difficult still to estimate the likelihood or the consequences of a terrorist group's acquiring enough fissionable material to fabricate atomic weapons. While nuclear power has an enormous advantage with regard to calculable health costs and externalities, it would be foolhardy not to attach high weights to these less quantifiable hazards in making a decision regarding coal versus nuclear power.

CONCLUSION: Direct externalities, beneficial or harmful, lead the Invisible Hand astray. In the interests of efficiency, the agent generating the externality ought, if the externality is beneficial, to be induced to engage in the process even more than private self-interest would dictate. If the externality is harmful, the generating agent ought of course to be induced to diminish the scale of polluting activity in comparison with what self-interest would dictate.

Chapter 17
WELFARE
ECONOMICS:
THE THEORY OF
ECONOMIC
POLICY

Externalities, therefore, represent sources of social gain or loss that do not get translated into the market signals that constitute the Invisible Hand. Traditional policy analysis has recognized a number of alternative remedies for this problem.

1. TAX-SUBSIDY ADJUSTMENTS: A tax placed on the generation of a harmful externality will tend to reduce the amount of externality imposed on others. An ideal

corrective tax would add to the private Marginal Cost, the cost recognized by the polluting producer in terms of self-interest, a penalty that is just enough to equal the Marginal Externality suffered by others. Thus the sum of the tax and the private Marginal Cost would bring home to the generating agent the total true social Marginal Cost of carrying on the polluting activity. For a beneficial externality, correspondingly, a corrective *subsidy* would be called for to induce an ideal (greater) level of the externality-generating activity.

2. UNITIZATION: If the upstream and the downstream productive processes using the river water were merged or "unitized" under the control of a single economic agent, what was previously an externality would be *internalized*. The single integrated water-using enterprise would now carry on the polluting activity at a socially efficient level, i.e., it would pollute only so long as the marginal upstream gain exceeded the marginal downstream loss. A particularly important instance of unitization occurs in oilfield operations. The externality here is a congestion effect: the fact that pumping at any well adversely affects the output of other wells in the same field (by drawing away the fugitive oil, and by reducing gas pressure). Under diversified ownership, the consequence is inefficient over-drilling and over-pumping. At any given well the owner is motivated to pump faster than he otherwise would, to capture oil under others' land and to prevent others from capturing the oil under his land. And in any given land tract, the owner is similarly induced to drill more wells than would otherwise be the case—locating wells all along the boundaries of the tract so as to minimize oil loss to others. With unitization, on the other hand, the sole ownerships of individual wells are exchanged for *pro rata* shares in the overall operation of the oilfield. This eliminates the motivation to over-pump or to over-drill. The unitized incentive is simply to produce most efficiently from the integrated field, as it no longer makes any difference on whose land the oil is brought to the surface.

3. PROPERTY REASSIGNMENT: The fundamental source of the externality problem is inappropriate assignment of legal property rights. If the span of actual effect always coincided with the span of legally-recognized control, externalities would not occur. In the river-water example, the downstream user should ideally be assigned a property right to receive water of some specified quality from the hands of the upstream user. A first user who degrades the quality below this level should be liable for the damages suffered by later users. Conversely, the upstream user who leaves the water in better condition than legally required should in principle be entitled to compensation from later users. An assignment of property entitlements to water quality would not, as might first be thought, simply freeze the pattern of uses in accordance with the legally defined rights. Should some other arrangement be mutually preferred, the parties concerned could negotiate an exchange of property rights. If the downstream user was initially entitled to absolutely pure water, for example, the upstream producer could nevertheless buy from him the right to pollute the river to some specified degree.

Chapter 17
WELFARE
ECONOMICS:
THE THEORY OF
ECONOMIC
POLICY

This last concept has been generalized into what is known as *Coase's Theorem*,[10] which can be stated as follows:

COASE'S THEOREM: Regardless of the specific initial assignment of property rights, in market equilibrium the final outcome will be efficient—provided that the initial legal assignment is well-defined and that transactions involving exchange of rights are costless.

The thrust of Coase's Theorem is that the Invisible Hand is much more effective than the argument about externalities at first suggests. For there are natural market forces at work tending to bring the "external" effects into the calculations of the responsible parties. If a producer initially owns the right to generate a harmful externality, those adversely affected can offer him a financial reward for *not* exercising that right. Or if the other parties are initially entitled to be safe from the externality, it is up to the producer to offer terms of compensation at which they will accept a degree of harm. (In the case of a beneficial externality, of course, the argument applies in reverse.) So long as the legal rights are well-defined and marketable, the Invisible Hand will tend to lead the parties to an efficient outcome, i.e., to a result that exhausts all possibilities for further mutual gain.

EXAMPLE 17.2
THE APPLES AND
THE BEES

One of the classical illustrations used in economists' discussions of externalities has been a tale of the apples and the bees. The apple-grower's orchard provides the beneficial externality of nectar for his neighbor's bees, a contribution to the production of honey for which the orchardist receives no reward. And the bees return the compliment by pollinating the apple blossoms *gratis,* thus contributing to the output of the orchard. These interacting externalities were assumed to represent a clear case of inadequate guidance by the Invisible Hand. Government action was supposed to be necessary to induce the orchardist to optimally cooperate with the beekeeper, i.e., to grow *more* nectar-yielding apple blossoms than the orchardist's self-interested calculation would dicate. And similarly, it was supposed, something had to be done to induce the beekeeper to provide *more* pollination benefits to his apple-growing neighbor than would ensue as a merely incidental side-effect of profitable honey production.

Upon looking into beekeeping in the state of Washington, however, Steven N. S. Cheung found the Invisible Hand alive and well! In actual fact, beekeepers and orchardists do not produce beneficial externalities for one another in a state of ignorance. On the contrary, active market dealings govern the placement of hives. The market terms depend upon the relative values of the two interacting "external" benefits: the honey yield to the beekeeper, as against the pollination services gained by the grower. The table here illustrates that where honey yield is great, the beekeeper ordinarily pays an "apiary rent" for the right to place his hive on the grower's

[10] R. H. Coase, "The Problem of Social Cost," *The Journal of Law & Economics,* v. 3 (Oct. 1960).

land. Where the honey yield is small, the grower pays pollination fees for the privilege of having hives placed on his land. Washington bees are even exported to California to help pollinate the early-season almond crop. Evidently, market processes are at work to bring "externalities" into private economic calculations.

Honey Yields and Pricing Arrangements, Washington (1970–71)

SEASON	CROP	SURPLUS HONEY (POUNDS PER HIVE)	POLLINATION FEES	APIARY RENT PER HIVE
Early Spring	Almond (Calif.)	0	$5–$8	—
	Cherry	0	$6–$8	—
Late Spring (major pollination season)	Apples and Soft Fruits	0	$9–$10	—
	Blueberry (with maple)	40	$5	—
	Cabbage	15	$8	—
	Cherry	0	$9–$10	—
	Cranberry	5	$9	—
Summer and Early Fall (major honey season)	Alfalfa	60	—	13¢–60¢
	Alfalfa (with pollination)	25–35	$3–$5	—
	Fireweed	60	—	25¢–63¢
	Mint	70–75	—	15¢–65¢
	Pasture	60	—	15¢–65¢
	Red Clover	60	—	65¢
	Red Clover (with pollination)	0–35	$3–$6	—
	Sweet Clover	60	—	20¢–25¢

Source: Steven N. S. Cheung, "The Fable of the Bees: An Economic Investigation," *The Journal of Law & Economics,* v. 16 (April 1973), p. 23.

Alas for the economists' fable, apple growing yields little or no honey. (The "apple honey" sold in markets seems to be an instance of imaginative labelling.)

So far so good. But Coase's Theorem seems to prove too much. Consider the case of simple monopoly, which (by the standard analysis) leads to an inefficient outcome—underproduction of the monopolized good. But wherever there is inefficiency there must be a mutual advantage of trade. Then, according to Coase's Theorem, the Invisible Hand should lead the monopolist and his customers to get together in some efficient arrangement; the monopolist can be made at least as well off as before, while the customers will do better. So monopoly should disappear, along with externalities!

The problem with the application of Coase's Theorem to "solve" the problem of monopoly, as in its application to "solve" the problem of externalities, is that the negotiations required may be impracticable. Where large numbers are involved, it may be impossible to secure a sufficient degree of unanimity. *Unitization,* for example, as an efficient solution of the externality problem in oilfields

Chapter 17
WELFARE
ECONOMICS:
THE THEORY OF
ECONOMIC
POLICY

537

should, according to Coase's Theorem, tend to come about simply in response to the Invisible Hand. But in practice it has been necessary to pass special legislation whereby hold-out minority tract-owners in an oilfield are compelled to comply with a unitization agreement favored by a sufficiently large majority. It is the "free rider" problem that makes unanimity almost impossible. If the majority agree to cease overpumping their wells, it pays to be a member of the non-complying minority. The latter secure the advantage of others' pumping reductions, while still pumping as hard as they wish themselves.[11]

If the numbers involved are small, on the other hand, the problem becomes one of *strategic behavior* (as discussed in Chapter 13). When a small number of bargainers face each other, the mere possibility of a mutually advantageous agreement does not guarantee that such an agreement will be reached.

Nevertheless, Coase's Theorem does clarify our ideas as to the fundamental meaning of so-called "externalities." From a policy point of view, it suggests that *the unambiguous assignment of exchangeable property rights,* whatever the specific nature of the assignment may be, might be an important step in promoting the achievement of efficiency.

EXAMPLE 17.3
WATER LAW[12]

In the eastern states, the law governing the use of flowing streams is based mainly upon the "riparian" doctrine; in the West, the "appropriation" doctrine dominates.

While the legislation of each state has unique features, the basic idea of the riparian principle is that every owner of land bordering a stream has an equal right to reasonable use of the flow. The riparian doctrine of property rights in water is defective *both* in terms of ambiguity and exchangeability. What is a "reasonable" use for one party relative to others is a subject of continual contention before administrative agencies and law courts. Water-users are deterred from making costly investments, however efficient, for fear that a judicial or administrative redetermination of "reasonable" uses may later deprive them of supply. Nor can any user buy another's water right, since all are equally entitled to the flow. In particular, it is generally impossible to buy the right to transfer water away from the stream onto "non-riparian" land, however productive such a transfer may be.

In the relatively arid western states, scarcity of water made the riparian doctrine intolerable. The appropriation doctrine that tended to be adopted instead is based upon the concept that "first in time is first in right." Subject to qualifications and conditions that vary from state to state, first users were given the right to appropriate specified quantities of flow, sometimes limited also as to time, place, or manner of diversion. In particular, appropriated water was no longer tied to "riparian" uses but could be transferred away

[12]Discussion based upon J. Hirshleifer, J. C. DeHaven, and J. W. Milliman, *Water Supply: Economics, Technology, and Policy* (Chicago: University of Chicago Press, 1960), Chap. 9.

---

[11]The motivation is essentially the same as that of the "chisellers" in a cartel situation (see Section 11.F). But, it should be noted, absolutely unanimous cooperation is not strictly necessary for a workable degree of agreement in either the unitization or cartel contexts.

from the stream. The appropriation doctrine represented a considerable improvement from the point of view of *certainty* of rights. However, the *exchangeability* of rights has remained subject to erratic legal intervention.

In recent years there has been a tendency, even in the western states, to empower administrative agencies or courts to determine what constitutes "reasonable" use for the award or deprivation of water rights. In consequence, the ambiguity of rights to water use has been increasing rather than decreasing. Recent legislation has also tended to be increasingly hostile to market exchanges of water rights. Under the statutes of Colorado, for example, it is illegal to sell water found in the state outside its boundaries. Colorado legislators seem to lack confidence in the ability of naive Coloradans to exact an appropriate price from wily out-of-staters.

PUBLIC GOODS

A commodity is called a "public good" if its consumption by any one economic agent does not reduce the amount available for others in the community. Or putting it another way, a good is "public" if providing the good for *anyone* makes it possible to provide it for *everyone,* without additional cost. Public goods thus represent a particular type of beneficial externality. A private good (e.g., a banana) is used or consumed *exclusively*; a public good is (or may be) used *concurrently* by many economic agents.

The traditional example is the lighthouse. If one ship receives the benefit of the warning signal, that in no way deprives others from doing so. Or in radio or television, a broadcast program is available non-exclusively to any and all persons equipped with suitable receivers.[13]

If Z is a public good, with the numeraire commodity Y remaining a private good, the efficiency condition as between a producing firm f and two consumers John (j) and Karl (k) can be expressed as:

$$(17.4) \qquad MC_z^f = MRSC_{ZY}^j + MRSC_{ZY}^k$$

That is, the Marginal Cost of the producing firm must be set equal to the *sum* of the consumers' marginal valuations of the public good. Geometrically, the picture is as in Figure 17.5. The two individuals' separate demand curves (each showing

[13]Since there are *some* costs to users (stationing a lookout to watch for the lighthouse, buying a receiving set for the broadcasts), the goods mentioned are not absolutely "pure" public goods. This qualification is minor in the cases given. But many goods lie in the intermediate range of the spectrum between wholly private and wholly public. A stage performance, for example, is "public" as among the members of a given audience. But the capacity of the theater sets a limit on the number who can be concurrently served, all others being excluded. In this discussion only "pure" public goods will be considered.

Chapter 17
WELFARE
ECONOMICS:
THE THEORY OF
ECONOMIC
POLICY

539

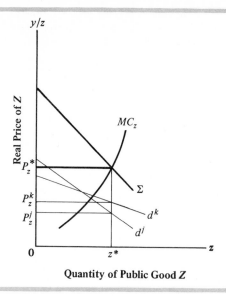

y/z

Real Price of Z

MC_z

P_z^*

Σ

P_z^k

P_z^j

d^k

d^j

0 z^* z

Quantity of Public Good Z

Figure 17.5

Public Good. MC_z represents the Marginal Cost of producing a public good Z, cost being measured in terms of amounts of the real numeraire good Y sacrificed. If John has demand curve d^j and Karl has demand curve d^k, the relevant total demand for the two consumers is the *vertical* summation curve Σ—since John and Karl consume the public good concurrently rather than exclusively. If the price P_z^j were charged to John, and P_z^k to Karl, and if the supplying firm behaved as a price-taker with regard to the summation price P_z, correct signals would be given to both supplier and demanders. The efficient output z^* would be produced, and that same quantity would be concurrently purchased and consumed by each demander.

the quantity of Z that would be purchased by that consumer, as a function of the real price of Z in units of numeraire Y) are shown as d^j and d^k. The demand curves are derived by the same logic as in the case of private goods (see Section 4.B); from the point of view of any one individual, the "publicness" of the commodity is irrelevant. At any given price P_z quoted to him, the consumer will purchase additional units until his Marginal Rate of Substitution in Consumption $MRSC_{ZY}$ falls to equality with P_z. Thus, the demand curve d^j can be regarded as a schedule of John's $MRSC_{ZY}^j$, and d^k as a corresponding schedule for Karl. The aggregate value of any additional unit of Z, produced for concurrent consumption by the two consumers together, is then shown in the diagram by the social valuation function Σ—the *vertical* summation[14] of d^j and d^k. The intersection of the MC_z and Σ curves represents the satisfaction of condition (17.4) above, so that z^* is the efficient level of output.[15]

Chapter 17
WELFARE
ECONOMICS:
THE THEORY OF
ECONOMIC
POLICY

540

[14]The familiar market demand curve applicable to private goods is the *horizontal* summation of the individual demand curves (see Section 4.D). The curve Σ is *not* a market demand curve in this usual sense.

[15]If one individual's d schedule were such as to make his $MRSC_{ZY}$ actually negative for sufficiently great public-good output, on the margin Z would be a *bad* rather than a good for him. Given a "free disposal" possibility (as in the case of broadcasting, where one can simply turn off his receiver), any

The problem for the Theorem of the Invisible Hand is: Can achievement of the efficiency condition (17.4) be mediated by market prices? First of all let us assume that, in principle at least, it is possible to charge for the use of the public good and to *exclude* those who do not pay. In television, for example, a coded or "scrambled" message could be broadcast that is only interpretable with the aid of a paid descrambling device.[16] Then private firms can contemplate producing public goods for market sale.[17] The market prices that would serve the needs of mediation are P_z^j and P_z^k in Figure 17.5, each price being equal to the respective consumer's separate $MRSC_{ZY}$ at the efficient output level z^*. The price-mediating conditions are:

$$(17.5) \qquad \begin{cases} MRSC_{ZY}^j = P_z^j \\ MRSC_{ZY}^k = P_z^k \end{cases} \text{ and } \quad MC_z = P_z^* \equiv P_z^j + P_z^k$$

It is evident that equations (17.5) imply satisfaction of the efficiency condition (17.4).

So there is a set of prices that would fill the bill. But could these prices be arrived at by a market-equilibrium process?

Note, first, that *price discrimination* is required since, in general, $P_z^j \neq P_z^k$. It was shown above (in Section 11.E), that a monopolist seller could—where resale of the good between consumers is impossible—segment the market so as to be able to charge different prices to different consumers. In the case of public goods, it may again be possible to segment the market (to prevent resale). Then a monopolist *could* arrive at the solution (17.5), corresponding to the intersection of MC_z and Σ in Figure 17.5. But there would be no motivation to do so. The monopolist would want to choose an output such that Marginal Cost MC_z equals the sum of the *Marginal Revenues* mr_z^j and mr_z^k in the segmented markets represented by the two individuals, rather than the sum of the prices P_z^j and P_z^k. Each person's Marginal Revenue curve mr would of course lie below the associated demand (Average Revenue) curve d, so that the vertical sum $mr_z^j + mr_z^k$ would lie below the vertical sum of the prices represented by the Σ curve. If follows that the monopolist, as we would expect, chooses an output *smaller* than that required by the efficiency condition (17.5).

Suppose, on the other hand, that the monopolist was somehow induced to act as a price-taker, calculating in terms of $P_z^j + P_z^k$ rather than $mr_z^j + mr_z^k$. But if

---

negative $MRSC_{ZY}$ need not be suffered, so that the social valuation function Σ would be a summation only of the *positive* ranges of the individual d curves. But if it were not possible for an individual to evade consumption of a public good, even after it becomes a bad, the Σ curve would be the *algebraic* sum of both positive and negative values along the individual d curves. (A possible example is national defense. This may be a public good for the majority, but a public bad for a minority of traitors who favor the enemy!) In what follows, it will be assumed that public goods do not ever become bads.

[16]Sometimes, however, this may be impracticable. Consider mosquito abatement. This is clearly a public good. But to exclude non-payers from the benefit, it would be necessary to somehow train or signal the mosquitoes that some targets were permissible.

[17]Radio and television broadcasts are provided privately even *without* explicit charge to the consumer. But of course the listeners are really paying something, in being willing to have their time and attention captured by commercial messages. (See the discussion of "time-prices" of goods in Section 6.B.)

Chapter 17
WELFARE
ECONOMICS:
THE THEORY OF
ECONOMIC
POLICY

price discrimination was ruled out, the monopolist would have to set $P_z^j = P_z^k$ at whatever level of output is chosen. (Even if discrimination were technically and legally feasible, the monopolist might not be able to secure the information about individual demand functions necessary for doing so.) Then the effective vertical summation curve Σ' from a revenue point of view (not shown in the diagram) would lie somewhat *below* the true Σ. The consequence, as before, would be a less than efficient output of the public good.

A public good might, conceivably at least, be provided *competitively* rather than monopolistically. Television broadcasting is a case where we see hot competition among firms (channels). However, the product differentiation as among competing broadcasters makes the instance closer to "monopolistic competition" (see Section 12.B) than to pure competition. As in the case of a monopolist supplier, the information necessary for effective price discrimination, even apart from legal or technical difficulties, poses a serious obstacle. So even a hypothetical competitively supplied public good is likely to be "under-produced."

CONCLUSION: The efficiency conditions for public goods require price discrimination in accordance with consumers' Marginal Rates of Substitution in Consumption. Because of the difficulty and costs of excluding non-payers, and of charging correct discriminatory prices, public goods are likely to be under-supplied by private firms.

One other consideration reinforcing this conclusion is the existence of *transaction costs* associated with the conversion of a public good into excludable private property. If a television broadcast is "scrambled" to permit charging a fee for receiving the program, society is bearing a cost in terms of the resources used for scrambling and unscrambling, as well as for the efforts involved in negotiating over price, billing, and all other costs of the market-exchange process. Again, these costs lead to under-production.

According to some welfare theorists, the various difficulties in private supply of public goods dictate that they be "publicly" (i.e., governmentally) provided instead. Indeed, some have thought that the concept of public goods serves to define the proper scope of government: "Private goods" ought to be privately supplied, and "public goods" ought to be publicly supplied. But in fact we do observe private firms supplying public goods. Television broadcasting is the obvious example, but even lighthouse services have at times been privately provided. And on the other hand government agencies, while supplying public goods like national defense, are also in the business of producing a vast range of private goods. Among the many examples are electric power (TVA), irrigation water (the U.S. Bureau of Reclamation), insurance (Social Security), education (public schools), and of course postal services (the U.S. Mail).

Government provision is inevitable only for those public goods for which *exclusion* of non-payers is unfeasible. Here the same "free rider" problem arises as already discussed under the heading of "Externalities" in Section C.3 above. If a non-payer can derive benefits on essentially the same terms as someone who

Chapter 17
WELFARE
ECONOMICS:
THE THEORY OF
ECONOMIC
POLICY

542

does pay, each and every person will be motivated to let the others foot the bill. In such circumstances provision of the public good by private firms may be impossible. But the difficulty is due to the *non-exclusionary* aspect rather than to the *public-good* aspect. Even a perfectly ordinary private good, not collectively consumed (e.g., food in a restaurant), could not be profitably provided on a private basis if non-payers could invade the premises and obtain service on the same basis as the paying customers!

Coase's Theorem, as introduced in Section C.3 above, asserted that market equilibrium would constitute an efficient outcome provided, among other things, that property rights are "well-defined." What does this mean, and what happens when the condition is not met?

For the purposes of the Theorem, property rights can be said to be "well-defined" if: (a) all resources are *appropriated* (belong legally to someone), and (b) legal rights to property are perfectly and costlessly *enforced*.

Taking up the latter condition first, if legal rights are *not* perfectly and costlessly enforced then some individuals may find it possible and advantageous to acquire the property of others without offering their own property in exchange. An obvious instance is theft. But even without violating the law, individuals could unilaterally attempt to gain control over resources now owned by others by means such as: instituting more or less groundless lawsuits, inducing legislators to change the law (or inducing bureaucrats to re-interpret the law) on their behalf, or even appealing to the charitable impulses of the present owners. Given that such options exist on the part of those desiring to acquire resources, it then follows that those presently vested with property rights may be induced to undertake defensive or protective measures: patrolling their property to prevent theft or invasion, hiring expensive lawyers to fight lawsuits, lobbying in Washington, and so forth. All such proceedings, both offensive or defensive, come under the heading of "appropriative" activities—efforts to change or to prevent changes in the structure of ownership of property. Such efforts are not costless, and will surely absorb resources that could have been devoted to production and exchange activities instead.

Turning back now to the first condition, suppose existing property rights are enforced but that some resources are not presently appropriated at all. If those resources are valuable, the consequence again will be appropriative activity. A dramatic historical instance was the Oklahoma land rush of 1889. When the settlers raced to stake out former Indian territories, the resources devoted to "rushing" so as to gain possession ahead of others constituted a social efficiency loss. Some of the externality problems of Section 17.C.3 were also associated with attempts to gain control of unappropriated resources: each owner of an oil well pumps faster because failure to do so would encourage neighbors to "rush" to drain away the petroleum underlying that owner's land. Settling new territories or pumping oil are themselves productive actions; what is inefficient is the waste in "rushing" to act before the resource involved is captured by others. The efficiency loss due to appropriative activity is therefore not generally due to the

Chapter 17
WELFARE
ECONOMICS:
THE THEORY OF
ECONOMIC
POLICY

543

existence of property rights under law, but rather to *imperfections* in their assignment or enforcement. A totally lawless society would not avoid appropriative activity; indeed, such activity would become everyone's main occupation.

Even costless transactions among the parties, were they possible, cannot in general eliminate appropriative activities in the absence of well-defined property rights. For, every transaction involves a *quid pro quo*—each party gives up a right to the other reciprocally. But appropriative activity is by definition not reciprocal; one party's gain is the other's loss. The upshot is that Coase's Theorem would not be applicable.[18]

17.D

THE PROBLEM OF EQUALITY

Equality of income has historically been an important political objective, especially in democratically governed societies. Attempts have been made to defend equality on utilitarian grounds. Suppose that individuals had cardinal and interpersonally comparable utility functions, characterized by diminishing Marginal Utility, and furthermore that *all these utility functions were essentially identical*. Then the total social aggregate of utility would be maximized by dividing income equally. This argument involves strong assumptions, of course, over and above acceptance of the philosophical premises of utilitarianism.

Alternatively, equality of income might be proclaimed as an "ethical" postulate in its own right, free of any utilitarian underpinnings. (But if a poor person favors equality, is that ethics or envy?)

17.D.1
An Application: Rawls' Concept of "Justice"

The philosopher John Rawls has recently proposed a strongly egalitarian criterion of "social justice."[19] The criterion deals primarily with distribution of the measurable goods of society, and so can best be regarded as mappable on the objective income axes I^j, I^k of Figure 17.1 rather than on the subjective utility axes U^j, U^k of Figure 17.2.

Rawls' key concept is what he calls "the difference principle." Inequality in a society, he asserts, is justified *only* to the extent that it benefits the *least* advantaged. In Figure 17.6, the 45° line shows all the conceivable income allocations I^j, I^k for which equality holds, i.e., for which $I^j = I^k$. Now consider the shaded social opportunity set bounded by the curve II'. The best attainable point on the 45° line is evidently the point F; this is the equality optimum. In moving from F toward the point S along the Social Opportunity Frontier II', a degree of inequality is being created (since, northwest of the 45° line, John's income I^j exceeds Karl's

Chapter 17
WELFARE
ECONOMICS:
THE THEORY OF
ECONOMIC
POLICY

544

[18]In certain special circumstances, agreement may still be possible to forego appropriative activity, each party accepting some recognized division of the resource at stake. The *quid pro quo* here is that each gives up the right or power to appropriate the resource, in return for the other's doing the same. Examples are settling out of court to end a lawsuit, or a negotiated peace to halt a war. Needless to say, despite such possibilities, lawsuits and wars still occur.

[19]John Rawls, *A Theory of Justice* (Cambridge, Mass.: Harvard University Press, 1971).

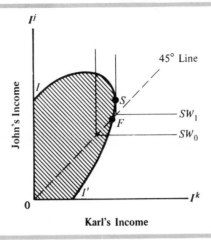

Figure 17.6
Rawls' Social Optimum. The philosopher John Rawls regards as "just" only those departures from equality of income that benefit the least advantaged. If *II'* is the Social Opportunity Frontier, *F* is the highest attainable point of equal incomes (along the 45° line). At *S*, in contrast, incomes are unequal. But, since even the less well-off party (Karl) has gained in moving from *F* to *S*, that move is supposedly "justified." In effect, Rawls' conception has indifference curves of "social welfare" like SW_0 and SW_1; right-angled, with the corners on the 45° equality line.

income I^k). But this is *justified*, according to Rawls, in that even the poorer individual (Karl) is thereby made better off.

It will be evident that the application of Rawls' difference principle leads to selection of the point *S* as the social optimum in Figure 17.6. More generally, his rule is equivalent to asserting a particular shape for the interpersonal or social "welfare" function (compare Figure 17.2). Here, the isoquants of social welfare or of Rawlsian "justice"[20] are rectangular with corners on the 45° line, as exemplified by SW_0 and SW_1 in the diagram.

Now consider instead a social opportunity set like that portrayed in Figure 17.1, where the frontier *II'* has negative slope throughout (i.e., where John cannot gain unless Karl loses, and vice versa). Under these circumstances the Rawlsian optimum always requires *absolute equality of income.*

A different approach to the problem of equality emphasizes that purely private motivation, in a world of individuals who are not completely selfish, will suffice to bring about a certain degree of equality. And indeed, the equality thus voluntarily achieved will represent an efficient (Pareto-optimal) allocation of incomes.

In Section 6.A.1, the "demand for charity" was studied. Apart from minor

17.D.2
Equality and Pareto-Optimality

---

[20]Rawls' identification of the word "justice" with "equality" is questionable terminology. Our ordinary understanding of "justice" is as a proper *relationship between a man's actions and his rewards*. The Biblical "eye for an eye" may be a primitive concept of justice, but it is the sort of thing that we mean by justice. In contrast, Rawls' concept concerns the distribution of rewards to individuals *independent of any actions on their part*. This is not justice, but bounty.

changes in notation, Figure 17.7 here is essentially equivalent to Figure 6.1 in the earlier chapter. I have preferences as between "My income" I^m and "His income" I^h, such that *both* I^h and I^m are "goods" for me when $I^h < I^m$ (i.e., I am benevolent to someone poorer than myself). Given an initial endowment allocation E of incomes such that $I^h < I^m$, the opportunity locus or "budget line" EK shows the allocations I can attain by unilaterally transferring my income to him.[21]

In the situation of Figure 17.7, my transfer optimum is the tangency T^*. Furthermore, if his preference function is like mine, the circumstances that impel me to donate to him (I am richer than he) also motivate him to accept the gift (he is poorer than I). Being mutually desired, the transfer is Pareto-optimal.

17.D.3
Equality as a Public Good

Still another approach emphasizes that equality can be regarded as a "public good," in the sense of Section 17.C.4. For, an increased degree of equality that satisfies the benevolent desires of any one individual will, without additional cost, also increase utility for any other person who is similarly situated and has similar benevolent preferences.

Returning to Figure 17.7, suppose that, before I make my individual voluntary transfer changing the income allocation from the endowment position E to

Figure 17.7

The Economics of Charity. My preferences shown here represent benevolence to others when they are poorer than myself. Given an initial endowment allocation of incomes E, and if I can transfer income to the other party along the line EK, my private optimum is at T^*. If he has similar preferences, since he is poorer than I he will also surely gain in utility terms. Thus, the move from E to T^* is Pareto-preferred. If a third party were to give him a contribution EF, the revised endowment allocation from my point of view becomes point F. I will then move along FK' to point T^{**}, making a somewhat smaller contribution.

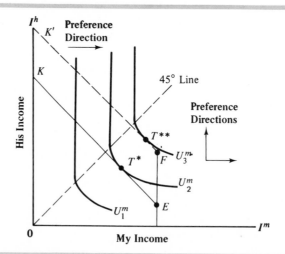

Chapter 17
WELFARE
ECONOMICS:
THE THEORY OF
ECONOMIC
POLICY

546

[21]As explained in Chapter 6, in the absence of taxes EK would have a slope of -1, an angle of $135°$ with the horizontal.

the optimum T^*, some third party A were to make a gift to my prospective beneficiary H. Specifically, if A's gift to H is in the amount EF, the initial endowment allocation of income between H and myself shifts upward to point F. My opportunity locus then becomes the dashed line FK'. Thus I could clearly attain a higher level of satisfaction (tangency T^{**} with a higher indifference curve on I^m, I^h axes) than before. A's gift has, to some degree, enabled me to satisfy my taste for benevolence without cost to myself.

Furthermore, this is an example of a *non-excludable* public good. Having made the gift to H, the third party A is in no way able to prevent me from enjoying the effects of that act. The consequence is, once again, a "free rider" problem. I transfer to H only the amount of income needed to move from F to T^{**}, whereas without A's intervention I would have been willing to make the larger transfers required to move from E to T^*. To some extent, therefore, as a potential donor I am free-riding on others' contributions. Similarly, the third party A (and other potential donors as well) may contribute less than they otherwise would, expecting to free-ride on my contribution. Following the familiar free-rider theme, it follows that a less-than-efficient amount of income transfers would be undertaken by private individuals. This analysis therefore provides a rationale for government intervention via *fiscal redistribution*, whereby taxes levied on the wealthier classes are collected for transfer to poorer groups.

To fit ideally into the model of benevolence as a public good, however, the redistributive taxes would have to be voluntarily levied upon themselves by the wealthier groups! A more cynical explanation of the phenomenon of fiscal redistribution would not make any use of benevolence as a motive, but would run simply in terms of political realities. This topic is considered further in Chapter 18.

But in any case, *private* charity is an important phenomenon. Hence, benevolent preferences surely do exist, and so cannot be entirely dismissed as motivation for fiscal redistribution.

17.E

WELFARE ECONOMICS—CONCLUSION

Welfare economics has been primarily preoccupied with the problem of *efficiency*, i.e., with the determination of the conditions leading to allocations on the Social Opportunity Frontier (as shown, for example, by the curve LL' in Figure 17.2). Any such allocation is characterized by the condition that there exists no other that is Pareto-preferred to it.

Achievement of efficiency is, however, neither necessary nor sufficient as a criterion of ideal social policy. The *distribution* of income as among individuals and social classes is another important criterion. Even granting the appropriateness of a certain tilt toward *equality* of income, the question remains as to how far to go in sacrificing efficiency for equality. And there are, of course, many other criteria with some claim to be considered in social policy: liberty to retain and use

Chapter 17
WELFARE
ECONOMICS:
THE THEORY OF
ECONOMIC
POLICY

lawfully acquired talents or property, communitarian versus individualistic values, and other non-utilitarian considerations.

Nevertheless, economists' emphasis upon the efficiency criterion has probably played a useful social role. The political processes that determine social policy tend to overlook considerations of efficiency almost entirely. Whether the issue be the progressive income tax, the protection of some industries by tariffs and quotas, penalization of others for "excessive" profits, combating monopoly, or choosing the proper scale of government, it has become a function of the economist to point out that there are efficiency implications that need to be evaluated as one input into the social decision process.

An older generation of welfare economists tended to think in terms of a policy shotgun with two barrels: (1) a presumption in favor of *laissez faire,* based on the Theorem of the Invisible Hand as discussed in Section 17.B above, but modified by (2) a presumption in favor of government intervention to remedy the specific failures and distortions of the Invisible Hand reviewed in Section 17.C. Neither barrel of the shotgun quite hits the target. The efficiency ideally attainable by the Invisible Hand is, as we have seen, not a fully satisfactory guide to policy. On the other hand, a failure of the Invisible Hand to achieve efficiency does not of itself provide any warrant for belief that the alternative of government intervention will improve matters.

To gain some understanding of this last question, it would be desirable to subject the process of political or governmental decision-making to an analytic investigation that parallels our treatment of the market process. Economists have indeed, though only very recently, turned to serious *positive* analysis of government, i.e., to the economic consequences of what government actually does as opposed to what in some ideal sense it "ought" to do. Recent developments in this field of inquiry will be examined in the following chapter.

SUMMARY OF CHAPTER 17

The study of the principles underlying correct public policy is called "welfare economics."

While there are many possible goals of policy, attention has traditionally been concentrated on only two: efficiency, and distributive equity. Efficiency is increased by making any change that is Pareto-preferred, i.e., that increases the utility of any person or persons without decreasing the utility of any other. An outcome is said to be efficient or Pareto-optimal when there are no other outcomes Pareto-preferred to it. (However, it is not true that every efficient outcome is Pareto-preferred to every outcome that is not efficient.) Distributive equity is ordinarily interpreted as *equality*. But while equality may be definable in terms of objective incomes, there is no way to say when two individuals' utilities are equal. Both efficiency and equality are goals based on utilitarian philosophy. Non-utilitarians have criticized such goals as, among other things, excessively individualistic and excessively materialistic.

The Theorem of the Invisible Hand states that, under ideal conditions, a *laissez-faire* economy will achieve an efficient utilization of resources. As economic agents respond to the ruling equilibrium prices, efficiency will be at-

Chapter 17
WELFARE
ECONOMICS:
THE THEORY OF
ECONOMIC
POLICY

548

tained among consumers in the allocation of finished products, among factor-owners in the choice between market employment and reservation uses of their resources, and among firms in using resources and producing final products.

However, there are several grounds on which the Invisible Hand might fail in the actual world: (1) Monopolies of many types exist, all leading to inefficient outcomes if operated for private gain. (2) Disequilibrium prices do not give the correct signals to buyers and sellers. (3) If the existing structure of property rights allows some agents to impose direct externalities on others, the incentives for the use of resources are distorted. Coase's Theorem asserts that property rights will be exchanged to eliminate inefficient externalities, but this holds only under ideal conditions: property rights must be well-defined, and transactions costless. (4) Public goods represent a special type of externality, where a commodity is concurrently rather than exclusively consumed—so that if a public good is provided for one person, there is no additional cost in providing it to others. If a public good is or can be made excludable in the market, it can be privately provided. There is a pattern of discriminatory prices that can achieve efficiency in the production and use of excludable public goods, but in practice such goods are likely to be under-supplied in the market. If a public good is non-excludable, on the other hand, it can scarcely be provided by the market at all. (But neither could a non-excludable private good.) (5) Where property rights are not well-defined, individuals will be motivated to undertake activities aimed at changing the effective structure of rights (or at preventing such changes). Resources devoted to such "appropriative" activities represent a loss of efficiency.

The ethical position associated with the philosopher Rawls demands absolute equality of income, except where a move in the direction of inequality would help the worst off. If potential donors have benevolent motivations, private incentives tend to bring about some Pareto-preferred moves toward equality of income. But such equality becomes a kind of non-excludable public good, and so under-provided by private incentives.

In view of the uncertainties of distributive equity (or its usual practical counterpart, equality) as goals, economists have tended to concentrate upon achievement of efficiency. This has probably served a socially useful function. While one must treat with reserve the proposition that an actual *laissez-faire* economy would approximate an efficient outcome, it remains to be seen whether actual government interventions normally tend to correct such an economy's failure to do so.

QUESTIONS FOR CHAPTER 17

Chapter 17
WELFARE
ECONOMICS:
THE THEORY OF
ECONOMIC
POLICY

Mainly for Review

R1. Explain and justify the normally "concave" shape of the Social Opportunity Frontier in income terms (Figure 17.1). What can be said about the shape of the Social Opportunity Frontier in utility terms (Figure 17.2)?

*The answers to asterisked questions appear at the end of the book.

*R2. Show how a Social Opportunity Frontier in utility terms for two individuals may be derived from the *contract curve* of the Edgeworth box diagram (discussed in Section 7.B).

*R3. What meaning, if any, can be given to the concept of a "social optimum"? How valid is "efficiency" or Pareto-optimality as a criterion of social optimality?

R4. What is the Theorem of the Invisible Hand?

*R5. What are the conditions of "efficiency" reached under ideal conditions by the unregulated market process? Can the conditions be achieved, in principle, without use of the market?

R6. Why does disequilibrium of markets lead to inefficiency?

*R7. Explain why a firm that is a monopolist in the product market is said to hire "too little" of the factors it uses for production. Explain why a firm that is a monopsonist in the factor market is also said to hire "too little." Given these effects, does it follow that too large a proportion of the community's resources are employed by competitive firms, or are retained for reservation uses by resource-owners, or both?

R8. What are public goods? What are externalities? Is a public good a special case of an externality?

R9. How would inability to exclude non-payers affect the private supply of public goods? The private supply of private goods?

*R10. What is the efficiency condition for optimal provision of a public good? In what sense is it appropriate in the case of public goods to sum individual demand curves *vertically*, whereas for private goods the summation takes place *horizontally*?

*R11. What limits the possibility of private supply of public goods? Will public provision mean that a more nearly optimal amount will be supplied?

R12. What is the Coase Theorem? Explain the relevance of each of the following conditions for the actual empirical applicability of the theorem: (a) well-defined property rights, and (b) low-costs of negotiating and enforcing agreements.

R13. What is "appropriative" activity? What are the implications of such activities for economic efficiency?

For Further Thought and Discussion

*T1. Fragment of a conversation based upon Robert Browning's poem, "My Last Duchess":

> But my dear Dr. H., your own textbook proves that in terms of economic efficiency I was amply justified in taking the life of my last duchess. For, being of not inconsiderable means, I was willing to pay more for her death than she could have afforded to pay to prevent it.
>
> —The Duke of Ferrara

Is the Duke's analysis correct?

*T2. "An efficient allocation of resources maximizes the dollar value of national income." True or false? Explain.

Chapter 17
WELFARE
ECONOMICS:
THE THEORY OF
ECONOMIC
POLICY

550

T3. In the apples – bees example in the text, the externality is mutually beneficial. Provide an example of a reciprocal relation in which the mutually imposed externalities are harmful. Can there be a case in which in one direction the effect is beneficial but in the other direction harmful?

*T4. What sorts of real-world considerations may forestall the working of Coase's Theorem by making property rights ambiguous or uncertain? By raising the costs of negotiating and enforcing contracts?

T5. What are the major considerations bearing upon the likelihood or effectiveness of achieving efficiency through market versus nonmarket means?

*T6. "An ideal market would achieve a Pareto-efficient outcome, but only one that is Pareto-preferred to the endowment situation; an ideal dictatorship would not be so limited." True or false? Explain.

*T7. Recently, steps have been taken in the United States to ban the commercial market in human blood. (One of the arguments given was that commercially provided blood is more likely to be infected with hepatitis than volunteered blood.) Can this ban be justified on efficiency grounds, or any other grounds?

18.A THEORIES OF THE STATE, 554

18.B THE VOLUNTARIST POLITY AND ITS IMPERFECTIONS, 556
  18.B.1 The Problem of Delegation, 557
  18.B.2 Majority and Minority, 558
  18.B.3 The Problem of Voting, 560

18.C COLLECTIVE ACTION, FREE RIDERS, AND PRESSURE GROUPS, 561

18.D BUREAUCRACY, 565

18.E THE SCOPE OF GOVERNMENT, 567
  18.E.1 Functions of Government, 567
  18.E.2 Instruments of Government Policy, 572
  18.E.3 A Scientific Issue in Political Economy: Growth of Government, 573

Examples
  18.1 DETERMINANTS OF VOTER TURNOUT, 560
  18.2 THE ECONOMICS OF ALLIANCE, 563
  18.3 REGULATED ELECTRICITY RATES, 564
  18.4 TAXICAB REGULATION, 566
  18.5 TAX-EXPENDITURE REDISTRIBUTION, 570
  18.6 GROWTH OF GOVERNMENT, 573

18

GOVERNMENT AND THE ECONOMY: A POSITIVE ANALYSIS

Supplementary Chapter

It is sometimes thought that the difference between behavior in the marketplace and behavior in the political sphere lies in the realm of *motives*: self-interest is expected to be the governing force in economic decisions, while in their political decisions people are supposedly concerned primarily with the public interest. This naive view is rejected here. The individuals who interact in their economic decisions are the same people, with the same motives, as those engaging in or subject to political decisions. To compare and contrast political and economic behavior we must look not to differences of motives but to differences in the *processes of human interaction*—differences in "the rules of the game."

In the economic sphere individuals interact primarily through the market, whose key feature is *contract*. One party agrees to sell, and the other to buy. In the political sphere the primary mode of human interaction is through *government*. What is the difference? You contract with your bank, your employer, your grocer. But parents govern their minor children. The warden governs prisoners. And all of us are governed by legislators, judges, and others in positions of political authority. Contractual association, being voluntary, is a relation of equality. But the essence of government is *subordination*: some persons are empowered, with the ultimate sanction of force, to impose their will upon others.

Political theorists have been at pains to justify, or at any rate to explain, why human societies must have or do have such subordination. Some of the leading theories are reviewed in Section 18.A. Section 18.B turns to the fundamental logic of *voluntary (contractual) political associations,* which come closest to the economic model in that subordination occurs "with the consent of the governed." Afterward, we will use the results obtained to examine a number of the ways in which economic and political decisions interact.

18.A

THEORIES OF THE STATE

Government, in the most general sense of the word, arises as has been noted in many contexts, including families, prisons, universities, and monasteries. But when we speak of "the" government we specifically mean the *state*. The state is a system of subordination that organizes all the individuals in a given geographical area, within which it possesses an effective monopoly of physical force. The all-inclusiveness of the state means that the political association is an *involuntary* one; a disaffected individual can escape it only by becoming an exile or outlaw. The edicts of those in state authority are enforced (where not voluntarily accepted) by coercion, i.e., by the threat of violence. It is the effectiveness of the *threat* that characterizes the functioning state. If *actual* violence must be continually used we have either war (between contending governments) or anarchy (the absence of government).

In the history of political thought the "positive" question of what the state *is* has often been confused with the "normative" issue of what it *should be*. Our interest here is solely in the positive or scientific aspect. Why do individuals accept a role of subordination in the political system (the "polity")? What functions does the state perform that promote the interests of the governed individuals? These two questions, which are at bottom the same, can be approached in terms of alternative "theories of the state."

1. DIVINE ORDINANCE: If the authority of kings (or other rulers) over lesser mortals is generally believed to be divinely ordained, there is no problem in explaining why the governed accept subordination. The divine-right doctrine seems a handy one for rulers, but there is another side of the coin. Under this theory the *function* of the governor can only be to carry out God's will, not his or her own will. Should the ruler fail to carry out God's will, it seems plausible that such a person forfeits authority, for which there is good Biblical precedent—beginning with the story of Saul. So even kings may have been uncomfortable with a theory in which their credential for power is the debatable matter of God's will.

For our purposes, the point is that the divinely ordained state (whether monarchy or republic or other) exists to serve *neither* the purposes of the ruler nor of the ruled, but rather those of God. However out of fashion intellectually, this belief is still ingrained to some degree in popular thinking. Our modern rulers still retain some useful shreds of the mystic aura once attached to sanctified leadership. Hence our shock when we learn of their all too human failings.

Chapter 18
GOVERNMENT
AND THE
ECONOMY:
A POSITIVE
ANALYSIS

554

2. NAKED POWER: At the other extreme from divine ordinance lies the view that government represents nothing but ability to seize and hold power—to coerce others into obedience. Dominance among humans, on this view, is not fundamentally different from the dominance observable in a pack of wolves. What limits any human ruler's domain is, ultimately, the fact of diminishing returns to the activity of organizing a system of coercion. Even Alexander's Macedonians eventually mutinied, forcing him to set a limit to his empire; it was Napoleon's refusal to accept any limit that led to his downfall.

A system of government based on naked power may still gain wide support, simply by being profitable to enough participants. The Third Reich promised the Germans the role of master race in a conquered world. But as there will necessarily be large numbers of individuals assigned the role of slaves or victims, the military burden on the masters may be more than they can bear.

3. INSTINCTUAL-BIOLOGICAL: According to Aristotle, man is by nature a "political animal," a creature for whom society and government are not an incidental but an essential aspect. Plato held a more extreme view: an "organic" conception of human society, in which the individual is unimportant and only the community counts. The organic theory suggests that the function of the state is to promote *community* survival and growth, not individual interest. People allow themselves to be ruled by the state not to achieve private goals, but rather because their individual lives are purposeless apart from the interests of the community. As a matter of observed fact, this is surely too extreme. We do indeed see many instances of self-sacrifice for the community. But while there are saints and heroes in the real world, there are also cowards and traitors.

A more moderate view strikes a balance between individual and community objectives. People have individual goals, but a social instinct is also part of the human make-up. Evolution has selected such a social instinct for survival, just as it has selected the social characteristics of ants, bees, wolves, and monkeys. In particular, it is generally believed, over the long sweep of prehistoric ages man evolved the ability to cooperate in the hunting group.[1] At a later stage in the development of large social units, the main selective pressure upon human social organization has been *war*. With minor exceptions, only those races and strains of humanity and only those political and cultural forms have survived that were efficient at war. Leadership is critical for success in the hunt and in war, as is also the willingness to be led—to the point where the individual may be motivated to sacrifice, even to give his life, for the group. Thus, subordination and a degree of unselfishness are grounded on instincts formed by an evolutionary process. Leaders, so long as their behavior seems consistent with group survival, can often count on the self-sacrificing instincts of followers.

4. VOLUNTARY CONTRACT: One way of explaining the existence of government, without departing from individualistic premises, is to deny that there is any ultimate difference between voluntary contractual association and the state. This leads

Chapter 18
GOVERNMENT
AND THE
ECONOMY:
A POSITIVE
ANALYSIS

[1]Desmond Morris, *The Human Zoo* (New York: McGraw-Hill, 1969), Ch. 1.

to the contention that the state itself is founded upon a *social contract*. Historical instances of such contracts are rare; the Mayflower Compact (1620) is the leading example. Still, it might be claimed that a kind of implicit contract exists, in which any individual is bound to accept the obligations and penalties of citizenship if he has partaken of the benefits thereof.

Social-contract theorists have usually pitched their arguments in normative terms: How "ought" the citizens or the rulers behave? But the underlying hypothesis can also be regarded as a positive theory. It asserts that rational individuals, to escape anarchy, combine to subject themselves to a system of subordination in the form of a "constitution." Even though some actions adverse to their interests are bound to be adopted, they will support the constitution on the basis of an *overall* comparison of costs and benefits.[2] The social-contract or voluntary-association theory of government, in its democratic version, fits most naturally into the approach of the economist. Understanding contracts, the economist is already tooled up for dealing with the contractual state! Without passing judgment on the scientific merits of this explanation of government and subordination, the next section studies how the desires of individuals can be mediated and integrated through a government mechanism (a polity) of the voluntarist type.

18.B

THE VOLUNTARIST POLITY AND ITS IMPERFECTIONS

The essence of the voluntarist view of the state can be grasped by thinking of *political parties* as akin to *business firms*. Business firms offer goods and services, at specified prices, to the consumers. Political parties offer packages of government policies, at certain costs in the form of taxes and other burdens, to the citizens. Firms are groupings of individuals trying to make a profit by providing *consumers* with what they want. Political parties are groupings of individuals trying to make a "profit" (which might, in some degree, represent satisfactions like power or glory apart from pecuniary remuneration) by providing *citizens* with what they want.

Indeed, ideal *laissez faire* in the economy corresponds to ideal democracy in the polity.[3] In each case, the enforcement mechanism is *competition*. In the ideal market economy, perfect competition among firms drives profits to zero in long-run equilibrium (see Section 10.D). Then firms have no power to do anything other than what consumers want, since any firm that fails to satisfy consumers will be driven out of business by other firms. In the ideal polity, perfect competition among parties similarly drives political "profit" to zero. Parties have no power to do anything other than what citizens want, since any party that fails to satisfy

Chapter 18
GOVERNMENT
AND THE
ECONOMY:
A POSITIVE
ANALYSIS

[2] See, especially, J. M. Buchanan and G. Tullock, *The Calculus of Consent* (Ann Arbor: University of Michigan Press, 1962).

[3] See Gary S. Becker, "Competition and Democracy," *Journal of Law and Economics,* v. 1 (Oct. 1958).

citizens will be voted out of office. Thus, Adam Smith's Invisible Hand is operative, to some degree at least, in the political as well as in the economic arena.

In the chapter preceding, we reviewed (under the heading of "Welfare Economics") the various imperfections of real-world market economies—monopoly, disequilibrium, externalities, etc.—that lead to results falling short of the ideal. It was emphasized that these imperfections of markets do not imply the conclusion that government necessarily "ought" to intervene. For one thing, we need to know something first about possible imperfections of the *political* process. We now take up this topic, the imperfections of political mechanisms when viewed as systems by which citizens voluntarily associate to achieve desired ends.

The political process does allow citizens to choose policies, in a sense, but only under severe restrictions. Rare exceptions apart, it is impractical to have citizens vote directly on policies. They vote only (and possibly at one or more removes) for *delegates* in the legislative, executive, and judicial branches of government; it is these delegates who make the actual policy choices. But elections of delegates are relatively infrequent. Whereas individuals make a host of market decisions every single day, they can only choose or recall their political delegates over election intervals measured in years. Some of the most important political officeholders, such as U.S. Supreme Court justices, are only indirectly "elected" at all, and are beyond effective control thereafter. So delegates may have a considerable degree of "power" (i.e., of leeway to violate the preferences of their constituents) before or even without ever having to face a day of reckoning.

The *limited options* available further erode the control that citizens have over their delegates. There is considerable "bundling" of issues in the election process. A voter may prefer the position of one candidate for office on one question, of a competing candidate on a second issue, and so forth. But the delegate elected will be representing (or misrepresenting) the voter in *all* decisions to be made during his term of office.

Also, political competition is highly imperfect. There appear to be strong economies of scale in the political process, so that candidates rarely stand for office independently. Instead, they are almost always tied in with organized political parties. In some democratic countries, there are only two effective parties, a situation that would be called "duopoly" in the economic sphere (see Section 13.A), where it is considered a serious imperfection of markets.

A number of political devices may provide citizens with a somewhat greater range of options of governmental choice: (1) In some countries, political competition is more varied in that multi-party systems exist. (2) Some states permit citizens to propose laws outside the legislature (the *initiative*), and to *recall* elected officers between scheduled elections. (3) Within parties, the "primary" and other techniques of participation provide ways for citizens to influence final choices offered the voters in the actual election. (4) Under a federal system, the citizen may support one party for national office and a different one for local office. (5) Similarly, where there is separation of powers the voter may choose different parties to represent him in the legislative and executive branches of government.

But these are all highly imperfect arrangements. Indeed, while improve-

Chapter 18
GOVERNMENT
AND THE
ECONOMY:
A POSITIVE
ANALYSIS

557

ments from the single point of view of *representation* of citizen preferences, some or all of the devices may be objectionable on other grounds. They may be inconsistent, for example, with effectiveness of government—with simply getting things done. In any case, the scope of individual choice remains drastically less in the political arena than in the marketplace.

18.B.2
Majority and Minority

Modern democratic political systems operate (with some qualifications) on the principle of *majority rule*. The necessity of making decisions through delegates poses a problem, as we have seen, since the delegate may not faithfully serve constituents' interests. But what if the constituents differ among themselves? Then, to be elected, delegates need only serve the majority interest; they must please only 50%-plus-one of those who turn out to vote.

This obviously puts the minority at a grave disadvantage. Conceivably, even their most vital interests may be at the mercy of the majority. If on some policy issue 75% of the constituency prefer alternative #1 and 25% prefer alternative #2, the delegate's support will be unlikely to be divided in this proportion. Rather, the delegate will be motivated to give full support to the group majority, those favoring alternative #1. In contrast, majority and minority preferences are normally *both* provided for, in due proportion, in a market economy. If 75% of consumers prefer chocolate and 25% prefer vanilla, chocolate and vanilla flavors will tend, other things equal, to be provided in just about these proportions.

The majority–minority problem repeats itself at a higher level, since the delegates themselves normally decide policies by majority voting in the legislative process. It is therefore conceivable that the "majority" position may represent only a bare 50% of the voters in a bare 50% of the election districts, so that the "majority" may be the 25% and the "minority" the 75% of the national consituency. This is of course only a very remote possibility.

Devices have emerged tending to provide partial remedies for the majority-minority problem. *Constitutional protection* limits the types of laws a majority can pass, thus affording some minimal security for minority rights. A very interesting phenomenon, which arises most visibly on the higher or legislative level, is called "log-rolling." Suppose that the minority legislators feel very strongly on a particular issue *A*. Then to swing over votes on issue *A*, they may promise other legislators to support *their* positions on separate issues *B, C, D,* etc. In this way the *intensity* of minority preferences is registered, to some degree, as a counterweight to the mere numbers of the majority.

The process of log-rolling can be regarded as a partial injection of market considerations into the political process. Through "political market exchange," delegates' votes on some issues are "bought," to be "paid for" by votes on other issues. Log-rolling, though generally considered an evil,[4] reminds us of the Fundamental Theorem of Exchange (Section 7.A)—the *mutual advantage of trade.* Indeed, efficiency in the sense of a *Pareto-optimal* outcome—a result in which it is no longer possible to achieve any further gains to anyone without hurting others

Chapter 18
GOVERNMENT
AND THE
ECONOMY:
A POSITIVE
ANALYSIS

558

[4]Not without reason, as will be indicated in Section 18.C.

(see Section 17.A)—would be achieved if legislators' votes on issues could be openly purchased for money!

The underlying logic is this. Setting aside problems of transaction costs and strategic behavior, an ideal system of political market exchange would be one requiring *unanimous* consent for every action. To achieve concurrence, every dissenter's vote would have to be "bought" by the winning side. This would guarantee that all political actions undertaken are actually Pareto-preferred over the initial situation (i.e., constitute an improvement for some, and an injury for none). Those who suffer from the chosen action are compensated by the purchase of their votes. With majority rule and log-rolling, it is true that compensation is not paid to all those affected—only to a number sufficient to comprise a voting majority. Nevertheless, since *both* sides will be trying to buy votes, the winning side will be the one able to bid higher. Hence under a bought-vote system the more highly-valued alternative would always be chosen. The result is Pareto-*optimal*, though not in general unanimously preferred (Pareto-*preferred*)[5] over the status quo.

That the purchase of votes seems offensive is a consequence of the problem of *delegation* discussed above. In a *direct* democracy, offering compensation, to win the approval of those adversely affected by a proposed policy alternative, would surely be quite reasonable. But our knowledge of the world leads us to suspect that any compensation privately paid to the delegate in a *representative* democracy may be pocketed rather than translated into benefits for the constituents. That is true enough, but we should realize where the real objection lies: in the delegation of decision-making power, not in the process of offering compensation to win the approval (buy the votes) of those injured by proposed public decisions.

There is still another curious problem of majority decision. Suppose a majority prefer option #1 over #2, and a majority also prefer #2 over #3. Still, it does not follow that a majority will prefer #1 over #3! Imagine that three individuals must make a collective decision as to color, say of their joint living quarters. Two of them may favor red over green, two favor green over yellow, and yet two favor yellow over red.[6] This problem of "cycling" means that majority preferences are not necessarily *transitive*. (Recall that transitivity of *individual* preferences was treated as an Axiom in Section 3.A.) It follows that it is not in general possible to construct a consistent rank ordering of majority preferences. In such circumstances, the way in which the issues are presented for voting (the "agenda") can easily determine the outcome. (It has been said that "whoever controls the agenda, controls the meeting.")

[5]It was shown in Section 17.A that a *Pareto-optimal* outcome is not necessarily *Pareto-preferred* to any given initial situation. In Figure 17.2, the Social Opportunity Frontier LL' is the set of Pareto-optimal outcomes. Starting from position C in Figure 17.2 as status quo, under the unanimity rule Pareto-preferred improvements would be adopted until an outcome like B on the Frontier—both Pareto-optimal, and Pareto-preferred to C—is attained. With bought votes under *majority* rule, however, the tendency is to attain a point like D'. Position D' is Pareto-optimal, but *not* Pareto-preferred to the starting position C (because a dissenting minority may have been victimized).

[6]This is the situation if, for example, the first voter's preference ordering is RGY, the second's is GYR, and the third's is YRG.

Chapter 18
GOVERNMENT
AND THE
ECONOMY:
A POSITIVE
ANALYSIS

559

It is the *vote* that represents the ultimate discipline that individual citizens can exercise upon their delegates. But the effectiveness of a single vote is so minuscule that the ordinary citizen is scarcely motivated to go to the polls at all. Even if the election of the preferred candidate were worth an enormous sum to the voter, one person's voting will actually have an effect upon the outcome only in a fantastically improbable situation, i.e., the case where that ballot gives the candidate a majority of one. Or if the citizen is not so interested in electing a particular candidate as in swelling the poll for an ideological position, again one vote more or less would scarcely ever be noticeable. And even if the voter has no selfish aims at all but intends to cast a purely public-spirited ballot, that single vote will no more measurably serve the *public* interest than it would the voter's own *selfish* interest.

If it were possible and legal for a candidate to *buy* votes, there would be no problem of motivating the voter. Parallel to the argument for log-rolling, a surprisingly good case can be made for buying citizens' votes at election time. What this means is that the politicians will be paying the constituents in advance for the gains to be reaped in office. Competition for votes before election would compensate for the scarcely controllable power granted the delegates after their election.

If votes are not paid for, and if the chance of affecting the outcome is negligible, why are so many votes actually cast in elections? If citizens are rational, it can only be that the *costs of casting a ballot are low*. And indeed, at least for city-dwellers and when the weather is good, the cost is small. Voting may actually be fun; it provides sociability and a feeling of civic accomplishment to offset the small travel and time cost involved.

Another somewhat subtler consequence of the imperfections of the political representation process enters here. In the market-place you "get what you pay for." In the political arena, it is all too easy to vote in a candidate and not get desired results out. (The main cost to the individual of such an outcome is not the trivial effort of wasted voting, of course, but the taxes and other burdens of undesired policies.) In view of the problems of electing a candidate supporting the whole bundle of one's preferred policies, and of ensuring that he abides by the platform upon which he was elected, it simply is not worthwhile for the rational citizen to invest large resources in determining what *are* the best policies. Voting is cheap, but voting *intelligently* may be quite costly. And so, citizens typically find themselves ill-informed on the issues about which they are casting ballots.

EXAMPLE 18.1
DETERMINANTS
OF VOTER
TURNOUT

If a citizen rationally considers whether to turn out and vote, his decision to incur the costs thereof should depend in part upon (1) the importance of the election, and (2) the probability of affecting the outcome. Y. Barzel and E. Silberberg[7] investigated the impact of these determinants upon the proportion of citizens actually casting ballots in U.S. gubernatorial elections in the years 1962, 1964, 1966 and 1968 (122 elections).

Among other findings, they obtained the results that:

[7] Y. Barzel and E. Silberberg, "Is the Act of Voting Rational?" *Public Choice*, v. 16 (Fall 1973).

1. *The larger the population, the smaller the percent of turnout.* This represents rational behavior, since the larger the population the smaller is the probability of a single vote determining the election. An *increase* of 1,000,000 in voting-age population of the state was associated with a 6% *decline* in the percent voting.

2. *The more one-sided the election, the smaller the turnout.* Again rational, since if voters had some inkling in advance of the one-sidedness they would place lower credence upon their own single ballot affecting the outcome. Statistically a 10% *increase* in the majority fraction was associated with a 7.7% *decline* in percentage voting.

3. *Coincidence of non-gubernatorial with gubernatorial elections increased turnout.* Statistically, a Presidential candidacy raised the fraction voting by 11.1%; a Senatorial candidacy by 5.5%. Obviously, it is more rational to vote, the more important is the election.

COMMENT: It would have been of interest to see if the difficulty and cost of voting significantly affected turnout. One would anticipate a larger fraction voting the better the weather, the less the average distance to the polls, the more convenient the voting hours, etc. As another point, it is also reasonable to expect a larger turnout on the part of those who expect to be able to cast *intelligent* ballots. (College graduates? Economics students?)

COLLECTIVE ACTION, FREE RIDERS, AND PRESSURE GROUPS

According to the traditional "welfare-economics" view, anytime one could show an imperfection of the market process, there was a presumptive justification for government remedial action. But our survey of the drastic imperfections of the delegation process in the democratic polity (when that process is regarded as a voluntaristic way of achieving individual ends) might tempt us to swing to the other extreme. So the question arises: Can an affirmative case be made for decision-making through the institution of government, to explain why at least a *portion* of economic activity is channeled through the state rather than through the market?

The usual economic answer is connected most fundamentally with the existence of *public goods,* i.e., of goods such that provision for any one person in the community means provision for all.[8] It was already explained in Section 17.C.4 why and how the market tends to "under-provide" public goods. This topic will be briefly reviewed here, with emphasis upon the *free-rider* problem.

We have by now encountered the free-rider problem in several different

Chapter 18
GOVERNMENT
AND THE
ECONOMY:
A POSITIVE
ANALYSIS

[8]This defines the limiting case of a "pure" public good; more generally, a commodity might partake of publicness to some partial degree.

contexts. In the case of a *cartel* (see Section 11.F), all members gain if they can stick together, holding down output so as to be able to impose a higher price on consumers. But granted that all other sellers are cooperating, any single member of the cartel is motivated to "chisel"; there is a temptation to take advantage of the high price in order to produce more than one's assigned share. A similar case exists with a *productive externality,* as when oil is pumped from a pool underlying the lands of several owners (Section 17.C.3). Here again it is in the interests of all jointly to hold back output, but in the interests of any single producer to expand output once the others are holding back. In each case, the economic agent motivated by self-interest is tempted to be a *free rider* upon others who are subordinating self-interest to the group-interest. The paradox is that all lose when all pursue their sole self-interest, and yet each has no guarantee that his or her restraint will be matched by the restraint of others.

The essence of the free-rider problem is that private costs must be incurred for group benefits. If the group is *small* enough, it may nevertheless be rational for self-interested individuals to generate positive quantities of public goods. But two important propositions can be asserted: (1) A less than Pareto-optimal quantity of the public good will be supplied, and (2) those with larger stakes in the outcome (e.g., those endowed with larger proportions of the aggregate wealth) will tend to provide *more* than proportionately larger shares of the public good.

While these theorems can be formally proved, a commonsense justification will suffice here. An individual Robinson Crusoe alone on an island would choose a preferred balance between two goods—say, between fish and mosquito-abatement. Both of these must necessarily be private goods so long as Robinson is isolated. But now suppose that Robinson is joined by Friday. Any effort at all on Friday's part in the way of mosquito-abatement provides Robinson with some "free" amount of the latter good. Counting on Friday to do something in this direction, Robinson will rationally redirect his efforts, striking a new balance so as to self-provide more fish (private good) and less mosquito-abatement (public good). The argument applies reciprocally to Friday's decision, of course. Each cuts back on his provision of the public good, as he bears the full marginal cost of his own efforts but does not receive the full marginal benefits thereof (some of which "spill over" to the other party). So an aggregate amount of the public good is produced that is less than what the efficiency condition (17.5) calls for—which is what an omniscient and benevolent government would have provided.

As to the second theorem, suppose that Robinson owns 80% of the resources on the island and Friday only 20%. Then Robinson knows that whatever mosquito-abatement takes place will have to be pretty much his own doing. He will therefore act *almost* as if he were alone on the island. Friday knows that Robinson will in any case be providing relatively ample amounts of the public good, perhaps far more than Friday would ever be interested in or could afford to provide himself with. Hence Friday will cut back his mosquito-abatement efforts to little or nothing. Thus, Robinson will be supplying *more* than his proportionate 80% and Friday *less* than his proportionate 20% of whatever public good is produced.

Chapter 18
GOVERNMENT
AND THE
ECONOMY:
A POSITIVE
ANALYSIS

562

An *alliance* between independent nations is generally undertaken in the interests of mutual defense. But defense is, to an important degree at least, a "public good" for the allied powers. Destruction of an enemy's bombers, for example, reduces the threat against each and all of the possible target nations. Since each participating nation receives only a portion of the benefit of any marginal increment of expenditure, all are tempted to "free ride" on the efforts of the others. But the larger nations are not in a position to "free ride" to nearly the same degree as the smaller allies.

A study of the North Atlantic Treaty Organization (NATO) defense expenditures in 1964 verified the differential expenditures of larger and smaller participants. The following table compares the rankings of NATO nations as to size (measured by GNP) and as to proportion of budget devoted to defense expenditures. The association is evident to the eye, and statistical testing indicates a high degree of significance.[9]

EXAMPLE 18.2
THE ECONOMICS
OF ALLIANCE

NATO Statistics

	GNP, 1964		DEFENSE BUDGET AS % OF GNP	
	$ BILLION	RANK	PERCENT	RANK
United States	569.03	1	9.0	1
Germany	88.87	2	5.5	6
United Kingdom	79.46	3	7.0	3
France	73.40	4	6.7	4
Italy	43.63	5	4.1	10
Canada	38.14	6	4.4	8
Netherlands	15.00	7	4.9	7
Belgium	13.43	8	3.7	12
Denmark	7.73	9	3.3	13
Turkey	6.69	10	5.8	5
Norway	5.64	11	3.9	11
Greece	4.31	12	4.2	9
Portugal	2.88	13	7.7	2
Luxembourg	.53	14	1.7	14

Source: M. Olson, Jr., and R. Zeckhauser, "An Economic Theory of Alliances," *Review of Economics and Statistics*, v. 48 (August 1966), p. 267.

[9] The most conspicuous exception, Portugal, is explainable on other grounds. This nation, tiny in GNP, supported a large defense budget because of its colonial commitments in Africa rather than its participation in NATO.

It is conceivable, then, that collective wants can be provided for, given small numbers, even without a government. NATO may be performing adequately, for example, without being in any way a super-government capable of coercing its members. But where numbers are quite large, and no single agent is in a position to derive a significant portion of the benefit from private action in the group interest, little or none of the public good will be supplied on self-interested grounds. Hence, setting aside the possibility of benevolence,[10] if *any* of the public good is to be supplied a coercive collectivist institution will have to provide it. The free-rider problem is overcome because in voting (if only indirectly, through election of delegates) for the supply of certain public goods, citizens are also voting to impose the burden of the costs thereof *upon others as well as upon themselves.*

The difference between the effectiveness of large and small groups in achieving collective ends has an important implication for observed political behavior. Members of a compact "special interest" (for example, businessmen and workers in a particular industry) are few in number compared to the population at large. Nevertheless, they are often successful in achieving political favors like tariffs or subsidies at the expense of the general consuming public. The reason is that the effective influence of the individual citizen-voter upon government is, for the reasons outlined in Section 18.B, extremely weak. Filling the vacuum are "pressure groups," which are sub-collectives of individuals interested in pushing particular policies or points of view upon the delegated representatives of the voters. Special interests have two factors on their side in forming pressure groups. First, their motivation is stronger. Since their financial interest is concentrated (as in the case of a tariff affecting a single industry), they gain far more from appropriate political action than any comparably sized group of the general public stand to lose, even though the *entire* public may suffer in the aggregate a much greater loss. Second, being small in number they are more able to overcome the free-rider problem in organizing their pressure group.

EXAMPLE 18.3
REGULATED
ELECTRICITY
RATES

Electricity, as a "natural monopoly," is now governmentally regulated in almost all states. The problem of collective action suggests the hypothesis that the relatively small numbers of *large* consumers of electricity will have an advantage over the multitude of *small* consumers of electricity in forming a pressure group that can influence the political agencies responsible for regulating rates.

This hypothesis was tested by George Stigler and Claire Friedland, making use of data from earlier years when there were still a considerable number of unregulated states. Since it can be presumed that *industrial* users of electricity are relatively large in scale (and small in number) in comparison with *residential* users, the ratio of the residential price to the industrial price is a relevant measure of the hypothesis that large users are favored over small. This ratio alone is not a satisfactory criterion, however, since there may well be differences in the cost of service that would warrant some degree of rate inequality between industrial and residential users. But there is no obvious reason *for the ratio to differ as between regulated and unregulated states.*

[10]Public-interested benevolence is not entirely unknown, of course. In ancient Greece the civic institution of the drama was largely supported by individual donors, and of course analogous modern examples can be cited. (A reputation for unselfish benevolence may, in some people's preference functions, be a private good worth buying!)

Average Ratio $\frac{Residential\ Price}{Industrial\ Price}$ for Electricity		
	1917	1937
Regulated states	1.616	2.459
Unregulated states	1.445	2.047

Source: G. J. Stigler and C. Friedland, "What Can Regulators Regulate? The Case of Electricity," *Journal of Law and Economics*, v. 5 (Oct. 1962), p. 9.

The data showed that the ratio was indeed substantially higher for the regulated states, consistent with the hypothesis that regulation works to the comparative advantage of large consumers over small consumers.

Of course, the political strength of "special interest" groups is only one side of the picture. It is easier for a small specialized group to organize and bring its weight to bear, but it remains a group small in number. Landlords can organize *against* rent controls more effectively than tenants *for* them, but a politician cannot ignore the fact that there are many more tenant than landlord votes. The "pressure group" phenomenon counterbalances somewhat the tendency of the democratic polity to override the interest of minorities (see Section 18.B.2). But it does so in a rather capricious way, protecting only those minorities strategically positioned (by reason of concentration) to influence the political process. One point of interest is that since production is generally a *specialized* activity and consumption an *unspecialized* one, government interventions have historically tended to favor producers over consumers. As we are all *both* producers and consumers, it might be thought that the effects cancel out. But the political measures that favor producers (for example, permitting formation of a cartel) tend to be anti-competitive. This leads to a loss of economic efficiency, apart from possibly objectionable effects upon wealth distribution.

18.D

BUREAUCRACY

The categories of political decision-making agents considered to this point include citizen-voters, political parties, elected representatives or delegates, and pressure groups. But another important element of the picture, the governmental bureaucracy, has not yet been referred to.

The bureaucracy consists of that class of government personnel not responsible for *making* policy decisions but for *implementing* them. Supposedly impartial and neutral, bureaucrats are not subject to election or recall at the hands of the voters. It follows that if bureaucrats really do determine the actual outcomes of decisions, then the ability of citizens to achieve their desires through the political mechanism (i.e., through their control over elected delegates) is even weaker than has previously been indicated.

Chapter 18
GOVERNMENT
AND THE
ECONOMY:
A POSITIVE
ANALYSIS

Now it is an obvious fact of common knowledge that implementation is as important as decision. For all practical purposes, implementation *is* the actual decision. So the bureaucracy surely does have substantial power. We would expect leading bureaucrats, from their positions of strength, to negotiate with the other powerful actors on the political scene so as to participate importantly in actual governmental choices.

What are the interests of the bureaucracy? Apart from high wages for small effort, a critical aim is *tenure of office*. A bureaucrat who could be easily dismissed would not long survive any battle with powerful elected delegates or pressure groups. Hence a prime goal is the strengthening of civil service regulations so as to permit dismissal only "for cause," strictly interpreted. This aim has been very satisfactorily achieved; the spoils system is to a large degree a thing of the past.

A second plausible bureaucratic aim is *agency growth*. Officeholders in a position to influence decisions are motivated to build empires by increasing the size of the resources under their control. As has been shown first by Professor Parkinson,[11] this works out in a remarkably regular fashion. The British Admiralty bureaucracy increases, while the Royal Navy diminishes; let the colonies declare their independence, Her Majesty's Colonial Office continues to expand; and the U.S. Department of Agriculture goes on growing in budget and employment while the number of farmers shrinks.

EXAMPLE 18.4 TAXICAB REGULATION	The taxicab industry in different cities tends to be regulated under one of two alternative systems: (1) municipal agency, or (2) independent commission. In a study of 33 cities, Ross D. Eckert argued that these modes of regulation are associated with different incentive structures for the regulators.

The decision-making officeholders in a municipal agency have, one would expect, the typical motivations of bureaucrats. As the degree of detailed supervision of the taxicab industry increases, a larger budget and staff will be "needed," with correspondingly higher salaries for the directors of such a massive and important regulatory activity. Independent commissioners, however, are in quite a different position. They generally engage in other public or private activity; their commission service is only a part-time occupation. Complex and detailed taxicab regulation, with consequent need to supervise large staffs, hear complaints, grant exceptions, etc., would require costly sacrifice of their time and effort. And since commissioners normally hold office only for a limited term of years, any long-run return (e.g., an upward trend in salaries for commissioners) that may result from more energetic regulatory activity may go only to benefit their successors in office.

One way of *reducing* the level of regulatory effort is to have a single "responsible" operator of all the taxicabs in a city. Outright monopoly situations are indeed more common in commission-regulated than in agency-

[11]C. Northcote Parkinson, *Parkinson's Law* (Boston: Houghton Mifflin, 1957).

regulated cities. But, for a variety of reasons, literal monopoly is rare. Many cities, however, have partial degrees of regulation-imposed monopoly effected through division of the market by quotas, territory assignments, or exclusive taxistands. The hypothesis is that commissioners would prefer this situation, whereas agency bureaucrats would welcome the necessity for elaborate and detailed regulatory dealings with a multiplicity of small operators. The data below show that the hypothesis was verified.

Taxicab Regulatory Status in 1967, for 22 U.S. Cities

	MONOPOLY OR MARKET DIVISION (NUMBER OF CITIES)	NEITHER MONOPOLY NOR MARKET DIVISION (NUMBER OF CITIES)
Commissions	5	1
Agencies	5	22

Source: Ross D. Eckert, "On the Incentives of Regulators: The Case of Taxicabs," *Public Choice*, v. 14 (Spring 1973), p. 90.

THE SCOPE OF GOVERNMENT

Perhaps the key scientific questions in political economy are: What are the forces determining the *types* of activities carried on through government, and the *scale* on which those activities are conducted? The economic approach suggests that observed activities reflect the goals and the relative strengths of the persons and groups participating in the day-to-day decisions of government, interacting according to the constitutional "rules of the game" in the political sphere.

As we have seen, the categories exercising political power include political parties, elected delegates, pressure groups furthering special interests, and bureaucrats. In a democratic system the "will of the people" (enforced ultimately by delegates' desire to be reelected) also plays an important role, but only as one element in the picture. Thus, the problem for *positive* political economy is to work out the logic of the interaction of these groups, under alternative constitutional structures, so as to be able to predict and understand the actual functioning of the political mechanism.

Standard statistical classifications of the expenditures of federal, state, and local government units in the United States do not always permit an entirely satisfactory breakdown by function. Table 18.1 is condensed from official statistical data.

As a first step to understanding, we can classify the various types of observed government activities under four main functions: (1) defense, (2) law, (3) production, and (4) distribution.

18.E.1

Functions of Government

Table 18.1

Direct General Expenditure by Function, by Level of Government, 1971–72
(in Millions of Dollars)

	FEDERAL	STATE	LOCAL	ALL GOVERNMENTS	% OF TOTAL
Total	154,516	62,051	104,822	321,389	100.00
National Defense and International					
Relations	79,258	—	—	79,258	24.66
Postal Service	9,366	—	—	9,366	2.91
Space Research and Technology	3,369	—	—	3,369	1.05
Transportation					
Highways	432	12,747	6,263	19,442	6.05
Other	4,141	303	1,551	5,995	1.87
Sewerage and Sanitation	—	—	4,729	4,729	1.47
Police, Fire, and Correction	665	2,209	8,453	11,326	3.52
Education and Human Resources					
Education	5,104	17,153	47,734	69,990	21.78
Health and Hospitals	4,166	6,008	6,858	17,033	5.30
Housing and Urban Renewal	2,630	34	2,747	5,411	1.68
Other	—	63	3,074	3,137	.98
Natural Resources	11,105	2,470	640	14,215	4.42
Public Welfare	2,488	12,247	8,822	23,558	7.33
Administration	3,400	3,675	4,897	11,971	3.72
Interest on Public Debt	17,114	2,135	3,827	23,077	7.18
Other and Unallocable	11,278	3,008	5,228	19,514	6.07

Source: U.S. Bureau of the Census, *Governmental Finances in 1971–72,* Series GF 72-No. 5, U.S. Government Printing Office, Washington, D.C., 1973, p. 23.

1. DEFENSE: The absolutely essential minimal function that government must provide for any society is protection against external and internal enemies. The government *is* the group exercising dominant force; if the existing government group fails to provide protection in a trial of strength, the newcomers will then constitute the government. The data of Table 18.1 show that National Defense and International Relations accounted for about 25% of government general expenditures in 1971–72. To this should be added the bulk of expenses under the category Police, Fire, and Correction; also, Interest on Public Debt in large part represents past military expenditures; and finally, shares of Administration and Other might well be attributed to Defense. Overall, some 35% of government expenditures in 1971–72 can be regarded as accounted for by the Defense function.

2. LAW: To operate at any level of effectiveness, members of a society cannot live completely at the whim of the governors. Rather, there must be some system of rights or property defining how individuals are permitted to act, alone or in association with others. The efficiency of a system of market exchange, in particular, depends (as we have seen) upon a well-defined structure of property rights. This system of rights, with correlative duties thus placed on others not to interfere with those rights, is *law.* Since law must be enforced to be useful, it cannot exist without government. Hence the nullity of so-called *international law,* in the absence of a super-government prepared to coerce those regimes that tear up the "scraps of paper" (treaties) that represent contracts among nations.

Chapter 18
GOVERNMENT
AND THE
ECONOMY:
A POSITIVE
ANALYSIS

568

Apart from the expenditures already accounted for under the heading of Defense, the budgetary burden of the legal system (legislatures, courts, etc.) is not large. The costs constitute only some fractions of relatively small categories like Police, Fire, and Correction and Administration in the table. (In early times, law was actually dispensed at a profit by royal courts, with fees for provision of justice serving as an important source of government revenue.)

Provision of a system of defense, and the administration of justice, are universally recognized as *essential* functions of government. Beyond this, however, governments may take a more or less activist role in guiding the economic performance of society—the production and distribution of goods and services.

3. PRODUCTION: Government is, as explained in Section 18.C above, uniquely able to make the collective choices involved in the provision of non-excludable *public goods*. Individuals can be regarded as voluntarily demanding public goods through the institution of government, thus avoiding the free-rider problem that would otherwise lead to under-provision of these goods. (It is possible to consider Defense and Law also as types of public goods, but for our purposes they are kept separate.) In Table 18.1, the expenditures (apart from those already listed under Defense and Law) that contain important public-good elements include Education, Transportation, and Space Research and Technology. Even if all the expenditures so categorized could be regarded as going to the purchase of public goods, the total is only around 31% of the aggregate of government spending.

Evidently, government is also in the business of providing a vast range of ordinary *private* goods. Postal Service, Social Insurance,[12] and Housing all represent goods that are essentially similar to commodities or services that are also provided privately—or surely would be so provided were it not (as in the case of the government's postal monopoly) illegal to do so. Health and Hospitals contains a small public-good component (preventing epidemics), but for the most part the expenditure represents provision of a private good—personal medical care. Even Education (though counted above within the public-good category) is much more importantly a private than a public good; the benefits of governmental expenditures for education go *primarily* to the educated person, and only secondarily to the remainder of society.

Apart from the actual provision of public or private goods, modern governments affect the productive efficiency of the economy in a variety of important ways. The provision and control of *money* facilitates the process of exchange (see Chapter 8).[13] The *stabilization of economic activity*—prevention of depressions, inflations, etc.—is also generally recognized as an appropriate function of modern government.[14] Anti-monopoly activities of agencies like the Anti-trust Division of

[12]Social Security and other social insurance arrangements are not included in the data of Table 18.1. The receipts and expenditures for these activities are regarded as going into or coming out of "trust funds" rather than the regular government accounts.

[13]It is an interesting topic of monetary theory whether the government role is inherent in the existence of money. Privately-produced moneys, it might be argued, could serve as well as or better than government money.

[14]Unfortunately, it is easier to *recognize* this function than to achieve it! Some observers wonder whether governmental attempts to stabilize the economy have made things worse instead of better.

Chapter 18
GOVERNMENT
AND THE
ECONOMY:
A POSITIVE
ANALYSIS

569

the Department of Justice, and the regulation of "natural monopolies" through governmental commissions, are designed to or can be defended as tending to improve efficiency in the allocation of resources.

Government policy toward monopoly provides an interesting test case for observing the interaction of politically powerful groups. To the extent that the political process tends (as remarked above) to give more weight to *producer* than to *consumer* interests, we might well doubt the effectiveness of government in controlling monopoly. And indeed, the charge has been made that regulatory agencies are often captured by the special interests they are supposed to be guarding against. On the federal level the Interstate Commerce Commission (regulating surface transportation), the Civil Aeronautics Board (regulating the airlines), and the Federal Communications Commission (regulating radio and television) have all been the targets of such charges. And in cases like the cartelization of many sectors of agricultural marketing (see Example 11.5), the fact that the aim of government action is higher prices for producers at the expense of consumers is scarcely a secret. On the other hand, whatever the wisdom of the "trust-busting" activity of the Department of Justice and the Federal Trade Commission, these agencies are generally regarded as independent of producer control. How the observed differences of behavior stem from the motivations, legal status, and incentives of the participants is a topic largely remaining to be explained.

4. DISTRIBUTION: An important activity of modern government is redistribution of income or wealth—in democratic countries at least, primarily from richer to poorer classes. In Table 18.1, the category of Public Welfare (7.3% of aggregate expenditures) is explicitly redistributive. But redistribution is also an important aspect of other categories, and indeed helps explain what might otherwise be regarded as anomalies. Consider the expenditures under the heading of Health and Hospitals. A typical procedure here is for government agencies to provide a relatively low quality of hospital or medical care, at zero price or at a very low price, to all who choose to use that service. But since the rich can afford and generally will prefer to buy somewhat better health care privately, only the poor choose the government service. The effect is a redistribution of income "in kind" to the poor. To greater or lesser degree, this analysis applies to public housing (all but the very poor will prefer private housing), to public education (the rich can afford private schools), to subsidized public transit (the rich travel by private car), etc.

EXAMPLE 18.5
TAX-EXPENDITURE
REDISTRIBUTION

The Tax Foundation attempted, for the year 1961, to assess the overall redistributive effect of the tax-expenditure system (federal, state, and local). Making a number of rather heroic assumptions about the burden of taxes collected and the benefits of expenditures on behalf of the different income classes, the researchers were able to summarize the results as shown in the following table.

COMMENT: As government expenditures in the aggregate were more than 30% of GNP in 1961, a very significant amount of redistribution from the

Redistributive Effect of Government Budgets, 1961

INCOME CLASS (AFTER PERSONAL TAXES)	RATIO OF GOVERNMENT BENEFITS TO TAXES
Under $2000	4.1
$2000–2999	2.6
$3000–3999	1.7
$4000–4999	1.2
$5000–5999	1.1
$6000–7499	.9
$7500–9999	.8
$10,000–14,999	.7
$15,000 and over	.4

Source: Tax Foundation, Inc., *Allocating Tax Burdens and Government Benefits by Income Class,* Government Brief No. 8, 1967, p. 2.

rich to the poor evidently took place through the tax-expenditure system in that year. And, more recently, both the proportionate level of government spending in relation to GNP and the fraction of that spending directed toward the redistribution function have been increasing.

The redistributive activity revealed by the preceding example suggests that the power of the vote is not as feeble as might have been inferred from the discussion in Section 18.B. In a democratic polity, electoral strength will be distributed more equally than income. It then seems reasonable that the poor will be able to use the governmental process to convert some of their comparatively greater political potency into money income. And the higher the income bracket, the greater the weight of numbers and political power in the hands of those lower down on the ladder. Hence, the more punitive the burden of fiscal redistribution that can be expected by those in that bracket.

Surprisingly, perhaps, this argument is not ironclad. In a system of self-interested majority voting, and if we rule out political coalitions of both ends against the middle, the *median* voter—the one half-way up the wealth distribution—is in a position of exceptional power. By allying with those of less wealth, this voter can bring about a redistribution of wealth downward; by voting with those of greater wealth, a redistribution upward. If wealth is initially distributed unequally, there must be more wealth above the median voter than below. Thus, one would think, an inevitable tendency exists for the median citizen to vote with the poor against the rich. But a simple numerical example shows that such an outcome is not at all inevitable. Suppose there is one rich voter R with wealth 300, one median voter M with wealth 200, and one poor voter P with wealth 100—i.e., a wealth distribution (300, 200, 100). Now, let M form a coalition with P. Then almost the best M can do for himself by political redistribution would be a revised arrangement of the total wealth of 600 units such as (250, 249, 101). Here, of the 50 wealth units confiscated from R only 1 went to P, with M gaining the remaining 49. This seems quite profitable but, even so, M might do better combining with R against P! Specifically, a voting coalition of M and R might achieve the

Chapter 18
GOVERNMENT
AND THE
ECONOMY:
A POSITIVE
ANALYSIS

571

revised distribution (301, 299, 0). Here the median voter gains 99 units going along with *R,* far better than the 49 won by lining up with *P.* This perhaps explains why, even in democratic polities, throughout much of history government has often served to grind the faces of the poor in favor of those above them on the wealth scale. Just why democratic societies in modern times have generally engaged in governmental redistribution in favor of the poor is somewhat of an unresolved problem.

It ought to be remembered, also, that expenditures *on behalf of* the poor are not necessarily payments *to* the poor. In a program like federally funded job training, for example, the bulk of the actual payments may go to middle-class bureaucrats—specifically, to teachers and administrators. The benefits to poor trainees are ''in kind,'' and may or may not be translatable by them into higher future cash incomes. Hence the interests of the poor and of the bureaucratic class in the redistributive process are intertwined.

Government can carry out its functions either directly or indirectly. Given the objective of achieving a higher level of education of the population, for example, there are still policy choices to be made. Government might subsidize education (in the limit, make it free) thus *inducing* consumers to choose more education voluntarily. Or government might declare education compulsory, thus *forcing* consumers to buy more—or accept more, if free. Current practice in the United States is to have education both free and compulsory up to a certain school-leaving age, and optional (but still more or less subsidized) thereafter.

Perhaps an even more important policy choice is whether or not government is actually to *provide* the service. Education might be made free and compulsory, and yet provided entirely through a system of private schools (see the discussion of subsidies versus vouchers in Section 4.E). The government could reimburse private schools for students enrolled, setting standards and monitoring performance, without actually being in the business of hiring teachers, erecting buildings, etc. Even pure public goods like lighthouse services could be provided privately, on contract with government.

At various times and places, a surprising variety of what we customarily think of as government-provided goods have actually been produced privately, sometimes at state expense, sometimes not. The bounty-hunters of the pioneer West tracked down criminals. Toll roads and canals can be and have been private businesses. There are private arbitration courts today that reduce the need to use public justice. There is one single service that, one would suppose, *must* be provided by government itself if it is to remain government—defense. Yet even this service has at times been provided commercially, by firms supplying mercenary soldiers. (Experience on this score has been largely unfavorable, however; a mercenary chief strong enough to be useful in defense is all too inclined to take over the government himself.)[15] Still, at least military *research* today is largely produced privately, on government contract.

Chapter 18
GOVERNMENT
AND THE
ECONOMY:
A POSITIVE
ANALYSIS

[15]Machiavelli, *The Prince,* Chap. 12.

The interests of the bureaucracy, it is clear, lie in the larger scale of agency activity made possible by *direct* government provision of goods and services. The incentives of the other major actors on the political scene are mixed, however. The choice between direct and indirect instruments for carrying out government functions, like the scope of the functions themselves, remains a largely unexplored scientific question.

18.E.3
A Scientific
Issue in
Political
Economy:
Growth of
Government

A striking phenomenon of modern times has been the steady growth of the government sector. Despite the hot political debates that have greeted the successive steps of government expansion, there is surprisingly little scientific understanding of the forces tending to bring it about.

The first and most obvious explanation is the increasing burden of the Defense function. As the technology of attack and destruction has improved so fantastically (nuclear bombs, intercontinental missiles, etc.), the complexity and cost of defense have grown correspondingly. But suppose we entirely exclude the Defense function. The scope of government has grown enormously in the nondefense sector as well.

Various stages in the expansion of the overall government sector in the United States are shown in the following table.

EXAMPLE 18.6
GROWTH OF
GOVERNMENT

Growth of Government in the United States

DATE	TOTAL EXPENDITURES		CIVILIAN EXPENDITURES	
	$ BILLIONS	% OF GNP	$ BILLIONS	% OF GNP
1890	$ 0.8	6.5%	$ 0.7	5.0%
1902	1.5	7.3	1.2	5.8
1913	3.2	7.8	2.8	6.8
1922	9.3	12.6	7.9	10.7
1929	10.7	10.4	9.5	9.2
1940	17.6	17.6	15.5	15.5
1950	65.9	23.1	42.2	14.8
1960	136.1	27.0	84.4	16.7
1970	313.0	32.2	225.1	23.1

Source: R. A. Musgrave and P. B. Musgrave, *Public Finance in Theory and Practice* (New York: McGraw-Hill, 1973), p. 118.

As may be seen, government expenditures have more than kept up with both the real growth of the economy and the inflation of prices, so as to constitute a steadily increasing fraction of GNP. Apart from the obvious fact that big jumps in expenditures have typically taken place in wartime, peacetime civilian expenditures as a percentage of GNP have also grown steadily.

Basically, there are two possible lines of explanation for the phenomenon of expansion of government. The first gives primary weight to the *voluntarist* aspect of political decision. In this view, government has expanded in response to desires on the part of the community for the types of services government can best provide. The second approach emphasizes, in contrast, *changes in the balance of political power* possessed by organized groups on the political scene.

Voluntaristic explanations might run in terms of some or all of the following points: (1) Public goods, in contrast with private goods, might have income elasticity greater than unity (see Section 5.A). Then with rising national income over time, citizen-voters have desired more of the public goods that government characteristically provides. (2) With increasing wealth and population, the limited geographical space we inhabit has become more and more crowded. In our daily lives we are therefore increasingly imposing *externalities* (see Section 17.C.3) upon one another. Hence the need for more government control of activities that could have safely been left private in a more dispersed and isolated society. (3) The technical efficiency of government may have grown relative to the private sector. With advances like computers, it has become possible to conduct enterprises on a much larger scale than previously. Government, as the largest-scale enterprise in society, may have gained in relative effectiveness.

Explanations that run in terms of political power, on the other hand, might point to considerations like the following: (1) The government bureaucracy, as it grows in numbers, becomes an increasingly potent political force. Wars and defense crises that require gigantic budgetary expansions leave in their wake a mass of officeholders, with sufficient political clout to resist budgetary contraction when the crises pass. (2) An important sociological development with consequences for the political structure has been the growth of the *educated class* in the population (say, those with college degrees). Educated persons are *relatively* better equipped to achieve positions of status and power in government rather than in business. Legislators, bureaucrats, and other important actors on the political scene are themselves members of the educated class and inclined to be responsive to its interests, especially as the educated are much more politically active than the population at large. (3) A related point is that the extraordinary and continuing advances in ability to communicate with large audiences—due to improvements in printing, the spread of literacy, and of course the recent development of radio and television—have made it increasingly possible to weld large numbers of people into political movements and pressure groups. Hence, demands for government services have expanded, or at any rate whatever demands exist have become more effectively voiced.

The degree of truth in each of these points, and the comparative explanatory values of the vountarist and the political-power approaches, unfortunately cannot be explored here. Indeed, the state of our knowledge as to major issues of political economy hardly goes beyond the formulation of hypotheses such as those outlined.

SUMMARY
OF CHAPTER
18

Behavior in the marketplace and behavior in politics are not subject to different motives. The people involved are the same; it is the "rules of the game" that are different. In the market, interactions in the form of reciprocal exchange take place through *contract*. But political interactions involve *government,* which is the subordination of some people to the will of others.

The *state* is an all-inclusive system of government in a given area, within which it has an effective monopoly of force. There are several "theories of the state": individuals may accept subordination to the state because they believe it is divinely ordained, because they are simply cowed by superior force, because they have a biological instinct to follow leaders who are working toward group ends, or because they are abiding by an explicit or implicit "social contract." The contractual or voluntarist theory of the state fits most naturally into the approach of the economist, though it is surely not a full explanation of political behavior.

In the voluntarist polity, political parties are like business firms in the economy. *Laissez faire* in the economy is like ideal democracy in the polity. Just as competition for sales forces firms to satisfy consumers' desires, competition for office forces parties to satisfy voters' wishes. Market competition has serious imperfections, but so has political competition. Citizens vote to choose their political delegates at relatively rare intervals; there is only a limited choice of candidates (commonly, just two), and many issues are bundled together in the position of each candidate. Under majority rule, there is the very serious problem of adequate provision for minority desires. A constitution may provide such protection; in addition, "log-rolling" allows intense minority preferences on some issues to be exchanged for votes on other issues. In principle, log-rolling or even direct purchase of votes will lead to Pareto-optimal outcomes. Another source of imperfection is the fact that a voter has little motivation to incur the necessary costs so as to cast an intelligent ballot.

An important function of government is the provision of public goods, since the free-rider problem limits the amounts of public goods that privately motivated individuals will supply. If public goods are furnished by government, all citizens can be made to bear their costs.

Citizens favoring any given public policy have a similar public-good problem in attempting to influence government. Compact special interests, with concentrated financial incentives and with a relatively small number of people to organize, find it easier to overcome this problem by forming "pressure groups."

Policies are actually *implemented* by the governmental bureaucracy, whose members have motives different from both voters and political delegates. Bureaucrats are motivated to achieve tenure in office, and also usually to increase the size of their agencies.

Among the key questions of political economy are the determinants of the types of activities conducted by government, and of the scale of such activities. Government has a special advantage in providing public goods, and the traditional minimal functions of government—defense and justice—are indeed public goods. But present-day governments also supply a vast range of what are mainly private goods: postal services, housing, insurance, education, etc. Government also regulates the private economy in a variety of ways, sometimes in response to public-good motivations (prevention of depression), sometimes to help certain private interests (tariffs on imports). Redistribution of income or wealth is another important governmental activity with public-good aspects. Detailed scientific expla-

Chapter 18
GOVERNMENT
AND THE
ECONOMY:
A POSITIVE
ANALYSIS

575

nations of the nature and scope of government, and in particular of the seemingly irrepressible tendency of the modern state apparatus to grow in size and in influence over the private sector, remain largely unresolved problems for political economy.

QUESTIONS FOR CHAPTER 18

Mainly for Review

*R1. Why is the "voluntarist" approach to the problem of political behavior particularly amenable to economic analysis? What other approaches are there?

*R2. What are some of the major obstacles preventing the expression of the "will of the people" through the political process? How are these analogous to, and how different from, the difficulties of the market process?

R3. How may *delegation* of decision-making power to political representatives lead to decisions diverging from the desires of constituents? Considering the corporation as a kind of political system, what protections and escape hatches do stockholders have that may not be available to members of the polity?

*R4. Under what circumstances does the "free rider" problem emerge? How valid is the assertion that all government is fundamentally a response to the free-rider problem?

R5. How do the goals and opportunities of bureaucrats differ from those of elected officials? How do they differ from those of managers of private firms?

R6. How are the administrative decisions of a commissioner with a limited period of office likely to differ from those of a lifetime civil servant?

*R7. Would the fidelity of the political system to citizen desires be improved by any or all of the following: more frequent elections, more numerous legislatures, elected rather than appointed judges, the spoils system rather than the merit system in civil service? Comment.

*R8. Is a unanimous consent rule, in which dissident votes must be purchased, an ideal political system—apart from transaction costs? Does the process of "log-rolling" provide some approximation of this result? What are some objections to log-rolling?

R9. Under what political mechanisms or situations do majorities tend to exploit minorities? Under what mechanisms or situations is it the other way around?

Chapter 18
GOVERNMENT
AND THE
ECONOMY:
A POSITIVE
ANALYSIS

For Further Thought and Discussion

*T1. If votes could be bought for money, would *both* the rich and the poor be better off in accordance with the mutual advantage of trade? What is the objection to buying votes for money?

* The answers to asterisked questions appear at the end of the book.

*T2. In market competition among firms, economic profit tends to be eliminated (the "zero-profit theorem" of Chapter 10). Does something analogous tend to occur in political competition between parties? Why or why not?

*T3. Which is more likely to gain legislative approval: a bill that would simply redistribute cash from the rich to the poor, or one to establish a bureaucracy to provide services to the poor? Explain.

*T4. Services that are *financed* by government need not actually be *produced* in the government sector. Give an example where government arranges with private enterprise for production of government-financed services. Give examples of activities paid for by the private sector but actually produced by government. Can you explain these developments?

T5. Why is there a risk that a regulatory agency may be "captured" by the industry it is intended to supervise?

*T6. Suppose there were a sudden unexpected increase in demand for a product now provided through the government sector. Would you expect any systematic differences in the price–quantity response as compared with a product provided through the private sector? What about the response to a decrease in demand? What about responses to increases or decreases in cost of production?

T7. Under a system that might be called "open corruption," government officials (including judges) could sell their decisions to the highest bidder. How bad would this be?

*T8. What explains the steady growth of the government sector relative to the private sector in the past century? Why was there a relative decline in the government sector during the era of industrialization in Great Britain?

ANSWERS

CHAPTER 1

R1. (a) Economics is a set of models or theories whose implications provide testable propositions about the real world. These models must stand or fall on the accuracy of their predictions. It is this use of evidence to judge theories that is scientific.

(b) Vegetables will be cheaper in season than out of season. People will seldom be observed throwing money away. Advertisers will claim that their products are better than competitors' products. To take a more extended example: sharply higher gasoline prices will tend to reduce auto travel generally, and also to lower average highway speeds (with a consequent reduction in accidents). It will also encourage sales of smaller cars, and thus lead Detroit to produce new models aiming at gas economy. In the longer run a trend to more compact cities will be observed. (Of course, all such predictions must be understood in an "other things equal" sense.)

(c) Certainly, economic science cannot predict everything. We have little or no idea as to causes of changes in tastes or social attitudes (the Protestant ethic vs. "Consciousness III"), or as to determinants of ideological movements like fascism or Marxism or Christianity, or as to social trends like growth of government. And even important issues of a more narrowly defined "economic" nature, such as causes of business fluctuations, remain unresolved.

R2. (a) Behavior may be defined as rational either in terms of *method* of decision (the choice is made by calculating the costs and benefits of alternative actions) or in terms of *results* (the action chosen turns out to be well-suited for achieving one's goals).

(b) In terms of *method*, a prospective wagerer at roulette might calculate the odds and observe the behavior of the wheel before choosing a number. It would be irrational to place a bet on the basis of a dream or heavenly vision. In terms of *results*, it's probably irrational to bet at all.

(c) Aggregated over many individuals, a limited degree of individual rationality will show up as a tendency toward rational behavior for the group as a whole. Even if the rational element is small, it operates in a consistent and predictable direction.

R7 (a) In a market economy, self-interested individuals will devote their resources to satisfying others by providing desired goods and services. What others are willing to pay enables the sellers to earn higher income and so better satisfy their own desires.

(b)(c)(d) No. If their own income is not increased by serving others, self-interested individuals will not do so.

R9. (a) "Real" flow are flows of goods or services (e.g., lamb chops, labor). "Financial" flows are flows of general purchasing power (money). Each flow represents one side of a class of transaction. Goods or services are traded for general purchasing power.

(b) In the "product market," firms trade the goods and services that they produce to consumers for dollars. In the "factor market," consumers in their capacity as resource-owners trade their factor services to firms for dollars. The dollars that consumers trade for goods and services are those which they receive for their factor services. Similarly, the dollars that firms pay for factor services are those which they receive for the goods and services they produce.

T1. (a) Yes, *other things equal.* (If other things were not equal, a state or nation with capital punishment might also be found to have a high murder rate—if, for example, it was the high frequency of murder that led to the imposition of the death penalty in that jurisdiction.)

(b) Yes. Increasing this tax exemption lowers the cost of having children and so should result (other things equal) in an increase in the birth rate.

T2. If insurance companies refused to recognize "mental illness" as an insurable category of sickness, and if the government did not finance treatment under Medicare, doctors would be less motivated to diagnose patients' psychological problems as "disease." This would surely lower the reported incidence of "mental illness." Making medical treatment more costly would also induce potential patients to confront their problems rather than accept the dependent status of being "sick." Note that the predicted effects here do *not* depend upon whether Dr. Szasz's theory about mental illness is in fact correct.

T5. The principle of the Invisible Hand applies to *market* interactions, which are voluntary and mutual in nature. Since the kinds of interactions mentioned in this question (crime, etc.) are not voluntary market exchanges, self-serving behavior may not benefit others.

T6. Drivers, being safer than before, would probably take a little less care to avoid accidents. Thus, *pedestrian* deaths might rise, though *driver* deaths would not.

T7. Dr. Johnson probably had in mind the Invisible Hand. Charles Baudelaire probably had in mind his publisher's refusing to give him a bigger advance on his royalties.

CHAPTER 2

R2. The price of a good X is the amount of another good (usually money) that must be given up in order to acquire a unit of good X. Consequently, price is a ratio of amounts, or a ratio of quantities (money/X).

R5. Yes. Shifting the supply curve up by T leads to a solution at the intersection of the *gross* (of tax) supply curve with the original demand curve. Shifting the demand curve down by T leads to a solution at the intersection of the *net* (of tax) demand curve with the original supply curve. As the only difference between gross and net supply or demand curves is a vertical displacement of T, the intersections take place at the same quantity. The intersection of the gross supply curve with the demand curve determines the gross price. The intersection of the net demand curve with the supply curve determines the net (of tax) price. But, of course, it is unnecessary to carry out both constructions; either suffices since the gross price and net price are related by $P^+ = P^- + T$.

R6. (a) Both. (b) Raise price paid by consumers, (c), (d) Lower price received by sellers.

R8. (a) A meaningful price ceiling or price floor is one that prevents the market from moving to an equilibrium. A meaningful price ceiling must be set *below* the equilibrium price, and a meaningful price floor must be set *above* the equilibrium price.

(b) Because trade is voluntary, it is the *smaller* of the desired transaction magnitudes (quantity supplied or quantity demanded) that determines the actual quantity traded. Price ceilings decrease the quantity that sellers are willing to offer. Price floors decrease the quantity that consumers wish to buy. Both decrease the actual quantity traded in the market.

(c) If a "meaningful" price floor, above the equilibrium level, is supported, sellers are able to complete some sales for which there are no demanders (apart from the supporting agency). Transactions then depend solely on the existence of supply at that price. If the floor price is above equilibrium, the quantity sold will increase. The supporting agency, however, will accumulate inventories.

R11. (a) May be false. (b) True. (c) False. (d) May be false. (e) True. (f) May be false.

R12. The "better approximation" of Marginal Revenue assigns the per-unit incremental change in revenue that takes place over a quantity interval to the mid-point of the interval, rather than to one or other of the end-points. Since *MR* varies from point to point over the entire interval, this procedure almost always provides a much more accurate estimate.

T1. (a) The tax would have a *small* effect on quantity exchanged in the market, a *small* effect on the gross price paid by buyers, but a *large* effect on net price to sellers. (The result here is seen more clearly if the demand curve is shifted down, rather than the supply curve up.)

(b) The steep supply curve means that suppliers are willing to offer even a slightly larger quantity only at a much higher price. Since the tax reduces quantity sold by lowering the *net* demand, the net price received by sellers falls sharply. The gross price paid by consumers rises, but only slightly, since the market quantity declines just slightly.

T3. (a) Since it would be more costly to operate automobiles, the demand curve for cars would shift to the left, leading to a fall in their price.

(b) The effect on prices of big, heavy cars ("gas-guzzlers") would be greater.

T4. (a) A change in economic data occurs, affecting demand or supply (or both). The new supply–demand equilibrium is attained with no transactions taking place at "wrong" prices. In effect, the new equilibrium is arrived at instantaneously.

(b) In the real world, these conditions are never precisely met. But in a market where traders are well informed, the model may be a close approximation of reality.

T6. (a) Wherever the Roman armies marched, the demand for foodstuffs increased because of the addition of military demands to civilian demands. This increase in demand resulted in an increase in equilibrium price.

(b) Diocletian's edict set a price ceiling below the (new) equilibrium price. As a result, there must have been unsatisfied buyers. It is likely that Diocletian's armies made up a large portion of these un-satisfied buyers. So either efforts to evade the edict were successful or Diocletian's armies went hungry, unless indeed they simply confiscated the food they wanted. (See Jacob Burckhardt, *The Age of Constantine the Great* [New York: Pantheon, 1949], Ch. 2.)

T7. Average and marginal magnitudes are per-unit magnitudes. For income taxes, the appropriate per-unit dimensions are dollars per dollar. Be-cause the units are the same in the numerator and the denominator, they cancel and the resulting dimension is a pure percentage.

CHAPTER 3

R1. (a) violates the Axiom of Comparison. (b) expresses indifference, but does not violate the laws. (c) indicates *inconsistency*, and thus also violates the Axiom of Comparison.

R4. Utility is simply an indicator of preference ranking. Of two bundles, the fact that one is preferred indicates that its utility is higher.

R6. If Total Utility is given in *ordinal* terms, the Marginal Utility function is undefined (apart from having positive or negative sign). Marginal magnitudes are calculated from quantitative increments or differences in total magnitudes. Since ordinal utility indicates only direction of preference, only the *signs* and not the quantitative increments of utility can be determined as amount consumed rises. It follows that the Marginal Utility function cannot be calculated numerically.

R8. (a) Ordinal. (b) Cardinal. (c) Interpersonal comparability.

T1. No.

T3. Placement in a horse race, or a tennis ladder, or a job seniority list. An interesting scientific example is a measure commonly used for *hardness*, based on the relation "scratches." Thus, diamond is harder than glass, and glass is harder than chalk, but this measure does not indicate *how much* harder.

T5. Any shape that is symmetrical across the 45° line. This would indicate, for example, that I am indifferent between the combination "His Income is $2000 while My Income is $1000" and the combination "My Income is $2000 while His Income is $1000."

T7. (a) No.
(b) The preference map would take the form of rays out of the origin. Along any single ray, representing a fixed *ratio* of "My Income" to "His Income," the individual would be equally happy. For such an individual the Preference Directions would be such that "My Income" is a good, while "His Income" is a bad.

CHAPTER 4

R3. (a) The budget line is the northeast boundary of an individual's market opportunity set. It is the locus of the achievable consumption bundles if the individual spends all of his income.
(b) The equation of the budget line is $I = P_x x + P_y y$.
(c) The slope of the budget line depends upon the relative prices of the goods X and Y. This slope will be $-P_x/P_y$.

R4. The optimum of the consumer is found geometrically as the point on the budget line touching the highest achievable indifference curve. If both goods are consumed, this will be an interior solution. If only one good is consumed (if the budget line touches the highest indifference curve at one axis), this will be a corner solution.

R6. (a) The Consumption Balance Equation is $MU_x/P_x = MU_y/P_y$. The Substitution Equivalence Equation is $MRS_C = MRS_E$ (or, slope of indifference curve = slope of budget line). The Consumption Balance Equation can be reduced to the Substitution Equivalence Equation, but not vice versa. This is because the CBE requires cardinal utility and the SEE requires only ordinal utility. Cardinal utility implies ordinal utility, but not vice versa.

(b) For the appropriate measure of utility, both equations will hold at an interior solution. But at a corner solution an *inequality* will ordinarily hold, dictating spending as much as possible on one of the commodities. In terms of geometry, a corner solution is not ordinarily a point of tangency between the budget line and an indifference curve. (As a very special case, however, it is conceivable that a tangency occurs exactly at a corner, in which case SEE would also hold for a corner solution.)

R9. (a) If the IEP has a positive slope, the Engel Curve for each good will have a positive slope.
(b) The Engel Expenditure Curve for each good will have a positive slope, but this slope will not exceed unity (the slope of the 45° line).
(c) If X is an inferior good, the Engel Curve will have a negative slope.

R12. If the Law of Demand holds, the PEP never curls back (toward the northwest).

R16. As long as a commodity X is a *good* (rather than a neuter or a bad), those receiving vouchers for purchase of X will consume at least the voucher equivalent. For those previously consuming less than this, the voucher will always increase consumption. For this reason, vouchers are particularly effective (relative to subsidies) in increasing consumption among persons who would otherwise have consumed little or none of X.

T1. (a) An experiment could reveal the *maximum* amount of Y an individual might be willing to pay for a small increment of X. This would be an approximation of the MRS_C.
(b) No known experiment could reveal Marginal Utility.

T3. (a) In moving northwest, the PEP is entering regions of higher y but lower x. Since utility is increasing along the PEP, it must be that y is increasing fast enough to more than compensate for the decrease in x. But the amount of y it is possible to acquire is bounded by the horizontal line through the starting-point K. So this process can continue only over a limited range of the PEP—which must soon turn northeast.
(b) This is impossible. Utility is increasing everywhere along the PEP, and the same starting-point cannot have both lower and higher utility.

T4. (a) An increase in P_x would tend to shift the IEP to the northwest.
(b) An increase in I would tend to displace the PEP toward the northeast (assuming X and Y are both normal superior goods).

T6. Since usually only a limited fraction of income is spent on any single good X, the income effect (enrichment or impoverishment) due to a change in P_x will be relatively small.

T8. The market base price (before deduction of subsidy) should *rise*, because increased quantities will be demanded. The effect will be to partially cancel the impact of the subsidy or voucher.

T10. (a) Coach travel is an inferior good here, since the purchased quantity of coach travel falls as income rises. Specifically, if income were to rise above $100, more first-class travel and less coach travel would be purchased.

(b) If the traveler's budget is so small that he can complete the trip only by traveling entirely in coach, then he will do so. If the traveler's budget permits the trip to be completed by traveling entirely in first-class, then only first-class travel will be purchased.

CHAPTER 5

R2. Such Engel Curves (of different steepness, but all being straight lines through the origin) do depict the same *proportionate response* of changes in consumption to changes in income. Steepness being greater for one commodity shows not greater income elasticity but rather that x/I is higher, i.e., that the commodity is absolutely more important in the consumer's budget. In some cases, we *would* want to distinguish between steeper and less steep Engel Curves, in which case the elasticity concept is unhelpful.

R5. (a) "Elastic demand" means that the absolute value of the price elasticity of demand exceeds one. "Inelastic demand" means that the absolute value of the price elasticity of demand is less than one.

(b) For a linear demand curve, the elasticity at any point is the ratio of two slopes: the slope of a ray from the origin *to* that point on the curve, divided by the constant slope *along* the curve. For a nonlinear demand curve, the slope *along* the curve is interpreted as the slope of a tangent to the curve at that point.

R6. (a) Negative infinity. (b) Zero. (c) −1.

R9. Price elasticity is −1. Income elasticity is +1.

T1. Assuming for simplicity just two goods X and Y, the equation (5.2) that we want to prove can be written in more detail as:

$$\frac{P_x x}{I} \left(\frac{\Delta x}{\Delta I} \frac{I}{x} \right) + \frac{P_y y}{I} \left(\frac{\Delta y}{\Delta I} \frac{I}{y} \right) = 1$$

After cancellations:

$$\frac{P_x \Delta x + P_y \Delta y}{\Delta I} = 1$$

But since $I = P_x x + P_y y$, with P_x and P_y as constants, $\Delta I = P_x \Delta x + P_y \Delta y$. So the numerator and denominator of the fraction above are equal, proving that their ratio does indeed equal unity.

T2. (a) This argument is based upon the substitution effect of a price change and is valid. Indifference curves drawn for a commodity and its close substitute will have very little curvature. A small proportionate price decrease (a small tilt of the budget line) will then tend to result in a large proportionate increase in quantity (a large shift in the consumer's optimum).

(b) This argument is based upon the income effect of a price change and is valid, increasingly so as the good accounts for a bigger portion of the budget. A luxury is a commodity with a strong positive income effect. Since a price decrease tends to enrich the consumer, the income effect will strongly reinforce the substitution effect and so lead to a relatively large proportionate increase in quantity. However, if the luxury commodity accounts for very little of the budget, the enrichment will be small and so the income effect will be insubstantial.

(c) This argument is based upon the income effect of a price change, but is invalid. The argument asserts that, since the commodity accounts for a large portion of an individual's budget, a price decrease will have a large enriching effect and so will lead to a large increase in the quantity purchased. Up to this point the argument is correct, but what it implies is a large *absolute* increase in quantity. Since a large proportion of the consumer's budget is already being spent on this good, a large absolute increase in quantity does not generally imply the large *proportionate* increase required for high elasticity. (See Question R9 for the price elasticity of a commodity that accounts for 100% of the consumer's budget.)

(d) This argument is valid for a linear demand curve (or approximately linear). Here the slope is the same at high or low prices, but at high prices there is a high ratio P/Q and at low prices a low ratio P/Q. Since elasticity equals the reciprocal of the slope times this ratio, the proposition follows. But if the slope is not constant—in particular, if it is high at high prices and low at low prices (as would be true for a constant-elasticity demand curve)—the proposition would not be valid.

T3. (a) At low incomes consumers are likely to be interested only in nutrition. High-quality and low-quality beef are good substitutes as far as nutrition is concerned. At high incomes other characteristics such as taste become increasingly important to consumers. Here, low quality beef is not a good substitute for high quality beef. Higher-up indifference curves would therefore have greater curvature.

(b) Because high-quality beef appears to be a luxury (it has a stronger positive income effect than low-quality beef), the price elasticity of demand for high-quality beef should be high relative to the price elasticity for low-quality beef.

T5. The secretary is mistaken. The prof would undoubtedly be *willing* to pay something more in total for 3 tickets than for 2. But if the price is only $10, *he does not have to* pay more for 3 tickets than he would have paid for 2 at a price of $20 each. Looking at this another way, the $10 is the worth of a *third* ticket to the prof, not the worth of each of three tickets. (If the objection were valid, it would never make sense for a consumer to have an inelastic demand for a good.)

T6. This is indeed possible, though opinions may differ about how likely it is. Consumers seeking "snob appeal" gain utility from *exclusiveness*. At a high price, they are getting not only the commodity but also the exclusivity. The fact that the price is high guarantees that not many people can afford the commodity, and therefore makes "snob" consumers more willing to buy than at a low price. But if the exclusiveness were provided in some other way (as by the medieval Statute of Dress that made it illegal for the lower orders to wear upper-class clothes), presumably the Law of Demand would hold.

T7. This is very much like the previous question, but here the additional element gained by the consumer from the high-price product (or so he believes) is *quality*. There is of course nothing paradoxical if someone prefers high quality even at a high price over low quality at a low price. Again, if the quality were guaranteed in some other way than by high price (perhaps by a consumer organization's rating of the product), presumably the Law of Demand would hold—a high-quality product at a low price would be chosen over the *same* high-quality product at a high price.

CHAPTER 6

R1. (a) A "luxury" was defined above as a strongly superior good; an implication would be that the income elasticity is at least unity. For none of the income groups investigated by Schwartz was the income elasticity of demand for charitable giving this large.

   (b) The price of charitable giving is the amount one individual must pay (the income the person must forego) to give a dollar to another person. Since charitable giving is tax-deductible, this price is (1 − marginal tax rate).

R2. Permitting the sale of coupons would benefit both the wealthy and the poor. The poor could sell coupons for dollars, shift their income constraint outward, and attain a more preferred position. The wealthy could buy coupons for dollars, shift their ration constraint upward (and their income constraint inward), and attain a more preferred position. Voluntary trade is mutually beneficial. If such trade occurs, it must benefit both parties.

R4. This corresponds to the statement that the income index $\mathscr{I}$ is greater than the Laspeyres index of prices $\mathscr{L}_P$—which implies also that the Paasche index of quantities $\mathscr{P}_Q$ is greater than one. The statement is true.

T2. (a) The usual justification is that rationed commodities tend to be those that are "essential" to life or health. If ration allowances were exchangeable, rich people might end up with more than "their fair share" of these essential commodities. Note that this assumes that the poorer people who sell their allowances are foolish in giving up some "essentials" for non-essentials—or else possibly that poorer people have to be forced to remain in good working condition for the sake of the war effort, though they themselves might prefer otherwise!

   (b) The adverse consequences include the loss of the gains from trade, plus the diversion of resources into black-market activities and the policing efforts required to minimize such activities.

T3. Consumption requires both income and time. A consumer will choose a most preferred position subject to both an income constraint and a time constraint. When relatively poor, the income constraint will tend to be binding. When relatively rich, the time constraint will tend to be binding. While "time-saving" devices in effect allow outward shifts of the time constraint, this has not occurred as rapidly as rising incomes have shifted out the income constraint. So the time constraint is increasingly the binding one upon individuals' consumption. Rich people simply do not have enough time to consume all the things they might enjoy and be able to pay for.

CHAPTER 7

R2. (a) It does not follow. Mutually beneficial trade can occur as long as their MRS_C's differ at their endowed positions (or at their Crusoe optimum positions, if production is possible).

(b) If individuals have identical preferences and identical endowments in a world of pure exchange, each individual's MRS_C will be the same and no mutually beneficial trade can occur.

(c) Similarly, if they have identical preferences and identical production opportunities, each individual's MRS_C at the Crusoe optimum will be the same and no mutually beneficial trade can occur.

R3. (a) Asymmetrical Production-Possibility Curves will tend to lead to specialization in production. An individual who is relatively well-suited to producing one good will tend to specialize in production of that good. Symmetrical indifference curves tend to lead to diversification in consumption.

(b) Yes. In the absence of trade an individual's degrees of specialization in production and in consumption would have to be identical. Trade allows the simultaneous existence of productive specialization and consumptive diversification.

R6. In a world of production and exchange (assuming interior solutions), at the productive optimum each individual must be producing at a point along his Production-Possibility Curve such that his MRS_T equals the ratio of market prices. Similarly, at the consumptive optimum each individual's MRS_C must equal the ratio of market prices. Additionally, for each good, the sum over all individuals of the produced quantities must equal the sum of the consumed quantities.

R8. The intersection of the full demand and supply curves determines the point at which the total quantity desired for consumption just equals the total quantity available for consumption. The intersection of the net (transaction) demand and supply curves determines the point at which the quantity desired in exchange equals the quantity offered for exchange. Since the two pairs of curves differ only by the *non-traded* amounts of the good (endowed and self-consumed quantities in pure exchange, or produced and self-consumed quantities in a world of production), the price that brings desired transaction quantities into equilibrium must also bring desired full quantities into equilibrium.

T2. A tax on *consumption* will reduce the incentive to acquire the taxed good either by production or by exchange. There will be less consumption and less production, whether for self-supply or for the market. A tax on *production* will have quite similar effects. A tax on *exchange*, in contrast, will tend to reduce production for the market but to increase production for self-supply. On balance, consumption of the good will also be reduced since the cost-reducing advantages of specialization will have been lost.

T3. Diminishing MRS_T is a reflection of the general law of diminishing returns that applies to all *productive* activities. Ideally, exchange does not involve any sacrifice of resources and so is not subject to diminishing returns. (However, the next chapter deals with *costly* exchange, in which case diminishing returns might be expected to apply.)

T5. (a) The Commission seems to assume (with no evident justification) that the demand for forests is necessarily inelastic.

(b) The President's Commission appears to be saying that plenty is better than scarcity, even if the *market value* of the resource would be greater if it were scarce. This is correct. (The concept of Consumer Surplus would have clarified the discussion.) The Commission seems to be afraid that economists, making use of "analysis in commercial terms," might go about recommending that we burn down half the nation's forests!

T6. Clearly, at least one of the two parties must be better off, since there is more of C and no less of Y available. But *i* (the seller of C) might end up worse off; if the demand for corn is inelastic, *i* will get less revenue in Y-units for any given amount of C sold. More surprisingly, *j* (the buyer of C) might alternatively end up worse off—if Y is an inferior good for *i*. (Work this out!)

CHAPTER 8

R1. If individual suppliers or demanders *view* their actions as having only a negligible effect on market price, the market price will *appear* fixed to them. Then they will exhibit price-taking behavior.

R3. (a) Yes, but only in a very special case. Autarky will occur in costless exchange if, for every individual, the ratio of market prices exactly equals the MRS_C and MRS_T at his or her Crusoe solution.

(b) Transaction costs create a spread between the gross and net price ratios. Any time an individual's MRS_C and MRS_T at the Crusoe solution fall inside this spread, the individual will choose an autarky solution (the Crusoe solution). The higher the transaction costs, the greater this spread and the more likely the autarky solution.

(c) Both payroll taxes and sales taxes can be viewed as transaction costs. Each type of tax creates a spread between the buyer's (gross) price and the seller's (net) price for goods and services traded in the market. But neither tax bears upon *self-supplied* goods and services. The increasing weight of payroll and sales taxes, by increasing the spread between buy and sell prices, raises the attractiveness and likelihood of self-supply (autarky) solutions as exemplified by the "do-it-yourself" trend.

R6. A command economy could avoid transaction costs by dispensing with markets, but it might incur larger enforcement costs than the transaction costs saved. While market economies must use resources to integrate individual decisions, command economies must use resources to enforce central decisions. At least as important, the commanders would require an enormous input of information if the economy is to function rationally—information automatically provided by price signals in market economies. Most important of all, what the command economy will aim at is "efficiency" in carrying out the desires of the commanders, which may be quite different from the desires of consumers.

T1. Some markets have disappeared mainly because of reduction in demand. Leeches are no longer sold to physicians, since bleeding has lost favor as a medical practice. Other markets have disappeared because supply has become excessively costly. An example might be the market for handmade shoes. One historically important market that has disappeared, mainly because of higher *transaction costs* (in the form of legal penalties), is the international slave trade.

T3. (a) Integration might be achieved by commands of a central authority. Or by mutual love and helpfulness, as within a family. Or even by instinct (see the next question).
  (b) Barter markets can and do function without the use of money.

T4. A Martian observer, unfamiliar with the mental limitations of flowers and bees, might indeed fail to appreciate the difference as compared with human exchange. Perhaps we're kidding ourselves, but we like to think that our exchanges are the result of *choice*. Presumably, the behavior of the bees is governed entirely by blind instinct, while the flowers are even farther from having any choice as to whether or not to offer their nectar to bees.

T7. Where both ration coupons and cash are required for trade, traders must maintain inventories of coupons as well as cash. In addition, traders must transport, authenticate, and physically transfer ration coupons as well as cash. If coupons can be bought and sold, there is also the cost of the coupon market. If coupons cannot be bought and sold there are the costs of enforcing (and the costs of evading) the restrictions on the sale of coupons.

T8. All these qualities reduce the cost of using money as medium of exchange or as store of value. A somewhat less obvious but very important quality, illustrated by the prisoner-of-war example, is that the monetary commodity should not also be a consumption good. Also, of course, the money should be cheap to produce.

CHAPTER 9

R3. (a) Economic profit is the difference between revenues and economic costs, i.e., costs inclusive of implicit payments for self-supplied resources.
  (b) Since owners receive profits, maximization of profit (owner wealth) is an appropriate goal for owners. Managers, if they are not also

owners, have no claim on profits and so if not watched by owners would be uninterested in maximizing profit. Managers might be interested in power, growth, stability, and a favorable corporate image as well as in larger salaries and more pleasant working conditions.

(c) If owners are not managers, owners and managers will seek different goals. Since it is owners who ultimately make decisions, mechanisms tend to be developed by owners to impose their profit-maximizing goal upon managers. Lawsuits and proxy fights can punish managers who are not pursuing owners' goals. Similarly, profit-sharing and stock-option plans reward managers for pursuing owners' goals. These mechanisms are imperfect, though, so the likely result is that the firm will pursue some mixture of owner and manager goals.

R5. (a) If a tp_a curve with a zero intercept on the output axis were shifted upward so as to make the intercept positive, the mp_a curve would be unaffected but the ap_a curve would be higher everywhere—the difference being greatest for very small quantities of the factor. (In fact, with a positive intercept of the tp_a curve, ap_a would approach infinity as a approaches zero.)

(b) If tp_a is initially increasing at an increasing rate, mp_a and ap_a will each have a rising range before diminishing returns set in. If tp_a is rising but at a decreasing rate throughout, mp_a and ap_a will be falling throughout.

R7. A firm will make short-run adjustments to changes in economic conditions if such changes are viewed as temporary. A firm will make long-run adjustments to changes in economic conditions if such changes are viewed as permanent.

T1. (a) Firms tend to diversify in the employment of factors, although not all factors are employed by each firm.

(b) If output isoquants are convex to the origin, minimizing the cost of producing a given output may yield interior solutions (positive employment) for some factors and corner solutions (zero employment) for other factors. This is consistent with the observation that more than one, but not necessarily all, factors are hired by a firm.

(c) If output isoquants were concave to the origin, minimizing the cost of producing a given output would always yield a corner solution. The firm would hire only one factor.

T2. Taking on additional traffic at a price lower than Average Cost would be financially advantageous if the price exceeds *Marginal* Cost. Even if *AVC* is only one-third of *AC,* Marginal Cost might not be low enough to warrant taking on the new traffic. (In fact, *MC* might even be above *AC.*)

T3. (a) If changing conditions are viewed as temporary, some factors may be held fixed in the face of a contraction of output to avoid the transaction costs incurred in selling the factors and then buying them back when conditions return to normal—or, for an expansion of output, to avoid the costs of buying factors and then selling them back. A similar result holds to the extent that the firm's operations involve *specializing* resources to the firm. Such specialized resources can only be sold at a low price to others, yet must be purchased at a high price. Then these resources may be held fixed during temporary changes in output.

(b) The factors that are held fixed are those which are highly specialized to the firm, or for which transaction costs are high.

T7. The short-run Marginal Cost is the additional cost of increasing output, holding some factors fixed. Whether these costs are paid immediately (operator over-time pay, increased usage of power, etc.) or at a later time (deferred maintenance), they are all costs of a short-run increase in output. The factory manager is confusing short-run costs with costs that must be *paid* immediately. They are not the same.

T9. (a) The Marginal Cost of providing service to more passengers when trains are running empty is quite low. Another passenger can be transported at very little additional cost. When trains are running full, however, the Marginal Cost of providing service to more passengers is much higher. Additional trains must be run, or further unpleasant crowding imposed on passengers. Since Marginal Cost is very low in off-hours, the transit line should encourage off-hour business, not discourage it. The management consultant is confusing Marginal Cost with Average Cost.

(b) "Commutation tickets" will increase ridership at rush hours, but it is during these times that the trains are already running full. If the cost of running additional trains, or of imposing crowding on customers, is high then the transit line is likely to be worse off by selling "commutation tickets." Discount tickets for *off-hour* riders, on the other hand, would likely increase revenues without a commensurate increase in cost. This type of discount would be a good idea.

CHAPTER 10

R1. Yes. Steepness and elasticity of supply, at a given point, must be inversely related.

R2. Whether the proposition (that doubling *all* inputs would always double output) is or is not true is arguable, but in any case it is not economically relevant. In the real world, it is never possible to double *all* relevant inputs.

R4. Where there are no "external" effects, the industry supply curve will be less steep than the firm supply curve but will have the same elasticity (the *proportionate* response of output to price will be the same).

R6. (a) In long-run equilibrium, the marginal firm is just on the borderline between staying in the industry and leaving. If product price were slightly lower, the firm would leave the industry. Consequently, the economic profit of the marginal firm will be (only negligibly above) zero.

(b) Infra-marginal firms have access to some special resources particularly suited to producing in this industry. As product price rises or falls, other firms will bid higher or lower for the right to use these special resources. Consequently, their opportunity cost to the firms will change in such a way as to leave each surviving firm with zero economic profit.

T1. True. A competitive firm will produce positive output only if Marginal Cost exceeds Average Variable Cost (in the short run) or Average Cost (in the long run). So AVC in the former case, or AC in the latter case, must be rising.

T4. No. All firms may be earning zero economic profit, and yet some may be able to survive even if product price falls. These will be the "inframarginal" firms (see Question R6).

T6. (a) Only if some coupons were initially unused would sale of coupons tend to raise the price of petroleum and elicit more supply. If all coupons were used initially, allowing sales would only redistribute coupons and would not elicit a greater quantity supplied since the legal maximum quantity was already being purchased.

(b) Salability, though, would cause a redistribution of coupons to those having the highest demand prices for gasoline—at least as high as the sum of the product price and the price paid for a coupon. Only those valuing a unit of gasoline at or greater than this sum would be purchasers of gasoline.

(c) Without the sale of coupons, some buyers may receive little or no Consumer Surplus from their purchases of gasoline while others who would receive great Consumer Surplus may be unable to make purchases. Salability will allow those previously unable to make purchases to bid away the coupons from those currently receiving little Consumer Surplus from gasoline.

T8. No. The output from existing wells is based, even in the short run, upon a calculation of the price received for oil versus the cost of pumping. The higher the price, the more it pays to pump. In the longer run the life of an existing well can also be extended by heating, flooding, re-drilling, etc.

CHAPTER 11

R1. To maximize profit, a monopolist will produce that rate of output at which $MR = MC$. Since Marginal Cost is always positive, the monopolist will always produce where Marginal Revenue is positive. Using formula (11.5), $MR > 0$ implies $|\eta| > 1$.

R3. Relative to a competitive outcome, monopoly results in a smaller rate of output as well as a transfer from consumers to producer. It is the smaller rate of output which implies an efficiency loss. Because less is produced and traded, some of the gains from specialization and trade are lost— the sum of Consumer Surplus and Producer Surplus is smaller. This is an efficiency loss.

R5. Owners of monopolies may not be any more interested in non-profit goals than owners of competitive firms, but the absence of competitive pressure allows indulging such goals. As another matter, they may be less able to successfully impose the goal of profit maximization upon managers, since owners of monopolies cannot measure their managers' performance by looking at the performance of rival firms. So owners may not know when profits are being maximized. Also anti-trust policy may act as a threat. (If profits are too large, perhaps an anti-trust suit will be forthcoming.) Finally, many monopolies are regulated and so legally constrained from maximizing profits. For any of these reasons, monopolies may not pursue profits as vigorously as competitive firms.

R6. (a) The *simple monopolist* maximizes profit by producing where $MR = MC$ and selling this output at a single price. This single price will always exceed Marginal Cost. The *market-segmentation monopolist* maximizes profit by producing where the Marginal Revenues for the several segments are equal to each other and to the Marginal Cost of producing. A different price is set in each market segment, but (unless demand is perfectly elastic in one or more segments) each of these prices exceeds Marginal Cost. The *perfectly-discriminating monopolist* maximizes profit by producing where the Marginal Revenues from sales to the various individuals are equal to each other and to Marginal Cost. Here, since individuals are charged different prices for each unit they purchase, the Marginal Revenue equals the marginal price (the price for the last unit). So the marginal price faced by each individual equals Marginal Cost.

(b) In both simple monopoly and market-segmentation monopoly, price exceeds Marginal Cost, and so there are potential efficiency gains from increasing output further. In perfect-discrimination monopoly, marginal price equals Marginal Cost; as there are no efficiency gains from increasing (or decreasing) output, the solution is already efficient.

R7. Any point on the supply curve of a competitive industry shows the Marginal Cost of industry output at that price. In deriving the supply curve we assume that each separate firm will have set Marginal Cost equal to price. The height of the point on the supply curve therefore shows the Marginal Cost of each and every firm for that level of industry output.

T1. Yes. A monopolist always operates in the range of elastic demand (see Question R1). But if demand is elastic, higher prices will substantially reduce quantity demanded.

T3. (a) A simple monopolist produces where demand price exceeds Marginal Cost. A perfectly discriminating monopolist can appropriate any difference between demand price and Marginal Cost and so will always expand output until demand price equals Marginal Cost. A perfectly discriminating monopolist, then, will tend to produce more than a simple monopolist. However, if the *income effect* is very strong, this conclusion may not hold (the discriminating monopolist extracts more income from the consumer at any level of output, which tends to reduce demand for additional units).

(b) A market-segmentation monopolist will charge a price higher than the simple monopoly price to some market segments and so sell less in these segments, but will also charge a price lower than the simple monopoly price to the other segments and so sell more there. The total produced and sold by a market segmentation monopolist, then, may be more or less than that of a simple monopolist.

(c) While a multi-part pricing monopolist will charge a price higher than the simple monopoly price for small purchases, he will charge a price lower than the simple monopoly price for purchases beyond a certain size. Some customers will buy less because they purchase too little to receive the lower marginal price. Other customers will purchase enough to receive the lower marginal price and so will purchase more (in the absence of a strong income effect) than if faced with a single monopoly price. The multi-part pricing monopolist, therefore, may or may not produce less than a simple monopolist.

T4. For a price-discriminating selling scheme to be effective, resale of the commodity must be difficult. If resale were easy, those buying at a low price would resell to those facing a high price. Such arbitrage would tend to eliminate any price differences. Resale of services is inherently more difficult than resale of manufactured goods.

T5. Many customers will lie about their age.

T6. One explanation: couples have better alternatives (closer substitutes for achieving thrills), so their demand is more elastic. Another explanation turns upon cost rather than demand considerations. Customers of such theaters like a degree of privacy, and so want a vacant seat on either side. The theater will then be undesirably crowded for singles when only half the seats are taken, whereas couples can fill two-thirds of the seats before crowding becomes uncomfortable. In effect, 2 seats have to be provided for every singles customer, but only 1½ seats per person for couples.

T10. Yes. Consider theft, for example. The marginal yield to the "industry" as a whole is probably less than that perceived by the individual competitive thief. Any increase in the scale of thievery tends to raise the intensity of defensive actions by potential victims, thereby reducing the returns to thieves in the aggregate. This is like a reduction in price. A monopolized theft industry would take this effect into account, and therefore engage in fewer (but more remunerative, on the average) crimes.

CHAPTER 12

R1. The locational metaphor states that the greater the number of plants, the closer plants are on the average to customers, and so the smaller the transport losses incurred. This will lead to a larger aggregate demand for the product itself. Similarly, the greater the number of varieties, the more closely the available products match customer preferences, and so the smaller the satisfaction loss to consumers. Again, this will lead to a larger aggregate demand.

R2. (a) While increased variety does raise the aggregate demand curve, it does so at a decreasing rate. Consequently, the *incremental* benefits to the monopoly firm in the form of increased revenues from offering greater and greater variety are decreasing. On the other hand, the incremental cost of providing increased variety—in the text example, this is the fixed cost associated with each added plant—is ordinarily non-decreasing. There will be some point, then, where still greater variety raises costs more than it raises revenues. The monopolist will not choose to increase variety beyond that point.

(b) If individuals' desires are for very similar products, there will be little benefit to the firm if it offers increased variety. And if there are large economies of scale, increased variety can only be offered at high cost. These two considerations may be powerful enough to induce the monopolist to offer only a single variety.

R6. Where a single attribute is desired by consumers, a monopolist will select that quality (amount of attribute per unit of product) which makes it possible to produce a chosen quantity of attribute at the lowest cost. While the monopolist will produce less aggregate quantity of attribute than a competitive industry, there is no reason to believe that the cost of producing this smaller quantity will be minimized when a lower-quality product is produced. In particular, if there is a single quality of product that provides attribute at lower cost of production throughout, this same quality of product would be offered either by a monopolist or a competitive industry.

R7. (a) A monopolist would obviously not suppress an invention that lowered the costs of producing a given product. Nor, if consumers are fully informed, would it pay to suppress an invention that raised quality at a given cost. (The only possible exception would be if the invention somehow destroyed the monopoly.)

(b) Consumers would not necessarily be better off. It is conceivable that adoption of a cost-reducing invention would lead the monopolist to produce a smaller amount than before, at a higher price. A similar result may come about for a quality-increasing invention.

T1. No, monopolistic competition emerges when consumers' tastes for different *varieties* provide each supplier with a degree of monopoly power over a "clientele" for each product. In contrast, if there is a single generally recognized *quality* attribute desired by all consumers, they will purchase from whichever firm offers this attribute at the lowest price. If there are many firms, each can survive only by offering the same price as the others per unit of quality attribute. As price-taking suppliers of the single quality attribute, the firms are engaging in pure competition.

T3. The discussion of "Suppression of Inventions" (Section 12.E) showed that an invention lowering Total and Average Cost at every level of output *might* conceivably raise Marginal Cost in some ranges of output. If so, even for a competitive industry, a cost-reducing invention *might* reduce the quantity offered at some prices. (This could happen only over a limited range, and even so seems a rather unlikely possibility.) Since a quality-improving invention is logically equivalent to a cost-reducing invention (in terms of the cost of producing the attribute desired by consumers), a corresponding analysis applies: the invention *might* conceivably (though this seems improbable) be adverse to consumers' interests.

T4. Think of oranges as providing various amounts of a desired attribute.

High-quality oranges contain more attribute than low-quality oranges. The cost of providing attribute to distant markets is the production cost plus a constant per-orange shipping cost. That is, it costs no more to ship a high-quality than a lower-quality orange. Then shipping costs *per unit of quality attribute* will be less if higher-quality oranges are shipped. Consequently, oranges shipped to distant locations tend to be of higher quality.

T5. The explanation seems to be that transportation itself (or the time that transport takes) degrades the quality of lobsters. If so, top-quality lobsters simply cannot be found except near the source. California oranges, in contrast, seem to retain their quality even when shipped long distances.

T6. This is similar to the situation with oranges. As a result of the tax, it becomes *relatively* cheaper than before to supply high-quality (high-mileage) gasoline. Some firms who previously found it more advantageous to produce a lower grade of gasoline are likely now to shift over to a better grade.

T8. No, this is not consistent with the analysis in the chapter. If consumers are interested only in the quality attribute (e.g., mileage), poorer consumers would tend to buy less mileage but there's no reason for them to buy a lower *grade* of gasoline. To the extent that the observation is correct, the explanation seems to be that purchase of higher-quality articles may yield a "luxury-good" attribute in the form of social distinction or prestige in addition to whatever material quality attribute the article contains. Chinchilla may not keep the wearer any warmer than squirrel, but there is something to be said for being seen in chinchilla. (See also Chapter 5, Question T6.)

CHAPTER 13

R2. The "Prisoners' Dilemma" is a social interaction situation in which each participant is motivated to adopt a shortsightedly selfish strategy—with the result that all parties lose. The source of the difficulty is that an individual choosing a cooperative strategy has no way to induce or compel the others to do the same, so the unselfish player ends up worse off than the others. Evidently, there is an unexploited mutual gain from exchange here, due to *inability to make binding agreements.*

R3. Monopolistic competition is a market structure in which each firm's product is differentiated from the others, but the relatively large number of firms rules out strategic behavior. In contrast, strategic behavior is the essence of oligopoly (competition among the few). Under oligopoly, products of the different firms may or may not be differentiated (the heterogeneous versus homogeneous cases).

R4. In the Nash solution of game theory, each party is doing the best he can *given* the strategies of the others. The Cournot solution for oligopoly similarly assumes that each firm adopts the best choice for its decision variable (price or quantity) given the choices made by the others.

R7. (a) If the demand curve is "kinked," the Marginal Revenue curve will have a vertical gap at the rate of output at which this kink exists. To maximize profit, the firm will set $MR = MC$. Assuming that MC initially cuts through the gap in MR, moderate changes in MC will still leave MC cutting through this gap in MR. As long as this is the case, the firm will not change its rate of output or price. If the kink is due to responses of other firms' prices as this firm changes its own price, then moderate shifts in the demand curve to the left or right may also leave MC cutting through the gap in MR—now at a smaller rate of output. Again, price will tend to be rigid.

(b) One method of enforcing a collusive agreement is for "loyal" firms to match any price cut by a defecting firm, but to refrain from matching any price increase. This leads to each potential defector viewing its demand curve as kinked at the agreed level of prices.

T2. Unfortunately from the analytical point of view, "learning" on the part of the firms opens up many new possibilities and the final outcome is not easily predictable. Suppose first that at each output of the other firm, the "learned" duopolist produces more than the simple duopolist—realizing that such increases in output will tend to bring about decreases in the other firm's output. If both firms "learn", the Reaction Curve of each will shift to the right relative to the Reaction Curves of simple duopolists. The consequence is that the outcome approaches the competitive solution—both firms are worse off than before! So they may "learn" by this to behave more cooperatively instead, holding back on output so as to approach the monopoly solution instead. But if one firm learns that the other is inclined to hold back, the first is tempted to "free ride" and produce more. So the final result is unclear.

T3. Yes. The kink would have a more extreme form under homogeneous oligopoly. A firm that raised its price, while other firms were keeping their prices constant, would lose *all* its business—so above the kink the demand curve would be flat (perfectly elastic). A firm that lowered price would find that other firms follow, so its demand below the kink would be no more elastic than the overall industry demand.

T5. (a) Table 13.2 shows that the symmetrical collusive solution is not generally better than the threat solution for *both* parties. If the threat can be made effective without having to be enforced very often, the "predatory price cutter" can do better than under collusion.

(b) Predatory price cutting is more likely to emerge where one firm is much more powerful or aggressive than the other, so that the threat is highly credible.

T6. (a) If consumers are uniformly distributed around a ring, then no matter how two producers locate they will each be closer to exactly half the consumers. Hence the locational equilibrium is indeterminate.

(b) If demand is not absolutely inelastic, each firm can gain by moving some distance away from the back-to-back solution. Even though the first firm to move does lose to the other firm some customers located near the middle, the saving in transport cost enables it to reduce price and thus make more sales to its remaining customers.

(c) If there are more than two oligopolists, the back-to-back solution along a line breaks down. Each firm will be trying to "jump" to an outside position that no more than two of them can attain. (But if the customers were distributed over a circular plane area instead, a generalized back-to-back solution for any number of firms could be found in which each firm has as "clientele" an equal angular sector of the circle.)

CHAPTER 14

R2. (a) For a monopolist in the product market, Marginal Revenue is always less than product price. Consequently, for such a monopolist mrp_a will always lie below (to the left of) vmp_a. For a competitor in the product market, Marginal Revenue equals product price. For such a competitor, mrp_a will be identical to vmp_a. So only for a monopolist in the product market will the mrp_a lie to the left of vmp_a.

(b) Whether the firm is a monopolist or a competitor in the product market, mrp_a is the firm's demand curve for factor A. But in the latter case, $vmp_a \equiv mrp_a$.

R4. (a) Since mrp_a must be declining for $mrp_a = h_a$ to be an optimum, for a competitor in the product market it will never be rational *not* to be in the region of diminishing *marginal* returns (mp_a declining). For a monopolist in the product market, MR is also declining so it *may* be possible to achieve declining mrp_a even with rising mp_a.

(b) $mrp_a = h_a$ may hold in the region of diminishing marginal returns but rising *average* returns (where mp_a lies above ap_a). But in this region $h_a = mrp_a = MR(mp_a) > MR(ap_a)$. Then for a competitive firm, $h_a > P(q/a)$, or $h_a a > Pq$. This means that the expenditure on factor A alone exceeds Total Revenue! So a competitive firm would *always* operate in the region of diminishing average returns.

(c) $mrp_a = h_a$ could never hold in the region of diminishing *total* returns. Here mp_a is negative and so mrp_a must also be negative. Since factor hire-price h_a can never be negative, a profit-maximizing firm would never hire so much factor as to be in the region of diminishing total returns.

R5. The conditions $mrp_a = h_a$ and $mrp_b = h_b$ imply that $mp_a/h_a = mp_b/h_b$. This equation states that an extra dollar spent on either factor A or factor B will increase output by the same amount. Consequently, factor proportions are optimal. And $mrp_a/h_a = mrp_b/h_b = 1$ is also implied, which is equivalent to $MR/MC = 1$. Consequently, the scale of output is also optimal.

R6. (a) Yes. The slope of the output isoquant shows the rate at which factor B can be substituted for factor A while maintaining output. If one unit less of factor A is employed, the fall in output will be (approximately) mp_a. The number of units of factor B which must be hired to maintain output will be (approximately) mp_a/mp_b. The approximation approaches exactness for very small changes. So the absolute value of the slope at a point on the output isoquant is mp_a/mp_b.

(b) The absolute value of the slope along a cost isoquant is the rate at which factor B can be traded for factor A in the market—equal to h_a/h_b.

R8. No, because firms can enter or leave the industry. The entry – exit effect tends to make the industry's demand for a factor more elastic.

R9. (a) True. A drop in the hire-price of factor A will lead to an increase in the employment of factor A and so to an increase in output. If the demand curve for product is inelastic, this will induce a relatively large fall in product price. So the industry will respond to a fall in the hire-price with only a small increase in the employment of factor A (and a small increase in output). The demand curve for factor A will be steep and so tend to be inelastic.

(b) True. The weaker the operation of the Law of Diminishing Returns, the more gradual the decline in the mp_a as more A is hired. When this decline is more gradual, firm demand curves for factor A and the resulting market demand curve will be relatively flat and so tend to be elastic.

(c) True. The more elastic the supply curves of factors complementary to factor A, the greater the increase in employment of these factors when the demand for them increases. As the hire-price of factor A falls, more A will be hired and so the demand for complementary factors will increase. If this results in a large increase in the quantity of complementary factors hired, there will be a large upward shift in mrp_a and so a relatively large increase in the quantity of factor A employed. Consequently, each firm's demand curve (and so the market demand curve) for factor A will be flatter and so tend to be more elastic, the more elastic the supply of complementary factors.

T1. (a) See Examples 9.4 through 9.8.

(b) This is a question of fact. The Laws of Diminishing Returns appear to be founded upon certain very general physical aspects of the world. Note, however, that economists admit a range of exceptions when they say only that Marginal or Average or Total returns *eventually* diminish as employment of one factor increases relative to others. It is possible that in a practical situation the "eventual" point is not yet reached, so that increasing returns apply in the relevant range.

T2. No. Here, the employer is not a price-taker. Consequently, there is no fixed relation between quantity employed and hire-price.

T4. (a) Even if two factors are anti-complementary, it is quite possible that each has positive Marginal Product. For each factor it is its mp that enters into $mrp \equiv MR \ (mp)$, to be compared with its hire-price h in making the employment decision.

(b) If interference is defined as a situation where hiring more of factor A reduces the *Total* Product tp_b of factor B (or, equivalently, the *Average* Product $ap_b \equiv q/b$), then output q must have fallen and so mp_a must be negative. This can never be rational.

T7. This chapter examines aspects of the *demand* for labor. Supply considerations (to be studied in the next chapter) also have a bearing upon whether wages are high or low. Demand for labor has been high in the U.S. as a result mainly of the presence of large amounts of complementary factors. In the early years these took the form of rich natural resources (fertile land, mineral wealth, navigable rivers). In more recent years, accumulations of complementary manufactured resources (machines, roads) have contributed to the demand for labor. Other possible sources of high demand for labor in the U.S. include rapid technological progress (see next question), relatively strong competition in product markets (so that *mrp* does not diverge very much from *vmp* for labor), and comparative absence of firms with effective monopsony power in the labor markets.

T8. Technological progress by definition tends to raise the *Average* Product of labor. It will tend to raise wages if the *Marginal* Product of labor increases. While the effects on Average Product and Marginal Product are usually parallel, there are exceptions. A "labor-saving" invention may raise the productivity of the first few workers employed so much that the Marginal Product for larger numbers falls. There is another line of causation, however, associated with the general enrichment that technological progress brings about. With higher wealth, there will be more demand for products involving labor of all types. So wages will tend to rise as a result of "revenue" considerations (see Question R1) even if the "productivity" considerations are affected adversely.

CHAPTER 15

R2. No. The supply curve can only bend backward if the income effect opposes the substitution effect. If leisure is an inferior good, the enrichment due to a wage increase would lead to less consumption of leisure (more supply of labor), thus *reinforcing* the substitution effect of the wage increase.

R3. At very low wage rates, few hours are being worked. A wage increase, multiplied by only a small number of hours, will have only a small enrichment effect compared to the substitution effect.

R4. The supply curve to a particular employment is likely to be much more elastic. Different employments of labor are probably, from the worker's point of view, close substitutes in his or her preference function. Then a relatively small change in the wage differential between two employments will induce a relatively large shift in labor supply from the now less attractive to the more attractive employment.

R6. If the wage rate increases, so will the price of leisure, and the individual will likely consume less leisure. Indeed, if the investment decision just leaves the individual as well off as before (on the same indifference curve), that person will always work more, as shown in Figure 15.14. Here only the substitution effect of the wage increase is effective; the income effect is exactly cancelled by the income loss due to the cost of training. If the individual ends up on a higher indifference curve as a result of the investment, then there will be a net income effect which may lead to working less. For this to be the case, though, the income effect of the wage increase upon leisure must be very strong. It must overwhelm both the substitution effect and the income loss from the investment in training.

R8. Each is a source of productive services, and thus a portion of society's real-capital.

R9. This relationship is $h_a = rP_a$. The hire price of the factor is equal to the interest yield on the capital-value or purchase price of the factor. This is an *equilibrium* relation. The purchase price of the factor will be bid up or down until the relation holds.

R11. Economic rent is that portion of payment to a factor in excess of the amount required to call it into employment. Economic rent is a measure of the resource-owner's (seller's) net gain from trade in the factor market. It is, then, analogous to Producer Surplus which is a measure of the seller's net gain from trade in the product market.

T2. Most resources can be viewed as having some reservation uses. An obvious example is land. If not leased on the market, land could be used as a homesite, or a garden, or a private game reserve.

T4. (a) Such a change in taste would lead to an outward shift of the supply curve of female labor. More labor would be offered at each wage rate.
   (b) If males and females make up at least partially distinguishable types of labor, the outward shift in the supply of female labor would lead to a *decrease* in the equilibrium wage rate for female workers relative to male workers.

T5. As long as leisure is a normal good, rising per-capita *wealth* in the form of nonlabor income (vertical shifts in E) will lead to an increase in leisure and so to a decrease in the number of hours worked. Rising real *wages* embody both an income and a substitution effect. The pure substitution effect always implies a decrease in leisure and an increase in hours worked, but the income effect works in the opposite direction. Since hours worked have been steadily falling as real wages have risen, the pure substitution effect of rising real wages appears to have been overwhelmed by the sum of the two income effects: that due to rising per-capita wealth (property income), plus the income effect of rising real wages.

T6. (a) The preferred position $S*$ of the slave would be an all-leisure solution, assuming that leisure is always a good for him. The position $M*$ preferred by the master would be the all-work solution, so long as the slave's labor yields any positive Marginal Product.
   (b) The master has two instruments to move the slave toward $M*$. One is force; the other, incentive payments or wages. It is likely that both will have a diminishing marginal effect. That is, additional units of either force or incentive payments will eventually motivate smaller and smaller increases in work. Consequently, it is likely that the master will choose a policy that includes both force and incentive payments to move the slave toward $M*$.
   (c) If additional units of incentive payments are *always* more effective than the first unit of force, the master would choose to use no force—which is equivalent to freeing the slave and paying wages. Otherwise, the master would choose to use some force.

T9. (a) The supply curve of land to *all* uses (including reservation uses) can be regarded as vertical, in the short run. But the supply of land to *market* uses will not be strictly vertical, even in the short run, since owners will have alternative reservation uses for their land. Both an income tax and a wealth tax on land would therefore have effects upon market supply in the short run. A *wealth tax* normally leads to increased market supply, since owners will suffer impoverishment and will then cut down on their reservation uses of land (apart from the unlikely case that such uses are an inferior good). An *income tax* will, however, also have a strong substitution effect in the opposite direction, and this will probably dominate so that less land will be offered in the market for productive services. (For either type of tax there will also be a *long-run* adverse effect on market supply, as the reduced returns will tend to induce owners not to maintain or develop land as a productive resource.)

(b) The effects on the supply of labor are entirely parallel. For labor, however, alternative (leisure) uses are probably much more important. Thus, a wealth tax upon labor capacity may have a significant effect in inducing more market supply of labor. And an income tax will have more equally countervailing income and substitution effects, with the final result indeterminate.

T10. If labor supply were more effectively cartelized in the U.S., wages would tend to be higher. This seems unlikely, however. It may be that U.S. laborers are willing to work harder, which would tend to raise their wages. Probably most important, there is more educational and training investment ("human capital") bound up in typical U.S. workers, making them more productive.

T12. Wage rates are high in New York City mainly because in that area a very unusual combination of natural and manufactured resources (the harbor, buildings and streets, railroads and subways, etc.) raises workers' productivity. If not balanced by other considerations, workers would flow in from the rest of the country to take advantage of these high wages. As they do so, however, crowding of the New York area tends to raise the cost of living there until the net advantage of such movement disappears and the population stabilizes.

CHAPTER 16

R2. (b) is correct. The ratio P_0/P_1 is the rate at which current consumption claims can be traded for one-year future consumption claims. If a current consumption claim is foregone, the market will pay back that claim plus interest next year. So $P_0/P_1 = 1 + r$. Consequently, $r = (P_0/P_1) - 1$. The annual rate of interest is the *premium* on the relative value of current over one-year future consumption claims.

R4. At equilibrium in pure exchange, lending equals borrowing. Lenders could be regarded as savers, and borrowers as dis-savers, but the aggregate of saving necessarily equals zero. Investment must always equal zero in a world of pure exchange. So at equilibrium, aggregate saving equals aggregate investment at zero.

R5. At equilibrium in a productive situation, aggregate saving equals aggregate investment. It is also true that aggregate borrowing equals aggregate lending, but the total of borrowing or lending need not equal the total of saving or investment.

R7. (a) The Present Value Rule directs decision-makers to adopt any incremental project for which the Present Value is positive, and to reject projects for which Present Value is negative.

(b) As long as the Separation Theorem holds, productive optimization is equivalent to wealth maximization. Since the Present Value Rule is a wealth-maximizing rule, decision-makers will then be led to the productive optimum. If the Separation Theorem does not hold, however, wealth maximization and productive optimization are not identical. Here, not only wealth but its distribution over time becomes important, and so the Present Value Rule will not necessarily lead to a productive optimum.

R8. (a) Project M is an investment project.

(b) The Present Value of M is 13.64 if r is 10%, 4.17 if r is 20%, and -3.85 if r is 30%.

(c) The highest interest rate at which M should be adopted is that at which Present Value becomes zero. This interest rate is 25%.

R9. (a) If only one project can be adopted, it should be project N. Both projects have positive Present Values, but the Present Value V_0 of project N is 25, whereas for project M the V_0 is 4.17.

(b) Even if both projects could be adopted together, they should not be. If both projects are adopted the combined Present Value is 15.83—less than the V_0 for project N alone.

T2. At equilibrium it must be true that—even though saving need not equal investment for any individual—both actual and desired saving equal actual and desired investment in the aggregate. If this were not the case, the interest rate would adjust to bring about the equality. If a floor or ceiling were placed upon the interest rate, it will still be true that *actual* aggregate saving equals *actual* investment. Here, the smaller of desired aggregate saving and desired aggregate investment will determine the actual quantity of saving and investment. It will not be true, however, that *desired* aggregate saving equals *desired* aggregate investment at the "frozen" market interest rate.

T3. (a) Because time-productivity will be relatively great in such a newly settled country, the real interest rate will tend to be high.

(b) The more isolated such a country is, the higher its real interest rate will be. Close contact with the rest of the world will lead to an inflow of investments from outside when the new country's rate of interest exceeds that existing elsewhere. Close contact with other countries, then, will tend to lower the real rate of interest in the new country.

(c) The lower the rate of interest, the more investment projects that will have a positive Present Value, and so the more investment will take place. Consequently, more investment will occur in a new country if it is in close contact with and so can draw resources from the rest of the world.

T4. If little investment is taking place because of low time-productivity, real interest rates will be low—reflecting this low time-productivity. If little investment is taking place because of high time-preference, interest rates will be high—reflecting this high time-preference. So the first (unproductive) country would tend to have a low real rate of interest and the other (impatient) country would tend to have a high real rate of interest.

T6. Negative rates of interest are not impossible. As equation (16.1) indicates, all that is required is that future claims exchange at a premium against current claims ($P_0 < P_1$). Negative interest rates are rarely observed, however. In most situations there are attractive investment opportunities which increase the investment demand for current funds, while time-preference (impatience) raises the consumptive demand for current funds. The combination assures that current funds will almost always exchange at a premium against future funds. Only a society expecting to be impoverished in the future, and lacking investment opportunities to correct this situation, is likely to be characterized by a negative real rate of interest.

CHAPTER 17

R2. The contract curve of the Edgeworth box diagram defined those allocations from which no mutually beneficial trade can occur. Consequently, the utilities of the two individuals at a point on the contract curve become the coordinates for a point on the utility Social Opportunity Frontier.

R3. (a) A "social optimum" can only be defined in terms of a social criterion. Given a social criterion, the "social optimum" is simply that allocation which best achieves the criterion. Where the criterion does not exist, allocations cannot be compared and so no meaning can be attached to the concept of a "social optimum." Currently, there seems to be no agreement as to a social criterion, and so the term "social optimum" lacks meaning. For example, some people regard unlimited abortion as social progress, others as social calamity.

(b) Efficiency is certainly a valid goal, in part, but there are many reasons why it should not be the only element in a social criterion. For one thing, considerations of equity may indicate some sacrifice of efficiency. Also, efficiency is based upon the satisfaction of individual wants as the measure of well-being. It might be argued that individuals are poor judges of what will actually benefit them, or that wants are not autonomous but really socially determined, or that supra-individualistic policy goals (liberty, justice, community) are also important.

R5. (a) The efficiency conditions are three. First, $MRSC_{XY}^j = P_X = MRSC_{XY}^k$, so that goods are allocated efficiently between consumers. Second, $MRSR_{AI}^j = h_a = MRSR_{AI}^k$, so reservation uses of resources are allocated efficiently between resource-owners. Third, $vmp_a^f = h_a = vmp_a^g$, so that resource services are used efficiently by firms in producing goods.

(b) These conditions could in principle be achieved without the market process. Efficient allocation might be directly imposed by a dictator.

R7. (a) The product-market monopolist and the factor-market monopsonist both violate the efficiency condition $vmp_a = h_a$. The product-market monopolist sets $h_a = mrp_a < vmp_a$. The factor-market monopsonist sets mrp_a (which may equal vmp_a) $= mfc_a > h_a$. That both produce "too little" follows, since in either case $vmp_a > h_a$. This causes an efficiency loss because these firms could, by producing more, convert units of resource A into a larger product value than competitive firms satisfying the condition $vmp_a = h_a$.

(b) Yes, it follows that "too much" of resource A is used by competitive firms, and that "too much" A is retained for reservation uses that could more efficiently be devoted to market employment.

R10. (a) This efficiency condition is $MC_Z^f = MRSC_{ZY}^j + MRSC_{ZY}^k$, i.e., the Marginal Cost of providing the public good Z must equal the sum of each consumer's marginal valuation of the public good (Marginal Rate of Substitution in Consumption between the public and private goods).

(b) For a public good, since *every* consumer can receive the same unit, the vertical summation of individual demand curves for a public good shows the social marginal valuation. For a private good, only one consumer receives each unit—so the social marginal valuation of the private good is simply the marginal valuation of the consumer receiving the marginal unit. Horizontal summation of individual demand curves for a private good generates the market demand curve for that good. It is, however, incorrect to view the vertical summation of individual demand curves for a public good as a *demand curve* for the public good. This vertical summation does *not* indicate the quantity that would be purchased at any price; all it shows is the social marginal valuation of the public good.

R11. (a) The private supply of public goods is limited, first, by the difficulty and cost of exclusion. Non-payers would have to be excluded for private provision to be feasible, and this may be impossible or quite costly. Where exclusion costs are sufficiently low a private firm may provide a public good, but will not likely provide an efficient quantity. For efficient provision, firms would have to charge different prices to different individuals. Such price discrimination might be illegal or simply too costly.

(b) Public provision *may* result in a more nearly optimal quantity, but this depends upon the forces determining governmental decisions (to be studied in Chapter 18). Where exclusion is impossible or very costly, private provision is unlikely, and so public provision may be inevitable.

T1. The Duke has not read the text carefully enough. If the Duchess were initially endowed with a property right in her own life, a Pareto-preferred movement toward an efficient solution would have to be *mutually* beneficial. It seems unlikely that the Duke could have paid enough to have the Duchess agree to her own death. If the Duke initially possessed the right to take the Duchess' life, on the other hand, his argument would be valid on efficiency grounds. Even then, however, he was not necessarily "justified" in terms of moral criteria.

T2. Definitely false. First of all, conventional national income measures fail to allow for a whole variety of sources of utility and disutility: for example, homemakers' services are not counted, nor is the value of leisure, nor are deductions made for degradation of the environment. But the statement would not be true even if there were a perfect national income measure. Monopolization of a good, for example, might raise the market value of national income while reducing efficiency.

T4. Property rights will be ill-defined when laws or court rulings are ambiguous and where legal precedents are conflicting or in a state of flux. Also, if it is costly to learn about one's rights, subjective uncertainty may persist even if the underlying legal theory is settled. The costs of transacting (negotiating and enforcing contracts) will tend to be high when multilateral contracting is required, or when individuals have incentives to behave strategically in order to capture more of the gains from an agreement. Some potential trades are hampered by the difficulty of describing the good or service in advance, or of measuring delivery performance thereafter. For example, contracts for labor service cannot generally guarantee in advance how devotedly the worker will perform, and this may even be hard to measure afterward. A perhaps clearer example is the used-car business, where prior determination of quality is notoriously difficult and where writing a level of agreed quality into the contract is almost impossible.

T6. True, since market reallocations of resources must be mutually beneficial. A dictator, in contrast, might achieve a Pareto-*efficient* outcome that was not Pareto-*preferred* to the original situation.

T7. Such a ban is certainly inefficient. The justification, if any, seems to be a paternalistic one: that poor people might be tempted to sell their blood and use the proceeds unwisely, and ought to be prevented from doing so. To the extent that such an argument is valid, less extreme measures than a total ban on sales of blood would seem to be more appropriate. The hepatitis problem is not a sufficient reason for banning the market in blood, since buyers are at liberty to use whatever method they deem appropriate in screening commercial donors. (As might have been anticipated, the prohibition of blood sales has caused dangerous blood "shortages.")

CHAPTER 18

R1. (a) The voluntarist approach to political behavior views individuals as accepting subordination in exchange for the benefits of government. Citizens in a sense shop for that government which provides them the largest increase in welfare. Political parties compete to become the government and so to capture the rewards of being in power. Since utility-maximization, exchange, and competition are all involved, this approach is particularly amenable to economic analysis.

(b) Three alternative approaches are suggested in the text. "Divine ordinance" views subordination to government as the result of a heavenly command. "Naked power" views subordination as the result simply of force. "Instinctual-biological" views this subordination as an inherited human pattern of association, which is a biological adaptation evolved by the human species.

R2. The imperfections of the political process, regarded as a mechanism designed to satisfy citizen desires, are somewhat analogous to the imperfections of the market process—but are, often, even more pervasive. In the political process citizens almost never make choices directly on substantive issues; actual decisions are made by imperfectly controllable delegates. Second, in the political process citizens have only a very narrow range of choice even of delegates. They must select from a very limited number of candidates (i.e., political competition is highly imperfect) at widely separated election intervals. In the market process individuals may select from a vast menu of choices almost continuously over time. Third, the political process makes decisions based upon some form of majority rule. If the majority prefer an alternative (e.g., war or peace), that decision is likely to be binding on all. In the market process, even though most people consume Chevys, the minority may still consume Fords. Fourth, the cost of acquiring information relative to the benefit derived therefrom by any single individual is much higher for political choices than for market choices.

R4. (a) A free-rider problem in the provision of goods will tend to arise whenever it is difficult to exclude non-payers from the benefits of group action—as when cartels drive up prices even for non-member firms, or when public goods are provided even to those who do not contribute to defray the costs.

(b) Not very valid. While much of government activity appears to be concerned with the provision of public goods where the free-rider problem is encountered—defense, law, and redistribution all can be viewed as having public-good characteristics—governments are also heavily involved with the provision of private goods. Far more important an objection is the question of whether it is true (as postulated in the voluntarist approach) that government is "fundamentally" concerned with providing goods at all. To the extent that the naked-power conception is valid, government is a system of organized exploitation rather than an instrument of the governed.

R7. More frequent elections, more numerous legislatures, and elected judges would all give citizens the *potential* of more control over government officials. The more frequent are elections and the more numerous the legislatures, though, the less important is any single election and so the less informed voters will typically be. Similarly, the election of one delegate responsible for appointing judges may lead to judges more in line with citizen desires than citizen election of individual judges. So it is not clear whether or not any of these proposals would actually improve the fidelity of the political system to citizen desires. Replacing the merit system in civil service by the spoils system gives citizens some control (though indirect) over bureaucrats. The spoils system would therefore make the governmental mechanism more accountable to citizen desires, but may still be unacceptable for other reasons.

R8. (a) Apart from the difficulties of striking bargains (transaction costs and strategic behavior), unanimous consent with the purchase of dissident votes would always result in decisions that improve the welfare of every voter—Pareto-preferred moves. In terms of Pareto-efficiency, this would be an ideal political system.

(b) Log-rolling allows voters to trade votes on one issue for votes on another issue, and so would indeed tend to lead to Pareto-preferred outcomes—series of decisions which together leave each voter better off. The objections to log-rolling are due primarily to the fact that *delegates*, not citizens, actually vote on policies and secondarily to the fact that only a majority is required to decide an issue. Because delegates vote, pressure groups with a strongly concentrated stake in a particular issue will be able to influence delegate votes unduly—in extreme cases, log-rolling might represent outright bribery. And because unanimity is not required, log-rolling might not make all participants better off—but only a majority of them.

T1. Any voluntary trade is mutually beneficial. So if the poor traded votes to the rich for money, both would gain in comparison with the initial situation. Objections to this practice are probably based on objections to the initial situation, in which the rich have more money to begin with.

T2. Yes, there is a certain tendency in this direction. A political party in office might "profit" by simply looting the taxpayers, or more subtly by carrying out ideological programs in opposition to voters' desires. The potential competition of other parties limits how far a party in power can go in this direction. But political competition is a much weaker force than economic competition (see Question R2), and so "political profit" is surely not driven to zero.

T3. Cash redistributions are not unknown. Social Security comes close to falling in this category, being a redistribution from the working age-group to the retired age-group. But that politicians prefer to establish service programs to "help" the poor (by health care, job training, education, etc.) has become increasingly evident in recent years. The advantage to legislators of being in on the ground floor when a large new bureaucracy is established to staff a service program (jobs to political supporters) seems clear.

T4. (a) Government construction is a service very often provided by contract with private suppliers, rather than by government employees. Perhaps the irregular extent and timing of construction work does not fit in so well with the security of employment tenure which is typical of government service. The political influence of private construction interests, in heading off competition from the government sector, also plays a role. But a full explanation does not seem at hand.

(b) Private customers pay (apart from possible elements of subsidy) for government-provided services like the post office, TVA, and in many countries railroad and telephone, etc. The explanation is not well understood. What is true is that once a service has been provided by government, a bureaucratic constituency develops tending to perpetuate that situation. So if first historical provision of telephone service, for example, happened to be by a government agency, it is likely to remain that way.

T6. Viewing government in a voluntarist framework, changes in demand or costs should have the same qualitative effects upon price and output for a governmentally-provided good as for a privately-provided good. The strength of the effects, however, will differ. Bureaucrats tend to have an interest in larger output and so in keeping prices low to users. With an increase in demand, therefore, government provision will tend to result in a greater increase in quantity and a smaller increase in price than in the case of private provision. For a decrease in demand, government provision will probably result in a smaller decrease in quantity and a larger fall in price than private provision. Similarly, if costs fall, government provision will tend to result in a larger increase in output and a larger fall in price than private provision. For a rise in costs, government provision will probably result in a smaller rise in price and a smaller decrease in output than private provision.

T8. (a) Voluntarist explanations look for reasons why voters would prefer larger government. For example, a high income elasticity of demand for government-provided goods coupled with rising incomes would generate increases in the demand for such goods. Non-voluntarist explanations might look for shifts in *political power* toward those who prefer larger governments. For example, the enlargement of bureaucracy in wartime might so increase the relative political power of bureaucrats as to preclude a return to a smaller level of government thereafter.

(b) Here again, there are various explanations. A possible one is that the new factory-provided private goods became cheaper relative to government-provided goods, and so the former sector grew relative to the latter.

INDEX

INDEX OF NAMES

Acton, Jan, 170
Ambrosius, John, 280–81
Aristotle, 8, 455
Ayllon, T., 9
Azrin, N. H., 9

Barzel, Y., 560
Basmann, R. L., 146
Battalio, R. C., 146, 461
Baudelaire, Charles, 580
Becker, Gary S., 556
Bell, F. W., 32, 142–43
Ben-Porath, Y., 78
Bentham, Jeremy, 66, 524
Boskin, Michael J., 453–54
Bradburn, N. M., 70
Brozen, Y., 440
Buchanan, J. M., 556
Bunkers, E. W., 232
Burckhardt, Jacob, 581
Burns, Robert, 9

Campbell, James D., 502
Caplovitz, D., 70

Chapman, D., 135
Charnov, Eric L., 50
Cheung, Steven N. S., 536–37
Chow, G. C., 35, 36
Clay, Lucius D., 42
Coase, Ronald H., 536
Cochrane, W. W., 232
Cody, Martin L., 13, 205
Cogan, John F., 459
Cohen, Jerome B., 42
Colberg, M. R., 440
Cournot, A. A., 393
Cowie, Richard J., 51

Dangerfield, R., 312
Darwin, Charles, 261
DeHaven, J. C., 503, 538
Demmert, H. G., 381
Demsetz, H., 237, 266–67
Diocletian, 57, 342, 581

Easterlin, R. A., 86
Eaton, Clement, 194
Eckert, Ross D., 566–67

Edgeworth, Francis Y., 72
Ehrlich, Isaac, 12, 13
Engel, Ernst, 104, 107–08
Epstein, L. A., 166

Fechner, G. T., 70
Feldstein, Martin, 497
Fisher, Irving, 153, 512
Frech, H. E., III, 320
Freeburg, L. C., 533
Friedland, Claire, 564–65
Friedman, M., 321
Fuchs, Y., 273

Galbraith, J. K., 266–67
Gibson, William E., 509
Giffen, Sir Robert, 111
Ginsberg, P., 320
Givson, W. L., Jr., 471
Goldschmidt, W., 34–35
Gordon, D. I., 312
Green, L., 146
Grossbard, Amyra, 105

Hamilton, W. D., 84
Harberger, A. C., 346
Heady, E. O., 282
Hedrick, J. L., 471
Hicks, J. R., 115, 180–81
Hinrichs, A. F., 439
Hirshleifer, J., 7, 194, 324, 464, 503, 538
Horvitz, P. M., 344
Hotelling, H., 403–04
Houthakker, H., 108
Huettner, D., 297

Ibbotson, Roger G., 505

Jamison, John A., 359

Kagel, John H., 146, 461
Kain, J. F., 131
Kalant, H., 113
Kalant, O. J., 113
Kamerschen, D. R., 346
Kirwan, Albert D., 193
Klemm, W. R., 146

Lamson, R. D., 380
Lave, L. B., 533
Lea, S. E. G., 112
Lee, F. Y., 244–45
Lewis, H. Gregg, 469, 470
Lindsay, C. M., 474
Livingston, Joseph, 509

MacCrimmon, K. R., 79
Machiavelli, N., 572
Maier, F. H., 471
Malthus, T. R., 261
Marani, A., 273

McGee, J. S., 396
Mendershausen, H., 325
Meyer, J. T., 131
Michaely, Michael, 211
Milliman, J. W., 7, 538
Mintz, Ilse, 219
Moore, T. G., 440
Mount, T., 135
Musgrave, P. B., 573
Musgrave, R. A., 573

Nash, J. F., 390
Nicols, Alfred, 267–68

Oi, W. Y., 423–24, 479
Olson, M., Jr., 563
Owen, Bruce M., 342

Pareto, Vilfredo, 73, 523
Parkinson, C. Northcote, 566
Peterson, J. M., 439–40
Phelps, C. E., 53
Phillips, E. L., 263
Phillips, K. E., 244–45

Rachlin, H., 146
Radford, R. A., 96–97, 103
Rapport, David J., 13, 205
Rawls, John, 544–45
Razin, Assaf, 501
Robbins, H., 464
Rockefeller, John D., 395
Rose, L., 475
Rosen, Sherwin, 161
Rottenberg, Simon, 470

Sahlins, Marshall, 253
Scherer, Joseph, 469
Schwartz, R. A., 159, 160, 586
Scully, Gerald W., 434
Seagraves, James A., 471
Seers, Dudley, 178
Shubik, M., 392
Silberberg, E., 560
Simon, Julian L., 69, 399
Sinquefield, Rex A., 505
Slutsky, Eugen, 179–81
Smith, Adam, 14–15, 21, 214, 464, 526, 557
Smith, R. T., 53
Smith, Vernon L., 235, 461
Sobell, L. C., 113
Sobell, M. B., 113
Stigler, George J., 310, 319, 321, 346,
    398–99, 405, 564–65
Szasz, T. S., 23, 579

Thaler, Richard, 161
Thales, 8
Tinic, S. M., 341
Toda, M., 79
Tullock, G., 556

Turner, James E., 13
Tyrrell, T., 135

Wales, T. J., 140, 141
Weber, E. H., 70
Weinstein, Arnold A., 64
Welch, Finis, 78

Westfield, Fred M., 287
Whitney, Eli, 31
Wise, Donald E., 462
Wohl, M., 131
Worcester, D. A., Jr., 346

Zeckhauser, R., 563

A

AFL-CIO, 441
Agricultural marketing orders, 358–59
Agricultural parity prices, 43–44
Alcoholic beverages, 140–41
Alcoholics, 113–14
Alliance, economics of, 563
American Medical Association (AMA), 469, 473
Animal labor supply, 461
Animal Robinson Crusoes, 205–06
Apples and the bees, 536–37
Appropriative activity, 543–44
Attributes (*see* Product, quality)
Autarky, 238–43, 247–49, 493 (*see also* Price, autarky)
Author versus publisher, 342–44
Average magnitudes, 44–55 (*see also* Cost; Revenue; etc.)

B

"Backward-bending" supply curve, 460–62, 482 (*see also* Supply curve, factor)
Bads, 78–83, 85, 93, 120
Ball-point pens, 79–80
Barter, 250–54, 261, 324
Baseball, 381–82, 434
Birds, 50
Black Death, 464
Black market, 41–42, 178, 323, 327
Borrowing, 489, 512 (*see also* Intertemporal choice)
Braceros, 461–62
Brides, 34–35
Budget line, 90–92, 121–22, 179–81, 449–50, 488, 490–91
Bureaucracy, 565–67, 575
Business firms (*see* Firm)

C

Capital, 471–72, 474–77, 481, 483
  capital goods (real-capital), 463, 487, 492
  capital-value, 475–77, 480
  human, 472–73, 475
Cardinal vs. ordinal magnitudes, 67–74, 84, 278 (*see also* Utility)
Cartels, 357–61, 362, 391–92, 468–71, 483
Catholics, 32, 142
"Ceilings" (*see* Price, ceilings)
Charity, 81–83, 157–60, 183, 545–46
Children, preferences for, 77–78

Circular flow of economic activity, 17–19, 21, 27, 62, 260–62, 412, 447, 480–81
Civil War, American, 193–94
Coase's Theorem, 536–38, 549
Collusion (*see* Cartels; Oligopoly)
Command economy, 230–31, 249–50
Commodities (*see* Goods; Product)
Comparative statics, 29–30 (*see also* Equilibrium, shift of)
Comparison, Axiom of, 63, 65
Competition, 195–97, 201, 232–36, 288–92, 560, 575 (*see also* Firm, competitive; Trader, competitive; Price-taker; Industry)
  monopolistic (*see* Monopolistic competition)
  perfect, 232–36, 260, 332
Complementarity
  in consumption, 144–46, 152
  in production, 426–28, 443
Computing power, 35–36
Consumer Surplus, 212–24, 225, 235 (*see also* Exchange, gains from)
Consumers Union, 506
Consumption, 16, 19, 480
  decision, 20, 88–122, 480
  diversity in, 93, 223, 450, 452
  intertemporal (*see* Intertemporal choice)
  "new theory," 170–71, 366
  opportunities, 89–94, 115–16 (*see also* Opportunity set)
  optimum, 89–115, 196, 222–23
    corner solution, 93, 95, 110, 120, 121
    interior solution, 93–95, 98, 121, 122
    variation with income, 100–08
    variation with prices, 108–11, 115–16 (*see also* Income effect; Substitution effect)
Consumption-Balance Equation, 94–96, 98–99
Contracts, 262–64, 298, 553, 555–56, 575
Contract curve, 196
Controls, price (*see* Price, ceilings; Price, floors; Markets, government intervention)
Corn production experiment, 280–82
Corner solution, 94
Corporation, 264–68
Cost, 265, 270, 337, 350
  Average, 44, 51–53, 276–77, 290–92, 299
  Average Variable, 276–77, 291–92, 299
  derivation of function, 274–77
  economic (opportunity), 204, 265
  fixed vs. variable, 274–77, 291–92
  of living, 178–79
  long-run, 292–98, 299–300
  Marginal, 44, 51–53, 276–77, 288–92, 298, 305–06, 308, 528, 535
  of the Marginal Unit, 435